Sociology tHROUGH LiTERATURE

Second edition

Sociology THROUGH LiTERATURE

Edited by

Lewis A. Coser

State University of New York
Stony Brook

Prentice-Hall, Inc., Englewood Cliffs, New Jersey

Library of Congress Cataloging in Publication Data

Coser, Lewis A. ed.
  Sociology through literature.

  (Prentice-Hall sociology series)
    1. Literature—Collections. I. Title.
PN6014.C64 1972   808.8   76-38997
ISBN   0-13-821538-3

Prentice-hall sociology series

Herbert Blumer, Editor

© 1972, 1963 Prentice-Hall, Inc.
Englewood Cliffs, New Jersey

10   9   8   7   6   5   4   3

Printed in the United States of America

Prentice-Hall International, Inc., London
Prentice-Hall of Australia, Pty. Ltd., Sydney
Prentice-Hall of Canada, Ltd., Toronto
Prentice-Hall of India Private Limited, New Delhi
Prentice-Hall of Japan, Inc., Tokyo

For Ellen

CONTENTS

Preface

In the introduction to the first edition of this reader I stated that this was an experimental venture and that only its use in the classroom would show whether the teaching of sociology through literature would prove to be a useful approach. Now, nine years later, the experiment seems to have succeeded, judging from the reviews, the sales, and the comments colleagues and students have been good enough to make to me.

For a number of years I resisted the entreaties of my editors who urged me to revise this volume—it would serve little purpose just to replace one selection with another. But developments in American society in recent years, and the development of American sociology as well, have changed my mind. In the last decade, American society has gone through a series of historical changes that have called attention to problems hitherto neglected or barely perceived, and sociologists have begun to consider issues and problems that previously had not been encompassed in their field of vision.

In an effort to keep abreast of these trends, I have included in this revised edition four entirely new sections dealing with *poverty, sex roles, youth,* and *total institutions.* Although these are not the only new topics that recently have stirred the sociological imagination, I venture to think that they are the most salient ones. I also have added selections in the sections on *race relations, the crowd and revolution, status and role,* and *the self and the other.* Among the authors now included for the first time are Gustave Flaubert, Virginia Woolf, O. Henry, Oscar Wilde, E. E. Cummings, Hendrik Ibsen, and a variety of both American and European contemporary writers.

Without the sensitive and critical comments that came from colleagues and students over the years, this new edition would not have seen the light of day. I am thankful to all of them.

Introduction

"There is no impression of life, no manner of seeing it and feeling it," Henry James once wrote, "to which the plan of the novelist may not offer a place."

Not only novelists, but most literary artists have endeavored, according to Henry James' prescription, to "try and catch the color of life itself."

In so doing, they have provided their readers with an immense variety of richly textured commentaries on man's life in society, on his involvement with his fellow-men.

Literature, though it may also be many other things, is social evidence and testimony. It is a continuous commentary on manners and morals. Its great monuments, even as they address themselves to the eternal existential problems which are at the root of the perennial tensions between men and their society, preserve for us the precious record of modes of response to peculiar social and cultural conditions.

Sociologists have but rarely utilized works of literature in their investigations. And yet it would appear obvious that the trained sensibilities of a novelist or a poet may provide a richer source of social insight than, say, the impressions of untrained informants on which so much sociological research currently rests. There is an intensity of perception in the first-rate novelist when he describes a locale, a sequence of action, or a clash of characters which can hardly be matched by those observers on whom sociologists are usually wont to rely. The literary creator has the ability to identify with wide ranges of experience, and he has the trained capacity to articulate through his fantasy the existential problems of his contemporaries. Why then should not sociology harness to its use, for the understanding of man and his society, those untapped sources in the rich accumulation of literature?

Fiction is not a substitute for systematically accumulated, certified knowledge. But it provides the social scientist with a wealth of sociologically relevant material, with manifold clues and points of departure for sociological theory and research. The creative imagination of the literary artist often has achieved insights into social processes which have remained unexplored in social science. This has been so, perhaps, because social scientists have but too often felt it is somewhat beneath their dignity to show an interest in literature. One may easily understand such a reaction on the part of practitioners of sciences which are as yet in their formative state and are hence especially concerned with asserting their scientific purity. But here, as elsewhere, to understand need not imply endorsement or condonation. The fact of the matter seems to be that this self-denying ordinance on the part of sociologists has hampered them in their tasks.

The great traditions of sociology are humanistic. The calling of sociology is to contribute to the self-interpretation of man. "Sociological analysis," as Edward Shils has recently argued, "is a continuation in a contemporary idiom of the great efforts of the human mind to render judgment on man's vicissitudes on earth." To the extent that the sociologist lives up to the ancient injunction to "know thyself," to that extent he cannot afford to cut himself off from any sources from which knowledge about man can be derived. If literature is one of these sources, then the social scientist who neglects its contributions narrows and confines his vision. The sociologist who ignores literature is bound to be not merely a much impoverished man, but a worse social scientist. Sociologists who, to use Veblen's telling phrase, dream of a "highly sterilized, germ-proof system of knowledge, kept in a cool dry place," ought to realize that such preoccupations, if pursued exclusively, may retard the progress of sociology as a humanistic discipline far more than they advance it. Nothing human ought to be alien to the social scientist; if a novel, a play or a poem is a personal and direct impression of social life, the sociologist should respond to it with the same openness and willingness to learn that he displays when he interviews a respondent, observes a community, or classifies and analyzes survey data.

As it is, there are likely to be few sociologists whose scientific concerns have not profited from some extra-curricular reading of fiction. When sociologists talk, say, about post-Napoleonic France, they surely have in mind a picture drawn for them by Balzac's *Comédie Humaine* rather than by some social historian. When they lecture on Victorian society, they are apt to think of the novels of Dickens or George Eliot.. Few, I think, would deny that their image of nineteenth-century Russia was formed in large part by Tolstoi or Dostoevski. Why then not make manifest and explicit what has been latent all along? A union of sociology and literature need not be a misalliance; on the contrary, there is a chance for a legitimate union.

Literary insight cannot replace scientific and analytical knowledge, but it can profit them immensely. Just as no psychologist would believe that knowledge of Nietzsche or Dostoevski replaces the contributions of Sigmund Freud, so no sociologist could possibly believe that Balzac's startling discussion of the impact of money on interpersonal relations dispenses one from reading Marx on the fetishism of commodities or Georg Simmel on the sociology of money. Yet a knowledge of the concreteness of the social process in the works of Proust or Flaubert, for example, can significantly enhance one's understanding of the more complex and abstract theoretical schemes of the great sociologists. We need to read Marx *and* Balzac. Max Weber *and* Proust. The understanding of one will be illuminated by the understanding of the other.

This book is not meant to be a contribution to the sociology of literature. Sociology of literature is a specialized area of study which focuses upon the relation between a work of art, its public, and the social structure in which it is produced and received. It seeks to explain the emergence of a particular art work in a particular form of society, and the ways in which the creative imagination of the writer is shaped by cultural traditions and social arrangements. The attempt here is to use the work of literature for an understanding of society, rather than to illuminate artistic production by reference to the society in which it arose. This collection, then, should help to teach modern sociology through illustrative material from literature. Such an approach, one may hope, does not only have pedagogical value. It may also contribute to the refinement and clarification of the concepts of sociology.

Robert K. Merton has argued that empirical research goes far beyond the passive role of verifying and testing theory; it initiates, reformulates, deflects and clarifies theory so that "the unanticipated, anomalous and strategic datum exerts pressure for initiating theory." One ventures to think that literary perceptions may upon occasion perform a similar role for sociological theory; certain types of knowledge, attained by intuitive methods, may be harnessed for use in theoretical systematization.

What has been said about the profit that the practice of sociology might derive from familiarity with literature applies even more strongly to the teaching of sociology. The college student who is first exposed to sociological research and theory is apt to feel that these works, to the extent that they are pitched on a relatively high level of abstraction, are remote from the concrete reality which he has so far known. Those of us who have taught classes in introductory sociology are well acquainted with the initial bewilderment of students when faced with what they conceive to be a gap between what sociologists seem to be talking about and the styles of thought with which they have been familiar. They find it hard to move back and forth between conceptually mediated knowledge and the immediacy of concrete experience. One of the aims of this book is to help the teacher of beginning students to overcome such initial resistance by affording him an opportunity to clothe the dry bones of social theory with the living and plastic tissue which grows from literary imagination. A student who has read Dickens' descriptions of London city life or Balzac's anatomy of Paris life styles will have a more ready understanding of Simmel's or Park's or Mumford's discussion of modern urban civilization. The beginning student of collective behavior, and not he exclusively, will surely benefit from reading Zola or Nathanael West on the subtle and complicated social process through which a crowd is transformed into a mob.

Any selection is incomplete and hence lays itself open to criticism on that count. Invariably every reader will think that another author, or another piece of literature ought to have been included. This is as it should be, for it will give the teacher who uses this book the opportunity to venture beyond, and to search for other literary materials to illustrate the uses of literature for sociology. To the extent that this selection stimulates such a quest, to that extent it will have fulfilled some of its main purposes. It is to be hoped that students, similarly, may be moved to explore on their own initiative in that vast store house of sociologically relevant materials which literature provides for them. Therefore, a certain amount of dissatisfaction with the selection provided in this book is not only anticipated but even welcome. Nevertheless, a word as to the principles of selection is in order.

Not all authors lend themselves to the uses of the anthologist. Many of them require long development of characterization, description or narrative in order to make a point or illustrate an idea. It is thus impossible to select from these authors relatively short passages to highlight a sociological concept. This is often the case with certain Victorian novelists or with, for example, Henry James or Joseph Conrad, who therefore are neglected in these pages. In other cases, especially among contemporary writers, copyright considerations forced abandonment of initial plans to select a particular piece of writing.

The bulk of the materials included here has been taken from nineteenth- and twentieth-century literature, although the eighteenth-century has not been neglected; a few selections from earlier periods have also been included. This emphasis on relatively recent literary work flowed from the desire to include only those writings that would not require extended exegesis to be understood. It followed also from the fact that, as Erich Auerbach has shown in his monumental *Mimesis*, it is within the last two centuries that European literature has reached a level of "realism" in literary representation that has not been equaled in earlier periods.

Most selections have been drawn from English and American literature, but the French and Russian also are represented rather fully. A number of selections represent other European literary traditions and a few derive from oriental literature. This selection is based on the assumption that the realistic tradition is more developed in Anglo-American and in French and Russian literature than in other European and extra-European literary cultures. Moreover, there are more translations available of French and Russian than of the other European literature; and, finally, the editor happens to be more acquainted with these literatures than with some others.

Although this volume contains a few poems, and one or two excerpts from plays, most selections of fiction are from short stories and novels. In addition, autobiography and travel literature, as well as essays by men of letters, have been used rather fully even though the purist might not consider some of them works meant to display the literary imagination. In these instances, acuteness of observation seemed to compensate amply, at least for the purposes of this book, for purely literary value. In general, however, the endeavor has been to include only selections from works which can be considered to rank as literary art of a high order. Sub-literary reportage, though possible of great documentary value (the work of John P. Marquand, for example) has not been drawn upon here.

This book is divided into chapters, each of which centers upon one of the major concepts of sociology. Most, though not all, of the major areas usually discussed in introductory textbooks have been covered, and the chapters have been so organized as to allow a fairly easy synchronization with the treatment in most such texts. The introductions to the different sections are meant to give a succinct overview of the concepts covered and a brief discussion of the selections. These introductions do not explain or analyze the text. Many of the selections, perhaps the very best of them, can be read on several levels of meaning. It would have been insulting to the reader and a barbarous misuse of literature to reduce a work of art to a simple example of sociology. What is provided here are some hints which may be useful for the beginner. For a more detailed explanation the student will have to address himself to the literary critic.

This book is frankly experimental; only its use in the classroom will show whether the teaching of sociology through literature can indeed enrich and enliven the subject, whether the literary imagination can stimulate the sociological imagination. The editor believes that the life of art illuminates the social life of man.

Sociology
THROUGH
LiTERATURE

Culture

All societies, whether animal or human, have things in common. This is why social thinkers of all ages so often have been tempted, in whimsy or in earnest, to compare human societies to bee hives, ant colonies or hunting packs. And this is also presumably why the social life of monkeys and apes has been so fascinating for generations of visitors to zoos and animal farms. Yet, human society differs from animal societies in one crucial way. In the non-human world each animal responds to the various life situations in which it may be placed in a fixed manner determined by heredity, though the higher sub-human mammals and the primates in particular are also capable of a great deal of learning through direct experience. But humans alone are capable of symbolic communication. Hence, only men can transcend *present* situations and establish cumulative bodies of knowledge as well as codes of conduct. Moreover, they can transmit them from generation to generation. Human societies alone possess *culture*.

Following the great British pioneer of anthropology Edward B. Tyler, culture can be defined as "that complex whole which includes knowledge, belief, art, morals, law, custom, and any other capabilities and habits acquired by man as a member of society." Men are organisms who are in symbolic communication with each other; they are a symbol-making and symbol-using species whose social inheritance, or culture, allows them to transcend the shortcomings of biological inheritance.

Later selections will include the discussion of many specific cultural traits. In this first section we aim only at conveying the general importance of culture in shaping human behavior. Denis Diderot, the great French *philosophe* and man of letters, one of the major figures of the Enlightenment, introduces the notion of cultural relativism in his imaginary and whimsical discussion of the differences between the culture of Tahiti and the West. One need not accept his notion that Tahitian culture is somehow more rational than our own and yet find his argument as to the relativity of moral standards quite persuasive. Herman Melville's description of the culture of the Marquesas Islands, which he visited as a young sailor, and where he spent several months as a captive of the natives, is taken from his first book *Typee* (1846). The student might find it rewarding to compare this account with studies by modern anthropologists, especially Ralph Linton, of the same islanders a century later. D. H. Lawrence's evocation of the ceremonial culture of the Indians of the American Southwest and of Mexico ranks among his best work. Even though he may have been mistaken in matters of detail, he seems to have been able, in the selection reprinted here, to capture some of the essential elements of the life styles of the Pueblo Indians.

Finally, lest one be led to believe that cultural analysis applies only to the relatively static conditions in which non-literate peoples play out their social roles, F. Scott Fitzgerald's description of changing cultural styles in near-contemporary America have been included here. Not quite everybody, as he seems to be suggesting, may have been caught by the spirit of the Jazz Age, but enough urban middle-class and upper-middle-class youths were indeed caught by it to make a difference in the cultural climate of America. The Jazz Age contributed greatly in transforming the moral atmosphere and in bringing about a decided shift in moral sensibilities. The young men and women who were having a gay time in the twenties could hardly have anticipated that their high-spirited fascination with extra-marital sex and extra-legal alcohol would contribute to a major cultural change in America—but it did.

Denis Diderot (1713–1784)

Blissful isles

A: Have you seen the Tahitian whom Bougainville took on board and brought to this country?

B: I've seen him; he is named Aotourou. The first land he saw he took for the native land of the explorers. Either they had deceived him about the length of the voyage, or, naturally misled by the apparent short distance from the shore of the sea where he lived to where the sky seemed to limit it at the horizon, he was ignorant of the real extent of the earth. The idea of the communal enjoyment of women was so well established in his mind that he threw himself upon the first European woman he met and prepared very seriously to treat her with true Tahitian courtesy. He was bored among us. The Tahitian alphabet having no b, c, d, f, g, q, x, y, nor z, he could never learn to speak our language, which presented too many foreign articulations and new sounds for his inflexible organs of speech. He never ceased to sigh for his own country, and I am not surprised. Bougainville's *Voyage* is the only one which has given me a taste for any other country than my own. Until reading this I had thought that nowhere was there anything so good as at home, with the result that I believed the same for every inhabitant of the earth: a natural effect of the attraction of the soil, an attraction which holds for good things which one enjoys at home and which one has not the same certainty of finding elsewhere.

A: What! Don't you think that the Parisian is convinced that he might grow corn in the Roman Campagna as in the fields of the Beauce?

B: Indeed, no. Bougainville sent Aotourou back, after having provided for his expenses and ensured his return.

A: Oh, Aotourou! How glad you will be to see your father and mother again, and your brothers, sisters, lovers and fellow-countrymen! What will you tell them about us?

B: Only a little, and that they won't believe.

A: Why only a little?

B: Because he has understood only a few things, and because he will not find in his language any terms corresponding to those things which he has understood.

From *Supplement to Bougainville's Voyage* (1796), in *Diderot, Interpreter of Nature*, translated by Jean Stewart and Jonathan Kemp. Copyright by International Publishers, 1943.

A: And why won't they believe him?

B: Because after comparing their ways with ours, they would much rather take Aotourou for a liar, than believe us to be so mad.

A: Really?

B: I don't doubt it. The life of a savage is simple, and our societies are such complex mechanisms. The Tahitian is at a primary stage in the development of the world, the European is at its old age. The interval separating us is greater than that between the new-born child and the decrepit old man. He understands nothing of our customs, our laws, or he sees in them only fetters disguised in a hundred ways; fetters which can only excite indignation and hatred in a being for whom liberty is one of the most profound of feelings.

A: Are you wanting to make a fable about Tahiti?

B: It is not a fable; and you would have no doubt of the sincerity of Bougainville, if you knew the *Supplement* to his *Voyage*.

A: Where is this *Supplement* to be found?

B: There on the table.

A: Won't you entrust it to me? . . .

B: Hold on! read. Let's skip this preamble which doesn't matter and go straight to the farewell of one of the island chiefs to our explorers. This will give you some idea of the eloquence of these people.

A: How did Bougainville understand these farewells spoken in a language of which he was ignorant?

B: You will see. It is an old man speaking.

The old man's farewell

He was the father of a large family. At the arrival of the Europeans, he looked disdainfully at them, showing neither astonishment, fear nor curiosity. They accosted him. He turned his back on them, and withdrew into his hut. His silence and his anxiety revealed his thoughts only too well: he lamented within himself for the great days of his country, now eclipsed. At the departure of Bougainville, when the inhabitants ran in a crowd to the shore, clinging to his garments, embracing his companions and weeping, the old man came forward with a stern air and said:

"Weep, poor folk of Tahiti, weep! Would that this were the arrival and not the departure of these ambitious and wicked men. One day you will know them better. One day they will return, in one hand the piece of wood you now see attached to the belt of this one, and the other grasping the blade you now see hanging from the belt of another. And with these they will enslave you, murder you or subject you to their extravagances and vices. One day you will serve under them, as corrupted, as vile, as loathsome as themselves.

"But I console myself; I am reaching the end of my journey; I shall not live to see the calamity I foretell. Oh people of Tahiti! Oh my friends! You have a means to escape the tragic future; but I would rather die than counsel it. Let them go their ways, let them live."

Then, addressing himself to Bougainville, he continued:

"And you, chief of these brigands who obey you, quickly take your vessel from our shores. We are innocent, we are happy; and you can only spoil our happiness. We follow the pure instincts of nature; and you have tried to wipe its impress from our shores. Here everything belongs to everybody. You have preached to us I know not what distinctions between "mine" and "thine." Our daughters and our wives are common to us all. You have shared this privilege with us; and you have lighted passions in them before unknown. They have become maddened in your arms; you have become ferocious in theirs. They have begun to hate each other; you have slain each other for them, and they have returned to us stained with your blood.

"We are a free people; and now you have planted in our country the title deeds of our future slavery. You are neither god nor demon; who are you, then, to make slaves? Orou! You understand the language of these men, tell us all, as you have told me, what they have written on this sheet of metal: 'This country is ours.' This country yours? And why? Because you have walked thereon? If a Tahitian landed one day on your shores, and scratched on one of your rocks or on the bark of your trees: 'This country belongs to the people of Tahiti'—what would you think?

"You are the strongest! And what of that? When someone took one of the contemptible trifles with which your vessel is filled, you cried out and you were revenged. Yet at the same time in the depths of your heart you plotted the theft of a whole country! You are not a slave; you would suffer death rather than be one; yet you want to enslave us. Do you think the Tahitian does not know how to defend his liberty and to die? The Tahitian you want to seize like a wild animal is your brother. You are both children of nature; what right have you over him that he has not over you? When you came, did we rush upon you, did we pillage your ship? Did we seize you and expose you to the arrows of our enemies? Did we yoke you with the animals for toil in our fields? No. We respected our own likeness in you. Leave us to our ways; they are wiser and more honest than yours. We do not want to barter what you call our ignorance for your useless civilization. Everything that is necessary and good for us we possess. Do we deserve contempt, because we have not known how to develop superfluous wants? When we hunger, we have enough to eat; when we are cold we have wherewith to clothe us. You have been in our huts; what is lacking there, in your opinion? You may pursue as far as you like what you call the comforts of life; but allow sensible people to stop, when they would only have obtained imaginary good from the continuation of their painful efforts. If you persuade us to exceed the narrow limits of our wants, when shall we ever finish toiling? When shall we enjoy ourselves? We have reduced the sum of our annual and daily labours to the least possible, because nothing seems to us preferable to repose. Go to your own country to agitate and torment yourself as much as you like; leave us in peace. Do not worry us with your artificial needs, nor with your imaginary virtues. Look on these men; see how upright, healthy and robust they are. Look on these women; see how upright, healthy, fresh and beautiful they are. Take this bow; it is my own. Call one, two, three or four of your friends to help you try to bend it. I can bend it myself, alone. I till the soil. I climb mountains. I pierce the forest. I can run a league on the plains in less than an hour. Your young companions would be hard put to follow me, yet I am more than ninety years old.

"Woe unto this island! Woe to these people to Tahiti and to all who will come after them, woe from the day you first visited us! We should know only one disease; that to which all men, animals and plants are subject—old age; but you have brought us another; you have infected our blood.

"It will perhaps be necessary to exterminate our daughters, wives, children, with our own hands; all those who have approached your women; those who have approached your men.

"Our fields shall be soaked with the foul blood which has passed from your veins into ours; or else our children, condemned to nourish and perpetuate the evil which you have given to the fathers and mothers, will transmit it forever to their descendants. Villains! You will be the guilty ones; guilty either of the ravages of disease that will follow the fatal embraces of your people, or of the murders which we shall commit to stop the spread of the poison.

"You speak of crimes! Do you know any more enormous than your own? What is your punishment for him who kills his neighbour?—death by the sword; what is your punishment for the coward who poisons?—death by fire. Compare your crime to his; tell us then, poisoner of whole people, what should be the torment you deserve? But a short while ago, the young Tahitian girl yielded herself to the transports and embraces of the Tahitian youth; waited impatiently until her mother, authorized by her having reached the age of marriage, should remove her veil and make naked her breast. She was proud to excite the desire and to attract the amorous glances of unknown men, of relatives, of her brother. Without dread and without shame, in our presence, in the midst of a circle of innocent Tahitians, to the sound of flutes, between the dances, she accepted the caresses of the one to whom her young heart and the secret voice of her senses urged her. The idea of crime, and the peril of disease came with you. Our enjoyments, once so sweet, are now accompanied by remorse and terror. That man in black who stands near you listening to me, has spoken to our lads. I do not know what he has said to our girls. But our lads are hesitant; our girls blush. Plunge if you will into the dark depths of the forest with the perverse companion of your pleasure; but let the good and simple Tahitians reproduce themselves without shame, under the open sky, in the full light of day. What finer and more noble feeling could you put in place of that with which we have inspired them, and which animates them now? They think that the moment to enrich the nation and the family with a new citizen is come, and they glory in it. They eat to live and to grow; they grow in order to multiply and they find in it nothing vicious nor shameful.

"Listen to the continuation of your crimes. You had scarcely come among our people than they became thieves. You had scarcely landed on our soil, than it reeked with blood. That Tahitian who ran to meet you, to receive you crying 'Taio! friend, friend,' you slew. And why did you slay him? . . . because he had been taken by the glitter of your little serpents' eggs. He gave you of his fruits; he offered you his wife and daughter, he ceded you his hut; yet you killed him for a handful of beads which he had taken without being asked. And the people? At the noise of your murderous shot, terror seized them, and they fled to the mountains. But be assured that they would not have waited long to descend again. Then you would all have perished, but for me. Ah! why did I pacify them, why do I still restrain them, even now? I do not know; for you deserve no pity; for you have a ferocious soul which will never feel it. You have wandered, you and yours, everywhere in our island. You have been respected; you have enjoyed all things; you have found neither barrier nor refusal in your ways; you have been invited within, you have sat, and all the abundance of our country has been spread before you. When you desired young girls, only excepting those who had not yet the privilege of unveiling their faces and breasts, their mothers have presented to you all the others, quite naked. You have possessed the tender victim of the duties of hospitality; flowers and leaves were heaped up for you and her; musicians sounded their instruments; nothing has spoiled the sweetness, nor hindered the freedom of your caresses nor of hers. They have sung the anthem exhorting you to be a man, and our child to be a woman, yielding and voluptuous. They danced around your couch. And it was when you came from the arms of this woman, after experiencing on her breast the sweetest of all intoxications, that you slew her brother, friend or father.

"You have done still worse. Look over there, see that enclosure bristling with weapons. These arms which have menaced only your enemies are now turned against our own children. See these unhappy companions of our pleasure. See their sadness, the grief of their fathers and the despair of their mothers. They are those condemned to die, either by our hands or by the diseases you have given them.

"Away now, unless your cruel eyes revel in the spectacle of death. Go now, go; and may the guilty seas which spared you on your voyage hither, absolve themselves and avenge us, by engulfing you before you return. . . ."

Discussion between the almoner and orou

B: In the sharing of Bougainville's crew among the Tahitians, the almoner was allotted to Orou; they were about the same age, thirty-five to thirty-six. Orou had then only his wife and three daughters, called Asto, Palli, and Thia. They undressed the almoner, bathed his face, hands and feet, and served him a wholesome and frugal meal. When he was about to go to bed, Orou, who had been absent with his family, reappeared, and presenting to him his wife and three daughters, all naked, said: "You have eaten, you are young and in good health; if you sleep alone you will sleep badly, for man needs a companion beside him at night. There is my wife, there are my daughters; choose the one who pleases you best. But if you wish to oblige me you will give preference to the youngest of my daughters, who has not yet had any children." The mother added: "Alas! But it's no good complaining about it; poor Thia! it is not her fault."

The almoner answered that his religion, his office, good morals and decency would not allow him to accept these offers.

Orou replied: "I do not know what this thing is that you call 'religion'; but I can only think ill of it, since it prevents you from tasting an innocent pleasure to which nature, the sovereign mistress, invites us all; prevents you from giving existence to one of your own kind, from doing a service which a father, mother, and children all ask of you, from doing something for a host who has received you well, and from enriching a nation, by giving it one more citizen. I do not know what this thing is which you call your 'office' but your first duty is to be a man and to be grateful. I do not suggest that you should introduce into your country the ways of Orou, but Orou, your host and friend, begs you to lend yourself to the ways of Tahiti. Whether the ways of Tahiti are better or worse than yours is an easy question to decide. Has the land of your birth more people than it can feed? If so your ways are neither worse nor better than ours. But can it feed more than it has? Our ways are better than yours. As to the sense of decency which you offer as objection, I understand you; I agree that I was wrong, and I ask your pardon. I do not want to injure your health; if you are tired, you must have rest; but I hope that you will not continue to sadden us. See the care you have made appear on all these faces; they fear lest you should have found blemishes on them which merit your disdain. But when it is only the pleasure of doing honour to one of my daughters, amidst her companions and sisters, and of doing a good action, won't that suffice you? Be generous!''

The Almoner: It's not that: they are all equally beautiful, but my religion! my office!

Orou: They are mine and I offer them to you; they are their own and they give themselves to you. Whatever may be the purity of conscience which the thing 'religion' and the thing 'office' prescribe, you can accept them without scruple. I am not abusing my authority at all; be sure that I know and respect the rights of the individual.''

Here the truthful almoner agrees that Providence had never exposed him to such violent temptation. He was young, he became agitated and tormented; he turned his eyes away from the lovely suppliants, and then regarded them again; he raised his hands and eyes to the sky. Thia, the youngest, clasped his knees and said: "Stranger, do not distress my father and mother, do not afflict me. Honour me in the hut, among my own people; raise me to the rank of my sisters, who mock me. Asto, the eldest, already had three children; the second, Palli, has two; but Thia has none at all. Stranger, honest stranger, do not repulse me; make me a mother, make me a child that I can one day lead by the hand, by my side, here in Tahiti; who may be seen held at my breast in nine months' time; one of whom I shall be so proud and who will be part of my dowry when I go from my parents' hut to another's. I shall perhaps be more lucky with you than with our young Tahitians. If you will grant me this favour I shall never forget you; I shall bless you all my life. I shall write your name on my arm and on your son's; we shall pronounce it always with joy. And when you leave these shores, my good wishes will go with you on the seas till you reach your own land.''

The candid almoner said that she clasped his knees, and gazed into his eyes so expressively and so touchingly; that she wept; that her father, mother and sisters withdrew; that he remained alone with her, and that, still saying, "my religion, my office," he found himself the next morning lying beside the young girl, who overwhelmed him with caresses, and who invited her parents and sisters, when they came to their bed in the morning, to join their gratitude to hers. Asto and Palli, who had withdrawn, returned bringing food, fruits and drink. They kissed their sister and made vows over her. They all ate together.

Then Orou, left alone with the almoner, said to him:

"I see that my daughter is well satisfied with you and I thank you. But would you teach me what is meant by this word 'religion' which you have repeated so many times and so sorrowfully?"

The almoner, after having mused a moment answered:

"Who made your hut and the things which furnish it?"

Orou: I did.

The Almoner: Well then, we believe that this world and all that it contains is the work of a maker.

Orou: Has he feet, hands and a head then?

The Almoner: No.

Orou: Where is his dwelling-place?

The Almoner: Everywhere.

Orou: Here too?

The Almoner: Here.

Orou: We have never seen him.

The Almoner: One doesn't see him.

Orou: That's an indifferent father, then! He must be old, for he will at least be as old as his work.

The Almoner: He does not age. He spoke to our ancestors, gave them laws, prescribed the manner in which he wished to be honoured; he ordered a certain behaviour as being good, and he forbade them certain other actions as being wicked.

Orou: I follow you; and one of the actions he forbade them, as wicked, was to lie with a woman or a girl? Why, then, did he make two sexes?

The Almoner: That they might be united; but with certain requisite conditions, after certain preliminary ceremonies in consequence of which the man belongs to the woman and only to her; and the woman belongs to the man, and only to him.

Orou: For their whole lives?

The Almoner: For the whole of their lives.

Orou: So that if it happened that a woman should lie with a man other than her husband, or a husband with another woman . . . but that couldn't happen. Since the maker is there and this displeases him, he will know how to prevent them doing it.

The Almoner: No; he lets them do it, and they sin against the law of God (for it is thus we call the great maker) against the law of the country; and they commit a crime.

Orou: I should be sorry to offend you by what I say, but if you would permit me, I would give you my opinion.

The Almoner: Speak.

Orou: I find these singular precepts opposed to nature and contrary to reason, made to multiply crimes and to plague at every moment this old maker, who has made everything, without help of hands, or head, or tools, who is everywhere and is not seen anywhere, who exists today and tomorrow and yet is not a day older, who commands and is not obeyed, who can prevent and yet does not do so. Contrary to nature because these precepts suppose that a free, thinking and sentient being can be the property of a being like himself. On what is this law founded? Don't you see that in your country they have confused the thing which has neither consciousness nor thought, nor desire, nor will; which one picks up, puts down, keeps or exchanges, without injury to it, or without its complaining, have confused this with the thing which cannot be exchanged or acquired, which has liberty, will, desire, which can give or refuse itself for a moment or for ever, which laments and suffers, and which cannot become an article of commerce, without its character being forgotten and violence done to its nature; contrary to the general law of existence? In fact, nothing could appear to you more senseless than a precept which refuses to admit that change which is a part of us, which commands a constancy which cannot be found there and which violates the liberty of the male and female by chaining them for ever to each other; more senseless than a fidelity which limits the most capricious of enjoyments to one individual; than an oath of the immutability of two beings made of flesh; and all that in the face of a sky which never for a moment remains the same, in caverns which threaten destruction, below a rock which falls to powder, at the foot of a tree which cracks, on a stone which rocks? Believe me, you have made the condition of man worse than that of animals. I do not know what your great maker may be; but I rejoice that he has never spoken to our forefathers, and I wish that he may never speak to our children; for he might tell them the same foolishness, and they commit the folly of believing it. Yesterday, at supper, you mentioned 'magistrates' and 'priests,' whose authority regulates your conduct; but, tell me, are they the masters of good and evil? Can they make what is just to be unjust and unjust, just? Does it rest with them to attribute good to harmful actions, and evil to innocent or useful actions? You could not think it, for, at that rate, there would be neither true nor false, good nor bad, beautiful nor ugly; or at any rate only what pleased your great maker, your magistrates and your priests to pronounce so. And from one moment to another you would be obliged to change your ideas and your conduct. One day someone would tell you, on behalf of one of your three masters, to kill, and you would be obliged by your conscience to kill; another day, "steal," and you would have to steal; or "do not eat this fruit" and you would not dare to eat it; "I forbid you this vegetable or animal" and you would take care not to touch them. There is no good thing that could not be forbidden you, and no wickedness that you could not be ordered to do. And what would you be reduced to, if your three masters, disagreeing among themselves, should at once permit, enjoin and forbid you the same thing, as I believe must often happen. Then, to please the priest you must become embroiled with the magistrate; to satisfy the magistrate you must displease the great maker; and to make yourself agreeable to the great maker you must renounce nature. And do you know what will happen then? You will neglect all of them, and you will be neither man, nor citizen nor pious; you will be nothing; you will be out of favour with all the kinds of authorities, at odds even with yourself, tormented by your heart, persecuted by your enraged masters; and wretched as I saw you yesterday evening when I offered my wife and daughters to you, and you cried out, "But my religion, my office!"

Do you want to know what is good and what is bad in all times and in all places? Hold fast to the nature of things and of actions; to your relations with your fellows; to the influence of your conduct on your individual usefulness and the general good. You are mad if you believe that there is anything, high or low in the universe, which can add to or subtract from the laws of nature. Her eternal will is that good should be preferred to evil, and the general good to the individual good. You may ordain the opposite but you will not be obeyed. You will multiply the number of malefactors and the wretched by fear, punishment and remorse. You will deprave consciences; you will corrupt minds. They will not know what to do or what to avoid. Disturbed in their state of innocence, at ease with crime, they will have lost their guiding star."

Herman Melville (1819–1891)

Domestic manners on the marquesas

During the second day of the Feast of Calabashes, Kory-Kory—being determined that I should have some understanding on these matters—had, in the course of his explanations, directed my attention to a peculiarity I had frequently remarked among many of the females;—principally those of a mature age and rather matronly appearance. This consisted in having the right hand and the left foot most elaborately tattooed, while the rest of the body was wholly free from the operation of the art, with the exception of the minutely dotted lips and slight marks on the shoulders, to which I have previously referred as comprising the sole tattooing exhibited by Fayaway, in common with other young girls of her age. The hand and foot thus embellished were, according to Kory-Kory, the distinguishing badge of wedlock, so far as that social and highly commendable institution is known among these people. It answers, indeed, the same purpose as the plain gold ring worn by our fairer spouses.

After Kory-Kory's explanation of the subject, I was for some time studiously respectful in the presence of all females thus distinguished, and never

---

From *Typee* by Herman Melville (1846).

ventured to indulge in the slightest approach to flirtation with any of their number. Married women, to be sure!—I knew better than to offend them.

A further insight, however, into the peculiar domestic customs of the inmates of the valley did away, in a measure, with the severity of my scruples, and convinced me that I was deceived in some, at least, of my conclusions. A regular system of polygamy exists among the islanders, but of a most extraordinary nature—a plurality of husbands, instead of wives; and this solitary fact speaks volumes for the gentle disposition of the male population. Where else, indeed, could such a practice exist, even for a single day?—Imagine a revolution brought about in a Turkish seraglio, and the harem rendered the abode of bearded men; or conceive some beautiful woman in our own country running distracted at the sight of her numerous lovers murdering one another before her eyes, out of jealousy for the unequal distribution of her favours! —Heaven defend us from such a state of things! —We are scarcely amiable and forbearing enough to submit to it.

I was not able to learn what particular ceremony was observed in forming the marriage contract, but am inclined to think that it must have been of a very simple nature. Perhaps the mere 'popping the question,' as it is termed with us, might have been followed by an immediate nuptial alliance. At any rate, I have more than one reason to believe that tedious courtships are unknown in the valley of Typee.

The males considerably outnumber the females. This holds true of many of the islands of Polynesia, although the reverse of that is the case in most civilised countries. The girls are first wooed and won, at a very tender age, by some stripling in the household in which they reside. This, however, is a mere frolic of the affections, and no formal engagement is contracted. By the time this first love has a little subsided, a second suitor presents himself, of graver years, and carries both boy and girl away to his own habitation. This disinterested and generous-hearted fellow now weds the young couple—marrying damsel and lover at the same time—and all three thenceforth live together as harmoniously as so many turtles. I have heard of some men who, in civilised countries, rashly marry large families with their wives, but had no idea that there was any place where people married supplementary husbands with them. Infidelity on either side is very rare. No man has more than one wife, and no wife of mature years has less than two husbands—sometimes she has three, but such instances are not frequent. The marriage tie, whatever it may be, does not appear to be indissoluble, for separations occasionally happen. These, however, when they do take place, produce no unhappiness, and are preceded by no bickerings, for the simple reason that an ill-used wife or a henpecked husband is not obliged to file a bill in Chancery to obtain a divorce. As nothing stands in the way of a separation, the matrimonial yoke sits easily and lightly, and a Typee wife lives on very pleasant and sociable terms with her husbands. On the whole, wedlock, as known among these Typees, seems to be of a more distinct and enduring nature than is usually the case with barbarous people. A baneful promiscuous intercourse of the sexes is hereby avoided, and virtue, without being clamorously invoked, is, as it were, unconsciously practised. . . .

Notwithstanding the existence of wedlock among the Typees, the Scriptural injunction to increase and multiply seems to be but indifferently attended to. I never saw any of those large families, in arithmetical or stepladder progression, which one often meets with at home. I never knew of more than two youngsters living together in the same home, and but seldom even that number. As for the women, it was very plain that the anxieties of the nursery but seldom disturbed the serenity of their souls, and they were never to be seen going about the valley with half a score of little ones tugging at their apron-strings, or rather at the bread-fruit leaf they usually wore in the rear.

The ratio of increase among all the Polynesian nations is very small; and in some places as yet uncorrupted by intercourse with Europeans, the births would appear but very little to outnumber the deaths; the population in such instances remaining nearly the same for several successive generations, even upon those islands seldom or never desolated by wars, and among people with whom the crime of infanticide is altogether unknown. This would seem expressly ordained by Providence to prevent the overstocking of the islands with a race too indolent to cultivate the ground, and who, for that reason alone, would, by any considerable increase in their numbers, be exposed to the most deplorable misery. During the entire period of my stay in the valley of Typee, I never saw more than ten or twelve children under the age of six months, and only became aware of two births.

It is to the absence of the marriage tie that the late rapid decrease of the population of the Sandwich Islands and of Tahiti is in part to be ascribed. The vices and diseases introduced among these unhappy people annually swell the ordinary mortality of the islands, while, from the same cause, the originally small number of births is proportionally decreased. Thus the progress of the Hawaiians and Tahitians to utter extinction is accelerated in a sort of compound ratio.

I have before had occasion to remark that I never saw any of the ordinary signs of a place of sepulture in the valley, a circumstance which I attributed, at the time, to my living in a particular part of it, and being forbidden to extend my rambles to any considerable distance towards the sea. I have since thought it probable, however, that the Typees either desirous of removing from their sight the evidences of mortality, or prompted by a taste for rural beauty, may have some charming cemetery situated in the shadowy recesses along the base of the mountains. At Nukuheva, two or three large quadrangular pi-pis, heavily flagged, enclosed with regular stone walls, and shaded over and almost hidden from view by the interlacing branches of enormous trees, were pointed out to me as burial-places. The bodies, I understood, were deposited in rude vaults beneath the flagging, and were suffered to remain there without being disinterred. Although nothing could be more strange and gloomy than the aspect of these places, where the lofty trees threw their dark shadows over rude blocks of stone, a stranger in looking at them would have discerned none of the ordinary evidences of a place of sepulture.

During my stay in the valley, as none of its inmates were so accommodating as to die and be buried, in order to gratify my curiosity with regard to their funeral rites, I was reluctantly obliged to remain in ignorance of them. As I have reason to believe, however, that the observances of the Typees in these matters are the same with those of all the other tribes on the island, I will here relate a scene I chanced to witness at Nukuheva.

A young man had died, about daybreak, in a house near the beach. I had been sent ashore that morning, and saw a good deal of the preparations they were making for his obsequies. The body, neatly wrapped in new white tappa, was laid out in an open shed of cocoa-nut boughs, upon a bier constructed of elastic bamboos ingeniously twisted together. This was supported, about two feet from the ground, by large canes planted upright in the earth. Two females of a dejected appearance, watched by its side, plaintively chanting, and beating the air with large grass fans whitened with pipe-clay. In the dwelling-house adjoining, a numerous company were assembled, and various articles of food were being prepared for consumption. Two or three individuals, distinguished by headdresses of beautiful tappa, and wearing a great number of ornaments, appeared to officiate as masters of the ceremonies. By noon the entertainment had fairly begun, and we were told that it would last during the whole of the two following days. With the exception of those who mourned by the corpse, every one seemed disposed to drown the sense of the late bereavement in convivial indulgence. The girls, decked out in their savage finery, danced; the old men chanted; the warriors smoked and chatted; and the young and lusty, of both sexes, feasted plentifully, and seemed to enjoy themselves as pleasantly as they could have done had it been a wedding.

The islanders understand the art of embalming, and practice it with such success that the bodies of their great chiefs are frequently preserved for many years in the very houses where they died. I saw three of these in my visit to the Bay of Tior. One was enveloped in immense folds of tappa, with only the face exposed, and hung erect against the side of the dwelling. The others were stretched out upon biers of bamboo, in open, elevated temples, which seemed consecrated to their memory. The heads of enemies killed in battle are invariably preserved and hung up as trophies in the house of the conqueror. I am not acquainted with the process which is in use, but believe that fumigation is the principal agency employed. All the remains which I saw presented the appearance of a ham after being suspended for some time in a smoky chimney.

But to return from the dead to the living: The late festival had drawn together, as I had every reason to believe, the whole population of the vale, and consequently I was enabled to make some estimate with regard to its numbers. I should imagine that there were about two thousand inhabitants in Typee; and no number could have been better adapted to the extent of the valley. The valley is some nine miles in length, and may average one in breadth, the houses being distributed at wide intervals throughout its whole extent, principally, however, towards the head of the vale. There are no villages; the houses stand here and there in the shadow of the groves, or are scattered along the banks of the winding stream, their golden-hued bamboo sides and gleaming white thatch forming a beautiful contrast to the perpetual verdure in which they are embowered. There are no roads of any kind in the valley—nothing but a labyrinth of footpaths twisting and turning among the thickets without end.

The penalty of the Fall presses very lightly upon the valley of Typee; for, with the one solitary exception of striking a light, I scarcely saw any piece of work performed there which caused the sweat to stand upon a single brow. As for digging and delving for a livelihood, the thing is altogether unknown. Nature had planted the bread-fruit and the banana, and in her own good time she brings them to maturity, when the idle savage stretches forth his hand, and satisfies his appetite.

Ill-fated people! I shudder when I think of the change a few years will produce in their paradisiacal abode; and probably when the most destructive vices, and the worst attendances on civilisation, shall have driven all peace and happiness from the valley, the magnanimous French will proclaim to the world that the Marquesas Islands have been converted to Christianity! And this the Catholic world will doubtless consider as a glorious event. Heaven help the "Isles of the Sea"! The sympathy which Christendom feels for them has, alas! in too many instances proved their bane.

D. H. Lawrence (1885–1930)

The dance of the sprouting corn

Pale, dry, baked earth, that blows into dust of fine sand. Low hills of baked earth, sinking heavily, and speckled sparsely with dark dots of cedar bushes.

A river on the plain of drought, just a cleft of dark, reddish-brown water, almost a flood. And over all, the blue, uneasy, alkaline sky.

A pale, uneven, parched world, where a motor-car rocks and lurches and churns in sand. A world pallid with dryness, inhuman with a faint taste of alkali. Like driving in the bed of a great sea that dried up unthinkable ages ago, and now is drier than any other dryness, yet still reminiscent of the bottom of the sea, sand-hills sinking, and straight, cracked mesas, like cracks in the dry-mud bottom of the sea.

So, the mud church standing discreetly outside, just outside the pueblo, not to see too much. And on its facade of mud, under the timbered mud-eaves, two speckled horses rampant, painted by the Indians, a red piebald and a black one.

Swish! Over the logs of the ditch-bridge, where brown water is flowing full. There below is the pueblo, dried mud like mud-pie houses, all squatting in a jumble, prepared to crumble into dust and be invisible, dust to dust returning, earth to earth.

That they don't crumble is the mystery. That these little squarish mud-heads endure for centuries, while Greek marble tumbles asunder, and cathedrals totter, is the wonder. But then, the naked human hand with a bit of new soft mud is quicker than time, and defies the centuries.

Roughly the low, square, mud-pie houses make a wide street where all is naked earth save a doorway or a window with a pale-blue sash. At the end of the street, turn again into a parallel wide, dry street. And there, in the dry, oblong aridity, there tosses a small forest that is alive; and thud-thud goes the drum, and the deep sound of men singing is like the deep soughing of the wind, in the depths of a wood.

You realize that you had heard the drum from the distance, also the deep, distant roar and boom of the singing, but that you had not heeded, as you don't heed the wind.

It tosses like young, agile trees in a wind. This is the dance of the sprouting corn, and everybody holds a little, beating branch of green pine. Thud-thud-thud-thud-thud! goes the drum, heavily the men hop and hop and hop, sway, sway, sway, sway go the little branches of green pine. It tosses like a little forest, and the deep sound of men's singing is like the booming and tearing of a wind deep inside a forest. They are dancing the spring corn dance.

This is the Wednesday after Easter, after Christ Risen and the corn germinated. They danced on Monday and on Tuesday. Wednesday is the third and last dance of this green resurrection.

You realize the long lines of dancers, and a solid cluster of men singing near the drum. You realize the intermittent black-and-white fantasy of the hopping Koshare, the jesters, the Delight-Makers. You become aware of the ripple of bells on the knee-garters of the dancers, a continual pulsing ripple of the little bells; and of the sudden wild, whooping yells from near the drum. Then you become aware of the seed-like shudder of the gourd rattles, as the dance changes, and the swaying of the tufts of green pine-twigs stuck behind the arms of all the dancing men, in the broad green arm-bands.

Gradually comes through to you the black, stable solidity of the dancing women, who poise like solid shadow, one woman behind each rippling, leaping male. The long, silky black hair of the women, streaming down their backs, and the equally long, streaming, gleaming hair of the males, loose over broad, naked, orange-brown shoulders.

Then the faces, the impassive, rather fat, golden-brown faces of the women, with eyes cast down, crowned above with the green tableta, like a flat tiara. Something strange and noble about the impassive, barefoot women in the short black cassocks, as they subtly tread the dance, scarcely moving, and yet edging rhythmically along, swaying from each hand the green spray of pine-twig out-out-out-out, to the thud of the drum, immediately behind the leaping fox-skin of the men dancers. And all the emerald-green, painted tabletas, the flat wooden tiaras shaped like a castle gateway, rise steady and noble from the soft, slightly bowed heads of the women, held by a band under the chin. All the tabletas down the line, emerald green, almost steady, while the bright black heads of the men leap softly up and down, between.

Bit by bit you take it in. You cannot get a whole impression, save of some sort of wood tossing, a little forest of trees in motion, with gleaming black hair and gold-ruddy breasts that somehow do not destroy the illusion of forest.

When you look at the women, you forget the men. The bare-armed, bare-legged, barefoot women with streaming hair and lofty green tiaras, impassive, downward-looking faces, twigs swaying outwards from subtle, rhythmic wrists; women clad in the black, prehistoric short gown fastened over one shoulder, leaving the other shoulder bare, and showing at the arm-place a bit of pink or white undershirt; belted also round the waist with a woven woollen sash, scarlet and green on the hand-woven black cassock. The noble, slightly submissive bending of the tiara-ed head. The subtle measure of the bare, breathing, bird-like feet, that are flat, and seem to cleave to earth softly, and softly lift away. The continuous outward swaying of the pine-sprays.

But when you look at the men, you forget the women. The men are naked to the waist, and ruddy-golden, and in the rhythmic, hopping leap of the dance their breasts shake downwards, as the strong, heavy body comes down, down, down, down, in the downward plunge of the dance. The black hair streams loose and living down their backs, the black brows are level, the black eyes look out unchanging from under the silky lashes. They are handsome, and absorbed with a deep rhythmic absorption, which still leaves them awake and aware. Down, down, down they drop, on the heavy, ceaseless leap of the dance, and the great necklaces of shell-cores spring on the naked breasts, the neck-shell flaps up and down, the short white kilt of woven stuff, with the heavy woollen embroidery, green and red and black, opens and shuts slightly to the strong lifting of the knees: the heavy whitish cords that hang from the kilt-band at the side sway and coil forever down the side of the right leg, down to the ankle, the bells on the red-woven garters under the knees ripple without end, and the feet, in buckskin boots furred round the ankle with a beautiful band of skunk fur, black with a white tip, come down with a lovely, heavy, soft precision, first one, then the other, dropping always plumb to earth. Slightly bending forward, a black gourd rattle in the right hand, a small green bough in the left, the dancer dances the eternal drooping leap, that brings his life down, down, down, down from the mind, down from the broad, beautiful, shaking breast, down to the powerful pivot of the knees, then to the ankles, and plunges deep from the ball of the foot into the earth, towards the earth's red centre, where these men belong, as is signified by the red earth with which they are smeared.

And meanwhile, the shell-cores from the Pacific sway up and down, ceaselessly, on their breasts.

Mindless, without effort, under the hot sun, unceasing, yet never perspiring nor even breathing heavily, they dance on and on. Mindless, yet still listening, observing. They hear the deep, surging singing of the bunch of old men, like a great wind soughing. They hear the cries and yells of the man waving his bough by the drum. They catch the word of the song, and at a moment, shudder the black rattles, wheel, and the line breaks, women from men, they thread across to a new formation. And as the men wheel round, their black hair gleams and shakes, and the long fox-skin sways, like a tail.

And always, when they form into line again, it is a beautiful long straight line, flexible as life, but straight as rain.

The men round the drum are old, or elderly. They are all in a bunch, and they wear day dress, loose cotton drawers, pink or white cotton shirt, hair tied up behind with the red cords, and banded round the head with a strip of pink rag, or white rag, or blue. There they are, solid like a cluster of bees, their black heads with the pink rag circles all close together, swaying their pine-twigs with rhythmic, wind-swept hands, dancing slightly, mostly on the right foot, ceaselessly, and singing, their black bright eyes absorbed, their dark lips pushed out, while the deep strong sound rushes like wind, and the unknown words form themselves in the dark.

Suddenly the solitary man pounding the drum swings his drum round, and begins to pound on the other end, on a higher note, pang-pang-pang! instead of the previous brumm! brumm! brumm! of the bass note. The watchful man next the drummer yells and waves lightly, dancing on bird-feet. The Koshare make strange, eloquent gestures to the sky.

And again the gleaming bronze-and-dark men dancing in the rows shudder their rattles, break the rhythm, change into a queer, beautiful two-step, the long lines suddenly curl into rings, four rings of dancers, the leaping, gleaming-seeming men between the solid, subtle, submissive blackness of the women who are crowned with emerald-green tiaras, all going subtly round in rings. Then slowly they change again, and form a star. Then again, unmingling, they come back into rows.

And all the while, all the while the naked Koshare are threading about. Of bronze-and-dark men dancers there are some forty-two, each with a dark, crowned woman attending him like a shadow. The old men, the bunch of singers in shirts and tied-up black hair, are about sixty in number, or sixty-four. The Koshare are about twenty-four.

They are slim and naked, daubed with black-and-white earth, their hair daubed white and gathered upwards to a great knot on top of the head, whence springs a tuft of corn-husks, dry corn leaves. Though they wear nothing but a little black square cloth, front and back, at their middle, they do not seem naked, for some are white with black spots, like a leopard, and some have broad black lines or zigzags on their smeared bodies, and all their faces are blackened with triangles or lines till they look like weird masks. Meanwhile their hair, gathered straight up and daubed white and sticking up from the top of the head with corn-husks, completes the fantasy. They are anything but natural. Like blackened ghosts of a dead corn-cob, tufted at the top.

And all the time, running like queer spotted dogs, they weave nakedly through the unheeding dance, comical, weird, dancing the dance-step naked and fine, prancing through the lines, up and down the lines, and making fine gestures with their flexible hands, calling something down from the sky, calling something up from the earth, and dancing forward all the time. Suddenly as they catch a word from the singers, name of a star, of a wind, a name for the sun, for a cloud, their hands soar up and gather in the air, soar down with a slow motion. And again, as they catch a word that means earth, earth deeps, water within the earth, or red-earth-quickening, the hands flutter softly down, and draw up the water, draw up the earth quickening, earth to sky, sky to earth, influences above to influences below, to meet in the germ-quick of corn, where life is.

And as they dance, the Koshare watch the dancing men. And if a fox-skin is coming loose at the belt, they fasten it as the man dances, or they stoop and tie another man's shoe. For the dancer must not hesitate to the end.

And then, after some forty minutes, the drum stops. Slowly the dancers file into one line, women behind men, and move away, threading towards their kiva, with no sound but the tinkle of knee-bells in the silence.

But at the same moment the thud of an unseen drum, from beyond, the soughing of deep song approaching from the unseen. It is the other half, the other half of the tribe coming to continue the dance. They appear round the kiva—one Koshare and one dancer leading the rows, the old men all abreast, singing already in a great strong burst.

So, from ten o'clock in the morning till about four in the afternoon, first one-half then the other. Till at last, as the day wanes, the two halves meet, and the two singings like two great winds surge one past the other, and the thicket of the dance becomes a real forest. It is the close of the third day.

Afterwards, the men and women crowd on the roofs of the two low round towers, the kivas, while the Koshare run round jesting and miming, and taking big offerings from the women, loaves of bread and cakes of blue-maize meal. Women come carrying big baskets of bread and guayaba, on two hands, an offering.

And the mystery of germination, not procreation, but putting forth, resurrection, life springing within the seed, is accomplished. The sky has its fire, its waters, its stars, its wandering electricity, its winds, its fingers of cold. The earth has its reddened body, its invisible hot heart, its inner waters and many juices and unaccountable stuffs. Between them all, the little seed: and also man, like a seed that is busy and aware. And from the heights and from the depths man, the caller, calls: a man, the knower, brings down the influences and brings up the influences, with his knowledge: man, so vulnerable, so subject, and yet even in his vulnerability and subjection, a master, commands the invisible influences and is obeyed. Commands in that song, in that rhythmic energy of dance, in that still-submissive mockery of the Koshare. And he accomplishes his end, as master. He partakes in the springing of the corn, in the rising and budding and earing of the corn. And when he eats his bread, at last, he recovers all he once sent forth, and partakes again of the energies he called to the corn, from out of the wide universe.

F. Scott Fitzgerald (1896–1940)

Echoes of the jazz age

It is too soon to write about the Jazz Age with perspective, and without being suspected of premature arteriosclerosis. Many people still succumb to violent retching when they happen upon any of its characteristic words—words which have since yielded in vividness to the coinages of the underworld. It is as dead as were the Yellow Nineties in 1902. Yet the present writer already looks back to it with nostalgia. It bore him up, flattered him and gave him more money than he had dreamed of, simply for telling people that he felt as they did, that something had to be done with all the nervous energy stored up and unexpended in the War.

The ten-year period that, as if reluctant to die outmoded in its bed, leaped to a spectacular death in October, 1929, began about the time of the May Day riots in 1919. When the police rode down the demobilized country boys gaping at the orators in Madison Square, it was the sort of measure bound to alienate the more intelligent young men from the prevailing order. We didn't remember anything about the Bill of Rights until Mencken began plugging it, but we did know that such tyranny belonged in the jittery little countries of South Europe. If goose-livered businessmen had this effect on the government, then maybe we had gone to war for J. P. Morgan's loans after all. But, because we were tired of Great Causes, there was no more than a short outbreak of moral indignation, typified by Dos Passos' *Three Soldiers*. Presently we began to have slices of the national cake and our idealism only flared up when the newspapers made melodrama out of such stories as Harding and the Ohio Gang or Sacco and Vanzetti. The events of 1919 left us cynical rather than revolutionary, in spite of the fact that now we are all rummaging around in our trunks wondering where in hell we left the liberty cap—"I know I had it"—and the moujik blouse. It was characteristic of the Jazz Age that it had no interest in politics at all.

It was an age of miracles, it was an age of art, it was an age of excess, and it was an age of satire. A Stuffed Shirt, squirming to blackmail in a lifelike way, sat upon the throne of the United States; a stylish young man hurried over to represent to us the throne of England. A world of girls yearned for the young Englishman; the old American groaned in his sleep as he waited to be poisoned by his wife, upon the advice of the female Rasputin who then made the ultimate decision in our national affairs. But such matters apart, we had things our way at last. With Americans ordering suits by the gross in London, the Bond Street tailors perforce agreed to moderate their cut to the American long-waisted figure and loose-fitting taste, something subtle passed to America, the style of man. During the Renaissance, Francis the First looked to Florence to trim his leg. Seventeenth-century England aped the court of France, and fifty years ago the German Guards officer bought his civilian clothes in London. Gentlemen's clothes—symbol of "the power that man must hold and that passes from race to race."

We were the most powerful nation. Who could tell us any longer what was fashionable and what was fun? Isolated during the European War, we had begun combing the unknown South and West for folkways and pastimes, and there were more ready to hand.

The first social revelation created a sensation out of all proportion to its novelty. As far back as 1915 the unchaperoned young people of the smaller cities had discovered the mobile privacy of that automobile given to young Bill at sixteen to make him "self-reliant." At first petting was a desperate adventure even under such favorable conditions, but presently confidences were exchanged and the old commandment broke down. As early as 1917 there were references to such sweet and casual dalliance in any number of the Yale Record or the Princeton Tiger.

But petting in its more audacious manifestations was confined to the wealthier classes—among other young people the old standard prevailed until after the War, and a kiss meant that a proposal was expected, as young officers in strange cities sometimes discovered to their dismay. Only in 1920 did the veil finally fall—the Jazz Age was in flower.

Scarcely had the staider citizens of the republic caught their breaths when the wildest of all generations, the generation which had been adolescent during the confusion of the War, brusquely shouldered my contemporaries out of the way and danced into the limelight. This was the generation whose girls dramatized themselves as flappers, the generation that corrupted its elders and eventually overreached itself less through lack of morals than through lack of taste. May one offer in exhibit the year 1922! That was the peak of the younger generation, for though the Jazz Age continued, it became less and less an affair of youth.

The sequel was like a children's party taken over by the elders, leaving the children puzzled and rather neglected and rather taken aback. By 1923 their elders, tired of watching the carnival with ill-concealed envy, had discovered that young liquor will take the place of young blood, and with a whoop the orgy began. The younger generation was starred no longer.

A whole race going hedonistic, deciding on pleasure. The precocious intimacies of the younger generation would have come about with or without prohibition—they were implicit in the attempt to adapt English customs to American conditions. (Our South, for example, is tropical and early maturing—it has never been part of the wisdom of France and Spain to let young girls go unchaperoned at sixteen and seventeen.) But the general decision to be amused that began with the cocktail parties of 1921 had more complicated origins.

The word jazz in its progress toward respectability has meant first sex, then dancing, then music. It is associated with a state of nervous stimulation, not unlike that of big cities behind the lines of a war. To many English the War still goes on because all the forces that menace them are still active— Wherefore eat, drink and be merry, for tomorrow we die. But different causes had now brought about a corresponding state in America—though there were entire classes (people over fifty, for example) who spent a whole decade denying its existence even when its puckish face peered into the family circle. Never did they dream that they had contributed to it. The honest citizens of every class, who believed in a strict public morality and were powerful enough to enforce the necessary legislation, did not know that they would necessarily be served by criminals and quacks, and do not really believe it today. Rich righteousness had always been able to buy honest and intelligent servants to free the slaves or the Cubans, so when this attempt collapsed our elders stood firm with all the stubbornness of people involved in a weak case, preserving their righteousness and losing their children. Silver-haired women and men with fine old faces, people who never did a consciously dishonest thing in their lives, still assure each other in the apartment hotels of New York and Boston and Washington that "there's a whole generation growing up that will never know the taste of liquor." Meanwhile their granddaughters pass the well-thumbed copy of *Lady Chatterley's Lover* around the boarding-school and, if they get about at all, know the taste of gin or corn at sixteen. But the generation who reached maturity between 1875 and 1895 continue to believe what they want to believe.

Even the intervening generations were incredulous. In 1920 Heywood Broun announced that all this hubbub was nonsense, that young men didn't kiss but told anyhow. But very shortly people over twenty-five came in for an intensive education. Let me trace some of the revelations vouch-safed them by reference to a dozen works written for various types of mentality during the decade. We begin with the suggestion that Don Juan leads an interesting life (*Jurgen*, 1919); then we learn that there's a lot of sex around if we only knew it (*Winesburg, Ohio*, 1920) that adolescents lead very amorous lives (*This Side of Paradise*, 1920), that there are a lot of neglected Anglo-Saxon words (*Ulysses*, 1921), that older people don't always resist sudden temptations (*Cytherea*, 1922), that girls are sometimes seduced without being ruined (*Flaming Youth*, 1922), that even rape often turns out well (*The Sheik*, 1922), that glamorous English ladies are often promiscuous (*The Green Hat*, 1924), that in fact they devote most of their time to it (*The Vortex*, 1926), that it's a damn good thing too (*Lady Chatterley's Lover*, 1928), and finally that there are abnormal variations (*The Well of Loneliness*, 1928, and *Sodom and Gomorrah*, 1929).

In my opinion the erotic element in these works, even *The Sheik* written for children in the key of *Peter Rabbit*, did not one particle of harm. Everything they described, and much more, was familiar in our contemporary life. The majority of the theses were honest and elucidating—their effect was to restore some dignity to the male as opposed to the he-man in American life. ("And what is a 'He-man'?" demanded Gertrude Stein one day. "Isn't it a large enough order to fill out to the dimensions of all that 'a man' has meant in the past? A 'He-man'!") The married woman can now discover whether she is being cheated, or whether sex is just something to be endured and her compensation should be to establish a tyranny of the spirit, as her mother may have hinted. Perhaps many women found that love was meant to be fun. Anyhow the objectors lost their tawdry little case, which is one reason why our literature is now the most living in the world.

Contrary to popular opinion, the movies of the Jazz Age had no effect upon its morals. The social attitude of the producers was timid, behind the times and banal—for example, no picture mirrored even faintly the younger generation until 1923, when magazines had already been started to celebrate it and it had long ceased to be news. There were a few feeble splutters and then Clara Bow in *Flaming Youth;* promptly the Hollywood hacks ran the theme into its cinematographic grave. Throughout the Jazz Age the movies got no farther than Mrs. Jiggs keeping up with its most blatant superficialities. This was no doubt due to the censorship as well as to innate conditions in the industry. In any case, the Jazz Age now raced along under its own power, served by great filling stations full of money.

The people over thirty, the people all the way up to fifty, had joined the dance. We graybeards (to tread down F.P.A.) remember the uproar when in 1912 grandmothers of forty tossed away their crutches and took lessons in the Tango and the Castle-Walk. A dozen years later a woman might pack the *Green Hat* with her other affairs as she set off for Europe or New York, but Savonarola was too busy flogging dead horses in Augean stables of his own creation to notice. Society, even in small cities, now dined in separate chambers, and the sober table learned about the gay table only from hearsay. There were very few people left at the sober table. One of its former glories, the less sought-after girls who had become resigned to sublimating a portable celibacy, came across Freud and Jung in seeking their intellectual recompense and came tearing back into the fray.

By 1926 the universal preoccupation with sex had become a nuisance. (I remember a perfectly mated, contented young mother asking my wife's advice about "having an affair right away," though she had no one especially in mind, "because don't you think it's sort of undignified when you get much over thirty?") For a while bootleg Negro records with their phallic euphemisms made everything suggestive, and simultaneously came a wave of erotic plays—young girls from finishing schools packed the galleries to hear about the romance of being a Lesbian and George Jean Nathan protested. Then one young producer lost his head entirely, drank a beauty's alcoholic bath-water and went to the penitentiary. Somehow his pathetic attempt at romance belongs to the Jazz Age, while his contemporary in prison, Ruth Snyder, had to be hoisted into it by the tabloids—she was, as the Daily News hinted deliciously to gourmets, about "to cook, and sizzle, *AND FRY!*" in the electric chair.

The gay elements of society had divided into two main streams, one flowing toward Palm Beach and Deauville, and the other, much smaller, toward the summer Riviera. One could get away with more on the summer Riviera, and whatever happened seemed to have something to do with art. From 1926 to 1929, the great years of the Cap d'Antibes, this corner of France was dominated by a group quite distinct from that American society which is dominated by Europeans. Pretty much of anything went at Antibes —by 1929, at the most gorgeous paradise for swimmers on the Mediterranean no one swam any more, save for a short hang-over dip at noon. There was a picturesque gradation of steep rocks over the sea and somebody's valet and an occasional English girl used to dive from them, but the Americans were content to discuss each other in the bar. This was indicative of something that was taking place in the homeland—Americans were getting soft. There were signs everywhere; we still won the Olympic games but with champions whose names had few vowels in them—teams composed, like the fighting Irish combination of Notre Dame, of fresh overseas blood. Once the French became really interested, the Davis Cup gravitated automatically to their intensity in competition. The vacant lots of the Middle-Western cities were built up now—except for a short period in school, we were not turning out to be an athletic people like the British, after all. The hare and the tortoise. Of course if we wanted to we could be in a minute; we still had all those reserves of ancestral vitality, but one day in 1926 we looked down and found we had flabby arms and a fat pot and couldn't say boop-boop-a-doop to a Sicilian. Shades of Van Bibber!—no utopian ideal, God knows. Even golf, once considered an effeminate game, had seemed very strenuous of late—an emasculated form appeared and proved just right.

By 1927 a wide-spread neurosis began to be evident, faintly signalled, like a nervous beating of the feet, by the popularity of cross-word puzzles. I remember a fellow ex-patriate opening a letter from a mutual friend of ours, urging him to come home and be revitalized by the hardy, bracing qualities of the native soil. It was a strong letter and it affected us both deeply, until we noticed that it was headed from a nerve-sanitarium in Pennsylvania.

By this time contemporaries of mine had begun to disappear into the dark maw of violence. A classmate killed his wife and himself on Long Island, another tumbled "accidentally" from a skyscraper in Philadelphia, another purposely from a skyscraper in New York. One was killed in a speak-easy in Chicago; another was beaten to death in a speak-easy in New York and crawled home to the Princeton Club to die; still another had his skull crushed by a maniac's axe in an insane asylum where he was confined. These are not catastrophes that I went out of my way to look for—these were my friends; moreover, these things happened not during the depression but during the boom.

In the spring of '27, something bright and alien flashed across the sky. A young Minnesotan who seemed to have had nothing to do with his generation did a heroic thing, and for a moment people set down their glasses in country clubs and speakeasies and thought of their old best dreams. Maybe there was a way out by flying, maybe our restless blood could find frontiers in the illimitable air. But by that time we were all pretty well committed; and the Jazz Age continued; we would all have one more.

Nevertheless, Americans were wandering ever more widely—friends seemed eternally bound for Russia, Persia, Abyssinia and Central Africa. And by 1928 Paris had grown suffocating. With each new shipment of Americans spewed up by the boom the quality fell off, until toward the end there was something sinister about the crazy boatloads. They were no longer the simple pa and ma and son and daughter, infinitely in their qualities of kindness and curiosity to the corresponding class in Europe, but fantastic neanderthals who believed something, something vague, that you remembered from a very cheap novel. I remember an Italian on a steamer who promenaded the deck in an American Reserve Officer's uniform picking quarrels in broken English with Americans who criticised their own institutions in the bar. I remember a fat Jewess, inlaid with diamonds, who sat behind us at the Russian ballet and said as the curtain rose, "Thad's luffly, dey ought to baint a bicture of it." This was low comedy, but it was evident that money and power were falling into the hands of people in comparison with whom the leader of a village Soviet would be a gold-mine of judgement and culture. There were citizens travelling in luxury in 1928 and 1929 who, in the distortion of their new condition, had the human value of Pekinese, bivalves, cretins, goats. I remember the Judge from some New York district who had taken his daughter to see the Bayeux Tapestries and made a scene in the papers advocating their segregation because one scene was immoral. But in those days life was like the race in *Alice in Wonderland*, there was a prize for every one.

The Jazz Age had had a wild youth and a heady middle age. There was the phase of the necking parties, the Leopold-Loeb murder (I remember the time my wife was arrested on Queensborough Bridge on the suspicion of being the "Bob-haired Bandit"), and the John Held Clothes. In the second phase such phenomena as sex and murder became more mature, if much more conventional. Middle age must be served and pajamas came to the beach to save fat thighs and flabby calves from competition with the one-piece bathing-suit. Finally skirts came down and everything was concealed. Everybody was at scratch now. Let's go—

But it was not to be. Somebody had blundered and the most expensive orgy in history was over.

It ended two years ago,* because the utter confidence which was its

*1929.

essential prop received an enormous jolt, and it didn't take long for the flimsy structure to settle earthward. And after two years the Jazz Age seems as far away as the days before the War. It was borrowed time anyhow—the whole upper tenth of a nation living with the insouciance of grand ducs and the casualness of chorus girls. But moralizing is easy now and it was pleasant to be in one's twenties in such a certain and unworried time. Even when you were broke you didn't worry about money, because it was in such profusion around you. Toward the end one had a struggle to pay one's share; it was almost a favor to accept hospitality that required any travelling. Charm, notoriety, mere good manners, weighed more than money as a social asset. This was rather splendid, but things were getting thinner and thinner as the eternal necessary human values tried to spread over all that expansion. Writers were geniuses on the strength of one respectable book or play; just as during the War officers of four months' experience commanded hundreds of men, so there were now many little fish lording it over great big bowls. In the theatrical world extravagant productions were carried by a few second-rate stars, and so on up the scale into politics, where it was difficult to interest good men in positions of the highest importance and responsibility, importance and responsibility far exceeding that of business executives but which paid only five or six thousand a year.

Now once more the belt is tight and we summon the proper expression of horror as we look back at our wasted youth. Sometimes, though, there is a ghostly rumble among the drums, an asthmatic whisper in the trombones that swings me back into the early twenties when we drank wood alcohol and every day in every way grew better and better, and there was a first abortive shortening of the skirts, and girls all looked alike in sweater dresses, and people you didn't want to know said "Yes, we have no bananas," and it seemed only a question of a few years before the older people would step aside and let the world be run by those who saw things as they were— and it all seems rosy and romantic to us who were young then, because we will never feel quite so intensely about our surroundings any more.

Social control

The term *social control* refers to those social mechanisms by which a group or society exercises its dominion over component individuals and enforces conformity to its norms. It refers to those regulative institutions that insure that individual behavior be in conformity with group demands. The range of mechanisms for such control is wide indeed. Not only law, but customs, folkways and even fashions operate to enforce conformity. Furthermore, modern sociological thought, following the lead of Durkheim and Freud, has now fully understood that social control, far from involving only external regulation of the person's conduct becomes in fact *internalized* in the individual so that the moral demands of society become constitutive elements of the individual's personality. While there may never be a perfect fit between individual demands and societal requirements, social control mechanisms insure that most individuals in most situations like to do the things they have to do.

The selection from the contemporary American novelist John Steinbeck illustrates the gradual emergence of social control mechanisms and of a normative structure among the fluid living conditions of migratory workers who are partly emancipated from the ordinary controls of American society. The short excerpt from the fourteenth-century Italian writer Franco Sacchetti indicates that the "tyranny of fashion" is by no means a modern phenomenon. Lev Tolstoi shows us that in nineteenth-century Russia "other directed men" were tuned in to the demands of public opinion. Nathaniel Hawthorne illustrates the control functions of legal punishment and their anchorage in group opinion.

Our selections from Dostoevski and Thomas Campanella, insofar as they discuss the philosophy behind a deliberate imposition of total social control, are of a somewhat different character. In his powerful parable, "The Grand Inquisitor," the great Russian novelist evokes in most imaginative a manner one of the central questions of human life in society: do men strive for freedom or do they not rather flee from freedom in order to gain controlled security? "The Grand Inquisitor," which is part of Dostoevski's great novel *The Brothers Karamazov*, pictures the return of Christ to earth and his encounter with the Grand Inquisitor, the representative of the hierarchy of Christ's Church. The Grand Inquisitor accuses Christ of having brought to men a freedom which they cannot endure. The Church represents the principle of order and authority; once men will be fully controlled, they will be secured against the temptations of freedom, the Grand Inquisitor argues. His arguments represent, so-to-speak, the extreme embodiment of the principle of social control.

When the Calabrian rebel monk, Thomas Campanella, wrote his utopian description of an ideal state, *The City of the Sun*, he meant to impress his readers with a picture of a society organized according to philosophical principles. The chief ruler, Metaphysicus, assisted by three subsidiary princes, Power, Wisdom and Love, rules the City according to the demands of total rationality. Yet, the modern reader will not be slow to discern in this picture so lovingly sketched by a rebel who spent many years in imprisonment, a frightening anticipation of the totalitarian state. *The City of the Sun* can be read as a kind of unwitting depiction of the principle of social control gone mad.

John Steinbeck (1902–1968)

The world of migratory workers

The cars of the migrant people crawled out of the side roads onto the great cross-country highway, and they took the migrant way to the West. In the daylight they scuttled like bugs to the westward; and as the dark caught them, they clustered like bugs near to shelter and to water. And because they were lonely and perplexed, because they had all come from a place of sadness and worry and defeat, and because they were all going to a new mysterious place, they huddled together; they talked together; they shared their lives, their food, and the things they hoped for in the new country. Thus it might be that one family camped near a spring, and another camped for the spring and for company, and a third because two families had pioneered the place and found it good. And when the sun went down, perhaps twenty families and twenty cars were there.

In the evening a strange thing happened: the twenty families became one family, the children were the children of all. The loss of home became one loss, and the golden time in the West was one dream. And it might be that a sick child threw despair into the hearts of twenty families, of a hundred people; that a birth there in a tent kept a hundred people quiet and awestruck through the night and filled a hundred people with a birth-joy in the morning. A family which the night before had been lost and fearful might search its goods to find a present for a new baby. In the evening, sitting about the fires, the twenty were one. They grew to be units of the camps, units of the evenings and the nights. A guitar unwrapped from a blanket and tuned— and the songs, which were all of the people, were sung in the nights. Men sang the words, and women hummed the tunes.

Every night a world created, complete with furniture—friends made and enemies established; a world complete with braggarts and with cowards, with quiet men, with humble men, with kindly men. Every night relationships that make a world, established; and every morning the world torn down like a circus.

At first the families were timid in the building and tumbling worlds, but gradually the technique of building worlds became their technique. Then leaders emerged, then laws were made, then codes came into being. And as the worlds moved westward they were more complete and better furnished, for their builders were more experienced in building them.

The families learned what rights must be observed—the right of privacy in the tent; the right to keep the black past hidden in the heart; the right to talk and to listen; the right to refuse help or to accept, to offer help or to decline it; the right of son to court and daughter to be courted; the right of the hungry to be fed; the rights of the pregnant and the sick to transcend all other rights.

And the families learned, although no one told them, what rights are monstrous and must be destroyed: the right to intrude upon privacy, the right to be noisy while the camp slept, the right of seduction or rape, the right of adultery and theft and murder. These rights were crushed, because the little worlds could not exist for even a night with such rights alive.

And as the worlds moved westward, rules became laws, although no one told the families. It is unlawful to foul near the camp; it is unlawful in any way to foul the drinking water; it is unlawful to eat good rich food near one who is hungry, unless he is asked to share.

And with the laws, the punishments—and there were only two—a quick and murderous fight or ostracism; the ostracism was the worst. For if one broke the laws his name and face went with him, and he had no place in any world, no matter where created.

In the worlds, social conduct became fixed and rigid, so that a man must say "Good morning" when asked for it, so that a man might have a willing girl if he stayed with her, if he fathered her children and protected them. But a man might not have one girl one night and another the next, for this would endanger the worlds.

The families moved westward, and the technique of building the worlds improved so that the people could be safe in their worlds; and the form was so fixed that a family acting in the rules knew it was safe in the rules.

There grew up government in the worlds, with leaders, with elders. A man who was wise found that his wisdom was needed in every camp; a man who was a fool could not change his folly with his world. And a kind of insurance developed in these nights. A man with food fed a hungry man, and thus insured himself against hunger. And when a baby died a pile of silver coins grew at the door flap, for a baby must be well buried, since it has had nothing else of life. An old man may be left in a potter's field, but not a baby.

A certain physical pattern is needed for the building of a world—water, a river bank, a stream, a spring, or even a faucet unguarded. And there is needed enough flat land to pitch the tents, a little brush or wood to build the fires. If there is a garbage dump not too far off, all the better; for there can be found equipment—stove tops, a curved fender to shelter the fire, and cans to cook in and to eat from.

And the worlds were built in the evening. The people, moving in from the highways, made them with their tents and their hearts and their brains.

In the morning the tents came down, the canvas was folded, the tent poles tied along the running board, the beds put in place on the cars, the pots in their places. And as the families moved westward, the technique of building up a home in the evening and tearing it down with the morning light became fixed; so that the folded tent was packed in one place, the cooking pots counted in their box. And as the cars moved westward, each member of the family grew into his proper place, grew into his duties; so that each member, old and young, had his place in the car; so that in the weary, hot evenings, when the cars pulled into the camping places, each member had his duty and went to it without instruction: children to gather wood, to carry water; men to pitch the tents and bring down the beds; women to cook the supper and to watch while the family fed. And this was done without command. The families, which had been units of which the boundaries were a house at night, a farm by day, changed their boundaries. In the long hot light, they were silent in the cars moving slowly westward; but at night they integrated with any group they found.

Franco Sacchetti (1335–1409)

Fashions in fourteenth century Italy

But was not this fashion of wearing gorgets the most extraordinary of all the fashions in the world? Of all that were ever seen in the world, this was the strangest and the most tiresome. And I, the writer, remember hearing Salvestro Brunelleschi relate that, after having dwelt a long time in Friuli, he returned to Florence just when his kindred were engaged in a very great quarrel with a neighbouring family called Agli. It so happened that one of these Agli, named Guernizo, returned home from Germany at this time; and either on account of the name, or because he was reputed a very fierce man, all the Brunelleschi armed themselves in such a manner that Salvestro was made to wear a gorget. And that morning at dinner a dish of beans was placed before him, and taking a spoonful to put them into his mouth, he dropped them down inside his gorget. The beans were very hot, and scalded his neck and throat so badly that he cried, "I put on the gorget for fear of Guernizo, and it hath caused me to burn my whole throat!" and rising up from the table he took off the gorget and cast it on the floor, saying, "I would rather be put to death by mine enemies than kill myself."

How many fashions have been altered in my time by the changeableness of those persons now living, and especially in mine own city! Formerly the women wore their bodices cut so open that they were uncovered to beneath

---

From *Tales of Sacchetti*, translated by M. G. Steegmann.

their armpits! Then with one jump, they wore their collars right up to their ears. And these are all outrageous fashions. I, the writer, could recite as many more of the customs and fashions which have been changed in my days as would fill a book as large as this whole volume. But although they were constantly changing in this city of ours, they were not invariable either in most of the other great cities of the world. And although formerly the Genoese never altered the fashion of their dress, and neither the Venetians nor the Catalans altered theirs, nor did their women either, nowadays it seemeth to me that the whole world is united in having but little firmness of mind; for the men and women of Florence, Genoa, Venice, Catalonia, indeed of all the Christian world, go dressed in the same manner, not being able to distinguish one from another. And would to Heaven they all remained fixed upon the same manner, but quite the contrary! For if one jay do but appear with a new fashion, all the world doth copy it. So that the whole world, but most especially Italy, is variable and hastens to adopt the new fashions. The young maidens, who used to dress with so much modesty, have now raised the hanging ends of their hoods and have twisted them into caps, and they go attired like common women, wearing caps, and collars and strings round their necks, with divers kinds of beasts hung upon their breasts. And what more wretched, dangerous, and useless fashion ever existed than that of wearing such sleeves as they do, or great sacks, as they might rather be called? They cannot raise a glass or take a mouthful without soiling both their sleeves and the tablecloth by upsetting the glasses on the table. Likewise do youths wear these immense sleeves, but still worse is it when even sucklings are dressed in them. The women wear hoods and cloaks. The young men for the most part go without cloaks and wear their hair long; they need but divest themselves of their breeches and they will then have left off everything they can, and truly these are so small that they could easily do without them. They put their legs into tight socks and upon their wrists they hang a yard of cloth; they put more cloth into the making of a glove than into a hood. Perchance they will thereby all do penance for their many vanities. For whoever liveth but one day in this world changeth his fashions a thousand times; each one seeketh liberty and yet depriveth himself of it. The Lord created our feet free, yet many persons are unable to walk on account of the long points of their shoes. He created legs with joints, but many have so stiffened them with strings and laces that they can scarcely sit down; their bodies are drawn in tightly, their arms are burdened with a train of cloth, their necks are squeezed into their hoods and their heads into a sort of nightcap, whereby all day they feel as though their heads were being sawn off. Truly there would be no end to describing the women's attire, considering the extravagance of their dress from their feet up to their heads, and how every day they are up on the roofs, some curling their hair, some smoothing it, and some bleaching it, so that often they die of the colds they catch!

Oh, the vanity of human power! Through thee true glory it lost! But I will speak no more of these things, for I should so engross myself in their misdeeds that I should be able to discourse of nothing else.

Lev Tolstoi (1828–1910)

An other directed man

Having finished his letters, Stepan Arkadevich moved up the papers from the court, rapidly turned over the leaves of two cases, made a few remarks on them with a large pencil, and, pushing the papers aside, betook himself to his coffee: while drinking it, he unfolded the still damp morning paper and began to read it.

Stepan Arkadevich subscribed to a liberal paper,—not of the extreme, but of the tendency to which the majority belonged. And although neither science, nor art, nor politics especially interested him, he firmly held to those opinions on all these subjects which the majority and his gazette professed, and changed them only when the majority changed them, or, to be more correct,—he did not change them, but they themselves changed in him imperceptibly.

Stepan Arkadevich chose neither direction nor views, but these directions and views came to him of their own accord, just as he did not choose the shape of his hat or coat, but took those that everybody wore. For him, living as he was in a certain society, with the need of some mental activity, which generally is developed at maturity, it was as necessary to have views as it was to have a hat. If there was a reason why he preferred the liberal tendency to the conservative, to which many of his circle belonged, it was not due to his finding the liberal tendency more sensible, but because it more nearly fitted in with his mode of life. The liberal party said that in Russia everything was bad, and, indeed, Stepan Arkadevich had many debts, while there was a definite want of money. The liberal party said that marriage was an obsolete institution and that it was necessary to reconstruct it, and, indeed, his domestic life gave him little pleasure and compelled him to lie and pretend, which was so contrary to his nature. The liberal party said, or rather implied, that religion was only a check for the barbarous part of the population, and, indeed, he could not endure even a short divine service without a pain in his legs, and could not comprehend what those terrible and turgid words about the world to come were for, when he was happy enough in this.

At the same time, Stepan Arkadevich, who was fond of a merry joke,

From *Anna Karenina* by Lev Tolstoi (1876), translated by Leo Wiener.

now and then took pleasure in baffling some inoffensive man by telling him that, if a man is to take any pride at all in his genealogy, there was no sense in stopping at Rurik and rejecting the first ancestor, the ape. Thus the liberal tendency became his habit, and he was fond of his gazette, as of a cigar after dinner, for the light mist which it raised in his head.

Nathaniel Hawthorne (1804–1864)

In the pillory

The grass-plot before the jail, in Prison-lane, on a certain summer morning, not less than two centuries ago, was occupied by a pretty large number of the inhabitants of Boston; all with their eyes intently fastened on the iron-clamped oaken door. Among any other population, or at a later period in the history of New England, the grim rigidity that petrified the bearded physiognomies of these good people would have augured some awful business in hand. It could have betokened nothing short of the anticipated execution of some noted culprit, on whom the sentence of a legal tribunal had but confirmed the verdict of public sentiment. But, in that early severity of the Puritan character, an inference of this kind could not so indubitably be drawn. It might be that a sluggish bond-servant, or an undutiful child, whom his parents had given over to the civil authority, was to be corrected at the whipping-post. It might be, that an Antinomian, a Quaker, or other heterodox religionist, was to be scourged out of the town, or an idle and vagrant Indian, whom the white man's fire-water had made riotous about the streets, was to be driven with stripes into the shadow of the forest. It might be, too, that a witch, like old Mistress Hibbins, the bitter-tempered widow of the magistrate, was to die upon the gallows. In either case, there was very much the same solemnity of demeanor on the part of the spectators; as befitted a people among whom religion and law were almost identical, and in whose character both were so thoroughly interfused, that the mildest and the severest acts of public discipline were alike made venerable and awful. Meager, indeed, and cold, was the sympathy that a transgressor might look for, from such bystanders, at the scaffold. On the other hand, a penalty which, in our days, would infer a degree of mocking infamy and ridicule, might then be invested with almost as stern a dignity as the punishment of death itself.

It was a circumstance to be noted, on the summer morning when our story begins its course, that the women, of whom there were several in the

From *The Scarlet Letter* by Nathaniel Hawthorne (1850).

crowd, appeared to take a peculiar interest in whatever penal infliction might be expected to ensue. The age had not so much refinement, that any sense of impropriety restrained the wearers of petticoat and farthingale from stepping forth into the public ways, and wedging their not unsubstantial persons, if occasion were, into the throng nearest to the scaffold at an execution. . . .

"Goodwives," said a hard-featured dame of fifty, "I'll tell ye a piece of my mind. It would be greatly for the public behoof, if we women, being of mature age and church-members in good repute, should have the handling of such malefactresses as this Hester Prynne. What think ye, gossips? If the hussy stood up for judgement before us five, that are now here in a knot together, would she come off with such a sentence as the worshipful magistrates have awarded? Marry, I trow not!"

"People say," said another, "that the Reverend Master Dimmesdale, her godly pastor, takes it very grievously to heart that such a scandal should have come upon his congregation."

"The magistrates are God-fearing gentlemen, but merciful overmuch, that is the truth," added a third autumnal matron. "At the very least, they should have put the brand of a hot iron on Hester Prynne's forehead. Madam Hester would have winced at that, I warrant me. But she, the naughty baggage, little will she care what they put upon the bodice of her gown! Why, look you, she may cover it with a brooch, or such like heathenish adornment, and so walk the streets as brave as ever!"

"Ah, but," interposed, more softly, a young wife, holding a child by the hand, "let her cover the mark as she will, the pang of it will be always in her heart."

"What do we talk of marks and brands, whether on the bodice of her gown, or the flesh of her forehead?" cried another female, the ugliest as well as the most pitiless of these self-constituted judges. "This woman has brought shame upon us all, and ought to die. Is there not law for it? Truly there is, both in the Scripture and the statute-book. Then let the magistrates, who have made it of no effect, thank themselves if their own wives and daughters go astray!"

"Mercy on us, good wife," exclaimed a man in the crowd, "is there no virtue in woman, save what springs from a wholesome fear of the gallows? That is the hardest word yet! Hush, now, gossips! for the lock is turning in the prison door, and here comes Mistress Prynne herself."

The door of the jail being flung open from within, there appeared, in the first place, like a black shadow emerging into sunshine, the grim and grisly presence of the town-beadle, with a sword by his side, and his staff of office in his hand. This personage prefigured and represented in his aspect the whole dismal severity of the Puritanic code of law, which it was his business to administer in its final and closest application to the offender.

Stretching forth the official staff in his left hand, he laid his right upon the shoulder of a young woman, whom he thus drew forward. . . .

The grim beadle now made a gesture with his staff.

"Make way, good people, make way, in the King's name!" cried he. "Open a passage, and, I promise ye, Mistress Prynne shall be set where man, woman and child may have a fair sight of her brave apparel, from this time till an hour past meridian. A blessing on the righteous colony of the Massachusetts, where iniquity is dragged out into the sunshine! Come along, Madam Hester, and show your scarlet letter in the market-place!"

A lane was forthwith opened through the crowd of spectators. Preceded by the beadle, and attended by an irregular procession of stern-browed men and unkindly-visaged women, Hester Prynne set forth toward the place appointed for her punishment. . . .

With almost a serene deportment . . . Hester Prynne passed through this portion of her ordeal, and came to a sort of scaffold at the western extremity of the market-place. It stood nearly beneath the eaves of Boston's earliest church, and appeared to be a fixture there.

In fact, this scaffold constituted a portion of a penal machine, which now, for two or three generations past, has been merely historical and traditionary among us, but was held, in the old time, to be as effectual an agent, in the promotion of good citizenship, as ever was the guillotine among the terrorists of France. It was, in short, the platform of the pillory; and above it rose the framework of that instrument of discipline so fashioned as to confine the human head in its tight grasp, and thus hold it up to the public gaze. The very ideal of ignominy was embodied and made manifest in this contrivance of wood and iron. There can be no outrage, methinks, against our common nature—whatever be the delinquencies of the individual—no outrage more flagrant than to forbid the culprit to hide his face for shame; as it was the essence of this punishment to do. In Hester Prynne's instance, however, as not unfrequently in other cases, her sentence bore, that she should stand a certain time upon the platform, but without undergoing that gripe about the neck and confinement of the head, the proneness to which was the most devilish characteristic of this ugly engine. Knowing well her part, she ascended a flight of wooden steps, and was thus displayed to the surrounding multitude, at about the height of a man's shoulders above the street. . . .

The scene was not without a mixture of awe, such as must always invest the spectacle of guilt and shame in a fellow-creature, before society shall have grown corrupt enough to smile, instead of shuddering at it. The witnesses of Hester Prynne's disgrace had not yet passed beyond their simplicity. They were stern enough to look upon her death, had that been the sentence, without a murmur at its severity, but had none of the heartlessness of another social state, which would find only a theme for jest in an exhibition like the present. Even if there had been a disposition to turn the matter into ridicule, it must have been repressed and overpowered by the solemn presence of men no less dignified than the Governor, and several of his counsellors, a judge, a general, and the ministers of the town; all of whom sat or stood in a balcony of the meeting-house, looking down upon the platform. When such personages could constitute a part of the spectacle, without risking the majesty or reverence of rank and office, it was safely to be inferred that the infliction of a legal sentence would have an earnest and effectual meaning. Accordingly, the crowd was somber and grave. . . .

Fedor Dostoevski (1821–1881)

The grand inquisitor

The Grand Inquisitor speaks to Christ returned to earth.

" 'For fifteen centuries we have been wrestling with Thy freedom, but now it is ended and over for good. Dost Thou not believe that it's over for good? Thou lookest meekly at me and deignest not even to be wroth with me. But let me tell Thee that now, to-day, people are more persuaded than ever that they have perfect freedom, yet they have brought their freedom to us and laid it humbly at our feet. But that has been our doing. Was this what Thou didst? Was this Thy freedom?' "

"I don't understand again," Alyosha broke in. "Is he ironical, is he jesting?"

"Not a bit of it! He claims it as a merit for himself and his Church that at last they have vanquished freedom and have done so to make men happy. 'For now' (he is speaking of the Inquisition, of course) 'for the first time it has become possible to think of the happiness of men. Man was created a rebel; and how can rebels be happy? Thou wast warned,' he says to Him. 'Thou hast had no lack of admonitions and warnings, but Thou didst not listen to those warnings; Thou didst reject the only way by which men might be made happy. But, fortunately, departing Thou didst hand on the work to us. Thou hast promised, Thou hast established by Thy word, Thou hast given to us the right to bind and to unbind, and now, of course, Thou canst not think of taking it away. Why, then, hast Thou come to hinder us?' "

"And what's the meaning of 'no lack of admonitions and warnings'?" asked Alyosha.

From *The Brothers Karamazov* by Fedor Dostoevski (1880), translated by Constance Garnett.

"Why, that's the chief part of what the old man must say."

" 'The wise and dread Spirit, the spirit of self-destruction and non-existence,' the old man goes on, 'the great spirit talked with Thee in the wilderness, and we are told in the books that he "tempted" Thee. Is that so? And could anything truer be said than what he revealed to Thee in three questions and what Thou didst reject, and what in the books is called "the temptation"? And yet if there has ever been on earth a real stupendous miracle, it took place on that day, on the day of the three temptations. The statement of those three questions was itself the miracle. If it were possible to imagine simply for the sake of argument that those three questions of the dread spirit had perished utterly from the books, and that we had to restore them and to invent them anew, and to do so had gathered all the wise men of the earth—rulers, chief priests, learned men, philosophers, poets—and had set them the task to invent three questions, such as would not only fit the occasion but express in three words, three human phrases, the whole future history of the world and of humanity—dost Thou believe that all the wisdom of the earth united could have invented anything in depth and force equal to the three questions which were actually put to Thee then by the wise and mighty spirit in the wilderness? From those questions alone, from the miracle of their statement, we can see that we have here to do not with the fleeting human intelligence but with the absolute and eternal. For in those three questions the whole subsequent history of mankind is, as it were, brought together into one whole, and foretold, and in them are united all the unsolved historical contradictions of human nature. At the time it could not be so clear, since the future was unknown; but now that fifteen hundred years have passed, we see that everything in those three questions was so justly divined and foretold, and has been so truly fulfilled, that nothing can be added to them or taken from them.

" 'Judge Thyself who was right—Thou or he who questioned Thee then? Remember the first question; its meaning, in other words, was this: "Thou wouldst go into the world, and art going with empty hands, with some promise of freedom which men in their simplicity and their natural unruliness cannot even understand, which they fear and dread—for nothing has ever been more insupportable for a man and a human society than freedom. But seest Thou these stones in this parched and barren wilderness? Turn them into bread, and mankind will run after Thee like a flock of sheep, grateful and obedient, though for ever trembling, lest Thou withdraw Thy hand and deny them Thy bread." But Thou wouldst not deprive man of freedom and didst reject the offer, thinking, what is that freedom worth, if obedience is bought with bread? Thou didst reply that man lives not by bread alone. But dost Thou know that for the sake of that earthly bread the spirit of the earth will rise up against Thee and will strive with Thee and overcome Thee, and all will follow him, crying, "Who can compare with this beast? He has given us fire from heaven!" Dost Thou know that the ages will pass, and humanity will proclaim by the lips of their sages that there is no crime, and therefore no sin; there is only hunger? "Feed men, and then ask of them virtue!" that's what they'll write on the banner, which they will raise against Thee, and with which they will destroy Thy temple. Where Thy temple stood will rise a new building; the terrible tower of Babel will be built again, and though, like the one of old, it will not be finished, yet Thou mightest have prevented that new tower and have cut short the sufferings of men for a thousand years; for they will come back to us after a thousand years of agony with their tower. They will seek us again, hidden underground in the catacombs, for we shall be again persecuted and tortured. They will find us and cry to us, "Feed us, for those who have promised us fire from heaven haven't given it!" And then we shall finish building their tower, for he finishes the building who feeds them. And we alone shall feed them in Thy name, declaring falsely that it is Thy name. Oh, never, never can they feed themselves without us! No science will give them bread so long as they remain free. In the end they will lay their freedom at our feet, and say to us, "Make us your slaves, but feed us." They will understand themselves, at last, that freedom and bread enough for all are inconceivable together, for never, never will they be able to share between them! They will be convinced, too, that they can never be free, for they are weak, vicious, worthless and rebellious. Thou didst promise them the bread of Heaven, but, I repeat again, can it compare with earthly bread in the eyes of the weak, ever-sinful and ignoble race of man? And if for the sake of the bread of Heaven thousands and tens of thousands shall follow Thee, what is to become of the millions and tens of thousands of millions of creatures who will not have the strength to forgo the earthly bread for the sake of the heavenly? Or dost Thou care only for the tens of thousands of the great and strong, while the millions, numerous as the sands of the sea, who are weak but love Thee, must exist only for the sake of the great and strong? No, we care for the weak too. They are sinful and rebellious, but in the end they too will become obedient. They will marvel at us and look on us as gods, because we are ready to endure the freedom which they have found so dreadful and to rule over them—so awful it will seem to them to be free. But we shall tell them we are Thy servants and rule them in Thy name. We shall deceive them again, for we will not let Thee come to us again. That deception will be our suffering, for we shall be forced to lie.

" 'This is the significance of the first question in the wilderness, and this is what Thou hast rejected for the sake of that freedom which Thou hast exalted above everything. Yet in this question lies hid the great secret of this world. Choosing "Bread," Thou wouldst have satisfied the universal and everlasting craving of humanity—to find someone to worship. So long as man remains free he strives for nothing so incessantly and so painfully as to find someone to worship. But man seeks to worship what is established beyond dispute, so that all men would agree at once to worship it. For these pitiful creatures are concerned not only to find what one or the other can worship, but to find something that all would believe in and worship; what is essential is that all may be together in it. This craving for community of worship is the chief misery of every man individually and of all humanity from the beginning of time. For the sake of common worship they've slain each other with the sword. They have set up gods and challenged one another, "Put away your gods and come and worship ours, or we will kill you and your gods!" And so it will be to the end of the world, even when gods disappear from the earth; they will fall down before idols just the same. Thou didst know, Thou couldst not but have known, this fundamental secret of human nature, but Thou didst reject the one infallible banner which was offered Thee to make all men bow down to Thee alone—the banner of earthly bread; and Thou hast rejected it for the sake of freedom and the bread of Heaven. Behold what Thou didst further. And all again in the name of freedom! I tell Thee that man is tormented by no greater anxiety than to find someone quickly to whom he can hand over that gift of freedom with which the ill-fated creature is born. But only one who can appease their conscience can take over their freedom. In bread there was offered Thee an invincible banner; give bread, and man will worship thee, for nothing is more certain than bread. But if someone else gains possession of his conscience—oh! then he will cast away Thy bread and follow after him who has ensnared his conscience. In that Thou wast right. For the secret of man's being is not only to live but to have something to live for. Without a stable conception of the object of life, man would not consent to go on living, and would rather destroy himself than remain on earth, though he had bread in abundance. That is true, but what happened? Instead of taking man's freedom from them, Thou didst make it greater than ever! Didst Thou forget that man prefers peace, and even death, to freedom of choice in the knowledge of good and evil? Nothing is more seductive for man than his freedom of conscience, but nothing is a greater cause of suffering. And behold instead of giving a firm foundation for setting the conscience of man at rest for ever, Thou didst choose all that is exceptional, vague and enigmatic; Thou didst choose what was utterly beyond the strength of man, acting as though Thou didst not love them at all—Thou who didst come to give Thy life for them! Instead of taking possession of men's freedom, Thou didst increase it, and burdened the spiritual kingdom of mankind with its sufferings for ever. Thou didst desire man's free love, that he should follow Thee freely, enticed and taken captive by Thee. In place of the rigid ancient law, man must hereafter with free heart decide for himself what is good and what is evil, having only Thy image before him as a guide. But didst Thou not know that he would at last reject even Thy image and Thy truth, if he is weighed down with the fearful burden of free choice? They will cry aloud at last that the truth is not in Thee, for they could not have been left in greater confusion and suffering than Thou hast caused, laying upon them so many cares and unanswerable problems.

" 'So that, in truth, Thou didst Thyself lay the foundation for the destruction of Thy Kingdom, and no one is more to blame for it. Yet what was offered Thee? There are three powers, three powers alone, able to conquer and to hold captive for ever the conscience of these impotent rebels for their happiness—those forces are miracle, mystery and authority. Thou hast rejected all three and hast set the example for doing so. When the wise and dread spirit set Thee on the pinnacle of the temple and said to Thee, "If Thou wouldst know whether Thou art the Son of God then cast Thyself down, for it is written: the angels shall hold him up lest he fall and bruise himself, and Thou shalt know then whether Thou art the Son of God and shalt prove then how great is thy faith in Thy Father." But Thou didst refuse and wouldst not cast Thyself down. Oh! of course, Thou didst proudly and well, like God; but the weak, unruly race of men, are they gods? Oh, Thou didst know then that in taking one step, in making one movement to cast Thyself down, Thou wouldst be tempting God and have lost all Thy faith in Him and wouldst have been dashed to pieces against that earth which Thou didst come to save. And the wise spirit that tempted Thee would have rejoiced. But I ask again, are there many like Thee? And couldst Thou believe for one moment that men, too, could face such a temptation? Is the nature of men such that they can reject miracle, and at the great moments of their life, the moments of their deepest, most agonising spiritual difficulties, cling only to the free verdict of the heart? Oh, Thou didst know that Thy deed would be recorded in books, would be handed down to remote times and the utmost ends of the earth, and Thou didst hope that man, following Thee, would cling to God and not ask for a miracle. But Thou didst not know that when man rejects miracle he rejects God too; for man seeks not so much God as the miraculous. And as man cannot bear to be without the miraculous, he will create new miracles of his own for himself, and will worship deeds of sorcery and witchcraft, though he might be a hundred times over a rebel, heretic and infidel. Thou didst not come down from the Cross when they shouted to Thee, mocking and reviling Thee, "Come down from the Cross and we will believe that Thou art He." Thou didst not come down, for again Thou wouldst not enslave man by a miracle, and didst crave faith given freely, not based on miracle. Thou didst crave for free love and not the base raptures of the slave before the might that has overawed him for ever. But Thou didst think too highly of men therein, for they are slaves, of course, though rebellious by nature. Look round and judge, fifteen centuries have passed, look upon them. Whom hast Thou raised up to Thyself? I swear, man is weaker and baser by nature than Thou hast believed him! Can he, can he do what Thou didst? By showing him so much respect, Thou didst, as it were, cease to feel for him, for Thou didst ask far too much from him—Thou who hast loved him more than Thyself! Respecting him less, Thou wouldst have asked less of him. That would have been more like love, for his burden would have been lighter. He is weak and vile. What though he is everywhere now rebelling against our power, and proud of his rebellion? It is the pride of a child and a schoolboy. There are little children rioting and barring out the teacher at school. But their childish delight will end; it will cost them dear. They will cast down temples and drench the earth with blood. But they will see at last, the foolish children, that, though they are rebels, they are impotent rebels, unable to keep up their own rebellion. Bathed in their foolish tears, they will recognise at last that He who created them rebels must have meant to mock at them. They will say this in despair, and their utterance will be a blasphemy which will make them more unhappy still, for man's nature cannot bear blasphemy, and in the end always avenges it on itself. And so unrest, confusion and unhappiness—that is the present lot of man after Thou didst bear so much for their freedom! Thy great prophet tells, in vision and in image, that he saw all those who took part in the first resurrection and that there were of each tribe twelve thousand. But if there were so many of them, they must have been not men but gods. They had borne Thy cross, they had endured scores of years in the barren, hungry wilderness, living upon locusts and roots—and Thou mayest indeed point with pride at those children of freedom, of free love, of free and splendid sacrifice for Thy name. But remember that they were only some thousands; and what of the rest? And how are the other weak ones to blame, because they could not endure what the strong have endured? How is the weak soul to blame that it is unable to receive such terrible gifts? Canst Thou have simply come to the elect and for the elect? But if so, it is a mystery and we cannot understand it. And if it is a mystery, we too have a right to preach a mystery, and to teach them that it's not the free judgement of their hearts, not love that matters, but a mystery which they must follow blindly, even against their conscience. So we have done. We have corrected Thy work and have founded it upon miracle, mystery and authority. And men rejoiced that they were again led like sheep, and that the terrible gift that had brought them such suffering was, at last, lifted from their hearts. Were we right teaching them this? Speak! Did we not love mankind, so meekly acknowledging their feebleness, lovingly lightening their burden, and permitting their weak nature even sin with our sanction? Why hast Thou come now to hinder us? And why dost Thou look silently and searchingly at me with Thy mild eyes? Be angry. I don't want Thy love, for I love Thee not. And what use is it for me to hide anything from Thee? Don't I know to Whom I am speaking? All that I can say is known to Thee already. And is it for me to conceal from Thee our mystery? Perhaps it is Thy will to hear it from my lips. Listen, then. We are not working with Thee but with him—that is our mystery. It's long—eight centuries—since we have been on his side and not on Thine. Just eight centuries ago we took from him what Thou didst reject with scorn, that last gift he offered Thee, showing Thee all the kingdoms of the earth. We took from him Rome and the sword of Caesar, and proclaimed our selves sole rulers of the earth, though hitherto we have not been able to complete our work. But whose fault is that? Oh, the work is only beginning, but it has begun. It has long to await completion and the earth has yet much to suffer, but we shall triumph and shall be Caesars, and then we shall plan the universal happiness of man. But Thou mightest have taken even then the sword of Caesar. Why didst Thou reject that last gift? Hadst Thou accepted that last counsel of the mighty spirit, Thou wouldst have accomplished all that man seeks on earth—that is, someone to worship, someone to keep his conscience, and some means of uniting all in one unanimous and harmonious ant-heap, for the craving for universal unity is the third and last anguish of men. Mankind as a whole has always striven to organise a universal state. There have been many great nations with great histories, but the more highly they were developed the more unhappy they were, for they felt more acutely than other people the craving for worldwide union. The great conquerors, Timours and Genghis Khans, whirled like hurricanes over the face of the earth striving to subdue its people, and they too were but the unconscious expression of the same craving for universal unity. Hadst Thou taken the world and Caesar's purple, Thou wouldst have founded the universal state and have given universal peace. For who can rule men if not he who holds their conscience and their bread in his hands? We have taken the sword of Caesar, and in taking it, of course have rejected Thee and followed him. Oh, ages are yet to come of the confusion of free thought, of their science and cannibalism. For having begun to build their tower of Babel without us, they will end, of course, with cannibalism. But then the beast will crawl to us and lick our feet and spatter them with tears of blood. And we shall sit upon the beast and raise the cup, and on it will be written, "Mystery." But then, and only then, the reign of peace and happiness will come for men. Thou art proud of Thine elect, but Thou hast only the elect, while we give rest to all. And besides, how many of those elect, those mighty ones who could become elect, have grown weary waiting for Thee, and have transferred and will transfer the powers of their spirit and the warmth on their heart to the other camp, and end by raising their free banner against Thee! Thou didst Thyself lift up that banner. But with us all will be happy and will no more rebel nor destroy one another as under Thy freedom. Oh, we shall persuade them that they will only become free when they renounce their freedom to us and submit to us. And shall we be right or shall we be lying? They will be convinced that we are right, for they will remember the horrors of slavery and confusion to which Thy freedom brought them. Freedom, free thought and science will lead them into such straits and will bring them face to face with such marvels and insoluble mysteries, that some of them, the fierce and rebellious, will destroy themselves; others, rebellious but weak, will destroy one another, while the rest, weak and unhappy, will crawl fawning to our feet and whine to us: "Yes, you were right, you alone possess His mystery, and we come back to you, save us from ourselves!"

" 'Receiving bread from us, they will see clearly that we take the bread made by their hands from them, to give it to them, without any miracle. They will see that we do not change the stones to bread, but in truth they will be more thankful for taking it from our hands than for the bread itself! For they will remember only too well in old days, without our help, even the bread they made turned to stones in their hands, while since they have come back to us, the very stones have turned to bread in their hands. Too, too well will they know the value of complete submission! And until men know that, they will be unhappy. Who is most to blame for their not knowing it, speak? Who scattered the flock and sent it astray on unknown paths? But the flock will come together again and will submit once more, and then it will be once for all. Then we shall give them the quiet humble happiness of weak creatures such as they are by nature. Oh, we shall persuade them at last not to be proud, for Thou didst lift them up and thereby taught them to be proud. We shall show them that they are weak, that they are only pitiful children, but that childlike happiness is the sweetest of all. They will become timid and will look to us and huddle close to us in fear, as chicks to a hen. They will marvel at us and will be awe-stricken before us, and will be proud at our being so powerful and clever, that we have been able to subdue such a turbulent flock of thousands of millions. They will tremble impotently before our wrath, their minds will grow fearful, they will be quick to shed tears like women and children, but they will be just as ready at a sign from us to pass to laughter and rejoicing, to happy mirth and childish song. Yes, we shall set them to work, but in their leisure hours we shall make their life like a child's game, with children's songs and innocent dance. Oh, we shall allow them every sin, they are weak and helpless, and they will love us like children because we allow them to sin. We shall tell them that every sin will be expiated, if it is done with our permission, that we allow them to sin because we love them, and the punishment for these sins we take upon ourselves. And we shall take it upon ourselves, and they will adore us as their saviours who have taken on themselves their sins before God. And they will have no secrets from us. We shall allow or forbid them to live with their wives and mistresses, to have or not to have children—according to whether they have been obedient or disobedient—and they will submit to us gladly and cheerfully. The most painful secrets of their conscience, all, all they will bring to us, and we shall have an answer for all. And they will be glad to believe our answer, for it will save them from the great anxiety and terrible agony they endure at present in making a free decision for themselves. And all will be happy, all the millions of creatures except the hundred thousand who rule over them. For only we, we who guard the mystery, shall be unhappy. There will be thousands of millions of happy babes, and a hundred thousand sufferers who have taken upon themselves the curse of the knowledge of good and evil. Peacefully they will die, peacefully they will expire in Thy name, and beyond the grave they will find nothing but death. But we shall keep the secret, and for their happiness we shall allure them with the reward of heaven and eternity. Though if there were anything in the other world, it certainly would not be for such as they. It is prophesied that Thou wilt come again in victory, Thou wilt come with Thy chosen, the proud and strong, but we will say that they have only saved themselves, but we have saved all. We are told that the harlot who sits upon the beast, and holds in her hands the mystery, shall be put to shame, that the weak will rise up again, and will rend her royal purple and will strip naked her loathsome body. But then I will stand up and point out to Thee the thousand millions of happy children who have known no sin. And we who have taken their sins upon us for their happiness will stand up before Thee and say: "Judge us if Thou canst and darest." Know that I fear Thee not. Know that I too have been in the wilderness, I too have lived on roots and locusts, I too prized the freedom with which Thou hast blessed men, and I too was striving to stand among Thy elect, among the strong and powerful, thirsting "to make up the number." But I awakened and would not serve madness. I turned back and joined the ranks of those who have corrected Thy work. I left the proud and went back to the humble, for the happiness of the humble. What I say to Thee will come to pass, and our dominion will be built up. I repeat, to-morrow Thou shalt see that obedient flock who at a sign from me will hasten to heap up the hot cinders about the pile on which I shall burn Thee for coming to hinder us. For if anyone has ever deserved our fires, it is Thou. To-morrow I shall burn Thee. Dixi.' "

Thomas Campanella (1568–1639)

The city of the sun

A dialogue between a Grand Master of the Knights Hospitalers and a
Genoese Sea Captain.

G.M. Tell me, I pray you, is there no jealousy among them or disappointment to that one who has not been elected to a magistracy, or to any other
dignity to which he aspires?

Capt. Certainly not. For not one wants either necessaries or luxuries.
Moreover, the race is managed for the good of the commonwealth, and not
of private individuals, and the magistrates must be obeyed. They deny what
we hold—viz., that it is natural to man to recognize his off-spring and to
educate them, and to use his wife and house and children as his own. For
they say that children are bred for the preservation of the species and not
for individual pleasure, as St. Thomas also asserts. Therefore the breeding
of children has reference to the commonwealth, and not to individuals,
except in so far as they are constituents of the commonwealth. And since
individuals for the most part bring forth children wrongly and educate them
wrongly, they consider that they remove destruction from the State, and
therefore for this reason, with most sacred fear, they commit the education
of the children, who, as it were, are the element of the republic, to the care
of magistrates; for the safety of the community is not that of a few. And
thus they distribute male and female breeders to the best natures according
to philosophical rules. Plato thinks that this distribution ought to be made
by lot, lest some men seeing that they are kept away from the beautiful
women, should rise up with anger and hatred against the magistrates; and
he thinks further that those who do not deserve cohabitation with the more
beautiful women, should be deceived while the lots are being led out of the
city by the magistrates, so that at all times the women who are suitable
should fall to their lot, not those whom they desire.

This shrewdness, however, is not necessary among the inhabitants of the
City of the Sun. For with them deformity is unknown. When the women
are exercised they get a clear complexion, and become strong of limb, tall
and agile, and with them beauty consists in tallness and strength. Therefore,
if any woman dyes her face, so that it may become beautiful, or uses high-
heeled boots so that she may appear tall, or garments with trains to cover
her wooden shoes, she is condemned to capital punishment. But if the

From *The City of the Sun* by Thomas Campanella (1623), translated by
Thomas W. Halliday.

women should even desire them, they have no facility for doing these things. For who indeed would give them this facility? Further, they assert that among us abuses of this kind arise from the leisure and sloth of women. By these means they lose their color and have pale complexions, and become feeble and small. For this reason they are without proper complexions, use high sandals, and become beautiful not from strength, but from slothful tenderness. And thus they ruin their own tempers and natures, and consequently those of their offspring. Furthermore, if at any time a man is taken captive with ardent love for a certain woman, the two are allowed to converse and joke together, and to give one another garlands of flowers or leaves, and to make verses. But if the race is endangered, by no means is further union between them permitted. Moreover, the love born of eager desire is not known among them; only that born of friendship.

Domestic affairs and partnerships are of little account, because, excepting the sign of honor, each one receives what he is in need of. To the heroes and heroines of the republic, it is customary to give the pleasing gifts of honor, beautiful wreaths, sweet food, or splendid clothes, while they are feasting. In the daytime all use white garments within the city, but at night or outside the city they use red garments either of wool or silk. They hate black as they do dung, and therefore they dislike the Japanese, who are fond of black. Pride they consider the most execrable vice, and one who acts proudly is chastised with the most ruthless correction. Wherefore no one thinks it lowering to wait at table or to work in the kitchen or fields. All work they call discipline, and thus they say that it is honorable to go on foot, to do any act of nature, to see with the eye, and to speak with the tongue; and when there is need they distinguish philosophically between tears and spittle.

Every man who, when he is told off to work, does his duty, is considered very honorable. It is not the custom to keep slaves For they are enough, and more than enough, for themselves. But with us, alas! it is not so. In Naples there exist 70,000 souls, and out of these scarcely 10,000 or 15,000 do any work, and they are always lean from overwork and are getting weaker every day. The rest become prey to idleness, avarice, ill-health, lasciviousness, usury, and other vices, and contaminate and corrupt very many families by holding them in servitude for their own use, by keeping them in poverty and slavishness, and by imparting to them their own vices. Therefore public slavery ruins them; useful works, in the field, in military service, and in arts, except those which are debasing, are not cultivated, the few who do practise them doing so with much aversion.

But in the City of the Sun, while duty and work are distributed among all, it only falls to each one to work for about four hours every day. The remaining hours are spent in learning joyously, in debating, in reading, in reciting, in writing, in walking, in exercising the mind and body, and with play. They allow no game which is played while sitting, neither the single die nor dice, nor chess, nor others like these. But they play with the ball, with the sack, with the hoop, with wrestling, with hurling at the stake. They say, moreover, that grinding poverty renders men worthless, cunning, sulky, thievish, insidious, vagabonds, liars, false witnesses, etc.; and that wealth makes them insolent, proud, ignorant, traitors, assumers of what they know not, deceivers, boasters, wanting in affection, slanderers, etc. But with them all the rich and poor together make up the community. They are rich because they want nothing, poor because they possess nothing; and consequently they are not slaves to circumstances, but circumstances serve them. And on this point they strongly recommend the religion of the Christians, and especially the life of the apostles.

G.M. This seems excellent and sacred, but the community of women is a thing too difficult to attain. The holy Roman Clement says that wives ought to be common in accordance with the apostolic institution, and praises Plato and Socrates, who thus teach, but the Glossary interprets this community with regard to obedience. And Tertullian agrees with the Glossary, that the first Christians had everything in common except wives.

Capt. These things I know little of. But this I saw among the inhabitants of the City of the Sun, that they did not make this exception. And they defend themselves by the opinion of Socrates, of Cato, of Plato, and St. Clement; but, as you say, they misunderstand the opinions of these thinkers. And the inhabitants of the solar city ascribe this to their want of education, since they are by no means learned in philosophy. Nevertheless, they send abroad to discover the customs of nations, and the best of these they always adopt. Practice makes the women suitable for war and other duties. Thus they agree with Plato, in whom I have read these same things. The reasoning of our Cajetan does not convince me, and least of all that of Aristotle. This thing, however, existing among them is excellent and worthy of imitation—viz., that no physical defect renders a man incapable of being serviceable except the decrepitude of old age, since even the deformed are useful for consultation. The lame serve as guards, watching with the eyes which they possess. The Blind card wool with their hands, separating the down from the hairs, with which latter they stuff the couches and sofas; those who are without the use of eyes and hands give the use of their ears or their voice for the convenience of the State, and if one has only one sense he uses it in the farms. And these cripples are well treated, and some become spies, telling the officers of the State what they have heard. . . .

G.M. What about their judges?

Capt. This is the point I was just thinking of explaining. Everyone is judged by the first master of his trade, and thus all the head artificers are judges. They punish with exile, with flogging, with blame, with deprivation of the common table, with exclusion from the church and from the company of women. When there is a case in which great injury has been done, it is punished by death, and they repay an eye with an eye, a nose for a nose, a tooth for a tooth, and so on, according to the law of retaliation. If the offence is wilful the Council decides. When there is strife and it takes place undesignedly the sentence is mitigated; nevertheless, not by the judge but by the triumvirate, from whom even it may be referred to Hoh, not on account of justice but of mercy, for Hoh is able to pardon. They have no prisons, except one tower for shutting up rebellious enemies, and there is no written statement of a case, which we commonly call a lawsuit. But the accusation and witnesses are produced in the presence of the judge and Power; the accused person makes his defence, and he is immediately acquitted or condemned by the judge; and if he appeals to the triumvirate, on the following day he is acquitted or condemned. On the third day he is dismissed through the mercy and clemency of Hoh, or receives the inviolable rigor of his sentence. An accused person is reconciled to his accuser and to his witnesses, as it were, with the medicine of his complaint, that is, with embracing and kissing.

No one is killed or stoned unless by the hands of the people, the accuser and the witnesses beginning first. For they have no executioners and lictors, lest the State should sink into ruin. The choice of death is given to the rest of the people, who enclose the lifeless remains in little bags and burn them by the application of fire, while exhorters are present for the purpose of advising concerning a good death. Nevertheless, the whole nation laments and beseeches God that his anger may be appeased, being in grief that it should, as it were, have to cut off a rotten member of the State. Certain officers talk to and convince the accused man by means of arguments until he himself acquiesces in the sentence of death passed upon him, or else he does not die. But if a crime has been committed against the liberty of the republic, or against God, or against the supreme magistrates, there is immediate censure without pity. These only are punished with death. He who is about to die is compelled to state in the presence of the people and with religious scrupulousness the reasons for which he does not deserve death, and also the sins of the others who ought to die instead of him, and further the mistakes of the magistrates. If, moreover, it should seem right to the person thus asserting, he must say why the accused ones are deserving of less punishment than he. And if by his arguments he gains the victory he is sent into exile, and appeases the State by means of prayers and sacrifices and good life ensuing. They do not torture those named by the accused person, but they warn them. Sins of frailty and ignorance are punished only with blaming, and with compulsory continuation as learners under the law and discipline of those sciences or arts against which they have sinned. And all these things they have mutually among themselves, since they seem to be in very truth members of the same body, and one of another.

This further I would have you know, that if a transgressor, without waiting to be accused, goes of his own accord before a magistrate, accusing himself and seeking to make amends, that one is liberated from the punishment of a secret crime, and since he had not been accused of such a crime, his punishment is changed into another. They take special care that no one should invent slander, and if this should happen they meet the offence with the punishment of retaliation. Since they always walk about and work in crowds, five witnesses are required for the conviction of a transgressor. If the case is otherwise, after having threatened him, he is released after he has sworn an oath as the warrant of good conduct. Or if he is accused a second or third time, his increased punishment rests on the testimony of three or two witnesses. They have but few laws, and these short and plain, and written upon a flat table, and hanging to the doors of the temple, that is between the columns. And on single columns can be seen the essences of things described in the very terse style of Metaphysic—viz., the essences of God, of the angels, of the world, of the stars, of man, of fate, of virtue, all done with great wisdom. The definitions of all the virtues are also delineated here, and here is the tribunal, where the judges of all the virtues have their seat. The definition of a certain virtue is written under that column where the judges for the aforesaid virtue sit, and when a judge gives judgment he sits and speaks thus: O son, thou hast sinned against this sacred definition of beneficence, or of magnanimity, or of another virtue, as the case may be. And after discussion the judge legally condemns him to the punishment for the crime of which he is accused—viz., for injury, for despondency, for pride, for ingratitude, for sloth, etc. But the sentences are certain and true correctives, savoring more of clemency than of actual punishment.

G.M. Now you ought to tell me about their priests, their sacrifices, their religion, and their belief.

Capt. The chief priest is Hoh, and it is the duty of all the superior magistrates to pardon sins. Therefore the whole State by secret confession, which we also use, tell their sins to the magistrates, who at once urge their souls and teach those that are inimical to the people. Then the sacred magistrates themselves confess their own sinfulness to the three supreme chiefs, and together they confess the faults of one another, though no special one is named, and they confess especially the heavier faults and those harmful to the State. At length the triumvirs confess their sinfulness to Hoh himself, who forthwith recognizes the kinds of sins that are harmful to the State and succors with timely remedies. Then he offers sacrifices and prayers to God. And before this he confesses the sins of the whole people, in the presence of God, and publicly in the temple, above the altar, as often as it had been necessary that the fault should be corrected. Nevertheless, no transgressor is spoken of by his name. In this manner he absolves the people by advising them that they should beware of sins of the aforesaid kind. Afterward he offers sacrifice to God, that he should pardon the State and absolve it of its sins, and to teach and defend it. Once in every year the chief priests of each separate subordinate State confess their sins in the presence of Hoh. Thus he is not ignorant of the wrongdoings of the provinces, and forthwith he removes them with all human and heavenly remedies.

Socialization

Socialization may be defined as the process by which an individual is fitted into the social framework and induced to play his assigned roles. The major agency in the process of socialization is usually the family which inculcates in the growing child the basic disciplines necessary for social living. The family, then, is the main link between child and society; it leads the child to internalize social norms by creating in it the desire to live up to the expectations of significant others. The attitudes of significant others— typically the parents—towards the child mark his primary self-image and self-conception and fashion his moral orientation. As the child grows up and his field of social vision and social contact widens, other adults such as teachers, as well as peers, become significant others to him. Finally the perceived appraisals of many particular others are organized into a pattern, thus forming a "generalized other" or internalized "conscience."

The internalized constraints that prompt men to live up to society's rules and so to acquire uniquely human attributes become part of the individual in the process of socialization. Society imposes on the biological organism a series of restricting injunctions; but it must be understood at the same time that human potentialities can be realized only in and through society so that a certain amount of repression is the very condition of human growth. Man is human only to the extent that he is socialized and can participate in the specifically human achievement which we call culture. Yet, lest we subscribe to an over-socialized view of man, we must bear in mind that certain conflicts between cultural requirements and biological drives are also the distinctive mark of the human animal.

While in relatively undifferentiated societies the family usually is the only major agency of socialization, in modern societies more specialized agencies such as schools, voluntary associations, and churches assume a considerable burden in the socialization process. Moreover, when persons are being inducted into more specialized roles, there exist specialized agencies of socialization preparing the neophyte for the specialized tasks he is about to undertake. To the extent that persons necessarily change some of their roles as they move through the life cycle it may be said that the process of socialization is never completed—from infancy to death men must continually learn new roles into which they must be socialized.

Our selection from Samuel Butler's bitter novel about the stultifying impact on children of Victorian authoritarian families, *The Way of All Flesh,* highlights some aspects of repressive types of socialization. Stephen Crane is now mainly remembered as a novelist of war; yet the short story which we here reprint in a somewhat abridged form reveals him as an extraordinarily acute observer of children. He shows here how tyrannically the peer group can oppress a child and how an adult "significant other" may restore the child's self-esteem by holding before him the image of a future time in which the child will have become a man. Sherwood Anderson's magnificent short story, one of a series of brilliant sketches about the pains of adolescence, highlights the importance of role models in socialization. He shows the profoundly disturbing consequences which follow upon the realization of a boy that his adored hero is in fact a frail and "sinful" human being. The selection from Mark Twain's *Life on the Mississippi* illustrates the process of socialization into a specialized occupation through exposure to its practices rather than through a formal process of education.

Samuel Butler (1825–1902)

An authoritarian father

I used to stay at Battersby for a day or two sometimes, while my godson and his brother and sister were children. I hardly know why I went, for Theobald

From *The Way of All Flesh* by Samuel Butler (1903).

and I grew more and more apart, but one gets into grooves sometimes, and the supposed friendship between myself and the Pontifexes continued to exist, though it was now little more than rudimentary. My godson pleased me more than either of the other children, but he had not much of the buoyancy of childhood, and was more like a puny, sallow little old man than I liked. The young people, however, were very ready to be friendly.

I remember Ernest and his brother hovered around me on the first day of one of these visits with their hands full of fading flowers, which they at length proffered me. On this I did what I suppose was expected: I inquired if there was a shop near where they could buy sweeties. They said there was, so I felt in my pockets, but only succeeded in finding two pence halfpenny in small money. This I gave them, and the youngsters, aged four and three, toddled off alone. Ere long they returned, and Ernest said, "We can't get sweeties for all this money" (I felt rebuked, but no rebuke was intended); "we can get sweeties for this" (showing a penny), "and for this" (showing another penny), "but we cannot get them for all this," and he added the halfpenny to the two pence. I suppose they had wanted a twopenny cake, or something like that. I was amused, and left them to solve the difficulty their own way, being anxious to see what they would do.

Presently Ernest said, "May we give you back this" (showing the halfpenny), "and not give you back this and this?" (showing the pence). I assented and they gave a sigh of relief and went on their way rejoicing. A few presents of pence and small toys completed the conquest and they began to take me into their confidence.

They told me a good deal which I am afraid I ought not to have listened to. They said that if grandpapa had lived longer he would most likely have been made a Lord, and that then papa would have been the Honourable and Reverend, but that grandpapa was now in heaven singing beautiful hymns with Grandmamma Allaby to Jesus Christ, who was very fond of them; and that when Ernest was ill, his mamma told him he need not be afraid of dying, for he would go straight to heaven, if he would only be sorry for having done his lessons so badly and vexed his dear papa, and if he would promise never, never to vex him any more; and that when he got to heaven Grandpapa and Grandmamma Allaby would meet him, and he would be always with them, and they would be very good to him and teach him to sing ever such beautiful hymns, more beautiful by far than those which he was now so fond of, etc., etc., but he did not wish to die, and was glad when he got better for there were no kittens in heaven, and he did not think there were cowslips to make cowslip tea with.

Their mother was plainly disappointed in them. "My children are none of them geniuses, Mr. Overton," she said to me at breakfast one morning. "They have fair abilities, and thanks to Theobald's tuition, they are forward for their years, but they have nothing like genius: genius is a thing apart from this, is it not?"

Of course I said it was "a thing quite apart from this," but if my thoughts had been laid bare, they would have appeared as "Give me my coffee immediately, ma'am, and don't talk nonsense." I have no idea what genius is, but so far as I can form any conception about it, I should say it was a stupid word which cannot be too soon abandoned to scientific and literary claqueurs.

I do not know what exactly Christina expected, but I should imagine it was something like this: "My children ought to be all geniuses, because they are mine and Theobald's, and it is naughty of them not to be; but, of course, they cannot be so good and clever as Theobald and I were, and if they show signs of being so it will be naughty of them. Happily, however, they are not this, and yet it is very dreadful that they are not. As for genius—hoity-toity, indeed—why, a genius should turn intellectual somersaults as soon as it is born, and none of my children have yet been able to get into the newspapers. I will not have children of mine give themselves airs—it is enough for them that Theobald and I should do so."

She did not know, poor woman, that the true greatness wears an invisible cloak, under cover of which it goes in and out among men without being suspected; if its cloak does not conceal it from itself always, and from all others for many years, its greatness will ere long shrink to very ordinary dimensions. What then, it may be asked, is the good of being great? The answer is that you may understand greatness better in others, whether alive or dead, and choose better company from these and enjoy and understand that company better when you have chosen it—also that you may be able to give pleasure to the best people and live in the lives of those who are yet unborn. This, one would think, was substantial gain enough for greatness without its wanting to ride roughshod over us, even when disguised as humility.

I was there on a Sunday, and observed the rigour with which the young people were taught to observe the Sabbath; they might not cut out things, nor use their paintbox on a Sunday, and this they thought rather hard, because their cousins the John Pontifexes might do these things. Their cousins might play with their toy train on Sunday, but though they had promised that they would run none but Sunday trains, all traffic had been prohibited. One treat only was allowed them—on Sunday evenings they might choose their own hymns.

In the course of the evening they came into the drawing room, and, as an especial treat, were to sing some of their hymns to me, instead of saying them, so that I might hear how nicely they sang. Ernest was to choose the first hymn, and he chose one about some people who were to come to the sunset tree. I am no botanist, and do not know what kind of tree a sunset tree is, but the words began, "Come, come, come; come to the sunset tree, for the day is past and gone." The tune was rather pretty and had taken Ernest's fancy, for he was unusually fond of music and had a sweet little child's voice which he liked using. He was, however, very late in being able to sound a hard "C" or "k" and, instead of saying "Come," he said "Tum, tum, tum."

"Ernest," said Theobald, from the armchair in front of the fire, where he was sitting with his hands folded before him, "don't you think it would be very nice if you were to say 'come' like other people, instead of 'tum'?"

"I do say tum," replied Ernest, meaning that he had said "come."

Theobald was always in a bad temper on Sunday evening. Whether it is that they are as much bored with the day as their neighbours, or whether they are tired, or whatever the cause may be, clergymen are seldom at their best on Sunday evening; I had already seen signs that evening that my host was cross, and was a little nervous at hearing Ernest say so promptly, "I do say tum," when his papa had said he did not say it as he should.

Theobald noticed the fact that he was being contradicted in a moment. He got up from his armchair and went to the piano.

"No, Ernest, you don't," he said, "you say nothing of the kind, you say 'tum,' not 'come.' Now say 'come' after me, as I do."

"Tum," said Ernest, at once; "is that better?" I have no doubt he thought it was, but it was not.

"Now, Ernest, you are not taking pains; you are not trying as you ought to do. It is high time you learned to say 'come'; why, Joey can say 'come,' can't you, Joey?"

"Yeth, I can," replied Joey, and he said something which was not far off "come."

"There, Ernest, do you hear that? There's no difficulty about it, nor shadow of difficulty. Now take your own time, think about it, and say 'come' after me."

The boy remained silent for a few seconds and then said "tum" again.

I laughed, but Theobald turned to me impatiently and said, "Please do not laugh, Overton; it will make the boy think it does not matter, and it matters a great deal"; then turning to Ernest he said, "Now, Ernest, I will give you one more chance, and if you don't say 'come,' I shall know that you are self-willed and naughty."

He looked very angry, and a shade came over Ernest's face, like that which comes upon the face of a puppy when it is being scolded without understanding why. The child saw well what was coming now, was frightened, and, of course, said "tum" once more.

"Very well, Ernest," said his father, catching him angrily by the shoulder. "I have done my best to save you, but if you will have it so, you will," and he lugged the little wretch, crying by anticipation, out of the room. A few minutes more and we could hear screams coming from the dining-room, across the hall which separated the drawing-room from the dining-room, and knew that poor Ernest was being beaten.

"I have sent him up to bed," said Theobald, as he returned to the drawing-room, "and now, Christina, I think we will have the servants in to prayers," and he rang the bell for them, red-handed as he was.

Stephen Crane (1870–1900)

Shame

When he arrived in the outskirts of the grove he heard a merry clamour, and when he reached the top of the knoll he looked down the slope upon a scene which almost made his little breast burst with joy. They actually had two camp-fires! Two camp-fires! At one of them Mrs. Earl was making some-thing—chocolate, no doubt—and at the other a young lady in white duck and a sailor hat was dropping eggs into boiling water. Other grown-up people had spread a white cloth and were laying upon it things from baskets. In the deep cool shadow of the trees the children scurried, laughing. Jimmie hastened forward to join his friends.

Homer Phelps caught first sight of him. "Ho!" he shouted; "here comes Jimmie Trescott! Come on, Jimmie; you be on our side!" The children had divided themselves into two bands for some purpose of play. The others of Homer Phelps' party loudly endorsed his plan. "Yes, Jimmie, you be on our side." Then arose the usual dispute. "Well, we got the weakest side."

"Tain't any weaker'n ours."

Homer Phelps suddenly started and, looking hard, said, "What you got in the pail, Jim?"

Jimmie answered, somewhat uneasily, "Got m'lunch in it."

Instantly that brat of Minnie Phelps simply tore down the sky with her shrieks of derision. "Got his lunch in it! In a pail!" She ran screaming to her mother. "Oh, mamma! Oh, mamma! Jimmie Trescott's got his picnic in a pail!"

Now there was nothing in the nature of this fact to particularly move the others—notably the boys, who were not competent to care if he had brought his luncheon in a coal-bin; but such is the instinct of childish society that they all immediately moved away from him. In a moment he had been made a social leper. All old intimacies were flung into the lake, so to speak. They dared not compromise themselves. At a safe distance the boys shouted, scornfully: 'Huh! Got his picnic in a pail!" Never again

---

From *Whilomville Stories* by Stephen Crane (1899).

during that picnic did the little girls speak of him as Jimmie Trescott. His name now was Him.

His mind was dark with pain as he stood, the hang-dog, kicking the gravel, and muttering as defiantly as he was able, "Well, I can have it in a pail if I want to." This statement of freedom was of no importance, and he knew it, but it was the only idea in his head.

He had been baited at school for being detected in writing a letter to little Cora, the angel child, and he had known how to defend himself, but this situation was in no way similar. This was a social affair, with grown people on all sides. It would be sweet to catch the Margate twins, for instance, and hammer them into a state of bleating respect for his pail; but that was a matter for the jungles of childhood, where grown folks seldom penetrated. He could only glower.

The amiable voice of Mrs. Earl suddenly called: "Come, children! Everything's ready!" They scampered away, glancing back for one last gloat at Jimmie standing there with his pail.

He did not know what to do. He knew that the grown people expected him at the spread, but if he approached he would be greeted by a shameful chorus from the children—more especially from some of those damnable little girls. Still, luxuries beyond all dreaming were heaped on that cloth. One could not forget them. Perhaps if he crept up modestly, and was very gentle and very nice to the little girls, they would allow him peace. Of course it had been dreadful to come with a pail to such a grand picnic, but they might forgive him.

Oh no, they would not! He knew them better. And then suddenly he remembered with what delightful expectations he had raced to this grove, and self-pity overwhelmed him, and he thought he wanted to die and make every one feel sorry.

The young lady in white duck and a sailor hat looked at him, and then spoke to her sister, Mrs. Earl. "Who's that hovering in the distance, Emily?"

Mrs. Earl peered. "Why, it's Jimmie Trescott! Jimmie, come to the picnic! Why don't you come to the picnic, Jimmie?" He began to sidle toward the cloth.

But at Mrs. Earl's call there was another outburst from many of the children. "He's got his picnic in a pail! In a pail! Got it in a pail!"

Minnie Phelps was a shrill fiend. "Oh, mamma, he's got it in that pail! See! Isn't it funny? Isn't it dreadful funny?"

"What ghastly prigs children are, Emily!" said the young lady. "They are spoiling that boy's whole day, breaking his heart, the little cats! I think I'll go over and talk to him."

"Maybe you had better not," answered Mrs. Earl, dubiously. "Somehow these things arrange themselves. If you interfere, you are likely to prolong everything."

"Well, I'll try, at least," said the young lady.

At the second outburst against him Jimmie had crouched down by a tree, half hiding behind it, half pretending that he was not hiding behind it. He turned his sad gaze toward the lake. The bit of water seen through the shadows seemed perpendicular, a slate-coloured wall. He heard a noise near him, and turning he perceived the young lady looking down at him. In her hand she held plates. "May I sit near you?" she asked, coolly.

Jimmie could hardly believe his ears. After disposing herself and the plates upon the pine needles, she made brief explanation. "They're rather crowded, you see, over there. I don't like to be crowded at a picnic, so I thought I'd come here. I hope you don't mind."

Jimmie made haste to find his tongue. "Oh, I don't mind! I like to have you here." The ingenuous emphasis made it appear that the fact of his liking to have her there was in the nature of a law-dispelling phenomenon, but she did not smile.

"How large is that lake?" she asked.

Jimmie falling into the snare, at once began to talk in the manner of a proprietor of the lake. "Oh, it's almost twenty miles long, an' in one place it's almost four miles wide! an' it's deep too—awful deep—an' it's got real steamboats on it, an'—oh—lots of other boats, an'—an'—an'—"

"Do you go out on it sometimes?"

"Oh, lots of times! My father's got a boat," he said, eyeing her to note the effect of his words.

She was correctly pleased and struck with wonder. "Oh, has he?" she cried, as if she never before had heard of a man owning a boat.

Jimmie continued: "Yes, an' it's a grea' big boat, too, with sails, real sails; an' sometimes he takes me out in her too; an' once he took me fishin', an' we had sandwiches, plenty of 'em, and my father he drank beer right out of the bottle—right out of the bottle!"

The young lady was properly overwhelmed by this amazing intelligence. Jimmie saw the impression he had created, and he enthusiastically resumed his narrative: "An' after, he let me throw the bottles in the water, and I throwed 'em 'way, 'way, 'way out. An' they sank, an'— never comed up," he concluded, dramatically.

His face was glorified; he had forgotten all about the pail; he was absorbed in this communion with a beautiful lady who was so interested in what he had to say.

She indicated one of the plates, and said, indifferently: "Perhaps you would like some of those sandwiches. I made them. Do you like olives? And there's a devilled egg. I made that also."

"Did you really?" said Jimmie, politely. His face gloomed for a moment because the pail was recalled to his mind, but he timidly possessed himself of a sandwich.

"Hope you are not going to scorn my devilled egg," said his goddess. "I am very proud of it." He did not; he scorned little that was on the plate.

Their gentle intimacy was ineffable to the boy. He thought he had a friend, a beautiful lady, who liked him more than she did anybody at the picnic, to say the least. This was proved by the fact that she had flung aside the luxuries of the spread cloth to sit with him, the exile. Thus early did he fall a victim to woman's wiles.

"Where do you live?" he asked, suddenly.

"Oh, a long way from here! In New York."

His next question was put very bluntly. "Are you married?"

"Oh no!" she answered, gravely.

Jimmie was silent for a time, during which he glanced shyly and furtively up at her face. It was evident that he was somewhat embarrassed. Finally he said, "When I grow up to be a man—"

"Oh, that is some time yet!" said the beautiful lady.

"But when I do, I—I should like to marry you."

"Well, I will remember it," she answered; "but don't talk of it now, because it's such a long time; and—I wouldn't wish you to consider yourself bound." She smiled at him.

He began to brag. "When I grow up to be a man, I'm goin' to have lots an' lots of money, an' I'm goin' to have a grea' big house, an' a horse an' a shotgun, an' lots an' lots of books 'bout elephants an' tigers, an' lots an' lots of ice-cream an' pie an'—carmels." As before, she was impressed; he could see it. "An' I'm goin' to have lots an' lots of children—'bout three hundred, I guess—an' there won't none of 'em be girls. They'll all be boys—like me."

"Oh, my!" she said.

His garment of shame was gone from him. The pail was dead and well buried. It seemed to him that months elapsed as he dwelt in happiness near the beautiful lady and trumpeted his vanity.

At last there was a shout. "Come on! we're going home." The picnickers trooped out of the grove. The children wished to resume their jeering, for Jimmie still gripped his pail, but they were restrained by the circumstances. He was walking at the side of the beautiful lady.

During the journey he abandoned many of his habits. For instance, he never travelled without skipping gracefully from crack to crack between the stones, or without pretending that he was a train of cars, or without some mumming device of childhood. But now he behaved with dignity. He made no more noise than a little mouse. He escorted the beautiful lady to the gate of the Earl home, where he awkwardly, solemnly, and wistfully shook hands in good-bye. He watched her go up the walk; the door clanged.

On his way home he dreamed. One of these dreams was fascinating.

Supposing the beautiful lady was his teacher in school! Oh, my! wouldn't he be a good boy, sitting like a statuette all day long, and knowing every lesson to perfection, and—everything. And then supposing that a boy should sass her. Jimmie painted himself waylaying that boy on the homeward road, and the fate of the boy was a thing to make strong men cover their eyes with their hands. And she would like him more and more—more and more. And he—he would be a little god. . . .

Sherwood Anderson (1876–1941)

I want to know why

We got up at four in the morning, that first day in the east. On the evening before we had climbed off a freight train at the edge of town, and with the true instinct of Kentucky boys had found our way across town and to the race track and the stables at once. Then we knew we were all right. Hanley Turner right away found a nigger we knew. It was Bildad Johnson who in the winter works at Ed Becker's livery barn in our home town, Beckersville. Bildad is a good cook as almost all our niggers are and of course he, like everyone in our part of Kentucky who is anyone at all, likes the horses. In the spring Bildad begins to scratch around. A nigger from our country can flatter and wheedle anyone into letting him do most anything he wants. Bildad wheedles the stable men and the trainers from the horse farms in our country around Lexington. The trainers come into town in the evening to stand around and talk and maybe get into a poker game. Bildad gets in with them. He is always doing little favors and telling about things to eat, chicken browned in a pan, and how is the best way to cook sweet potatoes and corn bread. It makes your mouth water to hear him.

When the racing season comes on and the horses go to the races and there is all the talk on the streets in the evenings about the new colts, and everyone says when they are going over to Lexington or to the spring meeting at Churchill Downs or to Latonia, and the horsemen that have been down to New Orleans or maybe at the winter meeting at Havana in Cuba come home to spend a week before they start out again, at such a time when everything talked about in Beckersville is just horses and nothing else and the outfits start out and horse racing is in every breath of air you breathe, Bildad shows up with a job as cook for some outfit. Often when

I think about it, his always going all season to the races and working in the livery barn in the winter where horses are and where men like to come and talk about horses, I wish I was a nigger. It's a foolish thing to say, but that's the way I am about being around horses, just crazy. I can't help it.

Well, I must tell you about what we did and let you in on what I'm talking about. Four of us boys from Beckersville, all whites and sons of men who live in Beckersville regular, made up our minds we were going to the races, not just to Lexington or Louisville, I don't mean, but to the big eastern track we were always hearing our Beckersville men talk about, to Saratoga. We were all pretty young then. I was just turned fifteen and I was the oldest of the four. It was my scheme. I admit that and I talked the others into trying it. There was Hanley Turner and Henry Rieback and Tom Tumberton and myself. I had thirty-seven dollars I had earned during the winter working nights and Saturdays in Enoch Myer's grocery. Henry Rieback had eleven dollars and the others, Hanley and Tom had only a dollar or two each. We fixed it all up and laid low until the Kentucky spring meetings were over and some of our men, the sportiest ones, the ones we envied the most, had cut out—then we cut out too.

I won't tell you the trouble we had beating our way on freights and all. We went through Cleveland and Buffalo and other cities and saw Niagara Falls. We bought things there, souvenirs and spoons and cards and shells with pictures of the falls on them for our sisters and mothers, but thought we had better not send any of the things home. We didn't want to put the folks on our trail and maybe be nabbed.

We got into Saratoga as I said at night and went to the track. Bildad fed us up. He showed us a place to sleep in hay over a shed and promised to keep still. Niggers are all right about things like that. They won't squeal on you. Often a white man you might meet, when you had run away from home like that, might appear to be all right and give you a quarter or a half dollar or something, and then go right and give you away. White men will do that, but not a nigger. You can trust them. They are squarer with kids, I don't know why.

At the Saratoga meeting that year there were a lot of men from home. Dave Williams and Arthur Mulford and Jerry Myers and others. Then there was a lot from Louisville and Lexington Henry Rieback knew but I didn't. They were professional gamblers and Henry Rieback's father is one too. He is what is called a sheet writer and goes away most of the year to tracks. In the winter when he is home in Beckersville he don't stay there much but goes away to cities and deals faro. He is a nice man and generous, is always sending Henry presents, a bicycle and a gold watch and a Boy Scout suit of clothes and things like that.

My own father is a lawyer. He's all right, but don't make much money and can't buy me things and anyway I'm getting so old now I don't expect it.

He never said nothing to me against Henry, but Hanley Turner and Tom Tumberton's fathers did. They said to their boys that money so come by is no good and they didn't want their boys brought up to hear gamblers' talk and be thinking about such things and maybe embrace them.

That's all right and I guess the men know what they are talking about, but I don't see what it's got to do with Henry or with horses either. That's what I'm writing this story about. I'm puzzled. I'm getting to be a man and want to think straight and be O.K., and there's something I saw at the race meeting at the eastern track I can't figure out.

I can't help it, I'm crazy about thoroughbred horses. I've always been that way. When I was ten years old and saw I was going to be big and couldn't be a rider I was so sorry I nearly died. Harry Hellinfinger in Beckersville, whose father is Postmaster, is grown up and too lazy to work, but likes to stand around in the street and get up jokes on boys like sending them to a hardware store for a gimlet to bore square holes and other jokes like that. He played one on me. He told me that if I would eat a half a cigar I would be stunted and not grow any more and maybe could be a rider. I did it. When father wasn't looking I took a cigar out of his pocket and gagged it down some way. It made me awful sick and the doctor had to be sent for, and then it did no good. I kept right on growing. It was a joke. When I told what I had done and why most fathers would have whipped me, but mine didn't.

Well, I didn't get stunted and didn't die. It serves Harry Hellinfinger right. Then I made up my mind I would like to be a stable boy, but had to give that up too. Mostly niggers do that work and I knew father wouldn't let me go into it. No use to ask him.

If you've never been crazy about thoroughbreds it's because you've never been around where they are much and don't know any better. They're beautiful. There isn't anything so lovely and clean and full of spunk and honest and everything as some race horses. On the big horse farms that are all around our town Beckersville there are tracks and the horses run in the early morning. More than a thousand times I've got out of bed before daylight and walked two or three miles to the tracks. Mother wouldn't of let me go but father always says, "Let him alone." So I got some bread out of the bread box and some butter and jam, gobbled it and lit out.

At the tracks you sit on the fence with men, whites and niggers, and they chew tobacco and talk, and then the colts are brought out. It's early and the grass is covered with shiny dew and in another field a man is plowing and they are frying things in a shed where the track niggers sleep, and you know how a nigger can giggle and laugh and say things that make you laugh. A white man can't do it and some niggers can't but a track nigger can every time.

And so the colts are brought out and some are just galloped by stable boys, but almost every morning on a big track owned by a rich man who lives maybe in New York, there are always, nearly every morning, a few colts and some of the old race horses and geldings and mares that are cut loose.

It brings a lump into my throat when a horse runs. I don't mean all horses but some. I can pick them nearly every time. It's in my blood like in the blood of race track niggers and trainers. Even when they just go slop-jogging along with a little nigger on their backs I can tell a winner. If my throat hurts and it's hard for me to swallow, that's him. He'll run like Sam Hill when you let him out. If he don't win every time it'll be a wonder and because they've got him in a pocket behind another or he was pulled or got off bad at the post or something. If I wanted to be a gambler like Henry Rieback's father I could get rich. I know I could and Henry says so too. All I would have to do is to wait 'til that hurt comes when I see a horse and then bet every cent. That's what I would do if I wanted to be a gambler, but I don't.

When you're at the tracks in the morning—not the race tracks but the training tracks around Beckersville—you don't see a horse, the kind I've been talking about, very often, but it's nice anyway. Any thoroughbred, that is sired right and out of a good mare and trained by a man that knows how, can run. If he couldn't what would he be there for and not pulling a plow?

Well, out of the stables they come and the boys are on their backs and it's lovely to be there. You hunch down on top of the fence and itch inside you. Over in the sheds the niggers giggle and sing. Bacon is being fried and coffee made. Everything smells lovely. Nothing smells better than coffee and manure and horses and niggers and bacon frying and pipes being smoked out of doors on a morning like that. It just gets you, that's what it does.

But about Saratoga. We was there six days and not a soul from home seen us and everything came off just as we wanted it to, fine weather and horses and races and all. We beat our way home and Bildad gave us a basket with fried chicken and bread and other eatables in, and I had eighteen dollars when we got back to Beckersville. Mother jawed and cried but Pop didn't say much. I told everything we done except one thing. I did and saw that alone. That's what I'm writing about. It got me upset. I think about it at night. Here it is.

At Saratoga we laid up nights in the hay in the shed Bildad had showed us and ate with the niggers early and at night when the race people had all gone away. The men from home stayed mostly in the grandstand and betting field, and didn't come out around the places where the horses are kept except to the paddocks just before a race when the horses are saddled. At Saratoga they don't have paddocks under an open shed as at Lexington and Churchill

Downs and other tracks down in our country, but saddle the horses right out in an open place under trees on a lawn as smooth and nice as Banker Bohon's front yard here in Beckersville. It's lovely. The horses are sweaty and nervous and shine and the men come out and smoke cigars and look at them and the trainers are there and the owners, and your heart thumps so you can hardly breathe.

Then the bugle blows for post and the boys that ride come running out with their silk clothes on and you run to get a place by the fence with the niggers.

I always am wanting to be a trainer or owner, and at the risk of being seen and caught and sent home I went to the paddocks before every race. The other boys didn't but I did.

We got to Saratoga on a Friday and on Wednesday the next week the big Mullford Handicap was to be run. Middlestride was in it and Sunstreak. The weather was fine and the track fast. I couldn't sleep the night before.

What had happened was that both these horses are the kind it makes my throat hurt to see. Middlestride is long and looks awkward and is a gelding. He belongs to Joe Thompson, a little owner from home who only has a half dozen horses. The Mullford Handicap is for a mile and Middlestride can't untrack fast. He goes away slow and is always way back at the half, then he begins to run and if the race is a mile and a quarter he'll just eat up everything and get there.

Sunstreak is different. He is a stallion and nervous and belongs on the biggest farm we've got in our country, the Van Riddle place that belongs to Mr. Van Riddle of New York. Sunstreak is like a girl you think about sometimes but never see. He is hard all over and lovely too. When you look at his head you want to kiss him. He is trained by Jerry Tillford who knows me and has been good to me lots of times, lets me walk into a horse's stall to look at him close and other things. There isn't anything as sweet as that horse. He stands at the post quiet and not letting on, but he is just burning up inside. Then when the barrier goes up he is off like his name, Sunstreak. It makes you ache to see him. It hurts you. He just lays down and runs like a bird dog. There can't anything I ever see run like him except Middlestride when he gets untracked and stretches himself.

Gee! I ached to see that race and those two horses run, ached and dreaded it too. I didn't want to see either of our horses beaten. We had never sent a pair like that to the races before. Old men in Beckersville said so and the niggers said so. It was a fact.

Before the race I went over to the paddocks to see. I looked a last look at Middlestride, who isn't such a much standing in a paddock that way, then I went to see Sunstreak.

It was his day. I knew when I see him. I forgot all about being seen myself and walked right up. All the men from Beckersville were there and no one noticed me except Jerry Tillford. He saw me and something happened. I'll tell you about that.

I was standing looking at that horse and aching. In some way, I can't tell how, I knew just how Sunstreak felt inside. He was quiet and letting the niggers rub his legs and Mr. Van Riddle himself put the saddle on, but he was just a raging torrent inside. He was like the water in the river at Niagara Falls just before its goes plunk down. That horse wasn't thinking about running. He don't have to think about that. He was just thinking about holding himself back 'til the time for the running came. I knew that. I could just in a way see right inside him. He was going to do some awful running and I knew it. He wasn't bragging or letting on much or prancing or making a fuss, but just waiting. I knew it and Jerry Tillford his trainer knew. I looked up and then that man and I looked into each other's eyes. Something happened to me. I guess I loved that man as much as I did the horse because he knew what I knew. Seemed to me there wasn't anything in the world but that man and the horse and me. I cried and Jerry Tillford had a shine in his eyes. Then I came away to the fence to wait for the race. The horse was better than me, more steadier, and now I know better than Jerry. He was the quietest and he had to do the running.

Sunstreak ran fast of course and he busted the world's record for a mile. I've seen that if I never see anything more. Everything came out just as I expected. Middlestride got left at the post and was way back and closed up to be second, just as I knew he would. He'll get a world's record too some day. They can't skin the Beckersville country on horses.

I watched the race calm because I knew what would happen. I was sure. Hanley Turner and Henry Rieback and Tom Tumberton were all more excited than me.

A funny thing had happened to me. I was thinking about Jerry Tillford the trainer and how happy he was all through the race. I liked him that afternoon even more than I even liked my own father. I almost forgot the horses thinking that way about him. It was because of what I had seen in his eyes as he stood in the paddocks beside Sunstreak before the race started. I knew he had been watching and working with Sunstreak since the horse was a baby colt, had taught him to run and be patient and when to let himself out and not to quit, never. I knew that for him it was like a mother seeing her child do something brave or wonderful. It was the first time I ever felt for a man like that.

After the race that night I cut out from Tom and Hanley and Henry. I wanted to be by myself and I wanted to be near Jerry Tillford if I could work it. Here is what happened.

The track in Saratoga is near the edge of town. It is all polished up and trees around, the evergreen kind, and grass and everything painted and nice. If you go past the track you get to a hard road made of asphalt for automobiles, and if you go along this for a few miles there is a road turns off to a little rummy-looking farm house set in a yard.

That night after the race I went along that road because I had seen Jerry and some other men go that way in an automobile. I didn't expect to find them. I walked for a ways and then sat down by a fence to think. It was the direction they went in. I wanted to be as near Jerry as I could. I felt close to him. Pretty soon I went up the side road—I don't know why—and came to the rummy farm house. I was just lonesome to see Jerry, like wanting to see your father at night when you are a young kid. Just then an automobile came along and turned in. Jerry was in it and Henry Rieback's father, and Arthur Bedford from home, and Dave Williams and two other men I didn't know. They got out of the car and went into the house, all but Henry Rieback's father who quarreled with them and said he wouldn't go. It was only about nine o'clock, but they were all drunk and the rummy looking farm house was a place for bad women to stay in. That's what it was. I crept up along a fence and looked through a window and saw.

It's what give me the fantods. I can't make it out. The women in the house were all ugly mean-looking women, not nice to look at or be near. They were homely too, except one who was tall and looked a little like the gelding Middlestride, but not clean like him, but with a hard ugly mouth. She had red hair. I saw everything plain. I got up by an old rose bush by an open window and looked. The women had on loose dresses and sat around in chairs. The men came in and some sat on the women's laps. The place smelled rotten and there was rotten talk, the kind a kid hears around a livery stable in a town like Beckersville in the winter but don't ever expect to hear talked when there are women around. It was rotten. A nigger wouldn't go into such a place.

I looked at Jerry Tillford. I've told you how I had been feeling about him on account of his knowing what was going on inside of Sunstreak in the minute before he went to the post for the race in which he made a world's record.

Jerry bragged in that bad woman house as I know Sunstreak wouldn't never have bragged. He said that he made that horse, that it was him that won the race and made the record. He lied and bragged like a fool. I never heard such silly talk.

And then, what do you suppose he did! He looked at the woman in there, the one that was lean and hard-mouthed and looked a little like the gelding Middlestride, but not clean like him, and his eyes began to shine just as they did when he looked at me and at Sunstreak in the paddocks at the track in the afternoon. I stood there by the window—gee!—but I wished I hadn't gone away from the tracks, but had stayed with the boys and the niggers and the horses. The tall rotten looking woman was between us just as Sunstreak was in the paddocks in the afternoon.

Then, all of a sudden, I began to hate that man. I wanted to scream and rush in the room and kill him. I never had such a feeling before. I was so mad clean through that I cried and my fists were doubled up so my finger nails cut my hands.

And Jerry's eyes kept shining and he waved back and forth, and then he went and kissed that woman and I crept away and went back to the tracks and to bed and didn't sleep hardly any, and then next day I got the other kids to start home with me and never told them anything I seen.

I been thinking about it ever since. I can't make it out. Spring has come again and I'm nearly sixteen and go to the tracks mornings same as always, and I see Sunstreak and Middlestride and a new colt named Strident I'll bet will lay them all out, but no one thinks so but me and two or three niggers.

But things are different. At the tracks the air don't taste as good or smell as good. It's because a man like Jerry Tillford, who knows what he does, could see a horse like Sunstreak run, and kiss a woman like that the same day. I can't make it out. Darn him, what did he want to do like that for? I keep thinking about it and it spoils looking at horses and smelling things and hearing niggers laugh and everything. Sometimes I'm so mad about it I want to fight someone. It gives me the fantods. What did he do it for? I want to know why.

Mark Twain (1835–1910)

Learning a trade

. . . What with lying on the rocks four days at Louisville, and some other delays, the poor old *Paul Jones* fooled away about two weeks in making the voyage from Cincinnati to New Orleans. This gave me a chance to get acquainted with one of the pilots, and he taught me how to steer the boat, and thus made the fascination of river life more potent than ever for me.

It also gave me a chance to get acquainted with a youth who had taken deck passage—more's the pity; for he easily borrowed six dollars of me on a promise to return to the boat and pay it back to me the day after we should arrive. But he probably died or forgot, for he never came. It was doubtless the former, since he said his parents were wealthy, and he only traveled deck passage because it was cooler.

I soon discovered two things. One was that a vessel would not be likely to sail for the mouth of the Amazon under ten or twelve years; and the other

---

From *Life on the Mississippi* by Mark Twain (1883).

was that the nine or ten dollars still left in my pocket would not suffice for so impossible an exploration as I had planned, even if I could afford to wait for a ship. Therefore it followed that I must contrive a new career. The *Paul Jones* was now bound for St. Louis. I planned a siege against my pilot, and at the end of three hard days he surrendered. He agreed to teach me the Mississippi River from New Orleans to St. Louis for five hundred dollars, payable out of the first wages I should receive after graduating. I entered upon the small enterprise of "learning" twelve or thirteen hundred miles of the great Mississippi River with the easy confidence of my time of life. If I had really known what I was about to require of my faculties, I should not have had the courage to begin. I supposed that all a pilot had to do was to keep his boat in the river, and I did not consider that that could be much of a trick, since it was so wide.

The boat backed out from New Orleans at four in the afternoon, and it was "our watch" until eight. Mr. Bixby, my chief, "straightened her up," plowed her along past the sterns of the other boats that lay at the Levee, and then said, "Here, take her; shave those steamships as close as you'd peel an apple." I took the wheel, and my heartbeat fluttered up into the hundreds; for it seemed to me that we were about to scrape the side off every ship in the line, we were so close. I held my breath, and began to claw the boat away from the danger; and I had my own opinion of the pilot who had known no better than to get us into such peril, but I was too wise to express it. In half a minute I had a wide margin of safety intervening between the *Paul Jones* and the ships; and within ten seconds more I was set aside in disgrace, and Mr. Bixby was going into danger again and flaying me alive with abuse of my cowardice. I was stung, but I was obliged to admire the easy confidence with which my chief loafed from side to side of his wheel, and trimmed the ships so closely that disaster seemed ceaselessly imminent. When he had cooled a little he told me that the easy water was close ashore and the current outside, and therefore we must hug the bank, up-stream, to get the benefit of the former, and stay well out, down-stream, to take advantage of the latter. In my own mind I resolved to be a down-stream pilot and leave the up-streaming to people dead to prudence.

Now and then Mr. Bixby called my attention to certain things. Said he, "This is Six-Mile Point." I assented. It was pleasant enough information, but I could not see the bearing of it. I was not conscious that it was a matter of any interest to me. Another time he said, "This is Nine-Mile Point." Later he said, "This is Twelve-Mile Point." They were all about level with the water's edge; they all looked alike to me; they were monotonously unpicturesque. I hoped Mr. Bixby would change the subject. But no; he would crowd up around a point, hugging the shore with affection, and then say: "The slack water ends here, abreast this bunch of China trees; now we cross over." So he crossed over. He gave me the wheel once or twice, but

I had no luck. I either came near chipping off the edge of a sugar-plantation, or I yawed too far from shore, and so dropped back into disgrace again and got abuse.

The watch was ended at last, and we took supper and went to bed. At midnight the glare of a lantern shone in my eyes, and the night watchman said:

"Come, turn out!"

And then he left. I could not understand this extraordinary procedure; so I presently gave up trying to, and dozed off to sleep. Pretty soon the watchman was back again, and this time he was gruff. I was annoyed. I said:

"What do you want to come bothering around here in the middle of the night for? Now, as like as not, I'll not get to sleep again tonight."

The watchman said:

"Well, if this ain't good, I'm blessed."

The "off-watch" was just turning in, and I heard some brutal laughter from them, and such remarks as "Hello, watchman! ain't the new cub turned out yet? He's delicate, likely. Give him some sugar in a rag, and send for the chambermaid to sing 'Rock-a-by Baby,' to him."

About this time Mr. Bixby appeared on the scene. Something like a minute later I was climbing the pilot-house steps with some of my clothes on and the rest in my arms. Mr. Bixby was close behind, commenting. Here was something fresh—this thing of getting up in the middle of the night to go to work. It was a detail in piloting that had never occurred to me at all. I knew that boats ran all night, but somehow I had never happened to reflect that somebody had to get up out of a warm bed to run them. I began to fear that piloting was not quite so romantic as I had imagined it was; there was something very real and worklike about this new phase of it.

It was rather a dingy night, although a fair number of stars were out. The big mate was at the wheel, and he had the old tub pointed at a star and was holding her straight up the middle of the river. The shores on either hand were not much more than half a mile apart, but they seemed wonderfully far away, and ever so vague and indistinct. The mate said:

"We've got to land at Jones's plantation, sir."

The vengeful spirit in me exulted. I said to myself, "I wish you joy of your job, Mr. Bixby; you'll have a good time finding Mr. Jones's plantation such a night as this; and I hope you never *will* find it as long as you live."

Mr. Bixby said to the mate:

"Upper end of the plantation, or the lower?"

"Upper."

"I can't do it. The stumps there are out of water at this stage. It's no great distance to the lower, and you'll have to get along with that."

"All right, sir. If Jones don't like it, he'll have to lump it, I reckon."

And then the mate left. My exultation began to cool and my wonder to come up. Here was a man who not only proposed to find this plantation on such a night, but to find either end of it you preferred. I dreadfully wanted to ask a question, but I was carrying about as many short answers as my cargo-room would admit of, so I held my peace. All I desired to ask Mr. Bixby was the simple question whether he was ass enough to really imagine he was going to find that plantation on a night when all plantations were exactly alike and all of the same color. But I held in. I used to have fine inspirations of prudence in those days.

Mr. Bixby made for the shore and soon was scraping it, just the same as if it had been daylight. And not only that, but singing:

"Father in heaven, the day is declining," etc.

It seemed to me that I had put my life in the keeping of a peculiarly reckless outcast. Presently he turned on me and said:

"What's the name of the first point above New Orleans?"

I was gratified to be able to answer promptly, and I did. I said I didn't know.

"Don't *know?*"

This manner jolted me. I was down at the foot again in a moment. But I had to say just what I had said before.

"Well, you're a smart one!" said Mr. Bixby. "What's the name of the *next* point?"

Once more I didn't know.

"Well this beats anything. Tell me the name of *any* point or place I told you."

I studied awhile and decided that I couldn't.

"Look here! What do you start out from, above Twelve-Mile Point, to cross over?"

"I—I—don't know."

"You—you—don't know?" mimicking my drawling manner of speech. "What *do* you know?"

"I—I—nothing, for certain."

"By the great Caesar's ghost, I believe you! You're the stupidest dunderhead I ever saw or ever heard of, so help me Moses! The idea of *you* being a pilot—*you!* Why, you don't know enough to pilot a cow down a lane."

Oh, but his wrath was up! He was a nervous man, and he shuffled from one side of his wheel to the other, as if the floor was hot. He would boil awhile to himself, and then overflow and scald me again.

"Look here! What do you suppose I told you the names of those points for?"

I tremblingly considered a moment, and then the devil of temptation provoked me to say:

"Well to—to—be entertaining, I thought."

This was a red rag to the bull. He raged and stormed so (he was crossing the river at the time) that I judged it made him blind, because he ran over the steering-oar of a trading-scow. Of course the traders sent up a volley of red-hot profanity. Never was a man so grateful as Mr. Bixby was; because he was brimful, and here were subjects who could *talk back*. He threw open a window, thrust his head out, and such an eruption followed as I never had heard before. The fainter and farther away the scowmen's curses drifted, the higher Mr. Bixby lifted his voice and the weightier his adjectives grew. When he closed the window he was empty. You could have drawn a seine through his system and not caught curses enough to disturb your mother with. Presently he said to me in the gentlest way:

"My boy, you must get a little memorandum book; and every time I tell you a thing, put it down right away. There's only one way to be a pilot, and that is to get this entire river by heart. You have to know it just like A B C."

That was a dismal revelation to me; for my memory was never loaded with anything but blank cartridges. However, I did not feel discouraged long. I judged that it was best to make some allowances, for doubtless Mr. Bixby was "stretching." Presently he pulled a rope and struck a few strokes on the big bell. The stars were all gone now, and the night was as black as ink. I could hear the wheels churn along the bank, but I was not entirely certain that I could see the shore. The voice of the invisible watchman called up from the hurricane-deck:

"What's this, sir?"

"Jones's plantation."

I said to myself, "I wish I might venture to offer a small bet that it isn't." But I did not chirp. I only waited to see. Mr. Bixby handled the engine-bells, and in due time the boat's nose came to the land, a torch glowed from the forecastle, a man skipped ashore, a darky's voice on the bank said: "Gimme de k'yarpet-bag, Mass' Jones," and the next moment we were standing up the river again, all serene. I reflected deeply awhile, and then said—but not aloud—"Well, the finding of that plantation was the luckiest accident that ever happened; but it couldn't happen again in a hundred years." And I fully believed it *was* an accident, too.

By the time we had gone seven or eight hundred miles up the river, I had learned to be a tolerably plucky up-stream steersman, in daylight; and before we reached St. Louis I had made a trifle of progress in night work, but only a trifle. I had a note-book that fairly bristled with the names of towns, "points," bars, islands, bends, reaches, etc.; but the information was to be found only in the note-book—none of it was in my head. It made my heart ache to think I had only got half of the river set down; for as our watch was four hours off and four hours on, day and night, there was a long four-hour gap in my book for every time I had slept since the voyage began.

My chief was presently hired to go on a big New Orleans boat, and I packed my satchel and went with him. She was a grand affair. When I stood in her pilot-house I was so far above the water that I seemed perched on a mountain; and her decks stretched so far away, fore and aft, below me, that I wondered how I could ever have considered the little *Paul Jones* a large craft. There were other differences, too. The *Paul Jones's* pilot-house was a cheap, dingy, battered rattletrap, cramped for room; but here was a sumptuous glass temple; room enough to have a dance in; showy red and gold window-curtains; an imposing sofa; leather cushions and a back to the high bench where visiting pilots sit, to spin yarns and "look at the river"; bright, fanciful "cuspidores," instead of a broad wooden box filled with sawdust; nice new oilcloth on the floor; a hospitable big stove for winter; a wheel as high as my head, costly with inlaid work; a wire tiller-rope; bright brass knobs for the bells, and a tidy, white-aproned, black "texas-tender," to bring up tarts and ices and coffee during mid-watch, day and night. Now this was "something like"; and so I began to take heart once more to believe that piloting was a romantic sort of occupation after all. The moment we were under way I began to prowl about the great steamer and fill myself with joy. She was as clean and as dainty as a drawing-room; when I looked down her long, gilded saloon, it was like gazing through a splendid tunnel; she had an oil-picture, by some gifted sign-painter, on every stateroom door; she flittered with no end of prism-fringed chandeliers; the clerk's office was elegant, the bar was marvelous, and the barkeeper had been barbered and upholstered at incredible cost. The boiler-deck (i.e., the second story of the boat, so to speak) was as spacious as a church, it seemed to me; so with the forecastle; and there was no pitiful handful of deck-hands, firemen, and roustabouts down there, but a whole battalion of men. The fires were fiercely glaring from a long row of furnaces, and over them were eight huge boilers! This was unutterable pomp. The mighty engines—but enough of this. I had never felt so fine before. And when I found that the regiment of natty servants respectfully "sir'd" me, my satisfaction was complete.

Youth

Section Three illustrated the process of socialization, that is, the mechanisms through which the child—and also the adult—is fitted into the general social framework and induced to live up to the norms which surround specific social roles. Section Four partially overlaps that topic. It examines the stages through which the young gradually develop into fully mature members of human communities. Whereas the previous section had its analytical focus in the operation of societal constraints, this section examines the process of socialization from the perspective of growing young men and women. Its focus is on the trials and tribulations, the joys and the tragedies, that typically attend the long and difficult road to adulthood.

The short section from William Wordsworth's great autobiographical poem *The Prelude* beautifully captures the transition from a state at which the baby in close touch and "mute dialogue" with the mother is still totally immersed in her, to the next developmental stage at which the properties and delights of the outside world are discovered, at which "every hour brings palpable access of knowledge." The second excerpt is from *High Wind in*

Jamaica, one of modern literature's most subtle studies of the mentality of children. Its author, the British novelist Richard Hughes, masterfully describes the birth of a feeling of individual autonomy.

The selection from Sherwood Anderson's autobiographical *Tar, a Midwestern Childhood*, sensitively deals with a later stage in the development of the young—when they discover the frightening yet attractive, the alluring yet anxiety-producing realities of sexual life. Anderson depicts the world of emerging sex through the eyes of a young boy. The same experience, as seen through the eyes of a girl, is described in the next selection. Anne Frank, an adolescent Jewish girl, in the intensely moving diary which she kept while hiding with her family from the Nazi occupiers in Holland during World War II, proved capable of profound insights into her own psychic development. The author and most of her family ultimately perished in a Nazi extermination camp.

The last two selections from Jeremy Larner's brilliant novel, and from James S. Kunen's engaging autobiographical account, *The Strawberry Statement*, need little comment. Students will have no difficulty in identifying with the heroes of these accounts. The selections show how confoundedly difficult it is to grow up in a contemporary world which makes very little sense to the young and in which most men, young or old, have a hard time finding their bearings. When much of the experienced world seems to come straight out of the theater of the absurd, it is understandable that many of the young today have the feeling that they indeed "grow up absurd." Moreover, when the young react to the decline of socially validated life styles by developing distinctive life styles of their own, only to find that adult society reacts by stigmatizing them, not only they themselves but also society is in for trouble. From such stuff comes radical change.

—————   **William Wordsworth (1770–1850)**   —————————

The prelude

> . . . From early days,
> Beginning not long after that first time
> In which, a Babe, by intercourse of touch,
> I held mute dialogues with my Mother's heart
> I have endeavour'd to display the means
> Whereby this infant sensibility,
> Great birthright of our Being, was in me
> Augmented and sustain'd. Yet is a path

—————

From *The Prelude* by William Wordsworth (1805–1806).

More difficult before me, and I fear
That in its broken windings we shall need
The chamois' sinews, and the eagle's wing:
For now a trouble came into my mind
From unknown causes. I was left alone,
Seeking the visible world, nor knowing why.
The props of my affections were remov'd,
And yet the building stood, as if sustain'd
By its own spirit! All that I beheld
Was dear to me, and from this cause it came,
That now to Nature's finer influxes
My mind lay open, to that more exact
And intimate communion which our hearts
Maintain with the minuter properties
Of objects which already are belov'd,
And of those only. Many are the joys
Of youth; but oh! what happens to live
When every hour brings palpable access
Of knowledge, when all knowledge is delight,
And sorrow is not there. The seasons came,
And every season to my notice brought
A store of transistory qualities
Which, but for this most watchful power of love
Had been neglected, left a register
Of permanent relations, else unknown,
Hence life, and change, and beauty, solitude
More active, even, than 'best society',
Society made sweet as solitude
By silent inobtrusive sympathies,
And gentle agitations of the mind . . .

Richard Hughes (1900–   )

I am emily

. . . And then an event did occur, to Emily, of considerable importance.
She suddenly realised who she was.

From pp. 188–95 in *A High Wind in Jamaica* by Richard Hughes. Copyright
1929, 1957 by Richard Hughes. Reprinted by permission of Harper & Row,
Publishers, Inc.

There is little reason that one can see why it should not have happened to her five years earlier, or even five later; and none, why it should have come that particular afternoon.

She had been playing houses in a nook right in the bows, behind the windlass (on which she had hung a devil's-claw as a door-knocker); and tiring of it was walking rather aimlessly aft, thinking vaguely about some bees and a fairy queen, when it suddenly flashed into her mind that she was *she*.

She stopped dead, and began looking over all of her person which came within the range of her eyes. She could not see much, except a foreshortened view of the front of her frock, and her hands when she lifted them for inspection; but it was enough for her to form a rough idea of the little body she suddenly realised to be hers.

She began to laugh, rather mockingly. "Well!" she thought, in effect. "Fancy *you*, of all people, going and getting caught like this!—You can't get out of it now, for a very long time: you'll have to go through with being a child, and growing up, and getting old, before you'll be quit of this mad prank!"

Determined to avoid any interruption of this highly important occasion, she began to climb the ratlines, on her way to her favourite perch at the masthead. Each time she moved an arm or a leg in this simple action, however, it struck her with fresh amazement to find them obeying her so readily. Memory told her, of course, that they had always done so before: but before, she had never realised how surprising this was.

Once settled on her perch, she began examining the skin of her hands with the utmost care: for it was *hers*. She slipped a shoulder out of the top of her frock; and having peeped in to make sure she really was continuous under her clothes, she shrugged it up to touch her cheek. The contact of her face and the warm bare hollow of her shoulder gave her a comfortable thrill, as if it was the caress of some kind friend. But whether the feeling came to her through her cheek or her shoulder, which was the caresser and which the caressed, that no analysis could tell her.

Once fully convinced of this astonishing fact, that she was now Emily Bas-Thornton (why she inserted the "now" she did not know, for she certainly imagined no transmigrational nonsense of having been anyone else before), she began seriously to reckon its implications.

First, what agency had so ordered it that out of all the people in the world who she might have been, she was this particular one, this Emily; born in such-and-such a year out of all the years in Time, and encased in this particular rather pleasing little casket of flesh? Had she chosen herself, or had God done it?

At this, another consideration: who was God? She had heard a terrible lot about Him, always: but the question of His identity had been left vague, as much taken for granted as her own. Wasn't she perhaps God, herself? Was it that she was trying to remember? However, the more she tried, the more it eluded her. (How absurd, to disremember such an important point as whether one was God or not!) So she let it slide: perhaps it would come back to her later.

Secondly, why had all this not occurred to her before? She had been alive for over ten years, now, and it had never once entered her head. She felt like a man who suddenly remembers at eleven o'clock at night, sitting in his own arm-chair, that he had accepted an invitation to go out to dinner that night. There is no reason for him to remember it now: but there seems equally little why he should not have remembered it in time to keep his engagement. How could he have sat there all the evening, without being disturbed by the slightest misgiving? How could Emily have gone on being Emily for ten years, without once noticing this apparently obvious fact?

It must not be supposed that she argued it all out in this ordered, but rather longwinded fashion. Each consideration came to her in a momentary flash, quite innocent of words; and in between her mind lazed along, either thinking of nothing or returning to her bees and the fairy queen. If one added up the total of her periods of conscious thought, it would probably reach something between four and five seconds; nearer five, perhaps; but it was spread out over the best part of an hour.

Well then, granted she was Emily, what were the consequences, besides enclosure in that particular little body (which now began on its own account to be aware of a sort of unlocated itch, most probably somewhere on the right thigh), and lodgement behind a particular pair of eyes?

It implied a whole series of circumstances. In the first place, there was her family, a number of brothers and sisters from whom, before, she had never entirely dissociated herself; but now she got such a sudden feeling of being a discrete person that they seemed as separate from her as the ship itself. However, willy-nilly she was almost as tied to them as she was to her body. And then there was this voyage, this ship, this mast round which she had wound her legs. She began to examine it with almost as vivid an illumination as she had studied the skin of her hands. And when she came down from the mast, what would she find at the bottom? There would be Jonsen, and Otto, and the crew: the whole fabric of a daily life which up to now she had accepted as it came, but which now seemed vaguely disquieting. What was going to happen? Were there disasters running about loose, disasters which her rash marriage to the body of Emily Thornton made her vulnerable to?

Sherwood Anderson

Tar is bothered

Something had been bothering Tar for a long time. It got worse during the summer of his thirteenth year. His mother had not been very well for a long time but that summer she seemed to get better. [*Now Tar, rather than John, sold the papers] but that did not take much time.[1] As his mother wasn't very well and had other younger children to take her time she couldn't pay much attention to [*Tar].

He and Jim Moore went off to the woods on afternoons. Sometimes they just lazied around and sometimes they went fishing or swimming. Up along the creek farmers were working in the fields. When they went swimming, in a place called "Mama Culver's Hole," other boys from town came.[2] Young men sometimes came down across the fields to the creek. There was one young man who was subject to fits. His father was the town blacksmith [*who had carried the dead woman out of the woods]. He went in swimming, just as the others did, but someone had to watch him [all the time]. Once he had a fit in the water and had to be pulled out so he wouldn't drown. Tar saw that, saw the man lying naked on the bank of the creek, saw the queer look in his eyes, the queer jerky movements of his legs, arms and body.

The man muttered words Tar couldn't understand. It might have been like a bad dream you have sometimes at night. [*He] only looked for a moment. Pretty soon the man got up and dressed. He walked slowly about in a field, his head hanging down, went to sit with his back against a tree. How pale he was.[3]

When the older boys and young men came to the swimming hole Tar and Jim Moore lit out. Older boys in such a place like to take it out on the youngsters. They throw mud on small boys' bodies after they come out from swimming and are partly dressed. When it hits you you have to go in and wash yourself off again. Sometimes they do it a dozen times.

Then they hide your clothes or dip them in the water and tie knots in the sleeve of your shirt. When you want to dress and go away you can't.

[1]In *Memoirs*, p. 36, Anderson describes his boyhood job as newsboy.
[2]This swimming hole is described in *Memoirs*, pp. 30–31.
[3]*Ibid.*

Reprinted by permission from *TAR: A Midwest Childhood*, Sherwood Anderson, edited with an Introduction by Ray Lewis White (Cleveland and London: The Press of Case University Western Reserve University, 1969), copyright © 1969 by the Press of Case Western Reserve University, Cleveland, Ohio 44106.

[*A gentle lot—small-town boys—sometimes.]

They take a shirt sleeve and dip it in the water. Then they tie a hard knot and pull as hard as they can and a boy has a hard time getting it untied. If he has to take his teeth to it the older boys in the water laugh and shout. There is a song about it full of words worse than you could hear in any livery stable. "Chaw beef," the older boys yell.[4] Then they shout out the song. The whole place rings with it. It isn't any fancy singing.

The thing that troubled Tar troubled Jim Moore too. Sometimes when they were alone together, in the woods away up the creek beyond the regular swimming hole, they went in together. Then they came out and lay naked on the bank of the creek on the grass in the sun. It felt good.

[*Then] they began to talk about things they had heard, at school, among the young men at the swimming hole.

"Suppose you ever got a chance with a girl, what then?" Maybe little girls going home together from school, no boys about, talk the same way.

"Oh, I won't get any such chance. I'd be afraid, I guess, wouldn't you?"

"I guess you get over being afraid. Let's go."[5]

You can talk and think about a lot of things and then, when you come home where your mother and sister are, it doesn't seem to count much against you. If you had a chance and did something it might be different.

Sometimes when Tar and Jim were lying like that, on the creek bank, one of them touched the other's body. It was a queer feeling. When it happened they both sprang up and began to run about. Some young trees grew by the creek bank up that way and they climbed the trees. The trees were small, smooth and slender and the boys pretended they were monkeys or some other kind of wild young animals. They kept on doing it for a long time, both acting rather crazy.

Once when they were doing it a man came along and they had to run and hide in some bushes. They were in a close place and had to lie close together. After the man passed they went at once to get their clothes, both feeling strange.

Strange about what? Well, how are you going to tell? All boys are that way sometimes.

There was a boy Jim and Tar both knew, who had the nerve to do anything. Once he was with a girl and they went into a barn. The girl's mother saw them go in and followed. The girl got a whipping. Neither Tar nor Jim thought anything really happened but the boy said it did. He bragged about it. "It isn't the first time."

Such talk. Tar and Jim thought the boy lied. "He wouldn't have the nerve—do you think?"

---

[4]The exact scene occurs in *Memoirs*, p. 31.

[5]On Anderson's early interest in sex, see *Memoirs*, pp. 61–74. Compare the ensuing episodes with "Nobody Knows," *Winesburg, Ohio*, pp. 58–62.

They talked about such things more than they wanted to. They couldn't help it. When they had talked a lot they both felt uncomfortable. Well, how are you going to find out anything? When men are talking you listen all you can. If the men see you hanging around they tell you to get out.

Tar saw things, taking papers to houses in the evening. There was a man used to come with a horse and buggy and wait in a certain place in a dark street and after a while he was joined by a woman. The woman was married and so was the man. Before the woman came the man had put on the side curtains to his buggy. They drove away together.

Tar knew who they were and after a time the man knew he knew. One day he met Tar on the street. The man stopped. He bought a paper. Then he stood looking at Tar with his hands thrust into his pockets. The man owned a large farm, several miles from town, and his wife and children lived out there but he was in town nearly all the time. He was a buyer of farm products, shipping them off to nearby cities. The woman Tar had seen get into the buggy was the wife of a merchant.

The man put a five dollar bill into Tar's hand. "I guess you know enough to keep your mouth shut," he said. That was all. After he said it the man turned and went away. Tar had never had so much money, had never before had any money he did not expect to account for. It was an easy way to get it. When any of the Moorehead children made any money they gave it to their mother. She never asked anything of the sort. It just seemed the natural thing to do.

Tar bought himself a quarter's worth of candy, he bought a package of Sweet Caporal cigarettes. He and Jim Moore would try smoking them sometime when they were off in the woods. Then he bought a swell necktie that cost fifty cents.

That was all right. He had a little more than four dollars in his pocket. He had got the change in silver dollars. Ernest Wright, who kept a small hotel in town, was always standing in front of his hotel with a pile of silver dollars in his hands, playing with them. At the fair, in the fall, when there were a lot of fakers from out of town come for the fair, they set up little booths for gambling. You could get a cane by throwing a ring over it or a gold watch or a revolver by picking out the right number on a wheel. There were lots of such places. One year Dick Moorehead, being out of work, got a job in one of them.

At all such places little piles of silver dollars were stacked about up where everyone could see them. Dick Moorehead said a farmer or a hired man had about as much chance to win any of the money as a snowball had in hell.

It was nice though to see the silver dollars piled up, nice to see Ernest Wright jingling silver dollars in his hands as he stood on the sidewalk before his hotel.

Nice for Tar to have four big silver dollars he did not feel he had to account for. They had just come down into his hand, out of the sky, as it were. The candy he could eat, the cigarettes he and Jim Moore would try smoking someday soon. The new necktie would be a little difficult. Where would he tell the others at home he had got it? Most boys of his age in town never got any fifty cent neckties. Dick didn't get but about two new ones a year—when there was a G.A.R. convention or something. Tar might say he had found it and found the four silver dollars, too. Then he could give the money to his mother and forget it. It was fine to feel the heavy silver dollars in his pocket but he had got them in a strange way. Silver is much better to have than bills. It feels like more.

When a man is married you see him with his wife and you do not think anything [about it] but a man like that, waiting in a buggy in a side street, and then a woman coming along trying to act as though she is going to call on some neighbor—it being night and supper over and her husband gone back to his store. Then the woman looking around and getting, quick, into the buggy. They driving off with the curtains drawn, that way.

Plenty Madame Bovaries in American small towns—what![6]

Tar wanted to tell Jim Moore but didn't dare. There was a kind of agreement between himself and the man from whom he had taken the five dollars.

The woman knew he knew as well as the man. He had come out of an alleyway bare-footed, making no sound, with a bundle of papers under his arm, had popped right out on them.

Maybe he did it purposely.

The woman's husband took a morning paper at his store and had an afternoon paper delivered at his house. It was a funny feeling to go into his store afterwards and see him there, talking to some man, knowing nothing, Tar, just a kid, knowing such a lot.

Well, what did he know?

The trouble is that such things set a boy thinking. You want to see a lot and when you see something it stirs you up and makes you almost wish you hadn't. The woman, when Tar took the paper to her house, never let on. She had a nerve all right.

Why did they go sneaking out that way? A boy knows but doesn't know. If Tar could only have talked it over with John or Jim Moore it would have been a relief. You can't talk about such things to someone in your own family. You have to go outside.

Tar saw other things. Win Connell, who worked in Cary's drug store, married Mrs. Grey, after her first husband died. She was taller than he was. They took a house and furnished it with her first husband's furniture. One

[6]Gustave Flaubert (1821–80) published *Madame Bovary* in 1857.

evening, when it was raining and dark, only about seven o'clock, Tar went along back of their house on his paper route and they had forgot to close the window blinds. They didn't have a thing on, either of them, and he was chasing her around. You would never think grown people could act like that.[7]

Tar was in the alleyway, just as he was that time he saw the people in the buggy. By cutting through alleyways you save time [*delivering papers] when a train is late. There he stood, holding his papers under his coat so they wouldn't get wet, and there were the two grown people acting like that.

There was a kind of living room and a stairway going upstairs and then some other rooms on the ground floor, without any lights in them.

What Tar saw first was the woman running like that, without any clothes on, across the room and her husband after her. It made Tar laugh. They were like monkeys. The woman ran upstairs and he after her. Then down she came again. They dodged into the dark rooms and then out again. He caught her sometimes but she must have been slippery. She got away every time. They kept it up and kept it up. Such a crazy thing to see. There was a couch in the room Tar was looking into and once she got behind it and he was in front. He put his hands on the top of the couch and sprang clear over. You wouldn't have thought [*a drug clerk] could do it.

Then he chased her into one of the dark rooms. Tar waited and waited but they did not come out.

---

[7]A similar scene of innocent voyeurism occurs in "Girl by the Stove," *Decision*, I (January, 1942), 19–22.

Anne Frank (1929–1945)

Anne discovers love

Wednesday, 5 January, 1944

Dear Kitty,

I have two things to confess to you today, which will take a long time. But I must tell someone and you are the best one to tell, as I know that, come what may, you always keep a secret.

The first is about Mummy. You know that I've grumbled a lot about Mummy, yet still tried to be nice to her again. Now it is suddenly clear to me what she lacks. Mummy herself has told us that she looked upon us

---

more as her friends than her daughters. Now that is all very fine, but still, a friend can't take a mother's place. I need my mother as an example which I can follow, I want to be able to respect her. I have the feeling that Margot thinks differently about these things and would never be able to understand what I've just told you. And Daddy avoids all arguments about Mummy.

I imagine a mother as a woman who, in the first place, shows great tact, especially towards her children when they reach our age, and who does not laugh at me if I cry about something—not pain, but other things—like "Mums" does.

One thing, which perhaps may seem rather fatuous, I have never forgiven her. It was on a day that I had to go to the dentist. Mummy and Margot were going to come with me, and agreed that I should take my bicycle. When we had finished at the dentist, and were outside again, Margot and Mummy told me that they were going into the town to look at something or buy something—I don't remember exactly what. I wanted to go, too, but was not allowed to, as I had my bicycle with me. Tears of rage sprang into my eyes, and Mummy and Margot began laughing at me. Then I became so furious that I stuck my tongue out at them in the street just as an old woman happened to pass by, who looked very shocked! I rode home on my bicycle, and I know I cried for a long time.

It is queer that the wound that Mummy made then still burns, when I think of how angry I was that afternoon.

The second is something that is very difficult to tell you, because it is about myself.

Yesterday I read an article about blushing by Sis Heyster. This article might have been addressed to me personally. Although I don't blush very easily, the other things in it certainly all fit me. She writes roughly something like this—that a girl in the years of puberty becomes quiet within and begins to think about the wonders that are happening to her body.

I experience that, too, and that is why I get the feeling lately of being embarrassed about Margot, Mummy, and Daddy. Funnily enough, Margot, who is much more shy than I am, isn't at all embarrassed.

I think what is happening to me is so wonderful, and not only what can be seen on my body, but all that is taking place inside. I never discuss myself or any of these things with anybody; that is why I have to talk to myself about them.

Each time I have a period—and that has only been three times—I have the feeling that in spite of all the pain, unpleasantness, and nastiness, I have a sweet secret, and that is why, although it is nothing but a nuisance to me in a way, I always long for the time that I shall feel that secret within me again.

Sis Heyster also writes that girls of this age don't feel quite certain of themselves, and discover that they themselves are individuals with ideas, thoughts, and habits. After I came here, when I was just fourteen, I began to think about myself sooner than most girls, and to know that I am a "person." Sometimes, when I lie in bed at night, I have a terrible desire to feel my breasts and to listen to the quiet rhythmic beat of my heart.

I already had these kinds of feelings subconsciously before I came here, because I remember that once when I slept with a girl friend I had a strong desire to kiss her, and that I did do so. I could not help being terribly inquisitive over her body, for she had always kept it hidden from me. I asked her whether, as a proof of our friendship, we should feel one another's breasts, but she refused. I go into ecstasies every time I see the naked figure of a woman, such as Venus, for example. It strikes me as so wonderful and exquisite that I have difficulty in stopping the tears rolling down my cheeks.

If only I had a girl friend!

Yours, Anne

Saturday, 15 July, 1944

Dear Kitty,

We have had a book from the library with the challenging title of: *What Do You Think of the Modern Young Girl?* I want to talk about this subject today.

The author of this book criticizes "the youth of today" from top to toe, without, however, condemning the whole of the young brigade as "incapable of anything good." On the contrary, she is rather of the opinion that if young people wished, they have it in their hands to make a bigger, more beautiful and better world, but that they occupy themselves with superficial things, without giving a thought to real beauty.

In some passages the writer gave me very much the feeling she was directing her criticisms at me, and that's why I want to lay myself completely bare to you for once and defend myself against this attack.

I have one outstanding trait in my character, which must strike anyone who knows me for any length of time, and that is my knowledge of myself. I can watch myself and my actions, just like an outsider. The Anne of every day I can face entirely without prejudice, without making excuses for her and watch what's good and what's bad about her. This "self-consciousness" haunts me, and every time I open my mouth I know as soon as I've spoken whether "that ought to have been different" or "that was right as it was." There are so many things about myself that I condemn; I couldn't begin to name them all. I understand more and more how true Daddy's words were when he said: "All children must look after their own upbringing." Parents can only give good advice or put them on the right paths. but the final forming of a person's character lies in their own hands.

In addition to this, I have lots of courage, I always feel so strong and as if I can bear a great deal, I feel so free and so young! I was glad when I first realized it, because I don't think I shall easily bow down before the blows that inevitably come to everyone.

But I've talked about these things so often before. Now I want to come to the chapter of "Daddy and Mummy don't understand me." Daddy and Mummy have always thoroughly spoiled me, were sweet to me, defended me, and have done all that parents could do. And yet I've felt so terribly lonely for a long time, so left out, neglected, and misunderstood. Daddy tried all he could to check my rebellious spirit, but it was no use, I have cured myself, by seeing for myself what was wrong in my behavior and keeping it before my eyes.

How is it that Daddy was never any support to me in my struggle, why did he completely miss the mark when he wanted to offer me a helping hand? Daddy tried the wrong methods, he always talked to me as a child who was going through difficult phases. It sounds crazy, because Daddy's the only one who has always taken me into his confidence, and no one but Daddy has given me the feeling that I'm sensible. But there's one thing he's omitted: you see, he hasn't realized that for me the fight to get on top was more important than all else. I didn't want to hear about "symptoms of your age," or "other girls," or "it wears off by itself"; I didn't want to be treated as a girl-like-all-others, but as Anne-on-her-own-merits. Pim didn't understand that. For that matter, I can't confide in anyone, unless they tell me a lot about themselves, and as I know very little about Pim, I don't feel that I can tread upon more intimate ground with him. Pim always takes up the older, fatherly attitude, tells me that he too has had similar passing tendencies. But still he's not able to feel with me like a friend, however hard he tries. These things have made me never mention my views on life nor my well-considered theories to anyone but my diary and, occasionally, to Margot. I concealed from Daddy everything that perturbed me; I never shared my ideals with him. I was aware of the fact that I was pushing him away from me.

I couldn't do anything else. I have acted entirely according to my feelings, but I have acted in the way that was best for my peace of mind. Because I should completely lose my repose and self-confidence, which I have built up so shakily, if, at this stage, I were to accept criticisms of my half-completed task. And I can't do that even from Pim, although it sounds very hard, for not only have I not shared my secret thoughts with Pim but I have often pushed him even further from me, by my irritability.

This is a point that I think a lot about: why is it that Pim annoys me? So much so that I can hardly bear him teaching me, that his affectionate ways strike me as being put on, that I want to be left in peace and would really prefer it if he dropped me a bit, until I felt more certain in my attitude towards him? Because I still have a gnawing feeling of guilt over that horrible letter that I dared to write him when I was so wound up. Oh, how hard it is to be really strong and brave in every way!

Yet this was not my greatest disappointment, no, I ponder far more over Peter than Daddy. I know very well that I conquered him instead of he conquering me. I created an image of him in my mind, pictured him as a quiet, sensitive, lovable boy, who needed affection and friendship. I needed a living person to whom I could pour out my heart; I wanted a friend who'd help to put me on the right road. I achieved what I wanted, and, slowly but surely, I drew him towards me. Finally, when I had made him feel friendly, it automatically developed into an intimacy which, on second thought, I don't think I ought to have allowed.

We talked about the most private things, and yet up till now we have never touched on those things that filled, and still fill, my heart and soul. I still don't know quite what to make of Peter, is he superficial, or does he still feel shy, even of me? But dropping that, I committed one error in my desire to make a real friendship: I switched over and tried to get at him by developing it into a more intimate relation, whereas I should have explored all other possibilities. He longs to be loved and I can see that he's beginning to be more and more in love with me. He gets satisfaction out of our meetings, whereas they just have the effect of making me want to try it out with him again. And yet I don't seem able to touch on the subjects that I'm so longing to bring out into the daylight. I drew Peter towards me, far more than he realizes. Now he clings to me, and for the time being, I don't see any way of shaking him off and putting him on his own feet. When I realized that he could not be a friend for my understanding, I thought I would at least try to lift him up out of his narrow-mindedness and make him do something with his youth.

"For in its innermost depths youth is lonelier than old age." I read this saying in some book and I've always remembered it, and found it to be true. Is it true then that grownups have a more difficult time here than we do? No. I know it isn't. Older people have formed their opinions about everything, and don't waver before they act. It's twice as hard for us young ones to hold our ground, and maintain our opinions, in a time when all ideals are being shattered and destroyed, when people are showing their worst side, and do not know whether to believe in truth and right and God.

Anyone who claims that the older ones have a more difficult time here certainly doesn't realize to what extent our problems weigh down on us, problems for which we are probably much too young, but which thrust themselves upon us continually, until, after a long time, we think we've found a solution, but the solution doesn't seem able to resist the facts which reduce it to nothing again. That's the difficulty in these times: ideals, dreams, and cherished hopes rise within us, only to meet the horrible truth and be shattered.

It's really a wonder that I haven't dropped all my ideals, because they seem so absurd and impossible to carry out. Yet I keep them, because in spite of everything I still believe that people are really good at heart. I simply can't build up my hopes on a foundation consisting of confusion, misery, and death. I see the world gradually being turned into a wilderness, I hear the ever approaching thunder, which will destroy us too, I can feel the sufferings of millions and yet, if I look up into the heavens, I think that it will all come right, that this cruelty too will end, and that peace and tranquility will return again.

In the meantime, I must uphold my ideals, for perhaps the time will come when I shall be able to carry them out.

Yours, Anne

Jeremy Larner (1937–)

Gabriel's search for the real thing

Gabriel was the only child of a careful-shrewed father who stayed comfortably middle-class even after investing himself past his first million dollars and a careful-clean mother who had nearly had a breakdown getting him born. (There was so much mess!) Strangely enough—despite his parents never giving him anything he didn't need and warning him how spoiled he was—little Gabriel became something of a problem child. Yes, he was a nasty kid all right, and for the well-being of the household he was sent to Arizona boarding schools in the wintertime and on supervised fishing treks etc to Canada in the summer. When Gabriel went trekking the counselors had to broil him steaks every night . . . or else Gabriel wouldn't eat. They tested him once and he went three days and started to die on them. Naturally his fellow trekkers hated him, but it was hard not to love him when he caught a fish: he was so deliriously happy.

In the form of a child, Gabriel could never quite pull himself together. But soon enough his life began to take a definite (& startling) shape: the revelation of Gabriel as the son of God. At twelve years of age Gabriel, to the despair of his would-be parents, declared himself an Anglo-Catholic.

Reprinted from *Drive He Said* by Jeremy Larner by permission of Robert Lantz-Candida Donadio Literary Agency. Copyright © 1964 by Jeremy Larner.

For the next three years he worshipped a life-size luminous crucifix on his bedroom wall and took private communion from an engraved silver chalice he had secured for $300 at an antiquary on 57th Street. (His life's savings —Gabriel played for keeps, even then.) Every Sunday Gabriel went unattended to the Anglican High Ceremony, where his great Hebrew eyes shone archangelic among the pallid Anglos & Saxons of the choir.

When Gabriel went to college he became Chairman of the Board. He possessed & displayed twenty-three cashmere sweaters, charcoal bermuda shorts with a belt in the back plus blazer, an initialed platinum hipflask, a car that played music of sophisticated violins and made up into a bed, and doll-girls to fit casually inside the car. Before long Gabriel was elected President of the Inter-Fraternity Social Committee, and suavely officiated at the Coronation of the Winter Passion Queen. For an instant he almost had his parents impressed (O vain dream of every dream-seized middle-class son!), and Gabriel grabbed that instant to insist that his father release certain monies deposited in Gabriel's name so Gabriel could use them to speculate in satellite missile stocks.

In the Spring of Gabriel's Sophomore year, alas, the Enemy launched a brief & devastating "peace offensive," which reduced Gabriel to farthings. Tired of himself, Gabriel took the disaster as a sign that the Gods, too, were bored with his corporate mode. And thus it came to pass that at the onset of the summer which would have marked the halfway point in his never-to-be-finished college career, Gabriel found himself with three months at home stretching ahead of him like an old age and the need to change his style becoming more anguished every day. His old friends revulsed him, but left alone he grew deeply depressed. For when the sons of God are not high, high as angels, they wallow in mucky despair and are as nothing to themselves. Gabriel felt himself incapable of emotion—neither thing nor person could arouse a sensation in him. When people tried to talk to him, he stared back in horror and retired to the bathroom where he would spend hours in reverie staring at the face imprisoned behind glass, puzzling who it was and what meant for. Once out of the bathroom, his anxiety took him anew: he was afraid that the face in the glass had been ripped out from behind and torn into shreds.

As usual it was a question of who would crack up first, Gabriel or his mother. He won: eight days after his homecoming she put on an incomparable display of hysterics. Rather pleased, Gabriel in the wake of her seconal readily promised to see a psychiatrist.

After a few days of searching, Gabriel walked into the office of a biotherapist.

"Sit down!" commanded Dr. Fulton Macher, watching him intently. "No, in that chair over there!"

Suddenly Dr. Macher jumped to his feet. "Why did you start?" he inquired. "Don't tell me, let me tell you. You don't know what role to take, do you? I can tell by mere observation of your body. You think you can't be seen through, but to the trained eye you give yourself away with every move of your musculature. You're beginning to resent me now, aren't you? You think perhaps I will reach across the desk and *strike you!*"

With the words *"strike you!"* Dr. Macher slammed an Oriental statuette against the wall, sending Gabriel leaping to the top of a hat tree. There followed a series of amazing revelations.

For Mrs. Reuben's $35/hr., the biotherapist began to ease Gabriel in the direction of Affirmative Posture and True Orgasm. In True Orgasm—the key to free-flowing love & creativity—the body moves as freely as a freely swinging leg. While Gabriel stood naked in the middle of the room, describing how beautifully bothered he was, the therapist moved around him, thumping and prodding. Occasionally Dr. Macher massaged Gabriel's leg muscles to loosen them up, and once he took off his shoes and worked on Gabriel's back with his bare feet.

Gabriel was willing and had much to say, but when results were slow appearing he was discouraged and talked of quitting and simply taking *karate* lessons. Perhaps it was his talent for meeting the right people at the destined time that pulled him through for the moment; at any rate it was the people he met who helped him turn more & more swinging, and his legs swung right along with him. The biotherapist's studio was located in a choice part of the Village, and hanging around certain bars Gabriel managed to contact newer & holier people than he had ever known existed. The first were the great actor Tony Valentine and his mad poet brother Billy-Gene Valentine. Tony was also an Orgasm man, but more than that he gave Gabriel his first fuzzy intimations of how the orgasm might be just one feature of a hitherto-unthoughtof psychic politics that could swing our desperate world into a new wild millennium of pleasure. Historically, said Tony, this had to be; the organism renews itself or perishes. For the individual, the title to such vision could come only through experience—and so Gabriel made himself available for a number of scenes with hookers, drag queens and certain selected studs. He did not kid himself that he was making it all the way.

It was enough to know that he was with it. Through Tony & Billy-Gene, Gabriel met painters, poets, hustlers, boosters, roosters, horse riders and magicians—all of whom seemed most *to exist*, and to exist so vividly that those who lived for any other reason became mute, impalpable and invisible to the young Gabriel. Jazz itself came to him, the Negro night come alive and *real*, not to be tricked, cutting in an edge of sheer hot beauty through the torpid blanket of daytime lies. When Gabriel shut his eyes and climbed inside, he *knew*—and, like the blues, he was a cure for himself. And when the music stopped, well, he still had something left, enough to go on with. . . . *Dayenu.*

When fall came Gabriel forswore his parents' support and went back to college car-less and nearly clothes-less. Immediately upon getting off the bus he resigned from his fraternity and got down to work. He knew he had a lot to learn. He wanted to travel the path of every revolutionary in history, to plot the spiral on which they swung, and to ride that curve out into the future. He studied hard, and before long he had earned himself his work-scholarship and his caretaker's room in the gym. The only problem was people. His former collegiate friends were as interesting to him as stiffs in a morgue. Equally dead were the officially good students, some of whom he knew were much more proficient than himself, because they tried so trustingly to be "rational"—i.e., to force whole sets of old learned vocabularies between themselves and the lives they were leading.... Open your eyes! screamed Gabriel, in every way he knew. Gabriel wasn't rational and he knew it. He was after something realer and larger than the definitions of words.

———   **James S. Kunen (1948–   )**   ———

Hitch-hiking

Thursday, July 4: I am going summer home to Hyannis for the weekend to write the entire book. Aside from the fact that I have no money, I want to hitch-hike anyway. Hitch-hiking is a way to look for America. Gallup takes polls; I take rides to find out where people are at.

I made a graphic-artsy sign to try to convey to the motoring public that I am an interesting person. In the corner I drew an American flag as a concession to the holiday. Also, I hope it may soften the effects of my hair somewhat. As a rule, hitch-hiking travel time is directly proportional to the length of your hair.

No sooner did I hit the road than a 1200c.c. dynamatic Harley-Davidson mammoth motorcycle approached me, with an officer of the law astride it. I considered making a break for it, but realized that would be an admission that I was doing something illegal, which is always a good thing to avoid, especially when you *are* doing something illegal. He didn't savagely beat me, but told me that hitching was prohibited on state roads *and* anywhere within New York City—double damning me. What should I do then, I wanted to know. He was of the opinion that that was my problem, which I suppose it was.

He left and I moved and I was picked up and I left. But the ride (two teen girls who were probably on their way to pick up a carton of Coke) only took me to New Rochelle. As I stood on the side of the road my thoughts centered around the prospect of the "Pokey"—where a state trooper had once threatened to put me when he caught me hitching at 3 A.M.

But the president-elect of the New Rochelle High School student government finally arrived and thought he knew me from somewhere. As he was moving me ten miles I explained that he'd seen me on the tube and he explained how things were at New Rochelle. He'd raised one hundred sixty-five bills to buy an anti-war ad in the school paper, and then the principal, who is widely held to be a bad person, refused to let the ad run. The paper, the principal said, must not be used for political ends, although he didn't say why. The students said "repression"—at that word, the American Civil Liberties Union came in. The left people threatened to walk out of the graduation exercises, which presumably would have embarrassed the principal. Meanwhile certain teachers were allegedly calling up football team members suggesting they pound the crap out of anybody who might spoil the commencement. The principal would not take any steps to protect the dissenting ones from this threat, but rather began selective enforcement of little school rules to harass the activists. Eventually a compromise was reached that was equally unsatisfactory to everybody, thus avoiding the walk-out.

I found all of this very interesting, because there seemed to be valid issues involved, some of them even relevant to education. (One complaint was that students could no longer get together and ask to be taught a course in anything they wanted, as they once had.) I had heard on the radio that kids were jumping around for no earthly reason at all at New Rochelle. I invited the kid to drop by the Liberation School and we parted friends.

Five rides and two hours later I was still nowhere. If you're ever hitchhiking, arrange not to be left off at Danny's Diner near Milford, Connecticut, because you'll *never* get out. You wouldn't believe the quality of the traffic there—all middle-aged, all couples, all on their way home to relax with the *Reader's Digest*. I was finally picked up by a Boston University business student who was smoking grass as he drove. He maintained that "It's the only way to drive," but he had a tendency to get in the way of other cars, and I was almost glad when he dropped me off.

Then a hippy-ish couple took me. The girl offered me a slice of watermelon. When I was through with it she urged me to throw the rind out of the window—inciting to litter. Just what I needed—get busted for a littering rap on top of six counts of hitchhiking with long hair. I avoided arrest, however, and they dropped me off in East Haven. "Have a good marriage," I said, as they had told me they were getting married.

I stood at the side of the road in East Haven for a terribly long time. I began to hallucinate, but not really—I remembered the date and realized it was fireworks I was seeing. Must have been 8:30 at least.

Soon it would be completely dark. I considered crossing over to the other side of the highway and trying to get back to New Haven for a bus. But that would be an incredible cop out. Besides, my magic ride might be on the way. If I quit now, think of the people I might have met but will never meet.

For the love of God, I said, somebody pick me up. But then I've got Laura, I can't ask for anything else. All right, but if it's all the same to You, *let* somebody pick me up without divine intervention.

A couple of times guys in cars gave me the finger. My reaction to that is generally one of relief that they didn't throw anything at me. Then a car came by and threw a beer can at me.

Then Wally and Jack stopped by. Wally and Jack were two high school grads returning to Fall River from a celebratory trip to New York. We immediately had to change a tire. That left one decent tire and three bald. Wally kept to around forty-five though, which is considerably faster than standing on the side of the road, so I was very happy.

But when we neared Fall River Wally hit ninety and I could smell the tire rubber burning. Okay, I asked myself—now, now are you sorry you hitched? When we crash, *then* I'll be sorry. Buses tip over, trains collide, planes fall down. (Ships sink.)

We didn't crash. It was midnight when they dropped me at the Fall River Bus Terminal. It was closed. I called my Fall River friend to find that there was no one home.

Fall River is an interesting city. It is a great cotton mill center from which all the cotton mills moved fifty years ago. It's quite a tough place to be in the nighttime.

I thought about calling home, because my parents had been expecting me during the day. But what could I say: "Hi Mom, I'm stranded in Fall River, with two dollars and nowhere to go. I'll try not to freeze to death and maybe I'll see you tomorrow."

I had resigned myself to being mugged when I brought myself up short. "Mugged, mugged, you're always going to be mugged. Did you ever consider getting knifed?"

I got back on the road and by 1 A.M. got one of those little rides that take you from somewhere to nowhere. At nowhere I stood and sat as a cold fog set in and it became 2 A.M. and then three.

I stood by a red light where people had a good chance to look me over. They would point at me and talk about me and drive away.

Please, please, please pick me up. What stories I could tell you. I could relate tales of Columbia to make your blood run cold. C'mon, pick me up somebody please I'm cold and I've nowhere to go can't you see that?

I threw myself at the mercy of the American people and was rebuffed completely.

I started singing "We shall not be moved." A guy came by with greased hair and a T-shirt and offered to take me half a mile to the bowling alley.

I thought I'd be better off staying at the intersection. He said "Okay, Peace," by which I thought he meant "Good luck fella," but then he gave the "V" and I gave it back saying "We will man," and knew it to be true. That was the trip for me.

But for all that I grew colder and cursed myself for forgetting that bowling alleys are invariably characterized by four walls and a roof.

A car slowed to a stop and when I moved to it, it sped off, the people inside laughing. That made me sad. I mean really if they don't want to pick me up, fine, I could be a crook. But why, why do that to me?

A car came by with a fishing pole hanging out and I yelled, "Good! Have a fishing rod sticking out the window. See if I care!" When you start talking like that you know you're going to be all right, because you're at your lowest. I readjusted my nice leather bag to show as prominently as possible on the roadside. Look everybody, I'm affluent, for Christ's sake.

Then came Reggie Andre, a black man from Falmouth who used to hitch all the time and can't stand to pass anybody up. I thanked him as much as I could short of saying I loved him, which might have been misconstrued. He bought me a cup of coffee, and not only was it a dime and good, but they refilled it free which is something I thought no longer existed. As we drove we talked about black power and the war and he was, I swear, much whiter than I am, which is good because if you accept the premise that blacks can be whiter than whites, then the whole color thing becomes quite confusing and maybe everyone will just forget about it.

He took me all the way to Falmouth, which is just fifteen miles through the woods from Hyannis. I was hoping he might say what the hell and take me home but that would have been a lot to ask. As he dropped me off in the blackness of night forest he said that I shouldn't have any trouble getting a ride there—lots of traffic. I thanked him again and swore he'd be in my book, which you see he is.

I decided to walk and was quite happy because it would be morning soon and I'd survived. The birds began to stir and I had them all to myself. I heard a hush and felt the gathering warm. The sun bobbed up from behind the edge of the world, into the bottom of the sky. "As the sun goes up over Cape Cod," I composed, "the gaseous ethery fog of morning drifts to the sky, and leaves the ground floor of Creation to Humanity." Also, "They rolled out the gray tar carpet for me, and I walked up it, and I walked down it and walked a long way on it, all the way home." I was quite giddy.

A summer kid milkman gave me a lift, and then some obnoxious rowdies, as it were, who wanted to know what could be expected from girls on the Cape, took me to my door, but not before I had walked six miles.

Friday, July 5, 6:30 A.M. Thirteen rides, thirteen hours. I felt the dawn walk was so beautiful it had made it all worth it. Something has to make it all worth it, and that's what I chose.

I creep into the house and go to sleep. Next my mother wakes me. "I assume," I say, "that you have been somewhat concerned regarding my whereabouts."

Radio: "The American fighter pilot who made the kill said, 'I've waited all my life for this.'" Waited all his life to kill someone. He said it took him about ninety seconds to fire the air-to-air missile. Took him about ninety seconds to kill someone.

Saturday, July 6: I tell my mother that I've been looking for a car to buy.

"I don't think you should buy a car," she says.

"Oh. Why not?"

"Because you've got just about enough money to pay for one year of college."

"Oh," I said, beginning to comprehend.

"And if you get kicked out of Columbia, you're going to have to pay for your own college."

"Oh, really," I said, thinking about what I was thinking. I was thinking that it would be pretty exciting being on my own. I could write and drive a cab parttime and get a loan and just barely get by. The whole starving artist scene. And I was thinking that was a silly thing to think.

I decided to leave. I said I was leaving because the house was too full of people for me to get anything done, which was true, but then I never get anything done under any circumstances. I left really because of the hostility. When I first arrived hostility embraced me and wouldn't let go as long as I stayed. You know—hair. They wanted me to get my hair cut.

Which leads me to write what I fervently hope will be the last words anyone bothers to write on the subject in twentieth-century American letters.

Hair

Hairs are filamentous chains of living cells which grow out of the epidermis. The very hairs of your head are all numbered (St. Matthew 10:30), but their length is a function only of how often they are cut—a matter of personal choice. Medical science has yet to discover any positive correlation between hair length and anything—intelligence, virility, morality, cavities, cancer—anything.

Long hair on men, however, has been known to make some people sick.

My father, for instance. On July 8, 1968, he alleged that long hair on his sons made him sick. "You look like a woman," he said. "I'll get a haircut," I said. That threw him off, but only for a moment. "If I were a girl," he continued, "I wouldn't like the way you look." "You are not a girl," I said, "and anyway, I said I'd get a haircut." "I don't see how your hair could possibly get any longer," he added. "Would you agree," I asked, "that if I let it grow for another two months, it would get longer?" "Maybe," he conceded, "but it just couldn't possibly be any longer."

My father talks about the bad associations people make when they see someone with hair. I come back with the bad associations people make when they see someone replete with a shiny new Cadillac that looks like it should have a silk-raimented coachman standing at each fender. But as for bad vibrations emanating from my follicles, I say great. I want the cops to sneer and the old ladies swear and the businessmen worry. I want everyone to see me and say "There goes an enemy of the state," because that's where I'm at, as we say in the Revolution biz.

Also, I like to have peace people wave me victory signs and I like to return them, and for that we've got to be able to recognize each other. And hair is an appropriate badge. Long hair should be associated with peace, because the first time American men wore short hair was after World War I, the first time great numbers of American men had been through the military.

Armies always shave hair to deprive the soldier of his individuality and his masculinity. (Yes, masculinity. Samson, much?) They want to depersonalize and humiliate you so that you aren't anybody any more and you'll have to prove yourself to them in their way, so that you have to develop new values, their values, and become a killer.

So if long hair just happens to be the peace thing, it's an appropriate happening.

I once read somewhere that older generatees who cast aspersions on the masculinity of hair people fear for their own masculinity.

Archibald Cox (crew-cut) told me that he thought anyone who made a big thing about kids' hair was loony as hell (or something to that effect. I don't remember his exact words).

Then there is the burn (side) question. "Are you going to let them grow or are you going to trim them?" my mother asked me in what I think was a tone of resigned curiosity. "I don't know," I said. "I haven't decided whether I want to emulate Martin Van Buren or Abraham Lincoln."

THE SELF
AND THE OTHER

"A man's social self," wrote William James, "is the recognition which he gets from his mates." This conception which was elaborated and refined by George Herbert Mead and Charles Horton Cooley who followed James' lead, has become a central tenet of modern sociology and social psychology. The self, far from being some ineffable essence, is now commonly seen to mature in and through commerce with others. It is in the context of social acts that the self arises. It is built up and reinforced in anticipation of the response of significant others; the self-conscious individual needs an audience. Isaac Babel the powerful Soviet short story writer, was wont in his stories of the Russian civil war to dwell on the theme of the relation between the self and the audience. Personal experience had led him to this emphasis: he had fought in the Red Army as a Jewish intellectual among Cossack peasant warriors. The story here reprinted shows the skilled effort of Babel's hero to adjust to the requirements of his new associates and to redefine his self in ways judged appropriate by them. George Orwell's essay illustrates the compulsions that others exercise over self. The lucid moralist, essayist, and novelist who has had such a major influence on modern literary sensibilities describes a situation in which an actor is forced into playing a role expected by an audience even though all his personal inclinations make it distasteful to him.

The remaining four selections all deal with instances in which the expected adjustment between the action of self and the reaction of others fails to occur. Luigi Pirandello's old man, his self image already shattered by the death of his wife and the attendant redefinition of his role, receives a further, perhaps fatal, blow to his self-esteem when his tender, fatherly feelings, his admiration for the sheer loveliness of a girl encountered in a park are interpreted by her as lewd behavior. Sherwood Anderson, one of the masters of the modern American short story, echoes his Italian contemporary, when he stresses the tragic implications of a lack of mutuality between the self and others.

Dorothy Parker in her *Arrangement in Black and White* offers a highly perceptive treatment of the theme of self and role as mask. She shows what may happen when the mask slips from the actor's face and leaves the audience aghast. Franz Kafka's sketch *A Little Woman* is one of the most subtle depictions of the failure of smooth adjustment between self and an other ever written.

Isaac Babel (1894– ?)

My first goose

Savitsky, Commander of the VI Division, rose when he saw me, and I wondered at the beauty of his giant's body. He rose, the purple of his riding breeches and the crimson of his little tilted cap and the decorations stuck on his chest cleaving the hut as a standard cleaves the sky. A smell of scent and the sickly sweet freshness of soap emanated from him. His long legs were like girls sheathed to the neck in shining riding boots.

He smiled at me, struck his riding whip on the table, and drew toward him an order that the Chief of Staff had just finished dictating. It was an order for Ivan Chesnokov to advance on Chugunov-Dobryvodka with the regiment entrusted to him, to make contact with the enemy and destroy the same.

"For which destruction," the Commander began to write, smearing the whole sheet, "I make this same Chesnokov entirely responsible, up to and including the supreme penalty, and will if necessary strike him down on the spot; which you, Chesnokov, who have been working with me at the front for some months now, cannot doubt."

The Commander signed the order with a flourish, tossed it to his orderlies and turned upon me gray eyes that danced with merriment.

I handed him a paper with my appointment to the Staff of the Division.

"Put it down in the Order of the Day," said the Commander. "Put him down for every satisfaction save the front one. Can you read and write?"

"Yes, I can read and write," I replied, envying the flower and iron of that youthfulness. "I graduated in law from St. Petersburg University."

"Oh, are you one of those grinds?" he laughed. "Specs on your nose, too! What a nasty little object! They've sent you along without making any enquiries; and this is a hot place for specs. Think you'll get on with us?"

"I'll get on all right," I answered, and went off to the village with the quartermaster to find a billet for the night.

The quartermaster carried my trunk on his shoulder. Before us stretched the village street. The dying sun, round and yellow as a pumpkin, was giving up its roseate ghost to the skies.

We went up to a hut painted over with garlands. The quartermaster stopped, and said suddenly, with a guilty smile:

"Nuisance with specs. Can't do anything to stop it, either. Not a life for the brainy type here. But you go and mess up a lady, and a good lady too, and you'll have the boys patting you on the back."

He hesitated, my little trunk on his shoulder; then he came quite close to me, only to dart away again despairingly and run to the nearest yard. Cossacks were sitting there, shaving one another.

"Here, you soldiers," said the quartermaster, setting my little trunk down on the ground. "Comrade Savitsky's orders are that you're to take this chap in your billets, so no nonsense about it, because the chap's been through a lot in the learning line."

The quartermaster, purple in the face, left us without looking back, I raised my hand to my cap and saluted the Cossacks. A lad with long straight flaxen hair and the handsome face of the Ryazan Cossacks went over to my little trunk and tossed it out at the gate. Then he turned his back on me and with remarkable skill emitted a series of shameful noises.

"To your guns—number double-zero!" an older Cossack shouted at him, and burst out laughing. "Running fire!"

His guileless art exhausted, the lad made off. Then crawling over the ground, I began to gather together the manuscripts and tattered garments that had fallen out of the trunk. I gathered them up and carried them to the other end of the yard. Near the hut, on a brick stove, stood a cauldron in which pork was cooking. The steam that rose from it was like the far-off smoke of home in the village, and it mingled hunger with desperate loneliness in my head. Then I covered my little broken trunk with hay, turning it into a pillow, and lay down on the ground to read in PRAVDA Lenin's speech at the Second Congress of the Comintern. The sun fell upon me from behind the toothed hillocks, the Cossacks trod on my feet, the lad made fun of me untiringly, the beloved lines came toward me along a thorny path and could not reach me. Then I put aside the paper and went out to the landlady, who was spinning on the porch.

"Landlady," I said, "I've got to eat."

The old woman raised to me the diffused whites of her purblind eyes and lowered them again.

"Comrade," she said, after a pause, "what with all this going on, I want to go and hang myself."

"Christ!" I muttered, and pushed the old woman in the chest with my fist. "You don't suppose I'm going to go into explanations with you, do you?"

And turning around I saw somebody's sword lying within reach. A severe-looking goose was waddling about the yard, inoffensively preening its feathers. I overtook it and pressed it to the ground. Its head cracked beneath my boot, cracked and emptied itself. The white neck lay stretched out in the dung, the wings twitched.

"Christ!" I said, digging into the goose with my sword. "Go and cook it for me, landlady."

Her blind eyes and glasses glistening, the old woman picked up the slaughtered bird, wrapped it in her apron, and started to bear it off toward the kitchen.

"Comrade," she said to me, after a while, "I want to go and hang myself." And she closed the door behind her.

The Cossacks in the yard were already sitting around their cauldron. They sat motionless, stiff as heathen priests at a sacrifice, and had not looked at the goose.

"The lad's all right," one of them said, winking and scooping up the cabbage soup with his spoon.

The Cossacks commenced their supper with all the elegance and restraint of peasants who respect one another. And I wiped the sword with sand, went out at the gate, and came in again, depressed. Already the moon hung above the yard like a cheap earring.

"Hey, you," suddenly said Surovkov, an older Cossack. "Sit down and feed with us till your goose is done."

He produced a spare spoon from his boot and handed it to me. We supped up the cabbage soup they had made, and ate the pork.

"What's in the newspaper?" asked the flaxen-haired lad, making room for me.

"Lenin writes in the paper," I said, pulling out PRAVDA. "Lenin writes that there's a shortage of everything."

And loudly, like a triumphant man hard of hearing, I read Lenin's speech out to the Cossacks.

Evening wrapped about me the quickening moisture of its twilight sheets; evening laid a mother's hand upon my burning forehead. I read on and rejoiced, spying out exultingly the secret curve of Lenin's straight line.

"Truth tickles everyone's nostrils," said Surovkov, when I had come to the end. "The question is, how's it to be pulled from the heap. But he goes and strikes at it straight off like a hen pecking at a grain!"

This remark about Lenin was made by Surovkov, platoon commander of the Staff Squadron; after which we lay down to sleep in the hayloft. We slept, all six of us, beneath a wooden roof that let in the stars, warming one another, our legs intermingled. I dreamed: and in my dreams saw women. But my heart, stained with bloodshed grated and brimmed over.

George Orwell (1903–1950)

Shooting an elephant

In Moulmein, in lower Burma, I was hated by large numbers of people—the only time in my life that I have been important enough for this to happen to me. I was sub-divisional police officer of the town, and in an aimless, petty kind of way anti-European feeling was very bitter. No one had the guts to raise a riot, but if a European woman went through the bazaars alone somebody would probably spit betel juice over her dress. As a police officer I was an obvious target and was baited whenever it seemed safe to do so. When a nimble Burman tripped me up on the football field and the referee (another Burman) looked the other way, the crowd yelled with hideous laughter. This happened more than once. In the end the sneering yellow faces of young men that met me everywhere, the insults hooted after me when I was at a safe distance, got badly on my nerves. The young Buddhist priests were the worst of all. There were several thousand of them in the town and none of them seemed to have anything to do except stand on street corners and jeer at Europeans.

All this was perplexing and upsetting. For all the time I had already made up my mind that imperialism was an evil thing and the sooner I chucked up my job and got out of it the better. Theoretically—and secretly, of course—I was all for the Burmese and all against their oppressors, the British. As for the job I was doing, I hated it more bitterly than I can perhaps make clear. In a job like that you see the dirty work of Empire at close quarters. The wretched prisoners huddling in the stinking cages of the lock-ups, the gray, cowed faces of the long-term convicts, the scarred buttocks of the men who had been flogged with bamboos—all these oppressed me with an intolerable sense of guilt. But I could get nothing into perspective. I was young and ill educated and I had had to think out my problems in the utter silence that is imposed on every Englishman in the East. I did not even know that the British Empire is dying, still less did I know that it is a great deal better than the younger empires that are going to supplant it. All I knew was that I was stuck between my hatred of the empire I served and my rage against the evil-spirited little beasts who tried to make my job impossible. With one part of my mind I thought of the British Raj as an unbreakable tyranny, as something clamped down, in *saecula saeculorum*, upon the will of prostrate peoples; with another part I thought that the greatest joy in the world would be to drive a bayonet into a Buddhist priest's guts. Feelings like these are the normal by-products of imperialism; ask any Anglo-Indian official, if you can catch him off duty.

One day something happened which in a roundabout way was enlightening. It was a tiny incident in itself, but it gave me a better glimpse than I had had before of the real nature of imperialism—the real motives for which despotic governments act. Early one morning the sub-inspector at a police station the other end of the town rang me up on the 'phone and said that an elephant was ravaging the bazaar. Would I please come and do something about it? I did not know what I could do, but I wanted to see what was happening and I got on to a pony and started out. I took my rifle, an old .44 Winchester and much too small to kill an elephant, but I thought the noise might be useful *in terrorem*. Various Burmans stopped me on the way and told me about the elephant's doing. It was not, of course, a wild elephant, but a tame one which had gone "must." It had been chained up, as tame elephants always are when their attack of "must" is due, but on the previous night it had broken its chain and escaped. Its mahout, the only person who could manage it when it was in that state, had set out in pursuit, but had taken the wrong direction and was now twelve hours' journey away, and in the morning the elephant had suddenly reappeared in the town. The Burmese population had no weapons and were quite helpless against it. It had already destroyed somebody's bamboo hut, killed a cow and raided some fruit-stalls and devoured the stock; also it had met the municipal rubbish van and, when the driver jumped out and took to his heels, turned the van over and inflicted violences upon it.

The Burmese sub-inspector and some Indian constables were waiting for me in the quarter where the elephant had been seen. It was a very poor quarter, a labyrinth of squalid bamboo huts, thatched with palm-leaf, winding all over a steep hillside. I remember that it was a cloudy, stuffy morning at the beginning of the rains. We began questioning the people as to where the elephant had gone and, as usual, failed to get any definite information. That is invariably the case in the East; a story always sounds clear enough at a distance, but the nearer you get to the scene of events the vaguer it becomes. Some of the people said that the elephant had gone in one direction, some said that he had gone in another, some professed not even to have heard of any elephant. I had almost made up my mind that the whole story was a pack of lies, when we heard yells a little distance away. There was a loud, scandalized cry of "Go away, child! Go away this instant!" and an old woman with a switch in her hand came round the corner of a hut, violently shooing away a crowd of naked children. Some more women followed, clicking their tongues and exclaiming; evidently there was something that the children ought not to have seen. I rounded the hut and saw a man's dead body sprawling in the mud. He was an Indian, a black Dravidian coolie, almost naked, and he could not have been dead many minutes. The people said that the elephant had come suddenly upon him round the corner of the hut, caught him with its trunk, put its foot on his back and ground him into the earth. This was the rainy season and the ground was soft, and his face had scored a trench a foot deep and a couple of yards long. He was lying on his belly with arms crucified and head sharply twisted to one side. His face was coated with mud, the eyes wide open, the teeth bared and grinning with an expression of unendurable agony. (Never tell me, by the way, that the dead look peaceful. Most of the corpses I have seen looked devilish.) The friction of the great beast's foot had stripped the skin from his back as neatly as one skins a rabbit. As soon as I saw the dead man I sent an orderly to a friend's house nearby to borrow an elephant rifle. I had already sent back the pony, not wanting it to go mad with fright and throw me if it smelt the elephant.

The orderly came back in a few minutes with a rifle and five cartridges, and meanwhile some Burmans had arrived and told us that the elephant was in the paddy fields below, only a few hundred yards away. As I started forward practically the whole population of the quarter flocked out of the houses and followed me. They had seen the rifle and were all shouting excitedly that I was going to shoot the elephant. They had not shown much interest in the elephant when he was merely ravaging their homes, but it was different now that he was going to be shot. It was a bit of fun to them, as it would be to an English crowd; besides they wanted the meat. It made me vaguely uneasy. I had no intention of shooting the elephant—I had merely sent for the rifle to defend myself if necessary— and it is always unnerving to have a crowd following you. I marched down the hill, looking and feeling a fool, with the rifle over my shoulder and an ever-growing army of people jostling at my heels. At the bottom, when you got away from the huts, there was a metalled road and beyond that a miry waste of paddy fields a thousand yards across, not yet ploughed but soggy from the first rains and dotted with coarse grass. The elephant was standing eight yards from the road, his left side toward us. He took not the slightest notice of the crowd's approach. He was tearing up branches of grass, beating them against his knees to clean them, and stuffing them into his mouth.

I had halted on the road. As soon as I saw the elephant I knew with perfect certainty that I ought not to shoot him. It is a serious matter to shoot a working elephant—it is comparable to destroying a huge and costly piece of machinery—and obviously one ought not to do it if it can possibly be avoided. And at that distance, peacefully eating, the elephant looked no more dangerous than a cow. I thought then and I think now that his attack of "must" was already passing off; in which case he would merely wander harmlessly about until the mahout came back and caught him. Moreover, I did not in the least want to shoot him. I decided that I would watch him for a little while to make sure that he did not turn savage again, and then go home.

But at that moment I glanced round at the crowd that had followed me. It was an immense crowd, two thousand at the least and growing every minute. It blocked the road for a long distance on either side. I looked at the sea of yellow faces above the garish clothes—faces all happy and excited over this bit of fun, all certain that the elephant was going to be shot. They were watching me as they would watch a conjurer about to perform a trick. They did not like me, but with the magical rifle in my hands I was momentarily worth watching. And suddenly I realized that I should have to shoot the elephant after all. The people expected it of me and I had got to do it; I could feel their two thousand wills pressing me forward, irresistibly. And it was at this moment, as I stood there with the rifle in my hands, that I first grasped the hollowness, the futility of the white man's dominion in the East. Here was I, the white man with his gun, standing in front of the unarmed native crowd—seemingly the leading actor of the piece; but in reality I was only an absurd puppet pushed to and fro by the will of those yellow faces behind. I perceived in this moment that when the white man turns tyrant it is his own freedom that he destroys. He becomes a sort of hollow, posing dummy, the conventionalized figure of a sahib. For it is the condition of his rule that he shall spend his life in trying to impress the "natives," and so in every crisis he has got to do what the "natives" expect of him. He wears a mask, and his face grows to fit it. I had got to shoot the elephant. I had committed myself to doing it when I sent for the rifle. A sahib has got to act like a sahib; he has got to appear resolute, to know his own mind and do definite things. To come all that way, rifle in hand, with two thousand people marching at my heels, and then to trail feebly away, having done nothing—no, that was impossible. The crowd would laugh at me. And my whole life, every white man's life in the East, was one long struggle not to be laughed at.

But I did not want to shoot the elephant. I watched him beating his bunch of grass against his knees with that preoccupied grandmotherly air that elephants have. It seemed to me that it would be murder to shoot him. At that age I was not squeamish about killing animals, but I had never shot an elephant and never wanted to. (Somehow it always seems worse to kill a *large* animal.) Besides, there was the beast's owner to be considered. Alive, the elephant was worth at least a hundred pounds; dead, he would only be worth the value of his tusks, five pounds, possibly. But I had got to act quickly. I turned to some experienced-looking Burmans who had been there when he arrived, and asked them how the elephant had been behaving. They all said the same thing: he took no notice of you if you left him alone, but he might charge if you went too close to him.

It was perfectly clear to me what I ought to do. I ought to walk up to within, say, twenty-five yards of the elephant and test his behavior. If he charged, I could shoot; if he took no notice of me, it would be safe to leave him until the mahout came back. But also I knew that I was going to do no such thing. I was a poor shot with a rifle and the ground was soft mud into which one would sink at every step. If the elephant charged and I missed him, I should have about as much chance as a toad under a steam-roller. But even then I was not thinking particularly of my own skin, only of the watchful yellow faces behind. For at that moment, with the crowd watching me, I was not afraid in the ordinary sense, as I would have been if I had been alone. A white man mustn't be frightened in front of "natives"; and so, in general, he isn't frightened. The sole thought in my mind was that if anything went wrong those two thousand Burmans would see me pursued, caught, trampled on, and reduced to a grinning corpse like that Indian up the hill. And if that happened it was quite probable that some of them would laugh. That would never do. There was only one alternative. I shoved the cartridges into the magazine and lay down on the road to get a better aim.

The crowd grew very still, and a deep, low, happy sigh, as of people who see the theater curtain go up at last, breathed from innumerable throats. They were going to have their bit of fun after all. The rifle was a beautiful German thing with cross-hair sights. I did not then know that in shooting an elephant one should shoot to cut an imaginary bar running from ear-hole to ear-hole. I ought, therefore, as the elephant was sideways on, to have aimed straight at his ear-hole; actually I aimed several inches in front of this, thinking the brain would be further forward.

When I pulled the trigger I did not hear the bang or feel the kick—one never does when a shot goes home—but I heard the devilish roar of glee that went up from the crowd. In that instant, in too short a time, one would have thought, even for the bullet to get there, a mysterious, terrible change had come over the elephant. He neither stirred nor fell, but every line of his body altered. He looked suddenly stricken, shrunken, immensely old, as though the frightful impact of the bullet had paralyzed him without knocking him down. At last, after what seemed a long time—it might have been five seconds, I dare say—he sagged flabbily to his knees. His mouth slobbered. An enormous senility seemed to have settled upon him. One could have imagined him thousands of years old. I fired again into the same spot. At the second shot he did not collapse but climbed with desperate slowness to his feet and stood weakly upright, with legs sagging and head drooping. I fired a third time. That was the shot that did for him. You could see the agony of it jolt his whole body and knock the last remnant of strength from his legs. But in falling he seemed for a moment to rise, for as his hind legs collapsed beneath him he seemed to tower upward like a huge rock toppling, his trunk reaching skyward like a tree. He trumpeted, for the first and only time. And then down he came, his belly toward me, with a crash that seemed to shake the ground even where I lay.

I got up. The Burmans were already racing past me across the mud. It was obvious that the elephant would never rise again, but he was not dead. He was breathing very rhythmically with long rattling gasps, his great mound of a side painfully rising and falling. His mouth was wide open—I could see far down into caverns of pale pink throat. I waited a long time for him to die, but his breathing did not weaken. Finally I fired my two remaining shots into the spot where I thought his heart must be. The thick blood welled out of him like red velvet, but still he did not die. His body did not even jerk when the shots hit him, the tortured breathing continued without a pause. He was dying, very slowly and in great agony, but in some world remote from me where not even a bullet could damage him further. I felt that I had got to put an end to that dreadful noise. It seemed dreadful to see the great beast lying there, powerless to move and yet powerless to die, and not even to be able to finish him. I sent back for my small rifle and poured shot after shot into his heart and down his throat. They seemed to make no impression. The tortured gasps continued as steadily as the ticking of a clock.

In the end I could not stand it any longer and went away. I heard later that it took him half an hour to die. Burmans were bringing dahs and baskets even before I left, and I was told they had stripped his body almost to the bones by the afternoon.

Afterward, of course, there were endless discussions about the shooting of the elephant. The owner was furious, but he was only an Indian and could do nothing. Besides, legally I had done the right thing, for a mad elephant has to be killed, like a mad dog, if its owner fails to control it. Among the Europeans opinion was divided. The older men said I was right, the younger men said it was a damn shame to shoot an elephant for killing a coolie, because an elephant was worth more than any damn Coringhee coolie. And afterward I was very glad that the coolie had been killed; it put me legally in the right and it gave me a sufficient pretext for shooting the elephant. I often wondered whether any of the others grasped that I had done it solely to avoid looking a fool.

Luigi Pirandello (1867–1936)

The soft touch of grass

They went into the next room, where he was sleeping in a big chair, to ask if he wanted to look at her for the last time before the lid was put on the coffin.

"It's dark. What time is it?" he asked.

It was nine-thirty in the morning, but the day was overcast and the light dim. The funeral had been set for ten o'clock.

Signor Pardi stared up at them with dull eyes. It hardly seemed possible that he could have slept so long and well all night. He was still numb with sleep and the sorrow of these last days. He would have liked to cover his face with his hands to shut out the faces of his neighbors grouped about his chair in the thin light; but sleep had weighted his body like lead, and although there was a tingling in his toes urging him to rise, it quickly went away. Should he still give way to his grief? He happened to say aloud, "Always . . ." but he said it like someone settling himself under the covers to go back to sleep. They all looked at him questioningly. Always what?

Always dark, even in the daytime, he had wanted to say, but it made no sense. The day after her death, the day of her funeral, he would always remember this wan light and his deep sleep, too, with her lying dead in the next room. Perhaps the windows . . .

"The windows?"

Yes they were still closed. They had not been opened during the night, and the warm glow of those big dripping candles lingered. The bed had been taken away and she was there in her padded casket, rigid and ashen against the creamy satin.

No. Enough. He had seen her.

He closed his eyes, for they burned from all the crying he had done these past few days. Enough. He had slept and everything had been washed away with that sleep. Now he was relaxed, with a sense of sorrowful emptiness. Let the casket be closed and carried away with all it held of his past life.

But since she was still there. . . .

He jumped to his feet and tottered. They caught him and, with eyes still closed, he allowed himself to be led to the open casket. When he opened his eyes and saw her, he called her by name, her name that lived for him alone, the name in which he saw her and knew her in all the fullness of the life they had shared together. He glared resentfully at the others daring to stare at her lying still in death. What did they know about her? They could not even imagine what it meant to him to be deprived of her. He felt like screaming, and it must have been apparent for his son hurried over to take him away. He was quick to see the meaning of this and felt a chill as though he were stripped bare. For shame—those foolish ideas up to the very last, even after night-long sleep. Now they must hurry so as not to keep the friends waiting who had come to follow the coffin to the church.

"Come on, Papa. Be reasonable."

With angry, piteous eyes, the bereaved man turned back to his big chair.

Reasonable, yes; it was useless to cry out the anguish that welled within him and that could never be expressed by words or deeds. For a husband who is left a widower at a certain age, a man still yearning for his wife, can the loss be the same as that of a son for whom—at a certain point—it is almost timely to be left an orphan? Timely, since he was on the point of getting married and would, as soon as the three months' mourning were passed, now that he had the added excuse that it was better for both of them to have a woman to look after the house.

"Pardi! Pardi!" they shouted from the entrance hall.

His chill became more intense when he understood clearly for the first time that they were not calling him but his son. From now on their surname would belong more to his son than to him. And he, like a fool, had gone in there to cry out the living name of his mate, like a profanation. For shame! Yes, useless, foolish ideas, he now realized, after that long sleep which had washed him clean of everything.

Now the one vital thing to keep him going was his curiosity as to how their new home would be arranged. Where, for example, were they going to have him sleep? The big double bed had been removed. Would he have a small bed? he wondered. Yes, probably his son's single bed. Now he would have the small bed. And his son would soon be lying in a big bed, his wife beside him within arm's reach. He, alone, in his little bed, would stretch out his arms into thin air.

He felt torpid, perplexed, with a sensation of emptiness inside and all around him. His body was numb from sitting so long. If he tried now to get up he felt sure that he would rise light as a feather in all that emptiness, now that his life was reduced to nothing. There was hardly any difference between himself and the big chair. Yet that chair appeared secure on its four legs, whereas he no longer knew where his feet and legs belonged nor what to do with his hands. What did he care about his life? He did not care particularly about the lives of others, either. Yet as he was still alive he must go on. Begin again—some sort of life which he could not yet conceive and which he certainly would never have contemplated if things had not changed in his own world. Now, deposed like this all of a sudden, not old and yet no longer young . . .

He smiled and shrugged his shoulders. For his son, all at once, he had become a child. But after all, as everyone knows, fathers are children to their grown sons who are full of worldly ambition and have successfully outdistanced them in positions of importance. They keep their fathers in idleness to repay all they have received when they themselves were small, and their fathers in turn become young again.

The single bed. . . .

But they did not even give him the little room where his son had slept. Instead, they said, he would feel more independent in another, almost hidden on the courtyard; he would feel free there to do as he liked. They refurnished it with all the best pieces, so it would not occur to anyone that it had once been a servant's room. After the marriage, all the front rooms were pretentiously decorated and newly furnished, even to the luxury of carpets. Not a trace remained of the way the old house had looked. Even with his own furniture relegated to that little dark room, out of the mainstream of the young people's existence, he did not feel at home. Yet, oddly enough, he did not resent the disregard he seemed to have reaped along with the old furniture, because he admired the new rooms and was satisfied with his son's success.

But there was another deeper reason, not too clear as yet, a promise of another life, all shining and colorful, which was erasing the memory of the old one. He even drew a secret hope from it that a new life might begin for him too. Unconsciously, he sensed the luminous opening of a door at his back whence he might escape at the right moment, easy enough now that no one bothered about him, leaving him as if on holiday in the sanctuary of his little room "to do as he pleased." He felt lighter than air. His eyes had a gleam in them that colored everything, leading him from marvel to marvel, as though he really were a child again. He had the eyes of a child— lively and open wide on a world which was still new.

He took the habit of going out early in the morning to begin his holiday which was to last as long as his life lasted. Relieved of all responsibilities, he agreed to pay his son so much every month out of his pension for his maintenance. It was very little. Though he needed nothing, his son thought he should keep some money for himself to satisfy any need he might have. But need for what? He was satisfied now just to look on at life.

Having shaken off the weight of experience, he no longer knew how to get along with oldsters. He avoided them. And the younger people considered him too old, so he went to the park where the children played.

That was how he started his new life—in the meadow among the children in the grass. What an exhilarating scent the grass had, and so fresh where it grew thick and high. The children played hide-and-seek there. The constant trickle of some hidden stream outpurled the rustle of the leaves. Forgetting their game, the children pulled off their shoes and stockings. What a delicious feeling to sink into all that freshness of soft new grass with bare feet!

He took off one shoe and was stealthily removing the other when a young girl appeared before him, her face flaming. "You pig!" she cried, her eyes flashing.

Her dress was caught up in front on a bush, and she quickly pulled it down over her legs, because he was looking up at her from where he sat on the ground.

He was stunned. What had she imagined? Already she had disappeared. He had wanted to enjoy the children's innocent fun. Bending down, he put his two hands over his hard, bare feet. What had she seen wrong? Was he too old to share a child's delight in going barefoot in the grass? Must one immediately think evil because he was old? Ah, he knew that he could change in a flash from being a child to becoming a man again, if he must. He was still a man, after all, but he didn't want to think about it. He refused to think about it. It was really as a child that he had taken off his shoes. How wrong it was of that wretched girl to insult him like that! He threw himself face down on the grass. All his grief, his loss, his daily loneliness had brought about this gesture interpreted now in the light of vulgar malice. His gorge rose in disgust and bitterness. Stupid girl! If he had wanted that— even his son admitted he might have "some desires"—he had plenty of money in his pocket for such needs.

Indignant he pulled himself upright. Shamefacedly, with trembling hands, he put on his shoes again. All the blood had gone to his head and the pulse now beat hot behind his eyes. Yes, he knew where to go for that. He knew.

Calmer now, he got up and went back to the house. In the welter of furniture which seemed to have been placed there on purpose to drive him mad, he threw himself on the bed and turned his face to the wall.

Sherwood Anderson

The egg

At Pickleville father and mother worked hard as they always had done. At first there was the necessity of putting our place into shape to be a restaurant. That took a month. Father built a shelf on which he put tins of vegetables. He painted a sign on which he put his name in large red letters. Below his name was the sharp command—*eat here*—that was so seldom obeyed. A show case was bought and filled with cigars and tobacco. Mother scrubbed the floor and the walls of the room. I went to school in the town and was glad to be away from the farm and from the presence of the discouraged, sad-looking chickens. Still I was not very joyous. In the evening I walked home from school along Turner's Pike and remembered the children I had seen playing in the town school yard. A troop of little girls had gone hopping about and singing. I tried that. Down along the frozen road I went hopping solemnly on one leg. "Hippity Hop To The Barber Shop," I sang shrilly. Then I stopped and looked doubtfully about. I was afraid of being seen in my gay mood. It must have seemed to me that I was doing a thing that should not be done by one who, like myself, had been raised on a chicken farm where death was a daily visitor.

Mother decided that our restaurant should remain open at night. At ten in the evening a passenger train went north past our door followed by a local freight. The freight crew had switching to do in Pickleville and when the work was done they came to our restaurant for hot coffee and food. Sometimes one of them ordered a fried egg. In the morning at four they returned north-bound and again visited us. A little trade began to grow up. Mother slept at night and during the day tended the restaurant and fed our boarders while father slept. He slept in the same bed mother had occupied during the night and I went off to the town of Bidwell and to school. During the long nights, while mother and I slept, father cooked meats that were to go into sandwiches for the lunch baskets of our boarders. Then an idea in regard to getting up in the world came into his head. The American spirit took hold of him. He also became ambitious.

In the long nights when there was little to do father had time to think. That was his undoing. He decided that he had in the past been an unsuccessful man because he had not been cheerful enough and that in the future he would adopt a cheerful outlook on life. In the early morning he came upstairs and got into bed with mother. She woke and the two talked. From my bed in the corner I listened.

It was father's idea that both he and mother should try to entertain the people who came to eat at our restaurant. I cannot now remember his words, but he gave the impression of one about to become in some obscure way a kind of public entertainer. When people, particularly young people from the town of Bidwell, came into our place, as on very rare occasions they did, bright entertaining conversation was to be made. From father's words I gathered that something of the jolly inn-keeper effect was to be sought. Mother must have been doubtful from the first, but she said nothing discouraging. It was father's notion that a passion for the company of himself and mother would spring up in the breasts of the younger people of the town of Bidwell. In the evening bright happy groups would come singing down Turner's Pike. They would troop shouting with joy and laughter into our place. There would be song and festivity. I do not mean to give the impression that father spoke so elaborately of the matter. He was as I have said an uncommunicative man. "They want some place to go. I tell you they want some place to go," he said over and over. That was as far as he got. My own imagination has filled in the blanks.

For two or three weeks this notion of father's invaded our house. We did not talk much, but in our daily lives tried earnestly to make smiles take the place of glum looks. Mother smiled at the boarders and I, catching the infection, smiled at our cat. Father became a little feverish in his anxiety to please. There was no doubt, lurking somewhere in him, a touch of the spirit of the showman. He did not waste much of his ammunition on the railroad men he served at night but seemed to be waiting for a young man or woman from Bidwell to come in to show what he could do. On the counter in the restaurant there was a wire basket kept always filled with eggs, and it must have been before his eyes when the idea of being entertaining was born in his brain. There was something prenatal about the way eggs kept themselves connected with the development of his idea. At any rate an egg ruined his new impulse in life. Late one night I was awakened by a roar of anger coming from father's throat. Both mother and I sat upright in our beds. With trembling hands she lighted a lamp that stood on a table by her head. Downstairs the front door of our restaurant went shut with a bang and in a few minutes father tramped up the stairs. He held an egg in his hand and his hand trembled as though he were having a chill. There was a half insane light in his eyes. As he stood glaring at us I was sure he intended throwing the egg at either mother or me. Then he laid it gently on the table beside the lamp and dropped on his knees beside mother's bed. He began to cry like a boy and I, carried away by his grief, cried with him. The two of us filled the little upstairs room with our wailing voices. It is ridiculous, but of the picture we made I can remember only the fact that mother's hand continually stroked the bald path that ran across the top of his head. I have forgotten what mother said to him and how she induced him to tell her of what had happened downstairs. His explanation also has gone out of my mind. I remember only my own grief and fright and the shiny path over father's head glowing in the lamp light as he knelt by the bed.

As to what happened downstairs. For some unexplainable reason I know the story as well as though I had been a witness to my father's discomfiture. One in time gets to know many unexplainable things. On that evening young Joe Kane, son of a merchant of Bidwell, came to Pickleville to meet his father, who was expected on the ten o'clock evening train from the South. The train was three hours late and Joe came into our place to loaf about and to wait for its arrival. The local freight train came in and the freight crew were fed. Joe was left alone in the restaurant with father.

From the moment he came into our place the Bidwell young man must have been puzzled by my father's actions. It was his notion that father was angry at him for hanging around. He noticed that the restaurant keeper was apparently disturbed by his presence and he thought of going out. However, it began to rain and he did not fancy the long walk to town and back. He bought a five-cent cigar and ordered a cup of coffee. He had a newspaper in his pocket and took it out and began to read. "I'm waiting for the evening train. It's late," he said apologetically.

For a long time father, whom Joe Kane had never seen before, remained silently gazing at his visitor. He was no doubt suffering from an attack of stage fright. As so often happens in life he had thought so much and so often of the situation that now confronted him that he was somewhat nervous in its presence.

For one thing, he did not know what to do with his hands. He thrust one of them nervously over the counter and shook hands with Joe Kane. "How-de-do," he said. Joe Kane put his newspaper down and stared at him. Father's eye lighted on the basket of eggs that sat on the counter and he began to talk. "Well," he began hesitantly, "well, you have heard of Christopher Columbus, eh?" He seemed to be angry. "That Christopher Columbus was a cheat," he declared emphatically. "He talked of making an egg stand on its end. He talked, he did, and then he went and broke the end of the egg."

My father seemed to his visitor to be beside himself at the duplicity of Christopher Columbus. He muttered and swore. He declared it was wrong to teach children that Christopher Columbus was a great man when, after all, he cheated at the critical moment. He had declared he would make an egg stand on end and then when his bluff had been called he had done a trick. Still grumbling at Columbus, father took an egg from the basket on the counter and began to walk up and down. He rolled the egg between the palms of his hands. He smiled genially. He began to mumble words regarding the effect to be produced on an egg by the electricity that comes out of the human body. He declared that without breaking its shell and by virtue of rolling it back and forth in his hands he could stand the egg on its end. He explained that the warmth of his hands and the gentle rolling movement he gave the egg created a new center of gravity, and Joe Kane was mildly interested. "I have handled thousands of eggs," father said. "No one knows more about eggs than I do."

He stood the egg on the counter and it fell on its side. He tried the trick again and again, each time rolling the egg between the palms of his hands and saying the words regarding the wonders of electricity and the laws of gravity. When after a half hour's effort he did succeed in making the egg stand for a moment he looked up to find that his visitor was no longer watching. By the time he had succeeded in calling Joe Kane's attention to the success of his effort the egg had again rolled over and lay on its side.

Afire with the showman's passion and at the same time a good deal disconcerted by the failure of his first effort, father now took the bottles containing the poultry monstrosities down from their place on the shelf and began to show them to his visitor. "How would you like to have seven legs and two heads like this fellow?" he asked, exhibiting the most remarkable of his treasures. A cheerful smile played over his face. He reached over the counter and tried to slap Joe Kane on the shoulder as he had seen men do in Ben Head's saloon when he was a young farmhand and drove to town on Saturday evenings. His visitor was made a little ill by the sight of the body of the terribly deformed bird floating in the alcohol bottle and got up to go. Coming from behind the counter father took hold of the young man's arm and led him back to his seat. He grew a little angry and for a moment had to turn his face away and force himself to smile. Then he put the bottles back on the shelf. In an outburst of generosity he fairly compelled Joe Kane to have a fresh cup of coffee and another cigar at his expense. Then he took a pan and filling it with vinegar, taken from a jug that sat beneath the counter, he declared himself about to do a new trick. "I will heat this egg in this pan of vinegar," he said. "Then I will put it through the neck of a bottle without breaking the shell. When the egg is inside the bottle it will resume its normal shape and the shell will become hard again. Then I will give the bottle with the egg in it to you. You can take it about with you wherever you go. People will want to know how you got the egg in the bottle. Don't tell them. Keep them guessing. That is the way to have fun with this trick."

Father grinned and winked at his visitor. Joe Kane decided that the man who confronted him was mildly insane but harmless. He drank the cup of coffee that had been given him and began to read his paper again. When the egg had been heated in vinegar father carried it on a spoon to the counter and going into a back room got an empty bottle. He was angry because his visitor did not watch him as he began to do his trick, but nevertheless went cheerfully to work. For a long time he struggled, trying to get the egg to go through the neck of the bottle. He put the pan of vinegar back on the stove, intending to reheat the egg, then picked it up and burned his fingers. After a second bath in the hot vinegar the shell of the egg had been softened a little but not enough for his purpose. He worked and worked and a spirit of desperate determination took possession of him. When he thought that at last the trick was about to be consummated the delay train came in at the station and Joe Kane started to go nonchalantly out at the door. Father made a last desperate effort to conquer the egg and make it do the thing that would establish his reputation as one who knew how to entertain guests who came into his restaurant. He worried the egg. He attempted to be somewhat rough with it. He swore and the sweat stood out on his forehead. The egg broke under his hand. When the contents spurted over his clothes, Joe Kane, who had stopped at the door, turned and laughed.

A roar of anger rose from my father's throat. He danced and shouted a string of inarticulate words. Grabbing another egg from the basket on the counter, he threw it, just missing the head of the young man as he dodged through the door and escaped.

Father came upstairs to mother and me with an egg in his hand. I do not know what he intended to do. I imagine he had some idea of destroying it, of destroying all eggs, and that he intended to let mother and me see him begin. When, however, he got into the presence of mother something happened to him. He laid the egg gently on the table and dropped on his knees by the bed as I have already explained. He later decided to close the restaurant for the night and to come upstairs and get into bed. When he did so he blew out the light and after much muttered conversation both he and mother went to sleep. I suppose I went to sleep also, but my sleep was troubled. I awoke at dawn and for a long time looked at the egg that lay on the table. I wondered why eggs had to be and why from the egg came the hen who again laid the egg. The question got into my blood. It has stayed there, I imagine, because I am the son of my father. At any rate, the problem remains unsolved in my mind. And that, I conclude, is but another evidence of the complete and final triumph of the egg—at least as far as my family is concerned.

Dorothy Parker (1893–1967)

Arrangement in black and white

The woman with the pink velvet poppies wreathed round the assisted gold of her hair traversed the crowded room at an interesting gait combining a skip with a sidle, and clutched the lean arm of her host.

"Now I got you!" she said. "Now you can't get away!"

"Why, hello," said her host. "Well. How are you?"

"Oh, I'm finely," she said. "Just simply finely. Listen. I want you to do me the most terrible favor. Will you? Will you please? Pretty please?"

"What is it?" said her host.

"Listen," she said. "I want to meet Walter Williams. Honestly, I'm just simply crazy about that man. Oh, when he sings! When he sings those spirituals! Well, I said to Burton, 'It's a good thing for you Walter Williams is colored,' I said 'or you'd have lots of reasons to be jealous.' I'd really love to meet him. I'd like to tell him I've heard him sing. Will you be an angel and introduce me to him?"

"Why, certainly," said her host. "I thought you'd met him. The party's for him. Where is he, anyway?"

"He's over there by the bookcase," she said. "Let's wait till those people get through talking to him. Well, I think you're simply marvellous, giving this perfectly marvellous party for him, and having him meet all these people, and all. Isn't he terribly grateful?"

"I hope not," said her host.

"I think it's really terribly nice," she said. "I do. I don't see why on earth it isn't perfectly all right to meet colored people. I haven't any feeling at all about it—not one single bit. Burton—oh, he's just the other way. Well, you know, he comes from Virginia, and you know how they are."

"Did he come tonight?" said her host.

"No, he couldn't," she said. "I'm a regular grass widow tonight. I told him when I left, 'There's no telling what I'll do,' I said. He was just so tired out, he couldn't move. Isn't it a shame?"

"Ah," said her host.

"Wait till I tell him I met Walter Williams!" she said. "He'll just about die. Oh, we have more arguments about colored people. I talk to him like I don't know what, I get so excited. 'Oh, don't be so silly,' I say. But I must say for Burton, he's heaps broader-minded than lots of these Southerners. He's really awfully fond of colored people. Well, he says himself, he wouldn't have white servants. And you know, he had this old colored nurse, this regular old nigger mammy, and he just simply loves her. Why, every time he goes home, he goes out in the kitchen to see her. He does, really, to this day. All he says is, he says he hasn't got a word to say against colored people as long as they keep their place. He's always doing things for them—giving them clothes and I don't know what all. The only thing he says, he says he wouldn't sit down at the table with one for a million dollars. 'Oh,' I say to him, 'you make me sick, talking like that.' I'm just terrible to him. Aren't I terrible?"

"Oh, no, no, no," said her host. "No, no."

"I am," she said. "I know I am. Poor Burton! Now, me, I don't feel that way at all. I haven't the slightest feeling about colored people. Why, I'm just crazy about some of them. They're just like children—just as easy-going, and always singing and laughing and everything. Aren't they the happiest things you ever saw in your life? Honestly, it makes me laugh just to hear them. Oh, I like them. I really do. Well, now, listen, I have this colored laundress, I've had her for years, and I'm devoted to her. She's a real character. And I want to tell you, I think of her as my friend. That's the way I think of her. As I say to Burton, 'Well, for Heaven's sakes, we're all human beings!' Aren't we?"

"Yes," said her host. "Yes, indeed."

"Now this Walter Williams," she said. "I think a man like that's a real artist. I do. I think he deserves an awful lot of credit. Goodness, I'm so crazy about music or anything, I don't care what color he is. I honestly think if a person's an artist, nobody ought to have any feeling at all about meeting them. That's absolutely what I say to Burton. Don't you think I'm right?"

"Yes," said her host. "Oh, yes."

"That's the way I feel," she said. "I just can't understand people being narrow-minded. Why, I absolutely think it's a privilege to meet a man like Walter Williams. Now, I do. I haven't any feeling at all. Well, my goodness, the good Lord made him, just the same as He did any of us. Didn't He?"

"Surely," said her host. "Yes, indeed."

"That's what I say," she said. "Oh, I get so furious when people are narrow-minded about colored people. It's just all I can do not to say something. Of course, I do admit when you get a bad colored man, they're simply terrible. But as I say to Burton, there are some bad white people, too, in this world. Aren't there?"

"I guess there are," said her host.

"Why, I'd really be glad to have a man like Walter Williams come to my house and sing for us, some time," she said. "Of course, I couldn't ask him on account of Burton, but I wouldn't have any feeling about it at all. Oh, can't he sing! Isn't it marvellous, the way they all have music in them?

It just seems to be right IN them? Come on, let's us go over and talk to him. Listen, what shall I do when I'm introduced? Ought I to shake his hand? Or what?"

"Why, do whatever you want," said her host.

"I guess maybe I'd better," she said. "I wouldn't for the world have him think I had any feeling. I think I'd better shake hands, just the way I would with anybody else. That's just exactly what I'll do."

They reached the tall young Negro, standing by the bookcase. The host performed introductions; the Negro bowed.

"How do you do?" he said. "Isn't it a nice party?"

The woman with the pink velvet poppies extended her hand at the length of her arm and held it so, in fine determination, for all the world to see, until the Negro took it, shook it, and gave it back to her.

"Oh, how do you do, Mr. Williams," she said. "Well, how do you do. I've just been saying, I've enjoyed your singing so awfully much. I've been to your concerts, and we have you on the phonograph and everything. Oh, I just enjoy it!"

She spoke with great distinctness, moving her lips meticulously, as if in parlance with the deaf.

"I'm so glad," he said.

"I'm just simply crazy about that 'Water Boy' thing you sing," she said. "Honestly, I can't get it out of my head. I have my husband nearly crazy, the way I go around humming it all the time. Oh, he looks just as black as the ace of—er. Well, tell me, where on earth do you get all those songs of yours? How do you ever get hold of them?"

"Why," he said, "there are so many different—"

"I should think you'd love singing them," she said. "It must be more fun. All those darling old spirituals—oh, I just love them! Well, what are you doing now? Are you still keeping up your singing? Why don't you have another concert, some time?"

"I'm having one the sixteenth of this month," he said.

"Well, I'll be there," she said. "I'll be there, if I possibly can. You can count on me. Goodness, here comes a whole raft of people to talk to you. You're just a regular guest of honor! Oh, who's that girl in white? I've seen her some place."

"That's Katherine Burke," said her host.

"Good Heavens," she said, "is that Katherine Burke? Why, she looks entirely different off the stage. I thought she was much better-looking. I had no idea she was so terribly dark. Why, she looks almost like— Oh, I think she's a wonderful actress! Don't you think she's a wonderful actress, Mr. Williams? Oh, I think she's marvellous. Don't you?"

"Yes, I do," he said.

"Oh, I do, too," she said. "Just wonderful. Well, goodness, we must give someone else a chance to talk to the guest of honor. Now, don't forget, Mr. Williams, I'm going to be at that concert if I possibly can. I'll be there applauding like everything. And if I can't come, I'm going to tell everybody I know to go, anyway. Don't you forget!"

"I won't" he said. "Thank you so much."

The host took her arm and piloted her firmly into the next room.

"Oh, my dear," she said. "I nearly died! Honestly, I give you my word, I nearly passed away. Did you hear that terrible break I made? I was just going to say Katherine Burke looked almost like a nigger. I just caught myself in time. Oh, do you think he noticed?"

"I don't believe so," said her host.

"Well, thank goodness," she said, "because I wouldn't have embarrassed him for anything. Why, he's awfully nice. Just as nice as he can be. Nice manners, and everything. You know, so many colored people, you give them an inch, and they walk all over you. But he doesn't try any of that. Well, he's got more sense, I suppose. He's really nice. Don't you think so?"

"Yes," said her host.

"I liked him," she said. "I haven't any feeling at all because he's a colored man. I felt just as natural as I would with anybody. Talked to him just as naturally, and everything. But honestly, I could hardly keep a straight face. I kept thinking of Burton. Oh, wait till I tell Burton I called him 'Mister'!"

Franz Kafka (1883–1924)

A little woman

She is a little woman; naturally quite slim, she is tightly laced as well; she is always in the same dress when I see her, it is made of grayish-yellow stuff something the color of wood and is trimmed discreetly with tassels or button-like hangings of the same color; she never wears a hat, her dull, fair hair is smooth and not untidy, but worn very loose. Although she is tightly laced she is quick and light in her movements, actually she rather overdoes the quickness, she loves to put her hands on her hips and abruptly turn the upper part of her body sideways with a suddenness that is surprising. The impression her hand makes on me I can convey only by saying that I have never seen a hand with the separate fingers so sharply differentiated from each other as hers; and yet her hand has no anatomical peculiarities, it is an entirely normal hand.

This little woman, then, is very ill-pleased with me, she always finds something objectionable in me, I am always doing the wrong thing to her, I annoy her at every step; if a life could be cut into the smallest of small pieces and every scrap of it could be separately assessed, every scrap of my life would certainly be an offense to her. I have often wondered why I am such an offense to her; it may be that everything about me outrages her sense of beauty, her feeling for justice, her habits, her traditions, her hopes, there are such completely incompatible natures, but why does that upset her so much? There is no connection between us that could force her to suffer because of me. All she has to do is to regard me as an utter stranger, which I am, and which I do not object to being, indeed I should welcome it, she only needs to forget my existence, which I have never thrust upon her attention, nor ever would, and obviously her torments would be at an end. I am not thinking of myself, I am quite leaving out of account the fact that I find her attitude of course rather trying, leaving it out of account because I recognize that my discomfort is nothing to the suffering she endures. All the same I am well aware that hers is no affectionate suffering; she is not concerned to make any real improvement in me, besides whatever she finds objectionable in me is not of a nature to hinder my development. Yet she does not care about my development either, she cares only for her personal interest in the matter, which is to revenge herself for the torments I cause her now and to prevent any torments that threaten her from me in the future. I have already tried once to indicate the best way of putting a stop to this perpetual resentment of hers, but my very attempt wrought her up to such a pitch of fury that I shall never repeat it.

I feel too a certain responsibility laid upon me, if you like to put it that way, for strangers as we are to each other, the little woman and myself, and however true it is that the sole connection between us is the vexation I cause her, or rather the vexation she lets me cause her, I ought not to feel indifferent to the visible physical suffering which this induces in her. Every now and then, and more frequently of late, information is brought to me that she has risen of a morning pale, unslept, oppressed by headache and almost unable to work; her family are worried about her, they wonder what can have caused her condition, and they have not yet found the answer. I am the only one who knows that it is her settled and daily renewed vexation with me. True, I am not so worried about her as her family; she is hardy and tough; anyone who is capable of such strong feeling is likely also to be capable of surviving its effects; I have even a suspicion that her sufferings— or some of them, at least—are only a pretense put up to bring public suspicion on me. She is too proud to admit openly what a torment my very existence is to her; to make any appeal to others against me she would consider beneath her dignity; it is only disgust, persistent and active disgust, that drives her to be preoccupied with me; to discuss in public this unclean affliction of hers would be too shameful. But to keep utterly silent about something that so persistently rankles would be also too much for her. So with feminine guile she steers a middle course; she keeps silent but betrays all the outward signs of a secret sorrow in order to draw public attention to the matter. Perhaps she even hopes that once public attention is fixed on me a general public rancor against me will rise up and use all its great powers to condemn me definitively much more effectively and quickly than her relatively feeble private rancor could do; she would then retire into the background, draw a breath of relief and turn her back on me. Well, if that is what her hopes are really set on, she is deluding herself. Public opinion will not take over her role; public opinion would never find me so infinitely objectionable, even under its most powerful magnifying glass. I am not so altogether useless a creature as she thinks; I don't want to boast and especially not in this connection; but if I am not conspicuous for specially useful qualities, I am certainly not conspicuous for the lack of them; only to her, only to her almost bleached eyes, do I appear so, she won't be able to convince anyone else. So in this respect I can feel quite reassured, can I? No, not at all; for if it becomes generally known that my behavior is making her positively ill, which some observers, those who most industriously bring me information about her, for instance, are not far from perceiving, or at least look as if they perceived it, and the world should put questions to me, why am I tormenting the poor little woman with my incorrigibility, and do I mean to drive her to her death, and when am I going to show some sense and have enough decent human feeling to stop such goings-on—if the world were to ask me that, it would be difficult to find an answer. Should I admit frankly that I don't much believe in these symptoms of illness, and thus produce the unfavorable impression of being a man who blames others to avoid being blamed himself, and in such an ungallant manner? And how could I say quite openly that even if I did believe that she were really ill, I should not feel the slightest sympathy for her, since she is a complete stranger to me and any connection between us is her own invention and entirely one-sided. I don't say that people wouldn't believe me; they wouldn't be interested enough to get so far as belief; they would simply note the answer I gave concerning such a frail, sick woman, and that would be little in my favor. Any answer I made would inevitably come up against the world's incapacity to keep down the suspicion that there must be a love affair behind such a case as this, although it is as clear as daylight that such a relationship does not exist, and that if it did it would come from my side rather than hers, since I should be really capable of admiring the little woman for the decisive quickness of her judgment and her persistent vitality in leaping to conclusions, if these very qualities were not always turned as weapons against me. She, at any rate, shows not a trace of friendliness towards me; in that she is honest and true; therein lies my last hope; not even to help on her campaign would she so far forget herself as to let any such suspicion arise. But public opinion which is wholly insensitive in such matters would abide by its prejudices and always denounce me.

So the only thing left for me to do would be to change myself in time, before the world could intervene, just sufficiently to lessen the little woman's rancor, not to wean her from it altogether, which is unthinkable. And indeed I have often asked myself if I am so pleased with my present self as to be unwilling to change it, and whether I could not attempt some changes in myself, even although I should be doing so not because I found them needful but merely to propitiate the little woman. And I have honestly tried, taking some trouble and care, it even did me good, it was almost a diversion; some changes resulted which were visible a long way off, I did not need to draw her attention to them, she perceives all that kind of thing much sooner than I do, she can even perceive by my expression beforehand what I have in mind; but no success crowned my efforts. How could it possibly do so? Her objection to me, as I am now aware, is a fundamental one; nothing can remove it, not even the removal of myself; if she heard that I had committed suicide she would fall into transports of rage.

Now I cannot imagine that such a sharp-witted woman as she is does not understand as well as I do both the hopelessness of her own course of action and the helplessness of mine, my inability, with the best will in the world, to conform to her requirements. Of course she understands it, but being a fighter by nature she forgets it in the lust of battle, and my unfortunate disposition, which I cannot help since it is mine by nature, conditions me to whisper gentle admonitions to anyone who flies into a violent passion. In this way, naturally, we shall never come to terms. I shall keep on leaving the house in the gay mood of early morning only to meet that countenance of hers, lowering at the sight of me, the contemptuous curl of her lips, the measuring glance, aware beforehand of what it is going to find, that sweeps over me and however fleeting misses nothing, the sarcastic smile furrowing her girlish cheek, the complaining lift of the eyes to Heaven, the planting of the hands on the hips, to fortify herself, and then the access of rage that brings pallor with it and trembling.

Not long ago I took occasion, for the very first time as I realized with some astonishment, to mention the matter to a very good friend of mine, just in passing, casually, in a word or two, reducing it to even less than its just proportions, trivial as it is in essence when looked at objectively. It was curious that my friend all the same did not ignore it, indeed of his own accord he even made more of it than I had done, would not be sidetracked and insisted on discussing it. But it was still more curious that in one important particular he underestimated it, for he advised me seriously to go away for a short time. No advice could be less understandable; the matter was simple enough, anyone who looked closely at it could see right through it, yet it was not so simple that my mere departure would set all of it right, or even the greater part of it. On the contrary, such a departure is just what I must avoid; if I am to follow a plan at all it must be that of keeping the affair within its present narrow limits which do not yet involve the outside world, that is to say, I must stay quietly where I am and not let it affect my behavior as far as can be seen, and that includes mentioning it to no one, but not at all because it is a kind of dangerous mystery, merely because it is a trivial, purely personal matter and as such to be taken lightly, and to be kept on that level. So my friend's remarks were not profitless after all, they taught me nothing new yet they strengthened my original resolution.

And on closer reflection it appears that the developments which the affair seems to have undergone in the course of time are not developments in the affair itself, but only in my attitude to it, insofar as that has become more composed on the one hand, more manly, penetrating nearer the heart of the matter, while on the other hand, under the influence of the continued nervous strain which I cannot overcome, however slight, it has increased in irritability.

I am less upset by the affair now that I think I perceive how unlikely it is to come to any decisive crisis, imminent as that sometimes seems to be; one is easily disposed, especially when one is young, to exaggerate the speed with which decisive moments arrive; whenever my small critic, grown faint at the very sight of me, sank sideways into a chair, holding on to the back of it with one hand and plucking at her bodice strings with the other, while tears of rage and despair rolled down her cheeks, I used to think that now the moment had come and I was just on the point of being summoned to answer for myself. Yet there was no decisive moment, no summons, women faint easily, the world has no time to notice all their doings. And what has really happened in all these years? Nothing except that such occasions have repeated themselves, sometimes more and sometimes less violently, and that their sum total has increased accordingly. And that people are hanging around in the offing and would like to interfere if they could find some way of doing it; but they can find none, so up till now they have had to rely on what they could smell out, and although that by itself is fully qualified to keep the owners of the noses busy it can't do anything more. Yet the situation was always like that, fundamentally, always provided with superfluous bystanders and nosy onlookers, who always justified their presence by some cunning excuse, for preference claiming to be relatives, always stretching their necks and sniffing trouble, but all they have achieved is to be still standing by. The only difference is that I have gradually come to recognize them and distinguish one face from another; once upon a time I believed that they had just gradually trickled in from outside, that the affair was having wider repercussions, which would themselves compel a crisis; today I think I know that these onlookers were always there from the beginning and have little or nothing to do with the imminence of a crisis. And the crisis itself, why should I dignify it by such a name? If it ever should happen—and certainly not tomorrow or the day after tomorrow, most likely never—that public opinion concerns itself with the affair, which, I must repeat, is beyond its competence, I certainly won't escape unharmed, but on the other hand people are bound to take into account that I am not unknown to the public, that I have lived for long in the full light of publicity, trustingly and trustworthily, and that this distressed little woman, this latecomer in my life, who, let me remark in passing, another man might have brushed off like a burr and privately trodden underfoot without a sound, that this woman at the very worst could add only an ugly little flourish to the diploma in which public opinion long ago certified me to be a respectable member of society. That is how things stand today, little likely to cause me any uneasiness.

The fact that in the course of years I have all the same become somewhat uneasy has nothing to do with the real significance of this affair; a man simply cannot endure being a continual target for someone's spite, even when he knows well enough that the spite is gratuitous; he grows uneasy, he begins, in a kind of physical way only, to expect final decisions, even when like a sensible man he does not much believe that they are forthcoming. Partly, too, it is a symptom of increasing age; youth sheds a bloom over everything; awkward characteristics are lost to sight in the endless upwelling of youthful energy; if as a youth a man has a somewhat wary eye it is not counted against him, it is not noticed at all, even by himself; but the things that survive in old age are residues, each is necessary, none is renewed, each is under scrutiny, and the wary eye of an aging man is clearly a wary eye and is not difficult to recognize. Only, as also in this case, it is not an actual degeneration of his condition.

So from whatever standpoint I consider this small affair, it appears, and this I will stick to, that if I keep my hand over it, even lightly, I shall quietly continue to live my own life for a long time to come, untroubled by the world, despite all the outbursts of the woman.

STATUS AND ROLE

The concepts *status* and *role* have come to play a central and indispensable part in modern sociological inquiry. They refer to positions within the social structure and to expectations concerning the behavior of persons who occupy such positions. A person in the position of physician is expected to live up to certain expectations in his professional conduct; the occupancy of this position entitles him to certain licenses and enjoins on him a certain mandate. Any person occupies a number of statuses within a social structure and hence has to play a variety of social roles appropriate to these statuses. Yet we sometimes also refer to the total status of a person in society, denoting thereby a kind of informal summing up of all the particular status positions he may occupy. In this sense the status of a Mr. Smith derives, as Ralph Linton argued in a seminal chapter of *The Study of Man,* from a combination of all the statuses which he holds as a citizen, as an attorney, as a Mason, as a Methodist, as a husband, and so on. A later chapter on stratification will further explore this notion.

Marcel Proust, one of the greatest modern French novelists, had no peer in his admirable ability to delineate upper-class status positions and the attendant subtleties of role behavior. The selections from his work barely suggest the power of his description and analysis of shades of conduct, expectations, and role-playing in these strata. He is the acknowledged master painter of the presentation of self among the high and mighty.

When we know the status of a person, we adjust our behavior toward him accordingly. But we may misjudge in this respect; we may, for example, make mistakes in perceiving status symbols. Such mistakes may lead to richly amusing results. Sholom Aleichem, the great Yiddish short story writer, the Russian master of the short story, Anton Chekhov, and the American short story writer, O. Henry, exploit such mistakes in status identification for highly comic effect in the three short stories here reprinted.

Bureaucracies are especially rich in complicated gradations of status among their personnel. Here status symbols, such as access to exclusive mess halls, or subtle gradations of deference, are highly elaborated. Herman Melville's *White Jacket* describes the status distinctions in a man-of-war on which he took to sea as a young sailor; George Orwell worked in the Parisian restaurants which he depicts in *Down and Out in Paris and London*. The very fact that both writers participated actively in the social systems which they describe may perhaps have allowed them to capture shades of meaning in the realm of status and role behavior which might well have remained hidden from an outside analyst.

The famous passage from Shakespeare's *As You Like It*, with its brilliant delineation of the concept of role, might have some sobering effects on budding sociologists who might be inclined to believe that sociological insights date only from the days in which systematic sociological theorizing became possible.

Marcel Proust (1871–1922)

The art of marking distances

A single point at which Guermantes and Courvoisiers converged was the art (one, for that matter, of infinite variety) of marking distances. The Guermantes' manners were not absolutely uniform towards everyone. And yet, to take an example, all the Guermantes, all those who really were Guermantes, when you were introduced to them proceeded to perform a sort of ceremony almost as though the fact that they held out their hands to you had been as important as the conferring of an order of knighthood. At the moment when a Guermantes, were he no more than twenty, but treading already in the footsteps of his ancestors, heard your name uttered by the person who introduced you, he let fall on you as though he had by no means made up his mind to say "How d'ye do?" a gaze generally blue, always of the coldness of a steel blade which he seemed ready to plunge into the deepest recesses of your heart. Which was as a matter of fact what the Guermantes imagined themselves to be doing, each of them regarding himself as a psychologist of the highest order. They thought moreover that they increased by this inspection the affability of the salute which was to follow it, and would not be rendered you without full knowledge of your deserts. All this occurred at a distance from yourself which, little enough had it been a question of a passage of arms, seemed immense for a handclasp, and had as chilling effect in this connexion as in the other, so that when the Guermantes, after a rapid twisting thrust that explored the most intimate secrets of your soul and laid bare your title to honour, had deemed you worthy to associate with him thereafter, his hand, directed towards you at the end of an arm stretched out to its fullest extent, appeared to be presenting a rapier at you for a single combat, and that hand was in fact placed so far in advance of the Guermantes himself at that moment that when he afterwards bowed his head it was difficult to distinguish whether it was yourself or his own hand that he was saluting. Certain Guermantes, lacking the sense of proportion, or being incapable of refraining from repeating themselves incessantly, went further and repeated this ceremony afresh every time they met you. Seeing that they had no longer any need to conduct the preliminary psychological investigation for which the "familiar spirit" had delegated its powers to them and the result of which they had presumably kept in mind, the insistence of the perforating gaze preceding the handclasp could be explained only by the automatism which their gaze had acquired or by some power of fascination which they believed themselves to possess. The Courvoisiers, whose physique was different, had tried in vain to assimilate that searching gaze and had had to fall back upon a lordly stiffness or a rapid indifference. On the other hand, it was from the Courvoisiers that certain very exceptional Guermantes of the gentler sex seemed to have borrowed the feminine form of greeting. At the moment when you were presented to one of these, she made you a sweeping bow in which she carried towards you, almost to an angle of forty-five degrees, her head and bust, the rest of her body (which came very high, up to the belt which formed a pivot) remaining stationary. But no sooner had she projected thus towards you the upper part of her person than she flung it backwards beyond the vertical line by a sudden retirement through almost the same angle. This subsequent withdrawal neutralised what appeared to have been conceded to you; the ground which you believed yourself to have gained did not even remain a conquest, as in a duel; the original positions were retained. This same annulment of affability by the resumption of distance (which was Courvoisier in origin and intended to shew that the advances made in the first movement were no more than a momentary feint) displayed itself equally clearly, in the Courvoisier ladies as in the Guermantes, in the letters which you received from them, at any rate in the first period of your acquaintance. The 'body' of the letter might contain sentences such as one writes only (you would suppose) to a friend, but in vain might you have thought yourself entitled to boast in that relation to the lady, since the letter began with 'Monsieur,' and ended with 'Croyez monsieur à mes sentiments distingués.' After which, between this cold opening and frigid conclusion which altered the meaning of all the rest, there might come in succession (were it a reply to a letter of condolence from yourself) the most touching pictures of the grief which the Guermantes lady had felt on losing her sister, of the intimacy that had existed between them, of the beauty of the place in which she was staying, of the consolation that she found in the charm of her young children, all this amounted to no more than a letter such as one finds in printed collections, the intimate character of which implied, however, no more intimacy between yourself and the writer than if she had been the Younger Pliny or Mme. de Simiane.

It is true that certain Guermantes ladies wrote to you from the first as 'My Dear Friend,' or 'My Friends'; these were not always the most simple natured among them, but rather those who, living only in the society of kings and being at the same time 'light,' assumed in their pride the certainty that everything which came from themselves gave pleasure and in their corruption the habit of setting no price upon any of the satisfactions that they had to offer. However, since to have had a common ancestor in the reign of Louis XIII was enough to make a young Guermantes say, in speaking of the Marquise de Guermantes: "My aunt Adam," the Guermantes were so numerous a clan that, even among these simple rites, that for example of the bow upon introduction to a stranger, there existed a wide divergence. Each subsection of any refinement had its own, which was handed down from parents to children like the prescription for a liniment or a special way of making jam. Thus it was that we saw Saint-Loup's handclasp thrust out as though involuntarily at the moment of his hearing one's name, without any participation by his eyes, without the addition of a bow. Any unfortunate commoner who for a particular reason —which, for that matter, very rarely occurred— was presented to anybody of the Saint-Loup subsection racked his brains over this abrupt minimum of a greeting, which deliberately assumed the appearance of non-recognition, to discover what in the world the Guermantes—male or female—could have against him. And he was highly surprised to learn that the said Guermantes had thought fit to write specially to the introducer to tell him how delighted he or she had been with the stranger, whom he or she looked forward to meeting again. As specialised as the mechanical gestures of Saint-Loup were the complicated and rapid capers (which M. de Charlus condemned as ridiculous) of the Marquis de Fierbois, the grave and measured paces of the Prince de Guermantes. But it is impossible to describe here the richness of the choreography of the Guermantes ballet owing to the sheer length of the cast. . . .

*   *   *

As she strolled by my side, the Duchesse de Guermantes allowed the azure light of her eyes to float in front of her, but vaguely, so as to avoid the people with whom she did not wish to enter into relations, whose presence she discerned at times, like a menacing reef in the distance. We advanced between a double hedge of guests, who conscious that they would never come to know 'Oriane,' were anxious at least to point her out, as a curiosity, to their wives: "Quick, Ursule, come and look at Madame de Guermantes talking to that young man." And one felt that in another moment they would be clambering upon the chairs, for a better view, as at the Military Review on the 14th of July, or the Grand Prix. Not that the Duchesse de Guermantes had a more aristocratic salon than her cousin. The former's was frequented by people whom the latter would never have been willing to invite, principally on account of her husband. She would never have been at home to Mme. Alphonse de Rothschild, who, an intimate friend of Mme. de la Trémoïlle and of Mme. de Sagan, as was Oriane herself, was constantly to be seen in the house of the last-named. It was the same with Baron Hirsch, whom the Prince of Wales had brought to see her, but not to the Princess, who would not have approved of him, and also with certain outstandingly notorious Bonapartists or even Republicans, whom the Duchesse found interesting but whom the Prince, a convinced Royalist, would not have allowed inside his house. His antisemitism also being founded on principle did not yield before any social distinction, however strongly accredited, and if he was at home to Swann, whose friend he had been since their boyhood, being, however, the only one of the Guermantes who addressed him as Swann and not as Charles, this was because, knowing that Swann's grandmother, a Protestant married to a Jew, had been the Duc de Berri's mistress, he endeavoured, from time to time, to believe in the legend which made out Swann's father to be a natural son of that Prince. By this hypothesis, which incidentally was false, Swann, the son of a Catholic father, himself the son of a Bourbon by a Catholic mother, was a Christian to his finger-tips. . . .

*   *   *

"Look, I shall be able to shew you his flowers now," she said to me, seeing that her husband was making signals to her to rise. And she took M. de Cambremer's arm again. M. Verdurin tried to apologise for this to M. de Charlus, as soon as he had got rid of Mme. de Cambremer, and to give him his reasons, chiefly for the pleasure of discussing these social refinements with a gentleman of title, momentarily the inferior of those who assigned to him the place to which they considered him entitled. But first of all he was anxious to make it clear to M. de Charlus that intellectually he esteemed him too highly to suppose that he could pay any attention to these trivialities. "Excuse my mentioning so small a point," he began, "for I can understand how little such things mean to you. Middle-class minds pay attention to them, but the others, the artists, the people who are really of our sort, don't give a rap for them. Now, from the first words we exchanged, I realised that you were one of us!" M. de Charlus, who gave a widely different meaning to this expression, drew himself erect. After the doctor's oglings, he found his host's insulting frankness suffocating. "Don't protest, my dear Sir, you are one of us, it is plain as daylight," replied M. Verdurin. "Observe that I have no idea whether you practise any of the arts, but that is not necessary. It is not always sufficient. Dechambre, who has just died, played exquisitely, with the most vigorous execution, but he was not one of us, you felt at once that he was not one of us. Brichot is not one of us. Morel is, my wife is, I can feel that you are . . ." "What were you going to tell me?" interrupted M. de Charlus, who was beginning to feel reassured as to M. Verdurin's meaning, but preferred that he should not utter these misleading remarks quite so loud. "Only that we put you on the left," replied M. Verdurin. M. de Charlus, with a comprehending, genial, insolent smile, replied: "Why! That is not of the slightest importance, here!" And he gave a little laugh that was all his own—a laugh that came to him probably from some Bavarian or Lorraine grandmother, who herself had inherited it, in identical form, from an ancestress, so that it had been sounding now, without change, for not a few centuries in little old-fashioned European courts, and one could relish its precious quality like that of certain old musical instruments that have now grown rare. There are times when, to paint a complete portrait of some one, we should have to add a phonetic imitation to our verbal description, and our portrait of the figure that M. de Charlus presented is liable to remain incomplete in the absence of that little laugh, so delicate, so light, just as certain compositions are never accurately rendered because our orchestras lack those 'small trumpets,' with a sound so entirely their own, for which the composer wrote this or that part. "But," M. Verdurin explained, stung by his laugh, "we did it on purpose. I attach no importance whatever to title of nobility," he went on, with that contemptuous smile which I have seen so many people whom I have known, unlike my grandmother and my mother, assume when they spoke of anything that they did not possess, before others who thus, they supposed, would be prevented from using that particular advantage to crow over them. "But don't you see, since we happened to have M. de Cambremer here, and he is a Marquis, while you are only a Baron. . . ." "Pardon me," M. de Charlus replied with an arrogant air to the astonished Verdurin, "I am also Duc de Brabant, Damoiseau de Montargis, Prince d'Oloron, de Carency, de Viareggio and des Dunes. However, it is not of the slightest importance. Please do not distress yourself," he concluded, resuming his subtle smile which spread itself over these final words: "I could see at a glance that you were not accustomed to society."

Sholom Aleichem (1859–1916)

On account of a hat

"Did I hear you say absent-minded? Now, in our town, that is, in Kasrilevke, we've really got someone for you—do you hear what I say? His name is Sholem Shachnah, but we call him Sholem Shachnah Rattlebrain, and is he absent-minded, is this a distracted creature, Lord have mercy on us! The stories they tell about him, about this Sholem Shachnah—bushels and baskets of stories—I tell you, whole crates full of stories and anecdotes! It's too bad you're in such a hurry on account of the Passover, because what I could tell you, Mr. Sholem Aleichem—do you hear what I say?—you could go on writing it down forever. But if you can spare a moment I'll tell you a story about what happened to Sholem Shachnah on a Passover eve—a story about a hat, a true story, I should live so, even if it does sound like someone made it up."

These were the words of a Kasrilevke merchant, a dealer in stationery, that is to say, snips of paper. He smoothed out his beard, folded it down over his neck, and went on smoking his thin little cigarettes, one after the other.

I must confess that this true story, which he related to me, does indeed sound like a concocted one, and for a long time I couldn't make up my mind whether or not I should pass it on to you. But I thought it over and decided that if a respectable merchant and dignitary of Kasrilevke, who

From *A Treasury of Yiddish Stories* edited by Irving Howe and Eliezer Greenberg. Copyright 1954 by The Viking Press, Inc., and reprinted by their permission.

deals in stationery and is surely no *literateur*—if he vouches for a story, it must be true. What would he be doing with fiction? Here it is in his own words. I had nothing to do with it.

This Sholem Shachnah I'm telling you about, whom we call Sholem Shachnah Rattlebrain, is a real-estate broker—you hear what I say? He's always with landowners, negotiating transactions. Transactions? Well, at least he hangs around the landowners. So what's the point? I'll tell you. Since he hangs around the landed gentry, naturally some of their manner has rubbed off on him, and he always has a mouth full of farms, home-steads, plots, acreage, soil, threshing machines, renovations, woods, timber, and other such terms having to do with estates.

One day God took pity on Sholem Shachnah, and for the first time in his career as a real-estate broker—are you listening?—he actually worked out a deal. That is to say, the work itself, as you can imagine, was done by others, and when the time came to collect the fee, the big rattler turned out to be not Sholem Shachnah Rattlebrain, but Drobkin, a Jew from Minsk province, a great big fearsome rattler, a real-estate broker from way back—he and his two brothers, also brokers and also big rattlers. So you can take my word for it, there was quite a to-do. A Jew has contrived and connived and has finally, with God's help, managed to cut himself in—so what do they do but come along and cut him out! Where's Justice? Sholem Shachnah wouldn't stand for it—are you listening to me? He set up such a holler and an outcry—"Look what they've done to me!"—that at last they gave in to shut him up, and good riddance it was too.

When he got his few cents Sholem Shachnah sent the greater part of it home to his wife, so she could pay off some debts, shoo the wolf from the door, fix up new outfits for the children, and make ready for the Passover holidays. And as for himself, he also needed a few things, and besides he had to buy presents for his family, as was the custom.

Meanwhile the time flew by, and before he knew it, it was almost Pass-over. So Sholem Shachnah—now listen to this—ran to the telegraph office and sent home a wire: *Arriving home passover without fail.* It's easy to say "arriving" and "without fail" at that. But you just try it! Just try riding out our way on the new train and see how fast you'll arrive. Ah, what a pleasure! Did they do us a favor! I tell you, Mr. Sholom Aleichem, for a taste of Paradise such as this you'd gladly forsake your own grandchildren! You see how it is: until you get to Zlodievka there isn't much you can do about it, so you just lean back and ride. But at Zlodievka the fun begins, because that's where you have to change, to get onto a new train, which they did us such a favor by running out to Kasrilevke. But not so fast. First, there's the little matter of several hours' wait, exactly as announced in the schedule—provided, of course, that you don't pull in after the Kasrilevke train has left. And at what time of night may you look forward to this treat?

The very middle, thank you, when you're dead tired and disgusted, without a friend in the world except sleep—and there's not one single place in the whole station where you can lay your head, not one. When the wise men of Kasrilevke quote the passage from the Holy Book, *"Tov shem meshemon tov,"* they know what they're doing. I'll translate it for you: We were better off without the train.

To make a long story short, when our Sholem Shachnah arrived in Zlodievka with his carpetbag he was half dead; he had already spent two nights without sleep. But that was nothing at all to what was facing him— he still had to spend the whole night waiting in the station. What shall he do? Naturally he looked around for a place to sit down. Whoever heard of such a thing? Nowhere. Nothing. No place to sit. The walls of the station were covered with soot, the floor was covered with spit. It was dark, it was terrible. He finally discovered one miserable spot on a bench where he had just room enough to squeeze in, and no more than that, be- cause the bench was occupied by an official of some sort in a uniform full of buttons, who was lying there all stretched out and snoring away to beat the band. Who this Buttons was, whether he was coming or going, he hadn't the vaguest idea, Sholem Shachnah, that is. But he could tell that Buttons was no dime-a-dozen official. This was plain by his cap, a military cap with a red band and a visor. He could have been an officer or a police official. Who knows? But surely he had drawn up to the station with a ringing of bells, had staggered in, full to the ears with meat and drink, laid himself out on the bench, as in his father's vineyard, and worked up a glorious snoring.

It's not such a bad life to be a gentile, and an official one at that, with buttons, thinks he, Sholem Shachnah, that is, and he wonders, dare he sit next to this Buttons, or hadn't he better keep his distance? Nowadays you never can tell whom you're sitting next to. If he's no more than a plain inspector, that's still all right. But what if he turns out to be a district inspector? Or a provincial commander? Or even higher than that? And supposing this is even Purishkevitch himself, the famous anti-Semite, may his name perish? Let someone else deal with him and Sholem Shachnah turns cold at the mere thought of falling into such a fellow's hands. But then he says to himself—now listen to this—Buttons, he says, who the hell is Buttons? And who gives a hang for Purishkevitch? Don't I pay my fare the same as Purishkevitch? So why should he have all the comforts of life and I none? If Buttons is entitled to a delicious night's sleep, then doesn't he, Sholem Shachnah that is, at least have a nap coming? After all, he's human too, and besides, he's already gone two nights without a wink. And so he sits down, on a corner of the bench, and leans his head back, not, God forbid, to sleep, but just like that, to snooze. But all of a sudden he remembers—he's supposed to be home for Passover, and to- morrow is Passover eve! What if, God have mercy, he should fall asleep and miss his train? But that's why he's got a Jewish head on his shoulders —are you listening to me or not?—so he figures out the answer to that one too, Sholem Shachnah, that is, and goes looking for a porter, a certain Yeremei, he knows him well, to make a deal with him. Whereas he, Sholem Shachnah, is already on his third sleepless night and is afraid, God forbid, that he may miss his train, therefore let him, Yeremei, that is, in God's name, be sure to wake him, Sholem Shachnah, because tomorrow night is a holiday, Passover. "Easter," he says to him in Russian and lays a coin in Yeremei's mitt. "Easter, Yeremei, do you understand, *goyisher kop?* Our Easter." The peasant pockets the coin, no doubt about that, and promises to wake him at the first sign of the train—he can sleep soundly and put his mind at rest. So Sholem Shachnah sits down in his corner of the bench, gingerly, pressed up against the wall, with his carpetbag curled around him so that no one should steal it. Little by little he sinks back, makes himself comfortable, and half shuts his eyes—no more than forty winks, you understand. But before long he's got one foot propped up on the bench and then the other; he stretches out and drifts off to sleep. Sleep? I'll say sleep, like God commanded us: with his head thrown back and his hat rolling away on the floor, Sholem Shachnah is snoring like an eight-day wonder. After all, a human being, up two nights in a row—what would you have him do?

He had a strange dream. He tells this himself, that is, Sholem Shachnah does. He dreamed that he was riding home for Passover—are you listening to me?—but not on the train, in a wagon, driven by a thievish peasant, Ivan Zlodi we call him. The horses were terribly slow, they barely dragged along. Sholem Shachnah was impatient, and he poked the peasant between the shoulders and cried, "May you only drop dead, Ivan darling! Hurry up, you lout! Passover is coming, our Jewish Easter!" Once he called out to him, twice, three times. The thief paid him no mind. But all of a sudden he whipped his horses to a gallop and they went whirling away, up hill and down, like demons. Sholem Shachnah lost his hat. Another minute of this and he would have lost God knows what. "Whoa, there, Ivan old boy! Where's the fire? Not so fast!" cried Sholem Shachnah. He covered his head with his hands—he was worried, you see, over his lost hat. How can he drive into town bareheaded? But for all the good it did him, he could have been hollering at a post. Ivan the Thief was racing the horses as if forty devils were after him. All of a sudden—tpprrru!—they came to a dead stop, right in the middle of the field—you hear me?—a dead stop. What's the matter? Nothing. "Get up," said Ivan, "time to get up."

Time? What time? Sholem Shachnah is all confused. He wakes up, rubs his eyes, and is all set to step out of the wagon when he realizes he has lost his hat. Is he dreaming or not? And what's he doing here? Sholem Shachnah finally comes to his senses and recognizes the peasant—this isn't Ivan Zlodi at all but Yeremei the porter. So he concludes that he isn't on the high road after all, but in the station at Zlodievka, on the way home for Passover, and that if he means to get there he'd better run to the window for a ticket, but fast. Now what? No hat. The carpetbag is right where he left it, but his hat? He pokes around under the bench, reaching all over, until he comes up with a hat—not his own, to be sure, but the official's, with the red band and the visor. But Sholem Shachnah has no time for details and he rushes off to buy a ticket. The ticket window is jammed, everybody and his cousins are crowding in. Sholem Shachnah thinks he won't get to the window in time, perish the thought, and he starts pushing forward, carpetbag and all. The people see the red band and the visor and they make way for him. "Where to, Your Excellency?" asks the ticket agent. What's this Excellency, all of a sudden? wonders Sholem Shachnah, and he rather resents it. Some joke, a gentile poking fun at a Jew. All the same he says, Sholem Shachnah, that is, "Kasrilevke." "Which class, Your Excellency?" The ticket agent is looking straight at the red band and the visor. Sholem Shachnah is angrier than ever. I'll give him an Excellency, so he'll know how to make fun of a poor Jew! But then he thinks, Oh, well, we Jews are in Diaspora—do you hear what I say?—let it pass. And he asks for a ticket third class. "Which class?" The agent blinks at him, very much surprised. This time Sholem Shachnah gets good and sore and he really tells him off. "Third!" says he. All right, thinks the agent, third is third.

In short, Sholem Shachnah buys his tickets, takes up his carpetbag, runs out onto the platform, plunges into the crowd of Jews and gentiles, no comparison intended, and goes looking for the third-class carriage. Again the red band and the visor work like a charm, everyone makes way for the official. Sholem Shachnah is wondering. What goes on here? But he runs along the platform till he meets a conductor carrying a lantern. "Is this third class?" asks Sholem Shachnah, putting one foot on the stairs and shoving his bag into the door of the compartment. "Yes, Your Excellency," says the conductor, but he holds him back. "If you please, sir, it's packed full, as tight as your fist. You couldn't squeeze a needle into that crowd." And he takes Sholem Shachnah's carpetbag—you hear what I'm saying?—and sings out. "Right this way, Your Excellency, I'll find you a seat." "What the Devil!" cries Sholem Shachnah. "Your Excellency and Your Excellency!" But he hasn't much time for the fine points; he's worried about his carpetbag. He's afraid, you see, that with all these Excellencies he'll be swindled out of his belongings. So he runs after the conductor with the lantern, who leads him into a second-class carriage. This is also packed to the rafters, no room even to yawn in there. "This way please, Your Excellency!" And again the conductor grabs the bag and Sholem Shachnah lights out after him. "Where in blazes is he taking me?" Sholem Shachnah is racking his brains over this Excellency business, but meanwhile he keeps his eye on the main thing—the carpetbag. They enter the first-class carriage, the conductor sets down the bag, salutes, and backs away, bowing. Sholem Shachnah bows right back. And there he is, alone at last.

Left alone in the carriage, Sholem Shachnah looks around to get his bearings—you hear what I say? He has no idea why all these honors have suddenly been heaped on him—first class, salutes, Your Excellency. Can it be on account of the real-estate deal he just closed? That's it! But wait a minute. If his own people, Jews, that is, honored him for this, it would be understandable. But gentiles! The conductor! The tickets agent! What's it to them? Maybe he's dreaming. Sholem Shachnah rubs his forehead, and while passing down the corridor glances into the mirror on the wall. It nearly knocks him over! He sees not himself but the official with the red band. That's who it is! "All my bad dreams on Yeremei's head and on his hands and feet, that lug! Twenty times I tell him to wake me and I even give him a tip, and what does he do, that dumb ox, may he catch cholera in his face, but wake the official instead! And me he leaves asleep on the bench! Tough luck, Sholem Shachnah old boy, but this year you'll spend Passover in Zlodievka, not at home."

Now get a load of this. Sholem Shachnah scoops up his carpetbag and rushes off once more, right back to the station where he is sleeping on the bench. He's going to wake himself up before the locomotive, God forbid, lets out a blast and blasts his Passover to pieces. And so it was. No sooner had Sholem Shachnah leaped out of the carriage with his carpetbag than the locomotive did let go with a blast—do you hear me?—one followed by another, and then, good night!

The paper dealer smiled as he lit a fresh cigarette, thin as a straw. "And would you like to hear the rest of the story? The rest isn't so nice. On account of being such a rattlebrain, our dizzy Sholem Shachnah had a miserable Passover, spending both Seders among strangers in the house of a Jew in Zlodievka. But this was nothing—listen to what happened afterward. First of all, he has a wife, Sholem Shachnah, that is, and his wife—how shall I describe her to you? I have a wife, *you* have a wife, we all have wives, we've had a taste of Paradise, we know what it means to be married. All I can say about Sholem Shachnah's wife is that she's A Number One. And did she give him a royal welcome! Did she lay into him! Mind you, she didn't complain about his spending the holiday away from home, and she said nothing about the red band and the visor. She let that stand for the time being; she'd take it up with him later. The only thing she complained about was—the telegram! And not so much the telegram—you hear what I say?—as the one short phrase, *without fail*. What possessed him to put that into the wire: *arriving home Passover without fail*. Was he trying to make the telegraph company rich? And besides, how dare a human being say "without fail" in the first place? It did him no good to answer and explain.

She buried him alive. Oh, well, that's what wives are for. And not that she was altogether wrong—after all, she had been waiting so anxiously. But this was nothing compared with what he caught from the town, Kasrilevke, that is. Even before he returned the whole town—you hear what I say?—knew all about Yeremei and the official and the red band and the visor and the conductor's Your Excellency—the whole show. He himself, Sholem Shachnah, that is, denied everything and swore up and down that the Kasrilevke smart-alecks had invented the entire story for lack of anything better to do. It was all very simple—the reason he came home late, after the holidays, was that he had made a special trip to inspect a wooded estate. Woods? Estate? Not a chance—no one bought *that!* They pointed him out in the streets and held their sides, laughing. And everybody asked him, 'How does it feel, Reb Sholem Shachnah, to wear a cap with a red band and a visor?' 'And tell us,' said others, 'what's it like to travel first class?' As for the children, this was made to order for them—you hear what I say? Wherever he went they trooped after him, shouting, 'Your Excellency! Your excellent Excellency! Your most excellent Excellency!'

"You think it's so easy to put one over on Kasrilevke?"

Anton Chekhov (1860–1904)

A chameleon

The police superintendent Otchumyelov is walking across the market square wearing a new overcoat and carrying a parcel under his arm. A red-haired policeman strides after him with a sieve full of confiscated gooseberries in his hands. There is silence all around. Not a soul in the square . . . The open doors of the shops and taverns look out upon God's world disconsolately, like hungry mouths; there is not even a beggar near them.

"So you bite, you damned brute?" Otchumyelov hears suddenly. "Lads, don't let him go! Biting is prohibited nowadays! Hold him! ah . . . ah!"

There is the sound of a dog yelping. Otchumyelov looks in the direction of the sound and sees a dog, hopping on three legs and looking about her, run out of Pitchugin's timber-yard. A man in a starched cotton shirt, with his waistcoat unbuttoned, is chasing her. He runs after her, and throwing his body forward falls down and seizes the dog by her hind legs. Once more there is a yelping and a shout of "Don't let go!" Sleepy countenances are protruded from the shops, and soon a crowd, which seems to have sprung out of the earth, is gathered round the timber-yard.

"It looks like a row, your honor . . ." says the policeman.

Translated by Constance Garnett.

Otchumyelov makes a half turn to the left and strides towards the crowd. He sees the aforementioned man in the unbuttoned waistcoat standing close by the gate of the timber-yard, holding his right hand in the air and displaying a bleeding finger to the crowd. On his half-drunken face there is plainly written: "I'll pay you out, you rogue!" and indeed the very finger has the look of a flag of victory. In this man Otchumyelov recognises Hryukin, the goldsmith. The culprit who has caused the sensation, a white borzoy puppy with a sharp muzzle and a yellow patch on her back, is sitting on the ground with her fore-paws outstretched in the middle of the crowd, trembling all over. There is an expression of misery and terror in her fearful eyes.

"What's it all about?" Otchumyelov inquires, pushing his way through the crowd. "What are you here for? Why are you waving your finger . . . ? Who was it shouted?"

"I was walking along here, not interfering with anyone, your honour," Hryukin begins, coughing into his fist. I was talking about firewood to Mitry Mitritch, when this low brute for no rhyme or reason bit my finger. You must excuse me, I am a working man . . . Mine is fine work. I must have damages, for I shan't be able to use this finger for a week, may be. It's not even the law, your honour, that one should put up with it from a beast. . . . If everyone is going to be bitten, life won't be worth living."

"H'm. Very good," says Otchumyelov sternly, coughing and raising his eyebrows. "Very good. Whose dog is it? I won't let this pass! I'll teach them to let their dogs run all over the place! It's time these gentry were looked after, if they won't obey the regulations! When he's fined, the blackguard, I'll teach him what it means to keep dogs and such stray cattle! I'll give him a lesson . . . ! Yeldyrin," cries the superintendent, addressing the policeman, "find out whose dog this is and draw up a report! And the dog must be strangled. Without delay! It's sure to be mad. . . . Whose dog is it, I ask?"

"I fancy it's General Zhgalov's," says someone in the crowd.

"General Zhigalov's, h'm . . . Help me off with my coat, Yeldyrin . . . it's frightfully hot! It must be a sign of rain . . . There's one thing I can't make out, how it came to bite you?" Otchumyelov turns to Hryukin. "Surely it couldn't reach your finger. It's a little dog, and you are a great hulking fellow! You must have scratched your finger with a nail, and then the idea struck you to get damages for it. We all know . . . your sort! I know you devils!"

"He put a cigarette in her face, your honour, for a joke, and she had the sense to snap at him . . . He is a nonsensical fellow, your honour!"

"That's a lie, Squinteye! You didn't see, so why tell lies about it? His honour is a wise gentleman, and will see who is telling lies and who is telling the truth, as in God's sight . . . And if I am lying let the court decide. It's written in the law . . . We are equal nowadays. My own brother is in the gendarmes . . . let me tell you . . ."

"Don't argue!"

"No, that's not the General's dog," says the policeman, with profound conviction, "the General hasn't got one like that. His are mostly setters."

"Do you know that for a fact?"

"Yes, your honour."

"I know it, too. The General has valuable dogs, thoroughbred, and this is goodness knows what! No coat, no shape . . . A low creature . . . And to keep a dog like that! . . . where's the sense of it. If a dog like that were to turn up in Petersburg or Moscow, do you know what would happen? They would not worry about the law, they would strangle it in a twinkling! You've been injured. . . . We must give them a lesson! It is high time . . . !"

"Yet maybe it is the General's," says the policeman, thinking aloud. "It's not written on its face . . . I saw one like it the other day in his yard."

"It is the General's, that's certain!" says a voice in the crowd.

"H'm, help me on with my overcoat, Yeldyrin, my lad . . . the wind's getting up . . . I am cold . . . You take it to the General's and inquire there. Say I found it and sent it. And tell them not to let it out into the street . . . It may be a valuable dog, and if every swine goes sticking a cigar in its mouth, it will soon be ruined. A dog is a delicate animal . . . And you put your hand down, you blockhead. It's no use your displaying your fool of a finger. It's your own fault . . ."

"Here comes the General's cook, ask him . . . Hi, Probor! Come here, my dear man! Look at this dog . . . Is it one of yours?"

"What an idea! We have never had one like that!"

"There's no need to waste time asking," says Otchumyelov. "It's a stray dog! There's no need to waste time talking about it . . . Since he says it's a stray dog, a stray dog it is . . . It must be destroyed, that's all about it."

"It is not our dog," Prohor goes on. "It belongs to the General's brother, who arrived the other day. Our master does not care for hounds. But his honour is fond of them . . ."

"You don't say his Excellency's brother is here? Vladimir Ivanitch?" inquires Otchumyelov, and his whole face beams with an ecstatic smile. "Well, I never! And I didn't know! Has he come on a visit?"

"Yes."

"Well, I never . . . He couldn't stay away from his brother . . . And there I didn't know! So this is his honour's dog? Delighted to hear it . . . Take it. It's not a bad pup . . . A lively creature . . . Snapped at this fellow's finger! Ha-ha-ha . . . Come, why are you shivering? Rrr . . . Rrr . . . The rogue's angry . . . a nice little pup."

Prohor calls the dog, and walks away from the timber-yard with her. The crowd laughs at Hyrukin.

"I'll make you smart yet!" Otchumyelov threatens him, and wrapping himself in his greatcoat, goes on his way across the square.

O. Henry (1862–1910)

While the auto waits

Promptly at the beginning of twilight, came again to that quiet corner of that quiet, small park the girl in gray. She sat upon a bench and read a book, for there was yet to come a half hour in which print could be accomplished.

To repeat: Her dress was gray, and plain enough to mask its impeccancy of style and fit. A large-meshed veil imprisoned her turban hat and a face that shone through it with a calm and unconscious beauty. She had come there at the same hour on the day previous, and on the day before that; and there was one who knew it.

The young man who knew it hovered near, relying upon burnt sacrifices to the great joss, Luck. His piety was rewarded, for, in turning a page, her book slipped from her fingers and bounded from the bench a full yard away.

The young man pounced upon it with instant avidity, returning it to its owner with that air that seems to flourish in parks and public places—a compound of gallantry and hope, tempered with respect for the policeman on the beat. In a pleasant voice, he risked an inconsequent remark upon the weather—that introductory topic responsible for so much of the world's unhappiness—and stood poised for a moment, awaiting his fate.

The girl looked him over leisurely; at his ordinary, neat dress and his features distinguished by nothing particular in the way of expression.

"You may sit down, if you like," she said, in a full, deliberate contralto. "Really, I would like to have you do so. The light is too bad for reading. I would prefer to talk."

The vassal of Luck slid upon the seat by her side with complaisance.

"Do you know," he said, speaking the formula with which park chairmen open their meetings, "that you are quite the stunningest girl I have seen in a long time? I had my eye on you yesterday. Didn't know somebody was bowled over by those pretty lamps of yours, did you, honeysuckle?"

"Whoever you are," said the girl, in icy tones, "you must remember that I am a lady. I will excuse the remark you have just made because the mistake was, doubtless, not an unnatural one—in your circle. I asked you

---

From *The Voice of the City* by O. Henry (1908).

to sit down; if the invitation must constitute me your honeysuckle, consider it withdrawn."

"I earnestly beg your pardon," pleaded the young man. His expression of satisfaction had changed to one of penitence and humility. "It was my fault, you know—I mean, there are girls in parks, you know—that is, of course, you don't know, but——"

"Abandon the subject, if you please. Of course I know. Now, tell me about these people passing and crowding, each way, along these paths. Where are they going? Why do they hurry so? Are they happy?"

The young man had promptly abandoned his air of coquetry. His cue was now for a waiting part; he could not guess the rôle he would be expected to play.

"It *is* interesting to watch them," he replied, postulating her mood. "It is the wonderful drama of life. Some are going to supper and some to—er—other places. One wonders what their histories are."

"I do not," said the girl; "I am not so inquisitive. I come here to sit because here, only, can I be near the great, common, throbbing heart of humanity. My part in life is cast where its beats are never felt. Can you surmise why I spoke to you, Mr.——?"

"Parkenstacker," supplied the young man. Then he looked eager and hopeful.

"No," said the girl, holding up a slender finger, and smiling slightly. "You would recognize it immediately. It is impossible to keep one's name out of print. Or even one's portrait. This veil and this hat of my maid furnish me with an *incog.* You should have seen the chauffeur stare at it when he thought I did not see. Candidly, there are five or six names that belong in the holy of holies, and mine, by the accident of birth, is one of them. I spoke to you, Mr. Stackenpot——"

"Parkenstacker," corrected the young man, modestly.

"—Mr. Parkenstacker, because I wanted to talk, for once, with a natural man—one unspoiled by the despicable gloss of wealth and supposed social superiority. Oh! you do not know how weary I am of it—money, money, money! And of the men who surround me, dancing like little marionettes all cut by the same pattern. I am sick of pleasure, of jewels, of travel, of society, of luxuries of all kinds."

"I always had an idea," ventured the young man, hesitatingly, "that money must be a pretty good thing."

"A competence is to be desired. But when you have so many millions that——!" She concluded the sentence with a gesture of despair. "It is the monotony of it," she continued, "that palls. Drives, dinners, theatres, balls, suppers, with the gilding of superfluous wealth over it all. Sometimes the very tinkle of the ice in my champagne glass nearly drives me mad."

Mr. Parkenstacker looked ingenuously interested.

"I have always liked," he said, "to read and hear about the ways of wealthy and fashionable folks. I suppose I am a bit of a snob. But I like to have my information accurate. Now, I had formed the opinion that champagne is cooled in the bottle and not by placing ice in the glass."

The girl gave a musical laugh of genuine amusement.

"You should know," she explained, in an indulgent tone, "that we of the non-useful class depend for our amusement upon departure from precedent. Just now it is a fad to put ice in champagne. The idea was originated by a visiting Prince of Tartary while dining at the Waldorf. It will soon give way to some other whim. Just as at a dinner party this week on Madison Avenue a green kid glove was laid by the plate of each guest to be put on and used while eating olives."

"I see," admitted the young man, humbly. "These special diversions of the inner circle do not become familiar to the common public."

"Sometimes," continued the girl, acknowledging his confession of error by a slight bow, "I have thought that if I ever should love a man it would be one of lowly station. One who is a worker and not a drone. But, doubtless, the claims of caste and wealth will prove stronger than my inclination. Just now I am besieged by two. One is a Grand Duke of a German principality. I think he has, or has had, a wife, somewhere, driven mad by his intemperance and cruelty. The other is an English Marquis, so cold and mercenary that I even prefer the diabolism of the Duke. What is it that impels me to tell you these things, Mr. Packenstacker?"

"Parkenstacker," breathed the young man. "Indeed, you cannot know how much I appreciate your confidences."

The girl contemplated him with the calm, impersonal regard that befitted the difference in their stations.

"What is your line of business, Mr. Parkenstacker?" she asked.

"A very humble one. But I hope to rise in the world. Were you really in earnest when you said that you could love a man of lowly position?"

"Indeed I was. But I said 'might.' There is the Grand Duke and the Marquis, you know. Yes; no calling could be too humble were the man what I would wish him to be."

"I work," declared Mr. Parkenstacker, "in a restaurant."

The girl shrank slightly.

"Not as a waiter?" she said, a little imploringly. "Labor is noble, but—personal attendance, you know—valets and——"

"I am not a waiter. I am cashier in"—on the street they faced that bounded the opposite side of the park was the brilliant electric sign "RESTAURANT" —"I am cashier in that restaurant you see there."

The girl consulted a tiny watch set in a bracelet of rich design upon her left wrist, and rose, hurriedly. She thrust her book into a glittering reticule suspended from her waist, for which, however, the book was too large.

"Why are you not at work?" she asked.

"I am on the night turn," said the young man; "it is yet an hour before my period begins. May I not hope to see you again?"

"I do not know. Perhaps—but the whim may not seize me again. I must go quickly now. There is a dinner, and a box at the play—and, oh! the same old round. Perhaps you noticed an automobile at the upper corner of the park as you came. One with a white body."

"And red running gear?" asked the young man, knitting his brows reflectively.

"Yes. I always come in that. Pierre waits for me there. He supposes me to be shopping in the department store across the square. Conceive of the bondage of the life wherein we must deceive even our chauffeurs. Good-night."

"But it is dark now," said Mr. Parkenstacker, "and the park is full of rude men. May I not walk———?"

"If you have the slightest regard for my wishes," said the girl, firmly, "you will remain at this bench for ten minutes after I have left. I do not mean to accuse you, but you are probably aware that autos generally bear the monogram of their owner. Again, good-night."

Swift and stately she moved away through the dusk. The young man watched her graceful form as she reached the pavement at the park's edge, and turned up along it toward the corner where stood the automobile. Then he treacherously and unhesitatingly began to dodge and skim among the park trees and shrubbery in a course parallel to her route, keeping her well in sight.

When she reached the corner she turned her head to glance at the motor car, and then passed it, continuing on across the street. Sheltered behind a convenient standing cab, the young man followed her movements closely with his eyes. Passing down the sidewalk of the street opposite the park, she entered the restaurant with the blazing sign. The place was one of those frankly glaring establishments, all white paint and glass, where one may dine cheaply and conspicuously. The girl penetrated the restaurant to some retreat at its rear, whence she quickly emerged without her hat and veil.

The cashier's desk was well to the front. A red-haired girl on the stool climbed down, glancing pointedly at the clock as she did so. The girl in gray mounted in her place.

The young man thrust his hands into his pockets and walked slowly back along the sidewalk. At the corner his foot struck a small, paper-covered volume lying there, sending it sliding to the edge of the turf. By its picturesque cover he recognized it as the book the girl had been readng. He picked it up carelessly, and saw that its title was "New Arabian Nights," the author being of the name of Stevenson. He dropped it again upon the grass, and lounged, irresolute, for a minute. Then he stepped into the automobile, reclined upon the cushions, and said two words to the chauffeur: "Club, Henri."

Herman Melville

Rank order aboard a man-of-war

Some account has been given of the various divisions into which our crew was divided; so it may be well to say something of the officers; who they are, and what are their functions.

Our ship, be it known, was the flag-ship; that is, we sported a *broad pennant*, or *bougee*, at the main, in token that we carried a Commodore—the highest rank of officers recognised in the American navy. The bougee is not to be confounded with the *long pennant* or *coach-whip*, a tapering, serpentine streamer worn by all men-of-war.

Owing to certain vague, republican scruples, about creating great officers of the navy, America has thus far had no admirals; though, as her ships of war increase, they may become indispensable. This will assuredly be the case, should she ever have occasion to employ large fleets; when she must adopt something like the English plan, and introduce three or four grades of flag-officers, above a Commodore—Admirals, Vice-Admirals, and Rear-Admirals of Squadrons; distinguished by the colors of their flags,—red, white, and blue, corresponding to the centre, van, and rear. These rank respectively with Generals, Lieutenant-Generals, and Major-Generals in the army; just as a Commodore takes rank with a Brigadier-General. So that the same prejudice which prevents the American Government from creating Admirals should have precluded the creation of all army officers above a Brigadier.

An American Commodore, like an English Commodore, or the French *Chef d'Escadre,* is but a senior Captain, temporarily commanding a small number of ships, detached for any special purpose. He has no permanent rank, recognised by Government, above his captaincy; though once employed as a Commodore, usage and courtesy unite in continuing the title.

Our Commodore was a gallant old man, who had seen service in his time. When a lieutenant, he served in the late war with England; and in the gunboat actions on the Lakes near New Orleans, just previous to the grand land engagements, received a musket-ball in his shoulder; which, with the two balls in his eyes, he carries about with him to this day.

Often, when I looked at the venerable old warrior, doubled up from the effect of his wound, I thought what a curious, as well as painful sensation,

From *White Jacket* by Herman Melville (1850).

it must be, to have one's shoulder a lead-mine; though, sooth to say, so many of us civilised mortals convert our mouths into Golcondas.

On account of this wound in his shoulder, our Commodore had a body-servant's pay allowed him, in addition to his regular salary. I cannot say a great deal, personally, of the Commodore; he never sought my company at all, never extended any gentlemanly courtesies.

But though I cannot say much of him personally, I can mention something of him in his general character, as a flagofficer. In the first place, then, I have serious doubts, whether, for the most part, he was not dumb; for, in my hearing, he seldom or never uttered a word. And not only did he seem dumb himself, but his presence possessed the strange power of making other people dumb for the time. His appearance on the quarter-deck seemed to give every officer the lock-jaw.

Another phenomenon about him was the strange manner in which every-one shunned him. At the first sign of those epaulets of his on the weather side of the poop, the officers there congregated invariably shrunk over to leeward, and left him alone. Perhaps he had an evil eye; may be he was the Wandering Jew afloat. The real reason probably was, that, like all high functionaries, he deemed it indispensable religiously to sustain his dignity, one of the most troublesome things in the world, and one calling for the greatest self-denial. And the constant watch, and many-sided guardedness, which this sustaining of a Commodore's dignity requires, plainly enough shows that, apart from the common dignity of manhood, Commodores, in general, possess no real dignity at all. True, it is expedient for crowned heads, generalissimos, Lord-high-admirals, and Commodores, to carry them-selves straight, and beware of the spinal complaint; but it is not the less veritable, that it is a piece of assumption, exceedingly uncomfortable to themselves, and ridiculous to an enlightened generation.

Now, how many rare good fellows there were among us main-top-men, who, invited into his cabin over a social bottle or two, would have rejoiced our old Commodore's heart, and caused that ancient wound of his to heal up at once.

Come, come, Commodore don't look so sour, old boy; step up aloft here into the *top*, and we'll spin you a sociable yarn.

Truly, I thought myself much happier in that white jacket of mine, than our old Commodore in his dignified epaulets.

One thing, perhaps, that more than anything else helped to make our Commodore so melancholy and forlorn, was the fact of his having so little to do. For as the frigate had a captain; of course, so far as *she* was con-cerned, our Commodore was a supernumerary. What abundance of leisure he must have had, during a three years' cruise; how indefinitely he might have been improving his mind!

But as every one knows that idleness is the hardest work in the world, so our Commodore was specially provided with a gentleman to assist him. This gentleman was called the *Commodore's secretary*. He was a remarkably urbane and polished man; with a very graceful exterior, and looked much like an Ambassador Extraordinary from Versailles. He messed with the Lieutenants in the Ward-room, where he had a state-room, elegantly furnished as the private cabinet of Pelham. His cot-boy used to entertain the sailors with all manner of stories about the silverkeyed flutes and flageolets, fine oil paintings, morocco bound volumes, Chinese chess-men, gold shirt-buttons, enamelled pencil cases, extraordinary fine French boots with soles no thicker than a sheet of scented note-paper, embroidered vests, incense-burning sealing-wax, alabaster statuettes of Venus and Adonis, tortoise-shell snuff-boxes, inlaid toiletcases, ivory-handled hair-brushes and mother-of-pearl combs, and a hundred other luxurious appendages scattered about this magnificent secretary's state-room.

I was a long time in finding out what this secretary's duties comprised. But it seemed, he wrote the Commodore's dispatches for Washington, and also was his general amanuensis. Nor was this a very light duty, at times; for some commodores, though they do not *say* a great deal on board ship, yet they have a vast deal to write. Very often, the regimental orderly, stationed at our Commodore's cabin-door, would touch his hat to the First Lieutenant, and with a mysterious air hand him a note. I always thought these notes must contain most important matters of state; until one day, seeing a slip of wet, torn paper in a scupper-hole, I read the following:

"Sir, you will give the people pickles to-day with their fresh meat.
"To Lieutenant Bridewell
          "By command of the Commodore
           "Adolphus Dashman, Priv. Sec."

This was a new revelation; for, from his almost immutable reserve, I had supposed that the Commodore never meddled immediately with the concerns of the ship, but left all that to the captain. But the longer we live, the more we learn of commodores.

Turn we now to the second officer in rank, almost supreme, however, in the internal affairs of his ship. Captain Claret was a large, portly man, a Harry the Eighth afloat, bluff and hearty; and as kingly in his cabin as Harry on his throne. For a ship is a bit of terra firma cut off from the main; it is a state in itself; and a captain is its king.

It is no limited monarchy, where the sturdy Commons have a right to petition, and snarl if they please; but almost a despotism, like the Grand Turk's. The captain's word is law; he never speaks but in the imperative mood. When he stands on his quarter-deck at sea, he absolutely commands as far as eye can reach. Only the moon and stars are beyond his jurisdiction. He is lord and master of the sun.

It is not twelve o'clock till he says so. For when the sailing-master, whose duty it is to take the regular observation at noon, touches his hat, and reports twelve o'clock to the officer of the deck, that functionary orders a midshipman to repair to the captain's cabin, and humbly inform him of the respectful suggestion of the sailing-master.

"Twelve o'clock reported, sir," says the middy.

"*Make* it so," replies the captain.

And the bell is struck eight by the messenger-boy, and twelve o'clock it is.

As in the case of the Commodore, when the captain visits the deck, his subordinate officers generally beat a retreat to the other side; and, as a general rule, would no more think of addressing him, except concerning the ship, than a lackey would think of hailing the Czar of Russia on his throne, and inviting him to tea. Perhaps no mortal man has more reason to feel such an intense sense of his own personal consequence, as the captain of the man-of-war at sea.

Next in rank comes the First or Senior Lieutenant, the chief executive officer. I have no reason to love the particular gentleman who filled that post aboard of our frigate, for it was he who refused my petition for as much black paint as would render water-proof that white-jacket of mine. All my soakings and drenchings lie at his state-room door. I hardly think I shall ever forgive him; every twinge of the rheumatism, which I still occasionally feel, is directly referable to him. The Immortals have a reputation for clemency; and *they* may pardon him; but he must not dun me to be merciful. But my personal feelings toward the man shall not prevent me from here doing him justice. In most things, he was an excellent seaman; prompt, loud, and to the point; and as such, was well fitted for his station. The First Lieutenancy of a frigate demands a good disciplinarian, and, every way, an energetic man. By the captain he is held respnsible for everything; by that magnate, indeed, he is supposed to be omnipresent; down in the hold, and up aloft, at one and the same time.

He presides at the head of the Ward-room officers' table, who are so called from their messing together in a part of the ship thus designated. In a frigate it comprises the after part of the berth-deck. Sometimes it goes by the name of the Gun-room, but oftener is called the Ward-room. Within, this Ward-room much resembles a long, wide corridor in a large hotel; numerous doors opening on both hands to the private apartments of the officers. I have never had a good interior look at it but once; and then the Chaplain was seated at the table in the centre, playing chess with the Lieutenant of Marines. It was mid-day, but the place was lighted by lamps.

Besides the First Lieutenant, the Ward-room officers include the junior lieutenants, in a frigate six or seven in number, the Sailing-master, Purser, Chaplain, Surgeon, Marine officers, and Midshipmen's Schoolmaster, or "the Professor." They generally form a very agreeable club of good fellows;

from their diversity of character, admirably calculated to form an agreeable social whole. The Lieutenants discuss sea-fights, and tell anecdotes of Lord Nelson and Lady Hamilton; the Marine officers talk of storming fortresses, and the siege of Gibraltar; the Purser steadies this wild conversation by occasional allusions to the rule of three; the Professor is always charged with a scholarly reflection, or an apt line from the classics, generally Ovid; the Surgeon's stories of the amputation-table judiciously serve to suggest the mortality of the whole party as men; while the good chaplain stands ready at all times to give them pious counsel and consolation.

Of course these gentlemen all associate on a footing of perfect social equality.

Next in order come the Warrant or Forward officers, consisting of the Boatswain, Gunner, Carpenter, and Sailmaker. Though these worthies sport long coats and wear the anchor-button; yet, in the estimation of the Ward-room officers, they are not, technically speaking, rated gentlemen. The First Lieutenant, Chaplain, or Surgeon, for example, would never dream of inviting them to dinner. In sea parlance, "they come in at the hawse holes"; they have hard hands; and the carpenter and sail-maker practically understand the duties which they are called upon to superintend. They mess by themselves. Invariably four in number, they never have need to play whist with a dummy.

In this part of the category now come the "reefers," otherwise "middies" or midshipmen. These boys are sent to sea, for the purpose of making commodores; and in order to become commodores, many of them deem it indispensable forthwith to commence chewing tobacco, drinking brandy and water, and swearing at the sailors. As they are only placed on board a sea-going ship to go to school and learn the duty of a Lieutenant; and until qualified to act as such, have few or no special functions to attend to, they are little more, while midshipmen, than supernumeraries on board. Hence, in a crowded frigate, they are so everlastingly crossing the path of both men and officers, that in the navy it has become a proverb, that a useless fellow is *as much in the way as a reefer.*

In a gale of wind, when all hands are called and the deck swarms with men, the little "middies" running about distracted and having nothing particular to do, make it up by vociferous swearing; exploding all about under foot like torpedoes. Some of them are terrible little boys, cocking their caps at alarming angles, and looking fierce as young roosters. They are generally great consumers of Macassar oil and the Balm of Columbia; they thirst and rage after whiskers; and sometimes, applying their ointments, lay themselves out in the sun, to promote the fertility of their chins.

As the only way to learn to command, is to learn to obey, the usage of a ship of war is such that the midshipmen are constantly being ordered about by the Lieutenants; though, without having assigned them their particular destinations, they are always going somewhere, and never arriving. In some things, they almost have a harder time of it than the seamen themselves. They are messengers and errand-boys to their superiors.

"Mr. Pert," cries an officer of the deck, hailing a young gentleman forward. Mr. Pert advances, touches his hat, and remains in an attitude of deferential suspense. "Go and tell the boatswain I want him." And with this perilous errand, the middy hurries away, looking proud as a king.

The middies live by themselves in the steerage, where, nowadays, they dine off a table, spread with a cloth. They have a castor at dinner; they have some other little boys (selected from the ship's company) to wait upon them; they sometimes drink coffee out of china. But for all these, their modern refinements, in some instances the affairs of their club go sadly to rack and ruin. The china is broken; the japanned coffee-pot dented like a pewter mug in an alehouse; the pronged forks resemble tooth-picks (for which they are sometimes used); the table-knives are hacked into hand-saws; and the cloth goes to the sail-maker to be patched. Indeed, they are something like collegiate freshmen and sophomores, living in the college buildings, especially so far as the noise they make in their quarters is concerned. The steerage buzzes, hums, and swarms like a hive; or like an infant-school of a hot day, when the school-mistress falls asleep with a fly on her nose.

In frigates, the ward-room—the retreat of the Lieutenants—immediately adjoining the steerage, is on the same deck with it. Frequently, when the middies, waking early of a morning, as most youngsters do, would be kicking up their heels in their hammocks, or running about with double-reefed night-gowns, playing *tag* among the "clews"; the Senior Lieutenant would burst among them with a—"Young gentlemen, I am astonished. You must stop this sky-larking. Mr. Pert, what are you doing at the table there, without your pantaloons? To your hammock, sir. Let me see no more of this. If you disturb the ward-room again, young gentleman, you shall hear of it." And so saying, this hoary-headed Senior Lieutenant would retire to his cot in his state-room, like the father of a numerous family after getting up in his dressing-gown and slippers, to quiet a daybreak tumult in his populous nursery.

Having now descended from Commodore to Middy, we come lastly to a set of nondescripts, forming also a "mess" by themselves, apart from the seamen. Into this mess, the usage of a man-of-war thrusts various subordinates—including the master-at-arms, purser's steward, ship's corporals, marine sergeants, and ships yeomen, forming the first aristocracy above the sailors.

The master-at-arms is a sort of high constable and school-master, wearing citizen's clothes, and known by his official rattan. He it is whom all sailors hate. His is the universal duty of a universal informer and hunter-up of delinquents. On the berth-deck he reigns supreme; spying out all grease-spots made by the various cooks of the seamen's messes, and driving the laggards up the hatches, when all hands are called. It is indispensable that he should be a very Vidocq in vigilance. But as it is a heartless, so is it a thankless office. Of dark nights, most masters-of-arms keep themselves in readiness to dodge forty-two pound balls, dropped down the hatchways near them.

The ship's corporals are this worthy's deputies and ushers.

The marine sergeants are generally tall fellows with unyielding spines and stiff upper lips, and very exclusive in their tastes and predilections.

The ship's yeoman is a gentleman who has a sort of counting-room in the tar-cellar down in the fore-hold. More will be said of him anon.

Except the officers above enumerated, there are none who mess apart from the seamen. The *petty officers*, so called; that is, the Boatswain's, Gunner's, Carpenter's and Sail-maker's mates, the Captains of the Tops, of the Forecastle, and of the After-Guard, and of the Fore and Main holds, and the Quarter-Masters, all mess in common with the crew, and in the American navy are only distinguished from the common seamen by their slightly additional pay. But in the English navy they wear crowns and anchors worked on the sleeves of their jackets, by way of badges of office. In the French navy they are known by strips of worsted worn in the same place, like those designating the Sergeants and Corporals in the army.

Thus it will be seen, that the dinner-table is the criterion of rank in our man-of-war world. The Commodore dines alone, because he is the only man of his rank in the ship. So too with the Captain; and the Wardroom officers, warrant officers, midshipmen, the master-at-arms' mess, and the common seamen;—all of them, respectively, dine together, because they are, respectively, on a footing of equality.

George Orwell

The pecking order of a restaurant

On my third day at the hotel the *chef du personnel*, who had generally spoken to me in quite a pleasant tone, called me up and said sharply:

"Here, you, shave that moustache off at once! *Nom de dieu*, who ever heard of a *plongeur* with a moustache?"

From *Down and Out in Paris and London* by George Orwell. Harcourt Brace Jovanovich, Inc. Copyright, 1933, by George Orwell. Reprinted by permission of Brandt & Brandt, Miss Sonia Brownell, and Secker & Warburg Ltd.

I began to protest, but he cut me short. "A *plongeur* with a moustache —nonsense! Take care I don't see you with it tomorrow."

On the way home I asked Boris what this meant. He shrugged his shoulders. "You must do what he says, *mon ami*. No one in the hotel wears a moustache, except the cooks. I should have thought you would have noticed it. Reason? There *is* no reason. It is the custom."

I saw that it was an etiquette, like not wearing a white tie with a dinner-jacket, and shaved off my moustache. Afterwards I found out the explanation of the custom, which is this: waiters in good hotels do not wear moustaches, and to show their superiority they decree that *plongeurs* shall not wear them either; and the cooks wear their moustaches to show their contempt for the waiters.

This gives some idea of the elaborate caste system existing in a hotel. Our staff, amounting to about a hundred and ten, had their prestige graded as accurately as that of soldiers, and a cook or waiter was as much above a *plongeur* as a captain above a private. Highest of all came the manager, who could sack anybody, even the cooks. We never saw the *patron*, and all we knew of him was that his meals had to be prepared more carefully than that of our customers; all the discipline of the hotel depended on the manager. Here was a conscientious man, and always on the lookout for slackness, but we were too clever for him. A system of service bells ran through the hotel, and the whole staff used these for signalling to one another. A long ring and a short ring, followed by two more long rings, meant that the manager was coming, and when we heard it we took care to look busy.

Below the manager came the *maître d'hotel*. He did not serve at table, unless to a lord or someone of that kind, but directed the other waiters and helped with the catering. His tips, and his bonus from the champagne companies (it was two francs for each cork he returned to them), came to two hundred francs a day. He was in a position quite apart from the rest of the staff, and took his meals in a private room, with silver on the table and two apprentices in clean white jackets to serve him. A little below the head waiter came the head cook, drawing about five thousand francs a month; he dined in the kitchen, but at a separate table, and one of the apprentice cooks waited on him. Then came the *chef du personnel*; he drew only fifteen hundred francs a month, but he wore a black coat and did no manual work, and he could sack *plongeurs* and fine waiters. Then came the other cooks, drawing anything between three thousand and seven hundred and fifty francs a month; then the waiters, making about seventy francs a day in tips, besides a small retaining fee; then the laundresses and sewing women; then the apprentice waiters, who received no tips, but were paid seven hundred and fifty francs a month; then the *plongeurs,* also at seven hundred and fifty francs; then the chambermaids, at five or six hundred francs a month; and lastly the cafetiers, at five hundred a month. We of the cafeterie were the very dregs of the hotel, despised and *tutoied* by everyone.

There were various others—the office employees, called generally couriers, the storekeeper, the cellarman, some porters and pages, the ice man, the bakers, the night-watchman, the doorkeeper. Different jobs were done by different races. The office employees and the cooks and sewing-women were French, the waiters Italians and Germans (there is hardly such a thing as a French waiter in Paris), the *plongeurs* of every race in Europe, beside Arabs and Negroes. French was the lingua franca, even the Italians speaking it to one another.

All the departments had their special perquisites. In all Paris hotels it is the custom to sell the broken bread to bakers for eight sous a pound, and the kitchen scraps to pigkeepers for a trifle, and to divide the proceeds of this among the *plongeurs*. There was much pilfering, too. The waiters all stole food—in fact, I seldom saw a waiter trouble to eat the rations provided for him by the hotel—and the cooks did it on a larger scale in the kitchen, and we in the cafeterie swilled illicit tea and coffee. The cellarman stole brandy. By a rule of the hotel the waiters were not allowed to keep stores of spirits, but had to go to the cellarman for each drink as it was ordered. As the cellarman poured out the drinks he would set aside perhaps a teaspoonful from each glass, and he amassed quantities in this way. He would sell the stolen brandy for five sous a swig if he thought he could trust you. . . .

What keeps a hotel going is the fact that the employees take a genuine pride in their work, beastly and silly though it is. If a man idles, the others soon find him out, and conspire against him to get him sacked. Cooks, waiters and *plongeurs* differ greatly in outlook, but they are all alike in being proud of their efficiency.

Undoubtedly the most workmanlike class, and the least servile, are the cooks. They do not earn quite so much as waiters, but their prestige is higher and their employment steadier. The cook does not look upon himself as a servant but as a skilled workman; he is generally called *un ouvrier,* which a waiter never is. He knows his power—knows that he alone makes or mars a restaurant, and that if he is five minutes late everything is out of gear. He despises the whole non-cooking staff, and makes it a point of honour to insult everyone below the head waiter. And he takes a genuine artistic pride in his work, which demands very great skill. It is not the cooking that is so difficult, but the doing everything to time. Between breakfast and luncheon the head cook at the Hotel X. would receive orders for several hundred dishes, all to be served at different times; he cooked a few of them himself, but he gave instructions about all of them and inspected them before they were sent up. His memory was wonderful. The vouchers were pinned on a board, but the head cook seldom looked at them; everything was stored in his mind, and exactly to the minute, as each dish fell due, he would call out, *"faites marcher une cotelette de veau"* (or whatever it was) unfailingly. He was an insufferable bully, but he was also an artist. It is for their punctuality, and not for any superiority in technique, that men cooks are preferred to women.

The waiter's outlook is quite different. He too is proud in a way of his skill, but his skill is chiefly in being servile. His work gives him the mentality, not of a workman, but of a snob. He lives perpetually in sight of rich people, stands at their tables, listens to their conversation, sucks up to them with smiles and discreet little jokes. He has the pleasure of spending money by proxy. Moreover, there is always the chance that he may become rich himself, for, though most waiters die poor, they have long runs of luck occasionally. At some cafes on the Grand Boulevard there is so much money to be made that the waiters actually pay the *patron* for their employment. The result is that between constantly seeing money, and hoping to get it, the waiter comes to identify himself to some extent with his employers. He will take pains to serve a meal in style, because he feels that he is participating in the meal himself.

I remember Valenti telling me of some banquet at Nice at which he had once served, and of how it cost two hundred thousand francs and was talked of for months afterwards. "It was splendid, *mon p'tit, mais magnifique!* Jesus Christ! The champagne, the silver, the orchids—I have never seen anything like them, and I have seen some things. Ah, it was glorious!"

"But," I said, "you were only there to wait?"

"Oh, of course. But still, it was splendid."

The moral is, never be sorry for a waiter. Sometimes when you sit in a restaurant, still stuffing yourself half an hour after closing time, you feel that the tired waiter at your side must surely be despising you. But he is not. He is not thinking as he looks at you, "What an overfed lout"; he is thinking, "One day, when I have saved enough money, I shall be able to imitate that man." He is ministering to a kind of pleasure he thoroughly understands and admires. And that is why waiters are seldom Socialists, have no effective trade union, and will work twelve hours a day—they work fifteen hours, seven days a week, in many cafes. They are snobs, and they find the servile nature of their work rather congenial.

The *plongeurs,* again, have a different outlook. Theirs is a job which offers no prospects, is intensely exhausting, and at the same time has not a trace of skill or interest; the sort of job that would always be done by women if women were strong enough. All that is required of them is to be constantly on the run, and to put up with long hours and a stuffy atmosphere. They have no way of escaping from this life, for they cannot save a penny from their wages, and working from sixty to a hundred hours a week leaves them no time to train for anything else. The best they can hope for is to find a slightly softer job as night-watchman or lavatory attendant.

And yet the *plongeurs*, low as they are, also have a kind of pride. It is the pride of the drudge—the man who is equal to no matter what quantity of work. At that level, the mere power to go on working like an ox is about the only virtue attainable. *Débrouillard* is what every *plongeur* wants to be called. A *débrouillard* is a man who, even when he is told to do the impossible, will *se débrouiller*—get it done somehow. One of the kitchen *plongeurs* at the Hotel X., a German, was well known as a *débrouillard*. One night an English lord came to the hotel, and the waiters were in despair, for the lord had asked for peaches, and there were none in stock; it was late at night, and the shops would be shut. "Leave it to me," said the German. He went out, and in ten minutes he was back with four peaches. He had gone into a neighboring restaurant and stolen them. That is what is meant by a *débrouillard*. The English lord paid for the peaches at twenty francs each.

Mario, who was in charge of the cafeterie, had the typical drudge mentality. All he thought of was getting through the *boulot,* and he defied you to give him too much of it. Fourteen years underground had left him with about as much natural laziness as a piston rod. *Faut être dur,* he used to say when anyone complained. You will often hear *plongeurs* boast, *je suis dur*—as though they were soldiers, not male charwomen.

Thus everyone in the hotel had his sense of honour, and when the press of work came we were all ready for a grand concerted effort to get through it. The constant war between the different departments also made for efficiency, for everyone clung to his own privileges and tried to stop the others idling and pilfering.

William Shakespeare (1564–1616)

The world as a stage

Jaques: All the world's a stage,
And all the men and women merely players.
They have their exits and their entrances;
And one man in his time plays many parts,
His acts being seven ages. At first the infant,
Mewling and puking in the nurse's arms.

From *As You Like It* by William Shakespeare.

Then the whining schoolboy, with his satchel
And shining morning face, creeping like snail
Unwillingly to school. And then the lover,
Sighing like furnace, with a woeful ballad
Made to his mistress' eyebrow. Then a soldier,
Full of strange oaths, and bearded like the pard,
Jealous in honour, sudden and quick in quarrel,
Seeking the bubble reputation
Even in the cannon's mouth. And then the justice,
In fair round belly with good capon lined,
With eyes severe and beard of formal cut,
Full of wise saws and modern instances;
And so he plays his part. The sixth age shifts
Into the lean and slippered pantaloon,
With spectacles on nose and pouch on side,
His youthful hose, well saved, a world too wide
For his shrunk shank; and his big manly voice,
Turning again toward childish treble, pipes
And whistles in his sound. Last scene of all,
That ends this strange eventful history,
Is second childishness and mere oblivion,
Sans teeth, sans eyes, sans taste, sans everything.

Sex roles

Among the many roles men and women play as they go through their lives and careers, sex roles are perhaps the most salient. Expectations pertaining to the distinctive behavior of men and of women shape each person's sense of self. Sexual identity is a key determinant of the overall sense of personal identity.

Sex roles tend to be socially defined on the basis of ascription; in only relatively rare and marginal cases is it possible for a person to "pass" from one sex role to another, to achieve a socially recognized sexual identity different from the original biologically given facts.

All known societies differentiate in some way between male and female sexual roles. The specific expectations surrounding sex roles vary, however, in different cultures and at different points in historical time. As Margaret Mead, among others, has shown in convincing detail, it is simply not true that all cultures, for example, define women as passive and men as active, males as aggressive and females as yielding and receptive.

The enormous variability in sex role definitions has perhaps been most apparent within the last hundred years—in the West and increasingly in the East, where female sex roles have changed with startling rapidity. The selections that follow illustrate this development.

Anton Chekhov's *The Darling* plastically depicts the sex role of the middle class woman as it prevailed in the nineteenth century. Women were seen by men, and largely also by themselves, as dependent on their husbands, as lacking personal autonomy. Their personalities were absorbed in the worlds in which their husbands moved; Chekhov's heroine changes her mental universe and her view of herself as she moves from one husband to another. The brief excerpt from a short story by the brilliant contemporary British novelist Doris Lessing (here entitled, *The Way You Get at Mum*) illustrates how in the traditional working-class family the personality of the mother was submerged in her family routines, in her devoted service to husband and children.

The famous final scene from Henrik Ibsen's *A Doll's House* marks the symbolic break with the Victorian sex role by a daring "new woman" who is no longer willing to accept the traditional subjection of the female to the male power. Banging the door behind her, Nora leaves Helmer and the echo of that bang still reverberates.

Yet banging of doors is not enough. As many "new women" have found, it is by no means easy to live up to or to keep up with the gradually emerging new role definitions for women when older definitions still surround us. Doris Lessing's *Martha Quest* finds it difficult to relate to men and to women who, modern and educated as they believe themselves to be, still cling to female role definitions which give saliency to domesticity, and are hence threatened and made uneasy by women who reject the primacy of domestic routines in the female sex role. Tess Slesinger, a highly gifted American writer of the thirties, illustrates the continued operation of the double standard even among sophisticated and "emancipated" American intellectuals. Finally, Virginia Woolf, the greatest woman writer of the twentieth century, describes the overwhelming difficulties that modern women face in their efforts to carve out a niche in the social world in which their personalities can freely flower without being absorbed by that of others.

Anton Chekhov

The darling

Olenka, the daughter of the retired collegiate assessor, Plemyanniakov, was sitting in her back porch, lost in thought. It was hot, the flies were persistent and teasing, and it was pleasant to reflect that it would soon be evening. Dark rainclouds were gathering from the east, and bringing from time to time a breadth of moisture in the air.

Kukin, who was the manager of an open-air theatre called the Tivoli, and who lived in the lodge, was standing in the middle of the garden looking at the sky.

"Again!" he observed despairingly. "It's going to rain again! Rain every day, as though to spite me! I might as well hang myself! It's ruin! Fearful losses every day."

He flung up his hands, and went on, addressing Olenka:

"There! that's the life we lead, Olga Semyonovna. It's enough to make one cry. One works and does one's utmost; one wears oneself out, getting no sleep at night, and racks one's brain what to do for the best. And then what happens? To begin with, one's public is ignorant, boorish. I give them the very best operetta, a dainty masque, first-rate music-hall artists. But do you suppose that's what they want! They don't understand anything of that sort. They want a clown; what they ask for is vulgarity. And then look at the weather! Almost every evening it rains. It started on the tenth of May, and it's kept it up all May and June. It's simply awful! The public doesn't come, but I've to pay the rent just the same, and pay the artists."

The next evening the clouds would gather again, the Kukin would say with an hysterical laugh:

"Well, rain away, then! Flood the garden, drown me! Damn my luck in this world and the next! Let the artists have me up! Send me to prison!— to Siberia!—the scaffold! Ha, ha, ha!"

And next day the same thing.

Olenka listened to Kukin with silent gravity, and sometimes tears came into her eyes. In the end his misfortunes touched her; she grew to love him. He was a small thin man, with a yellow face, and curls combed forward on his forehead. He spoke in a thin tenor; as he talked his mouth worked on one side, and there was always an expression of despair on his face; yet he aroused a deep and genuine affection in her. She was always fond of some-one, and could not exist without loving. In earlier days she had loved her

From Anton Chekhov, *The Darling and Other Stories*, translated by Constance Garnett.

papa, who now sat in a darkened room, breathing with difficulty; she had loved her aunt who used to come every other year from Bryansk; and before that, when she was at school, she had loved her French master. She was a gentle, soft-hearted, compassionate girl, with mild, tender eyes and very good health. At the sight of her full rosy cheeks, her soft white neck with a little dark mole on it, and the kind, naive smile, which came into her face when she listened to anything pleasant, men thought, "Yes, not half bad," and smiled too, while lady visitors could not refrain from seizing her hand in the middle of a conversation, exclaiming in a gush of delight, "You darling!"

The house in which she had lived from her birth upwards, and which was left her in her father's will, was at the extreme end of the town, not far from the Tivoli. In the evenings and at night she could hear the band playing, and the crackling and banging of fireworks, and it seemed to her that it was Kukin struggling with his destiny, storming the entrenchments of his chief foe, the indifferent public; there was a sweet thrill at her heart, she had no desire to sleep, and when he returned home at daybreak, she tapped softly at her bedroom window, and showing him only her face and one shoulder through the curtain, she gave him a friendly smile. . . .

He proposed to her, and they were married. And when he had a closer view of her neck and her plump, fine shoulders, he threw up his hands, and said:

"You darling!"

He was happy, but as it rained on the day and night of his wedding, his face still retained an expression of despair.

They got on very well together. She used to sit in his office, to look after things in the Tivoli, to put down the accounts and pay the wages. And her rosy cheeks, her sweet, naive, radiant smile, were to be seen now at the office window, now in the refreshment bar or behind the scenes at the theatre. And already she used to say to her acquaintances that the theatre was the chief and most important thing in life, and that it was only through the drama that one could derive true enjoyment and become cultivated and humane.

"But do you suppose the public understands that?" she used to say. "What they want is a clown. Yesterday we gave 'Faust Inside Out,' and almost all the boxes were empty; but if Vanitchka and I had been producing some vulgar thing, I assure you the theatre would have been packed. To-morrow Vanitchka and I are doing 'Orpheus in Hell.' Do come."

And what Kukin said about the theatre and the actors she repeated. Like him she despised the public for their ignorance and their indifference to art; she took part in the rehearsals, she corrected the actors, she kept an eye on the behaviour of the musicians, and when there was an unfavourable notice in the local paper, she shed tears, and then went to the editor's office to set things right.

The actors were fond of her and used to call her "Vanitchka and I," and "the darling"; she was sorry for them and used to lend them small sums of money, and if they deceived her, she used to shed a few tears in private, but did not complain to her husband.

They got on well in the winter too. They took the theatre in the town for the whole winter, and let it for short terms to a Little Russian company or to a conjurer, or to a local dramatic society. Olenka grew stouter, and was always beaming with satisfaction, while Kukin grew thinner and yellower, and continually complained of their terrible losses, although he had not done badly all the winter. He used to cough at night, and she used to give him hot raspberry tea or lime-flower water, to rub him with eau-de-Cologne and to wrap him in her warm shawls.

"You're such a sweet pet!" she used to say with perfect sincerity, stroking his hair. "You're such a pretty dear!"

Towards Lent he went to Moscow to collect a new troupe, and without him she could not sleep, but sat all night at her window, looking at the stars, and she compared herself with the hens, who are awake all night and uneasy when the cock is not in the hen-house. Kukin was detained in Moscow, and wrote that he would be back at Easter, adding some instructions about the Tivoli. But on the Sunday before Easter, late in the evening, came a sudden ominous knock at the gate; someone was hammering on the gate as though on a barrel—boom, boom, boom! The drowsy cook went flopping with her bare feet through the puddles, as she ran to open the gate.

"Please open," said someone outside in a thick bass. "There is a telegram for you."

Olenka had received telegrams from her husband before, but this time for some reason she felt numb with terror. With shaking hands she opened the telegram and read as follows:

"Ivan Petrovitch died suddenly to-day. Awaiting immate instructions funeral Tuesday."

That was how it was written in the telegram—"fufuneral," and the utterly incomprehensible word "immate." It was signed by the stage manager of the operatic company.

"My darling!" sobbed Olenka. "Vanitchka, my precious, my darling! Why did I ever meet you! Why did I know you and love you! Your poor heart-broken Olenka is all alone without you!"

Kukin's funeral took place on Tuesday in Moscow, Olenka returned home on Wednesday, and as soon as she got indoors she threw herself on her bed and sobbed so loudly that it could be heard next door, and in the street.

"Poor darling!" the neighbours said, as they crossed themselves. "Olga Semyonovna, poor darling! How she does take on!"

Three months later Olenka was coming home from mass, melancholy and in deep mourning. It happened that one of her neighbours, Vassily

Andreitch Pustovalov, returning home from church, walked back beside her. He was the manager at Babakayev's, the timber merchant's. He wore a straw hat, a white waistcoat, and a gold watch-chain, and looked more like a country gentleman than a man in trade.

"Everything happens as it is ordained, Olga Semyonovna," he said gravely, with a sympathetic note in his voice; "and if any of our dear ones die, it must be because it is the will of God, so we ought to have fortitude and bear it submissively."

After seeing Olenka to her gate, he said good-bye and went on. All day afterwards she heard his sedately dignified voice, and whenever she shut her eyes she saw his dark beard. She liked him very much. And apparently she had made an impression on him too, for not long afterwards an elderly lady, with whom she was only slightly acquainted, came to drink coffee with her, and as soon as she was seated at table began to talk about Pustovalov, saying that he was an excellent man whom one could thoroughly depend upon, and that any girl would be glad to marry him. Three days later Pustovalov came himself. He did not stay long, only about ten minutes, and he did not say much, but when he left, Olenka loved him—loved him so much that she lay awake all night in a perfect fever, and in the morning she sent for the elderly lady. The match was quickly arranged, and then came the wedding.

Pustovalov and Olenka got on very well together when they were married.

Usually he sat in the office till dinner-time, then he went out on business, while Olenka took his place, and sat in the office till evening, making up accounts and booking orders.

"Timber gets dearer every year; the price rises twenty per cent," she would say to her customers and friends. "Only fancy we used to sell local timber, and now Vassitchka always has to go for wood to the Mogilev district. And the freight!" she would add, covering her cheeks with her hands in horror. "The freight!"

It seemed to her that she had been in the timber trade for ages and ages, and that the most important and necessary thing in life was timber; and there was something intimate and touching to her in the very sound of words such as "baulk," "post," "beam," "pole," "scantling," "batten," "lath," "plank," etc.

At night when she was asleep she dreamed of perfect mountains of planks and boards, and long strings of waggons, carting timber somewhere far away. She dreamed that a whole regiment of six-inch beams forty feet high, standing on end, was marching upon the timber-yard; that logs, beams, and boards knocked together with the resounding crash of dry wood, kept falling and getting up again, piling themselves on each other. Olenka cried out in her sleep, and Pustovalov said to her tenderly: "Olenka, what's the matter, darling? Cross yourself!"

Her husband's ideas were hers. If he thought the room was too hot, or that business was slack, she thought the same. Her husband did not care for entertainments, and on holidays he stayed at home. She did likewise.

"You are always at home or in the office," her friends said to her. "You should go to the theatre, darling, or to the circus."

"Vassitchka and I have no time to go to theatres," she would answer sedately. "We have no time for nonsense. What's the use of these theatres?"

On Saturdays Pustovalov and she used to go to the evening service; on holidays to early mass, and they walked side by side with softened faces as they came home from church. There was a pleasant fragrance about them both, and her silk dress rustled agreeably. At home they drank tea, with fancy bread and jams of various kinds, and afterwards they ate pie. Every day at twelve o'clock there was a savoury smell of beetroot soup and of mutton or duck in their yard, and on fast-days of fish, and no one could pass the gate without feeling hungry. In the office the samovar was always boiling, and customers were regaled with tea and cracknels. Once a week the couple went to the baths and returned side by side, both red in the face.

"Yes, we have nothing to complain of, thank God," Olenka used to say to her acquaintances. "I wish everyone were as well off as Vassitchka and I."

When Pustovalov went away to buy wood in the Mogilev district, she missed him dreadfully, lay awake and cried. A young veterinary surgeon in the army, called Smirnin, to whom they had let their lodge, used sometimes to come in in the evening. He used to talk to her and play cards with her, and this entertained her in her husband's absence. She was particularly interested in what he told her of his home life. He was married and had a little boy, but was separated from his wife because she had been unfaithful to him, and now he hated her and used to send her forty roubles a month for the maintenance of their son. And hearing of all this, Olenka sighed and shook her head. She was sorry for him.

"Well, God keep you," she used to say to him at parting, as she lighted him down the stairs with a candle. "Thank you for coming to cheer me up, and may the Mother of God give you health."

And she always expressed herself with the same sedateness and dignity, the same reasonableness, in imitation of her husband. As the veterinary surgeon was disappearing behind the door below, she would say:

"You know, Vladimir Platonitch, you'd better make it up with your wife. You should forgive her for the sake of your son. You may be sure the little fellow understands."

And when Pustovalov came back, she told him in a low voice about the veterinary surgeon and his unhappy home life, and both sighed and shook their heads and talked about the boy, who, no doubt, missed his father, and by some strange connection of ideas, they went up to the holy ikons, bowed to the ground before them and prayed that God would give them children.

And so the Pustovalovs lived for six years quietly and peaceably in love and complete harmony.

But behold! one winter day after drinking hot tea in the office, Vassily Andreitch went out into the yard without his cap on to see about sending off some timber, caught cold and was taken ill. He had the best doctors, but he grew worse and died after four months' illness. And Olenka was a widow once more.

"I've nobody, now you've left me, my darling," she sobbed, after her husband's funeral. "How can I live without you, in wretchedness and misery! Pity me, good people, all alone in the world!"

She went about dressed in black with long "weepers," and gave up wearing hat and gloves for good. She hardly ever went out, except to church, or to her husband's grave, and led the life of a nun. It was not till six months later that she took off the weepers and opened the shutters of the windows. She was sometimes seen in the mornings, going with her cook to market for provisions, but what went on in her house and how she lived now could only be surmissed. People guessed, from seeing her drinking tea in her garden with the veterinary surgeon, who read the newspaper aloud to her, and from the fact that, meeting a lady she knew at the post-office, she said to her:

"There is no proper veterinary inspection in our town, and that's the cause of all sorts of epidemics. One is always hearing of people's getting infection from the milk supply, or catching diseases from horses and cows. The health of domestic animals ought to be as well cared for as the health of human beings."

She repeated the veterinary surgeon's words, and was of the same opinion as he about everything. It was evident that she could not live a year without some attachment, and had found new happiness in the lodge. In anyone else this would have been censured, but no one could think ill of Olenka; everything she did was so natural. Neither she nor the veterinary surgeon said anything to other people of the change in their relations, and tried, indeed, to conceal it, but without success, for Olenka could not keep a secret. When he had visitors, men serving in his regiment, and she poured out tea or served the supper, she would begin talking of the cattle plague, of the foot and mouth disease, and of the municipal slaughter-houses. He was dreadfully embarrassed, and when the guests had gone, he would seize her by the hand and hiss angrily:

"I've asked you before not to talk about what you don't understand. When we veterinary surgeons are talking among ourselves, please don't put your word in. It's really annoying."

And she would look at him with astonishment and dismay, and ask him in alarm: "But, Voloditchka, what *am* I to talk about?"

And with tears in her eyes she would embrace him, begging him not to be angry, and they were both happy. . . .

Doris Lessing (1919–   )

The way you get at mum

There were another five minutes to go. "I don't think it's right, the way you get at Mum," Lennie said, at last coming to the point.

"But I haven't said a bloody word," said Charlie, switching without having intended it into his other voice, the middle-class voice which he was careful never to use with his family except in joke. Lennie gave him a glance of surprise and reproach and said: "All the same. She feels it."

"But it's bloody ridiculous." Charlie's voice was rising. "She stands in that kitchen all day, pandering to our every whim, when she's not doing housework or making a hundred trips a day with that bloody coal. . . ." In the Christmas holidays, when Charlie had visited home last, he had fixed up a bucket on the frame of an old pram to ease his mother's work. This morning he had seen the contrivance collapsed and full of rainwater in the back yard. After breakfast Lennie and Charlie had sat at the table in their shirt-sleeves watching their mother. The door was open into the back yard. Mrs. Thornton carried a shovel whose blade was nine inches by ten, and was walking back and forth from the coalhole in the yard, through the kitchen, into the parlour. On each inward journey, a small clump of coal balanced on the shovel. Charlie counted that his mother walked from the coalhole to the kitchen fire and the parlour fire thirty-six times. She walked steadily, the shovel in front, held like a spear in both hands, and her face frowned with purpose. Charlie had dropped his head onto his arms and laughed soundlessly until he felt Lennie's warning gaze and stopped the heave of his shoulders. After a moment he had sat up, straight-faced. Lennie said: "Why do you get at Mum, then?" Charlie said: "But I haven't said owt." "No, but she's getting riled. You always show what you think, Charlie boy." As Charlie did not respond to this appeal—for far more than present charity— Lennie went on: "You can't teach an old dog new tricks." "Old! She's not fifty!"

Now Charlie said, continuing the early conversation: "She goes on as if she were an old woman. She wears herself out with nothing—she could get through all the work she has in a couple of hours if she organized herself. Or if just for once she told us where to get off."

"What'd she do with herself then?"

"Do? Well, she could do something for herself. Or see friends. Or something."

"She feels it. Last time you went off she cried."

"She *what?*" Charlie's guilt almost overpowered him, but the inner didactic voice switched on in time and he spoke through it: "What right have we to treat her like a bloody servant? Betty likes her food this way and that way, and Dad won't eat this and that, and she stands there and humours the lot of us—like a servant."

"And who was it last night said he wouldn't have fat on his meat and changed it for hers?" said Lennie smiling, but full of reproach.

"Oh, I'm just as bad as the rest of you," said Charlie, sounding false. "It makes me wild to see it," he said, sounding sincere. Didactically he said: "All the women in the village—they take it for granted. If someone organised them so that they had half a day to themselves sometimes, they'd think they were being insulted—they can't stop working. Just look at Mum, then. She comes into Doncaster to wrap sweets two or three times a week—well, she actually loses money on it, by the time she's paid bus fares. I said to her, 'You're actually losing money on it,' and she said 'I like to get out and see a bit of life.' A bit of life! Wrapping sweets in a bloody factory. Why can't she just come into town of an evening and have a bit of fun without feeling she has to pay for it by wrapping sweets, sweated bloody labour? And she actually loses on it. It doesn't make sense. They're human beings, aren't they? Not just. . . ."

Henrik Ibsen (1828–1906)

A doll's house cracks up

Nora. . . . When your terror was over—not for me, but for yourself—when there was nothing more to fear,—then it was to you as though nothing had happened. I was your lark again, your doll—whom you would take twice as much care of in future, because she was so weak and fragile. *(Stands up.)* Torvald, in that moment it burst upon me that I had been living here these eight years with a strange man, and had borne him three children. Oh! I can't bear to think of it—I could tear myself to pieces!

Helmer *(sadly).* I see it, I see it; an abyss has opened between us. But, Nora, can it never be filled up?

Nora. As I now am, I am no wife for you.

From *A Doll's House* by Henrik Ibsen (1879).

Helmer. I have strength to become another man.

Nora. Perhaps—when your doll is taken away from you.

Helmer. To part—to part from you! No, Nora, no; I can't grasp the thought.

Nora *(going into room, right).* The more reason for the thing to happen.

(She comes back with out-door things and a small travelling-bag, which she puts on a chair.)

Helmer. Nora, Nora, not now! Wait till to-morrow.

Nora *(putting on cloak).* I can't spend the night in a strange man's house.

Helmer. But can't we live here, as brother and sister?

Nora *(fastening her hat).* You know very well that wouldn't last long. Good-bye, Torvald. No, I won't go to the children. I know they're in better hands than mine. As I now am, I can be nothing to them.

Helmer. But some time, Nora; some time—

Nora. How can I tell? I have no idea what will become of me.

Helmer. But you are my wife, now and always!

Nora. Listen, Torvald—when a wife leaves her husband's house, as I am doing, I have heard that in the eyes of the law he is free from all duties towards her. At any rate, I release you from all duties. You must not feel yourself bound any more than I shall. There must be perfect freedom on both sides. There, there is your ring back. Give me mine.

Helmer. That too?

Nora. That too.

Helmer. Here it is.

Nora. Very well. Now it's all over. Here are the keys. The servants know about everything in the house, better than I do. To-morrow, when I have started, Christina will come to pack up my things. I will have them sent after me.

Helmer. All over! all over! Nora, will you never think of me again?

Nora. Oh, I shall often think of you, and the children, and this house.

Helmer. May I write to you, Nora?

Nora. No, never. You must not.

Helmer. But I must send you—

Nora. Nothing, nothing.

Helmer. I must help you if you need it.

Nora. No, I say. I take nothing from strangers.

Helmer. Nora, can I never be more than a stranger to you?

Nora *(taking her travelling-bag).* Oh, Torvald, then the miracle of miracles would have to happen.

Helmer. What is the miracle of miracles?

Nora. Both of us would have to change so that— Oh, Torvald, I no longer believe in miracles.

Helmer. But I will believe. We must so change that—

Nora. That communion between us shall be a marriage. Good-bye *(She goes out.)*

Helmer *(sinks in a chair by the door with his face in his hands).* Nora! Nora! *(He looks round and stands up.)* Empty. She's gone. *(A hope inspires him.)* Ah! The miracle of miracles—?!

(From below is heard the reverberation of a heavy door closing.)

Doris Lessing ————————————————————

Martha's quest

It was a beautiful afternoon: there had been a storm, and the sky was full and clear, with shining masses of washed clouds rolling lightly in bright sunlight. The trees in the park glistened a soft, clean green; the puddles on the pavements reflected foliage and sky; and as the car turned into the grounds of the school where Mr. Pyecroft was headmaster, these puddles became ruffled brown silk, and above them, all down the drive, grew massed shrubs, glistening with wet. On a deep-green lawn were several deck chairs. From them two men rose as Martha approached; and again she thought, disappointedly, But they are old.

They were, in fact, between thirty and forty; they wore flannels, open shirts, sandals; they were of the same type: all long, thin, bony men, with intellectual faces, spectacles, thinning hair. It would be untrue to say that Martha made any such observation, or even compared them with Joss. When she met people, she felt a dazzled and confused attraction of sympathy, or dislike. Now she was in sympathy; she responded to the half-grudging deference older men offer a young girl. She answered their questions brightly, and was conscious of her appearance, because they were.

Mr. Pyecroft said that his wife would not be long, she was giving the

---

children their tea; the other two men also apologized for the absence of their wives, and Martha accepted these social remarks not at their social value, but with the statement which she imagined sounded light and flippant, but actually sounded hostile: "Children are a nuisance, aren't they?"

Soon three women came from a verandah of the big school building, shepherding half a dozen children and two native nannies to another lawn, about a hundred yards away, which was sheltered by a big glossy cedrela-toona tree. As soon as the women appeared, the voices of the men acquired a touch of heartiness that had not been there before, grew louder; and they turned their shoulders on these domestic arrangements with an uneasy determination which at once struck Martha, for she felt it herself. She was watching the scolding and fussy women as if her eyes were glued to them in fierce horror; she said to herself, Never, never, I'd rather die; and she reclined in her deck chair with a deliberate coolness, a deliberately untroubled look.

When Mrs. Pyecroft, Mrs. Perr, and Mrs. Forester came to join the men, they apologized, laughing, together and separately, for being a nuisance, and explained how the children had been troublesome, and went into details (and in a way that made it seem as if it were an accusation against the men themselves) of how Jane was off her food, while Tommy was in a trying psychological phase. The men listened, politely, from their chairs; but they were not allowed to remain in them, for it appeared that the whole group must be rearranged, an operation which took a good deal of time. Martha was more and more hostile and critical—the womens seemed to her un-pleasant and absurd, with their fuss and their demands; she was as much on the defensive as if their mere presence were a menace to herself.

She looked at their dresses, as Donovan had taught her to look, but understood at once that here was a standard that refused to acknowledge Donovan. Their appearance had something in common which was difficult to define; Martha made no attempt to define it, she merely felt derisive. They were not at all the unashamedly housewifely women of "the district"; nor were they fashionable—clearly, they disdained fashion. Their dresses tended to be discordantly colourful, and too long for the year; their hair was looped or braided or fringed, in a consciously womanly way; they wore bright beads and "touches" of embroidery—Martha found herself fiddling with her embroidered belt and with her scarf, which was now uncomfortable. She was stifled by it.

A native servant rolled a waggon with tea things across the lawn, and there began a business of pouring, handing cups and passing cakes. Martha joked and lit a cigarette, and said she was slimming. The women looked sharply at her, and said that at her age it was ridiculous; they looked at the men for support, and did not find it. If there was an edge on their voices when they spoke to her, they could hardly be judged for it; for Martha's gaze was expressing the most frank criticism, even scorn; and she, in her turn, ranged herself with the men as if it were her due to have their support.

With the arrival of the ladies, the rights of the intellect were at once asserted; and Martha was informed of times of meetings, the origin of the Left Book Club, the courage and force and foresight of a Mr. Gollancz, and that "we" were trying to raise aid for Spain. But no sooner had this conversation begun than the children began to shriek, and all three women rushed off, as one, to the rescue, in spite of the two native nannies, who might have been considered sufficient to deal with them. And so it went on: the three women came back, hurriedly apologizing, firmly took up the threads of their respective remarks, a general conversation began to develop, and then either a child would come rushing across the lawn, shouting "Mummy, Mummy!" or one, or all, of the women found it necessary to go to the children.

And Martha heard that fierce and passionate voice repeating more and more loudly inside her, I will *not* be like this; for, comparing these intelligent ladies, who nevertheless expressed resentment against something (but what?) in every tone of their voices, every movement of their bodies, with the undemanding women of the district, who left their men to talk by themselves while they made a world of their own with cooking and domesticity—comparing them, there could be no doubt which were the more likeable. And if, like Martha, one had decided to be neither one nor the other, what could one be but fierce and unhappy and determined? . . .

Tess Slesinger (1915–1945)

Her second husband took a lover

To hell with philosophy, in short. "But what are you going to *do?*" he says, Dill says, and you discover that he too is lying without moving, as afraid as you that if a muscle twitches or a breath catches, something, or the whole of everything, will go smashing to small pieces in this life you share. What are you going to *do?* To *do?* Why, lie here, I suppose, for the rest of our married life, in your arms gone cold, in our bed gone cold, my heart gone cold as a philosopher's. What am I going to *do*, you think. It is a good question. One of the best questions, for there is never any answer to it.

Certainly, you think, you have a legalistic right to go out and get even . . . But you did that once, you matched Jimsie amour for amour, and what happened? Why, the string between you wore out, it got like old elastic and finally, because it would never snap any more for deadness, each of you let go his end and wandered off, too empty to feel pain, too dead to feel anything. You merely destroyed something that way, Cornelia, you didn't even save your self-respect when that bank closed. No, that's painless dentistry again, remote control, the Machine Age, Watson and the reflex, the Modern Generation. To derive *full* value out of anything, one must pay the price in pain; full beauty consists of pain as well as joy—and halving the pain cuts the joy in two. Let us not compromise, you think strongly; God send me pain again, God let me feel.

"I mean, can you love me in spite of anything?" If I love you at all, you think, if there is such a thing as love at all, then I suppose it is in spite of anything. "Oh sure," you hear yourself saying like a girl scout, but it sounds like the kind of records your grandfather used to play on his gramophone. "And how about you, my gay deceiver, would you love me in spite of anything, Dill? Would you now?" Impossible, clearly, to speak without lilting; try a drop of pallid humor first thing in the morning, nothing like it to aid digestion, avoid those infidelity blues, that early-morning tremolo.

"Anything, *but no gents*," he says, with fear piled up in his eyes and a sort of anticipatory hatred. "Don't ask me why, I don't *know* why, but it's different with a man."

He says and has said and will go on saying, *But no gents* for you, my girl, one gent and I am through. He will go on saying it until there has been one gent. (And the first is the only one that counts. After that, the elastic begins to stretch and go dead—we found that out between us, Jimsie and I.) Then it is a toss-up what he will do, when there has been one gent. But one thing is clear, Cornelia, you shrewd and calculating woman, one thing is clear: one gent, and you will have lost the large part of your power over him. For it is not true that men despise what they possess or what they have exclusive rights over; what is true is that they cannot love (in normal, masculine fashion) what they must share. No, there is no point to your going and doing likewise, not as long as there is any point to your relations with this man, this philandering second husband, this gay deceiver who tells the truth and looks so far from gay about it. As long as he can lie there with fear written on his face and say to you *But no gents*, you have a power which nothing can destroy. You gain thereby an integrity which exists not merely in his eyes, but which is actual, which is a fact. You become a whole person even in your sadness, while he stands before you, however male, a split one. He will know it, you will know it.

"The old Dolly Gray complex," you say. And evidently every man has the germs of it in him somewhere, the little woman waiting at home. It is even a little perverse that he can feel this way about you when he considers you were a bum (as he called it) out and out before he met you, ever since Jimsie in fact, and realizes that you were one on the very night he met you. But that's nice; that's what appeals to him; the very perversity of these strange facts: that you were a bastard (in his own language) and that now you sit at home and wait for him. He could not bear it if you were straight-out Dolly Gray, for he is a modern young man. But you have that whole rich background (rich! and supposing you have children and then grand-children, would that story about falling asleep in a fraternity house with two "brothers" be the kind kids would like to hear from dear old Granny?)—but you have it, and he can never quite forgive you, and this is enough to tease him and please him for the rest of his life; you can never be quite Dolly Gray in his eyes because you can never shake off your past and his memory of your complaisance (to put it mildly) on the very night on which he met you. All right, let him have the joy of reforming you, of capturing what was free and keeping it in a cage, of owning what used to belong to nobody. At least let him for the time being. See what happens. You can always go back to being a bum again. Hallelujah, bum again! "I couldn't stand it if I thought this changed things," says Dill—and of course he knows it has changed things, what he means is he can't stand it if it's going to change your staying at home and waiting for him.

"Ah, let's get up, nothing is changed, why should it be," you say quite gayly (and feeling it too), and spring stiffly out of his stiff arms. Well, it isn't quite the same as yesterday, it never will be. There is none of that pleasant, early-morning family-feeling now. You feel wicked a little as you run about with your pyjamas falling off one shoulder, getting breakfast but taking care to be rather attractive about it today as though you and Dill were not married yet. Ah yes, it is a very flirtatious breakfast that you have, flirtatious and a little bit precarious, for if the toast burns you might cry, and if the coffee is not done properly today he might fling it to the floor in a rage. But no, no; everything comes out all right because it *had* to come out all right, even the eggs get poached quite nicely instead of slipping out of their shells and allowing themselves to be parboiled—the toast turns out like the toast in a suave English comedy, and the coffee has never been better (you taste all this with your mind, with your weighing-machine, for your tongue has ceased to give a damn, and your alimentary canal is working like a derrick without a soul.) In fact the whole thing passes off rather like a fine English play, in which the husband has just murdered the child because he found out his wife had it by the butler, the wife is scheduled to murder the butler imme-diately after breakfast, and meantime the butler serves them an impeccable breakfast over an impeccable table with unimpeachable manners, and the husband and the wife delicately break their toast and wonder if the season will be a good one, if the Queen has got over her cold. Oh yes, yes, yes, it is all very nice, Dill flips over the pages of *The Times* (why is he wearing his good blue jacket and his natty grey trousers, he never starts that until May and here it is only April) and Cornelia does the wifely thing, she keeps his plate stacked with fresh toast and wipes the corners of her mouth (which she has rouged before breakfast, for a change) very nicely, with the edge of the fringed napkin (which belongs to the linen set they don't usually use when they are alone).

And it is all very nice (and a little bit formal), only that the house looks queerly different to you now, no longer quite your own, it no longer holds you as it held you yesterday. Yet there have been days when those four walls were so dear to you, too dear, times when they hemmed you in until you felt like a caged animal. Today you rather wish they pressed in closer. But the walls seem all made of doors today. Now the boredom that weighed pleasantly yesterday is gone. Why did you not whisper yesterday, while there was still time, why did you not shout it yesterday while you still had the voice—that that boredom was a good thing, let us preserve it, Dill, it is good, it is warm, it is real; it cannot be said today. No, no, and a good thing too, for this is life, life as it is spoken in the Twentieth Century, will you have a little toast dear? No? really not? then how about a second cup of coffee, well for heaven's sake, those politicians! when will they leave off cutting one another's throats?—all so very delicate and stilted, all so very fine and quiet, so civilized, so neat, the corpse inside in the bedroom but the play's the thing and let's not forget our very fine modern manners. (And why, with that impossibly gay suit, has he chosen that impossibly gay tie— a bow tie, does he think it's Spring?) but why in such a hurry, Dill, Dill darling—"You've left half your coffee, it's cold, Dill, let me pour you another cup? it's still hot." And you have the specious joy of seeing him stay against his will and drink his second cup of coffee, which he clearly doesn't want.

So he wipes his mouth and puts his fancy napkin down and stands there smiling at you quite politely. This is the moment for you to rise and casually murder the butler and come back and help your husband with his coat. But you can't make the grade. For you see it all suddenly, you see it there in his face, reluctant as he is to hurt you. He does have an actual existence outside of you, and he is anxious to leave you now and enter it. You see it in his face. It is clearer than any of the things you told yourself—and he cannot help revealing it to you. He will be lost to you the minute he walks out of your sight; he will be back, of course, but this time and forever after you will know that he has been away, clean away, on his own. You see it in his face, and your heart, which had sunk to the lowest bottom, suddenly sinks lower.

"Don't go yet." It is time to murder the butler, but you walk instead— or lilt, for you cannot trust yourself to walk—to your husband, and you begin a wretched game of opening up each button of his coat after he has fastened it. You go on playing the game together, both of you laughing, it may be a little ruefully. He lets you get all the buttons undone at last, and then when you press yourself against him like a very small girl suddenly, he puts his arms around you and holds you—oh *fairly* tight, you think, but you can feel his arms relaxing, you can feel goodbye in his fingertips. You indulge yourself anyway for a mad whirling second, you steal what he doesn't want to give you, the illusion of comfort against his apochryphal chest, the illusion that he is holding you so tightly that he will never let you go. And then you give up, quite nicely, and stand back surveying him with your head on one side. Very definitely you refrain from asking him why the Spring suit, the bow tie. Quite loudly you do not ask him what time he will be home.

He tells you, though, he tells you everything. "I'll be a little late," he says; "I've got to stop off someplace for a cocktail or something." I'll be a little late, he tells you, with his gay-deceiver's troubled eyes, with his blue serge coat and light grey pants, and with the tiny pause he gives his words, I'll be a little late because I've got to stop off for a cocktail or something—with my girl; because I'm helpless, Cornelia, helpless, caught in as strong a web as your misery makes for you . . .

In a minute now the pain will go tearing and surging through the veils, drop the curtain on the polished comedy—but hold it for another moment. "Oh, then," you say, reaching up, quite coy, quite gay, "you must let me fix your tie in a better bow, if you are stopping off someplace for a cocktail or something." Tweak, tweak, like an idiot, at his gay bow tie. "Which will you have, my darling, my blessing or my cake? And always remember, little one, that everything you do reflects on me," but this is bad, you realize, and turning with your hands raised in a rather silly gesture that is meant for mocking admiration, you wave him off, "There, there we are, now off with you in a cloud of dust."

B plus for that one, little sister, you tell yourself wearily, as you stand there hearing the door slam, and you wait there a minute but he doesn't come back, he isn't coming back, and if he were going to telephone you from the corner drug-store he would have done it by now, and you walk back past the laden table and you do not sweep the cups and saucers off the table, nor do you scream nor do you turn on the gas nor do you telephone the boy that used to take you dancing (though you think of all these things), nor do you fall in a heap sobbing on the empty bed (though that is what you thought you wanted to do)—you merely stand at the kitchen sink letting the hot water run to grow hotter, and you say to the cold walls reproachfully, "Oh Dill, Dill . . . oh Jimsie, Jimsie . . ." and when the doorbell rings at last you know that it is not Dill and not Jimsie but merely the man collecting last week's laundry.

Virginia Woolf (1882–1941)

A room of one's own

The British Museum was another department of the factory. The swing-doors swung open; and there one stood under the vast dome, as if one were a thought in the huge bald forehead which is so splendidly encircled by a band of famous names. One went to the counter; one took a slip of paper; one opened a volume of the catalogue, and . . . . . the five dots here indicate five separate minutes of stupefaction, wonder and bewilderment. Have you any notion how many books are written about women in the course of one year? Have you any notion how many are written by men? Are you aware that you are, perhaps, the most discussed animal in the universe? Here had I come with a notebook and a pencil proposing to spend a morning reading, supposing that at the end of the morning I should have transferred the truth to my notebook. But I should need to be a herd of elephants, I thought, and a wilderness of spiders, desperately referring to the animals that are reputed longest lived and most multitudinously eyed, to cope with all this. I should need claws of steel and beak of brass even to penetrate the husk. How shall I ever find the grains of truth embedded in all this mass of paper, I asked myself, and in despair began running my eye up and down the long list of titles. Even the names of the books gave me food for thought. Sex and its nature might well attract doctors and biologists; but what was surprising and difficult of explanation was the fact that sex—woman, that is to say—also attracts agreeable essayists, light-fingered novelists, young men who have taken the M.A. degree; men who have taken no degree; men who have no apparent qualification save that they are not women. Some of these books were, on the face of it, frivolous and facetious; but many, on the other hand, were serious and prophetic, moral and hortatory. Merely to read the titles suggested innumerable schoolmasters, innumerable clergymen mounting their platforms and pulpits and holding forth with a loquacity which far exceeded the hour usually allotted to such discourse on this one subject. It was a most strange phenomenon; and apparently—here I consulted the letter M—one confined to male sex. Women do not write books about men—a fact that I could not help welcoming with relief, for if I had first to read all that men have written about women, then all that women have written about men, the aloe that flowers once in a hundred years would flower twice before I could set pen to paper. So, making a perfectly arbitrary choice of a dozen volumes or so, I sent my slips of paper to lie in the wire tray, and waited in my stall, among the other seekers for the essential oil of truth.

What could be the reason, then, of this curious disparity, I wondered, drawing cart-wheels on the slips of paper provided by the British taxpayer for other purposes. Why are women, judging from this catalogue, so much more interesting to men than men are to women? A very curious fact it seemed, and my mind wandered to picture the lives of men who spend their time in writing books about women, whether they were old or young, married or unmarried, red-nosed or hump-backed—anyhow, it was flattering, vaguely, to feel oneself the object of such attention, provided that it was not entirely bestowed by the crippled and the infirm—so I pondered until all such frivolous thoughts were ended by an avalanche of books sliding down on to the desk in front of me. Now the trouble began. The student who has been trained in research at Oxbridge has no doubt some method of shepherding his question past all distractions till it runs into its answer as a sheep runs into its pen. The student by my side, for instance, who was copying assiduously from a scientific manual was, I felt sure, extracting pure nuggets of the essential ore every ten minutes or so. His little grunts of satisfaction indicated so much. But if, unfortunately, one has had no training in a university, the question far from being shepherded to its pen flies like a frightened flock hither and thither, helter-skelter, pursued by a whole pack of hounds. Professors, schoolmasters, sociologists, clergymen, novelists, essayists, journalists, men who had no qualification save that they were not women, chased my simple and single question—Why are women poor?—until it became fifty questions; until the fifty questions leapt frantically into mid-stream and were carried away. Every page in my notebook was scribbled over with notes. To show the state of mind I was in, I will read you a few of them, explaining that the page was headed quite simply, WOMEN AND POVERTY, in block letters; but what followed was something like this:

> Condition in Middle Ages of,
> Habits in the Fiji Islands of,
> Worshipped as goddesses by,
> Weaker in moral sense than,
> Idealism of,
> Greater conscientiousness of,
> South Sea Islanders, age of puberty among,
> Attractiveness of,
> Offered as sacrifice to,
> Small size of brain of,
> Profounder sub-consciousness of,
> Less hair on the body of,

Mental, moral and physical inferiority of,
Love of children of,
Greater length of life of,
Weaker muscles of,
Strength of affections of,
Vanity of,
Higher education of,
Shakespeare's opinion of,
Lord Birkenhead's opinion of,
Dean Inge's opinion of,
La Bruyère's opinion of,
Dr. Johnson's opinion of,
Mr. Oscar Browning's opinion of, . . .

Here I drew breath and added, indeed, in the margin, Why does Samuel Butler say, "Wise men never say what they think of women"? Wise men never say anything else apparently. But, I continued, leaning back in my chair and looking at the vast dome in which I was a single but by now somewhat harassed thought, what is so unfortunate is that wise men never think the same thing about women. Here is Pope:

Most women have no character at all.

And here is La Bruyère:

Les femmes sont extrêmes; elles sont
meilleures ou pires que les hommes—

a direct contradiction by keen observers who were contemporary. Are they capable of education or incapable? Napoleon thought them incapable. Dr. Johnson thought the opposite.[1] Have they souls or have they not souls? Some savages say they have none. Others, on the contrary, maintain that women are half divine and worship them on that account.[2] Some sages hold that they are shallower in the brain; others that they are deeper in the consciousness. Goethe honoured them; Mussolini despises them. Wherever one looked men thought about women and thought differently. It was impossible to make head or tail of it all, I decided, glancing with envy at the

[1] " 'Men know that women are an overmatch for them, and therefore they choose the weakest or the most ignorant. If they did not think so, they never could be afraid of women knowing as much as themselves.' . . . In justice to the sex, I think it but candid to acknowledge that, in a subsequent conversation, he told me that he was serious in what he said."—Boswell, *The Journal of a Tour to the Hebrides.*

[2] "The ancient Germans believed that there was something holy in women, and accordingly consulted them as oracles."—Frazer, *Golden Bough.*

reader next door who was making the neatest abstracts, headed often with an A or a B or a C, while my own notebook rioted with the wildest scribble of contradictory jottings. It was distressing, it was bewildering, it was humiliating. Truth had run through my fingers. Every drop had escaped.

I could not possibly go home, I reflected, and add as a serious contribution to the study of women and fiction that women have less hair on their bodies than men, or that the age of puberty among the South Sea Islanders is nine— or is it ninety?—even the handwriting had become in its distraction in-decipherable. It was disgraceful to have nothing more weighty or respect-able to show after a whole morning's work. And if I could not grasp the truth about W. (as for brevity's sake I had come to call her) in the past, why bother about W. in the future? It seemed pure waste of time to consult all those gentlemen who specialise in woman and her effect on whatever it may be—politics, children, wages, morality—numerous and learned as they are. One might as well leave their books unopened.

But while I pondered I had unconsciously, in my listlessness, in my desperation, been drawing a picture where I should, like my neighbour, have been writing a conclusion. I had been drawing a face, a figure. It was the face and the figure of Professor von X. engaged in writing his monu-mental work entitled *The Mental, Moral, and Physical Inferiority of the Female Sex.* He was not in my picture a man attractive to women. He was heavily built; he had a great jowl; to balance that he had very small eyes; he was very red in the face. His expression suggested that he was labouring under some emotion that made him jab his pen on the paper as if he were killing some noxious insect as he wrote, but even when he had killed it that did not satisfy him; he must go on killing it; and even so, some cause for anger and irritation remained. Could it be his wife, I asked, looking at my picture. Was she in love with a cavalry officer? Was the cavalry officer slim and elegant and dressed in astrachan? Had he been laughed at, to adopt the Freudian theory, in his cradle by a pretty girl? For even in his cradle the professor, I thought, could not have been an attractive child. Whatever the reason, the professor was made to look very angry and very ugly in my sketch, as he wrote his great book upon the mental, moral and physical inferiority of women. Drawing pictures was an idle way of finishing an unprofitable morning's work. Yet it is in our idleness, in our dreams, that the submerged truth sometimes comes to the top. A very elementary exercise in psychology, not to be dignified by the name of psycho-analysis, showed me, on looking at my notebook, that the sketch of the angry professor had been made in anger. Anger had snatched my pencil while I dreamt. But what was anger doing there? Interest, confusion, amusement, boredom— all these emotions I could trace and name as they succeeded each other throughout the morning. Had anger, the black snake, been lurking among them? Yes, said the sketch, anger had. It referred me unmistakably to the one book, to the one phrase, which had roused the demon; it was the professor's statement about the mental, moral and physical inferiority of women. My heart had leapt. My cheeks had burnt. I had flushed with anger. There was nothing specially remarkable, however foolish, in that. One does not like to be told that one is naturally the inferior of a little man— I looked at the student next me—who breathes hard, wears a ready-made tie, and has not shaved this fortnight. One has certain foolish vanities. It is only human nature, I reflected, and began drawing cartwheels and circles over the angry professor's face till he looked like a burning bush or a flaming comet—anyhow, an apparition without human semblance or significance. The professor was nothing now but a faggot burning on the top of Hampstead Heath. Soon my own anger was explained and done with; but curiosity remained. How explain the anger of the professors? Why were they angry? For when it came to analysing the impression left by these books there was always an element of heat. This heat took many forms; it showed itself in satire, in sentiment, in curiosity, in reprobation. But there was another element which was often present and could not immediately be identified. Anger, I called it. But it was anger that had gone underground and mixed itself with all kinds of other emotions. To judge from its odd effects, it was anger disguised and complex, not anger simple and open.

Whatever the reason, all these books, I thought, surveying the pile on the desk, are worthless for my purposes. They were worthless scientifically, that is to say, though humanly they were full of instruction, interest, boredom, and very queer facts about the habits of the Fiji Islanders. They had been written in the red light of emotion and not in the white light of truth. Therefore they must be returned to the central desk and restored each to his own cell in the enormous honeycomb. All that I had retrieved from that morning's work had been the one fact of anger. The professors—I lumped them together thus—were angry. But why, I asked myself, having returned the books, why, I repeated, standing under the colonnade among the pigeons and the prehistoric canoes, why are they angry? And, asking myself this question, I strolled off to find a place for luncheon. What is the real nature of what I call for the moment their anger? I asked. Here was a puzzle that would last all the time that it takes to be served with food in a small restaurant somewhere near the British Museum. Some previous luncher had left the lunch edition of the evening paper on a chair, and, waiting to be served, I began idly reading the headlines. A ribbon of very large letters ran across the page. Somebody had made a big score in South Africa. Lesser ribbons announced that Sir Austen Chamberlain was at Geneva. A meat axe with human hair on it had been found in a cellar. Mr. Justice ————— commented in the Divorce Courts upon the Shamelessness of Women. Sprinkled about the paper were other pieces of news. A film actress had been lowered from a peak in California and hung suspended in mid-air. The weather was going to be foggy. The most transient visitor to this planet,

I thought, who picked up this paper could not fail to be aware, even from this scattered testimony, that England is under the rule of a patriarchy. Nobody in their senses could fail to detect the dominance of the professor. His was the power and the money and the influence. He was the proprietor of the paper and its editor and sub-editor. He was the Foreign Secretary and the Judge. He was the cricketer; he owned the racehorses and the yachts. He was the director of the company that pays two hundred per cent to its shareholders. He left millions to charities and colleges that were ruled by himself. He suspended the film actress in mid-air. He will decide if the hair on the meat axe is human; he it is who will acquit or convict the murderer, and hang him, or let him go free. With the exception of the fog he seemed to control everything. Yet he was angry. I knew that he was angry by this token. When I read what he wrote about women I thought, not of what he was saying, but of himself. When an arguer argues dispassionately he thinks only of the argument; and the reader cannot help thinking of the argument too. If he had written dispassionately about women, had used indisputable proofs to establish his argument and had shown no trace of wishing that the result should be one thing rather than another, one would not have been angry either. One would have accepted the fact, as one accepts the fact that a pea is green or a canary yellow. So be it, I should have said. But I had been angry because he was angry. Yet it seemed absurd, I thought, turning over the evening paper, that a man with all this power should be angry. Or is anger, I wondered, somehow, the familiar, the attendant sprite on power? Rich people, for example, are often angry because they suspect that the poor want to seize their wealth. The professors, or patriarchs, as it might be more accurate to call them, might be angry for that reason partly, but partly for one that lies a little less obviously on the surface. Possibly they were not "angry" at all; often, indeed, they were admiring, devoted, exemplary in the relations of private life. Possibly when the professor insisted a little too emphatically upon the inferiority of women, he was concerned not with their inferiority, but with his own superiority. That was what he was protecting rather hot-headedly and with too much emphasis, because it was a jewel to him of the rarest price. Life for both sexes—and I looked at them, shouldering their way along the pavement—is arduous, difficult, a perpetual struggle. It calls for gigantic courage and strength. More than anything, perhaps, creatures of illusion as we are, it calls for confidence in oneself. Without self-confidence we are as babes in the cradle. And how can we generate this imponderable quality, which is yet so invaluable, most quickly? By thinking that other people are inferior to oneself. By feeling that one has some innate superiority—it may be wealth, or rank, a straight nose, or the portrait of a grandfather by Romney—for there is no end to the pathetic devices of the human imagination—over other people. Hence the enormous importance to a patriarch who has to conquer, who has to rule, of feeling that great numbers of people, half the human race indeed, are by nature inferior to himself. It must indeed be one of the chief sources of his power. But let me turn the light of this observation on to real life, I thought. Does it help to explain some of those psychological puzzles that one notes in the margin of daily life? Does it explain my astonishment the other day when Z, most humane, most modest of men, taking up some book by Rebecca West and reading a passage in it, exclaimed, "The arrant feminist! She says that men are snobs!" The exclamation, to me so surprising—for why was Miss West an arrant feminist for making a possibly true if uncomplimentary statement about the other sex?—was not merely the cry of wounded vanity; it was a protest against some infringement of his power to believe in himself. Women have served all these centuries as looking-glasses possessing the magic and delicious power of reflecting the figure of man at twice its natural size. Without that power probably the earth would still be swamp and jungle. The glories of all our wars would be unknown. We should still be scratching the outlines of deer on the remains of mutton bones and bartering flints for sheepskins or whatever simple ornament took our unsophisticated taste. Supermen and Fingers of Destiny would never have existed. The Czar and the Kaiser would never have worn their crowns or lost them. Whatever may be their use in civilised societies, mirrors are essential to all violent and heroic action. That is why Napoleon and Mussolini both insist so emphatically upon the inferiority of women, for if they were not inferior, they would cease to enlarge. That serves to explain in part the necessity that women so often are to men. And it serves to explain how restless they are under her criticism; how impossible it is for her to say to them this book is bad, this picture is feeble, or whatever it may be, without giving far more pain and rousing far more anger than a man would do who gave the same criticism. For if she begins to tell the truth, the figure in the looking-glass shrinks; his fitness for life is diminished. How is he to go on giving judgement, civilising natives, making laws, writing books, dressing up and speechifying at banquets, unless he can see himself at breakfast and at dinner at least twice the size he really is? So I reflected, crumbling my bread and stirring my coffee and now and again looking at the people in the street. The looking-glass vision is of supreme importance because it charges the vitality; it stimulates the nervous system. Take it away and man may die, like the drug fiend deprived of his cocaine. Under the spell of that illusion, I thought, looking out of the window, half the people on the pavement are striding to work. They put on their hats and coats in the morning under its agreeable rays. They start the day confident, braced, believing themselves desired at Miss Smith's tea party; they say to themselves as they go into the room, I am the superior of half the people here, and it is thus that they speak with that self-confidence, that self-assurance, which have had such profound consequences in public life and lead to such curious notes in the margin of the private mind.

Stratification

All known societies have classified their members into categories above or below one another on a scale of superiority or inferiority. This process of stratification involves the allocation of individuals to different levels enjoying unequal amounts of status, wealth, power, and prestige. The contrasts between higher and lower, rich and poor, powerful and powerless, between those who expect deference and those who give it, provide the substance of social stratification. Unequal rewards, privileges, and immunities, as well as unequal distributions of rights and duties, characterize all stratification systems. A stratified society is, by definition, a society of unequals. While stratification is an omnipresent fact in human society, the basis upon which it is established varies considerably. People may be ranked in terms of wealth or power, in terms of their access or lack of access to magical means, in terms of their degree of holiness, and so on. When the system of stratification is primarily based on position in the economic order and there exists the possibility of social mobility, one is in the presence of a class system of stratification. When no such movements are possible and membership in a stratum is based on heredity, we are in the presence of a caste system of stratification. When life styles, deference, honor and prestige are the central criteria for ranking people in a social order, we are in the presence of a system based on status. In modern America class and status stratification exist side by side and, in addition, the relations between the white majority and the Negro minority are based on a caste system.

The selections in this chapter cannot fully illustrate the complexity of stratification systems; they merely highlight a few major characteristics of them. Daniel Defoe, in his satirical poem, "The True-born Englishman," deflates the hereditary pretensions of the English nobility of his time by indicating that, given the fluidity of the English system of stratification, the bulk of British nobility, far from descending from Norman ancestors, were in fact the sons of successful tradesmen. There was much more mobility in the British system than its aristocratic ideologists were wont to consider. Oliver Goldsmith in *The Citizen of the World* continued Defoe's attack on the pretensions of the nobility. The book consists of a series of imaginary letters, patterned after Montesqieu's *Persian Letters* in which the fads and foibles of contemporary England are mercilessly exposed. The passage here reprinted attacks the uselessness of the nobility and thus constitutes a vindication of the bourgeois ethos of work against the aristocratic claim to deference based on such notions as honor.

Honoré de Balzac was a deeply conservative writer. *La Comédie Humaine*, his magnificent anatomy of post-revolutionary French society, is informed by his distaste of the disorder and *anomie* into which France had plunged, or so he thought, during the Restoration and the July monarchy. Yet his conservatism did not lead him into an uncritical adulation of those claiming aristocratic status. In the passage from his novel *The Thirteen* he shows that a nobility which has abandoned the ideal of service to the nation in favor of self-seeking and self-preservation abdicates its social functions and contributes to disorder and decadence.

William M. Thackeray's short sketch highlights the horrified discovery of proper Victorian gentlemen that the English poor are excluded from most of the benefits of English society, that they are in but not *of* English society, that there exist indeed, to use Disraeli's famous phrase, "two nations" in England. When Harriet Martineau, the British novelist and economist, visited America and described it in her *Society in America* (1837), she was especially struck by the fact that, despite pretensions to equality, status distinctions and tendency toward social closure were much more pronounced than European democrats had previously recognized. Finally, George Orwell in the autobiographical sketch from *The Road to Wigan Pier*, shows the sharp gulf which separated the British middle class from the working class in the first half of the twentieth century. He is especially acute in noting the status symbols, from speech to smell, which served to maintain and reinforce this gulf.

Daniel Defoe (1661–1731)

What makes a peer?

'Tis well that virtue gives nobility,
Else God knows where had we our gentry,
Since scarce one family is left alive,
Which does not from some foreigner derive.
Of sixty thousand English gentlemen,
Whose names and arms in registers remain,
We challenge all our heralds to declare
Ten families which English Saxons are.

France justly boasts the ancient noble lines
Of Bourbon, Montmorency, and Lorraine.
The Germans, too, their house of Austria show,
And Holland, their invincible Nassau.
Lines which in heraldry were ancient grown,
Before the name of Englishman was known.
Even Scotland, too, her elder glory show,
Her Gordons, Hamiltons, and her Monro's;
Douglas', Mackays, and Grahams, names well known,
Long before ancient England knew her own.

But England, modern to the last degree,
Borrows or makes her own nobility,
And yet she boldly boasts of pedigree;
Repines that foreigners are put upon her,
And talks of her antiquity and honour:
Her Sackvills, Savils, Cecils, Delamers,
Mohuns, Montagues, Duras, and Veeres,
Not one have English names, yet all are English peers.

Your Houblons, Papillons, and Lethuliers,
Pass now for true-born English knights and squires,
And make good senate-members, or lord-mayors.

From *The True-Born Englishman* by Daniel Defoe (1701).

Wealth, howsoever got, in England makes
Lords of mechanics, gentlemen of rakes.
Antiquity and birth are needless here;
'Tis impudence and money makes a peer.

Innumerable city knights we know,
From Blue-Coat Hospitals, and Bridewell flow.
Draymen and porters fill the city chair,
And foot-boys magisterial purple wear.
Fate has but very small distinction set
Betwixt the counter and the coronet.
Tarpaulin lords, pages of high renown,
Rise up by poor men's valour, not their own;
Great families of yesterday we show,
And lords, whose parents were the Lord knows who.

Oliver Goldsmith (1728–1774)

The flow of the mushroom-broth

In a late excursion with my friend into the country, a gentleman with a blue ribbon tied round his shoulder, and in a chariot drawn by six horses passed swiftly by us, attended with a numerous train of captains, lacquies and coaches filled with women. When we were recovered from the dust raised by this cavalcade, and could continue our discourse without danger of suffocation, I observed to my companion, that all this state and equipage, which he seemed to despise, would in China be regarded with the utmost reverence, because such distinctions were always the reward of merit; the greatness of a mandarin's retinue being a most certain mark of the superiority of his abilities or virtue.

The gentleman who has now passed us, replied my companion, has no claims from his own merit to distinction; he is possessed neither of abilities nor virtue: it is enough for him that one of his ancestors was possessed of these qualities two hundred years before him. There was a time, indeed, when his family deserved their title, but they are long since degenerated, and his ancestors for more than a century have been more and more solicitous to keep up the breed of their dogs and horses, than that of other children. This very nobleman, simple as he seems, is descended from a race of states-

From *Letters of a Citizen of the World to his Friends in the East* by Oliver Goldsmith (1762).

men and heroes; but unluckily his great-grandfather marrying a cook-maid, and she having a trifling passion for his lordship's groom, they some how crossed the strain, and produced an heir, who took after his mother in his great love to *good eating*, and his father in a violent affection for *horse-flesh*. These passions have for some generations passed on from father to son, and are now become the characteristics of the family, his present lordship being equally remarkable for his kitchen and his stable.

But such a nobleman, cried I, deserves our pity, thus placed in so high a sphere of life, which only the more exposes to contempt. A king may confer titles, but it is personal merit alone that insures respect. I suppose, added I, that such men are despised by their equals, neglected by their inferiors, and condemned to live among involuntary dependents in irksome solitude.

You are still under a mistake, replied my companion, for though this nobleman is a stranger to generosity; though he takes twenty opportunities in a day of letting his guests know how much he despises them; though he is possessed neither of taste, wit, nor wisdom; though incapable of improving others by his conversation, and never known to enrich any by his bounty; yet for all this, his company is eagerly sought after: he is a lord, and that is as much as most people desire in a companion. Quality and title have such allurements, that hundreds are ready to give up all their own importance, to cringe, to flatter, to look little, and to pall every pleasure in constraint, merely to be among the great, though without the least hopes of improving their understanding, or sharing their generosity; they might be happy among their equals, but those are despised for company, where they are despised in turn. You saw what a crowd of humble cousins, card-ruined beaus, and captains on half-pay, were willing to make up this great man's retinue down to his country-seat. Not one of all these that could not lead a more comfortable life at home in their little lodging of three shillings a week, with their luke-warm dinner, served up between two pewter plates from a cook's-shop. Yet poor devils, they are willing to undergo the impertinence and pride of their entertainer, merely to be thought to live among the great: they are willing to pass the summer in bondage, though conscious they are taken down only to approve his lordship's taste upon every occasion, to tag all his stupid observations with a very true, to praise his stable, and descant upon his claret and cookery.

The pitiful humiliations of the gentlemen you are now describing, said I, puts me in mind of a custom among the Tartars of Koreki, not entirely dissimilar to this we are now considering.[1] The Russians, who trade with them carry thither a kind of mushrooms, which they exchange for furs or squirrels, ermines, sables, and foxes. These mushrooms the rich Tartars

---

[1]Van Stralenberg, a writer of credit, gives the same account of this people. See *An Historico-geographical Description of the North-eastern parts of Europe and Asia*, p. 397.

lay up in large quantities for the winter; and when a nobleman makes a mushroom-feast, all the neighbours around are invited. The mushrooms are prepared by boiling, by which the water acquires an intoxicating quality, and is a sort of drink which the Tartars prize beyond all other. When the nobility and ladies are assembled, and the ceremonies usual between people of distinction over, the mushroom-broth goes freely round; they laugh, talk double entendre, grow fuddled, and become excellent company. The poorer sort, who love mushroom-broth to distraction as well as the rich, but cannot afford it at the first hand, post themselves on these occasions round the huts of the rich, and watch the opportunity of the ladies and gentlemen as they come down to pass their liquor, and holding a wooden bowl, catch the delicious fluid, very little altered by filtration, being still strongly tinctured with the intoxicating quality. Of this they drink with the utmost satisfaction, and thus they get as drunk and as jovial as their betters.

Happy nobility, cries my companion, who can fear no diminution of respect, unless by seing seized with strangury; and who when most drunk are most useful; though we have not this custom among us, I foresee, that if it were introduced, we might have many a toad-eater in England ready to drink from the wooden bowl on these occasions, and to praise the flavour of his lordship's liquor: As we have different classes of gentry, who knows but we may see a lord holding a bowl to a minister, a knight holding it to his lordship, and a simple squire drinking it double distilled from the loins of the knighthood? For my part, I shall never for the future hear a great man's flatterers haranguing in his praise that I shall not fancy I behold the wooden bowl; for I can see no reason why a man, who can live easily and happily at home, should bear the drudgery of decorum and the impertinence of his entertainer, unless intoxicated with a passion for all that was quality; unless he thought that whatever came from the great was delicious, and had the tincture of the mushroom in it. Adieu.

Honoré de Balzac (1799-1850)

The doom of the nobility

Given a certain number of families of unequal fortune in any given space, you will see an aristocracy forming under your eyes; there will be the patricians, the upper classes, and yet other ranks below them. Equality may be a *right*, but no power on earth can convert it into *fact*. It would be a good

---

From *The Thirteen* by Honoré de Balzac (1833), translated by Ellen Marriage.

thing for France if this idea could be popularized. The benefits of political harmony are obvious to the least intelligent classes. Harmony is, as it were, the poetry of order, and order is a matter of vital importance to the working population. And what is order, reduced to its simplest expression, but the agreement of things among themselves—unity, in short? Architecture, music, and poetry, everything in France more than in any other country, is based upon this principle; it is written upon the very foundations of her clear accurate language, and a language must always be the most infallible index of national character. In the same way you may note that the French popular airs are those most calculated to strike the imagination, the best modulated melodies are taken over by the people; clearness of thought, the intellectual simplicity of an idea attracts them; they like the incisive sayings that hold the greatest number of ideas. France is the one country in the world where a little phrase may bring about a great revolution. Whenever the masses have risen, it has been to bring men, affairs, and principles into agreement. No nation has a clearer conception of that idea of unity which should permeate the life of an aristocracy; possibly no other nation has so intelligent a comprehension of a political necessity; history will never find her behind the time. France has been led astray many a time, but she is deluded, woman-like, by generous ideas, by a glow of enthusiasm which at first outstrips sober reason.

So, to begin with, the most striking characteristic of the Faubourg [St. Germain] is the splendor of its great mansions, its great gardens, and a surrounding quiet in keeping with princely revenues drawn from great estates. And what is this distance set between a class and a whole metropolis but the visible and outward expression of the widely different attitude of mind which must inevitably keep them apart? The position of the head is well defined in every organism. If by any chance a nation allows its head to fall at its feet, it is pretty sure sooner or later to discover that this is a suicidal measure; and since nations have no desire to perish, they set to work at once to grow a new head. If they lack the strength for this, they perish as Rome perished, and Venice, and so many other states.

This distinction between the upper and lower spheres of social activity, emphasized by differences in their manner of living, necessarily implies that in the highest aristocracy there is real worth and some distinguishing merit. In any State, no matter what form of "government" is affected, so soon as the patrician class fails to maintain that complete superiority which is the condition of its existence, it ceases to be a force, and is pulled down at once by the populace. The people always wish to see money, power, and initiative in their leaders' hands, hearts, and heads; they must be the spokesmen, they must represent the intelligence and the glory of the nation. Nations, like women, love strength in those who rule them; they cannot give love without respect; they refuse utterly to obey those of whom they do not stand in awe.

An aristocracy fallen into contempt is a *roi fainéant*, a husband in petticoats; first it ceases to be itself, and then it ceases to be.

And in this way the isolation of the great, the sharply marked distinction in their manner of life, or in a word, the general custom of the patrician caste is at once the sign of a real power, and their destruction so soon as that power is lost. The Faubourg Saint-Germain failed to recognize the conditions of its being, while it would still have been easy to perpetuate its existence, and therefore was brought low for a time. The Faubourg should have looked the facts fairly in the face, as the English aristocracy did before them; they should have seen that every institution has its climacteric periods, when words lose their old meanings, and ideas reappear in a new guise, and the whole conditions of politics were a changed aspect, while the underlying realities undergo no essential alteration. . . .

The stateliness of the castles and palaces where nobles dwell; the luxury of the details; the constantly maintained sumptuousness of the furniture; the "atmosphere" in which the fortunate owner of landed estates (a rich man before he was born) lives and moves easily and without friction; the habit of mind which never descends to calculate the petty work-a-day gains of existence; the leisure; the higher education attainable at a much earlier age; and lastly, the aristocratic condition that makes of him a social force, for which his opponents, by dint of study and a strong will and tenacity of vocation, are scarcely a match—all these things should contribute to form a lofty spirit in a man, possessed of such privileges from his youth up; they should stamp his character with that high self-respect, of which the least consequence is a nobleness of heart in harmony with the noble name that he bears. And in some few families all this is realized. There are noble characters here and there in the Faubourg, but they are marked exceptions to a general rule of egoism which has been the ruin of this world within a world. The privileges above enumerated are the birthright of the French noblesse, as of every patrician efflorescence ever formed on the surface of a nation; and will continue to be theirs so long as their existence is based upon real estate, or money; *domaine-sol* and *domaine-argent* alike, the old solid bases of an organized society; but such privileges are held upon the understanding that the patricians must continue to justify their existence. There is a sort of moral *fief* held on a tenure of service rendered to the sovereign, and here in France the people are undoubtedly the sovereigns nowadays. The times are changed and so are the weapons. The knight-banneret of old wore a coat of chain armor and a hauberk; he could handle a lance well and display his pennon, and no more was required of him; to-day he is bound to give proof of his intelligence. A stout heart was enough in the days of old; in our days he is required to have a capacious brain-pan. Skill and knowledge and capital—these three points mark out a social triangle on which the scutcheon of power is blazoned; our modern aristocracy must take its stand on these.

A fine theorem is as good as a great name. The Rothschilds, the Fuggers of the nineteenth century, are princes *de facto*. A great artist is in reality an oligarch; he represents a whole century, and almost always he is a law to others. And the art of words, the high pressure machinery of the writer, the poet's genius, the merchant's steady endurance, the strong will of the statesman who concentrates a thousand dazzling qualities in himself, the general's sword,—all these victories, in short, which a single individual will win, that he may tower above the rest of the world, the patrician class is now bound to win and keep exclusively. They must head the new forces as they once headed the material forces; how should they keep the position unless they are worthy of it? How, unless they are the soul and brain of a nation, shall they set its hands moving? How lead a people without the power of command? And what is the marshal's *bâton* without the innate power of the captain in the man who wields it? The Faubourg Saint-Germain took to playing with *bâtons*, and fancied that all the power was in its hands. It inverted the terms of the proposition which called it into existence. And instead of flinging away the insignia which offended the people, and quietly grasping the power, it allowed the bourgeoisie to seize the authority, clung with fatal obstinacy to its shadow, and over and over again forgot the laws which a minority must observe if it would live. When an aristocracy is scarce a thousandth part of the body social, it is bound to-day, as of old, to multiply its points of action, so as to counterbalance the weight of the masses in a great crisis. And in our days those means of action must be living forces, and not historical memories.

In France, unluckily, the noblesse were still so puffed up with the notion of their vanished power, that it was difficult to contend against a kind of innate presumption in themselves. Perhaps this is a national defect. The Frenchman is less given than any one else to undervalue himself; it comes natural to him to go from his degree to the one above it; and while it is a rare thing for him to pity the unfortunates over whose heads he rises, he always groans in spirit to see so many fortunate people above him. He is very far from heartless, but too often he prefers to listen to his intellect. The national instinct which brings the Frenchman to the front, the vanity that wastes his substance, is as much a dominant passion as thrift in the Dutch. For three centuries it swayed the noblesse, who, in this respect, were certainly pre-eminently French. The scion of the Faubourg Saint-Germain, beholding his material superiority, was fully persuaded of his intellectual superiority. And everything contributed to confirm him in his belief; for ever since the Faubourg Saint-Germain existed at all—which is to say, ever since Versailles ceased to be the royal residence—the Faubourg, with some few gaps in continuity, was always backed up by the central power, which in France seldom fails to support that side. Thence its downfall in 1830.

At that time the party of the Faubourg Saint-Germain was rather like an army without a base of operation. It had utterly failed to take advantage of the peace to plant itself in the heart of the nation. It sinned for want of learning its lesson, and through an utter incapability of regarding its interests as a whole. A future certainly was sacrificed to a doubtless present gain. This blunder in policy may perhaps be attributed to the following cause.

The class-isolation so strenuously kept up by the noblesse brought about fatal results during the last forty years; even caste-patriotism was extinguished by it, and rivalry fostered among themselves. When the French noblesse of other times were rich and powerful, the nobles (*gentilhommes*) could choose their chiefs and obey them in the hour of danger. As their power diminished, they grew less amenable to discipline; and as in the last days of the Byzantine Empire, every one wished to be emperor. They mistook their uniform weakness for uniform strength.

Each family ruined by the Revolution and the abolition of the law of primogeniture thought only of itself, and not at all of the great family of the noblesse. It seemed to them that as each individual grew rich, the party as a whole would gain in strength. And herein lay their mistake. Money, likewise, is only the outward and visible sign of power. All these families were made up of persons who preserved a high tradition of courtesy, of true graciousness of life, of refined speech, with a family pride, and a squeamish sense of *noblesse oblige* which suited well with the kind of life they led; a life wholly filled with occupations which become contemptible so soon as they cease to be accessories and take the chief place in existence. There was a certain intrinsic merit in all these people, but the merit was on the surface, and none of them were worth their face-value.

Not a single one among those families had courage to ask itself the question, "Are we strong enough for the responsibility of power?" They were cast on the top, like the lawyers of 1830; and instead of taking the patron's place, like a great man, the Faubourg Saint-Germain showed itself greedy as an upstart. The most intelligent nation in the world perceived clearly that the restored nobles were organizing everything for their own particular benefit. From that day the noblesse was doomed.

William M. Thackeray (1811–1863)

Waiting at the station

We are amongst a number of people waiting for the Blackwall train at the Fenchurch Street Station. Some of us are going a little farther than Black-

From *Sketches and Travels in London* by William M. Thackeray.

wall—as far as Gravesend; some of us are going even farther than Gravesend —to Port Phillip, in Australia, leaving behind the *patriae fines* and the pleasant fields of Old England. It is rather a queer sensation to be in the same boat and station with a party that is going upon so prodigious a journey. One speculates about them with more than an ordinary interest, thinking of the difference between your fate and theirs, and that we shall never behold these faces again.

Some eight-and-thirty women are sitting in the large Hall of the station, with bundles, baskets, and light baggage, waiting for the steamer, and the orders to embark. A few friends are taking leave of them, bonnets are laid together; and whispering going on. A little crying is taking place;—only a very little crying,—and among those who remain, as it seems to me, not those who are going away. They leave behind them little to weep for; they are going from bitter cold and hunger, constant want and unavailing labour. Why should they be sorry to quit a mother who has been so hard to them as our country has been? How many of these women will ever see the shore again, upon the brink of which they stand, and from which they will depart in a few minutes more? It makes one sad and ashamed too, that they should not be more sorry. But how are you to expect love where you have given such scanty kindness? If you saw your children glad at the thought of leaving you, and for ever: would you blame yourselves or them? It is not that the children are ungrateful, but the home was unhappy, and the parents indifferent or unkind. You are in the wrong, under whose government they only had neglect and wretchedness; not they, who can't be called upon to love such an unlovely thing as misery, or to make any other return for neglect but indifference and aversion.

You and I, let us suppose again, are civilised persons. We have been decently educated: and live decently every day, and wear tolerable clothes, and practise cleanliness: and love the arts and graces of life. As we walk down this rank of eight-and-thirty female emigrants, let us fancy that we are at Melbourne, and not in London, and that we have come down from our sheep-walks, or clearings, having heard of the arrival of forty honest, well-recommended young women, and having a natural longing to take a wife home to the bush—which of these would you like? If you were an Australian Sultan, to which of these would you throw the handkerchief? I am afraid not one of them. I fear, in our present mood of mind, we should mount horse and return to the country, preferring a solitude, and to be a bachelor, than to put up with one of these for a companion. There is no girl here to tempt you by her looks: (and, world-wiseacre as you are, it is by these you are principally moved)—there is no pretty, modest, red-cheeked rustic,— no neat, trim little grisette, such as what we call a gentleman might cast his eyes upon without too much derogating, and might find favour in the eyes of a man about town. No; it is a homely bevy of women with scarcely any beauty amongst them—their clothes were decent, but not the least picturesque —their faces are pale and care-worn for the most part—how, indeed, should it be otherwise, seeing that they have known care and want all their days?— there they sit, upon bare benches, with dingy bundles, and great cotton umbrellas—and the truth is, you are not a hardy colonist, a feeder of sheep, feller of trees, a hunter of kangaroos—but a London man, and my lord the Sultan's cambric handkerchief is scented with Bond Street perfumery—you put it in your pocket, and couldn't give it to any one of these women.

They are not like you, indeed. They have not your tastes and feeling: your education and refinements. They would not understand a hundred things which seem perfectly simple to you. They would shock you a hundred times a day by as many deficiencies of politeness, or by outrages upon the Queen's English—by practices entirely harmless, and yet in your eyes actually worse than crimes—they have large hard hands and clumsy feet. The woman you love must have pretty soft fingers that you may hold in yours: must speak her language properly, and at least when you offer her your heart, must return hers with its *h* in the right place, as she whispers that it is yours, or you will have none of it. If she says, "Hedward, I ham so unappy to think I shall never behold you agin,"—though her emotion on leaving you might be perfectly tender and genuine, you would be obliged to laugh. If she said, "Hedward, my art is yours for hever and hever" (and anybody heard her), she might as well stab you,—you couldn't accept the most faithful affection offered in such terms—you are a town-bred man, I say, and your handkerchief smells of Bond Street musk and millefleur. A sun-burnt settler out of the Bush won't feel any of these exquisite tortures: or understand this kind of laughter: or object to Molly because her hands are coarse and her ankles thick: but he will take her back to his farm, where she will nurse his children, bake his dough, milk his cows, and cook his kangaroo for him.

But between you, an educated Londoner, and that woman, is not the union absurd and impossible? Would it not be unbearable for either? Solitude would be incomparably pleasanter than such a companion.—You might take her with a handsome fortune, perhaps, were you starving; but then it is because you want a house and carriage, let us say (your necessaries of life), and must have them even if you purchase them with your precious person. You do as much, or your sister does as much, every day. That, however, is not the point: I am not talking about the meanness to which your worship may be possibly obliged to stoop, in order, as you say, "to keep up your rank in society"—only stating that this immense social difference does exist. You don't like to own it: or don't choose to talk about it, and such things had much better not be spoken about at all. I hear your worship say, there must be differences in rank and so forth! Well! out with it at once: you don't think Molly is your equal—nor indeed is she in possession of many artificial acquirements. She can't make Latin verses, for example, as you used to do at school; she can't speak French and Italian, as your wife very likely can, etc.—and in so far she is your inferior, and your amiable lady's.

But what I note, what I marvel at, what I acknowledge, what I am ashamed of, what is contrary to Christian morals, manly modesty and honesty and to the national well-being, is that there should be that immense social distinction between the well-dressed classes (as, if you will permit me, we will call ourselves), and our brethren and sisters in the fustian jackets and pattens. If you deny it for your part, I say that you are mistaken, you deceive yourself wofully. I say that you have been educated to it through Gothic ages, and have had it handed down to you from your fathers (not that they were anybody in particular, but respectable, well-dressed progenitors, let us say for a generation or two)—from your well-dressed fathers before you. How long ago is it, that our preachers were teaching the poor "to know their station?" that it was the peculiar boast of Englishmen, that any man, the humblest among us, could, by talent, industry, and good luck, hope to take his place in the aristocracy of his country, and that we pointed with pride to Lord This, who was the grandson of a barber; and to Earl That, whose father was an apothecary? What a multitude of most respectable folks pride themselves on these things still! The gulf is not impassable, because one man in a million swims over it, and we hail him for his strength and success. He had landed on the happy island. He is one of the aristocracy. Let us clap hands and applaud. There's no country like ours for rational freedom.

If you go up and speak to one of these women, as you do (and very good-naturedly, and you can't help that confounded condescension), she curtsies and holds down her head meekly, and replies with modesty, as becomes her station, to your honour with the clean shirt and the well-made coat. "And so she should," what hundreds of thousands of us rich and poor say still. Both believe this to be bounden duty; and that a poor person should naturally bob her head to a rich one physically and morally.

Let us get her last curtsy from her as she stands here upon the English shore. When she gets into the Australian woods her back won't bend except to her labour; or, if it do, from old habit and the reminiscence of the old country, do you suppose her children will be like that timid creature before you? They will know nothing of that Gothic society, with its ranks and hierarchies, its cumbrous ceremonies, its glittering antique paraphernalia, in which we have been educated; in which rich and poor still acquiesce, and which multitudes of both still admire: far removed from these old-world traditions, they will be bred up in the midst of plenty, freedom, manly brotherhood. Do you think if your worship's grandson goes into the Australian woods, or meets the grandchild of one of yonder women by the banks of the Warrawarra, the Australian will take a hat off or bob a curtsy to the new comer? He will hold out his hand, and say, "Stranger, come into my house and take a shakedown and have a share of our supper. You come out of the old country, do you? There was some people were kind to my grandmother there, and sent her out to Melbourne. Times are changed since then—come in and welcome!"

What a confession it is that we have almost all of us been obliged to make! A clever and earnest-minded writer gets a commission from the *Morning Chronicle* newspaper, and reports upon the state of our poor in London; he goes amongst labouring people and poor of all kinds—and brings back what? A picture of human life so wonderful, so awful, so piteous and pathetic, so exciting and terrible, that readers of romances own they never read anything like to it; and that the griefs, struggles, strange adventures here depicted, exceed anything that any of us could imagine. Yes; and these wonders and terrors have been lying by your door and mine ever since we had a door of our own. We had but to go a hundred yards off and see for ourselves, but we never did. Don't we pay poor-rates, and are they not heavy enough in the name of patience? Very true; and we have our own private pensioners, and give away some of our superfluity, very likely. You are not unkind; not ungenerous. But of such wondrous and complicated misery as this you confess you had no idea. No. How should you?—you and I—we are of the upper classes; we have had hitherto no community with the poor. We never speak a word to the servant who waits on us for twenty years; we condescend to employ a tradesman, keeping him at a proper distance, mind, of course, at a proper distance—we laugh at his young men, if they dance, jug, and amuse themselves like their betters, and call them counter-jumpers, snobs, and what not? of his workmen we know nothing, how pitilessly they are ground down, how they live and die, here close by us at the backs of our houses; until some poet like Hood wakes and sings that dreadful *Song of the Shirt;* some prophet like Carlyle rises up and denounces woe; some clear-sighted, energetic man like the writer of the *Chronicle* travels into the poor man's country for us, and comes back with his tale of terror and wonder.

Awful, awful poor man's country! The bell rings, and these eight-and-thirty women bid adieu to it, rescued from it (as a few thousands more will be) by some kind people who are interested in their behalf. In two hours more, the steamer lies alongside the ship *Culloden,* which will bear them to their new home.

Harriet Martineau (1802–1876)

The first people in boston and philadelphia

This word [caste], at least its meaning, is no more likely to become obsolete in a republic than among the Hindoos themselves. The distinctive characteristics may vary; but there will be rank, and tenacity of rank, wherever there is society. As this is natural, inevitable, it is of course right. The question must be what is to entitle to rank.

As the feudal qualifications for rank are absolutely non-existent in America (except in the slave States, where there are two classes, without any minor distinctions), it seems absurd that the feudal remains of rank in Europe should be imitated in America. Wherever the appearance of a conventional aristocracy exists in America, it must arise from wealth, as it cannot from birth. An aristocracy of mere wealth is vulgar everywhere. In a republic, it is vulgar in the extreme.

This is the only kind of vulgarity I saw in the United States. I imagine that the English who have complained the most copiously of the vulgarity of American manners, have done so from two causes: from using their own conventional notions as a standard of manners (which is a vulgarism in themselves); and also from their intercourses with the Americans having been confined to those who consider themselves the aristocracy of the United States; the wealthy and showy citizens of the Atlantic ports. Foreign travellers are most hospitably received by this class of society; introduced to "the first people in Boston,"—"in New York,"—"in Philadelphia"; and taught to view the country with eyes of their hosts. No harm is intended here: it is very natural: but it is not the way for strangers to obtain an understanding of the country and the people. The traveller who chooses industriously to see for himself, not with European or aristocratic merely, but with human eyes, will find the real aristocracy of the country, not only in ball-rooms and bank-parlours, but also in fishing boats, in stores, in college chambers, and behind the plough. Till he has seen all this, and studied the natural manners of the natural aristocracy, he is no more justified in applying the word "vulgar" to more than a class, than an American would be who should call all the English vulgar, when he had seen only the London alderman class.

I had the opportunity of perceiving what errors might arise from this cause. I was told a great deal about "the first people in Boston": which is perhaps as aristocratic, vain, and vulgar a city, as described by its own "first people," as any in the world. Happily, however, Boston has merits

From *Society in America* by Harriet Martineau (1837).

which these people know not of. I am far from thinking it, as they do, the most religious, the most enlightened, and the most virtuous city in the world. There are other cities in the United States which, on the whole, I think more virtuous and more enlightened: but I certainly am not aware of so large a number of peculiarly interesting and valuable persons living in near neighbourhood, anywhere else but in London. But it happens that these persons belong chiefly to the natural, very few to the conventional, aristocracy. They have little perceptible influence. Society does not seem to be much the better for them. They save their own souls; but, as regards society, the salt appears to have lost its savour. It is so sprinkled as not to season the body. With men and women enough on the spot to redeem society from false morals, and empty religious profession, Boston is the headquarters of Cant. Notwithstanding its superior intelligence, its large provision of benevolent institutions, and its liberal hospitality, there is an extraordinary and most pernicious union, in more than a few scattered instances, of profligacy and the worst kind of infidelity, with a strict religious profession, and an outward demeanour of remarkable propriety. The profligacy and infidelity might, I fear, be found in all other cities, on both sides the water; but nowhere, probably, in absolute coexistence with ostensible piety. This is not the connexion in which to speak of the religious aspect of the matter; but, as regards the cant, I believe that it proceeds chiefly from the spirit of caste which flourishes in a society which on Sundays and holidays professes to have abjured it. It is true that the people of New England have put away duelling; but the feelings which used to vent themselves by the practice of duelling are cherished by the members of the conventional aristocracy. This is revealed, not only by the presence of cant, but by the confessions of some who are bold enough not to pretend to be either republicans or Christians. There are some few who openly desire a monarchy; and a few more who constantly insinuate the advantages of a monarchy, and the distastefulness of a republic. It is observable that such always argue on the supposition that if there were a monarchy, they should be the aristocracy: a point in which I imagine they would find themselves mistaken, if so impossible an event could happen at all. This class, or coterie, is a very small one, and not influential; though a gentleman of the kind once ventured to give utterance to his aspirations after monarchy in a Fourth of July oration; and afterwards to print them. There is something venerable in his intrepidity, at least. The reproach of cant does not attach to him.

The children are such faithful reflectors of this spirit as to leave no doubt of its existence, even amidst the nicest operations of cant. Gentlemen may disguise their aristocratic aspirations under sighs for the depressed state of literature and science; supposing that wealth and leisure are the constituents of literature, and station the proximate cause of science; and committing the slight mistake of assuming that the natural aristocracy of England, her philosophers and poets, have been identical with, or originated by, her conventional aristocracy. The ladies may conceal their selfish pride of caste, even from themselves, under pretensions to superior delicacy and refinement. But the children use no such disguises. Out they come with what they learn at home. A school-girl told me what a delightful "set" she belonged to at her school: how comfortable they all were once, without any sets, till several grocers' daughters began to come in, as their fathers grew rich; and it became necessary for the higher girls to consider what they should do, and to form themselves into sets. She told me how the daughter of a lottery office-keeper came to the school; and no set would receive her; how unkindly she was treated, and how difficult it was for any individual to help her, because she had not spirit or temper enough to help herself. My informant went on to mention how anxious she and her set, of about sixty young people, were to visit exclusively among themselves, how "delightful" it would be to have no grocers' daughters among them; but that it was found to be impossible.

Here is an education to be going on in the middle of a republic! Much solace, however, lies in the last clause of the information above quoted. The Exclusives do find their aims 'impossible.' They will neither have a monarchy, nor be able to complete and close their "sets": least of all will any republican functions be discharged by those who are brought up to have any respect of occupations,—to regard a grocer as beneath a banker. The chief effect of the aristocratic spirit in a democracy is to make those who are possessed by it exclusives in a double sense; in being excluded yet more than in excluding. The republic suffers no further than by having within it a small class acting upon anti-republican morals, and becoming thereby its perverse children, instead of its wise and useful friends and servants.

In Philadelphia, I was much in society. Some of my hospitable acquaintances lived in Chestnut Street, some in Arch Street, and many in other places. When I had been a few weeks in the city, I found to my surprise that some of the ladies who were my admiration had not only never seen or heard of other beautiful young ladies whom I admired quite as much, but never would see or hear of them. I inquired again and again for a solution of this mystery. One person told me that a stranger could not see into the usages of their society. This was just what I was feeling to be true; but it gave me no satisfaction. Another said it was the mutual ignorance from the fathers of the Arch Street ladies having made their fortunes, while the Chestnut Street ladies owed theirs to their grandfathers. Another, who was amused with a new fashion of curtseying, just introduced, declared it was from the Arch Street ladies rising twice on their toes before curtseying, while the Chestnut Street ladies rose thrice. I was sure of only one thing in the matter; that it was a pity that the parties should lose the pleasure of admiring each other, for no better reasons than these: and none better were apparent.

It is not to be supposed that the mere circumstance of living in a republic will ever eradicate that kind of self-love which takes the form of family pride. It is a stage in the transit from selfishness to benevolence; and therefore natural and useful in its proper time and place. As every child thinks his father the wisest man in the world, the loving member of a family thinks his relations the greatest, best and happiest of people, till he gets an intimate knowledge of some others. This species of exclusiveness exists wherever there are families. An eminent public man, travelling in a somewhat retired part of his State, told us how he had been amused with an odd instance of family pride which had just come under his notice. Some plain farmers, brothers, had claimed to be his cousins; and he found they were so. They introduced each other to him; and one brought his son,—a hideous little Flibbertigibbet, with a shock of carroty hair. His father complacently stroked his hair, and declared he was exactly like his uncle Richard: his uncle Richard over again; 'twas wonderful how like his uncle Richard he was in all respects: the hair was the very same; and his uncle Richard was dumb till very late, and then stammered: "and this little fellow," said the father, with a complacent smile,—"this little fellow is six years old, and he can't speak a word."

No one will find fault with the pride of connexion in this stage. Supposing it to remain in its present state, it is harmless from its extreme smallness. In a city, under the stimulus of society, the same pride may be either perverted into the spirit of caste, or exalted into the affection of pure republican brotherhood. The alternative is significant as to the state of the republic, and all-important to the individual.

The extent and influence of the conventional aristocracy in the United States are significant of the state of the republic so far as that they afford an accurate measure of the anti-republican spirit which exists. Such an aristocracy must remain otherwise too insignificant to be dangerous. It cannot choose its own members, restrict its own numbers, or keep its gentility from contamination; for it must be perpetuated, not by hereditary transmission, but by accessions from below. Grocers grow rich, and mechanics become governors of States; and happily there is no law, nor reason, nor desire that it should be otherwise. This little cloud will always overhang the republic, like the perpetual vapour which hovers above Niagara, thrown up by the force and regularity of the movement below. Some observers may be sorry that the heaven is never to be quite clear: but none will dread the little cloud. It would be about as reasonable to fear that the white vapour should drown the cataract from whence it issues as that the conventional aristocracy of America should swamp the republic.

George Orwell

The lower classes smell

I was born into what you might describe as the lower-upper-middle class. The upper-middle class, which had its heyday in the 'eighties and 'nineties, with Kipling as its poet laureate, was a sort of mound of wreckage left behind when the tide of Victorian prosperity receded. Or perhaps it would be better to change the metaphor and describe it not as a mound but as a layer—the layer of society lying between £2,000 and £300 a year: my own family was not far from the bottom. You notice that I define it in terms of money, because that is always the quickest way of making yourself understood. Nevertheless, the essential point about the English class-system is that it is *not* entirely explicable in terms of money. Roughly speaking it is a money-stratification, but it is also interpenetrated by a sort of shadowy caste-system; rather like a jerry-built modern bungalow haunted by medieval ghosts. Hence the fact that the upper-middle class extends or extended to incomes as low as £300 a year—to incomes, that is, much lower than those of merely middle-class people with no social pretensions. Probably there are countries where you can predict a man's opinions from his income, but it is never quite safe to do so in England; you have always got to take his traditions into consideration as well. A naval officer and his grocer very likely have the same income, but they are not equivalent persons and they would only be on the same side in very large issues such as a war or a general strike—possibly not even then.

Of course it is obvious now that the upper-middle class is done for. In every country town in Southern England, not to mention the dreary wastes of Kensington and Earl's Court, those who knew it in the days of its glory, are dying, vaguely embittered by a world which has not behaved as it ought. I never open one of Kipling's books or go into one of the huge dull shops which were once the favourite haunt of the upper-middle class, without thinking "Change and decay in all around I see." But before the war the upper-middle class, though already none too prosperous, still felt sure of itself. Before the war you were either a gentleman or not a gentleman, and if you were a gentleman you struggled to behave as such, whatever your income might be. Between those with £400 a year and those with £2,000 or even £1,000 a year there was a great gulf fixed, but it was a gulf which those with £400 a year did their best to ignore. Probably the distinguish-

From *The Road to Wigan Pier* by George Orwell (1937). Reprinted by permission of Harcourt Brace Jovanovich, Inc., Miss Sonia Brownell, and Secker & Warburg Ltd.

ing mark of the upper-middle class was that its traditions were not to any extent commercial, but mainly military, official, and professional. People in this class owned no land, but they felt that they were landowners in the sight of God and kept up a semi-aristocratic outlook by going into the professions and the fighting services rather than into trade. Small boys used to count the plum stones on their plates and foretell their destiny by chanting "Army, Navy, Church, Medicine, Law"; and even of these "Medicine" was faintly inferior to the others and only put in for the sake of symmetry. To belong to this class when you were at the £400 a year level was a queer business, for it meant that your gentility was almost purely theoretical. You lived, so to speak, at two levels simultaneously. Theoretically you knew all about servants and how to tip them, although in practice you had one or, at most, two resident servants. Theoretically you knew how to wear your clothes and how to order a dinner, although in practice you could never afford to go to a decent tailor or a decent restaurant. Theoretically you knew how to shoot and ride, although in practice you had no horses to ride and not an inch of ground to shoot over. It was this that explained the attraction of India (more recently Kenya, Nigeria, etc.) for the lower-upper-middle class. The people who went there as soldiers and officials did not go there to make money, for a soldier or an official does not make money; they went there because in India, with cheap horses, free shooting, and hordes of black servants, it was so easy to play at being a gentleman.

In the kind of shabby-genteel family that I am talking about there is far more *consciousness* of poverty than in any working-class family above the level of the dole. Rent and clothes and school-bills are an unending nightmare, and every luxury, even a glass of beer, is an unwarrantable extravagance. Practically the whole family income goes in keeping up appearances. It is obvious that people of this kind are in an anomalous position, and one might be tempted to write them off as mere exceptions and therefore unimportant. Actually, however, they are or were fairly numerous. Most clergymen and schoolmasters, for instance, nearly all Anglo-Indian officials, a sprinkling of soldiers and sailors and a fair number of professional men and artists, fall into this category. But the real importance of this class is that they are the shock-absorbers of the bourgeoisie. The real bourgeoisie, those in the £2,000 a year class and over, have their money as a thick layer of padding between themselves and the class they plunder; in so far as they are aware of the Lower Orders at all they are aware of them as employees, servants and tradesmen. But it is quite different for the poor devils lower down who are struggling to live genteel lives on what are virtually working-class incomes. These last are forced into close and, in a sense, intimate contact with the working class, and I suspect it is from them that the traditional upper-class attitude towards "common" people is derived.

And what is this attitude? An attitude of sniggering superiority punctuated by bursts of vicious hatred. Look at any number of *Punch* during the past thirty years. You will find it everywhere taken for granted that a working-class person, as such, is a figure of fun, except at odd moments when he shows signs of being too prosperous, whereupon he ceases to be a figure of fun and becomes a demon. It is no use wasting breath in denouncing this attitude. It is better to consider how it has arisen, and to do that one has got to realize what the working class look like to those who live among them but have different habits and traditions.

A shabby-genteel family is in much the same position as a family of "poor whites" living in a street where everyone else is a Negro. In such circumstances you have got to cling to your gentility because it is the only thing you have; and meanwhile you are hated for your stuck-up-ness and for the accent and manners which stamp you as one of the boss class. I was very young, not much more than six, when I first became aware of class-distinctions. Before that age my chief heroes had generally been working-class people, because they always seemed to do such interesting things, such as being fishermen and blacksmiths and bricklayers. I remember the farm hands on a farm in Cornwall who used to let me ride on the drill when they were sowing turnips and would sometimes catch the ewes and milk them to give me a drink; and the workmen building a new house next door, who let me play with the wet mortar and from whom I first learned the word "b_____"; and the plumber up the road with whose children I used to go out birdnesting. But it was not long before I was forbidden to play with the plumber's children; they were "common" and I was told to keep away from them. This was snobbish, if you like, but it was also necessary, for middle-class people cannot afford to let their children grow up with vulgar accents. So, very early, the working class ceased to be a race of friendly and wonderful beings and became a race of enemies. We realised that they hated us, but we could never understand why, and naturally we set it down to pure, vicious malignity. To me in my early boyhood, to nearly all children of families like mine, "common" people seemed almost sub-human. They had coarse faces, hideous accents and gross manners, they hated everyone who was not like themselves, and if they got half a chance they would insult you in brutal ways. That was our view of them, and though it was false it was understandable. For one must remember that before the war there was much more overt class-hatred in England than there is now. In those days you were quite likely to be insulted simply for looking like a member of the upper classes; nowadays, on the other hand, you are more likely to be fawned upon. Anyone over thirty can remember the time when it was impossible for a well-dressed person to walk through a slum street without being hooted at. Whole quarters of big towns were considered unsafe because of "hooligans" (now almost an extinct type), and the London gutter-boy everywhere, with his loud voice and lack of intellectual scruples, could make life a misery for people who considered it beneath their dignity to answer back. A recurrent terror of my holidays, when I was a small boy, was the gangs of "cads" who were liable to set upon you five or ten to one. In term time, on the other hand, it was we who were in the majority and the "cads" who were oppressed; I remember a couple of savage mass-battles in the cold winter of 1916–17. And this tradition of open hostility between upper and lower class had apparently been the same for at least a century past. A typical joke in *Punch* in the 'sixties is a picture of a small, nervous-looking gentleman riding through a slum street and a crowd of street-boys closing in on him with shouts of " 'Ere comes a swell! Let's frighten 'is 'oss!" Just fancy the street boys trying to frighten his horse now! They would be much likelier to hang round him in vague hopes of a tip. During the past dozen years the English working class have grown servile with a rather horrifying rapidity. It was bound to happen, for the frightful weapon of unemployment has cowed them. Before the war their economic position was comparatively strong, for though there was no dole to fall back upon, there was not much unemployment, and the power of the boss class was not so obvious as it is now. A man did not see ruin staring him in the face every time he cheeked a "toff," and naturally he did cheek a "toff" whenever it seemed safe to do so. G. J. Renier, in his book on Oscar Wilde, points out that the strange, obscene bursts of popular fury which followed the Wilde trial was essentially social in character. The London mob had caught a member of the upper classes on the hop, and they took care to keep him hopping. All this was natural and even proper. If you treat people as the English working class have been treated during the past two centuries, you must expect them to resent it. On the other hand the children of shabby-genteel families could not be blamed if they grew up with a hatred of the working class, typified for them by prowling gangs of "cads."

But there was another and more serious difficulty. Here you come to the real secret of class distinctions in the West—the real reason why a European of bourgeois upbringing, even when he calls himself a Communist, cannot without a hard effort think of a working man as his equal. It is summed up in four frightful words which people nowadays are chary of uttering, but which were bandied about quite freely in my childhood. The words were: *the lower classes smell.*

That was what we were taught—*the lower classes smell.* And here, obviously, you are at an impassable barrier. For no feeling of like or dislike is quite so fundamental as a *physical* feeling. Race-hatred, religious hatred, differences of education, of temperament, of intellect, even differences of moral code, can be got over; but physical repulsion cannot. You can have an affection for a murderer or a sodomite, but you cannot have an affection for a man whose breath stinks—habitually stinks, I mean. However well you may wish him, however much you may admire his mind and character, if his breath stinks he is horrible and in your heart of hearts you will hate him. It may not greatly matter if the average middle-class person is brought up to believe that the working classes are ignorant, lazy, drunken, boorish and dishonest; it is when he is brought up to believe that they are dirty that the harm is done. And in my childhood we *were* brought up to believe that they were dirty. Very early in life you acquired the idea that there was something subtly repulsive about a working-class body; you would not get nearer to it than you could help. You watched a great sweaty navvy walking down the road with his pick over his shoulder; you looked at his discoloured shirt and his corduroy trousers stiff with the dirt of a decade; you thought of those nests and layers of greasy rags below, and, under all, the unwashed body, brown all over (that was how I used to imagine it), with its strong, bacon-like reek. You watched a tramp taking off his boots in a ditch—ugh! It did not seriously occur to you that the tramp might not enjoy having black feet. And even "lower-class" people whom you knew to be quite clean—servants, for instance—were faintly unappetising. The smell of their sweat, the very texture of their skins, were mysteriously different from yours.

Everyone who has grown up pronouncing his aitches and in a house with a bathroom and one servant is likely to have grown up with these feelings; hence the chasmic, impassable quality of class-distinctions in the West. It is queer how seldom this is admitted. At the moment I can think of only one book where it is set forth without humbug, and that is Mr. Somerset Maugham's *On A Chinese Screen.* Mr. Maugham describes a high Chinese official arriving at a wayside inn and blustering and calling everybody names in order to impress upon them that he is a supreme dignitary and they are only worms. Five minutes later, having asserted his dignity in the way he thinks proper, he is eating his dinner in perfect amity with the baggage coolies. As an official he feels that he has got to make his presence felt, but he has no feeling that the coolies are of different clay from himself. I have observed countless similar scenes in Burma. Among Mongolians—among all Asiatics, for all I know—there is a sort of natural equality, an easy intimacy between man and man, which is simply unthinkable in the West. Mr. Maugham adds:

In the West we are divided from our fellows by our sense of smell. The working man is our master, inclined to rule us with an iron hand, but it cannot be denied that he stinks: none can wonder at it, for a bath in the dawn when you have to hurry to your work before the factory bell rings is no pleasant thing, nor does heavy labour tend to sweetness; and you do not change your linen more than you can help when the week's washing must be done by a sharp-tongued wife. I do not blame the working man because he stinks, but stink he does. It makes social intercourse difficult to persons of sensitive nostril. The matutinal tub divides the classes more effectually than birth, wealth or education.

Power And Authority

Power may be broadly defined as the ability to determine the behavior of others in accordance with one's own desires. There are but few social relationships in which the power element is totally absent, and it hence stands to reason that the concept of power is central to all sociological theorizing. Not only in such coercive organizations as concentration camps, military establishments or mental hospitals but also in voluntary organizations, in business or even in interpersonal relations, power is a key determinant of behavior. The exercise of social power may ultimately rest on the possible application of coercive sanctions in the case of noncompliance, but in the great majority of cases what is involved is not the unilateral imposition of the will of one actor on the other but rather the voluntary acceptance of the superordinate's decision by the subordinate. Such an acceptance may be mainly based on a purely utilitarian calculation, as in much of labor-management relations; it may be primarily based on the fear of reprisal as in concentration camps or mental hospitals, or it may involve the recognition by the subordinate that the superordinate has a right to exercise his power. Such granting of a right to power, that is legitimate power, is usually referred to as *authority*. Authority hence refers to that type of power which is considered in accord with norms accepted by both partners in the relationship. For many purposes it is furthermore necessary to distinguish between different grounds for legitimation. Max Weber's threefold classification of types of authority—legal, traditional and charismatic—though probably not exhaustive, is yet most often referred to in sociological theorizing and research.

The selection from Norman Mailer's brilliant novel about the Second World War, *The Naked and the Dead,* highlights the use of coercive power, but also points up the limitations of pure coercion. Arturo Barea, one of the major literary spokesmen of Republican Spain who lives in exile, describes in his autobiographical book *The Forging of A Rebel,* a somewhat similar case of the coercive exercise of power, but within a context in which charismatic elements, that is, extraordinary personal appeal, can be seen as a major determinant of compliance. George Bernard Shaw's preface to *Saint Joan* explains in some detail the basis for Joan's strong appeal to her followers as well as the resistance of traditional powerholders to the unwonted interference of her charisma with the traditional exercise of authority. Charles Dickens in the selection from his *Dombey and Son* describes the exercise of power within the context of a business organization. In addition to utilitarian considerations the fear of reprisal is seen as the major reason for the acceptance of the autocratic and capricious exercise of power by the head of the firm.

The selection from Ralph Waldo Emerson's essay on Napoleon will help illustrate the extent to which the extraordinary power of a charismatic leader depends on the ready acceptance of his followers. To Emerson, Napoleon's power flowed from the fact that he was a "representative man"—representative, that is, of the desires and aspirations of the French middle classes. The selection from Tolstoi's *War and Peace* also deals with Napoleon, but Tolstoi shows that in Russia, when no voluntary acceptance was forthcoming, pure coercion proved not feasible; there Napoleon lost all his power to influence men and events; Napoleon's failure in Moscow revealed the "poverty of power."

Norman Mailer (1923–   )

Power and its limits

Hearn looked at his watch. "It's time to go to chow." Outside the tent the earth was almost white in the glare of the overhead sun.

"You'll go to chow when I release you."

"Yes, sir." Hearn scraped his foot slowly against the floor, stared at him quietly, a little doubtfully.

"You threw that cigarette on my floor today, didn't you?"

Hearn smiled. "I figured that was going to be the point of all this talk."

"It was simple enough for you, wasn't it? You resented some of my actions, and you indulged a childish tantrum. But it's the kind of thing I don't care to permit." The General held his half-smoked cigarette in his hand, and waved it slightly as he spoke. "If I were to throw this down on the floor, would you pick it up?"

"I think I'd tell you to go to hell."

"I wonder. I've indulged you too long. You really can't believe I'm serious, can you? Suppose you understood that if you didn't pick it up, I would court-martial you, and you might have five years in a prison stockade."

"I wonder if you have the power for that?"

"I do. It would cause me a lot of difficulty, your court-martial would be reviewed, and after the war there might be a *bit* of a stink, it might even hurt me personally, but I would be upheld. I would have to be upheld. Even if you won eventually, you would be in prison for a year or two at least while it was all being decided."

"Don't you think that's a bit steep?"

"It's tremendously steep, it has to be. There was the old myth of divine intervention. You blasphemed, and a lightning bolt struck you. That was a little steep too. If punishment is at all proportionate to the offense, then power becomes watered. The only way you generate the proper attitude of awe and obedience is through immense and disproportionate power. With this in mind, how do you think you would react?"

Hearn was kneading his thighs again. "I resent this. It's an unfair proposition. You're settling a difference between us by . . ."

"You remember when I gave that lecture about the man with the gun?"

"Yes."

"It's not an accident that I have this power. Nor is it that you're in a situation like this. If you'd been more aware, you wouldn't have thrown down that cigarette. Indeed, you wouldn't have if I were a blustering profane General of the conventional variety. You don't quite believe I'm serious, that's all."

"Perhaps I don't."

Cummings tossed his cigarette at Hearns feet. "All right, Robert, suppose you pick it up," he said quietly.

There was a long pause. Under his breastbone, Cummings could feel his heart grinding painfully. "I hope, Robert, that you pick it up. For your sake." Once more he stared into Hearn's eye.

And slowly Hearn was realizing that he meant it. It was apparent in his expression. A series of emotions, subtle and conflicting, flowed behind the surface of his face. "If you want to play games," he said. For the first time Cummings could remember, his voice was unsteady. After a moment or two, Hearn bent down, picked up the cigarette, and dropped it in an ashtray. Cummings forced himself to face the hatred in Hearn's eyes. He was feeling an immense relief.

"If you want to, you can go to chow now."

"General, I'd like a transfer to another division." Hearn was lighting another cigarette, his hands not completely steady.

"Suppose I don't care to arrange it?" Cummings was calm, almost cheerful. He leaned back in his chair, and tapped his foot slowly. "Frankly, I don't particularly care to have you around as my aide any longer. You aren't ready to appreciate this lesson yet. I think I'm going to send you to the salt mines. Suppose after lunch you report over to Dalleson's section, and work under him for a while."

"Yes, sir." Hearn's face had become expressionless again. He started toward the exit of the tent, and then paused. "General?"

"Yes?" Now that it was over, Cummings wished that Hearn would leave. The victory was losing its edge, and minor regrets, delicate little reservations, were cloying him.

"Short of bringing in every man in the outfit, all six thousand of them, and letting them pick up cigarettes, how are you going to impress them?"

This was the thing that had sullied his pleasure. Cummings realized it now. There was still the other problem, the large one. "I'll manage that, Lieutenant. I think you'd better worry about your own concerns."

After Hearn had gone, Cummings looked at his hands. "When there are little surges of resistance, it merely calls for more power to be directed downward." And that hadn't worked with the line troops. Hearn he had been able to crush, any single man he could manage, but the sum of them was different still, resisted him still. He exhaled his breath, feeling a little weary. There was going to be a way, he would find it. There had been a time when Hearn had resisted him too.

And his elation, suppressed until now, stimulated him, eased to some extent the sores and frustrations of the past few weeks.

Hearn returned to his own tent, and missed lunch. For almost an hour he lay face down on his cot, burning with shame and self-disgust and an impossible impotent anger. He was suffering an excruciating humiliation which mocked him in its very intensity. He had known from the moment the General had sent for him that there would be trouble, and he had entered with the confidence that he wouldn't yield.

And yet he had been afraid of Cummings, indeed afraid of him from the moment he had come into the tent. Everything in him had demanded that he refuse to pick up the cigarette and he had done it with a sick numbed suspension of his will.

"The only thing to do is to get by on style." He had said that once, lived by it in the absence of anything else, and it had been a working guide, almost satisfactory until now. The only thing that had been important was to let no one in any ultimate issue ever violate your integrity, and this had been an ultimate issue. Hearn felt as if an immense cyst of suppuration and purulence had burst inside him, and was infecting his blood stream now, washing through all the conduits of his body in a sudden violent flux of change. He would have to react or die, effectively, and for one of the few times in his life he was quite uncertain of his own ability. It was impossible; he would have to do something, and he had no idea what to do. The moment was intolerable, the midday heat fierce and airless inside the tent, but he lay motionless, his large chin jammed into the canvas of his cot, his eyes closed, as if he were contemplating all the processes, all the things he had learned and unlearned in his life, and which were free now, sloshing about inside him with the vehemence and the agony of anything that had been suppressed for too long.

"I never thought I would crawfish to him."

That was the shock, that was the thing so awful to realize.

Arturo Barea (1897–1957)

Coercion and the lure of power

Lieut.-Colonel Millán Astray came out of the tent, followed by a couple of officers. The crowd fell silent. The Commander stretched his bony frame, while his hands mangled a glove until it showed the hairs of the fur lining. The whole might of his stentorian voice filled the encampment, and the

From *The Forging of a Rebel* by Arturo Barea (1946). Reprinted by permission of Hinshaw & Stuhlmann.

noises from the bivouacs of the other units died down. Eight thousand men tried to hear him, and they listened.

"*Caballeros Legionarios!*"

"Gentlemen of the Legion . . . yes, gentlemen! Gentlemen of the *tercio* of Spain, offspring of the Flanders *tercios* of old. Gentlemen! Some people say that before coming here you were I know not what! but anything rather than gentlemen: some murderers, others thieves, and all with your lives finished—dead! And it is true what they say. But here, since you are here, you are gentlemen. You have risen from the dead—for don't forget that you have been dead, that your lives were finished. You have come here to live a new life for which you must pay with death. You have come here to die. It is to die that one joins the Legion.

"What are you? The Betrothed of Death. You are the gentlemen of the Legion. You have washed yourselves clean, for you have come here to die. There is no other life for you than in this Legion. But you must understand that you are Spanish gentlemen, all of you, knights like those other legionaries who, conquering America, begat you. In your veins there are some drops of the blood of Pizarro and Cortés. There are drops of the blood of those adventurers who conquered a world and who, like you, were gentlemen—the Betrothed of Death. Long live Death . . . !

"*Viva la Muerte!*"

Millàn Astray's whole body underwent a hysterical transfiguration. His voice thundered and sobbed and shrieked. Into the faces of those men he spat all their misery, their shame, their ugliness, their crimes, and then he swept them along in fanatical fury to a feeling of chivalry, to a readiness to renounce all hope, beyond that of dying a death which would wash away their stains of cowardice in the splendor of courage. When the Standard shouted in wild enthusiasm, I shouted with them. Spanchiz pressed my arm:

"He's a grand fellow, isn't he?"

Millàn went round the circle of legionaries, stopping here or there before the most exotic or the most bestial faces. He stopped in front of a mulatto with thick lips, the liverish yellow-white of his rounded eyeballs shot with blood.

"Where do you come from, my lad?"

"What the devil's that to you?" the man answered.

Millàn Astray stared straight into the other's eyes.

"You think you're brave, don't you? Listen. Here, I am the Chief. If anyone like you speaks to me he stands to attention and says: 'At your orders, sir. I don't want to say where I come from.' And that's as it should be. You've a perfect right not to name your country, but you have no right to speak to me as if I were the likes of you."

"And in what are you more than I am?" The man spat it from lips wet with saliva as if they were on heat.

At times men can roar. At times men can pounce as though their muscles were of rubber and their bones steel rods.

"I . . . ?" roared the commander. "I am more than you, more of a man than you!" He sprang at the other and caught him by the shirt collar. He lifted him almost off the ground, hurled him into the center of the circle and smacked his face horribly with both hands. It lasted two or three seconds. Then the mulatto recovered from the unexpected assault and jumped. They hit each other as men in the primeval forest must have done before the first stone ax was made. The mulatto was left on the ground nearly unconscious, bleeding.

Millàn Astray, more erect, more terrifying than ever, rigid with a furious homicidal madness, burst into the shout:

"Attention!"

The eight hundred legionaries—and I—snapped into it like automatons. The mulatto rose, scraping the earth with his hands and knees. He straightened himself. His nose poured blood mixed with dirt like a child's mucus. The torn lip was more bloated than ever. He brought his heels together and saluted. Millàn Astray clapped him on his powerful back:

"I need brave men at my side tomorrow. I suppose I'll see you near me."

"At your orders, sir." Those eyes, more bloodshot than ever, more yellow with jaundice, held a fanatical flame.

George Bernard Shaw (1856–1950)

Saint joan's appeal

Having thus brought the matter home to ourselves, we may now consider the special feature of Joan's mental constitution which made her so unmanageable. What is to be done on the one hand with rulers who will not give any reason for their orders, and on the other with people who cannot understand the reasons when they are given? The government of the world, political, industrial, and domestic, has to be carried on mostly by the giving and obeying of orders under just these conditions. "Don't argue: do as you are told" has to be said not only to children and soldiers, but practically to everybody. Fortunately most people do not want to argue: they are only too glad to be saved the trouble of thinking for themselves. And the ablest and most independent thinkers are content to understand their own special department. In other departments they will unhesitatingly ask

From *Preface to Saint Joan* by G. B. Shaw (1923). Reprinted by permission of The Society of Authors and the Bernard Shaw Estate.

for and accept the instructions of a policeman or the advice of a tailor without demanding or desiring explanations.

Nevertheless, there must be some ground for attaching authority to an order. A child will obey its parents, a soldier his officer, a philosopher a railway porter, and a workman a foreman, all without question, because it is generally accepted that those who give the orders understand what they are about, and are duly authorised and even obliged to give them, and because, in the practical emergencies of daily life, there is no time for lessons and explanations, or for arguments as to their validity. Such obediences are as necessary to the continuous operation of our social system as the revolutions of the earth are to the succession of night and day. But they are not so spontaneous as they seem: they have to be very carefully arranged and maintained. A bishop will defer to and obey a king; but let a curate venture to give him an order, however necessary and sensible, and the bishop will forget his cloth and damn the curate's impudence. The more obedient a man is to accredited authority the more jealous he is of allowing any unauthorized person to order him about.

With all this in mind, consider the career of Joan. She was a village girl, in authority over sheep and pigs, dogs and chickens, and to some extent over her father's hired laborers when he hired any, but over no one else on earth. Outside the farm she had no authority, no prestige, no claim to the smallest deference. Yet she ordered everybody about, from her uncle to the king, the archbishop, and the military General Staff. Her uncle obeyed her like a sheep, and took her to the castle of the local commander, who, on being ordered about, tried to assert himself, but soon collapsed and obeyed. And so on up to the king, as we have seen. This would have been unbearably irritating even if her orders had been offered as rational solutions of the desperate difficulties in which her social superiors found themselves just then. But they were not so offered. Nor were they offered as the expression of Joan's arbitrary will. It was never "I say so," but always "God says so."

Leaders who take that line have no trouble with some people, and no end of trouble with others. They need never fear a lukewarm reception. Either they are messengers of God, or they are blasphemous imposters. In the Middle Ages the general belief in witchcraft greatly intensified this contrast, because when an apparent miracle happened (as in the case of the wind changing at Orleans) it proved the divine mission to the credulous, and proved a contract with the devil to the sceptical. All through, Joan had to depend on those who accepted her as an incarnate angel against those who added to an intense resentment of her presumption a bigoted abhorrence of her as a witch. To this abhorrence we must add the extreme irritation of those who did not believe in the voices, and regarded her as a liar and imposter. It is hard to conceive anything more infuriating to a statesman or a military commander, or to a court favorite, than to be over-ruled at every turn, or to be robbed of the ear of the reigning sovereign, by an impudent young upstart practising on the credulity of the populace and the vanity and silliness of an immature prince by exploiting a few of those lucky coincidences which pass as miracles with uncritical people. Not only were the envy, snobbery, and competitive ambition of the baser natures exacerbated by Joan's success, but among the friendly ones that were clever enough to be critical a quite reasonable scepticism and mistrust of her ability, founded on a fair observation of her obvious ignorance and temerity, were at work against her. And as she met all remonstrances and all criticisms, not with arguments or persuasion, but with a flat appeal to the authority of God and a claim to be in God's special confidence, she must have seemed, to all who were not infatuated by her, so insufferable that nothing but an unbroken chain of overwhelming successes in the military and political field could have saved her from the wrath that finally destroyed her.

—————   **Charles Dickens (1812–1870)**   —————

A business tyrant

Mr. Dombey's offices were in a court where there was an old-established stall of choice fruit at the corner: where perambulating merchants, of both sexes, offered for sale at any time between the hours of ten and five, slippers, pocket-books, sponges, dogs' collars, and Windsor soap; and sometimes a pointer or an oil-painting.

The pointer always came that way, with a view to the Stock Exchange, where a sporting taste (originating generally in bets of new hats) is much in vogue. The other commodities were addressed to the general public; but they were never offered by the venders to Mr. Dombey. When he appeared, the dealers in those wares fell off respectfully. The principal slipper and dogs' collar man—who considered himself a public character, and whose portrait was screwed on to an artist's door in Cheapside—threw up his fore-finger to the brim of his hat as Mr. Dombey went by. The ticket-porter, if he were not absent on a job, always ran officiously before, to open Mr. Dombey's office door as wide as possible, and hold it open, with his hat off, while he entered.

The clerks within were not a whit behind-hand in their demonstrations of respect. A solemn hush prevailed, as Mr. Dombey passed through the outer office. The wit of the counting-house became in a moment as mute as the row of leathern fire-buckets, hanging up behind them. Such vapid

———
From *Dombey and Son* by Charles Dickens (1848).

and flat daylight as filtered through the ground-glass windows, and skylights, leaving a black sediment upon the panes, showed the books and the figures bending over them, enveloped in a studious gloom, and as much abstracted in appearance, from the world without, as if they were assembled at the bottom of the sea; while a mouldy little strong room in the obscure perspective, where a shaded lamp was always burning, might have represented the cavern of some ocean-monster, looking on with a red eye at these mysteries of the deep.

When Perch, the messenger, whose place was on a little bracket, like a timepiece, saw Mr. Dombey come in—or rather, when he felt that he was coming, for he had usually an instinctive sense of his approach—he hurried into Mr. Dombey's room, stirred the fire, quarried fresh coals from the bowels of the coal box, hung the newspaper to air upon the fender, put the chair ready, and the screen in its place, and was round upon his heel on the instant of Mr. Dombey's entrance, to take his great-coat and hat, and hang them up. Then Perch took the newspaper, and gave it a turn or two in his hands before the fire, and laid it, deferentially, at Mr. Dombey's elbow. And so little objection had Perch to doing deferential in the last degree, that if he might have laid himself at Mr. Dombey's feet, or might have called him by some such title as used to be bestowed upon the Caliph Haroun Alraschid, he would have been all the better pleased.

As this honor would have been an innovation and an experiment, Perch was fain to content himself by expressing as well as he could, in his manner, You are the light of my Eyes. You are the breath of My Soul. You are the commander of the Faithful Perch! With this imperfect happiness to cheer him, he would shut the door softly, walk aways on tiptoe, and leave his great chief to be stared at, through a dome-shaped window in the leads, by ugly chimney pots and backs of houses, and especially by the bold window of a haircutting saloon on a first floor, where a waxen effigy, bald as a Mussulman in the morning, and covered after eleven o'clock in the day, with luxuriant hair and whiskers in the latest Christian fashion, showed him the wrong side of its head forever.

Between Mr. Dombey and the common world, as it was accessible through the medium of the outer office—to which Mr. Dombey's presence in his own room may be said to have struck like damp, or cold air—there were two degrees of descent. Mr. Carker in his own office was the first step; Mr. Morfin, in *his* own office, was the second. Each of these gentlemen occupied a little chamber like a bath-room, opening from the passage outside Mr. Dombey's door. Mr. Carker, as Grand Vizier, inhabited the room that was nearest to the Sultan. Mr. Morfin, as an officer of inferior state, inhabited the room that was nearest to the clerks.

The gentleman last mentioned was a cheerful-looking hazel-eyed elderly bachelor; gravely attired, as to his upper man, in black, and as to his legs, in pepper and salt color. His dark hair was just touched here and there with specks of gray, as though the tread of Time had splashed it: and his whiskers were already white. He had a mighty respect for Mr. Dombey, and rendered him due homage; but as he was of a genial temper himself, and never wholly at his ease in that stately presence, he was disquieted by no jealousy of the many conferences enjoyed by Mr. Carker, and felt a secret satisfaction in having duties to discharge, which rarely exposed him to be singled out for such distinction. He was a great musical amateur in his way—after business; and has a paternal affection for his violoncello, which was once in every week transported from Islington, his place of abode, to a certain club-room hard by the Bank, where quartets of the most tormenting and excruciating nature were executed every Wednesday evening by a private party. Mr. Carker was a gentleman thirty-eight or forty years old, of a florid complexion, and with two unbroken rows of glistening teeth, whose regularity and whiteness were quite distressing. It was impossible to escape the observation of them, for he showed them whenever he spoke; and bore so wide a smile upon his countenance (a smile, however, very rarely, indeed extending beyond his mouth), that there was something in it like the snarl of a cat. He affected a stiff white cravat, after the example of his principal, and was closely buttoned up and tightly dressed. His manner towards Mr. Dombey was deeply conceived and perfectly expressed. He was familiar with him, in the very extremity of his sense of the distance between them. "Mr. Dombey, to a man in your position from a man in mine, there is no show of subservience compatible with the transaction of business between us, that I should think sufficient. I frankly tell you, sir, I gave it up altogether. I feel that I could not satisfy my own mind; and Heaven knows, Mr. Dombey, you can afford to dispense with the endeavor." If he had carried these words about with him, printed on a placard, and had constantly offered it to Mr. Dombey's perusal on the breast of his coat, he could not have been more explicit than he was.

This was Carker the manager. Mr. Carker, the junior, Walter's friend, was his brother; two or three years older than he, but widely removed in station. The younger brother's post was on the top of the official ladder; the elder brother's at the bottom. The elder brother never gained a stave, or raised his foot to mount one. Young men passed above his head, and rose and rose; but he was always at the bottom. He was quite resigned to occupy that low condition; never complained of it: and certainly never hoped to escape from it.

"How do you do this morning?" said Mr. Carker the manager, entering Mr. Dombey's room soon after his arrival one day: with a bundle of papers in his hand.

"How do you do, Carker?" said Mr. Dombey, rising from his chair, and standing with his back to the fire. "Have you anything there for me?"

"I don't know that I need trouble you," returned Carker, turning over the papers in his hand. "You have a committee today at three, you know."

"And one at three, three-quarters," added Mr. Dombey.

"Catch you forgetting anything!" exclaimed Carker, still turning over his papers. "If Mr. Paul inherits your memory, he'll be a troublesome customer in the House. One of you is enough."

"You have an accurate memory of your own," said Mr. Dombey.

"Oh! *I*" returned the manager. "It's the only capital of a man like *me*."

Mr. Dombey did not look less pompous or at all displeased, as he stood leaning against the chimney-piece, surveying his (of course unconscious) clerk from head to foot. The stiffness and nicety of Mr. Carker's dress, and a certain arrogance of manner, either natural to him or imitated from a pattern not far off, gave great additional effect to his humility. He seemed a man who would contend against the power that vanquished him, if he could, but who was utterly borne down by the greatness and superiority of Mr. Dombey.

"Is Morfin here?" asked Mr. Dombey after a short pause, during which Mr. Carker had been fluttering his papers, and muttering little abstracts of their contents to himself.

"Morfin's here," he answered, looking up with his widest and most sudden smile; "humming musical recollections—of his last night's quartet party, I suppose—through the walls between us, and driving me half mad. I wish he'd make a bonfire of his violoncello, and burn his music books in it."

"You respect nobody, Carker, I think," said Mr. Dombey.

"No?" inquired Carker, with another wide and most feline show of his teeth. "Well! Not many people I believe. I wouldn't answer, perhaps," he murmured, as if he were only thinking it, "for more than one."

A dangerous quality, if real; and a not less dangerous one, if feigned. But Mr. Dombey hardly seemed to think so, as he still stood with his back to the fire, drawn up to his full height, and looking at his head clerk with a dignified composure, in which there seemed to lurk a stronger latent sense of power than usual.

"Talking of Morfin," resumed Mr. Carker, taking out one paper from the rest, "He reports a junior dead in the agency at Barbados, and proposes to reserve a passage in the Son and Heir—she'll sail in a month or so—for the successor. You don't care who goes, I suppose? We have nobody of that sort here."

Mr. Dombey shook his head with supreme indifference.

"It's no very precious appointment," observed Mr. Carker, taking up a pen, with which to indorse a memorandum on the back of the paper. "I hope he may bestow it on some orphan nephew of a musical friend. It may perhaps stop *his* fiddle-playing, if he has a gift that way. Who's that? come in!"

"I beg your pardon, Mr. Carker. I didn't know you were here, sir," answered Walter, appearing with some letters in his hand, unopened, and newly arrived. "Mr. Carker the junior sir"—

At the mention of this name, Mr. Carker the manager was, or affected to be, touched to the quick with shame and humiliation. He cast his eyes full on Mr. Dombey with an altered and apologetic look, abased them on the ground, and remained for a moment without speaking.

"I thought, sir," he said suddenly and angrily, turning on Walter, "that you had been before requested not to drag Mr. Carker the junior into your conversation."

"I beg your pardon," returned Walter. "I was only going to say that Mr. Carker the junior had told me he believed you were gone out, or I should not have knocked at the door when you were engaged with Mr. Dombey. These are letters for Mr. Dombey, sir."

"Very well, sir," returned Mr. Carker the manager, plucking them sharply from his hand. "Go about your business."

But in taking them with so little ceremony, Mr. Carker dropped one on the floor, and did not see what he had done; neither did Mr. Dombey observe the letter lying near his feet. Walter hesitated for a moment, thinking that one or other of them would notice it; but finding that neither did, he stopped, came back, picked it up, and laid it himself on Mr. Dombey's desk. The letters were post-letters; and it happened that the one in question was Mrs. Pipchin's regular report, directed as usual—for Mrs. Pipchin was but an indifferent pen-woman—by Florence. Mr. Dombey having his attention silently called to this letter by Walter, started, and looked fiercely at him, as if he believed that he had purposely selected it from all the rest.

"You can leave the room, sir!" said Mr. Dombey, haughtily.

He crushed the letter in his hand; and having watched Walter out at the door, put it in his pocket without breaking the seal.

"You want somebody to send to the West Indies, you were saying," observed Mr. Dombey, hurriedly.

"Yes," replied Carker.

"Send young Gay."

"Good, very good indeed. Nothing easier," said Mr. Carker, without any show of surprise, and taking up the pen to re-indorse the letter, as coolly as he had done before. " 'Send young Gay.' "

"Call him back," said Mr. Dombey.

Mr. Carker was quick to do so, and Walter was quick to return.

"Gay," said Mr. Dombey, turning a little to look at him over his shoulder. "Here is a"—

"An opening," said Mr. Carker, with his mouth stretched to the utmost.

"In the West Indies. At Barbados. I am going to send you," said Mr. Dombey, scorning to embellish the bare truth, "to fill a junior situation in the counting-house at Barbados. Let your uncle know from me, that I have chosen you to go to the West Indies."

Walter's breath was so completely taken away by his astonishment, that he could hardly find enough for the repetition of the words "West Indies."

"Somebody must go," said Mr. Dombey, "and you are young and healthy, and your uncle's circumstances are not good. Tell your uncle that you are appointed. You will not go yet. There will be an interval of a month—or two perhaps."

"Shall I remain there, sir?" inquired Walter.

"Will you remain there, sir!" repeated Mr. Dombey, turning a little more round towards him. "What do you mean? What does he mean, Carker?"

"Live there, sir," faltered Walter.

"Certainly," returned Mr. Dombey.

Walter bowed.

"That's all," said Mr. Dombey, resuming his letters. "You will explain to him in good time about the usual outfit and so forth, Carker, of course. He needn't wait, Carker."

"You needn't wait, Gay," observed Mr. Carker; bare to the gums.

"Unless," said Mr. Dombey, stopping in his reading without looking off the letter, and seeming to listen. "Unless he has anything to say."

"No, sir," returned Walter, agitated and confused, and almost stunned, as an infinite variety of pictures presented themselves to his mind; among which Captain Cuttle in his glazed hat, transfixed with astonishment at Mrs. Mac Stinger's and his uncle bemoaning his loss in the little back parlor, held prominent places. "I hardly know—I—I am much obliged, sir."

"He needn't wait, Carker," said Mr. Dombey.

And as Mr. Carker again echoed the words, and also collected his papers as if he were going away too, Walter felt that his lingering any longer would be an unpardonable intrusion—especially as he had nothing to say—and therefore walked out quite confounded.

——————   **Ralph Waldo Emerson (1803–1882)**   ——————

The basis of napoleon's power

Among the eminent persons of the nineteenth century, Bonaparte is far the best known and the most powerful; and owes his predominance to the fidelity with which he expresses the tone of thought and belief, the aims of the masses of active and cultivated men. It is Swedenborg's theory that every organ is made up of homogeneous particles; or as it is sometimes expressed, every whole is made of similars; that is, the lungs are composed of infinitely small lungs; the liver, of infinitely small livers; the kidney, of little

From "Napoleon; or the Man of the World," published in *Representative Men*, by Ralph Waldo Emerson (1850).

kidneys, etc. Following this analogy, if any man is found to carry with him the power and affections of vast numbers, if Napoleon is France, if Napoleon is Europe, it is because the people whom he sways are little Napoleons.

In our society there is a standing antagonism between the conservative and the democratic classes; between those who have made their fortunes, and the young and the poor who have fortunes to make; between the interests of dead labor—that is, the labor of hands long ago still in the grave, which labor is now entombed in money stocks, or in land and buildings owned by idle capitalists—and the interests of living labor, which seeks to possess itself of land and buildings and money stocks. The first class is timid, selfish, illiberal, hating innovation, and continually losing numbers by death. The second class is selfish also, encroaching, bold, self-relying, always outnumbering the other and recruiting its numbers every hour by births. It desires to keep open every avenue to the competition of all, and to multiply avenues: the class of business men in America, in England, in France and throughout Europe; the class of industry and skill. Napoleon is its representative. The instinct of active, brave, able men, throughout the middle class every where, has pointed out Napoleon as the incarnate Democrat. He had their virtues and their vices; above all, he had their spirit or aim. That tendency is material, pointing at a sensual success and employing the richest and most various means to that end; conversant with mechanical powers, highly intellectual, widely and accurately learned and skilful, but subordinating all intellectual and spiritual forces into means to a material success. To be the rich man, is the end. "God has granted," says the Koran, "to every people a prophet in its own tongue." Paris and London and New York, the spirit of commerce, of money and material power were also to have their prophet; and Bonaparte was qualified and sent.

Every one of the million readers of anecdotes or memoirs or lives of Napoleon, delights in the page, because he studies in it his own history. Napoleon is thoroughly modern, and, at the highest point of his fortunes, has the very spirit of the newspapers. He is no saint—to use his own word, "no capuchin," and he is no hero, in the high sense. The man in the street finds in him the qualities and powers of other men in the street. He finds him, like himself, by birth a citizen, who, by very intelligible merits, arrived at such a commanding position that he could indulge all those tastes which the common man possesses but is obliged to conceal and deny: good society, good books, fast travelling, dress, dinners, servants without number, personal weight, the execution of his ideas, the standing in the attitude of a benefactor to all persons about him, the refined enjoyments of pictures, statues, music, palaces and conventional honors—precisely what is agreeable to the heart of every man in the nineteenth century, this powerful man possessed.

It is true that a man of Napoleon's truth of adaptation to the mind of the masses around him, becomes not merely representative but actually a monopolizer and usurper of other minds. Thus Mirabeau plagiarized every good thought, every good word that was spoken in France. Dumont relates that he sat in the gallery of the Convention and heard Mirabeau make a speech. It struck Dumont that he could fit it with a peroration, which he wrote in pencil immediately, and showed it to Lord Elgin, who sat by him. Lord Elgin approved it, and Dumont, in the evening, showed it to Mirabeau. Mirabeau read it, pronounced it admirable, and declared he would incorporate it into his harangue tomorrow, to the Assembly. "It is impossible," said Dumont, "as unfortunately, I have shown it to Lord Elgin." "If you have shown it to Lord Elgin and to fifty persons beside, I shall still speak it to-morrow": and he did it with much effect, at the next day's session. For Mirabeau, with his over-powering personality, felt that these things which his presence inspired were as much his own as if he had said them, and that his adoption of them gave them their weight. Much more absolute and centralizing was the successor to Mirabeau's popularity and to much more than his predominance in France. Indeed, a man of Napoleon's stamp almost ceases to have a private speech and opinion. He is so largely receptive, and is so placed, that he comes to be a bureau for all the intelligence, wit and power of the age and country. He gains the battle; he makes the code; he makes the system of weights and measures; he levels the Alps; he builds the road. All distinguished engineers, servants, statists, report to him: so likewise do all good heads of every kind: he adopts the best measures, sets his stamp on them, and not these alone, but on every happy and memorable expression. Every sentence spoken by Napoleon and every line of his writing, deserves reading, as it is the sense of France.

Bonaparte was the idol of common men because he had in transcendent degree the qualities and powers of common men. There is a certain satisfaction in coming down to the lowest ground of politics, for we get rid of cant and hypocrisy. Bonaparte wrought, in common with that great class he represented for power and wealth—but Bonaparte, specially, without any scruple as to the means. All the sentiments which embarrass men's pursuit of these objects, he sets aside. The sentiments were for women and children. Fontanes, in 1804, expressed Napoleon's own sense, when in behalf of the Senate he addressed him—"Sire, the desire of perfection is the worst disease that ever afflicted the human mind." The advocates of liberty and of progress are "ideologists"—a word of contempt often in his mouth—"Necker is an ideologist"; "Lafayette is an ideologist."

An Italian proverb, too well known, declares that "if you would succeed, you must not be too good." It is an advantage, within certain limits, to have renounced the dominion of the sentiments of piety, gratitude and generosity; since what was an impassable bar to us, and still is to others, becomes a convenient weapon for our purposes; just as the river which was a formidable barrier, winter transforms into the smoothest of roads.

Napoleon renounced, once for all, sentiments and affections, and would help himself with his hands and his head. With him is no miracle and no magic. He is a worker in brass, in iron, in wood, in earth, in roads, in buildings, in money and in troops, and a very consistent and wise master-workman. He is never weak and literary, but acts with the solidity and the precision of natural agents. He has not lost his native sense and sympathy with things. Men give way before such a man, as before natural events. To be sure there are men enough who are immersed in things, as farmers, smiths, sailors and mechanics generally; and we know how real and solid such men appear in the presence of scholars and grammarians: but these men ordinarily lack the power of arrangement, and are like hands without a head. But Bonaparte superadded to this mineral and animal force, insight and generalization, so that men saw in him combined the natural and the intellectual power, as if the sea and land had taken flesh and begun to cipher. Therefore the land and sea seemed to presuppose him. He came unto his own and they received him. This ciphering operative knows what he is working with and what is the product. He knew the properties of gold and iron, of wheels and ships, of troops and diplomatists, and required that each should do after its kind.

The art of war was the game in which he exerted his arithmetic. It consisted, according to him, in having always more forces than the enemy, on the point where the enemy is attacked, or where he attacks: and his whole talent is strained by endless manoeuvre and evolution, to march always on the enemy at an angle, and destroy his forces in detail. It is obvious that a very small force, skilfully and rapidly manoeuvring so as always to bring two men against one at the point of engagement, will be an overmatch for a much larger body of men.

The times, his constitution and his early circumstances combined to develop this pattern democrat. He had the virtues of his class and the conditions for their activity. That common-sense which no sooner respects any end than it finds the means to effect it; the delight in the use of means; in the choice, simplification and combining the means; the directness and thoroughness of his work; the prudence with which all was seen and the energy with which all was done, make him the natural organ and head of what I may almost call, from its extent, the *modern* party.

Nature must have far the greatest share in every success, and so in his. Such a man was wanted, and such a man was born; a man of stone and iron, capable of sitting on horseback sixteen or seventeen hours, of going many days together without rest or food except by snatches, and with the speed and spring of a tiger in action; a man not embarrassed by any scruples; compact, instant, selfish, prudent, and of a perception which did not suffer itself to be baulked or misled by any pretences of others, or any superstition or any heat or haste of his own. "My hand of iron," he said, "was not at the extremity of my arm, it was immediately connected with my head." He respected the power of nature, and fortune, and ascribed to it his superiority, instead of valuing himself, like inferior men, on his opinionativeness, and waging war with nature. His favorite rhetoric lay in allusion to his star; and he pleased himself, as well as the people, when he styled himself the "Child of Destiny." "They charge me," he said, "with the commission of great crimes: men of my stamp do not commit crimes. Nothing has been more simple than my elevation, 'tis in vain to ascribe it to intrigue or crime; it was owing to the peculiarity of the times and to my reputation of having fought well against the enemies of my country. I have always marched with the opinion of great masses and with events. Of what use then would crimes be to me?" Again he said, speaking of his son, "My son cannot replace me; I could not replace myself. I am the creature of circumstances. . . ."

His grand weapon, namely the millions whom he directed, he owed to the representative character which clothed him. He interests us as he stands for France and for Europe; and he exists as captain and king only as far as the Revolution, or the interest of the industrious masses, found an organ and a leader in him. In the social interests, he knew the meaning and value of labor, and threw himself naturally on that side. I like an incident mentioned by one of his biographers at St. Helena. "When walking with Mrs. Balcombe, some servants, carrying heavy boxes, passed by on the road, and Mrs. Balcombe desired them, in rather an angry tone, to keep back. Napoleon interfered, saying 'Respect the burden, Madame.' " In the time of the empire he directed attention to the improvement and embellishment of the markets of the capital. "The market-place," he said, "is the Louvre of the common people." The principal works that have survived him are his magnificent roads. He filled the troops with his spirit, and a sort of freedom and companionship grew up between him and them, which the forms of his court never permitted between the officers and himself. They performed, under his eye, that which no others could do. The best document of his relation to his troops is the order of the day on the morning of the battle of Austerlitz, in which Napoleon promises the troops that he will keep his person out of reach of fire. This declaration, which is the reverse of that ordinarily made by generals and sovereigns on the eve of a battle, sufficiently explains the devotion of the army to their leader.

But though there is in particulars this identity between Napoleon and the mass of the people, his real strength lay in their conviction that he was their representative in his genius and aims, not only when he courted, but when he controlled, and even when he decimated them by his conscriptions. He knew, as well as any Jacobin in France, how to philosophize on liberty and equality; and when allusion was made to the precious blood of centuries, which was spilled by the killing of the Duc d'Enghien, he suggested, "Neither is my blood ditch-water." The people felt that no longer the throne was occupied and the land sucked of its nourishment, by a small class of legitimates, secluded from all community with the children of the soil, and holding the ideas and superstition of a long-forgotten state of society. Instead of the vampyre, a man of themselves held, in the Tuileries, knowledge and ideas like their own, opening of course to them and their children all places of power and trust. The day of sleepy, selfish policy, ever narrowing the means and opportunities of young men, was ended, and a day of expansion and demand was come. A market for all the powers and productions of man was opened; brilliant prizes glittered in the eyes of youth and talent. The old, iron-bound, feudal France was changed into a young Ohio or New York; and those who smarted under the immediate rigors of the new monarch, pardoned them as the necessary severities of the military system which had driven out the oppressor. And even when the majority of the people had begun to ask whether they had really gained any thing under the exhausting levies of men and money of the new master, the whole talent of the country, in every rank and kindred, took his part and defended him as its natural patron. In 1814, when advised to rely on the higher classes, Napoleon said to those around him, "Gentlemen, in the situation in which I stand, my only nobility is the rabble of the Faubourgs."

Napoleon met this natural expectation. The necessity of his position required a hospitality to every sort of talent, and its appointment to trust; and his feeling went along with this policy. Like every superior person, he undoubtedly felt a desire for men and compeers, and a wish to measure his power with other masters, and an impatience of fools and underlings. In Italy, he sought for men and found none. "Good God! he said, "how rare men are! There are eighteen millions in Italy, and I have with difficulty found two—Dandolo and Melzi." In later years, with larger experience, his respect for mankind was not increased. In a moment of bitterness he said to one of his oldest friends, "Men deserve the contempt with which they inspire me. I have only to put some gold-lace on the coat of my virtuous republicans and they immediately become just what I wish them." This impatience at levity was, however, an oblique tribute of respect to those able persons who commanded his regard not only when he found them friends and coadjutors but also when they resisted his will. He could not confound Fox and Pitt, Carnot, Lafayette and Bernadotte with the danglers of his court; and in spite of the detraction which his systematic egotism dictated toward the great captains who conquered with and for him, ample acknowledgments are made by him to Lannes, Duroc, Kleber, Dessaix, Massena, Murat, Ney and Augereau. If he felt himself their patron and the founder of their fortunes, as when he said "I made my generals out of mud"— he could not hide his satisfaction in receiving from them a seconding and support commensurate with the grandeur of his enterprise. In the Russian campaign he was so much impressed by the courage and resources of

Marshal Ney, that he said, "I have two hundred millions in my coffers, and I would give them all for Ney." The characters which he has drawn of several of his marshals are discriminating, and though they did not content the insatiable vanity of French officers, are no doubt substantially just. And in fact every species of merit was sought and advanced under his government. "I know," he said, "the depth and draught of water of every one of my generals." Natural power was sure to be well received at his court. Seventeen men in his time were raised from common soldiers to the rank of king, marshal, duke or general; and the crosses of his Legion of Honor were given to personal valor, and not to family connexion. "When soldiers have been baptized in the fire of a battlefield, they have all one rank in my eyes."

When a natural king becomes a titular king, everybody is pleased and satisfied. The Revolution entitled the strong populace of the Faubourg St. Antoine, and every horse-boy and powder-monkey in the army, to look on Napoleon as flesh of his flesh and creature of *his* party; but there is something in the success of grand talent which enlists an universal sympathy. For in the prevalence of sense and spirit over stupidity and malversation, all reasonable men have an interest; and as intellectual beings we feel the air purified by the electric shock, when material force is overthrown by intellectual energies. As soon as we are removed out of the reach of local and accidental partialities, Man feels that Napoleon fights for him; these are honest victories; this strong steam-engine does our work. Whatever appeals to the imagination, by transcending the ordinary limits of human ability, wonderfully encourages and liberates us. This capacious head, revolving and disposing sovereignly trains of affairs, and animating such multitudes of agents; this eye, which looked through Europe; this prompt invention; this inexhaustible resource—what events! what romantic pictures! what strange situations!—when spying the Alps, by a sunset in the Sicilian sea; drawing up his army for battle in sight of the Pyramids, and saying to his troops, "From the tops of those pyramids, forty centuries look down on you"; fording the Red Sea; wading in the gulf of the Isthmus of Suez. On the shore of Ptolemais, gigantic projects agitated him. "Had Acre fallen, I should have changed the face of the world." His army, on the night of the battle of Austerlitz, which was the anniversary of his inauguration as Emperor, presented him with a bouquet of forty standards taken in fight. Perhaps it is a little puerile, the pleasure he took in making these contrasts glaring; as when he pleased himself with making kings wait in his antechambers, at Tilsit, at Paris, and at Erfurt.

Lev Tolstoi

The poverty of power

Napoleon's activity in Moscow was as marvellous and as full of genius as anywhere else. Command upon command and plan upon plan was continually being issued by him from the time he entered Moscow to the time he left it. The absence of the citizens and of a deputation, and even the burning of Moscow, did not daunt him. He did not lose sight of the welfare of his army, nor of the doings of the enemy, nor of the welfare of the people of Russia, nor the conduct of affairs at Paris, nor of diplomatic negotiations as to the terms of peace.

On the military side, immediately on entering Moscow, Napoleon gives General Sebastiani strict orders to keep a watch on the movements of the Russian army, sends detachments along the various roads, and charges Murat to find Kutuzov. Then he gives careful instructions for the fortification of the Kremlin; then he makes a plan of the coming campaign over the whole map of Russia; that was a work of genius, indeed. On the diplomatic side, Napoleon summons to his presence Captain Yakovlev, who had been robbed and reduced to rags and did not know how to get out of Moscow, expounds to him minutely his whole policy and his magnanimity; and after writing a letter to the Emperor Alexander, in which he considers it his duty to inform his friend and brother that Rastoptchin had performed his duties very badly in Moscow, he despatches Yakovlev with it to Petersburg.

Expounding his views and his magnanimity with equal minuteness to Tutolmin, he despatches that old man too to Petersburg to open negotiations.

On the judicial side, orders were issued, immediately after the fires broke out, for the guilty persons to be found and executed. And the miscreant Rastoptchin was punished by the order to set fire to his houses.

On the administrative side, Moscow was presented with a constitution. A municipal council was instituted, and the following proclamation was issued:—

Citizens of moscow

Your misfortunes have been cruel, but his majesty the Emperor and King wishes to put an end to them. Terrible examples have shown you how he punishes crime and breach of discipline. Stern measures have been taken to put an end to disorder and to restore public security. A paternal council, chosen from

From *War and Peace* by Lev Tolstoi (1869), translated by Constance Garnett.

among yourselves, will compose your municipality or town council. It will care for you, for your needs and your interests. The members of it will be distinguished by a red ribbon, which they will wear across the shoulder, and the mayor will wear a white sash over it. But except when discharging their duties, they will wear only a red ribbon round the left arm.

The city police are established on their former footing, and they are already restoring order. The government has appointed two general commissioners, or superintendents of police, and twenty commissioners, or police inspectors, stationed in the different quarters of the town. You will recognise them by the white ribbon they will wear round the left arm. Several churches of various denominations have been opened, and divine service is performed in them without hindrance. Your fellow-citizens are returning every day to their dwellings, and orders have been given that they should find in them the aid and protection due to misfortune. These are the measures which the government has adopted to restore order and alleviate your position; but to attain that end, it is necessary that you should unite your efforts with them; should forget, if possible, the misfortunes you have suffered; should look hopefully at a fate that is not so cruel; should believe that a shameful death inevitably awaits those guilty of violence against your persons or your deserted property, and consequently leaves no doubt that they will be preserved, since such is the will of the greatest and most just of monarchs. Soldiers and citizens of whatever nation you may be! Restore public confidence, the source of the prosperity of a state; live like brothers, give mutual aid and protection to one another; unite in confounding the projects of the evil-minded; obey the civil and military authorities, and your tears will soon cease to flow.

On the commissariat side, Napoleon issued orders for all the troops to enter Moscow in turn, *à la maraude*, to gather supplies for themselves; so that in that way the army was provided with supplies for the future.

On the religious side, Napoleon ordered the priests to be brought back, and services to be performed again in the churches.

With a view to encouraging commerce and providing supplies for the troops, the following notice was placarded everywhere:—

Proclamation

You, peaceable inhabitants of Moscow, artisans, and working men, who have been driven out of the city by the disturbance, and you, scattered tillers of the soil, who are still kept in the fields by groundless error, hear! Tranquillity is returning to this capital, and order is being restored in it. Your fellow-countrymen are coming boldly out of their hiding-places, seeing that they are treated with respect. Every act of violence against them or their property is promptly punished. His majesty the Emperor and King protects them, and he reckons none among you his enemies but such as disobey his commands. He wishes to put an end to your trouble, and to bring you back to your homes and your families. Co-operate with his beneficent designs and come to us without apprehension. Citizens! Return with confidence to your habitations; you will soon find the means of satisfying your needs! Artisans and industrious handicraftsmen! Return to your employment; houses, shops, and guards to protect them are awaiting you, and you will receive the payment due to you for your toil! And you, too, peasants, come out of the forests where you have been hiding in terror, return without fear to your huts in secure reliance on finding protection. Markets have been established in the city, where peasants can bring their spare stores and country produce. The government has taken the following measures to secure freedom of sale for them: (1) From this day forward, peasants, husbandmen, and inhabitants of the environs of Moscow can, without any danger, bring their goods of any kind to two appointed markets—namely the Mohovaya and the Ohotny Ryad. (2) Goods shall be bought from them at such a price as seller and buyer shall agree upon together; but if the seller cannot get what he asks for at a fair price, he will be at liberty to take his goods back to his village, and no one can hinder his doing so on any pretext whatever. (3) Every Sunday and Wednesday are fixed for weekly market days: to that end a sufficient number of troops will be stationed on Tuesdays and Saturdays along all the high roads at such a distance from the town as to protect the carts coming in. (4) Similar measures will be taken that the peasants with their carts and horses may meet with no hindrance on their homeward way. (5) Steps will be immediately taken to re-establish the ordinary shops.

Inhabitants of the city and of the country, and you workmen and handicraftsmen of whatever nationality you may be! You are called upon to carry out the paternal designs of his majesty the Emperor and King, and to co-operate with him for the public welfare. Lay your respect and confidence at his feet, and do not delay to unite with us!

With a view to keeping up the spirits of the troops and the people, reviews were continually being held, and rewards were distributed.

The Emperor rode about the streets and entertained the inhabitants; and in spite of his preoccupation with affairs of state, visited in person the theatre set up by his orders.

As regards philanthropy, too—the fairest jewel in the conqueror's crown—Napoleon did everything that lay within him. On the benevolent institutions he ordered the inscription to be put up, *Maison de ma mère*, thereby combining a touching filial sentiment with a monarch's grandeur of virtue. He visited the Foundling Home; and as he gave the orphans he had saved his white hands to kiss, he conversed graciously with Tutolmin. Then, as Thiers eloquently recounts, he ordered his soldiers' pay to be distributed among them in the false Russian notes he had counterfeited:—

"Reinforcing the use of these methods by an act worthy of him and of the French army, he had assistance distributed to those who had suffered loss from the fire. But as provisions were too precious to be given to strangers, mostly enemies, Napoleon preferred to furnish them with money for them to provide themselves from without, and ordered paper roubles to be distributed among them."

With a view to maintaining discipline in the army, orders were continually being issued for severly punishing nonfulfilment of military duty and for putting an end to pillaging.

But, strange to say, all these arrangements, these efforts and plans, which were no whit inferior to those that had been made on similar occasions before, never touched the root of the matter; like the hands on the face of a clock, when detached from the mechanism, they turned aimlessly and arbitrarily, without catching the wheels.

The plan of campaign, that work of genius, of which Thiers says, that his genius never imagined anything more profound, more skilful, and more admirable, and entering into a polemical discussion with M. Fenn, proves that the composition of this work of genius is to be referred, not to the 4th, but to the 15th of October—that plan never was and never could be put into execution, because it had nothing in common with the actual facts of the position. The fortification of the Kremlin, for which it was necessary to pull down la Mosquée (as Napoleon called the church of Vassily the Blessed) turned out to be perfectly useless. The mining of the Kremlin was only of use for carrying out the desire the Emperor expressed on leaving Moscow, to blow up the Kremlin, like a child that beats the floor against which it has hurt itself. The pursuit of the Russian army, on which Napoleon laid so much stress, led to an unheard-of-result. The French generals lost sight of the sixty thousand men of the Russian army, and it was only, in the words of Thiers, thanks to the skill, and apparently also the genius, of Murat that they succeeded at last in finding, like a lost pin, this army of sixty thousand men.

On the diplomatic side, all Napoleon's expositions of his magnanimity and justice, both to Tutolmin and to Yakovlev (the latter was principally interested in finding himself a great-coat and a conveyance for travelling) turned out to be fruitless. Alexander would not receive these envoys, and made no reply to the message they brought.

On the side of the law, of order, after the execution of the supposed incendiaries, the other half of Moscow was burnt down.

The establishment of a municipal council did not check pillage, and was no benefit to any one but the few persons, who were members of it, and were able on the pretext of preserving order to plunder Moscow on their own account, or to save their own property from being plundered.

On the religious side, the difficulty had so easily been settled by Napoleon's visit to a mosque in Egypt, but here similar measures led to no results whatever. Two or three priests, picked up in Moscow, did attempt to carry out Napoleon's desire; but one of them was slapped in the face by a French soldier during the service, and in regard to the other, the following report was made by a French official: "The priest, whom I discovered and invited to resume saying the Mass, cleaned and closed the church. In the night they came again to break in the doors, break the padlocks, tear the books, and commit other disorders."

As for the encouragement of commerce, the proclamation to "industrious artisans and peasants," met with no response at all. Industrious artisans there were none in Moscow, and the peasants set upon the messengers who ventured too far from the town with this proclamation and killed them.

The attempts to entertain the people and the troops with theatres were equally unsuccessful. The theatres set up in the Kremlin and Poznyakov's house were closed again immediately, because the actors and actresses were stripped of their belongings by the soldiers.

Even philanthropy did not bring the desired results. Moscow was full of paper money, genuine and counterfeit, and the notes had no value. The French, accumulating booty, cared for nothing but gold. The counterfeit notes, which Napoleon so generously bestowed on the unfortunate, were of no value, and even silver fell below its standard value in relation to gold.

But the most striking example of the ineffectiveness of all efforts made by the authorities was Napoleon's vain endeavour to check plunder, and to maintain discipline.

Here are reports sent in by the military authorities:

"Pillage continues in the city, in spite of the orders to stop it. Order is not yet restored, and there is not a single merchant carrying on trade in a lawful fashion. But the canteen-keepers permit themselves to sell the fruits of pillage.

"Part of my district continues to be a prey to the pillaging of the soldiers of the 3rd corps who, not satisfied with tearing from the poor wretches, who have taken refuge in the underground cellars, the little they have left, have even the ferocity to wound them with sword-cuts, as I have seen in several instances.

"Nothing new, but the soldiers give themselves up to robbery and plunder. October 9th.

"Robbery and pillage continue. There is a band of robbers in our district, which would need strong guards to arrest it. October 11th.

"The Emperor is exceedingly displeased that, in spite of the strict orders to stop pillage, bands of marauders from the guards are continually returning to the Kremlin. In the Old Guards, the disorder and pillaging have been more violent than ever last night and to-day. The Emperor sees, with regret, that the picked soldiers, appointed to guard his person, who should set an example to the rest, are losing discipline to such a degree as to break into the cellars and stores prepared for the army. Others are so degraded that they refuse to obey sentinels and officers on guard, abuse them, and strike them.

"The chief marshal of the palace complains bitterly that, in spite of repeated prohibitions, the soldiers continue to commit nuisances in all the courtyards, and even before the Emperor's own windows."

The army, like a herd of cattle run wild, and trampling underfoot the fodder that might have saved them from starvation, was falling to pieces, and getting nearer to its ruin with every day it remained in Moscow.

But it did not move.

It only started running when it was seized by panic fear at the capture of a transport on the Smolensk road and the battle of Tarutino. The news of the battle of Tarutino reached Napoleon unexpectedly in the middle of a review, and aroused in him—so Thiers tells us—a desire to punish the Russians, and he gave the order for departure that all the army was clamouring for.

In their flight from Moscow, the soldiers carried with them all the plunder they had collected. Napoleon, too, carried off his own private *trésor*. Seeing the great train of waggons, loaded with the booty of the army, Napoleon was alarmed (as Thiers tells us). But with his military experience, he did not order all unnecessary waggons of goods to be burnt, as he had done with a marshal's baggage on the way to Moscow. He gazed at those carts and carriages, filled with soldiers, and said that it was very well, that those conveyances would come in useful for provisions, the sick, and the wounded.

The plight of the army was like the plight of a wounded beast, that feels its death at hand, and knows not what it is doing. Studying the intricate manoeuvres and schemes of Napoleon and his army from the time of entering Moscow up to the time of the destruction of that army is much like watching the death struggles and convulsions of a beast mortally wounded. Very often the wounded creature, hearing a stir, rushes to meet the hunter's shot, runs forward and back again, and itself hastens its end. Napoleon under the pressure of his army did likewise. Panic-stricken at the rumour of the battle of Tarutino, like a wild beast, the army made a rush towards the shot, reached the hunter, and ran back again; and at last, like every wild creature took the old familiar track, that was the worst and most disastrous way for it.

Napoleon is represented to us as the leader in all this movement, just as the figurehead in the prow of a ship to the savage seems the force that guides the ship on its course. Napoleon in his activity all this time was like a child, sitting in a carriage, pulling the straps within it, and fancying he is moving it along.

Bureaucracy

While popular usage often equates the term *bureaucracy* with such negative stereotypes as "red tape" or inefficiency and tends to apply it to governmental organizations alone, its sociological usage is very different. Sociologists mean by *bureaucracy* a type of hierarchical organization which is designed to coordinate the work of many individuals in the pursuit of large-scale administrative tasks, public or private. Specialization, hierarchy, impersonality and the dominance of specific rules characterize bureaucratic organization. The high degree of differentiation in the modern world has created the need for complex systems of hierarchical coordination, and such systems could not operate without clearcut rules governing the behavior of those performing administrative functions in impersonal ways. Many writers on the subject of bureaucracy have an ambivalent attitude toward it. Max Weber, the great German sociologist who initiated its systematic study, saw in it the most efficient and the most rational instrument for the accomplishment of large-scale tasks, but he also recoiled in horror from the vision of

232

a world progressively rationalized and demystified. He asked himself whether it would be possible "to keep a portion of mankind free from the parcelling-out of the soul, from this supreme mastery of the bureaucratic way of life." Karl Mannheim, at a somewhat later time, asked whether an increase in the functional rationality which bureaucratization brings in its wake, would not lead to a progressive decrease of substantial rationality, that is, "the capacity to act intelligently . . . on the basis of one's own insight into the interrelations of events." Most analysts who have at all reflected on the matter, have asked themselves whether bureaucracy, developed by men as a servant in the pursuit of their goals, might not in the end become their master, a kind of Frankenstein monster dominating its own creators.

Such considerations play only a secondary role in sociological analysis of bureaucratic structures, but they tend to become central in most literary treatments of the subject. While the selection from the British novelist Anthony Trollope, *The Three Clerks*, is in the main a dispassionate description of certain bureaucratic processes, the selection from Balzac's *The Functionaries* must be read as a mixture of description and polemic. Dickens' brilliant evocation of the Circumlocution Office, in his *Little Dorrit*, is tinged with violent hatred for what this author considered the dead hand of bureaucratic administration. Dickens here wrote a caricature rather than a description; but it must be understood that what he wanted to convey was not simple portrayal of normal activities but rather some insight into the pathology of bureaucratic practices. Here as elsewhere the pathological sheds some light on "normal" behavior also. Franz Kafka, the great modern novelist, from whose *The Castle* a typical passage has been selected, shared some of Dickens' preoccupations. By stressing the pathology of bureaucratic behavior, he aimed at representing in emblematic forms the nightmare of a fully rationalized world. Kafka's work can be read on many levels; the interest here is in his acute comprehensions of the dysfunctional aspects of bureaucracy and in his realization that, to paraphrase Robert K. Merton, rules originally conceived as a means may become, if rigidly adhered to, transformed into ends in themselves, so that an instrumental value becomes a terminal value. The danger of bureaucratic ritualism is dramatically explored in Ambrose Bierce's short story "One Kind of Officer." This little-known story from his sketches of the Civil War highlights the frightening consequences of literal adherence to rules; such ritualism defeats the very aims for the accomplishment of which the rules were originally conceived.

Anthony Trollope (1815–1882)

A succession crisis and its resolution

When it was declared to the world of Downing Street that Sir Gregory Hard-lines was to be a great man, to have an office of his own, and to reign over assistant-commissioners and subject secretaries, there was great commotion at the Weights and Measures; and when his letter of resignation was absolutely there, visible to the eyes of clerks, properly docketed and duly minuted, routine business was, for a day, nearly suspended. Gentlemen walked in and out from each other's rooms, asking this momentous question—Who was to fill the chair which had so long been honoured by the great Hardlines? Who was to be thought worthy to wear that divine mantle?

But even this was not the question of the greatest moment which at that period disturbed the peace of the office. It was well known that the chief clerk must be chosen from one of the three senior clerks, and that he would be so chosen by the voice of the Commissioners. There were only three men who were deeply interested in this question. But who would then be the new senior clerk, and how would he be chosen? A strange rumour began to be afloat that the new scheme of competitive examination was about to be tried in filling up this vacancy, occasioned by the withdrawal of Sir Gregory Hardlines. From hour to hour the rumour gained ground, and men's minds began to be much disturbed.

It was no wonder that men's minds should be disturbed. Competitive examinations at eighteen, twenty, and twenty-two may be very well, and give an interesting stimulus to young men at college. But it is a fearful thing for a married man with a family, who has long looked forward to rise to a certain income by the worth of his general conduct and by the value of his seniority—it is a fearful thing for such a one to learn that he has again to go through his school tricks, and fill up examination papers, with all his juniors round him using their stoutest efforts to take his promised bread from out of his mouth. *Detur digno* is a maxim which will make men do their best to merit rewards; every man can find courage within his heart to be worthy; but *detur digniori* is a fearful law for such a profession as the Civil Service. What worth can make a man safe against the possible greater worth which will come treading on his heels? The spirit of the age raises, from year to year, to a higher level the standard of education. The prodigy of 1857, who is now destroying all the hopes of the man who was well enough in 1855, will be a dunce to the tyro of 1860.

There were three or four in the Weights and Measures who felt all this

---

From *The Three Clerks* by Anthony Trollope (1857).

with the keenest anxiety. The fact of their being there, and of their having passed the scrutiny of Mr. Hardlines, was proof enough that they were men of high attainments; but then the question arose to them and others whether they were men exactly of those attainments which were *now* most required. Who is to say what shall constitute the merits of the *dignior?* It may one day be conic sections, another Greek iambics, and a third German philosophy. Rumour began to say that foreign languages were now very desirable. The three excellent married gentlemen who stood first in succession for the coveted promotion were great only in their vernacular.

Within a week from the secession of Sir Gregory, his immediate successor had been chosen, and it had been officially declared that the vacant situation in the senior class was to be thrown open as a prize for the best man in the office. Here was a brilliant chance for young merit! The place was worth £600 a-year, and might be gained by any one who now received no more than £100. Each person desirous of competing was to send in his name to the Secretary, on or before that day fortnight; and on that day month, the candidates were to present themselves before Sir Gregory Hardlines and his board of Commissioners.

And yet the joy of office was by no means great. The senior of those who might become competitors, was of course a miserable, disgusted man. He went about fruitlessly endeavouring to instigate rebellion against Sir Gregory, that very Sir Gregory whom he had for many years all but worshipped. Poor Jones was, to tell the truth, in a piteous case. He told the Secretary flatly that he would not compete with a lot of boys fresh from school, and his friends began to think of removing his razors. Nor were Brown and Robinson in much better plight. They both, it is true, hated Jones ruthlessly, and desired nothing better than an opportunity of supplanting him. They were, moreover, fast friends themselves; but not the less on that account had Brown a mortal fear of Robinson, as also had Robinson a mortal fear of Brown.

Then came the bachelors. First there was Uppinall, who, when he entered the office, was supposed to know everything which a young man had ever known. Those who looked most to dead knowledge were inclined to back him as first favourite. It had, however, been remarked, that his utility as a clerk had not been equal to the profundity of his acquirements. Of all the candidates he was the most self-confident.

The next to him was Mr. A. Minusex, a wondrous arithmetician. He was one who could do as many sums without pen and paper as a learned pig; who was so given to figures that he knew the number of stairs in every flight he had gone up and down in the metropolis; one who, whatever the subject before him might be, never thought but always counted. Many who knew the peculiar propensities of Sir Gregory's earlier days thought that Mr. Minusex was not an unlikely candidate.

The sixth in order was our friend Norman. The Secretary and the two Assistant-Secretaries, when they first put their heads together on the matter, declared that he was the most useful man in the office.

There was a seventh, named Alphabet Precis. Mr. Precis' peculiar forte was a singular happiness in official phraseology. Much that he wrote would doubtless have been considered in the purlieus of Paternoster Row as ungrammatical, if not unintelligible; but according to the syntax of Downing Street, it was equal to Macaulay, and superior to Gibbon. He had frequently said to his intimate friends, that in official writing, style was everything; and of his writing it certainly did form a very prominent part. He knew well, none perhaps so well, when to beg leave to lay before the Board—and when simply to submit to the Commissioners. He understood exactly to whom it behoved the secretary 'to have the honour of being a very humble servant,' and to whom the more simple 'I am, sir,' was a sufficiently civil declaration. These are qualifications great in official life, but were not quite so esteemed at the time of which we are speaking as they had been some few years previously.

There was but one other named as likely to stand with any probability of success, and he was Alaric Tudor. Among the very junior of the office he was regarded as the greatest star of the office. There was a dash about him and a quick readiness for any work that came to hand in which, perhaps, he was not equalled by any of his compeers. Then, too, he was the special friend of Sir Gregory. . . .

*   *   *

Norman made his appearance at the office on the first Monday of the new year. He had hitherto sat at the same desk with Alaric, each of them occupying one side of it; on his return he found himself opposite to a stranger. Alaric had, of course, been promoted to a room of his own.

The Weights and Measures had never been a noisy office; but now it became more silent than ever. Men there talked but little at any time, and now they seemed to cease from talking altogether. It was known to all that the Damon and Pythias of the establishment were Damon and Pythias no longer; that war waged between them, and that if all accounts were true, they were ready to fly each at the other's throat. Some attributed this to the competitive examination; others said it was love; others declared that it was money the root of evil; and one rash young gentleman stated his positive knowledge that it was all three. At any rate something dreadful was expected; and men sat anxious at their desks, fearing the coming evil.

On the Monday the two men did not meet, nor on the Tuesday. On the next morning, Alaric, having acknowledged to himself the necessity of breaking the ice, walked into the room where Norman sat with three or four others. It was absolutely necessary that he should make some arrangement with him as to a certain branch of office-work; and though it was competent for him, as the superior, to have sent for Norman as the inferior, he thought it best to abstain from doing so, even though he were thereby obliged to face his enemy, for the first time, in the presence of others.

'Well, Mr. Embryo,' said he, speaking to the new junior, and standing with his back to the fire in an easy way, as though there was nothing wrong under the sun, or at least nothing at the Weights and Measures, 'well, Mr. Embryo, how do you get on with those calculations?'

'Pretty well, I believe, sir; I think I begin to understand them now,' said the tyro, producing for Alaric's gratification five or six folio-sheets covered with intricate masses of figures.

'Ah! yes; that will do very well,' said Alaric, taking up one of the sheets, and looking at it with an assumed air of great interest. Though he acted his part pretty well, his mind was very far removed from Mr. Embryo's efforts.

Norman sat at his desk, as black as a thunder-cloud, with his eyes turned intently at the paper before him; but so agitated that he could not even pretend to write.

'By the by, Norman,' said Alaric, 'when will it suit you to look through those Scotch papers with me?'

'My name, sir, is Mr. Norman,' said Harry, getting up and standing by his chair with all the firmness of a Paladin of old.

'With all my heart,' said Alaric. 'In speaking to you I can have but one wish, and that is to do so in any way that may best please you.'

'Any instructions you may have to give I will attend to, as far as my duty goes,' said Norman.

And then Alaric, pushing Mr. Embryo from his chair without much ceremony, sat down opposite to his former friend, and said and did what he had to say and do with an easy unaffected air, in which there was, at any rate, none of the usual superciliousness of a neophyte's authority. Norman was too agitated to speak reasonably, or to listen calmly, but Alaric knew that though he might not do so today, he would tomorrow, or if not tomorrow, then the next day; and so from day to day he came into Norman's room and transacted his business. Mr. Embryo got accustomed to looking through the window at the Council Office for the ten minutes that he remained there, and Norman also became reconciled to the custom. And thus, though they never met in any other way, they daily had a kind of intercourse with each other, which at last, contrived to get itself arranged into a certain amount of civility on both sides.

Honoré de Balzac

The genus "clerk" and his natural habitat

M. Poiret junior was so called to distinguish him from an elder brother who had left the service. Poiret senior had retired to the Maison Vauquer, at which boarding-house Poiret junior occasionally dined, meaning likewise to retire thither some day for good. Poiret junior had been thirty years in the department. Every action in the poor creature's life was part of a routine; Nature herself is more variable in her revolutions. He always put his things in the same place, laid his pen on the same mark in the grain of the wood, sat down in his place at the same hour, and went to warm himself at the stove at the same minute; for his one vanity consisted in wearing an infallible watch, though he always set it daily by the clock of the Hotel de Ville, which he passed on his way from the Rue du Martroi.

Between six and eight o'clock in the morning Poiret made up the books of a large dry goods store in the Rue Saint-Antoine; from six to eight in the evening he again acted as book-keeper to the firm of Camusot in the Rue des Bourdonnais. In this way he made an income of a thousand crowns a year, including his salary. By this time he was within a few months of his retirement upon a pension, and therefore treated the office intrigues with much indifference. Retirement had already dealt Poiret senior his death-blow; and probably when Poiret junior should no longer be obliged to walk daily from Rue du Martroi to the office, to sit on his chair at a table and copy out documents daily, he too would age very quickly. Poiret junior collected back numbers of the "Moniteur" and of the newspaper to which the clerks subscribed. He achieved this with a collector's enthusiasm. If a number was mislaid, or if one of the clerks took away a copy and forgot to bring it back again, Poiret junior went forthwith to the newspaper office to ask for another copy, and returned delighted with the cashier's politeness. He always came in contact with a charming young fellow; journalists, according to him, were pleasant and little known people. Poiret junior was a man of average height, with dull eyes, a feeble, colorless expression, a tanned skin puckered into gray wrinkles with small bluish spots scattered over them, a snub nose, and a sunken mouth, in which one or two bad teeth still lingered on. . . .

His long, thin arms terminated in big hands without any pretension to whiteness; his gray hair, flattened down on his head by the pressure of his hat, gave him something of a clerical appearance; a resemblance the less welcome to him, because though he was not able to give an account of his

From *Les Employés* by Honoré de Balzac (1837), translated by Ellen Marriage.

religious opinions, he hated priests and ecclesiastics of every sort and description. This antipathy, however, did not prevent him from feeling an extreme attachment for the Government, whatever it might happen to be. Even in the very coldest weather, Poiret never buttoned his old-fashioned great-coat or wore any but laced shoes or black trousers. He had gone to the same stores for thirty years. When his tailor died, he asked for leave to go to the funeral, shook hands at the graveside with the man's son, and assured him of his custom. Poiret was on friendly terms with all his tradesmen; he took an interest in their affairs, chatted with them, listened to the tales of their grievances, and paid promptly. If he had occasion to write to make a change in an order, he observed the utmost ceremony, dating the letter, and beginning with "Monsieur" on a separate line; then he took a rough copy, and kept it in a pasteboard case, labeled *"my correspondence."*

No life could be more methodical. Poiret kept every receipted bill, however small the amount; and all his private account books, year by year, since he came into the office, were put away in paper covers. He dined for a fixed sum per month at the same eating-house (the sign of the Sucking Calf, in the Place du Châtelet), and at the same table (the waiters used to keep his place for him); and as he never gave The Golden Cocoon, the famous silk-mercer's establishment, so much as five minutes more than the due time, he always reached the Café David, the most famous café in the Quarter, at half-past eight, and stayed there till eleven o'clock. He had frequented that café likewise for thirty years, and punctually took his *bavaroise* at half-past ten; listening to political discussions with his arms crossed on his walking-stick, and his chin on his right hand, but he never took part in them. The lady at the desk was the one woman with whom he liked to converse; to her ears he confided all the little events of his daily existence, for he sat at a table close beside her. Sometimes he would play at dominoes, the one game that he had managed to learn; but if his partners failed to appear, Poiret was occasionally seen to doze, with his back against the panels, while the newspaper frame in his hand sank down on the slab of marble before him. . . . Baudoyer's office boasted various examples of the genus clerk in diverse, baldfronted, chilly mortals, with frames well wadded round with flannel. These individuals carried thorn-sticks, wore threadbare clothes, and were never seen without an umbrella. They perched, as a rule, on sixth floors, and cultivated flowers at that height. Clerks of this type rank half-way between the prosperous janitor and the needy artisan; they are too far from the administrative centre to hope for any promotion whatsoever; they are pawns upon the bureaucratic chessboard. When their turn comes to go on guard, they rejoice to get a day from the office. There is nothing that they will not do for extras. How they exist at all their very employers would be puzzled to say; their lives are an indictment against the State that assuredly causes the misery by accepting such a condition of things.

At sight of their strange faces it is hard to decide whether these quill-bearing mammals become cretinous at their task, or whether, on the other hand, they would never have undertaken it if they had not been, to some extent, cretins from birth. Perhaps Nature and the Government may divide the responsibility between them. "Villagers," according to an unknown writer, "are submitted to the influences of atmospheric conditions and surrounding circumstances. They do not seek to explain the fact to themselves. They are in a manner identified with their natural surroundings. Slowly and imperceptibly the ideas and ways of feeling awakened by those surroundings will permeate their being and come to the surface of their lives, in their personal appearance and in their actions, with variations for each individual organization and temperament. And thus, if any student feels attracted to the little known and fruitful field of physiological inquiry, which includes the effects produced by external natural agents upon human character, for him the villager becomes a most interesting and trustworthy book." But for the *employé*, Nature is replaced by the office; his horizon is bounded upon all sides by green pasteboard cases. For him atmospheric influences mean the air of the corridors, the stuffy atmosphere of unventilated rooms where men are crowded together; and the odor of paper and quills. A floor of bare bricks of parquetry, bestrewn with strange litter, and besprinkled from the messenger's watering-can, is the scene of his labors; his sky is the ceiling, to which his yawns are addressed; his element is dust. The above remarks on the villager might have been meant for the clerk; he too is "identified" with his surroundings. The sun scarcely shines into the horrid dens known as public offices; the thinking powers of their occupants are strictly confined to a monotonous round. Their prototype, the millhorse, yawns hideously over such work, and cannot stand it for long.

Charles Dickens

The circumlocution office

The Circumlocution Office was (as every body knows without being told) the most important Department under government. No public business of any kind could possibly be done at any time, without the acquiescence of the Circumlocution Office. Its finger was in the largest public pie, and in the smallest public tart. It was equally impossible to do the plainest right and to undo the plainest wrong without the express authority of the Circumlocution Office. If another Gunpowder Plot had been discovered half an hour

From *Little Dorrit* by Charles Dickens (1857).

before the lighting of the match, nobody would have been justified in saving the Parliament until there had been half a score of boards, half a bushel of minutes, several sacks of official memoranda, and a family-vaultful of ungrammatical correspondence, on the part of the Circumlocution Office.

This glorious establishment had been early in the field, when the one sublime principle involving the difficult art of governing a country was first distinctly revealed to statesmen. It had been foremost to study that bright revelation, and to carry its shining influence through the whole of the official proceedings. Whatever was required to be done, the Circumlocution Office was beforehand with all the public departments in the art of perceiving—*how not to do it.*

Through this delicate perception, through the tact with which it invariably seized it, and through the genius with which it always acted on it, the Circumlocution Office had risen to overtop all the public departments; and the public condition had risen to be—what it was.

It is true that How not to do it was the great study and object of all public departments and professional politicians all round the Circumlocution Office. It is true that every new premier and every new government, coming in because they had upheld a certain thing as necessary to be done, were no sooner come in than they applied their utmost faculties to discovering, How not to do it. It is true that from the moment when a general election was over, every returned man who had been raving on hustings because it hadn't been done, and who had been asking the friends of the honorable gentleman in the opposite interest on pain of impeachment to tell him why it hadn't been done, and who had been asserting that it must be done, and who had been pledging himself that it should be done, began to devise, How it was not to be done. It is true that the debates of both Houses of Parliament the whole session through, uniformly tended to the protracted deliberation, How not to do it. It is true that the royal speech at the opening of such session virtually said, My lords and gentlemen, you have a considerable stroke of work to do, and you will please to retire to your respective chambers, and discuss, How not to do it. It is true that the royal speech, at the close of such session, virtually said, My lords and gentlemen, you have through several laborious months been considering with great loyalty and patriotism, How not to do it, and you have found out; and with the blessing of Providence upon the harvest (natural, not political), I now dismiss you. All this is true, but the Circumlocution Office went beyond it.

Because the Circumlocution Office went on mechanically, every day, keeping this wonderful, all-sufficient wheel of statesmanship, How not to do it, in motion. Because the Circumlocution Office was down upon any ill-advised public servant who was going to do it, or who appeared to be by any surprising accident in remote danger of doing it, with a minute and a memorandum, and a letter of instructions that extinguished him.

It was this spirit of national efficiency in the Circumlocution Office that had gradually led to its having something to do with every thing. Mechanicians, natural philosophers, soldiers, sailors, petitioners, memorialists, people with grievances, people who wanted to prevent grievances, people who wanted to redress grievances, jobbing people, jobbed people, people who couldn't get rewarded for merit, and people who couldn't get punished for demerit, were all indiscriminately tucked up under the foolscap paper of the Circumlocution Office.

Numbers of people were lost in the Circumlocution Office. Unfortunates with wrongs, or with projects for the general welfare (and they had better have had wrongs at first, than have taken that bitter English recipe for certainly getting them), who in slow lapse of time and agony had passed safely through other public departments; who, according to rule, had been bullied in this, overreached by that, and evaded by the other; got referred at last to the Circumlocution Office, and never reappeared in the light of day. Boards sat upon them, secretaries minuted upon them, commissioners gabbled about them, clerks registered, entered, checked, and ticked them off, and they melted away. In short, all the business of the country went through the Circumlocution Office, except the business that never came out of it; and *its* name was Legion.

Sometimes angry spirits attacked the Circumlocution Office. Sometimes, parliamentary questions were asked about it, and even parliamentary motions made or threatened about it, by demagogues so low and ignorant as to hold that the real recipe of government was, How to do it. Then would the noble lord, or right honorable gentleman, in whose department it was to defend the Circumlocution Office, put an orange in his pocket, and make a regular field-day of the occasion. Then would he come down to that House with a slap upon the table, and meet the honorable gentleman foot to foot. Then would he be there to tell that honorable gentleman that the Circumlocution Office not only was blameless in this matter but was commendable in this matter, was extollable to the skies in this matter. Then would he be there to tell that honorable gentleman that, although the Circumlocution Office was invariably right, and wholly right, it never was so right as in this matter. Then would he be there to tell that honorable gentleman that it would have been more to his honor, more to his credit, more to his good taste, more to his good sense, more to half the dictionary of commonplaces, if he had left the Circumlocution Office alone, and never approached this matter. Then would he keep one eye upon a coach or crammer from the Circumlocution Office sitting below the bar, and smash the honorable gentleman with the Circumlocution Office account of this matter. And although one of two things always happened; namely, either that the Circumlocution Office had nothing to say and said it, or that it had something to say of which the noble lord, or right honorable gentleman, blundered one half and forgot the other; the Circumlocution Office was always voted im-maculate by an accommodating majority.

Such a nursery of statesmen had the Department become in virtue of a long career of this nature, that several solemn lords had attained the reputation of being quite unearthly prodigies of business, solely from having practiced How not to do it, at the head of the Circumlocution Office. As to the minor priests and acolytes of that temple, the result of all this was that they stood divided into two classes, and, down to the junior messenger, either believed in the Circumlocution Office as a heaven-born institution, that had an absolute right to do whatever it liked; or took refuge in total infidelity, and considered it a flagrant nuisance.

Franz Kafka (1883–1924)

In the maze of bureaucracy

We replied with thanks to the order that I've mentioned already, saying that we didn't need a land-surveyor. But this reply doesn't appear to have reached the original department—I'll call it A—but by mistake went to another department, B. So Department A remained without an answer, but unfortunately our full reply didn't reach B either; whether it was that the order itself was not enclosed by us, or whether it got lost on the way—it was certainly not lost in my department, that I can vouch for—in any case all that arrived at Department B was the covering letter, in which was merely noted that the enclosed order, unfortunately an impractical one, was con-cerned with the engagement of a land-surveyor. Meanwhile Department A was waiting for our answer; they had, of course, made a memorandum of the case, but as, excusably enough, often happens and is bound to happen even under the most efficient handling, our correspondent trusted to the fact that we would answer him, after which he would either summon the Land-Surveyor or else, if need be, write us further about the matter. As a result he never thought of referring to his memorandum, and the whole thing fell into oblivion. But in Department B the covering letter came into the hands of a correspondent famed for his conscientiousness, Sordini by name, an Italian; it is incomprehensible even to me, though I am one of the initi-ated, why a man of his capacities is left in an almost subordinate position. This Sordini naturally sent us back the unaccompanied covering letter for completion. Now months, if not years, had passed by this time since that first communication from Department A, which is understandable enough, for when—as is the rule—a document goes the proper route, it reaches the department at the outside in a day and is settled that day, but when it once in a while loses its way, then in an organization so efficient as ours its proper destination might be sought for literally with desperation; otherwise it mightn't be found; and then—well, then the search may last really for a long time. Accordingly, when we got Sordini's note we had only a vague memory of the affair; there were only two of us to do the work at that time, Mizzi and myself, the teacher hadn't yet been assigned to us; we only kept copies in the most important instances, so we could only reply in the most vague terms that we knew nothing of this engagement of a land-surveyor and that as far as we knew there was no need for one.

"But"—here the Mayor interrupted himself as if, carried on by his tale, he had gone too far, or as if at least it was possible that he had gone too far, "doesn't the story bore you?"

"No," said K., "it amuses me."

Thereupon the Mayor said: "I'm not telling it to amuse you."

"It only amuses me," said K., "because it gives me an insight into the ludicrous bungling that in certain circumstances may decide the life of a human being."

"You haven't been given any insight into that yet," replied the Mayor gravely, "and I can go on with my story. Naturally Sordini was not satisfied with our reply. I admire the man, though he is a plague to me. He literally distrusts everyone; even if, for instance, he has come to know somebody, through countless circumstances, as the most reliable man in the world, he distrusts him as soon as fresh circumstances arise, as if he didn't want to know him, or rather as if he wanted to know that he was a scoundrel. I consider that right and proper, an official must behave like that; unfortunately, with my nature I can't follow out this principle; you see yourself how frank I am with you, a stranger, about those things, I can't act in any other way. But Sordini, on the contrary, was seized by suspicion when he read our reply. Now a huge correspondence began to grow. Sordini inquired how I had suddenly recalled that a land-surveyor shouldn't be summoned. I replied, drawing on Mizzi's splendid memory, that the first suggestion had come from the bureau itself (but that it had come from a different department we had of course forgotten long before this). Sordini countered; why had I only mentioned this official order now? I replied: because I had just remembered it. Sordini: that was very extraordinary. Myself: it was not in the least extraordinary in such a long-drawn-out business. Sordini: yes, it was extraordinary, for the order that I remembered didn't exist. Myself: of course it didn't exist, for the whole document has been lost. Sordini: but there must be a memorandum extant relating to this first communication, and there wasn't one extant. That made me halt, for that an error should happen in Sordini's department I dared neither maintain nor believe. Perhaps, my dear Land-Surveyor, you'll make the reproach against Sordini in your mind that in consideration of my assertion he should have been moved at least to make inquiries in the other departments about the affair. But that is just what would have been wrong; I don't want any blame to attach to this man, no, not even in your thoughts. It's a working principle of the head bureau that the very possibility of error must be ruled out of account. This ground principle is justified by the consummate organization of the whole authority, and it is necessary if the maximum speed in transacting business is to be attained. So it wasn't within Sordini's power to make inquiries in other departments; besides, they simply wouldn't have answered, because they would have guessed at once that it was a case of hunting out a possible error."

"Allow me, Mr. Mayor, to interrupt you with a question," said K. "Did you not mention once before a Control Authority? From your description the whole economy is one that would rouse one's apprehensions if one could imagine the Control failing."

"You're very strict," said the Mayor, "but multiply your strictness a thousand times and it would still be nothing compared with the strictness that the Authority imposes on itself. Only a total stranger could ask a question like yours. Is there a Control Authority? There are only Control authorities. Frankly, it isn't their function to hunt out errors in the vulgar sense, for errors don't happen, and even when once in a while an error does happen, as in your case, who can say finally that it's an error?"

"This is news indeed!" cried K.

"It's very old news to me," said the Mayor. "Not unlike yourself, I'm convinced that an error has occurred, and as a result Sordini is quite ill with despair, and the first Control officials, whom we have to thank for discovering the source of error, recognize that there is an error. But who can guarantee that the second Control officials will decide in the same way, and the third and all the others?"

"That may be," said K. "I would much rather not mix in these speculations yet; besides, this is the first mention I've heard of those Control officials and naturally I can't understand them yet. But I fancy that two things must be distinguished here; first, what is transacted in the offices and can be construed again officially this way or that, and, secondly, my own actual person, me myself, situated outside of the offices and threatened by their encroachments, which are so meaningless that I can't even yet believe in the seriousness of the danger. The first evidently is covered by what you, Mr. Mayor, tell me in such extraordinary and disconcerting detail; all the same, I should like to hear a word now about myself."

"I'm coming to that too," said the Mayor, "but you couldn't understand it without my giving a few more preliminary details. My mentioning the Control officials just now was premature. So I must turn back to the discrepancies with Sordini. As I said, my defense gradually weakened. But whenever Sordini has in his hands even the slightest hold against anyone, he has as good as won, for then his vigilance, energy, and alertness are actually increased and it's a terrible moment for the victim, and a glorious one for the victim's enemies. It's only because in other circumstances I have experienced this last feeling that I'm able to speak of him as I do. All the same, I have never managed yet to come within sight of him. He can't get down here, he's so overwhelmed with work; from the descriptions I've heard of his room, every wall is covered with pillars of documents tied together, piled on top of one another; those are only the documents that Sordini is working on at the time, and as bundles of papers are continually being taken away and brought in, and all in great haste, those columns are always falling on the floor, and it's just those perpetual crashes, following fast on one another, that have come to distinguish Sordini's workroom. Yes, Sordini is a worker, and he gives the same scrupulous care to the smallest case as to the greatest."

"Mr. Mayor," said K., "you always call my case one of the smallest, and yet it has given hosts of officials a great deal of trouble, and if, perhaps, it was unimportant at the start, yet through the diligence of officials of Sordini's type it has grown into a great affair. Very much against my will, unfortunately, for my ambition doesn't run to seeing columns of documents, all about me, rising and crashing together, but to working quietly at my drawingboard as a humble land-surveyor."

"No," said the Superintendent, "it's not at all a great affair, in that respect you've no ground for complaint—it's one of the least important among the least important. The importance of a case is not determined by the amount of work it involves; you're far from understanding the authorities if you believe that. But even if it's a question of the amount of work, your case would remain one of the slightest; ordinary cases—those without any so-called errors, I mean—provide far more work and far more profitable work as well. Besides, you know absolutely nothing yet of the actual work that was caused by your case. I'll tell you about that now. Well, presently Sordini left me out of account, but the clerks arrived, and every day a formal inquiry involving the most prominent members of the community was held in the Herrenhof. The majority stuck by me, only a few held back—the question of a land-surveyor appeals to peasants—they scented secret plots and injustices and what not, found a leader, no less, and Sordini was forced by their assertions to the conviction that if I had brought the question forward in the Village Council, every voice wouldn't have been against the summoning of a land-surveyor. So a commonplace—namely, that a land-surveyor wasn't needed—was turned after all into a doubtful matter at least. A man called Brunswick distinguished himself especially—you don't know him, of course—probably he's not a bad man, only stupid and fanciful, he's a son-in-law of Lasemann's."

"Of the master tanner?" asked K., and he described the full-bearded man whom he had seen at Lasemann's.

"Yes, that's the man," said the Mayor.

"I know his wife, too," said K. a little at random.

"That's possible," replied the Mayor briefly.

"She's beautiful," said K., "but rather pale and sickly. She comes, of course, from the Castle?" It was half a question.

The Mayor looked at the clock, poured some medicine into a spoon, and gulped at it hastily.

"You only know the official side of the Castle?" asked K. bluntly.

"That's so," replied the Mayor, with an ironical and yet grateful smile, "and it's the most important. And as for Brunswick, if we could exclude him from the Council we would almost all be glad, and Lasemann not least. But at that time Brunswick gained some influence; he's not an orator of course, but a shouter; but even that can do a lot. And so it came about that I was forced to lay the matter before the Village Council; however, it was Brunswick's only immediate triumph, for of course the Village Council refused by a large majority to hear anything about a land-surveyor. That too was a long time ago, but the whole time since, the matter has never been allowed to rest, partly owing to the conscientiousness of Sordini, who by the most painful sifting of data sought to fathom the motives of the majority no less than the opposition; partly owing to the stupidity and ambition of Brunswick, who had several personal acquaintances among the authorities, whom he set working with fresh inventions of his fancy. Sordini, at any rate, didn't let himself be deceived by Brunswick—how could Brunswick deceive Sordini?—but simply to prevent himself from being deceived a new sifting of data was necessary, and long before it was ended Brunswick had already thought out something new; he's very, very versatile, no doubt of it; that goes with his stupidity. And now I come to a peculiar characteristic of our administrative apparatus. Along with its precision it's extremely sensitive as well. When an affair has been weighed for a very long time, it may happen, even before the matter has been fully considered, that suddenly in a flash the decision comes in some unforeseen place, which, moreover, can't be found any longer later on—a decision that settles the matter, if in most cases justly, yet all the same arbitrarily. It's as if the administrative apparatus were unable any longer to bear the tension, the year-long irritation caused by the same affair—probably trivial in itself—and had hit on the decision by itself, without the assistance of the officials. Of course, a miracle didn't happen and certainly it was some clerk who hit upon the solution or the unwritten decision, but in any case it couldn't be discovered by us at least, by us here, or even by the head bureau, which clerk had decided in this case and on what grounds. The Control officials only discovered that much later, but we shall never learn it; besides, by this time it would scarcely interest anybody. Now, as I said, it's just these decisions that are generally excellent. The only annoying thing about them—it's usually the case with such things—is that one learns too late about them and so in the meantime keeps on still passionately canvassing things that were decided long ago. I don't know whether in your case a decision of this kind happened—some people say yes, others no—but if it had happened, then the summons would have been sent to you and you would have made the long journey to this place, much time would have passed, and in the meanwhile Sordini would have been working away here all the time on the same case until he was exhausted, Brunswick would have been intriguing and I would have been plagued by both of them. I only indicate this possibility, but I know the following for a fact: a Central official discovered meanwhile that a query had gone out from Department A to the Village Council many years before regarding a land-surveyor, without having received a reply up to then. A new inquiry was sent to me, and now the whole business was really cleared up. Department A was satisfied with my answer that a land-surveyor was not needed, and Sordini was forced to recognize that he had not been equal to this case and, innocently it is true, had gone through so much nerve-racking work for nothing. If new work hadn't come rushing in as ever from every side, and if your case hadn't been a very unimportant case—one might almost say the least important among the unimportant—we might all of us have breathed freely again, I fancy even Sordini himself; Brunswick was the only one who grumbled, but that was only ridiculous. And now imagine to yourself, Land-Surveyor, my dismay when after the fortunate end of the whole business—and since then, too, a great deal of time had passed by—suddenly you appear and it begins to look as if the whole thing must begin all over again. You'll understand, of course, that I'm firmly resolved, so far as I'm concerned, not to let that happen in any case?"

Ambrose Bierce (1842–1914?)

One kind of officer

"Captain Ransome, it is not permitted to you to know *anything*. It is sufficient that you obey my order—which permit me to repeat. If you perceive any movement of troops in your front you are to open fire, and if attacked hold this position as long as you can. Do I make myself understood, sir?"

"Nothing could be plainer, Lieutenant Price,"—this to an officer of his own battery, who had ridden up in time to hear the order—"the general's meaning is clear, is it not?"

"Perfectly."

From *Tales of Soldiers and Civilians* by Ambrose Bierce (1891).

The lieutenant passed on to his post. For a moment General Cameron and the commander of the battery sat in their saddles, looking at each other in silence. There was no more to say; apparently too much had already been said. Then the superior officer nodded coldly and turned to his horse to ride away. The artillerist saluted slowly, gravely, and with extreme formality. One acquainted with the niceties of military etiquette would have said that by his manner he attested a sense of the rebuke that he had incurred. It is one of the important uses of civility to signify resentment.

When the general had joined his staff and escort, awaiting him at a little distance, the whole cavalcade moved off toward the right of the guns and vanished in the fog. Captain Ransome was alone, silent, motionless as an equestrian statue. The gray fog, thickening every moment, closed in about him like a visible doom.

The fighting of the day before had been desultory and indecisive. At the points of collision the smoke of battle had hung in blue sheets among the branches of the trees till beaten into nothing by the falling rain. In the softened earth the wheels of cannon and ammunition wagons cut deep, ragged furrows, and movements of infantry seemed impeded by the mud that clung to the soldiers' feet as, with soaken garments and rifles imperfectly protected by capes of overcoats they went dragging in sinuous lines hither and thither through dripping forest and flooded field. Mounted officers, their heads protruding from rubber ponchos that glittered like black armor, picked their way, singly and in loose groups, among the men, coming and going with apparent aimlessness and commanding attention from nobody but one another. Here and there a dead man, his clothing defiled with earth, his face covered with a blanket or showing yellow and claylike in the rain, added his dispiriting influence to that of the other dismal features of the scene and augmented the general discomfort with a particular dejection. Very repulsive these wrecks looked—not at all heroic, and nobody was accessible to the infection of their patriotic example. Dead upon the field of honor, yes; but the field of honor was so very wet! It makes a difference.

The general engagement that all expected did not occur, none of the small advantages accruing, now to this side and now to that, in isolated and accidental collisions being followed up. Half-hearted attacks provoked a sullen resistance which was satisfied with mere repulse. Orders were obeyed with mechanical fidelity; no one did any more than his duty.

"The army is cowardly to-day," said General Cameron, the commander of a Federal brigade, to his adjutant-general.

"The army is cold," replied the officer addressed, "and—yes, it doesn't wish to be like that."

He pointed to one of the dead bodies, lying in a thin pool of yellow water, its face and clothing bespattered with mud from hoof and wheel.

The army's weapons seemed to share its military delinquency. The rattle of rifles sounded flat and contemptible. It had no meaning and scarcely roused to attention and expectancy the unengaged parts of the line-of-battle and the waiting reserves. Heard at a little distance, the reports of cannon were feeble in volume and *timbre:* they lacked sting and resonance. The guns seemed to be fired with light charges, unshotted. And so the futile day wore on to its dreary close, and then to a night of discomfort succeeded a day of apprehension.

An army has a personality. Beneath the individual thought and emotions of its component parts it thinks and feels as a unit. And in this large, inclusive sense of things lies a wiser wisdom than the mere sum of all that it knows. On that dismal morning this great brute force, groping at the bottom of a white ocean of fog among trees that seemed as sea weeds, had a dumb consciousness that all was not well; that a day's manoeuvring had resulted in a faulty disposition of its parts, a blind diffusion of its strength. The men felt insecure and talked among themselves of such tactical errors as with their meager military vocabulary they were able to name. Field and line officers gathered in groups and spoke more learnedly of what they apprehended with no greater clearness. Commanders of brigades and divisions looked anxiously to their connections on the right and on the left, sent staff officers on errands of inquiry and pushed skirmish lines silently and cautiously forward into the dubious region between the known and the unknown. At some points on the line the troops, apparently of their own volition, constructed such defenses as they could without the silent spade and the noisy ax.

One of these points was held by Captain Ransome's battery of six guns. Provided always with intrenching tools, his men had labored with diligence during the night, and now his guns thrust their black muzzles through the embrasures of a really formidable earthwork. It crowned a slight acclivity devoid of undergrowth and providing an unobstructed fire that would sweep the ground for an unknown distance in front. The position could hardly have been better chosen. It had this peculiarity, which Captain Ransome, who was greatly addicted to the use of the compass, had not failed to observe: it faced northward, whereas he knew that the general line of the army must face eastward. In fact, that part of the line was "refused"—that is to say, bent backward, away from the enemy. This implied that Captain Ransome's battery was somewhere near the left flank of the army; for an army in line of battle retires its flanks if the nature of the ground will permit, they being its vulnerable points. Actually, Captain Ransome appeared to hold the extreme left of the line, no troops being visible in that direction beyond his own. Immediately in rear of his guns occurred that conversation between him and his brigade commander, the concluding and more picturesque part of which is reported above.

Captain Ransome sat motionless and silent on horseback. A few yards away his men were standing at their guns. Somewhere—everywhere within a few miles—were a hundred thousand men, friends and enemies. Yet he was alone. The mist had isolated him as completely as if he had been in the heart of a desert. His world was a few square yards of wet and trampled earth about the feet of his horse. His comrades in that ghostly domain were invisible and inaudible. These were conditions favorable to thought, and he was thinking. Of the nature of his thoughts his clear-cut handsome features yielded no attesting sign. His face was as inscrutable as that of the sphinx. Why should it have made a record which there was none to observe? At the sound of a footsteps he merely turned his eyes in the direction whence it came; one of his sergeants, looking a giant in stature in the false perspective of the fog, approached, and when clearly defined and reduced to his true dimensions by propinquity, saluted and stood at attention.

"Well, Morris," said the officer, returning his subordinate's salute.

"Lieutenant Price directed me to tell you, sir, that most of the infantry has been withdrawn. We have no sufficient support."

"Yes, I know."

"I am to say that some of our men have been out over the works a hundred yards and report that our front is not picketed."

"Yes."

"They were so far forward that they heard the enemy."

"Yes."

"They heard the rattle of the wheels of artillery and the commands of officers."

"Yes."

"The enemy is moving toward our works."

Captain Ransome, who had been facing to the rear of his line—toward the point where the brigade commander and his cavalcade had been swallowed up by the fog—reined his horse about and faced the other way. Then he sat motionless as before.

"Who are the men who made that statement?" he inquired, without looking at the sergeant; his eyes were directed straight into the fog over the head of his horse.

"Corporal Hassman and Gunner Manning."

Captain Ransome was a moment silent. A slight pallor came into his face, a slight compression affected the lines of his lips, but it would have required a closer observer than Sergeant Morris to note the change. There was none in the voice.

"Sergeant, present my compliments to Lieutenant Price and direct him to open fire with all the guns. Grape."

The sergeant saluted and vanished in the fog.

Searching for his division commander, General Cameron and his escort had followed the line of battle for nearly a mile to the right of Ransome's battery, and there learned that the division commander had gone in search of the corps commander. It seemed that everybody was looking for his immediate superior—an ominous circumstance. It meant that nobody was quite at ease. So General Cameron rode on for another half-mile, where by good luck he met General Masterson, the division commander, returning.

"Ah, Cameron," said the higher officer, reining up, and throwing his right leg across the pommel of his saddle in a most unmilitary way—"anything up? Found a good position for your battery, I hope—if one place is better than another in the fog."

"Yes, general," said the other, with the greater dignity appropriate to his less exalted rank, "my battery is very well placed, I wish I could say that it is as well commanded."

"Eh, what's that? Ransome? I think him a fine fellow. In the army we should be proud of him."

It was customary for officers of the regular army to speak of it as "the army." As the greatest cities are most provincial, so the self-complacency of aristocracies is most frankly plebeian.

"He is too fond of his opinion. By the way, in order to occupy the hill that he holds I had to extend my line dangerously. The hill is on my left—that is to say the left flank of the army."

"Oh, no, Hart's brigade is beyond. It was ordered up from Drytown during the night and directed to hook on to you. Better go and—"

The sentence was unfinished: a lively cannonade had broken out on the left, and both officers, followed by their retinues of aides and orderlies making a great jingle and clank, rode rapidly toward the spot. But they were soon impeded, for they were compelled by the fog to keep within sight of the line-of-battle, behind which were swarms of men, all in motion across their way. Everywhere the line was assuming a sharper and harder definition, as the men sprang to arms and the officers, with drawn swords, "dressed" the ranks. Color-bearers unfurled the flags, buglers blew the "assembly," hospital attendants appeared with stretchers. Field officers mounted and sent their impedimenta to the rear in care of Negro servants. Back in the ghostly spaces of the forest could be heard the rustle and murmur of the reserves, pulling themselves together.

Nor was all this preparation vain, for scarcely five minutes had passed since Captain Ransome's guns had broken the truce of doubt before the whole region was aroar: the enemy had attacked nearly everywhere.

Captain Ransome walked up and down behind his guns, which were firing rapidly but with steadiness. The gunners worked alertly, but without haste or apparent excitement. There was really no reason for excitement; it is not much to point a cannon into a fog and fire it. Anybody can do as much as that.

The men smiled at their noisy work, performing it with a lessening alacrity. They cast curious regards upon their captain, who had now mounted the banquette of the fortification and was looking across the parapet as if observing the effect of his fire. But the only visible effect was the substitution of wide, low-lying sheets of smoke for their bulk of fog. Suddenly out of the obscurity burst a great sound of cheering, which filled the intervals between the reports of the guns with startling distinctness! To the few with leisure and opportunity to observe, the sound was inexpressibly strange—so loud, so near, so menacing, yet nothing seen! The men who had smiled at their work smiled no more, but performed it with a serious and feverish activity.

From his station at the parapet Captain Ransome now saw a great multitude of dim gray figures taking shape in the mist below him and swarming up the slope. But the work of the guns was now fast and furious. They swept the populous declivity with gusts of grape and canister, the whirring of which could be heard through the thunder of the explosions. In this awful tempest of iron the assailants struggled forward foot by foot across their dead, firing into the embrasures, reloading, firing again, and at last falling in their turn, a little in advance of those who had fallen before. Soon the smoke was dense enough to cover all. It settled down upon the attack and, drifting back, involved the defense. The gunners could hardly see to serve their pieces, and when occasional figures of the enemy appeared upon the parapet—having had the good luck to get near enough to it, between two embrasures, to be protected from the guns—they looked so unsubstantial that it seemed hardly worth while for the few infantrymen to go to work upon them with the bayonet and tumble them back into the ditch.

As the commander of a battery in action can find something better to do than cracking individual skulls, Captain Ransome had retired from the parapet to his proper post in rear of his guns, where he stood with folded arms, his bugler beside him. Here, during the hottest of the fight, he was approached by Lieutenant Price, who had just sabred a daring assailant inside the work. A spirited colloquy ensued between the two officers— spirited, at least, on the part of the lieutenant, who gesticulated with energy and shouted again and again into his commander's ear in the attempt to make himself heard above the infernal din of the guns. His gestures, if coolly noted by an actor, would have been pronounced to be those of protestation: one would have said that he was opposed to the proceedings. Did he wish to surrender?

Captain Ransome listened without a change of countenance or attitude, and when the other man had finished his harangue, looked him coldly in the eyes and during a seasonable abatement of the uproar said:

"Lieutenant Price, it is not permitted to you to know *anything*. It is sufficient that you obey my orders."

The lieutenant went to his post, and the parapet being now apparently clear Captain Ransome returned to it to have a look over. As he mounted the banquette a man sprang upon the crest, waving a great brilliant flag. The captain drew a pistol from his belt and shot him dead. The body, pitching forward, hung over the inner edge of the embankment, the arms straight downward, both hands still grasping the flag. The man's few followers turned and fled down the slope. Looking over the parapet, the captain saw no living thing. He observed also that no bullets were coming into the work.

He made a sign to the bugler, who sounded the command to cease firing. At all other points the action had already ended with a repulse of the Confederate attack; with the cessation of this cannonade the silence was absolute.

General Masterson rode into the redoubt. The men, gathered in groups, were talking loudly and gesticulating. They pointed at the dead, running from one body to another. They neglected their foul and heated guns and forgot to resume their outer clothing. They ran to the parapet and looked over, some of them leaping down into the ditch. A score were gathered about a flag rigidly held by a dead man.

"Well, my men," said the general cheerily, "you have had a pretty fight of it."

They stared; nobody replied; the presence of the great man seemed to embarrass and alarm.

Getting no response to his pleasant condescension, the easy-mannered officer whistled a bar or two of a popular air, and riding forward to the parapet, looked over at the dead. In an instant he had whirled his horse about and was spurring along in rear of the guns, his eyes everywhere at once. An officer sat on the trail of one of the guns, smoking a cigar. As the general dashed up he rose and tranquilly saluted.

"Captain Ransome!"—the words fell sharp and harsh, like the clash of steel blades—"you have been fighting our own men—our own men, sir; do you hear? Hart's brigade!"

"General, I know that."

"You know it—you know that, and you sit here smoking? Oh, damn it, Hamilton, I'm losing my temper,"—this to his provost-marshal. "Sir— Captain Ransome, be good enough to say—to say why you fought our own men."

"That I am unable to say. In my orders that information was withheld."

Apparently the general did not comprehend.

"Who was the aggressor in this affair, you or General Hart?" he asked.

"I was."

"And could you not have known—could you not see, sir, that you were attacking our own men?"

The reply was astounding!

"I knew that, general. It appeared to be none of my business."

Then, breaking the dead silence that followed his answer, he said:

"I must refer you to General Cameron."

"General Cameron is dead, sir—as dead as he can be—as dead as any man in this army. He lies back yonder under a tree. Do you mean to say that he had anything to do with this horrible business?"

Captain Ransome did not reply. Observing the altercation his men had gathered about to watch the outcome. They were greatly excited. The fog, which had been partly dissipated by the firing, had again closed in so darkly about them that they drew more closely together till the judge on horseback and the accused standing calmly before him had but a narrow space free from intrusion. It was the most informal of courts-martial, but all felt that the formal one to follow would but affirm its judgment. It had no jurisdiction, but it had the significance of prophecy.

"Captain Ransome," the general cried impetuously, but with something in his voice that was almost entreaty, "if you can say anything to put a better light upon your incomprehensible conduct I beg you will do so."

Having recovered his temper this generous soldier sought for something to justify his naturally sympathetic attitude toward a brave man in the imminence of a dishonorable death.

"Where is Lieutenant Price?" the captain said.

That officer stood forward, his dark saturnine face looking somewhat forbidding under a bloody handkerchief bound about his brow. He understood the summons and needed no invitation to speak. He did not look at the captain, but addressed the general:

"During the engagement I discovered the state of affairs, and apprised the commander of the battery. I ventured to urge that the firing cease. I was insulted and ordered to my post."

"Do you know anything of the orders under which I was acting?" asked the captain.

"Of any orders under which the commander of the battery was acting," the lieutenant continued, still addressing the general, "I know nothing."

Captain Ransome felt his world sink away from his feet. In those cruel words he heard the murmur of the centuries breaking upon the shore of eternity. He heard the voice of doom; it said, in cold, mechanical, and measured tones: "Ready, aim, fire!" and he felt the bullets tear his heart to shreds. He heard the sound of the earth upon his coffin and (if the good God was so merciful) the song of a bird above his forgotten grave. Quietly detaching his sabre from its supports, he handed it up to the provost-marshal.

Total institutions

A few years ago a gifted modern sociologist, Irving Goffman, coined the term "Total Institutions" to denote organizations in which men or women are confined for all 24 hours of the day, so that their lives can be totally controlled. Prime examples of such total institutions are the army, mental or other hospitals, prisons, concentration camps, and boarding schools.

Under ordinary circumstances, modern men and women freely move between the several organizations and institutional settings in which they are involved. One may work in a factory or office, belong to one or more voluntary organizations, participate in a residential community, and spend considerable time in a household and family. All these settings typically demand a certain amount of loyalty and commitment, but none ask for exclusive allegiance. The many segmental types of involvements in which modern men are enmeshed allow them to develop a certain degree of personal autonomy in their freedom to move from one circle to another. Even though a person may be devoted to all of the circles, none can absorb his total personality.

Matters are fundamentally different in total institutions. Since their claim on their members or inmates is total, since they aim at controlling the whole man, rather than a segment of his personality, they tend to reduce or to obliterate personal autonomy. Here men and women are governed by the rhythms and regulations of the institution, rather than by their own wishes and desires. Such institutions attempt more or less successfully to strip people of their personal identities. The inmates are material, malleable putty, shaped and molded by the hands of their superiors or guardians.

Excerpts from Oscar Wilde's *The Ballad of Reading Gaol*, written in prison while he was confined on a morals charge, vividly convey the sense of human loss and abandonment of prisoners who feel that "by all forgot, we rot and rot." Few other literary treatments of the horrors of long-term imprisonment are as powerful indictments of an inhuman system as these lines.

e. e. cummings, the great American poet, was imprisoned during World War I in a French jail which he called *The Enormous Room*. His classical description of prison conditions, and particularly of the regulations and imposed routines that govern the life of prisoners, make up the second selection.

Arthur Koestler, the Hungarian-British writer perhaps best known for his political novel *Darkness at Noon*, was likewise imprisoned by the French. He spent a part of World War II as an "undesirable alien" in a French concentration camp. The excerpt from his book *Scum of the Earth* focuses on the internal organization of the prisoners. He stresses that a concentration camp, just like most prisons, is far from harboring a mass of undifferentiated inmates, that it has a "class structure" of its own. The class divisions and the struggles between the haves and the havenots that mark the outside society are here reproduced in a distorted microcosm.

The boarding school in which the young George Orwell grew up did not have all the coercive features of prisons or concentration camps. Yet, as the excerpt from his moving "Such, Such Were the Joys . . ." plainly indicates, the damage done to a sensitive boy by the brutality and callousness that prevailed, and probably still prevails, in such schools, was often as maiming to the psyche as a term of imprisonment.

The section closes with a selection from the great Russian novelist Alexander Solzhenitsyn's *One Day in the Life of Ivan Denisovich*. His description of the inhumanity of man to man in the Stalinist concentration camps in which he himself suffered for many years, vividly evokes the barrier between the inmates and their guardians, the institutionalized bar to the flow of human empathy between those "who live in the warm and those who live in the cold."

Oscar Wilde (1854–1900)

Reading gaol

I know not whether Laws be right,
   Or whether Laws be wrong;
All that we know who lie in gaol
   Is that the wall is strong;
And that each day is like a year
   A year whose days are long.

But this I know, that every Law
   That men have made for Man,
Since first Man took his brother's life,
   And the sad world began,
But straws the wheat and saves the chaff
   With a most evil fan.

This too I know—and wise it were
   If each could know the same—
That every prison that men build
   Is built with bricks of shame,
And bound with bars lest Christ should see
   How men their brothers maim.

With bars they blur the gracious moon,
   And blind the goodly sun:
And they do well to hide their Hell,
   For in it things are done
That Son of God nor son of Man
   Ever should look upon!

The vilest deeds like poison weeds,
   Bloom well in prison-air;
It is only what is good in Man
   That wastes and withers there:
Pale Anguish keeps the heavy gate,
   And the Warder is Despair.

From *The Ballad of Reading Gaol* by Oscar Wilde (1898).

For they starve the little frightened child
　　Till it weeps both night and day:
And they scourge the weak, and flog the fool,
　　And gibe the old and grey,
And some grow mad, and all grow bad,
　　And none a word may say.

Each narrow cell in which we dwell
　　Is a foul and dark latrine,
And the fetid breath of living Death
　　Chokes up each grated screen,
And all, but Lust, is turned to dust
　　In Humanity's machine.

The brackish water that we drink
　　Creeps with a loathsome slime,
And the bitter bread they weigh in scales
　　Is full of chalk and lime,
And Sleep will not lie down, but walks
　　Wild-eyed, and cries to Time.

But though lean Hunger and green Thirst
　　Like asp with adder fight,
We have little care of prison fare,
　　For what chills and kills outright
Is that every stone one lifts by day
　　Becomes one's heart by night.

With midnight always in one's heart,
　　And twilight in one's cell,
We turn the crank, or tear the rope,
　　Each in his separate Hell,
And the silence is more awful far
　　Than the sound of a brazen bell.

And never a human voice comes near
　　To speak a gentle word:
And the eye that watches through the door
　　Is pitiless and hard:
And by all forgot, we rot and rot,
　　With soul and body marred . . .

e. e. cummings (1894–1962)

The enormous room

We filed from the *cour*, through the door, past a little window which I was told belonged to the kitchen, down the clammy corridor, up the three flights of stairs, to the door of The Enormous Room. Padlocks were unlocked, chains rattled, and the door thrown open. We entered. The Enormous Room received us in silence. The door was slammed and locked behind us by the *planton*, whom we could hear descending the gnarled and filthy stairs.

In the course of a half-hour, which time as I was informed intervened between the just-ended morning promenade and the noon meal which was the next thing on the programme, I gleaned considerable information concerning the daily schedule of La Ferté. A typical day was divided by *planton*-cries as follows:

(1) *'Cafe.'* At 5:30 every morning a *planton* or *plantons* mounted to the room. One man descended to the kitchen, got a pail of coffee, and brought it up.

(2) *'Corvée d'eau.'* From time to time the occupants of the room chose one of their number to be *'maître de chambre,'* or roughly speaking Boss. When the *planton* opened the door, allowing the coffee-getter to descend, it was the duty of the *maître de chambre* to rouse a certain number of the men (generally six, the occupants of the room being taken in rotation), who forthwith carried the pails of urine and excrement to the door. Upon the arrival of coffee, the *maître de chambre* and his crew 'descended' said pails, together with a few clean pails for water, to the ground floor; where a *planton* was in readiness to escort them to a sort of sewer situated a few yards beyond the *cour des femmes*. Here the full pails were dumped: with the exception, occasionally, of one or two pails of urine which the *Surveillant* might direct to be thrown on the *Directeur's* little garden in which it was rumoured he was growing a rose for his daughter. From the sewer the *corvée* gang were escorted to a pump, where they filled their water pails. They then mounted to the room, where the emptied pails were ranged against the wall beside the door, with the exception of one which was returned to the *cabinet*. The water pails were placed hard by. The door was now locked, and the *planton* descended.

While the men selected for *corvée* had been performing their duties the other occupants had been enjoying coffee. The corvée men now joined them.

The *maître de chambre* usually allowed about fifteen minutes for himself and his crew to consume their breakfast. He then announced:

(3) *'Nettoyage de Chambre.'* Some one sprinkled the floor with water from one of the pails which had been just brought up. The other members of the crew swept the room, fusing their separate piles of filth at the door. This process consumed something like a half-hour.

(4) The sweeping completed, the men had nothing more to do till 7.30, at which hour a *planton* mounted, announcing *'A la promenade les hommes.'* The *corvée* crew now carried down the product of their late labours. The other occupants descended or not directly to the *cour*, according to their tastes; morning promenade being optional. At 9.30 the *planton* demanded:

(5) *'Montez les hommes.'* Those who had taken advantage of the morning stroll were brought upstairs to the room, the *corvée* men descended the excrement which had accumulated during promenade, and everybody was thereupon locked in for a half-hour, or until ten o'clock, when a *planton* again mounted and cried:

(6) *'A la soupe les hommes.'* Every one descended to a wing of the building opposite the *cour des hommes,* where the noon meal was enjoyed until 10.30 or thereabouts, when the order:

(7) *'Tout le monde en haut'* was given. There was a digestive interval of two and a half hours spent in the room. At one o'clock a *planton* mounted, announcing:

(8) *'Les hommes à la promenade'* (in which case the afternoon promenade was a matter of choice) or *'Tout le monde en bas,'* whereat every one had to descend, willy-nilly, *'plucher les pommes'*—potatoes (which constituted the *pièce de résistance* of *'la soupe'*) being peeled and sliced on alternate days by the men and the girls. At 3.30:

(9) *'Tout le monde en haut'* was again given, the world mounted, the *corvée* crew descended excrement, and every one was then locked in till 4, at which hour a *planton* arrived to announce:

(10) *'A la soupe,'* that is to say the evening meal, or dinner. After dinner anyone who wished might go on promenade for an hour; those who wished might return to the room. At eight o'clock the *planton* made a final inspection and pronounced:

(11) *'Lumières éteintes.'*

The most terrible cry of all, and which was not included in the regular programme of *planton*-cries, consisted of the words:

'A la douche les hommes'—when all, sick, dead and dying not excepted, descended to the baths. Although *les douches* came only once in *quinze jours*, such was the terror they inspired that it was necessary for the *planton* to hunt under *paillasses* for people who would have preferred death itself.

Upon remarking that *corvée d'eau* must be excessively disagreeable, I was informed that it had its bright side, viz. that in going to and from the sewer one could easily exchange a furtive signal with the women who always took pains to be at their windows at that moment. Influenced perhaps by this, Harree and Pompom were in the habit of doing their friends' *corvées* for a consideration. The girls, I was further instructed, had their *corvée* (as well as their meals) just after the men; and the miraculous stupidity of the *plantons* had been known to result in the coincidence of the two.

At this point somebody asked me how I had enjoyed my *douche?*

I was replying in terms of unmeasured opprobrium when I was interrupted by that gruesome clanking and rattling which announced the opening of the door. A moment later it was thrown wide, and the beefy-neck stood in the doorway, a huge bunch of keys in his paw, and shouted:

'A la soupe les hommes.'

The cry was lost in a tremendous confusion, a reckless thither-and-hithering of humanity, every one trying to be at the door, spoon in hand, before his neighbour. B. said calmly, extracting his own spoon from beneath his *paillasse*, on which we were seated: 'They'll give you yours downstairs, and when you get it you want to hide it or it'll be pinched'—and in company with Monsieur Bragard, who had refused the morning promenade, and whose gentility would not permit him to hurry when it was a question of such a low craving as hunger, we joined the dancing, roaring throng at the door. I was not too famished myself to be unimpressed by the instantaneous change which had come over The Enormous Room's occupants. Never did Circe herself cast upon men so bestial an enchantment. Among these faces convulsed with utter animalism I scarcely recognized my various acquaintances. The transformation produced by the *planton's* shout was not merely amazing; it was uncanny, and not a little thrilling. These eyes bubbling with lust, obscene grins sprouting from contorted lips, bodies unclenching and clenching in unctuous gestures of complete savagery, convinced me by a certain insane beauty. Before the arbiter of their destinies some thirty creatures, hideous and authentic, poised, cohering in a sole chaos of desire; a fluent and numerous cluster of vital inhumanity. As I contemplated this ferocious and uncouth miracle, this beautiful manifestation of the sinister alchemy of hunger, I felt that the last vestige of individualism was about utterly to disappear, wholly abolished in a gambolling and wallowing throb.

The beefy-neck bellowed:

'Est-ce que vous êtes tous ici?'

A shrill roar of language answered. He looked contemptuously around him, upon the thirty clamouring faces each of which wanted to eat him—puttees, revolver and all. Then he cried:

'Allez, descendez.'

Squirming, jostling, fighting, roaring, we poured slowly through the doorway. Ridiculously. Horribly. I felt like a glorious microbe in huge, absurd din irrevocably swathed. B. was beside me. A little ahead Monsieur Auguste's voice protested. Count Bragard brought up the rear.

When we reached the corridor nearly all the breath was knocked out of me. The corridor being wider than the stairs allowed me to inhale and look around. B. was yelling in my ear:

'Look at the Hollanders and the Belgians! They're always ahead when it comes to food!'

Sure enough: John the Bathman, Harree and Pompom were leading this extraordinary procession. Fritz was right behind them, however, and pressing the leaders hard. I heard Monsieur Auguste crying in his child's voice:

'Si tout-le-monde veut marcher dou-ce-ment nous allons ar-ri-ver plus tôt! Il faut pas faire comme ça!'

Then suddenly the roar ceased. The mêlée integrated. We were marching in orderly ranks. B. said:

'The *Surveillant!'*

At the end of the corridor, opposite the kitchen window, there was a flight of stairs. On the third stair from the bottom stood (teetering a little slowly back and forth, his lean hands joined behind him and twitching regularly, a *képi* tilted forward on his cadaverous head so that its visor almost hid the weak eyes sunkenly peering from under droopy eyebrows, his pompous rooster-like body immaculately attired in a shiny uniform, his puttees sleeked, his *croix* polished)—The Fencer. There was a renovated look about him which made me laugh. Also his pose was ludicrously suggestive of Napoleon reviewing the armies of France.

Our column's first rank moved by him. I expected it to continue ahead through the door and into the open air, as I had myself done in going from *les douches* to *le cour*; but it turned a sharp right and then sharp left, and I perceived a short hall, almost hidden by the stairs. In a moment I had passed the Fencer myself and entered the hall. In another moment I was in a room, pretty nearly square, filled with rows of pillars. On turning into the hall the column had come almost to a standstill. I saw now that the reason for this slowing-down lay in the fact that on entering the room every man in turn passed a table and received a piece of bread from the chef. When B. and I came opposite the table the dispenser of bread smiled pleasantly and nodded to B., then selected a large hunk and pushed it rapidly into B.'s hands with an air of doing something which he shouldn't. B. introduced me, whereupon the smile and selection was repeated.

'He thinks I'm a German,' B. explained in a whisper, 'and that you are a German too.' Then aloud, to the cook: 'My friend here needs a spoon. He just got here this morning and they haven't given him one.'

The excellent person at the bread table hereupon said to me: 'You shall go to the window and say I tell you to ask for spoon and you will catch one spoon'—and I broke through the waiting line, approached the kitchen-window, and demanded of a roguish face within:

'Une cuillère, s'il vous plait.'

The roguish face, which had been singing in a high faint voice to itself, replied critically but not unkindly:

'Vous êtes un nouveau?'

I said that I was, that I had arrived late last night.

It disappeared, reappeared, and handed me a tin spoon and cup, saying:

'Vous n'avez pas de tasse?'—'Non,' I said.

'Tiens. Prends ça. Vite.' Nodding in the direction of the *Surveillant,* who was standing all this time on the stairs behind me.

I had expected from the cook's phrase that something would be thrown at me which I should have to catch, and was accordingly somewhat relieved at the true state of affairs. On re-entering the *salle à manger* I was greeted by many cries and wavings, and looking in their direction perceived *tout le monde* uproariously seated at wooden benches which were placed on either side of an enormous wooden table. There was a tiny gap in one bench where a place had been saved for me by B. with the assistance of Monsieur Auguste, Count Bragard, Harree and several other fellow-convicts. In a moment I had straddled the bench and was occupying the gap, spoon and cup in hand, and ready for anything.

The din was perfectly terrific. It had a minutely large quality. Here and there, in a kind of sonal darkness, solid sincere unintelligible absurd wisps of profanity heavily flickered. Optically the phenomenon was equally remarkable: seated waggingly swaying corpse-like figures, swaggering, pounding with their little spoons, roaring hoarse unkempt. Evidently *Monsieur le Surveillant* had been forgotten. All at once the roar bulged unbearably. The roguish man, followed by the *chef* himself, entered with a suffering waddle, each of them bearing a huge bowl of steaming something. At least six people immediately rose, gesturing and imploring: *'Ici'—'Mais non, ici'—'Mettez le ici—'*

The bearers plumped their burdens carefully down, one at the head of the table and one in the middle. The men opposite the bowls stood up. Every man seized the empty plate in front of him and shoved it into his neighbour's hand; the plates moved toward the bowls, were filled amid uncouth protestations and accusations—*'Mettez plus que ça'—'C'est pas juste, alors'—'Donnez-moi encore des pommes'—'Nom de Dieu, il n'y en a pas assez'—'Cochon, qu'est-ce qu'il veut?'—*'Shut up'—*'Gottverdummer'—*and returned one by one. As each man received his own, he fell upon it with a sudden guzzle. Eventually, in front of me, solemnly sat a faintly-smoking urine-coloured circular broth, in which soggily hung half-suspended slabs of raw potato. Following the example of my neighbours, I too addressed myself to *La Soupe.* I found her luke-warm, completely flavourless. I examined the hunk of bread. It was almost bluish in colour; in taste mouldy, slightly sour. 'If you crumb some into the soup,' remarked B., who had been studying my reactions from the corner of his eye, 'they both taste better.' I tried the experiment. It was a complete success. At least one felt as if one were getting nourishment. Between gulps I smelled the bread furtively. It smelled rather much like an old attic in which kites and other toys gradually are forgotten in a gentle darkness.

B. and I were finishing our soup together when behind and somewhat to the left there came the noise of a lock being manipulated. I turned and saw in one corner of the *salle à manger* a little door, shaking mysteriously. Finally it was thrown open, revealing a sort of minute bar and a little closet filled with what appeared to be groceries and tobacco; and behind the bar, standing in the closet, a husky competent-looking lady. 'It's the canteen,' B. said. We rose, spoon in hand and breadhunk stuck on spoon, and made our way to the lady. I had, naturally, no money; but B. reassured me that before the day was over I should see the *Gestionnaire* and make arrangements for drawing on the supply of ready cash which the gendarmes who took me from Gré had confided to the *Surveillant's* care; eventually I could also draw on my account with Norton-Harjes in Paris; meantime he had *quelques sous* which might well go into *chocolat* and cigarettes. The large lady had a pleasant quietness about her, a sort of simplicity, which made me extremely desirous of complying with B.'s suggestion. Incidentally I was feeling somewhat uncertain in the region of the stomach, due to the unique quality of the lunch which I had just enjoyed, and I brightened at the thought of anything as solid as *chocolat.* Accordingly we purchased (or rather B. did) a *paquet jaune* and a cake of something which was not Menier. And the remaining *sous* we squandered on a glass apiece of red acrid *pinard*, gravely and with great happiness pledging the hostess of the occasion and then each other.

With the exception of ourselves hardly anyone patronized the canteen, noting which I felt somewhat conspicuous. When, however, Harree, Pompom and John the Bathman came rushing up and demanded cigarettes my fears were dispelled. Moreover the *pinard* was excellent.

'Come on! Arrange yourselves!' the bull-neck cried hoarsely as the five of us were lighting up; and we joined the line of fellow-prisoners with their breads and spoons, gaping, belching, trumpeting fraternally, by the doorway.

'Tout le monde en haut!' this *planton* roared.

Slowly we filed through the tiny hall, past the stairs (empty now of their Napoleonic burden), down the corridor, up the creaking, gnarled, damp flights, and (after the inevitable pause in which the escort rattled chains and locks) into The Enormous Room. . . .

Arthur Koestler (1905–   )

The world of the scum

It all began with the food parcels and the canteen. The nourishment provided by the camp was just sufficient to keep a man alive in a state of permanent, aching, stomach-burning hunger, with constant day-dreams of food.
Yet in the same barrack some of the crowd fed on tinned meats, sausage,
bacon, cheese, butter, chocolate, and fruit. The contrast between rich and
poor reached the pungency of a social satire. The dark tunnel of our barrack
became a nightmarish exaggerated model of human society, a kind of dis-
torting mirror.

Some dilettantish attempts to introduce practical Communism were nipped
in the bud: principally because, out of the 200 in our barrack, only about
ten belonged to the moneyed (or, more correctly, the 'parcelled') class—that
is, received food from outside regularly. Besides, the number of the parcels
was limited to one a week, and their weight to 10 lb. maximum. As to the
canteen, those who possessed some cash were only allowed to spend about
10s. a month. Thus, in a general share-out, one man's share would have
amounted to an average of 6 oz. of food per week, or practically nothing.
Besides, only three or four of the regular parcel-receivers were willing to
submit to such an extraordinary sacrifice. The collective sense, as it generally
is, was mainly a privilege of the have-nots.

The attempt at 'socialism'[1] having failed, 'capitalist' corruption and decay
took its inevitable course. In the beginning, for a few cigarettes or a bit of
sausage, one could bribe the cooks to give one hot water for tea, or hire
people to wash one's shirts and polish one's boots; later on, when the *milieu*
had established its rule over the barrack, one could by bribery obtain practically anything: exemption from work, larger living-space, alcoholic drinks,
and protection from denunciation to the authorities.

The *milieu* in our barrack had its recognized leader in the person of
Cyrano, a scarfaced young Spaniard with a high-pitched voice oddly con-
trasting with his sturdy build. He pretended to be a political refugee and
former member of the F.A.I., the Anarchist Federation, and had for the

___

[1]'Socialist' and 'capitalist' in inverted commas, as property in our community included no means of production, only goods for consumption. The pedantry of this
footnote may be excused by the fact that the majority of people still live in a state of
analphabetism as far as the economic functioning of society is concerned.

___

From *Scum of the Earth* by Arthur Koestler. Copyright 1941 by Arthur Koestler, renewed 1969 by Arthur Koestler. Reprinted with permission of the
Macmillan Company and A. D. Peters & Company.

past two years exercised the profession of *maquereau*, or pimp, in the rue du Faubourg Montmartre. We knew this from his friend Ornato, a dark, elegant Italian who had been a cocaine dealer in the same *quartier*, and went about day and night in a conspicuous, bright, and fluffy teddy-bear coat. They had as permanent hanger-on George, a little Armenian *minus habeans* of seventeen, who had made a living in Paris by alternately stealing bicycles and prostituting himself. His beat comprised the public conveniences between the Place Pigalle and Place Blanche, and the permanent amusements fair at the Palais Berlitz.

Cyrano and Ornato had proclaimed themselves *chefs de groupe* when Kuryatchuk was elected barrack chief. How exactly they had managed this nobody remembered clearly afterwards—they went about with some lists amidst the general excitement of the first day, when all the interest was centred on the election of the barrack chief and on the barber question; and next day they were firmly established in their posts. To be *chef de groupe* had considerable advantages: exemption from work, power to settle minor disputes concerning the distribution of vacant places whose tenants were in hospital, and custody of the lists of those temporarily exempted from work by the doctor. As at least one-quarter of the barrack was always ill with influenza and dysentery, and as only a fraction of them could be accommodated in hospital, it became mainly a question of a bribe to Cyrano or Ornato whether one had to join a working squad or was allowed to lie all day on the straw in the barrack. Adjutant Pernod and his staff never bothered about the lists; they found it simpler to rely upon the *chef de baraque* and the *chefs de groupe*, as long as they had the required number of men for work.

But to buy Cyrano's favour—Ornato only played a subsidiary role—was expensive and required a certain diplomacy. One couldn't simply put a box of sardines into his hands and ask to be let off work for a day. A certain code had to be observed, an indirect, roundabout language be used, an atmosphere of confidence and intimacy be created. Only a few had the means and the technique to obtain Cyrano's favour. Besides, he was touchy and proud. I had a row with him in the very first days, and he made life difficult for me, although as an *exempt définitif* he could not force me to work. Later, when Mario was on the verge of collapse and refused to go to see the doctor, I had to come to terms with Cyrano in order to buy Mario a couple of days of rest. The only occasion that I seriously quarrelled with Mario was when he found out about it. I never tried it again. Mario had one *idée fixe*: to avoid any occasion of being humiliated by those who had power over us. This obsession, result of nine years of prison life, determined his conduct in the camp and led him to a kind of masochistic, almost suicidal behaviour; to go on working with a temperature of 103.5; to refuse to write petitions for his release in the flowery French style required in such documents, and even to refuse a written declaration of his loyalty to the Allied cause—he had volunteered for the French Army from the first day of the war—for fear that it might be interpreted as an enforced and not a voluntary political act.

It was the ever-recurring and fatal constellation: the Cyranos and Ornatos and their patrons and *protégés* got on swimmingly in our rubbish heap of a camp, while the Marios and Tamàses played the eternal role of Don Quixote.

Yet one obstacle to Cyrano's prosperous ascent still remained: Kuryatchuk the elephant. Nominally at least he was still *chef de baraque*, and from time to time even his slow-moving brain discovered an irregularity on the lists and put a stop to one of Cyrano's clever combines. Cyrano tried everything to kick him out of the way, but Kuryatchuk just looked down at him with his sleepy eyes and occasionally gave a roar through his proboscis that made the barrack quiver.

One day, in the second month of our stay in Le Vernet, during the midday break, a troop of gendarmes suddenly raided our barrack, pushed everybody out, locked the doors and allowed nobody to approach. We stood around in a crowd, stunned. Then Adjudant Pernod, Fernandel, and the Corsican arrived in a solemn group, followed by Cyrano and Kuryatchuk. The rumour soon went round that they were searching the barrack for stolen goods; actually complaints of thefts had been multiplying during the last fortnight. Ornato remained outside; he moved from group to group in his bright teddy-bear coat and made one or two confidential hints that the search might lead to 'very unexpected results'. After half an hour or so the five emerged into the daylight, the officials looking very official, Cyrano with a triumphant wink, and Kuryatchuk carrying a large bundle in his hands and looking more stupid than ever. He lumbered along behind the staff and disappeared with them in the direction of the office. But Cyrano joined the crowd and, after letting himself be pressed for a while, he informed us confidentially that the 'stolen goods'—some two or three shirts and a few pairs of socks—had been found in the barrack chief's bag.

We suspected at once that the elephant was innocent and that Cyrano had played a dirty trick on him; and even Pernod and his staff guessed that something of the sort must have happened. The investigation was carried out secretly, but we learned that three compatriots of Kuryatchuk, amongst them the opera singer, had testified to having played cards the previous evening on Kuryatchuk's suitcase, which had been emptied for this purpose and found to contain nothing but a dirty pair of pants, strewn with tea-leaves and tobacco. He was acquitted, but nevertheless resigned from his post; he seemed to have taken the suspicion to heart, and henceforth led a shadowy and melancholy existence on his heap of straw in a corner, out of the limelight of public interest.

Against Cyrano nothing could be proved; yet his hopes of becoming Kuryatchuk's successor were cut short by Adjudant Pernod, who, abolishing the election system with a majestic and somewhat unsteady gesture, appointed a Swiss named Storfer, a queer man and a newcomer amongst us, to the post of *chef de baraque*.

Storfer had arrived at the camp only a fortnight before; he was about forty, under middle height and burly, with the twisted, stunted, and cunning face of a peasant from the mountains. He wore khaki trousers and a green hat with a feather which he never took off, not even when asleep. He went about alone, hardly talking to anybody, except to George, the Armenian nancy-boy. The first we learned about him was that he was liable to epileptic fits, as he had one the night after his arrival. The second, that he had spent twelve years in the Foreign Legion, and afterwards worked in a circus. The third, that he was an informer who reported everything that happened in the barrack to the Corsican.

Storfer's nomination inaugurated a new era in the barrack. He had us all in his power by the simple expedient of denouncing anybody he disliked to the gendarmes. His first victim was Cyrano himself, who had remained *chef de groupe* and was in Storfer's way. Cyrano had made a remark about the ceremony of 'saluting the flag'—every morning in turn twenty men were marched to the camp entrance and had to perform a sort of parade while the tricolor was hoisted on the flagpole; they had to get up half an hour earlier than the others, and Cyrano had said something to the effect that this was a bloody nuisance. The remark was made in Storfer's presence. An hour later three Guards came for Cyrano and marched him off. He was kept in jail for three weeks, terribly beaten up and transferred to Section B for having 'insulted the French flag'. We never saw him again.

Having got rid of Cyrano, Storfer methodically developed bribery into a system. We all more or less became his tributaries, according to our means. He 'took' money in any amount, from 10 sous to 100 francs, and bestowed favours accordingly. Cyrano's régime had been old-fashioned, nineteenth-century banditism; Storfer introduced the modern form of racket into our society, with its typical feature of collaboration between the gang and the authorities. For Pernod and his staff, of course, knew what went on, but the advantage of having their own informer as barrack chief outweighed their moral scruples if they had any; their only interest was not to be bothered with anything, and Storfer saw to that.

The new régime brought forth a marked development in the process of class differentiation. The privileges of the parcelled class were no longer confined to food and cigarettes, but gradually extended to housing conditions and the general style of living.

The first member of the plutocracy to have an entire five-man compartment to himself, and a valet to attend to him, was Mr. Goodman, agent of a well-known American armament firm in France. He was of Balkan origin, had worked for the French *Deuxième Bureau*, and was detained under suspicion of being a double agent, which I believe he actually was. There was always vacancies in the barrack, and Goodman, by paying a considerable weekly sum to Storfer, secured exclusive possession of the corner compartment on the upper platform opposite to ours. Parta, his valet, was a little Hungarian salesman who slaved for Goodman as maid-of-all-work in exchange for a share of Goodman's gorgeous meals of tinned foods and an occasional American cigarette or a glass of brandy, smuggled to Goodman by the gendarmes through the intermediary of Storfer.

Parta had transformed Goodman's compartment into a kind of cosy attic. There was no straw on the floor; Goodman slept on a pneumatic mattress and Parta on a palliasse. They had a table—the planks of an old crate nailed together—and stools, and shelves serving as a larder. In the evening they burnt smuggled candles. They had separated their compartment from the adjoining one with brown-paper pinned on to the wooden framework, and from the outer corridor by hanging blankets over a wire. From time to time Goodman gave parties to other members of the plutocracy.

Opposite to Goodman, in the upper corner compartment next to ours, lived Storfer with his two satellites: George, the little Armenian bicycle thief who had become Storfer's brat, and Emil, another Swiss and former *légionnaire*, also homosexual. They too had a table and candles to burn.

So had we. A table, five stools, a larder-shelf and even a bookshelf, all in a space of 2 by 3 yards. The straw was stuffed into five palliasses which we had been sent from home, all neatly piled on top of each other during the daytime. We couldn't afford candles, but we had two lamps made of old tins filled with oil and a wick steadied by a wire hook. We represented the lower ranks of the plutocracy, as between the five of us only two received parcels, which we shared. They usually arrived on Thursday and we had a rigid rationing system to make them last the whole week; every bar of chocolate and every biscuit was counted and divided into five times seven rations, and the skin of the sausages was marked with a scale like a thermometer. The same system of refined economy was applied to space. We had to share 6 square yards between the five of us, and to sit round the table was only possible if we arranged our limbs in one particular way, like a jig-saw puzzle.

The life we led was a proof of man's capacity for adaptation. I think that even the condemned souls in purgatory after a time develop a sort of homely routine. That is, by the way, why most prison memoirs are unreadable. The difficulty of conveying to the reader in his armchair an idea of the nightmare world from which he has emerged makes the author depict the prisoner's state of mind as an uninterrupted continuity of despair. He fears to appear frivolous or to spoil his effect by admitting that even in the depths of misery cheerfulness keeps breaking in.

On the other hand, the above-mentioned *douceurs de la vie,* such as tables, stools, palliasses, and light, were confined to a small fraction of the barrack—about twenty out of 200, and to five compartments out of a total of fifty. They were the five next to the door at the southern end of the barrack. There was Storfer's compartment and ours on the left-hand upper platform and the Eligulashwily clan below us; there was Goodman's compartment and the 'Carluccio group' facing us on the right-hand upper platform and some of the well-to-do White Russians under them. These first 6 yards of the barrack looked like a cross-section through some miniature Japanese hut, very primitive but still quite habitable; the remaining 24 yards were simply a stable, dirty and oppressing, the air unbreathable, for men smell worse than horses.

It was a revolting contrast and apparently irremediable. All the privileges the plutocracy enjoyed were illicit; the tables and stools were made of planks stolen from the Military Administration, candles and oil-lamps were officially prohibited. Their use by a few was tolerated, but it could not be generalized. By all their traditional standards, Fernandel and the Corsican found it natural that Mr. Goodman, who was dressed like a gentleman, or Mr. K., whose name had been 'printed in the papers', should enjoy privileges which Yankel and other have-nots were denied. One of the reasons for the bankruptcy of the European Left was their failure to realize how deep were the mental roots of class distinctions. They thought they could treat as a mere prejudice what in reality had come to be a conditioned reflex of mankind.

The only measure of levelling in which we succeeded was to provide all the inmates of our barrack with blankets and to introduce a weekly collection to improve the soup. The amount collected was spent entirely on potatoes, beans, lentils and noodles—that is, on the same foodstuffs as the soup was made of; all we could do was to make it a little thicker.

In No. 33, the German barrack, conditions were better and the class distinctions less sharp. It was a more homogeneous and more disciplined crowd.

Finally, there was Barrack 32, or the Leper Barrack. Its inmates had been there long before us; it was they whom we had seen on the road to the camp, as a horrifying revelation of the depths of abjectness and misery to which man can be reduced.

If the pauper section of our barrack was a purgatory, No. 32 was the real inferno. It was in complete darkness and the smell was appalling. None of its inhabitants possessed a change of shirt or socks, and many of them had actually sold their last shirt for a packet of cigarettes, and went about naked under a thin and ragged jacket. The barrack was infested with vermin and disease. Outside working hours, its inmates did odd jobs for others, washing their linen for the price of a few slices of bread, mending shoes, cleaning boots. They received no letters and wrote none. They lingered about the camp, picking up cigarette ends out of the mud and from the concrete floors of the latrines, where most were to be found. Even the most wretched in the other hutments looked upon these with a mixture of horror and dismay. . . .

Such, such were the joys

The differences between home and school were more than physical. That bump on the hard mattress, on the first night of term, used to give me a feeling of abrupt awakening, a feeling of: "This is reality, this is what you are up against." Your home might be far from perfect, but at least it was a place ruled by love rather than by fear, where you did not have to be perpetually on your guard against the people surrounding you. At eight years old you were suddenly taken out of this warm nest and flung into a world of force and fraud and secrecy, like a goldfish into a tank full of pike. Against no matter what degree of bullying you had no redress. You could only have defended yourself by sneaking, which, except in a few rigidly defined circumstances, was the unforgivable sin. To write home and ask your parents to take you away would have been even less thinkable, since to do so would have been to admit yourself unhappy and unpopular, which a boy will never do. Boys are Erewhonians: they think that misfortune is disgraceful and must be concealed at all costs. It might perhaps have been considered permissible to complain to your parents about bad food, or an unjustified caning, or some other ill-treatment inflicted by masters and not by boys. The fact that Sim never beat the richer boys suggests that such complaints were made occasionally. But in my own peculiar circumstances I could never have asked my parents to intervene on my behalf. Even before I understood about the reduced fees, I grasped that they were in some way under an obligation to Sim, and therefore could not protect me against him. I have mentioned already that throughout my time at Crossgates I never had a cricket bat of my own. I had been told this was because "your parents couldn't afford it." One day in the holidays, by some casual remark, it came out that they had provided ten shillings to buy me one: yet no cricket bat appeared. I did not protest to my parents, let alone raise the subject with Sim. How could I? I was dependent on him, and the ten shillings was merely a fragment of what I owed him. I realise now, of course, that it is immensely unlikely that Sim had simply stuck to the money. No doubt the matter had slipped his memory. But the point is that I assumed that he had stuck to it, and that he had a right to do so if he chose.

How difficult it is for a child to have any real independence of attitude could be seen in our behaviour towards Bingo. I think it would be true to say that every boy in the school hated and feared her. Yet we all fawned on her in the most abject way, and the top layer of our feelings towards her was a sort of guilt-stricken loyalty. Bingo, although the discipline of the school depended more on her than on Sim, hardly pretended to dispense justice. She was frankly capricious. An act which might get you a caning one day, might next day be laughed off as a boyish prank, or even commended because it "showed you had guts." There were days when everyone cowered before those deepset, accusing eyes, and there were days when she was like a flirtatious queen surrounded by courtier-lovers, laughing and joking, scattering largesse, or the promise of largesse ("And if you win the Harrow History Prize I'll give you a new case for your camera!"), and occasionally even packing three or four favoured boys into her Ford car and carrying them off to a teashop in town, where they were allowed to buy coffee and cakes. Bingo was inextricably mixed up in my mind with Queen Elizabeth, whose relations with Leicester and Essex and Raleigh were intelligible to me from a very early age. A word we all constantly used in speaking of Bingo was "favour." "I'm in good favour," we would say, or "I'm in bad favour." Except for the handful of wealthy or titled boys, no one was permanently in good favour, but on the other hand even the outcasts had patches of it from time to time. Thus, although my memories of Bingo are mostly hostile, I also remember considerable periods when I basked under her smiles, when she called me "old chap" and used my Christian name, and allowed me to frequent her private library, where I first made acquaintance with *Vanity Fair*. The high-water mark of good favour was to be invited to serve at table on Sunday nights when Bingo and Sim had guests to dinner. In clearing away, of course, one had a chance to finish off the scraps, but one also got a servile pleasure from standing behind the seated guests and darting deferentially forward when something was wanted. Whenever one had the chance to suck up, one did suck up, and at the first smile one's hatred turned into a sort of cringing love. I was always tremendously proud when I succeeded in making Bingo laugh. I have even, at her command, written *vers d'occasion*, comic verses to celebrate memorable events in the life of the school.

I am anxious to make it clear that I was not a rebel, except by force of circumstances. I accepted the codes that I found in being. Once, towards the end of my time, I even sneaked to Brown about a suspected case of homosexuality. I did not know very well what homosexuality was, but

I knew that it happened and was bad, and that this was one of the contexts in which it was proper to sneak. Brown told me I was "a good fellow," which made me feel horribly ashamed. Before Bingo one seemed as helpless as a snake before a snake-charmer. She had a hardly varying vocabulary of praise and abuse, a whole series of set phrases, each of which promptly called forth the appropriate response. There was *"Buck* up, old chap!"*, which inspired one to paroxysms of energy; there was "Don't *be* such a fool!" (or, "It's path*e*tic, isn't it?"), which made one feel a born idiot; and there was "It isn't very straight of you, is it?", which always brought one to the brink of tears. And yet all the while, at the middle of one's heart, there seemed to stand an incorruptible inner self who knew that whatever one did—whether one laughed or snivelled or went into frenzies of gratitude for small favours—one's only true feeling was hatred. . . .

Alexander Solzhenitsyn (1918–   )

The cold and the warm

The corridor in the hospital was so clean—it always was—that he was scared to walk along it. The walls were painted a shiny white, and the furniture was all white as well.

But the office doors were shut. The doctors must still be in bed. One of the medics—a young fellow by the name of Nikolay Vdovushkin—was sitting in the orderlies' room at a nice clean desk and he was wearing a nice clean white coat. He was writing something.

There was no one else around.

Shukhov took off his hat, as though this was one of the higher-ups, and in the good old camp fashion, looking at things you weren't supposed to see, he couldn't help noticing that Vdovushkin was writing in neat, straight lines, starting each line right under the one before with a capital letter and leaving a little room at the side. Shukhov saw at once, of course, that this wasn't work but some stuff of his own and none of Shukhov's business.

"Listen, Nikolay Semyonovich, I'm feeling kind of sick," he said, with a hangdog look, as if he was trying to scrounge something.

Vdovushkin looked up from his work, cool and wide-eyed. He wore a white cap, to match his coat, and he had no number tags.

"But why did you wait till now? And why didn't you come yesterday

From *One Day in the Life of Ivan Denisovich* by Alexander Solzhenitsyn. Reprinted by permission of Frederick Praeger, Publishers, Inc. 1963.

evening? You know we can't take people in the morning. We've already sent the sick list to the PPS."

Shukhov knew all this. And he knew it wasn't any easier to get on the sick list in the evening either.

"But the trouble is, Nikolay, it doesn't feel so bad in the evening, when it ought to."

"What's wrong with you?"

"Well, when you get down to it, it's nothing in particular. I just feel rotten all over."

Shukhov was not one of those who's always hanging around the hospital block, and Vdovushkin knew it. But he was allowed to excuse only two men in the morning and he'd already excused them. And their names were on the list under the greenish glass on the table. There was a line drawn under them.

"You should have thought of this before. What do you think you're doing—coming here just before roll call? Here!"

Vdovushkin took one of the thermometers sticking through gauze in a jar, wiped the solution off it, and gave it to Shukhov.

Shukhov sat down on a bench by the wall, keeping on the very edge of it but just far enough in not to tip it over. He didn't choose this awkward place on purpose, but this was how he showed he was out of his depth in the hospital block and didn't expect very much.

Vdovushkin went on writing.

The hospital block was in the most out-of-the-way corner of the compound, and there was no noise from outside. There were no clocks ticking here—the prisoners weren't supposed to have any. The powers that be kept time for them. You didn't even hear a mouse scratching. They'd all been caught by the hospital cat appointed for the purpose.

Shukhov felt odd sitting by a bright lamp in such a clean room, where it was so quiet, and doing nothing for five whole minutes. He studied all the walls, but there was nothing. He looked at his jacket. The number on his chest had gotten a little worn. He'd have to have it redone if he didn't want trouble. He felt his beard. It had gotten pretty rough since that last visit to the bathhouse about ten days ago. But what the hell! There'd be another bath in about three days, and he'd have a shave then. Why waste time waiting in line at the barber's? He didn't have to look his best for anyone.

Then, looking at Vdovushkin's nice white cap, Shukhov remembered the field hospital on the river Lovat, how he'd gone there with an injured jaw and—dope that he was!—returned to his unit of his own free will. And he could have had five whole days in bed!

Now his one dream was to get sick for a couple of weeks, not fatally or anything that needed an operation, but just sick enough to be sent to the hospital. He'd lie there, he thought, for three weeks without moving, and even if the soup they gave you was a little thin it would still be great.

But then Shukhov remembered that there was no peace even in the hospital nowadays. There was a new doctor who'd come with a recent batch of prisoners—Stepan Grigoryevich, a loudmouth know-it-all who never stayed still himself and never let the patients alone either. He'd had the bright idea of putting all the walking cases to work around the hospital, making fences and paths and carrying earth to the flowerbeds. And in the winter there was always snow to clear. He kept saying that work was the best cure for illness.

What he didn't understand was that work has killed many a horse. If he'd put in a little hard work laying bricks, he wouldn't go around shooting off his mouth so much.

Vdovushkin was still writing away. He really was doing something on the side, something that didn't mean much to Shukhov. He was copying out a long poem that he'd given the finishing touches to the day before and had promised to show Stepan Grigoryevich today—the man who believed in work as a cure-all.

This sort of thing could only happen in a camp. It was Stepan Grigoryevich who told Vdovushkin to say he was a medic and then gave him the job. So Vdovushkin started learning how to give injections to poor, ignorant prisoners who would never let it enter their simple, trusting minds that a medic might not be a medic at all. Nikolay had studied literature at the university and had been arrested in his second year. Stepan Grigoryevich wanted him to write the sort of thing here he couldn't write "outside."

The signal for roll call came faintly through the double windows. They were covered by ice. Shukhov sighed and stood up. He still felt feverish, but it looked as though he had no chance to get out of work. Vdovushkin reached for his thermometer and squinted at it.

"Look, it's hard to say—just under ninety-nine. If it were over a hundred, it'd be a clear case. But as things are I can't let you off. Take a chance and stay if you want. If the doctor takes a look at you and thinks you're sick, he'll let you off. But if not, it's the cooler for you. You'd be better off going to work."

Shukhov said nothing. He didn't even nod. He rammed on his cap and went out.

When you're cold, don't expect sympathy from someone who's warm.

The sociology of politics

In the modern world, in which differentiated social institutions have taken the place of what in earlier times were more diffuse structures of power and influence, the study of politics must focus on the state, the institution which claims, to quote Max Weber, "the monopoly of the legitimate use of physical force within a given territory." Hence, modern politics means essentially an activity striving to share power or striving to influence power, either among states or among groups within a state. He who is active in politics strives for power for its own sake or as a means for asserting ideological, economic and other claims. Yet power as such is always unstable; as Rousseau formulated it, "The strongest is never strong enough to be always the master unless he transforms his strength into right, and obedience into duty." Hence, the political process centers to a large extent on political symbols which legitimize systems of power. Political scientists traditionally have focused most of their attention upon the machinery of government. The sociological analysis of politics, on the other hand, concerns the interplay between politics and social structure. It deals with political activities within a broader perspective, stressing the underlying social conditions that affect political decisions. Consequently, the connections between, say, the stratification system and political behavior, or between ethnic cleavages and political processes, have more particularly attracted the attention of political sociologists. These sociologists have emphasized the ways in which a political order as well as specific political behavior—for example voting—must be studied with reference to non-political factors, such as socialization, primary groups, patterns of interaction, and so on. They have also dealt with the role of voluntary associations and political parties in the generation and mobilization of resources which can be brought to bear upon those wielding political power.

The selections attempt to convey a sense of variety of political settings. Theodore Dreiser, in the excerpt from *The Titan*, provides a vivid picture of the operation of urban political machines and ward politics around the turn of the century. Robert Penn Warren, the contemporary novelist, in *All the King's Men*, gives a thinly disguised account of the rise of Huey Long in Louisiana politics in the late twenties; he transcends the limitations of time and place by succeeding in giving us a classic picture of the demagogue. The English Victorian novelist George Meredith sketches in a few rapid strokes some major differences between the political styles of radical, liberals, and Tories. The long excerpt from Ignazio Silone's much neglected *The School for Dictators*, provides an imaginative dissection of the politics of totalitarianism through an imaginary set of conversations between an American aspirant dictator, his "scientific" advisor, and a "cynic" who is plainly the author's *alter ego*. Finally, Arthur Koestler's self-contained story within a story from his major work *Darkness at Noon* conveys within its restricted compass the destructive impact of Stalinist politics, not only on the Western labor movement but on the whole Western system of values.

Theodore Dreiser (1871–1945)

Ward politics, money, and organization

It so happened that by now another election was pending in Chicago, and Hand, along with Schryhart and Arneel—who joined their forces because of his friendship for Hand—decided to try to fight Cowperwood through this means.

Hosmer Hand, feeling that he had the burden of a great duty upon him, was not slow in acting. He was always, when aroused, a determined and able fighter. Needing an able lieutenant in the impending political conflict, he finally bethought himself of a man who had recently come to figure somewhat conspicuously in Chicago politics—one Patrick Gilgan, the same Patrick Gilgan of Cowperwood's old Hyde Park gas-war days. Mr. Gilgan was now a comparatively well-to-do man. Owing to a genial capacity for mixing with people, a close mouth, and absolutely no understanding of, and consequently no conscience in matters of large public import (in so far as they related to the so-called rights of the mass), he was a fit individual to succeed politically. His saloon was the finest in all Wentworth Avenue. It fairly glittered with the newly introduced incandescent lamp reflected in a perfect world of beveled and faceted mirrors. His ward, or district, was full of low, rain-beaten cottages crowded together along half-made streets; but Patrick Gilgan was now a state senator, slated for Congress at the next Congressional election, and a possible successor of the Hon. John J. McKenty as dictator of the city, if only the Republican party should come into power. (Hyde Park, before it had been annexed to the city, had always been Republican, and since then, although the larger city was normally Democratic, Gilgan could not conveniently change.) Hearing from the political discussion which preceded the election that Gilgan was by far the most powerful politician on the South Side, Hand sent for him. Personally, Hand had far less sympathy with the polite moralistic efforts of men like Haguenin, Hyssop, and others who were content to preach morality and strive to win by the efforts of the unco good, than he had with the cold political logic of a man like Cowperwood himself. If Cowperwood could work through McKenty to such a powerful end, he Hand, could find some one else who could be made as powerful as McKenty.

"Mr. Gilgan," said Hand, when the Irishman came in, medium tall, beefy, with shrewd, twinkling gray eyes and hairy hands, "you don't know me—"

"I know *of you* well enough," smiled the Irishman, with a soft brogue. "You don't need an introduction to talk to me."

"Very good," replied Hand, extending his hand. "I know of you, too. Then we can talk. It's the political situation here in Chicago I'd like to discuss with you. I'm not a politician myself, but I take some interest in what's going on. I want to know what you think will be the probable outcome of the present situation here in the city."

Gilgan, having no reason for laying his private political convictions bare to any one whose motive he did not know, merely replied: "Oh, I think the Republicans may have a pretty good show. They have all but one or two of the papers with them, I see. I don't know much outside of what I read and hear people talk."

Mr. Hand knew that Gilgan was sparring, and was glad to find his man canny and calculating.

"I haven't asked you to come here just to be talking over politics in general, as you may imagine, Mr. Gilgan. I want to put a particular problem before you. Do you happen to know either Mr. McKenty or Mr. Cowperwood?"

"I never met either of them to talk to," replied Gilgan. "I know Mr. McKenty by sight, and I've seen Mr. Cowperwood once." He said no more.

"Well," said Mr. Hand, "suppose a group of influential men here in Chicago were to get together and guarantee sufficient funds for a city-wide campaign; now, if you had the complete support of the newspapers and the Republican organization in the bargain, could you organize the opposition here so that the Democratic party could be beaten this fall? I'm not talking about the mayor merely and the principal city officers, but the council, too—the aldermen. I want to fix things so that the McKenty-Cowperwood crowd couldn't get an alderman or a city official to sell out, once they are elected. I want the Democratic party beaten so thoroughly that there won't be any question in anybody's mind as to the fact that it has been done. There will be plenty of money forthcoming if you can prove to me, or, rather, to the group of men I am thinking of, that the thing can be done."

Mr. Gilgan blinked his eyes solemnly. He rubbed his knees, put his thumbs in the armholes of his vest, took out a cigar, lit it, and gazed poetically at the ceiling. He was thinking very, very hard. Mr. Cowperwood and Mr. McKenty, as he knew, were very powerful men. He had always managed to down the McKenty opposition in his ward, and several others adjacent to it, and in the Eighteenth Senatorial District, which he represented. But to be called upon to defeat him in Chicago, that was different. Still, the thought of a large amount of cash to be distributed through him, and the chance of wresting the city leadership from McKenty by the aid of the so-called moral forces of the city, was very inspiring. Mr. Gilgan was a good politician. He loved to scheme and plot and make deals—as much for the fun of it as anything else. Just now he drew a solemn face, which, however, concealed a very light heart.

"I have heard," went on Hand, "that you have built up a strong organization in your ward and district."

"I've managed to hold me own," suggested Gilgan, archly. "But this winning all over Chicago," he went on, after a moment, "now, that's a pretty large order. There are thirty-one wards in Chicago this election, and all but eight of them are nominally Democratic. I know most of the men that are in them now, and some of them are pretty shrewd men, too. This Dowling in council is nobody's fool, let me tell you that. Then there's Duvanicki and Ungerich and Tiernan and Kerrigan—all good men." He mentioned four of the most powerful and crooked aldermen in the city. "You see, Mr. Hand, the way things are now the Democrats have the offices, and the small jobs to give out. That gives them plenty of political workers to begin with. Then they have the privilege of collecting money from those in office to help elect themselves. That's another great privilege." He smiled. "Then this man Cowperwood employs all of ten thousand men at present, and any ward boss that's favorable to him can send a man out of work to him and he'll find a place for him. That's a gre-a-eat help in building up a party following. Then there's the money a man like Cowperwood and others can contribute at election time. Say what you will, Mr. Hand, but it's the two, and five, and ten dollar bills paid out at the last moment over the saloon bars and at the polling-places that do the work. Give me enough money"—and at this noble thought Mr. Gilgan straightened up and slapped one fist lightly in the other, adjusting at the same time his half-burned cigar so that it should not burn his hand—"and I can carry every ward in Chicago, bar none. If I have money enough," he repeated, emphasizing the last two words. He put his cigar back in his mouth, blinked his eyes defiantly, and leaned back in his chair.

"Very good," commented Hand, simply; "but how much money?"

"Ah, that's another question," replied Gilgan, straightening up once more. "Some wards require more than others. Counting out the eight that are normally Republican as safe, you would have to carry eighteen others to have a majority in council. I don't see how anything under ten to fifteen thousand dollars to a ward would be safe to go on. I should say three hundred thousand dollars would be safer, and that wouldn't be any too much by any means."

Mr. Gilgan restored his cigar and puffed heavily the while he leaned back and lifted his eyes once more.

"And how would that money be distributed exactly?" inquired Mr. Hand.

"Oh, well it's never wise to look into such matters too closely," commented Mr. Gilgan, comfortably. "There's such a thing as cutting your cloth too close in politics. There are ward captains, leaders, block captains, workers. They all have to have money to do with—to work up sentiment— and you can't be too inquiring as to just how they do it. It's spent in saloons, and buying coal for mother, and getting Johnnie a new suit here and there. Then there are torch-light processions and club-rooms and jobs to look after. Sure, there's plenty of places for it. Some men may have to be brought into these wards to live—kept in boarding-houses for a week or ten days." He waved a hand deprecatingly.

Mr. Hand, who had never busied himself with the minutiae of politics, opened his eyes slightly. This colonizing idea was a little liberal, he thought.

"Who distributes this money?" he asked, finally.

"Nominally, the Republican County Committee, if it's in charge; actually, the man or men who are leading the fight. In the case of the Democratic party it's John J. McKenty, and don't you forget it. In my district it's me, and no one else."

Mr. Hand, slow, solid, almost obtuse at times, meditated under lowering brows. He had always been associated with a more or less silk-stocking crew who were unused to the rough usage of back-room saloon politics, yet every one suspected vaguely, of course, at times that ballot-boxes were stuffed and ward lodging-houses colonized. Every one (at least every one of any worldly intelligence) knew that political capital was collected from office-seekers, office-holders, beneficiaries of all sorts and conditions under the reigning city administration. Mr. Hand had himself contributed to the Republican party for favors received or about to be. As a man who had been compelled to handle large affairs in a large way he was not inclined to quarrel with this. Three hundred thousand dollars was a large sum, and he was not inclined to subscribe it alone, but fancied that at his recommendation and with his advice it could be raised. Was Gilgan the man to fight Cowperwood? He looked him over and decided—other things being equal—that he was. And forthwith the bargain was struck. Gilgan, as a Republican central committeeman—chairman, possibly—was to visit every ward, connect up with every available Republican force, pick strong, suitable anti-Cowperwood candidates, and try to elect them, while he, Hand, organized the money element and collected the necessary cash. Gilgan was to be given money personally. He was to have the undivided if secret support of all the high Republican elements in the city. His business was to win at almost any cost. And as a reward he was to have the Republican leadership in city and county.

"Anyhow," said Hand, after Mr. Gilgan finally took his departure, "things won't be so easy for Mr. Cowperwood in the future as they were in the past. And when it comes to getting his franchises renewed, if I'm alive, we'll see whether he will or not."

Robert Penn Warren (1905–   )

The voice of the demagogue

The candidate could still stand, at least with one thigh propped against the table. He had begun to talk by this time, too. He had called them his friends in two or three ways and had said he was glad to be there. Now he stood there clutching the manuscript in both hands, with his head lowered like a dehorned cow beset by a couple of fierce dogs in the barnyard, while the sun beat on him and the sweat dropped. Then he took a grip on himself, and lifted his head.

"I have a speech here," he said. "It is a speech about what this state needs. But there's no use telling you what this state needs. You are the state.

From *All the King's Men*, copyright, 1946, by Robert Penn Warren. Reprinted by permission of Harcourt Brace Jovanovich, Inc.

You know what you need. Look at your pants. Have they got holes in the knee? Listen to your belly. Did it ever rumble for emptiness? Look at your crop. Did it ever rot in the field because the road was so bad you couldn't get it to market? Look at your kids. Are they growing up ignorant as you and dirt because there isn't any school for them?"

Willie paused, and blinked around at the crowd. "No," he said, "I'm not going to read you any speech. You know what you need better'n I could tell you. But I'm going to tell you a story."

And he paused, steadied himself by the table, and took a deep breath while the sweat dripped.

I leaned toward Sadie. "What the hell's the bugger up to?" I asked.

"Shut up," she commanded, watching him.

He began again. "It's a funny story," he said. "Get ready to laugh. Get ready to bust your sides for it is sure a funny story. It's about a hick. It's about a red-neck, like you all, if you please. Yeah, like you. He grew up like any other mother's son on the dirt roads and gully washes of a north-state farm. He knew all about being a hick. He knew what it was to get up before day and get cow dung between his toes and feed and slop and milk before breakfast so he could set off by sunup to walk six miles to a one-room, slab-sided schoolhouse. He knew what it was to pay high taxes for that windy shack of a schoolhouse and those gully-washed red-clay roads to walk over— or to break his wagon axle or string-halt his mules on.

"Oh, he knew what it was to be a hick, summer and winter. He figured if he wanted to do anything he had to do it himself. So he sat up nights and studied books and studied law so maybe he could do something about changing things. He didn't study the law in any man's school or college. He studied it nights after a hard day's work in the field. So he could change things some. For himself and for folks like him. I am not lying to you. He didn't start out thinking about all the other hicks and how he was going to do wonderful things for them. He started out thinking of number one, but something came to him on the way. How he could not do something for himself and not for other folks or for himself without the help of other folks. It was going to be all together or none. That came to him.

"And it came to him with the powerful force of God's own lightning on a tragic time back in his own home county two years ago when the first brick schoolhouse ever built in his county collapsed because it was built of politics-rotten brick, and it killed and mangled a dozen poor little scholars. Oh, you know that story. He had fought the politics back of building that schoolhouse of rotten brick but he lost and it fell. But it started him thinking. Next time would be different.

"People were his friends because he had fought that rotten brick. And some of the public leaders down in the city knew that and they rode up to his pappy's place in a big fine car and said how they wanted him to run for Governor."

I plucked Sadie's arm. "You think he's going to—"

"Shut up," she said savagely.

I looked toward Duffy up there on the platform back of Willie. Duffy's face was worried. It was red and round and sweating, and it was worried.

"Oh, they told him," Willie was saying, "and that hick swallowed it. He looked in his heart and thought he might try to change things. In all humility he thought how he might try. He was just a human, country boy, who believed like we have always believed back here in the hills that even the plainest, poorest fellow can be Governor if his fellow citizens find he has got the stuff and the character for the job.

"Those fellows in the striped pants saw the hick and they took him in. They said how MacMurfee was a limber-back and a dead-head and how Joe Harrison was the tool of the city machine, and how they wanted that hick to step in and try to give some honest government. They told him that. But—" Willie stopped, and lifted his right hand clutching the manuscript to high heaven—"do you know who they were? They were Joe Harrison's hired hands and lickspittles and they wanted to get a hick to run to split MacMurfee's hick vote. Did I guess this? I did not. No, for I heard their sweet talk. And I wouldn't know the truth this minute if that woman right there—" and he pointed down at Sadie—"if that woman right there—"

I nudged Sadie and said, "Sister, you are out of a job."

"—if that fine woman right there hadn't been honest enough and decent enough to tell the foul truth which stinks in the nostrils of the Most High!"

Duffy was on his feet, edging uncertainly toward the front of the platform. He kept looking desperately toward the band as though he might signal them to burst into music and then at the crowd as though he were trying to think of something to say. Then he edged toward Willie and said something to him.

But the words, whatever they were, were scarcely out of his mouth before Willie had turned on him. "There!" Willie roared. "There!" And he waved his right hand, the hand clutching the manuscript of his speech. "There is the Judas Iscariot, the lickspittle, the nose-wiper!"

And Willie waved his right arm at Duffy, clutching the manuscript which he had not read. Duffy was trying to say something to him, but Willie wasn't hearing it, for he was waving the manuscript under Duffy's retreating nose and shouting, "Look at him! Look at him!"

Duffy, still retreating, looked toward the band and waved his arms at them and shouted, "Play, play! Play the 'Star-Spangled Banner'!"

But the band didn't play. And just then as Duffy turned back to Willie, Willie made a more than usually energetic pass of the fluttering manuscript under Duffy's nose and shouted, "Look at him, Joe Harrison's dummy!"

Duffy shouted, "It's a lie!" and stepped back from the accusing arm.

I don't know whether Willie meant to do it. But anyway, he did it. He didn't exactly shove Duffy off the platform. He just started Duffy doing a dance along the edge, a kind of delicate, feather-toed, bemused, slow-motion adagio accompanied by arms pinwheeling around a face which was like a surprised custard pie with a hole scooped in the middle of the meringue, and the hole was Duffy's mouth, but no sound came out of it. There wasn't a sound over that five-acre tract of sweating humanity. They just watched Duffy do his dance.

Then he danced right off the platform. He broke his fall and half lay, half sat, propped against the bottom of the platform with his mouth still open. No sound came out of it now, for there wasn't any breath to make a sound.

All of that, and me without a camera.

Willie hadn't even bothered to look over the edge. "Let the hog lie!" he shouted. "Let the hog lie, and listen to me, you hicks. Yeah, you're hicks, too, and they've fooled you, too, a thousand times, just like they fooled me. For that's what they think we're for. To fool. Well, this time I'm going to fool somebody. I'm getting out of this race. You know why?"

He paused and wiped the sweat off his face with his left hand, a flat scouring motion.

"Not because my little feelings are hurt. They aren't hurt, I never felt better in my life, because now I know the truth. What I ought to have known long back. Whatever a hick wants he's got to do for himself. Nobody in a fine automobile and sweet talking is going to do it for him. When I come back to run for Governor again, I'm coming on my own and I'm coming for blood. But I'm getting out now.

"I'm resigning in favor of McMurfee. By God, everything I've said about MacMurfee stands and I'll say it again, but I'm going to stump this state for him. Me and the other hicks, we are going to kill Joe Harrison so dead he'll never even run for dogcatcher in this state. Then we'll see what MacMurfee does. This is his last chance. The time has come. The truth is going to be told and I'm going to tell it. I'm going to tell it over this state from one end to the other if I have to ride the rods or steal me a mule to do it, and no man, Joe Harrison or any other man, can stop me. For I got me a gospel and I—..."

Willie kept his word. He stumped the state for MacMurfee. He didn't ride the rods or buy him a mule or steal him one. But he drove the pants off his pretty good secondhand car over the washboard and through the hub-deep dust and got mired in the black gumbo when a rain came and sat in his car waiting for the span of mules to come and pull him out. He stood on schoolhouse steps, and on the top of boxes borrowed from the drygoods stores and on the seats of farm wagons and on the porches of crossroads stores, and talked. "Friends, red-necks, suckers, and fellow hicks," he would say, leaning forward, leaning at them, looking at them. And he would pause, letting the words sink in. And in the quiet the crowd would be restless and resentful under these words, the words they knew people called them but the words nobody ever got up and called them to their face. "Yeah," he would say, "yeah," and twist his mouth on the word, "that's what you are, and you needn't get mad at me for telling you. Well, get mad, but I'm telling you. That's what you are. And me—I'm one, too. Oh, I'm a red-neck, for the sun has beat down on me. Oh, I'm a sucker, for I fell for that sweet-talking fellow in the fine automobile. Oh, I took the sugar tit and hushed my crying. Oh, I'm a hick and I am the hick they were going to try to use and split the hick vote. But I'm standing here on my own hind legs, for even a dog can learn to do that, give him time. I learned. It took me a time but I learned, and here I am on my own hind legs." And he would lean at them. And demand, "Are you, are you on your hind legs? Have you learned that much yet? You think you can learn that much?"

He told them things they didn't like. He called them the names they didn't like to be called, but always, almost always, the restlessness and resentment died and he leaned at them with his eyes bugging and his face glistening in the hot sunlight or the red light of a gasoline flare. They listened while he told them to stand on their own hind legs. Go and vote, he told them. Vote for MacMurfee this time, he told them, for he is all you have got to vote for. But vote strong, strong enough to show what you can do. Vote him in and then if he doesn't deliver, nail up his hide. "Yeah," he would say, leaning, "yeah, nail him up if he don't deliver. Hand me the hammer and I'll nail him." Vote, he told them. Put MacMurfee on the spot, he told them.

He leaned at them and said, "Listen to me, you hicks. Listen here and lift up your eyes and look on the God's blessed and unflyblown truth. If you've got the brain of a sapsucker left and can recognize the truth when you see it. This is the truth; you are a hick and nobody ever helped a hick but the hick himself. Up there in town they won't help you. It is up to you and God, and God helps those who help themselves!"

He gave them that, and they stood there in front of him, with a thumb hooked in the overall strap, and the eyes under the pulled down hat brim squinting at him as though he were something spied across a valley or cove, something they weren't quite easy in the mind about, too far away to make out good, or a sudden movement in the brush seen way off yonder across the valley or across the field and something might pop out of the brush, and under the eyes the jaw revolving worked the quid with a slow, punctilious, immitigable motion, like an historical process. And Time is nothing to a hog, or to History, either. They watched him, and if you watched close you might be able to see something beginning to happen. They stand so quiet, they don't even shift from one foot to the other—they've got a talent for being quiet, you can see them stand on the street corner when they come to town, not moving or talking, or see one of them squatting on his heels by the road, just looking off where the road drops over the hill—and their squinched eyes don't flicker off the man up there in front of them. They've got a talent for being quiet. But sometimes the quietness stops. It snaps all of a sudden, like a piece of string pulled tight. One of them sits quiet on the bench, at the brush-arbor revival, listening, and all of a sudden he jumps up and lifts up his arms and yells, "Oh, Jesus! I have seen His name!" Or one of them presses his finger on the trigger, and the sound of the gun surprised even him.

Willie is up there. In the sun, or in the red light of the gasoline flare. "You ask me what my program is. Here it is, you hicks. And don't you forget it. Nail 'em up! Nail up Joe Harrison. Nail up anybody who stands in your way. Nail up MacMurfee if he don't deliver. Nail up anybody who stands in your way. You hand me the hammer and I'll do it with my own hand. Nail 'em up on the barn door! And don't fan away the bluebottles with any turkey wing!"

It was Willie, all right. It was the fellow with the same name.

MacMurfee was elected. Willie had something to do with it, for the biggest vote was polled in the sections Willie had worked that they had any record of. But all the time MacMurfee didn't quite know what to make of Willie. He shied off him at first, for Willie had said some pretty hard things about him, and then when it did look as though Willie would make an impression, he shilly-shallied. And in the end Willie got on his hind legs and said how the MacMurfee people were offering to pay his expenses but he was on his own, he wasn't MacMurfee's man, even if he was saying to vote for MacMurfee. He was paying his way, he said, even if he had to put another mortgage on his pappy's farm and the last one it would hold. Yes, and if there was anybody who couldn't afford two dollars to pay his poll tax and came to him and said it straight out, he, Willie Stark, would pay that tax out of money he had got by mortgaging his pappy's farm. That was how much he believed in what he was saying.

———   **George Meredith (1828–1909)**   ———

The politics of radicalism

The brisk Election-day, unlike that wearisome but instructive canvass of the Englishman in his castle vicatim, teaches little; and its humours are those of a badly-managed Christmas pantomime without a columbine—old tricks, no graces. Nevertheless, things hang together so that it cannot be passed over with a bare statement of the fact of the Liberal-Radical defeat

From *Beauchamp's Career* by George Meredith (1874).

in Bevisham: the day was not without fruit in time to come for him whom his commiserating admirers of the non-voting sex all round the borough called the poor dear commander. Beauchamp's holiday out of England had incited Dr. Shrapnel to break a positive restriction put upon him by Jenny Denham, and actively pursue the canvass and the harangue in person; by which conduct, as Jenny had foreseen, many temperate electors were alienated from Commander Beauchamp, though no doubt the Radicals were made compact: for they may be the skirmishing faction—poor scattered fragments, none of them sufficiently downright for the other; each outstripping each; rudimentary emperors, elementary prophets, inspired physicians, nostrum-devouring patients, whatsoever you will; and still here and there a man shall arise to march them in close columns, if they can but trust him; in perfect subordination, a model even for Tories while they keep shoulder to shoulder. And to behold such a disciplined body is intoxicating to the eye of a leader accustomed to count ahead upon vapourish abstractions, and therefore predisposed to add a couple of noughts to every tangible figure in his grasp. Thus will a realized fifty become five hundred or five thousand to him: the very sense of numbers is instinct with multiplication in his mind; and those years far on in advance, which he has been looking to with some fatigue to the optics, will suddenly and rollickingly roll up to him at the shutting of his eyes in a temporary fit of gratification. So, by looking and by not looking, he achieves his phantom victory—embraces his cloud.

Dr. Shrapnel conceived that the day was to be a Radical success; and he, a citizen aged and exercised in reverses, so rounded by the habit of them indeed as to tumble and recover himself on the wind of the blow that struck him, was, it must be acknowledged, staggered and cast down when he saw Beauchamp drop, knowing full well his regiment had polled to a man. Radicals poll early; they would poll at cockcrow if they might; they dance on the morning. As for their chagrin at noon, you will find descriptions of it in the poet's Inferno. They are for lifting our clay soil on a level of Archimedes, and are not great mathematicians. They have perchance a foot of our earth, and perpetually do they seem to be producing an effect, perpetually does the whole land roll back on them. You have not surely to be reminded that it hurts them: the weight is immense. Dr. Shrapnel, however, speedily looked out again on his vast horizon, though prostrate. He regained his height of stature with no man's help. Success was but postponed for a generation or two. Is it so very distant? Gaze on it with the eye of our parent orb! 'I shall not see it here; you may,' he said to Jenny Denham; and he fortified his outlook by saying to Mr. Lydiard that the Tories of our time walked, or rather stuck, in the track of the Radicals of a generation back. Note, then, that Radicals, always marching to the triumph, never taste it; and for Tories it is Dead Sea fruit, ashes in their mouths! Those Liberals, those temporisers, compromisers, a concourse of atoms! glorify themselves in the animal satisfaction of sucking the juice of the fruit, for which they pay with their souls. They have no true cohesion, for they have no vital principle.

Mr. Lydiard being a Liberal, bade the doctor not to forget the work of the Liberals, who touched on Tory and Radical with a pretty steady swing, from side to side, in the manner of the pendulum of a clock, which is the clock's life, remember that. The Liberals are the professors of the practicable in politics.

'A suitable image for time-servers!' Dr. Shrapnel exclaimed, intolerant of any mention of the Liberals as a party, especially in the hour of Radical discomfiture, when the fact that compromisers should exist exasperates men of a principle. 'Your Liberals are the band of Pyrrhus, an army of bastards, mercenaries professing the practicable for pay. They know us as the motive force, the Tories the resisting power, and they feign to aid us in battering our enemy, that they may stop the shock. We fight, they profit. What are they? Stranded Whigs, crotchetty manufacturers; dissentient religionists; the half-minded, the hare-hearted; the I would and I would not—shifty creatures, with youth's enthusiasm decaying in them, and a purse beginning to jingle; fearing lest we do too much for safety, our enemy not enough for safety. They a party? Let them take action and see! *We* stand a thousand defeats; they not one! Compromise begat them. Once let them leave sucking the teats of compromise, yea, once put on the air of men who fight and die for a cause, they fly to pieces. And whither the fragments? Chiefly, my friend, into the *Tory* ranks. Seriously so I say. You between future and past are for the present—but with the hunted look behind of all godless livers in the present. You Liberals are Tories with foresight, Radicals without faith. You start, in fear of Toryism, on an errand of Radicalism, and in fear of Radicalism to Toryism you draw back. There is your pendulum-swing!'

Ignazio Silone (1900–   )

How to become a dictator

Thomas The Cynic: There is a chapter in the Bible to which I should like to call your attention on the way back to your hotel. You will perhaps remember that in the Book of Judges there is a description of the Fascist *coup d'état* carried out by Abimelech, the illegitimate son of Gideon, who paid and armed gangs of beggars and ne'er-do-wells for the purpose, and with their aid killed one by one "upon one stone," as the Bible says, the

---

threescore and ten sons whom Gideon had by his legal wives. The story of this misdeed is immediately followed by a really illuminating parable concerning the politician's vocation. With your permission I shall refresh your memory of it. One day, the parable relates, the trees went forth to anoint a king over them; and they said unto the olive tree, Reign thou over us. But the olive tree said unto them, Should I leave my fatness, wherewith by me they honor God and man, and go hither and thither, ever on the move, to be promoted over the trees? And the trees said to the fig tree, Come thou and reign over us. But the fig tree said unto them, Should I forsake my sweetness and my good fruit and bustle perpetually about the streets of the world, busying myself from morning to night with politics? Then said the trees unto the vine, Come thou and reign over us. And the vine said unto them, Should I leave my wine, which cheereth God and man, and go to be promoted over the trees and talk foolishness? Then said the trees unto the bramble, Come thou and reign over us. And the bramble said unto the trees, If in truth ye anoint me king over you, then come and put your trust in my shadow: and if not, let fire come out of the bramble and reduce you all to ashes. This extraordinary parable is rarely commented upon by the priests, and then they always misinterpret it, because it is, in my opinion, one of the most subversive in the Bible. The bramble is an utterly useless plant, and that is why it is fated to rule over the others.

Professor Pickup: The bramble of the Old Testament reminds me of the crown of thorns of the New. Do you think every crown is a crown of thorns?

Mr. W.: I certainly think that in comparison with the ordinary, normal man, whose interests and pleasures are manifold, your true politician can well be compared to the bramble, which is useless and sterile in comparison with the olive tree, the fig tree and the vine. In reality it belongs to a different species, a more self-centered species. Your born politician is unable to adapt himself to ordinary life, and when he eventually finds the path that leads to power, as he gradually advances along it, everything else becomes indifferent to him and his outlook becomes more and more restricted and concentrated on one, single ambition that is the source of all his joy and all his anguish. If there are politicians who desire power for the sake of realizing their ideals, as it is called, or for the sake of enriching themselves or acquiring women and racehorses and such things, they deserve our contempt, because such people are nothing but miserable intruders. Your true politician desires power for its own sake, and all his voluptuousness lies in the exercise of power. For him ideas, reforms, peace, war, women, horses are merely the instruments, the incidentals of power and not the reverse. A little while ago, while you two were arguing, I started wondering whether I was by any chance an extraordinary man. I assure you, without any false modesty, that I am not yet crazy enough to believe it, though when everybody else believes it I shall probably end by believing it too. Were the men who are now in power in Rome, Berlin, Moscow, really extraordinary men? All those who knew them in boyhood and youth deny it, and I have no difficulty in accepting what they say. The future dictators were not in the least extraordinary, but then they were not ordinary, either. The ordinary man is a hotchpotch of desires. He likes eating, drinking, smoking, sleeping, keeping a canary, playing tennis, going to the theater, being well dressed, having children, stamp-collecting, doing his job, and many other things besides. That is the reason he remains a nobody; he spreads himself over so many little things. But the born politician wants nothing but power and lives for nothing but power. It is his bread, his meat, his work, his hobby, his lover, his canary, his theater, his stamp-album, his life-sentence. The fact that all his powers and energies are concentrated upon one thing makes it easy for him to appear extraordinary in the eyes of the masses and thus become a leader, in the same way as those who really concentrate on God become saints and those who only live for money become millionaires.

Thomas The Cynic: That is why dictators, saints, and millionaires appear inhuman to the ordinary man. If everybody lived like them the world would be a lunatic asylum. The refusal of the olive tree, the fig tree, and the vine to become professional politicians in the parable well illustrates the ordinary man's repugnance and horror of such abnormality. Note that their answer is not that they do not wish to enter politics, but that they cannot enter politics, because, thank Heaven, their nature is to be useful and to live an ordered life and not to run hither and thither, talking foolishness, making an uproar in the market-place and giving themselves airs. You know there are many people who maintain that Hitler and Mussolini, for example, are mad, mad in the clinical sense. That is a thoroughly intelligible thing for normal, useful, and decent people to believe. (Incidentally, if an ordinary person looked out of the window and saw us arguing in the street at this time of night the first thing he would say would most likely be, "The poor fellows must be mad!") But if democratic politicians and Socialists hold the same opinion of the dictators it only proves that they themselves are amateurs and intruders on the political scene. The Fascist leader's superiority over his opponents consists above all in this: that he aspires to power, only to power, and to nothing but power. Whether he is on the side of the capitalists or the workers, the church or the devil, is a secondary matter to him. What matters to him is power. The fact that his whole life is politics gives him an incalculable advantage over his opponents, who are often good family men, sometimes even gentlemen, encumbered with "ideas," "principles," and "programs," tied to special interests, and bound to answer for their actions to congresses and committees; moreover, apart from politics, they often have other passions, such as literature or hunting or fishing or music or golf or pipe-smoking, not to speak of the passions which fill the pages of the picture papers. Politics for the Fascist leader is not a profession but a passion in the true sense of the word; an exclusive and totalitarian passion, like every true passion (the word means concentration of all the emotions on a single object, and comes from the Latin *passio*, which means suffering). As for the voluptuous satisfaction the dictators derive from the exercise of power, which largely compensates them for the lack of ordinary pleasures, one can detect it in the faces of Hitler, Mussolini, and Stalin in the rare photographs of those great men in which, perhaps in a moment of absentmindedness or in a fleeting interval between two poses, they have allowed themselves to be taken off their guard. Their expression on such occasions strikingly suggests the look of the half-drunk toper raising a glass of champagne to his lips, or the adulterous woman, blissfully tired, leaving the bedroom. The Greeks had no doubts about the voluptuous nature of tyranny. (In Plato's *Republic* Socrates asks, "Perhaps it was because of this that even in ancient times Eros was called a tyrant?") Even the sadism of tyrants obviously derives from Eros. In 1914, during the riots in the Ancona district, Mussolini wrote: "We record events with a little of that legitimate joy which the artist must feel in front of his own creation." He was then a militant Socialist, but that turn of phrase revealed the future Fascist leader. Pilsudski confesses in his war memories that for him "there was much poetical emotion in the first battles of the war, as in a first love-affair or a first kiss." Hitler's *Mein Kampf* is a very dismal book as a whole, but the description of the first meeting at which the stormtroopers beat up their opponents is noticeably gay. "The crop of bloodshed sprang up marvelously," Goering wrote in his book, *Aufbau einer Nation*, in connection with the Nazi *putsch* of 1923. There is a peasant proverb which says, "Rain in April means wine in the barrel." Stalin's character is mistrustful and retiring, but the only personal confidence of his that I have read is as follows: "There is nothing more delightful," he once said, "than to arrange in detail a trap into which one's enemy will inevitably fall, and then to go to bed."

Professor Pickup: Do you believe that a passion for a thing is sufficient to enable you to get it? I know many men who live only for money, but not one of them has become a millionaire.

Thomas The Cynic: Many are called, but few are chosen.

Professor Pickup: Let us leave aside the multitude who are called and concern ourselves only with the small band of the chosen, of the elect. That will bring us back from psychology to politics. Who are the elect? Neo-Sociology gives a clear and indisputable answer (truth is only truth if it is indisputable). Neo-Sociology tells us that the elect are the elect. Nothing could be clearer than that. All the theological speculation of the Calvinists on the problem of predestination failed to reach a clearer conclusion. But for you, who are devoid of all metaphysical sense, this is not sufficient. You want to know what distinguishes the true leader from the false . . .

Mr. W.: Here we are back at the hotel. If you are not sleepy, let us go up to our room and continue the discussion there. But we shall have to talk quietly in order not to disturb the neighbors.

Professor Pickup: What distinguishes the true leader from the false? You will not mind if I, too, refer to my anthology of quotations. I have here my *Breviary of Fascist Thought,* containing the answers to all the political problems of our time. What does Pilsudski tell us apropos of the leader? "For ten years I sought to discover in what the essence of leadership lay; in the midst of danger as Clausewitz says; in the midst of uncertainty, and finally, as I myself put it, in the midst of eternal and insoluble conflicts which one must cut through like a Gordian knot with the sword of decision and the sword of command." Max Weber distinguishes three types of sovereignty (each with its appropriate type of leader): "legal" sovereignty, "traditional" sovereignty, and "charismatic" sovereignty. It is the third of these which is of interest to us. "Charismatic" sovereignty, according to Weber, depends on "an individual's extraordinary sanctity or heroism or typicalness, or the things done or put forward by him." The mere presence of a "charismatic" leader is enough to rouse the enthusiasm of the people, in whose eyes he is the country's savior and only hope. He has disciples, sends messages, and speaks like an oracle. He is Stirner's "Individual," whose individualism, however, is not a-social and anarchist but authoritarian in character. "One man must emerge from the multitude of perhaps millions of people," Hitler wrote in *Mein Kampf,* "who with irresistible force will extract rock-firm beliefs from the flux of popular ideas and will fight for those beliefs, maintaining that they and they alone are right, until a granite rock of single-minded faith and will arises from the inconstant sea of unrestricted thought." Elsewhere in the same book he writes: "He who wishes to be a leader bears the ultimate responsibility and the heaviest responsibility as well as his supreme and unbounded authority. He who is not fit for this or is too cowardly to bear the consequences of his actions is not suitable to be a leader. Only a hero is suited to leadership." The true leader rules the masses and does not let himself be ruled by them. Nietzsche painted a vivid picture of the false leader. "The recipe for what the masses call a great man is easily given," he wrote. "Under all circumstances must they be given something that they find very pleasing, or they must be given the idea that they would find it very pleasing, and then they must be given it. But under no circumstances must they be given it at once; it must be struggled for with the greatest expenditure of effort, or at least seem to be so struggled for. The masses must be made to believe that a powerful, yea, an indomitable will is at work; at least such a will must seem to be at work.

Everyone admires a strong will, because nobody has one and everyone assures himself that if he had one there would be no limits to circumscribe him and his egoism. If it appears that such a strong will, instead of listening to its own appetites, is bringing about something very pleasing to the masses, more wonder is aroused and people congratulate themselves. Moreover let him (i.e., the owner of this will) have all the characteristics of the masses. The less ashamed they are in front of him the more popular he will be. Thus let him be violent, envious, domineering, designing, fawning, creeping, conceited, everything according to circumstances." The picture Nietzsche paints us of the true hero, the Superman, is very different, although you will readily understand that my ideas do not entirely coincide with his. Your true leader carries within himself the certainty of his own mission. One November evening at Fontainebleau Napoleon asked Cardinal Fesch, who had been deploring the arrest of Pius VII, if he could see anything in the clouded sky, and when the cardinal answered that he could not, Napoleon said: "Very well, you had better learn to hold your peace; for I can see my star." You will agree that it is difficult to answer a man who sees stars that are invisible to others. At the age of fifteen Henri de Saint-Simon ordered his servant to say to him every morning when he woke up, "Get up, *M. le Comte,* because you have great things to do." Later he sent Louis XVIII a letter that began with the words: "Prince, listen to the voice of God, Who talks through my mouth."

Mr. W.: Have you much more to read from your *Breviary,* professor?

Thomas The Cynic: In these discussions I wish to refrain as much as possible from answering quotation with quotation. Nothing is more ridiculous in my opinion than for men who are discussing contemporary facts to be everlastingly searching for explanations in dead authors instead of examining and analyzing what is in front of their eyes. Nevertheless, sometimes I shall be forced to quote, and for two reasons in particular. In the first place we shall often be discussing facts which have been so travestied by propaganda that your knowledge of them is bound to be imperfect. In these cases it will be necessary to correct your erroneous impressions and quote my sources in doing so. In the second place I shall sometimes find myself dealing with older ideas which have often been explained in the past but are no longer current because they are inconvenient to the propagandists; and when I recall them, so that they may enlighten us today, it is only just that I should attribute them to their rightful authors, so that they may get their due and I may not seem to be decking myself out in borrowed plumage. Your story about Count Henri de Saint-Simon suggests an interesting point, my dear professor. Why did he order his servant to repeat those words to him every morning? After all, he might have written them on a piece of paper and put it at his bedside or suspended it from the ceiling by a string so that it hung right over his nose. But neither of these stratagems would have been so effective. The servant was necessary because to a certain extent he represented society. "Individual greatness is always a social function," Trotsky has written. You cannot have a king without subjects or a leader without those who are willing to be led. We shall not arrive at any clear understanding of the dictator's function if we confine ourselves solely to the consideration of his personality, as we have been doing so far. We shall have also to consider the relations between the dictator and the masses. It is in the stormy vicissitudes of these that the multitude of those who are called is thinned down into the little band of the chosen. In connection with this you will notice how significant is the agreement between the thought of the divine Plato and the more recent discoveries of Freud. The Greeks believed that it was not the tyrant who made the slave, but the slave who made the tyrant, just as in certain primitive forms of life the subject is determined by the object. ("It is not the fish that takes the worm but the worm that takes the fish.") Every generation has the government it deserves. Have free peoples ever submitted to tyranny or servile peoples enjoyed liberty for long? In the *Republic* Plato describes how the various forms of government decay and succeed one another and how from extreme democracy there often arises its opposite, tyranny. He calls the demagogues who helped inflame the unruly passions of youth *tyrannopoioi*, tyrant-makers, and a "tyrannical" generation that which promoted the moral and political disorder of a city, thus facilitating a *coup d'état* by some adventurer. This fundamental idea of the intimate relationship between the organization of society and the way its members feel and behave, and the consequent internal significance of facts which are apparently entirely external and violent, such as the seizure of power by a band of ruffians, was for a long time lost sight of by students of political science, who laid all stress on the initiative, the energy, the will of the leader, as if he were all-important and as if the masses remained entirely passive or simply did not count. The ancient Greek idea is confirmed and amplified by the discoveries of modern psychology. In the years of infancy and adolescence, the external constraint represented by the father-figure, at first no doubt the real father and later, perhaps, a schoolmaster, a priest, or a policeman, is gradually absorbed and incorporated within us as a kind of moral supreme court which imposes itself on the self and the ego, the conscious and the unconscious mind. Freud calls it the ego-ideal or super-ego, and we end by adopting it so thoroughly that we feel it to be a part of ourselves. If a boy in whom this phenomenon has taken place is still afraid of disobeying his father even though there is not the slightest risk of discovery, it is not so much from fear of punishment as from fear of his own internal judge. This psychological mechanism, which is common to all mankind, plays a decisive part in the relations between a political leader and the people. The individuals who compose the people incorporate the leader-figure into their own ego-ideal, making it completely a part of themselves. At the same time they completely transfigure their leader (the real leader, that is to say, and not the leader inside them) bestowing upon him all the qualities desired by their ego-ideal. Thus a complete psychological exchange takes place. On the one hand the leader is introjected by his followers and becomes an integral part of their psychological make-up, the "better," the "ideal" part, while on the other their ego-ideal is externalized, projected outside them and incarnated in him. Thanks to this psychological process, by which the masses identify themselves completely with their leader, all the individuals of whom the masses consist, even the humblest and most wretched among them—I should say, especially the humblest and most wretched among them—are able to dismiss their own wretchedness and helplessness and take an illusory revenge on life; at the same time the leader's personality is promptly made to transcend the mediocrity of his real ego and is endowed with all the qualities which millions of poor devils would dearly love to have themselves, and he rockets up to the skies surrounded with the halo of a national hero, a mythical savior. He is the individualized product of a great collective dream. All that is required is for the Pope to declare him "a special envoy of Providence," and the fiction is complete. Those who escape the collective hypnosis and try to discuss or criticize him, or recall his origins, his misspent youth, his limited education, his cowardice, his inadaptability to ordinary life, are wasting their time, because there is very little connection between what the present leader of Italian Fascism, for example, represents in the imagination of many Italians and foreigners and the Mr. Benito Mussolini of the pre-war years. True, the first *fasci* were founded by this Mr. Benito Mussolini, but it was Fascism that created the Duce, investing the rather commonplace personality of the former Benito Mussolini with the virtues, failings, and aspirations of the ego-ideal of millions of Italians. If you attempt to criticize the Duce or discuss his character or behavior "objectively" with a convinced Fascist you expose yourself to the same sort of difficulties as you would if you entered a church and said: "Can't you see, my good woman, that the statue of St. Anthony before which you are kneeling lacks even artistic value and is a worthless piece of *papier maché?*" The good woman would scratch your eyes out. Criticizing the leader in the presence of a true Fascist is equivalent to attacking his greatest pride, the source from which he draws comfort and consolation to alleviate the difficulties of real life. He will react to you as though you had tried to stab him to the heart. The closeness of identification between the leader and the masses explains the solidarity of the Fascist organizations. Does the leader say and do today the very opposite of what he was saying and doing yesterday: It makes no difference, because the strongest tie that binds him to the masses is not a political idea or a political program. "If my leader acts in this manner, it must be right!" the rank-and-file Fascist thinks; and since he believes that he has not had the personal success in life he deserves only because he is not clever or cunning enough, his ego-ideal makes him proud to believe that "his" leader is so clever and cunning and so skillful at deceiving his enemies by frequent changes of policy. The Fascist leader is not only a political leader, he is not even first and foremost a political leader; first and foremost he takes the place of the father in the childish mind of the masses, the father who is protector, breadwinner, judge, master, and guide. Hence the Fascist leader's enormous advantage over the democratic politician, whom the electors generally see every four or five years at election times, that is, if they see him at all.

Arthur Koestler

The politics of stalinism

Two years ago the Party had called up the workers of the world to fight the newly established dictatorship in the heart of Europe by means of a political and economic boycott. No goods coming from the enemy's country should be bought, no consignments for its enormous armament industry should be allowed to pass. The sections of the Party executed these orders with enthusiasm. The dock workers in the small port refused to load or unload cargoes coming from that country or destined for it. Other trade unions joined them. The strike was hard to carry through; conflicts with the police resulted in wounded and dead. The final result of the struggle was still uncertain when a little fleet of five curious, old-fashioned black cargo boats sailed into the port. Each of them had the name of a great leader of the Revolution painted on its stern, in the strange alphabet used "over there," and from their bows waved the flag of the Revolution. The striking workers greeted them with enthusiasm. They at once began to unload the cargo. After several hours it came to light that the cargo consisted of certain rare minerals and was destined for the war industry of the boycotted country.

The dockers' section of the Party immediately called a committee meeting, where people came to blows. The dispute spread through the movement all over the country. The reactionary Press exploited the event with derision. The police ceased their attempts to break the strike, proclaimed their neutrality and let the harbour workers decide for themselves whether they would unload the cargo of the curious black fleet or not. The Party leadership called the strike off and gave orders to unload the cargo. They gave reasonable explanations and cunning argument for the behaviour of the Country of the Revolution, but few were convinced. The section split; the majority of the old members left. For months the Party led the shadow of an existence; but gradually, as the industrial distress of the country grew, it regained its popularity and strength.

Two years had passed. Another hungry dictatorship in the south of Europe began a war of plunder and conquest in Africa. Again the Party called for a boycott. They received an even more enthusiastic response than on the previous occasion. For this time the governments themselves in nearly every country in the world had decided to cut off the aggressor's supply of raw materials.

Without raw materials and particularly without petrol, the aggressor would be lost. This was the state of affairs, when again the curious little black fleet set out on her way. The biggest of the ships bore the name of a man who had raised his voice against war and had been slain; at their mastheads waved the flag of the Revolution and in their holds they carried the petrol for the aggressor. They were only a day's journey away from this port, and Little Loewy and his friends knew as yet nothing of their approach. It was Rubashov's task to prepare them for it.

On the first day he had said nothing—only felt his ground. On the morning of the second day the discussion began in the Party meeting-room.

This room was big, bare, untidy and furnished with that lack of care which made the Party's offices in every town in the world look exactly alike. It was partly a result of poverty, but chiefly of an ascetic and gloomy tradition. The walls were covered with old election posters, political slogans and typed notices. In one corner stood a dusty old duplicator. In another lay a heap of old clothes destined for the families of strikers; next to them piles of yellowing leaflets and brochures. The long table consisted of two parallel planks laid over a couple of trestles. The windows were smeared with paint as in an unfinished building. Over the table a naked electric bulb hung on a cord from the ceiling, and next to it a sticky paper fly-catcher. Round the table sat hunchbacked little Loewy, ex-wrestler Paul, the writer Bill and three others.

Rubashov spoke for some time. The surroundings were familiar to him; their traditional ugliness made him feel at home. In these surroundings he was again fully convinced of the necessity and utility of his mission and could not understand why, in the noisy pub the night before, he had had that feeling of uneasiness. He explained objectively and not without warmth the state of things, without as yet mentioning the practical object of his coming. The world boycott against the aggressor had failed because of the hypocrisy and greed of the European governments. Some of them still kept up an appearance of sticking to the boycott, the others not even that. The aggressor needed petrol. In the past the Country of the Revolution had covered a considerable part of this need. If now it stopped the supplies, other countries would greedily spring into the breach: indeed they asked nothing better than to push the Country of the Revolution from the world markets. Romantic gestures of that sort would only hamper the development of industry Over There, and with it the revolutionary movement all over the world. So the inference was clear.

Paul and the three dock-hands nodded. They were slow thinkers; everything the comrade from Over There was telling them sounded quite convincing; it was only a theoretical discourse, of no immediate consequence to them. They did not see the actual point he was aiming at; none of them thought of the black flotilla which was approaching their harbour. Only Little Loewy and the writer with the twisted face exchanged a quick glance. Rubashov noticed it. He finished a shade more drily, without warmth in his voice:

"That is really all I had to tell you as far as principle is concerned. You are expected to carry out the decisions of the C.C. and to explain the ins and outs of the matter to the politically less developed comrades, if any of them should have any doubts. For the moment I have no more to say."

There was silence for a minute. Rubashov took his pince-nez off and lit a cigarette. Little Loewy said in a casual tone of voice:

"We thank the speaker. Does anybody wish to ask any question?"

Nobody did. After a while one of the three dock workers said awkwardly:

"There is not much to be said to it. The comrades Over There must know what they are about. We, of course, must continue to work for the boycott. You can trust us. In our port nothing will get through for the swine."

His two colleagues nodded. Wrestler Paul confirmed: "Not here," made a bellicose grimace and waggled his ears for fun.

For a moment Rubashov believed he was faced by an oppositional faction; he only realized gradually that the others had really not grasped the point. He looked at Little Loewy, in the hope that he would clear up the misunderstanding. But Little Loewy held his eyes lowered and was silent. Suddenly the writer said with a nervous twitch:

"Couldn't you choose another harbour this time for your little transactions? Must it always be us?"

The dockers looked at him in surprise; they did not understand what he meant by "transaction"; the idea of the small black fleet which was approaching their coast through mist and smoke was further than ever from their minds. But Rubashov had expected this question:

"It is both politically and geographically advisable," he said. "The goods will be conveyed from here by land. We have, of course, no reason to keep anything secret: still, it is more prudent to avoid a sensation which the reactionary Press might exploit."

The writer again exchanged a glance with Little Loewy. The dock-hands looked at Rubashov uncomprehendingly; one could see them working it out slowly in their heads. Suddenly Paul said in a changed, hoarse voice:

"What, actually, are you talking about?"

They all looked at him. His neck was red, and he was looking at Rubashov with bulging eyes. Little Loewy said with restraint:

"Have you only just noticed?"

Rubashov looked from one to the other, and then said quietly:

"I omitted to tell you the details. The five cargo boats of the Commissariat for Foreign Trade are expected to arrive tomorrow morning, weather permitting."

Even now it took several minutes before they had all understood. Nobody said a word. They all looked at Rubashov. Then Paul stood up slowly, flung his cap to the ground, and left the room. Two of his colleagues turned their heads after him. Nobody spoke. Then Little Loewy cleared his throat and said:

"The Comrade speaker has just explained to us the reasons for this business: if they do not deliver the supplies, others will. Who else wishes to speak?"

The docker who had already spoken shifted on his chair and said:

"We know that tune. In a strike there are always people who say: if I don't do the work, someone else will take it. We've heard enough of that. That's how blacklegs talk."

Again there was a pause. One heard outside the front door being slammed by Paul. Then Rubashov said:

"Comrades, the interests of our industrial development Over There come before everything else. Sentimentality does not get us any further. Think that over."

The docker shoved his chin forward and said:

"We have already thought it over. We've heard enough of it. You Over There must give the example. The whole world looks to you for it. You talk of solidarity and sacrifice and discipline, and at the same time you use your fleet for plain blacklegging."

At that Little Loewy lifted his head suddenly; he was pale; he saluted Rubashov with his pipe and said low and very quickly:

"What the comrade said is also my opinion. Has anyone anything further to say? The meeting is closed."

Rubashov limped out of the room on his crutches. Events followed their prescribed and inevitable course. While the little old-fashioned fleet was entering the harbour, Rubashov exchanged a few telegrams with the competent authorities Over There. Three days later the leaders of the dockers' section were expelled from the Party and Little Loewy was denounced in the official Party organ as an *agent provocateur*. Another three days later Little Loewy had hanged himself.

Urban sociology

The city, wrote Robert Park, "is something more than a congeries of individual men and of social conveniences . . . something more, also, than a mere constellation of institutions and administrative devices. . . . The city is, rather, a state of mind, a body of customs and traditions, and of the organized attitudes and sentiments that inhere in these customs and are transmitted with this tradition." Urban sociologists have tended to live up to Park's injunction. They have not only tried to analyze the spatial patterns of the city, its economic and demographic structures and processes, its status order and institutional arrangements, they have also attempted to understand what characterizes urbanism as a way of life. They have attempted to study the ecology of the city but they have also asked: what kind of men live in the city? What type of personality adaptation, what mental attitudes are fostered in it? What is the character of the interpersonal relationship among urbanites?

Urban styles of life, when contrasted to their rural counterparts, typically involve a multiplicity of contacts with a variety of persons rather than a limited number of relationships with relatively few types of persons. The resultant segmentalization of human relationships in the city has struck many observers. People in the city are more widely differentiated among each other because the city offers more differentiated roles than does a rural civilization. The city levels traditional distinctions that have grown up in the countryside; it is hence a great emancipator. It allows the emergence of personal life styles and non-conformist behavior under the cover of that anonymity which it so readily provides. It fosters sophistication and rationality, cultural diversity and inventiveness, at the same time as it also may lead to a loosening of the bonds of community and the rise of *anomie*. As the city erodes traditional rhythms of human life, it creates its own mechanical rhythm and imposes it upon its denizens. The clock, the train schedule and the traffic light may govern the life of the city dweller with as tyrannical a force as the prescribed routines of tradition may govern the life of his rural brothers.

Many observers of the modern industrial city, as it emerged in the nineteenth century, were especially struck by its glaring extremes of opulence and poverty. This is what struck Herman Melville when he described Liverpool in the autobiographical narrative *Redburn* (1849). The Victorian poet James Thomson, not unmindful of poverty and misery from which he suffered himself, chose to dwell on the loneliness, the shallowness, the despair which seemed to him to characterize city life styles in his gloomy and deeply pessimistic poem "The City of the Dreadful Night." In contrast, the English essayist Thomas De Quincey as an observer emphasizes the powerful rhythms of the city in the passages from his *Autobiographical Sketches* which are here reprinted. He describes ways in which the city's energy radiates from its core and dominates the surrounding countryside. Jules Romains, the contemporary French novelist, shows in his major series of books, *Men of Good Will*, a great sensibility for city life styles and the ecological patterns of urban agglomerations. Romains, it may be noted, was a student of sociology at the Sorbonne, and is one of the most self-conscious sociological novelists of our day; the passages here reprinted rank among the best characterizations of a modern city. Honoré de Balzac remains to this day the most complete chronicler of the varieties of urban experience, as evidenced in this selection from *The Girl with the Golden Eyes*.

Herman Melville

The shame of liverpool

In going to our boarding-house, the Sign of the Baltimore Clipper, I generally passed through a narrow street called "Launcelott's-Hey," lined with dingy, prison-like cotton warehouses. In this street, or rather alley, you seldom see any one but a truck-man, or some solitary old warehouse-keeper, haunting his smoky den like a ghost.

Once, passing through this place, I heard a feeble wail, which seemed to come out of the earth. It was but a strip of crooked side-walk where I stood; the dingy wall was on every side, converting the mid-day into twilight; and not a soul was in sight. I started, and could almost have run, when I heard that dismal sound. At last I advanced to an opening which communicated downward with deep tiers of cellars beneath a crumbling old warehouse; and there, some fifteen feet below the walk, crouching in nameless squalor, with her head bowed over, was the figure of what had been a woman. Her blue arms folded to her livid bosom two shrunken things like children, that leaned toward her, one on each side. At first, I knew not whether they were alive or dead. They made no sign; they did not move or stir; but from the vault came that soul-sickening wail.

I made a noise with my foot, which, in the silence, echoed far and near; but there was no response. Louder still; when one of the children lifted its head, and cast upward a faint glance; then closed its eyes, and lay motionless. The woman also, now gazed up, and perceived me; but let fall her eye again. They were dumb and next to dead with want. How they had crawled into that den, I could not tell; but there they had crawled to die. At that moment I never thought of relieving them; for death was so stamped in their glazed and unimploring eyes, that I almost regarded them as already no more. I stood looking down on them, while my whole soul swelled within me; and I asked myself, What right had any body in the wide world to smile and be glad, when sights like this were to be seen? It was enough to turn the heart to gall; and make a man-hater of a Howard. For who were these ghosts that I saw? Were they not human beings? A woman and two girls? With eyes, and lips, and ears like any queen? with hearts which, though they did not pound with blood, yet beat with a dull, dead ache that was their life.

At last, I walked on toward an open lot in the alley, hoping to meet there some ragged old women, whom I had daily noticed groping amid

From *Redburn* by Herman Melville (1849).

foul rubbish for little particles of dirty cotton, which they washed out and sold for a trifle.

I found them; and accosting one, I asked if she knew of the persons I had just left. She replied, that she did not; nor did she want to. I then asked another, a miserable, toothless old woman, with a tattered strip of coarse baling stuff round her body. Looking at me for an instant, she resumed her raking in the rubbish, and said that she knew who it was that I spoke of; but that she had no time to attend to beggars and their brats. Accosting still another, who seemed to know my errand, I asked if there was no place to which the woman could be taken. "Yes," she replied, "to the church-yard." I said she was alive, and not dead.

"Then she'll never die," was the rejoinder. "She's been down there these three days, with nothing to eat;—that I know myself."

"She desarves it," said an old hag, who was just placing on her crooked shoulders her bag of pickings, and who was turning to totter off, "that Betsy Jennings desarves it—was she ever married? tell me that."

Leaving Launcelott's-Hey, I turned into a more frequented street; and soon meeting a policeman, told him of the condition of the woman and the girls.

"It's none of my business, Jack," said he. "I don't belong to that street."

"Who does, then?"

"I don't know. But what business is it of yours? Are you not a Yankee?"

"Yes," said I, "but come, I will help you remove that woman, if you say so."

"There, now, Jack, go on board your ship and stick to it; and leave these matters to the town."

I accosted two more policemen, but with no better success; they would not even go with me to the place. The truth was, it was out of the way, in a silent, secluded spot; and the misery of the three outcasts, hiding away in the ground, did not obtrude upon any one.

Returning to them, I again stamped to attract their attention; but this time, none of the three looked up, or even stirred. While I yet stood irresolute, a voice called to me from a high, iron-shuttered window in a loft over the way; and asked what I was about. I beckoned to the man, a sort of porter, to come down, which he did; when I pointed down into the vault.

"Well," said he, "what of it?"

"Can't we get them out?" said I, "haven't you some place in your warehouse where you can put them? have you nothing for them to eat?"

"You're crazy, boy," said he; "do you suppose, that Parkins and Wood want their warehouse turned into a hospital?"

I then went to my boarding-house, and told Handsome Mary of what I had seen; asking her if she could not do something to get the woman and girls removed; or if she could not do that, let me have some food for them. But though a kind person in the main, Mary replied that she gave away enough to beggars in her own street (which was true enough) without looking after the whole neighborhood.

Going into the kitchen, I accosted the cook, a little shriveled-up old Welsh-woman, with a saucy tongue, whom the sailors called Brandy-Nan; and begged her to give me some cold victuals, if she had nothing better, to take to the vault. But she broke out in a storm of swearing at the miserable occupants of the vault, and refused. I then stepped into the room where our dinner was being spread; and waiting till the girl had gone out, I snatched some bread and cheese from a stand, and thrusting it into the bosom of my frock, left the house. Hurrying to the lane, I dropped the food down into the vault. One of the girls caught at it convulsively, but fell back, apparently fainting; the sister pushed the other's arm aside, and took the bread in her hand; but with a weak uncertain grasp like an infant's. She placed it to her mouth; but letting it fall again, murmuring faintly something like "water." The woman did not stir; her head was bowed over, just as I had first seen her.

Seeing how it was, I ran down toward the docks to a mean little sailor tavern, and begged for a pitcher; but the cross old man who kept it refused, unless I would pay for it. But I had no money. So as my boarding-house was some way off, and it would be lost time to run to the ship for my big iron pot; under the impulse of the moment, I hurried to one of the Boodle Hydrants, which I remembered having seen running near the scene of a still smoldering fire in an old rag house; and taking off a new tarpaulin hat, which had been loaned to me that day, filled it with water.

With this, I returned to Launcelott's-Hey; and with considerable difficulty, like getting down into a well, I contrived to descend with it into the vault; where there was hardly space enough left to let me stand. The two girls drank out of the hat together; looking up at me with an unalterable, idiotic expression, that almost made me faint. The woman spoke not a word, and did not stir. While the girls were breaking and eating the bread, I tried to lift the woman's head; but, feeble as she was, she seemed bent upon holding it down. Observing her arms still clasped upon her bosom, and that something seemed hidden under the rags there, a thought crossed my mind, which impelled me forcibly to withdraw her hands for a moment; when I caught a glimpse of a meager little babe, the lower part of its body thrust into an old bonnet. Its face was dazzlingly white, even in its squalor; but the closed eyes looked like balls of indigo. It must have been dead some hours.

The woman refusing to speak, eat, or drink, I asked one of the girls who they were, and where they lived; but she only stared vacantly, muttering something that could not be understood.

The air of the place was now getting too much for me; but I stood deliberating a moment, whether it was possible for me to drag them out of the vault. But if I did, what then? They would only perish in the street, and here they were at least protected from the rain; and more than that might die in seclusion.

I crawled up into the street, and looking down upon them again, almost repented that I had brought them any food; for it would only tend to prolong their misery, without hope of any permanent relief: for die they must very soon; they were too far gone for any medicine to help them. I hardly know whether I ought to confess another thing that occurred to me as I stood there; but it was this—I felt an almost irresistible impulse to do them the last mercy, of in some way putting an end to their horrible lives; and I should almost have done so, I think, had I not been deterred by thoughts of the law. For I well knew that the law, which would let them perish of themselves without giving them one cup of water, would spend a thousand pounds, if necessary, in convicting him who should so much as offer to relieve them from their miserable existence.

The next day, and the next, I passed the vault three times, and still met the same sight. The girls leaning up against the woman on each side, and the woman with her arms still folding the babe, and her head bowed. The first evening I did not see the bread that I had dropped down in the morning; but the second evening, the bread I had dropped that morning remained untouched. On the third morning the smell that came from the vault was such, that I accosted the same policeman I had accosted before, who was patrolling the same street, and told him that the persons I had spoken to him about were dead, and he had better have them removed. He looked as if he did not believe me, and added, that it was not his street.

When I arrived at the docks on my way to the ship, I entered the guard-house within the walls, and asked for one of the captains, to whom I told the story; but, from what he said, was led to infer that the Dock Police was distinct from that of the town, and this was not the right place to lodge my information.

I could do no more that morning, being obliged to repair to the ship; but at twelve o'clock, when I went to dinner, I hurried into Launcelott's-Hey, when I found that the vault was empty. In place of the woman and children, a heap of quick-lime was glistening.

I could not learn who had taken them away, or whither they had gone; but my prayer was answered—they were dead, departed, and at peace.

But again I looked down into the vault, and in fancy beheld the pale, shrunken forms still crouching there. Ah! what are our creeds, and how do we hope to be saved? Tell me, oh Bible, that story of Lazarus again, that I may find comfort in my heart for the poor and forlorn. Surrounded as we are by the wants and woes of our fellow-men, and yet given to follow our own pleasures, regardless of their pains, are we not like people sitting up with a corpse, and making merry in the house of the dead?

I might relate other things which befell me during the six weeks and more that I remained in Liverpool, often visiting the cellars, sinks, and hovels of the wretched lanes and courts near the river. But to tell of them, would only be to tell over again the story just told; so I return to the docks.

The old women described as picking dirty fragments of cotton in the empty lot, belong to the same class of beings who at all hours of the day are to be seen within the dock walls, raking over and over the heaps of rubbish carried ashore from the holds of the shippings.

As it is against the law to throw the least thing overboard, even a rope yarn; and as this law is very different from similar laws in New York, inasmuch as it is rigidly enforced by the dock-masters; and, moreover, as after discharging a ship's cargo, a great deal of dirt and worthless dunnage remains in the hold, the amount of rubbish accumulated in the appointed receptacles for depositing it within the walls is extremely large, and is constantly receiving new accessions from every vessel that unlades at the quays.

Standing over these noisome heaps, you will see scores of tattered wretches, armed with old rakes and picking-irons, turning over the dirt, and making as much of a rope-yarn as if it were a skein of silk. Their findings, nevertheless, are but small; for as it is one of the immemorial perquisites of the second mate of a merchant ship to collect, and sell on his own account, all the condemned "old junk" of the vessel to which he belongs, he generally takes good heed that in the buckets of rubbish carried ashore, there shall be as few rope-yarns as possible.

In the same way, the cook preserves all the odds and ends of pork-rinds and beef-fat, which he sells at considerable profit; upon a six months' voyage frequently realizing thirty or forty dollars from the sale, and in large ships, even more than that. It may easily be imagined, then, how desperately driven to it must these rubbish-pickers be, to ransack heaps of refuse which have been previously gleaned.

Nor must I omit to make mention of the singular beggary practiced in the streets frequented by sailors; and particularly to record the remarkable army of paupers that beset the docks at particular hours of the day.

At twelve o'clock the crews of hundreds and hundreds of ships issue in crowds from the dock gates to go to their dinner in the town. This hour is seized upon by the multitudes of beggars to plant themselves against the outside of the walls, while others stand upon the curbstone to excite the charity of the seamen. The first time that I passed through this long lane of pauperism, it seemed hard to believe that such an array of misery could be furnished by any town in the world.

Every variety of want and suffering here met the eye, and every vice showed here its victims. Nor were the marvelous and almost incredible shifts and stratagems of the professional beggars, wanting to finish this picture of all that is dishonorable to civilization and humanity.

Old women, rather mummies, drying up with slow starving and age;

young girls, incurably sick, who ought to have been in the hospital; sturdy young boys, hollow-eyed and decrepit; and puny mothers, holding up puny babes in the glare of the sun, formed the main features of the scene.

But these were diversified by instances of peculiar suffering, vice, or art in attracting charity, which, to me at least, who had never seen such things before, seemed to the last degree uncommon and monstrous.

I remember one cripple, a young man rather decently clad, who sat huddled up against the wall, holding a painted board on his knees. It was a picture intending to represent the man himself caught in the machinery of some factory, and whirled about among spindles and cogs, with his limbs mangled and bloody. This person said nothing, but sat silently exhibiting his board. Next him, leaning upright against the wall, was a tall, pallid man, with a white bandage round his brow, and his face cadaverous as a corpse. He, too, said nothing; but with one finger silently pointed down to the square of flagging at his feet, which was nicely swept, and stained blue, and bore this inscription in chalk:

> I have had no food for three days;
> My wife and children are dying.

Farther on lay a man with one sleeve of his ragged coat removed, showing an unsightly sore; and above it a label with some writing.

In some places, for the distance of many rods, the whole line of flagging immediately at the base of the wall, would be completely covered with inscriptions, the beggars standing over them in silence.

But as you passed along these horrible records, in an hour's time destined to be obliterated by the feet of thousands and thousands of wayfarers, you were not left unassailed by the clamorous petitions of the more urgent applicants for charity. They beset you on every hand; catching you by the coat; hanging on, and following you along; and, for *Heaven's sake*, and for *God's sake*, and for *Christ's sake*, beseeching of you but one ha'penny. If you so much as glanced your eye on one of them, even for an instant, it was perceived like lightning, and the person never left your side until you turned into another street, or satisfied his demands. Thus, at least, it was with the sailors; though I observed that the beggars treated the town's people differently.

I can not say that the seamen did much to relieve the destitution which three times every day was presented to their view. Perhaps habit had made them callous; but the truth might have been that very few of them had much money to give. Yet the beggars must have had some inducement to infest the dock walls as they did.

As an example of the caprice of sailors, and their sympathy with suffering among members of their own calling, I must mention the case of an old man, who every day, and all day long, through sunshine and rain, occupied a particular corner, where crowds of tars were always passing. He was an uncommonly large, plethoric man, with a wooden leg, and dressed in the nautical garb; his face was red and round; he was continually merry; and with his wooden stump thrust forth, so as almost to trip up the careless wayfarer, he sat upon a great pile of monkey jackets, with a little depression in them between his knees, to receive the coppers thrown him. And plenty of pennies were tost into his poorbox by the sailors, who always exchanged a pleasant word with the old man, and passed on, generally regardless of the neighboring beggars.

The first morning I went ashore with my shipmates, some of them greeted him as an old acquaintance; for that corner he had occupied for many long years. He was an old man-of-war's man, who had lost his leg at the battle of Trafalgar; and singular to tell, he now exhibited his wooden one as a genuine specimen of the oak timbers of Nelson's ship, the *Victory*.

Among the paupers were several who wore old sailor hats and jackets, and claimed to be destitute tars; and on the strength of these pretensions demanded help from their brethren; but Jack would see through their disguise in a moment, and turn away, with no benediction.

As I daily passed through this lane of beggars, who thronged the docks as the Hebrew cripples did the Pool of Bethesda, and as I thought of my utter inability in any way to help them, I could not but offer up a prayer, that some angel might descend, and turn the waters of the docks into an elixir, that would heal all their woes, and make them, man and woman, healthy and whole as their ancestors, Adam and Eve, in the garden.

Adam and Eve! If indeed ye are yet alive and in heaven, may it be no part of your immortality to look down upon the world ye have left. For as all these sufferers and cripples are as much your family as young Abel, so, to you, the sight of the world's woes would be a parental torment indeed.

————   **James Thomson (1834–1882)**   ————

The city as nightmare

What men are they who haunt these fatal glooms,
    And fill their living mouths with dust to death,
And make their habitations in the tombs,
    And breathe eternal sighs with mortal breath,

From *The City of Dreadful Night* by James Thomson (1874).

And pierce life's pleasant veil of various error
To reach that void of darkness and old terror
  Wherein expire the lamps of hope and faith?

They have much wisdom yet they are not wise,
  They have much goodness yet they do not well,
(The fools we know have their own Paradise,
  The wicked also have their proper Hell);
They have much strength but still their doom is stronger,
Much patience but their time endureth longer,
  Much valour but life mocks it with some spell.

They are most rational and yet insane:
  An outward madness not to be controlled;
A perfect reason in the central brain,
  Which has no power, but sitteth wan and cold,
And sees the madness, and foresees as plainly
The ruin in its path, and trieth vainly
  To cheat itself refusing to behold.

And some are great in rank and wealth and power,
  And some renowned for genius and for worth;
And some are poor and mean, who brood and cower
  And shrink from notice, and accept all dearth
Of body, heart and soul, and leave to others
All boons of life: yet these and those are brothers,
  The saddest and the weariest men on earth.

        .   .   .   .

Wherever men are gathered, all the air
  Is charged with human feeling, human thought;
Each shout and cry and laugh, each curse and prayer,
  Are into its vibrations surely wrought;
Unspoken passion, wordless meditation,
Are breathed into it with our respiration;
  It is with our life fraught and overfraught.

So that no man there breathes earth's simple breath,
  As if alone on mountains or wide seas;
But nourishes warm life or hastens death
  With joys and sorrows, health and foul disease,
Wisdom and folly, good and evil labours,
Incessant of his multitudinous neighbours;
  He in his turn affecting all of these.

That City's atmosphere is dark and dense,
    Although not many exiles wander there,
With many a potent evil influence,
    Each adding poison to the poisoned air;
Infections of unutterable sadness,
Infections of incalculable madness,
    Infections of incurable despair.

Thomas De Quincey (1785–1859)

The powers and rhythms of london

It was a most heavenly day in May of this year (1800), when I first beheld and first entered this mighty wilderness, the city—no! not the city, but the nation—of London. Often since then, at distances of two and three hundred miles or more from this colossal emporium of men, wealth, arts, and intellectual power, have I felt the sublime expression of her enormous magnitude in one simple form of ordinary occurrence—viz., in the vast droves of cattle, suppose upon the great north roads, all with their heads directed to London, and expounding the size of the attracting body, together with the force of its attractive power, by the never ending succession of these droves, and the remoteness from the capital of the lines upon which they were moving. A suction so powerful, felt along radii so vast, and a consciousness, at the same time, that upon other radii still more vast, both by land and by sea, the same suction is operating, night and day, summer and winter, and hurrying for ever into one centre the infinite means needed for her infinite purposes, and the endless tributes to the skill or to the luxury of her endless population, crowds the imagination with a pomp to which there is nothing corresponding upon this planet, either amongst the things that have been, or the things that are. Or, if any exception there is, it must be sought in ancient Rome. We, upon this occasion, were in an open carriage, and, chiefly (as I imagine) to avoid the dust, we approached London by rural lanes, where any such could be found, or, at least, along by-roads, quiet and shady, collateral to the main roads. In the mode of approach, we missed some features of the sublimity belonging to any of the common approaches upon a main road; we missed the whirl and the uproar, the tumult and the agitation, which continually thicken and thicken throughout the last dozen miles before you reach the suburbs. Already at three stages' distance (say, 40 miles from London), upon some of the greatest roads, the dim presenti-

---

"The City of London" from *Autobiographical Sketches* by Thomas De Quincey (1834–1853).

ment of some vast capital reaches you obscurely, and like a misgiving. This blind sympathy with a mighty but unseen object, some vast magnetic range of Alps, in your neighbourhood, continues to increase, you know not how. Arrived at the last station for changing horses, Barnet, suppose, on one of the north roads, or Hounslow on the western, you no longer think (as in all other places) of naming the next stage; nobody says, on pulling up, "Horses on to London"—that would sound ridiculous; one mighty idea broods over all minds, making it impossible to suppose any other destination. Launched upon this final stage, you soon begin to feel yourself entering the stream as it were of a Norwegian *maelstrom;* and the stream at length becomes the rush of a cataract. What is meant by the Latin word *trepidatio?* Not anything peculiarly connected with panic; it belongs as much to the hurrying to and fro of a coming battle, as of a coming flight; to a marriage festival as much as to a massacre; *agitation* is the nearest English word. This *trepidation* increases both audibly and visibly at every half-mile, pretty much as one may suppose the roar of Niagara and the thrilling of the ground to grow upon the senses in the last ten miles of approach, with the wind in its favour, until at length it would absorb and extinguish all other sounds whatsoever. Finally, for miles before you reach a suburb of London such as Islington, for instance, a last great sign and augury of the immensity which belongs to the coming metropolis forces itself upon the dullest observer, in the growing sense of his own utter insignificance. Everywhere else in England, you yourself, horses, carriage, attendants (if you travel with any), are regarded with attention, perhaps even curiosity: at all events you are seen. But, after passing the final post-house on every avenue to London, for the latter ten or twelve miles, you become aware that you are no longer noticed: nobody sees you; nobody hears you; nobody regards you; you do not even regard yourself. In fact, how should you at the moment of first ascertaining your own total unimportance in the sum of things—a poor shivering unit in the aggregate of human life? Now, for the first time, whatever manner of man you were or seemed to be starting, squire or "squireen," lord or lordling, and however related to that city, hamlet, or solitary house, from which yesterday or to-day you slipped your cable—beyond disguise you find yourself but one wave in a total Atlantic, one plant (and a parasitical plant besides, needing alien props) in a forest of America.

These are feelings which do not belong by preference to thoughtful people—far less to people merely sentimental. No man was left to himself for the first time in the streets, as yet unknown, of London, but he must have been saddened and mortified, perhaps terrified, by the sense of desertion and utter loneliness which belong to his situation. No loneliness can be like that which weighs upon the heart in the centre of faces never-ending, without voice or utterance from him; eyes innumerable, that have "no speculation" in their orbs which *he* can understand; and hurrying figures of men and women weaving to and fro, with no apparent purposes intelligible to a stranger, seeming like a mask of maniacs, or, oftentimes, like a pageant of phantoms. The great length of the streets in many quarters of London; the continual opening of transient glimpses into other vistas equally far-stretching, going off at right angles to the one which you are traversing; and the murky atmosphere which, settling upon the remoter end of every long avenue, wraps its termination in gloom and uncertainty; all these are circumstances aiding that sense of vastness and illimitable proportions which for ever brood over the aspect of London in its interior. Much of the feeling which belongs to the outside of London, in its approaches for the last few miles, I had lost, in consequence of the stealthy route of by-roads, lying near Uxbridge and Watford, through which we crept into the suburbs. But for that reason, the more abrupt and startling had been the effect of emerging somewhere into the Edgeware Road, and soon afterwards into the very streets of London itself;—through *what* streets, or even what quarter of London, is now totally obliterated from my mind, having perhaps never been comprehended. All that I remember is one monotonous awe and blind sense of mysterious grandeur and Babylonian confusion, which seemed to pursue and to invest the whole equipage of human life, as we moved for nearly two hours through streets; sometimes brought to anchor for ten minutes or more, by what is technically called a "lock," that is, a line of carriages of every description inextricably massed and obstructing each other, far as the eye could stretch; and then, as if under an enchanter's rod, the "lock" seemed to thaw; motion spread with the fluent race of light or sound through the whole icebound mass, until the subtle influence reached *us* also; who were again absorbed into the great rush of flying carriages; or, at times, we turned off into some less tumultuous street, but of the same mile-long character; and finally, drawing up about noon, we alighted at some place, which is as little within my distinct remembrance as the route by which we reached it.

——————— **Jules Romains (1885–   )** ———————

Paris, the scene and the setting

In the centre of the city the mass movements of evening, those long ascensions towards the north and towards the east, like an interminable drawing of breath, were barely beginning. Activity had deserted the inside of the

Reprinted from *Men of Good Will* by Jules Romains, by permission of Alfred A. Knopf, Inc. Copyright 1933 by Alfred A. Knopf, Inc.

Bourse and the banks and was diminishing on the floors of business buildings, but only to increase and thicken in the streets. The shops were lighting up. The noise of the capital curled itself into knots. In the rue Lamarck, Louis Bastide, insinuating his hoop between fussy visitors to Paris and hawkers of medallions, was on the run again—a child coming down to merge once more into the mass of the city, where night was sparkling into birth.

Sirens hooted. The station clocks pointed to five o'clock. Four, seven, eleven express trains were on their way to Paris. The four which creeping along far away had barely emerged from the provinces. They had just left the last big cities which Paris allows to grow at a certain distance away from her. They stake out around her a circle which is like the shape of her shadow. As soon as you enter it, impalpably Paris has begun.

Three other expresses, much nearer, were crossing the countryside— impregnated with Paris and subject to her, but still beautiful, in the slanting rays of the russet sun. They were just reaching the second circle—the one which is drawn, a dozen leagues away from Notre-Dame, by the chief towns of the old land of Ile-de-France.

The four expresses which ran ahead of the others were already approaching the inner suburbs, slowing down as they plunged into them. One was coming from Lyons, another from Lille, a third from Bordeaux, and a fourth from Amsterdam.

Part of the centre of the city was beginning to relax. A brisk stream of vehicles was flowing towards the west, and a continuous swarming of pedestrians filled all the arteries which lead from the Place de la Concorde to the Bastille. It was the hour when the proportion of wealthy people in the streets is the highest; when the big shops, with their pitiless lights, are full of women; when women seem everywhere happier and more numerous than men; when, in the churches, there is a faint murmur of prayers by candlelight alone; and when the children of the poorer quarters chase one another shouting along the sidewalks.

In the Metro stations travellers, with one ear cocked for the approaching rumble of a train, were studying the map, looking for a street. Others, when they saw them doing so, noticed the map and looked at it too. For the first time, perhaps, they realized what the shape of the city was like, and really thought about it. They were surprised to discover which way such-and-such a boulevard ran, how big such-and-such a district was.

Cab-drivers and taxi-drivers were picking up fares and listening to the names of streets hitherto unknown to them. Then Paris unfolded in their heads, in their whole consciousness—a tangible Paris, made up of lines that were alive, of distances which were something that you actually felt; a Paris soaked with movement like a sponge and distorted by the perpetual flux of things that approached and receded. Suddenly, in this Paris which they identified with themselves, a street stung them somewhere quite definite, and they went after it as though it were an itch.

In the offices of the Prefecture, at the end of slatternly corridors, men in sleeve-guards were adding up births, cases of diphtheria, accidents caused by horse-drawn vehicles and by motor-vehicles, square yards of asphalt roadway, hundredweights of meat on the hoof, Metro tickets reckoned by station and by line, net costs of passenger miles. They bent like anatomists over a bloodless Paris, and sliced long strips of figures off her.

The people in the eleven expresses were thinking about Paris. Those who knew her already saw before them street-turnings, homes, faces; rehearsed how they were going to act, what they were going to do, what they were going to say in definite circumstances; lay down in advance in beds where sleep awaited them in a certain fashion. The new-comers interrogated themselves, put questions to the country outside the windows, to their baggage, to the stations that flitted past, to the round light in the compartment, to the faces of silent fellow-travellers. Uneasily they recalled, they marshalled, all their preconceived ideas about Paris. They invented imaginary settings for people whom they knew. They endowed names that somebody had scribbled for them on a scrap of paper with voices, faces, bodily presences.

On the outskirts of Paris, speculators in real estate tramped in the mud of unfinished roads, raised their heads to fix the direction of north and south by the light of the setting sun, cast an eye over an old woman passing by, a lamp-post, the corner cafe; listened to the rumbling of an omnibus; sniffed the wind, as though the future were going to whisper to them.

A pedlar of laces and pencils, abandoning the Porte Saint-Denis district, went down the boulevard Sébastopol towards the Châtelet and the Hotel de Ville, as though an instinct, like that of a fish, conveyed to him that certain waters were more or less favourable according to the time of day. Pickpockets, still more sensitive to shiftings of the shoal, devoted themselves to similar migrations; and prostitutes, who have no such caprices, dutifully set out to take up their posts in the line of the lust patrol.

Meanwhile schoolboys in class-rooms, chewing their penholders and running their hands through their hair, watched the last rays of daylight being chased by the gas-light over the shining surface of big maps. They could see the whole of France, and Paris stuck like a fat, slimy blob on the forty-eighth parallel, and making it bend under its weight. They could see Paris, funnily tied on to its river, held there by a stopper, cornered like a pearl on a twisted thread. You felt like untwisting the thread, and letting Paris slide upstream to the junction with the Marne, or downstream, as far as possible towards the sea.

Elsewhere, in a hotel room, in a clot of the crowd, in a compartment in an express, there was somebody who thought, just for a moment, about the shape or about the sheer size of Paris. Somebody groped in his memory for a figure, drew comparisons, was surprised. One or two people consulted note-books, guide-books. Visitors who had looked at Paris from the top of a tower, as they came down the spiral staircase again, estimated the extent of this horizon where everything was human. Others, who had come from abroad, asked themselves: "Are there going to be more people here than in the subway?" "Am I going to be more jostled about than when I try to walk along Cheapside?"

But the schoolboys had turned their eyes towards the map of Europe. They could still see France—see her, quite obviously, like something curvetting, almost rearing, ahead of the Continent; but at the same time something tucked away a little, something precious, something protected by more exposed salients. Asia and Europe turned their backs on each other; Europe trickled away towards the west; Europe was a march towards the Occident. Paris, reduced to a point, set too high for the convenience of France, seemed to be situated at a spot chosen by Europe.

Less well placed for the provinces of France than for the nations of Europe; less well placed for the safeguarding of any of them than for the meeting of all of them, Paris gave her name to the destined site of a world capital. Even her remoteness from the sea was, from this point of view, something that pleased the eyes. A capital on the coast always seems too far outside, too vulnerable, too much at the mercy of comings and goings by sea, too wide open to its traffic. To protect the heart of the West, you needed that thickness of French soil.

And during this time, among the last visitors to the towers and the high places, more than one, contemplating the real Paris under its October evening, thought that it looked like a kind of lake. A bend of the Seine had overflowed, had spread itself just as the ground allowed it. But, instead of water, there were three million people.

As a matter of fact, men had, indeed, replaced the prehistoric water. Many centuries after it had withdrawn, they had begun a similar overflowing. They had spread themselves in the same hollows, pushed out in the same directions. It was down there, towards Saint-Merri, the Temple, the Hôtel de Ville, towards the Halles, the Innocents' cemetery, and the Opéra, it was in the places where the water had found the greatest difficulty in running away, which had kept on oozing with infiltrations, with subterranean streams, that men also had most completely saturated the soil. The most densely populated and busiest quarters still lay over what had once been marsh.

Like the overflowing of the water, the overflowing of people had followed depressions in the surface, circumvented and avoided obstacles, and slowly spread as far as it could up the beds of valleys. But at the same time the human flood had spontaneous movements of its own, apparently capricious, and acted in obedience to tendencies which were foreign to the water. Sometimes it defied the law of gravity. After behaving like a lake, just when, like a lake, it had found its own level and might be expected to lapse into stagnation, it had proceeded to behave like a mouldy soil or like herbage. It had attached itself to certain slopes, crept up them, seemed attracted by the summits, and covered them little by little.

So it was that Paris, very gently, had climbed up her hills. Not only had she spread herself at an increasing distance from her river, but she had even forgotten it. The shape of its valley no longer controlled hers, or if it did, it was with the addition of more mysterious laws. To explain the growth of the city, it did not even suffice any more to think of it as a vegetal growth. You had to bring human eyes to bear on the site, to look up at the heights, to realize how the lie of the land worked on the mind.

The hill of Montmartre had represented, for centuries, a very visible goal, set away to the north, almost provocative. For a city that was still young, it was difficult to resist the temptation to reach it—at the beginning by pilgrimages, by Sunday walks. Little by little taverns spread out along the road to it. A string of houses linked the gate of Paris with the wine-shops in the gardens on the hill, and with the mills whence donkeys carried you along its paths.

When the basilica of the Sacré-Coeur began to rear itself aloft, enormous, bulging in all directions, made of a marvellously white stone in order to catch and diffuse all the light that was available above the mist and the smoke, it was more than a thousand years since Paris had dreamed of installing herself up there and marking her occupation by some trophy which could be seen from the other end of the plain of the Ile-de-France, as the trophy of La Turbie may be seen from ships at sea.

It was this trophy of the conquest of Montmartre that the people standing in the corridors of the Lille express were looking. They had passed Survilliers. The train, at a hundred and twenty kilometres an hour, was running down the gentle slope that leads to Saint-Denis. They had already put on their overcoats and taken their baggage down from the racks. But their eyes satiated themselves with the hugeness of the church, and they experienced a fearful pride in the fact that Paris should have devised this imposing way of watching their arrival.

It was at this trophy of Montmartre that the farm labourer was looking as he came on his bicycle from the fields along the road from Gonesse to Le Tremblay. He had some difficulty in keeping the soles of his boots, thick with clay, on the pedals. But when he sat down in a tavern a little later, the horizon of Montmartre would not have vanished from his mind altogether. The room, the tables, the glasses would take on a little of that pomp, that glory, which invests the leisure of the Parisian working man.

Within the same radius, Paris had not found any similar goal presented to her. Mont Valérien was too far away. It still remained so in 1908. It had never succeeded in inspiring anything more than ideas of military defence or an excursion right out into the country.

But between east and north-east one of the oldest extensions of Paris had long since encountered the first slopes of Ménilmontant-Belleville. In this direction there was no beckoning summit, no goal that you were moved to conquer and put your mark upon. The plain rose gently; then the slope became steeper and finally abrupt. A long spur of hill, rocky in places, led up to a very wide plateau, where you had only to advance a little to forget Paris and see nothing but the semi-country undulations that rolled away towards the east. The city had attacked this slope slowly. It had pushed its houses forward almost in line over a front a league long, with some outposts just a little advanced along the roads that led to the old suburbs or along miniature ravines, and with checks to the advance where it encountered an escarpment.

To the south of the river the Sainte-Geneviève hill, incorporated in Paris since ancient times, had served as a stage for her growth, a new point of departure. On this quiet close eminence the human mass, not yet very vigorous, has seized as a means of pulling itself up in order to be able to spread farther afterwards. It had thus gained the level of the long upper plain which stretches away toward Montrouge; and it had only to drop down a little to invade the whole of the left bank of the Seine as far as Grenelle.

Towards the west and the north-west another rising plain had let itself be won, little by little. In this direction, too, there was no goal to attain; none of those natural sites whose mere appearance provokes the growth of a city. There was not even a limit, an impressive boundary of the horizon, as there was to the east. There was simply a reserve of space, an outlet, a simple solution which seemed to repeat itself indefinitely. For about the next bend of the Seine and the hills that partly followed it Paris did not even think. They were situated outside her future.

Honoré de Balzac

The anatomy of paris

By dint of taking interest in everything, the Parisian ends by being interested in nothing. No emotion dominating his face, which friction has rubbed away, it turns gray like the faces of those houses upon which all kinds of dust and smoke have blown. In effect, the Parisian, with his indifference on the day for what the morrow will bring forth, lives like a child, whatever may be his age. He grumbles at everything, consoles himself for everything,

From *The Girl with the Golden Eyes* by Honoré de Balzac (1833), translated by Ellen Marriage.

jests at everything, forgets, desires, and tastes everything, seizes all with passion, quits all with indifference—his kings, his conquests, his glory, his idols of bronze or glass—as he throws away his stockings, his hats, and his fortune. In Paris no sentiment can withstand the drift of things, and their current compels a struggle in which the passions are relaxed: there love is a desire, and hatred a whim; there's no true kinsman but the thousand-franc note, no better friend than the pawnbroker. This universal toleration bears its fruits, and in the salon, as in the street, there is no one *de trop*, there is no one absolutely useful, or absolutely harmful—knaves or fools, men of wit or integrity. There everything is tolerated: the government and the guillotine, religion and the cholera. You are always acceptable to this world, you will never be missed by it. What, then, is the dominating impulse in this country without morals, without faith, without any sentiment, wherein, however, every sentiment, belief, and moral has its origin and end? It is gold and pleasure. Take those two words for a lantern, and explore that great stucco cage, that hive with its black gutters, and follow the windings of that thought which agitates, sustains, and occupies it! Consider! And, in the first place, examine the world which possesses nothing.

The artisan, the man of the proletariat, who uses his hands, his tongue, his back, his right arm, his five fingers, to live—well, this very man, who should be the first to economize his vital principle, outruns his strength, yokes his wife to some machine, wears out his child, and ties him to the wheel. The manufacturer—or I know not what secondary thread which sets in motion all these folk who with their foul hands mould and gild porcelain, sew coats and dresses, beat out iron, turn wood and steel, weave hemp, festoon crystal, imitate flowers, work woolen things, break in horses, dress harness, carve in copper, paint carriages, blow glass, corrode the diamond, polish metals, turn marble into leaves, labor on pebbles, deck out thought, tinge, bleach, or blacken everything—well, this middleman has come to that world of sweat and good-will, of study and patience, with promises of lavish wages, either in the names of the town's caprices or with the voice of the monster dubbed speculation. Thus, these *quadrumanes* set themselves to watch, work, and suffer, to fast, sweat, and bestir them. Then, careless of the future, greedy of pleasure, counting on their right arm as the painter on his palette, lords for one day, they throw their money on Monday's to the cabarets which gird the town like a belt of mud, haunts of the most shameless of the daughters of Venus, in which the periodical money of this people, as ferocious in their pleasures as they are calm at work, is squandered as it had been at play. For five days, then, there is no repose for this laborious portion of Paris! It is given up to actions which make it warped and rough, lean and pale, gush forth with a thousand fits of creative energy. And then its pleasure, its repose, are an exhausting debauch, swarthy and black with blows, white with intoxication, or yellow with indigestion. It lasts but two days, but it steals to-morrow's bread, the week's soup, the wife's dress, the child's wretched rags. Men, born doubtless to be beautiful—for all creatures have a relative beauty—are enrolled from their childhood beneath the yoke of force, beneath the rule of the hammer, the chisel, the loom, and have been promptly vulcanized. Is not Vulcan, with his hideousness and his strength, the emblem of this strong and hideous nation—sublime in its mechanical intelligence, patient in its season, and once in a century terrible, inflammable as gunpowder, and ripe with brandy for the madness of revolution, with wits enough, in fine, to take fire at a captious word, which signifies to it always: Gold and Pleasure! If we comprise in it all those who hold out their hands for an alms, for lawful wages, or the five francs that are granted to every kind of Parisian prostitution, in short, for all money well or ill earned, this people numbers three hundred thousand individuals. Were it not for the cabarets, would not the Government be overturned every Tuesday? Happily, by Tuesday, this people is glutted, sleeps off its pleasure, is penniless, and returns to its labor, to dry bread, stimulated by a need of material procreation, which has become a habit to it. None the less, this people has its phenomenal virtues, its complete men, unknown Napoleons, who are the type of its strength carried to its highest expression, and sum up its social capacity in an existence wherein thought and movement combine less to bring joy into it than to neutralize the action of sorrow.

Chance has made an artisan economical, chance has favored him with forethought, he has been able to look forward, has met with a wife and found himself a father, and, after some years of hard privation, he embarks in some little draper's business, hires a shop. If neither sickness nor vice blocks his way—if he has prospered—there is the sketch of this normal life.

And, in the first place, hail to that king of Parisian activity, to whom time and space give way. Yes, hail to that being, composed of saltpeter and gas, who makes children for France during his laborious nights, and in the day multiplies his personality for the service, glory, and pleasure of his fellow-citizens. This man solves the problem of sufficing at once to his amiable wife, to his hearth, to the *Constitutionnel*, to his office, to the National Guard, to the opera, and to God; but, only in order that the *Constitutionnel*, his office, the National Guard, the opera, his wife, and God may be changed into coin. In fine, hail to an irreproachable pluralist. Up every day at five o'clock, he traverses like a bird the space which separates his dwelling from the Rue Montmartre. Let it blow or thunder, rain or snow, he is at the *Constitutionnel*, and waits there for the load of newspapers which he had undertaken to distribute. He receives this political bread with eagerness, takes it, bears it away. At nine o'clock he is in the bosom of his family, flings a jest to his wife, snatches a loud kiss from her, gulps down a cup of coffee, or scolds his children. At a quarter to ten he puts in an appearance at the *Mairie*. There, stuck upon a stool, like a parrot on its perch, warmed by Paris town, he registers until four o'clock, with never a tear or a smile, the deaths and births of an entire district. The sorrow, the happiness, of the parish flow beneath his pen—as the essence of the *Constitutionnel* traveled before upon his shoulders. Nothing weighs upon him! He goes always straight before him, takes his patriotism ready made from the newspaper, contradicts no one, shouts or applauds with the world, and lives like a bird. Two yards from his parish, in the event of an important ceremony, he can yield his place to an assistant, and betake himself to chant a requiem from a stall in the church of which on Sundays he is the fairest ornament, where his is the most imposing voice, where he distorts his huge mouth with energy to thunder out a joyous *Amen*. So is he chorister. At four o'clock, freed from his official servitude, he reappears to shed joy and gaiety upon the most famous shop in the city. Happy is his wife, he has no time to be jealous: he is a man of action rather than of sentiment. His mere arrival spurs the young ladies at the counter; their bright eyes storm the customers; he expands in the midst of all the finery, the lace and muslin kerchiefs, that their cunning hands have wrought. Or, again, more often still, before his dinner he waits on a client, copies the page of a newspaper, or carries to the doorkeeper some goods that have been delayed. Every other day, at six, he is faithful to his post. A permanent bass for the chorus, he betakes himself to the opera, prepared to become a soldier or an arab, prisoner, savage, peasant, spirit, camel's leg or lion, a devil or a genie, a slave or a eunuch, black or white; always ready to feign joy or sorrow, pity or astonishment, to utter cries that never vary, to hold his tongue, to hunt, or fight for Rome or Egypt, but always at heart— a huckster still.

At midnight he returns—a man, the good husband, the tender father; he slips into the conjugal bed, his imagination still afire with the illusive forms of the operatic nymphs, and so turns to the profit of conjugal love the world's depravities, the voluptuous curves of Taglioni's leg. And, finally, if he sleeps, he sleeps apace, and hurries through his slumber as he does his life.

This man sums up all things—history, literature, politics, government, religion, military science. Is he not a living encyclopedia, a grotesque Atlas; ceaselessly in motion, like Paris itself, and knowing not repose? He is all legs. No physiognomy could preserve its purity amid such toils. Perhaps the artisan who dies at thirty, an old man, his stomach tanned by repeated doses of brandy, will be held, according to certain leisured philosophers, to be happier than the huckster is. The one perishes in a breath, and the other by degrees. From his eight industries, from the labor of his shoulders, his throat, his hands, from his wife and his business, the one derives— as from so many farms—children, some thousands of francs, and the most laborious happiness that has ever diverted the heart of man. This fortune and these children, or the children who sum up everything for him, become the prey of the world above, to which he brings his ducats and his daughter or his son, reared at college, who, with more education than his father, raises higher his ambitious gaze. Often the son of a retail tradesman would fain be something in the State.

Ambition of that sort carries on our thought to the second Parisian sphere. Go up one story, then, and descend to the *entresol:* or climb down from the attic and remain on the fourth floor: in fine, penetrate into the world which has possessions: the same result! Wholesale merchants, and their men—people with small banking accounts and much integrity—rogues and cats-paws, clerks old and young, sheriffs' clerks, barristers' clerks, solicitors' clerks; in fine, all the working, thinking, and speculating members of that lower middle class which honeycombs the interests of Paris and watches over its granary, accumulates the coin, stores the products that the proletariat have made, preserves the fruits of the South, the fishes, the wine from every sun-favored hill; which stretches its hands over the Orient, and takes from it the shawls that the Russ and the Turk despise; which harvests even from the Indies; crouches down in expectation of a sale, greedy of profit; which discounts bills, turns over and collects all kinds of securities, holds all Paris in its hand, watches over the fantasies of children, spies out the caprices and the vices of mature age, sucks money out of disease. Even so, if they drink no brandy, like the artisan, nor wallow in the mire of debauch, all equally abuse their strength, immeasurably strain their bodies and their minds alike, are burned away with desires, devastated with the swiftness of the pace. In their case the physical distortion is accomplished beneath the whip of interests, beneath the scourge of ambitions which torture the educated portion of this monstrous city, just as in the case of the proletariat it is brought about by the cruel see-saw of the material elaborations perpetually required from the despotism of the aristocratic "I *will.*" Here, too, then, in order to obey that universal master, pleasure or gold, they must devour time, hasten time, find more than four-and-twenty hours in the day and night, waste themselves, slay themselves, and purchase two years of unhealthy repose with thirty years of old age. Only, the working-man dies in hospital when the last term of his stunted growth expires; whereas the man of the middle class is set upon living, and lives on, but in a state of idiocy. You will meet him, with his worn, flat old face, with no light in his eyes, with no strength in his limbs, dragging himself with a dazed air along the boulevard—the belt of his Venus, of his beloved city. What was his want? The sabre of the National Guard, a permanent stock-pot, a decent plot in Père Lachaise, and, for his old age, a little gold honestly earned. *His* Monday is on Sunday, his rest a drive in a hired carriage—a country excursion during which his wife and children glut themselves merrily with dust or bask in the sun; his dissipation is at the restaurateur's, whose poisonous dinner has won reknown, or at some family ball, where he suffocates till midnight. Some fools are surprised at the phantasmagoria of the monads which they see with the aid of the microscope in a drop of water; but what would Rabelais' Gargantua,—that misunderstood figure of an audacity so sublime,—what would that giant say, fallen from the celestial spheres, if he amused himself by contemplating the motions of this secondary life of Paris, of which here is one of the formulae? Have you seen one of those little constructions—cold in summer, and with no other warmth than a small stove in winter—placed beneath the vast copper dome which crowns the Halle-au-blé? Madame is there by morning. She is engaged at the markets, and makes by this occupation twelve thousand francs a year, people say. Monsieur, when Madame is up, passes into a gloomy office, where he lends money till the week-end to the tradesmen of his district. By nine o'clock he is at the passport office, of which he is one of the minor officials. By evening he is at the box-office of the Théâtre Italien, or of any other theatre you like. The children are put out to nurse, and only return to be sent to college or to boarding school. Monsieur and Madame live on the third floor, have but one cook, give dances in a salon twelve foot by eight, lit by argand lamps; but they give a hundred and fifty thousand francs to their daughter, and retire at the age of fifty, an age when they begin to show themselves on the balcony of the opera, in a fiacre at Longchamps; or, on sunny days, in faded clothes on the boulevards—the fruit of all this sowing. Respected by their neighbors, in good odor with the government, connected with the upper middle classes, Monsieur obtains at sixty-five the Cross of the Legion of Honor, and his daughter's father-in-law, a parochial mayor, invites him to his evenings. These lifelong labors, then, are for the good of the children, whom these lower middle classes are inevitably driven to exalt. Thus each sphere directs all its efforts towards the sphere above it. The son of the rich grocer becomes a notary, the son of the timber merchant becomes a magistrate. No link is wanting in the chain, and everything stimulates the upward march of money.

Thus we are brought to the third circle of this hell, which, perhaps, will some day find its Dante. In this third social circle, a sort of Parisian belly, in which the interests of the town are digested, and where they are condensed into the form known as *business*, there moves and agitates, as by some acrid and bitter intestinal process, the crowd of lawyers, doctors, notaries, councilors, business men, bankers, big merchants, speculators, and magistrates. Here are to be found even more causes of moral and physical destruction than elsewhere. These people—almost all of them—live in unhealthy offices, in fetid antechambers, in little barred dens, and spend their days bowed down beneath the weight of affairs; they rise at dawn to be in time, not to be left behind, to gain all or not to lose, to overreach a man or his money, to open or wind up some business, to take advantage of some fleeting opportunity, to get a man hanged or set him free. They infect their horses, they overdrive and age and break them, like their own legs, before their time. Time is their tyrant: it fails them, it escapes them; they can neither expand it nor cut it short. What soul can remain great, pure, moral, and generous, and consequently, what face retain its beauty in this depraving practice of a calling which compels one to bear the weight of the public sorrows, to analyze them, to weigh them, estimate them, and mark them out by rule? Where do these folk put aside their hearts? . . . I do not know; but they leave them, somewhere or other, when they have any, before they descend each morning into the abyss of the misery which puts families on the rack. For them there is no such thing as mystery; they see the reverse side of society, whose confessors they are, and despise it. Then, whatever they do, owing to their contact with corruption, they either are horrified at it and grow gloomy, or else, out of lassitude, or some secret compromise, espouse it. In fine, they necessarily become callous to every sentiment, since man, his laws and his institutions, make them steal, like jackals, from corpses that are still warm. At all hours the financier is trampling on the living, the attorney on the dead, the pleader on the conscience. Forced to be speaking without a rest, they all substitute words for ideas, phrases for feelings, and their soul becomes a larynx. Neither the great merchant, nor the judge, nor the pleader preserves his sense of right; they feel no more, they apply set rules that leave cases out of count. Borne along by their headlong course, they are neither husbands nor fathers nor lovers; they glide on sledges over the facts of life, and live at all times at the high pressure conduced by business and the vast city. When they return to their homes they are required to go to a ball, to the opera, into society, where they can make clients, acquaintances, protectors. They all eat to excess, play and keep vigil, and their faces become bloated, flushed, and emaciated.

To this terrific expenditure of intellectual strength, to such multifold moral contradictions, they oppose—not, indeed, pleasure, it would be too pale a contrast—but debauchery, a debauchery both secret and alarming, for they have all means at their disposal, and fix the morality of society. Their genuine stupidity lies hid beneath their specialism. They know their business, but are ignorant of everything which is outside it. So that to preserve their self-conceit they question everything, are crudely and crookedly critical. They appear to be sceptics and are in reality simpletons; they swamp their wits in interminable arguments. Almost all conveniently adopt social, literary, or political prejudices, to do away with the need of having opinions, just as they adapt their conscience to the standard of the Code or the Tribunal of Commerce. Having started early to become men of note, they turn into mediocrities, and crawl over the high places of the world. So, too, their faces present the harsh pallor, the deceitful coloring, those dull, tarnished eyes, and garrulous, sensual mouths, in which the observer recognizes the symptoms of the degeneracy of the thought and its rotation in the circle of a special idea which destroys the creative faculties of the brain and the gift of seeing in large, of generalizing and deducing. No man who has allowed himself to be caught in the revolutions of the gear of these huge machines can ever become great. If he is a doctor, either he has practised little or he is an exception—a Bichat who dies young. If a great merchant, something remains—he is almost Jacques Coeur. Did Robespierre practise? Danton was an idler who waited. But who, moreover, has ever felt envious of the figures of Danton and Robespierre, however lofty they were? These men of affairs, par excellence, attract money to them, and hoard it in order to ally themselves with aristocratic families. If the ambition of the working-man is that of the small tradesman, here, too, are the same passions. In Paris, vanity sums up all the passions. The type of this class might be either an ambitious bourgeois, who, after a life of privation and continual scheming, passes into the Council of State as an ant passes through a chink; or some newspaper editor, jaded with intrigue, whom the king makes a peer of France—perhaps to revenge himself on the nobility; or some notary become mayor of his parish: all people crushed with business, who, if they attain their end, are literally *killed* in its attainment. In France the usage is to glorify wigs. Napoleon, Louis XVI, the great rulers, alone have always wished for young men to fulfil their projects.

Above this sphere the artist world exists. But here, too, the faces stamped with the seal of originality are worn, nobly indeed, but worn, fatigued, nervous. Harassed by a need of production, outrun by their costly fantasies, worn out by devouring genius, hungry for pleasure, the artists of Paris would all regain by excessive labor what they have lost by idleness, and vainly seek to reconcile the world and glory, money and art. To begin with, the artist is ceaselessly panting under his creditors; his necessities beget his debts, and his debts require of him his nights. After his labor, his pleasure. The comedian plays till midnight, studies in the morning, rehearses at noon; the sculptor is bent before his statue; the journalist is a marching thought, like the soldier when at war; the painter who is the fashion is crushed with work, the painter with no occupation, if he feels himself to be a man of genius, gnaws his entrails. Competition, rivalry, calumny assail talent. Some, in desperation, plunge into the abyss of vice, others die young and unknown because they have discounted their future too soon. Few of these figures, originally sublime, remain beautiful. On the other hand, the flagrant beauty of their heads is not understood. An artist's face is always exorbitant, it is always above or below the conventional lines of what fools call the *beau-idéal*. What power is it that destroys them? Passion. Every passion in Paris resolves into two terms: gold and pleasure. Now, do you not breathe again? Do you not feel air and space purified? Here is neither labor nor suffering. The soaring arch of gold has reached the summit. From the lowest gutters, where its stream commences, from the little shops where it is stopped by puny coffer-dams, from the heart of the counting-houses and great work-shops, where its volume is that of ingots—gold, in the shape of dowries and inheritances, guided by the hands of young girls or the bony fingers of age, courses towards the aristocracy, where it will become a blazing, expansive stream. But, before leaving the four territories upon which the utmost wealth of Paris is based, it is fitting, having cited the moral causes, to deduce those which are physical, and to call attention to a pestilence, latent, as it were, which incessantly acts upon the faces of the porter, the artisan, the small shopkeeper; to point out a deleterious influence the corruption of which equals that of the Parisian administrators who allow it so complacently to exist!

If the air of the houses in which the greater proportion of the middle classes live is noxious, if the atmosphere of the streets belches out cruel miasmas into stuffy back-kitchens where there is little air, realize that, apart from this pestilence, the forty thousand houses of this great city have their foundations in filth, which the powers that be have not yet seriously attempted to enclose with mortar walls solid enough to prevent even the most fetid mud from filtering through the soil, poisoning the wells, and maintaining subterraneously to Lutetia the tradition of her celebrated name. Half of Paris sleeps amidst the putrid exhalations of courts and streets and sewers. But let us turn to the vast salons, gilded and airy; the hotels in their gardens, the rich, indolent, happy, moneyed world. There the faces are lined and scarred with vanity. There nothing is real. To seek for pleasure is it not to find ennui? People in society have at an early age warped their nature. Having no occupation other than to wallow in pleasure, they have speedily misused their sense, as the artisan has misused brandy. Pleasure is of the nature of certain medical substances: in order to obtain constantly the same effects the doses must be doubled, and death or degradation is contained in the last. All the lower classes are on their knees before the wealthy, and watch their tastes in order to turn them into vices and exploit them. Thus you see in these folk at an early age tastes instead of passions, romantic fantasies and lukewarm loves. There impotence reigns; there ideas have ceased—they have evaporated together with energy amongst the affectations of the boudoir and the cajolements of women. There are fledglings of forty, old doctors of sixty years. The wealthy obtain in Paris ready-made wit and science—formulated opinions which save them from the need of having wit, science, or opinion of their own. The irrationality of this world is equaled by its weakness and its licentiousness. It is greedy of time to the point of wasting it. Seek in it for affection as little as for ideas. Its kisses conceal a profound indifference, its urbanity a perpetual contempt. It has no other fashion of love. Flashes of wit without profundity, a wealth of indiscretion, scandal, and above all, commonplace. Such is the sum of its speech; but these happy fortunates pretend that they do not meet to make and repeat maxims in the manner of La Rochefoucauld as though there did not exist a mean, invented by the eighteenth century, between a superfluity and absolute blank. If a few men of character indulge in witticism, at once subtle and refined, they are misunderstood; soon, tired of giving without receiving, they remain at home, and leave fools to reign over their territory. This hollow life, this perpetual expectation of a pleasure which never comes, this permanent ennui and emptiness of soul, heart, and mind, the lassitude of the upper Parisian world, is reproduced on its features, and stamps its parchment faces, its premature wrinkles, that physiognomy of the wealthy upon which impotence has set its grimace, in which gold is mirrored, and whence intelligence has fled.

Such a view of moral Paris proves that physical Paris could not be other than it is. This coroneted town is like a queen, who, being always with child, has desires of irresistible fury. Paris is the crown of the world, a brain which perishes of genius and leads human civilization; it is a great man, a perpetually creative artist, a politician with second-sight who must of necessity have wrinkles on his forehead, the vices of the great man, the fantasies of the artist, and the politician's disillusions. Its physiognomy suggests the evolution of good and evil, battle and victory; the moral combat of '89, the clarion calls of which still re-echo in every corner of the world; and also the downfall of 1814. Thus this city can no more be moral, or cordial, or clean, than the engines which impel those proud leviathans which you admire when they cleave the waves! Is not Paris a sublime vessel laden with intelligence? Yes, her arms are one of those oracles which fatality sometimes allows. The *City of Paris* has her great mast, all of bronze, carved with victories, and for watchman—Napoleon. The barque may roll and pitch, but she cleaves the world, illuminates it through the hundred mouths of her tribunes, ploughs the seas of science, rides with full sail, cries from the height of her tops, with the voice of her scientists and artists: "Onward, advance! Follow me!" She carries a huge crew, which delights in adorning her with fresh streamers. Boys and urchins laughing in the rigging; ballast of heavy bourgeoisie; working-men and sailor-men touched with tar; in her cabins the lucky passengers; elegant midshipmen smoke their cigars leaning over the bulwarks; then, on the deck, her soldiers, innovators or ambitious, would accost every fresh shore, and shooting out their bright lights upon it, ask for glory which is pleasure, or for love which needs gold.

Thus the exorbitant movement of the proletariat, the corrupting influence of the interests which consume the two middle classes, the cruelties of the artist's thought, and the excessive pleasure which is sought for incessantly by the great, explain the normal ugliness of the Parisian physiognomy. It is only in the Orient that the human race presents a magnificent figure, but that is an effect of the constant calm affected by those profound philosophers with their long pipes, their short legs, their square contour, who despise and hold activity in horror, whilst in Paris the little and the great and the mediocre run and leap and drive, whipped on by an inexorable goddess, Necessity —the necessity for money, glory, and amusement. Thus, any face which is fresh and graceful and reposeful, any really young face, is in Paris the most extraordinary of exceptions; it is met with rarely. Should you see one there, be sure it belongs either to a young and ardent ecclesiastic or to some good abbé of forty with three chins; to a young girl of pure life such as is brought up in certain middle-class families; to a mother of twenty, still full of illusions, as she suckles her first-born; to a young man newly embarked from the provinces, and intrusted to the care of some devout dowager who keeps him without a sou; or, perhaps, to some shop assistant who goes to bed at midnight wearied out with folding and unfolding calico, and rises at seven o'clock to arrange the window; often again to some man of science or poetry, who lives monastically in the embrace of a fine idea, who remains sober, patient, and chaste; else to some self-contented fool, feeding himself on folly, reeking of health, in a perpetual state of absorption with his own smile; or to the soft and happy race of loungers, the only folk really happy in Paris, which unfolds for them hour by hour its moving poetry.

Poverty

Poverty has always been with us. Under certain cultural conditions and in specific historical circumstances it has been seen as a problem and even as a scandal; at other times it has been taken for granted. Poverty is not simply a condition of deprivation; the poor occupy a special, usually stigmatized, status which is accorded them by the rest of society, and which varies with the prevailing standards and norms. The sociology of poverty is hence not so much concerned with determining the exact levels of deprivation or with establishing an income line below which poverty is said to emerge. Rather, it attempts to investigate the social consequences of the fact that society assigns certain persons to the despised category of the poor and hence evokes in them styles of life at variance with those that operate in 'respectable' society.

In nineteenth-century England and America, i.e., in industrial societies governed by the ethic of work and achievement, those who for one reason or another did not live up to the prevailing ethos were severely stigmatized.

If at all possible, they were relegated to workhouses where they were treated as barely tolerated outcasts. No matter how harsh their treatment, they were supposed to be grateful for the meager favors bestowed upon them. Charles Dickens' description of the orphanage in which *Oliver Twist* is raised conveys the atmosphere of condescension and terror in which the English poor, young and old, were typically treated by Victorian gentlemen, callous and self-righteous in their firm belief that the poor somehow did not belong to the same race as themselves.

Mid-Victorian callousness has given way to somewhat more humanitarian attitudes in the twentieth century, but the fate of the poor has not changed quite as much as would seem at first blush. They continue to be stigmatized and despised. Some years ago there appeared a translation of the diary of a Brazilian ragpicker woman, Carolina Maria De Jesus, under the title *Child of the Dark*. A few entries from this diary are reproduced to convey the horror of an existence in the interstices of an urban society which hardly has any concern for the social pariahs in its midst.

In contemporary American society the welfare poor, though at least given some minimal financial support, are treated with contempt. As *Barbara Dugan's Story*, an autobiographical account, transcribed in Richard M. Elman's *The Poorhouse State*, makes clear, the present welfare system is demeaning as well as inadequate, and fails to come to terms with the manifold problems that the welfare poor face in their miserable everyday lives.

By no means are all the poor in contemporary America black, but a much higher proportion of blacks than of whites are poor. Racial discrimination is an added burden. Thus a majority of American blacks suffer from the double handicap of being in the lowest class as well as in the lowest ethnic status. Until recently, as the excerpts from Claude Brown's autobiographical *Manchild in the Promised Land* show, blacks tended to be resigned to their status, fearful of demanding more equitable treatment. More recently they have begun to voice their demands in a more militant and forceful manner. The black woman described in the excerpt from *The Hit*, a fine novel by a young black writer, Julian Mayfield, wavers on the borderline between resignation and revolt. The excerpts from Ralph Ellison's *Invisible Man*, reprinted in Section seventeen, describe a ghetto riot in which previous restraints have been thrown off by the deprived who now openly defy those whom they count responsible for their misery.

Lest the impression is conveyed that poverty is exclusively an urban phenomenon, this section ends with a short excerpt about Southern white sharecroppers from a moving book by James Agee and Walker Evans, *Let Us Now Praise Famous Men*. Even though its authors use a lyrical language which might appear too emotive to the sociologist, they have captured some of the peculiar life styles of the rural poor.

Charles Dickens

I want some more

"Hush!" said the gentleman who had spoken first. "You know you've got no father or mother, and that you were brought up by the parish, don't you?"

"Yes, sir," replied Oliver, weeping bitterly.

"What are you crying for?" inquired the gentleman in the white waistcoat. And to be sure it was very extraordinary. What *could* the boy be crying for?

"I hope you say your prayers every night," said another gentleman in a gruff voice; "and pray for the people who feed you, and take care of you— like a Christian."

"Yes, sir," stammered the boy. The gentleman who spoke last was unconsciously right. It would have been *very* like a Christian, and a mar- vellously good Christian too, if Oliver had prayed for the people who fed and took care of *him*. But he hadn't, because nobody had taught him.

"Well! You have come here to be educated, and taught a useful trade," said the red-faced gentleman in the high chair.

"So you'll begin to pick oakum to-morrow morning at six o'clock," added the surly one in the white waistcoat.

For the combination of both these blessings in the one simple process of picking oakum, Oliver bowed low, by the direction of the beadle, and was hurried away to a large ward: where, on a rough hard bed, he sobbed him- self to sleep. What a noble illustration of the tender laws of England! They let the paupers go to sleep!

Poor Oliver! He little thought, as he lay sleeping in happy unconscious- ness of all around him, that the board had that very day arrived at a decision which would exercise the most material influence over all his future fortunes. But they had. And this was it:—

The members of this board were very sage, deep, philosophical men; and when they came to turn their attention to the workhouse, they found out at once, what ordinary folks would never have discovered—the poor people like it! It was a regular place of public entertainment for the poorer classes; a tavern where there was nothing to pay; a public breakfast, dinner, tea, and supper all the year round; a brick and mortar elysium, where it was all play and no work. "Oho!" said the board, looking very knowing; "we are the fellows to set this to rights; we'll stop it all, in no time." So, they established the rule, that all poor people should have the alternative (for they would compel nobody, not they), of being starved by a gradual process

From *Oliver Twist* by Charles Dickens (1838).

in the house, or by a quick one out of it. With this view, they contracted with the water-works to lay on an unlimited supply of water; and with a corn-factor to supply periodically small quantities of oatmeal; and issued three meals of thin gruel a day, with an onion twice a week, and half a roll on Sundays. They made a great many other wise and humane regulations, having reference to the ladies, which it is not necessary to repeat; kindly undertook to divorce poor married people, in consequence of the great expense of a suit in Doctors' Commons; and, instead of compelling a man to support his family, as they had theretofore done, took his family away from him, and made him a bachelor! There is no saying how many applicants for relief, under these last two heads, might have started up in all classes of society, if it had not been coupled with the workhouse; but the board were long-headed men, and had provided for this difficulty. The relief was inseparable from the workhouse and the gruel; and that frightened people.

For the first six months after Oliver Twist was removed, the system was in full operation. It was rather expensive at first, in consequence of the increase in the undertaker's bill, and the necessity of taking in the clothes of all the paupers, which fluttered loosely on their wasted, shrunken forms, after a week or two's gruel. But the number of workhouse inmates got thin as well as the paupers; and the board were in ecstasies.

The room in which the boys were fed, was a large stone hall, with a copper at one end: out of which the master, dressed in an apron for the purpose, and assisted by one or two women, ladled the gruel at meal-times. Of this festive composition, each boy had one porringer, and no more—except on occasions of great public rejoicing, when he had two ounces and a quarter of bread besides. The bowls never wanted washing. The boys polished them with their spoons till they shone again; and when they had performed this operation, (which never took very long, the spoons being nearly as large as the bowls) they would sit staring at the copper, with such eager eyes, as if they could have devoured the very bricks of which it was composed; employing themselves, meanwhile, in sucking their fingers most assiduously, with the view of catching up any stray splashes of gruel that might have been cast thereon. Boys have generally excellent appetites. Oliver Twist and his companions suffered the tortures of slow starvation for three months: at last they got so voracious and wild with hunger, that one boy, who was tall for his age, and hadn't been used to that sort of thing, (for his father had kept a small cook's shop); hinted darkly to his companions, that unless he had another basin of gruel *per diem*, he was afraid he might some night happen to eat the boy who slept next to him, who happened to be a weakly youth of tender age. He had a wild, hungry eye; and they implicitly believed him. A council was held, lots were cast who should walk up to the master after supper that evening, and ask for more; and it fell to Oliver Twist.

The evening arrived; the boys took their places. The master, in his cook's uniform, stationed himself at the copper; his pauper assistants ranged themselves behind him; the gruel was served out; and a long grace was said over the short commons. The gruel disappeared; the boys whispered each other, and winked at Oliver; while his next neighbors nudged him. Child as he was, he was desperate with hunger, and reckless with misery. He rose from the table; and advancing to the master, basin and spoon in hand, said: somewhat alarmed at his own temerity:

"Please, sir, I want some more."

The master was a fat, healthy man; but he turned very pale. He gazed in stupefied astonishment on the small rebel for some seconds; and then clung for support to the copper. The assistants were paralyzed with wonder; the boys with fear.

"What!" said the master at length, in a faint voice.

"Please, sir," replied Oliver, "I want some more."

The master aimed a blow at Oliver's head with the ladle; pinioned him in his arms; and shrieked aloud for the beadle.

The board were sitting in solemn conclave, when Mr. Bumble rushed into the room in great excitement, and addressing the gentleman in the high chair, said:

"Mr. Limbkins, I beg your pardon, sir! Oliver Twist has asked for more!"

There was a general start. Horror was depicted on every countenance.

"For *more!*" said Mr. Limbkins. "Compose yourself, Bumble, and answer me distinctly. Do I understand that he asked for more, after he had eaten the supper allotted by the dietary?"

"He did, sir," replied Bumble.

"That boy will be hung," said the gentleman in the white waistcoat. "I know that boy will be hung."

Nobody controverted the prophetic gentleman's opinion. An animated discussion took place. Oliver was ordered into instant confinement; and a bill was next morning pasted on the outside of the gate, offering a reward of five pounds to anybody who would take Oliver Twist off the hands of the parish. In other words, five pounds and Oliver Twist were offered to any man or woman who wanted an apprentice to any trade, business, or calling.

"I never was more convinced of anything in my life," said the gentleman in the white waistcoat, as he knocked at the gate and read the bill next morning: "I never was more convinced of anything in my life, than I am that that boy will come to be hung."

Carolina Maria de Jesus

Child of the dark

July 15, 1955   The birthday of my daughter Vera Eunice. I wanted to buy a pair of shoes for her, but the price of food keeps us from realizing our desires. Actually we are slaves to the cost of living. I found a pair of shoes in the garbage, washed them, and patched them for her to wear.

I didn't have one cent to buy bread. So I washed three bottles and traded them to Arnaldo. He kept the bottles and gave me bread. Then I went to sell my paper. I received 65 cruzeiros. I spent 20 cruzeiros for meat. I got one kilo of ham and one kilo of sugar and spent six cruzeiros on cheese. And the money was gone.

I was ill all day. I thought I had a cold. At night my chest pained me. I started to cough. I decided not to go out at night to look for paper. I searched for my son João. He was at Felisberto de Carvalho Street near the market. A bus had knocked a boy into the sidewalk and a crowd gathered. João was in the middle of it all. I poked him a couple of times and within five minutes he was home.

I washed the children, put them to bed, then washed myself and went to bed. I waited until 11:00 for a certain someone. He didn't come. I took an aspirin and laid down again. When I awoke the sun was sliding in space. My daughter Vera Eunice said: "Go get some water, Mother!"

July 16   I got up and obeyed Vera Eunice. I went to get the water. I made coffee. I told the children that I didn't have any bread, that they would have to drink their coffee plain and eat meat with *farinha*.[1] I was feeling ill and decided to cure myself. I stuck my finger down my throat twice, vomited, and knew I was under the evil eye. The upset feeling left and I went to Senhor Manuel, carrying some cans to sell. Everything that I find in the garbage I sell. He gave me 13 cruzeiros. I kept thinking that I had to buy bread, soap, and milk for Vera Eunice. The 13 cruzeiros wouldn't make it. I returned home, or rather to my shack, nervous and exhausted. I thought of the worrisome life that I led. Carrying paper, washing clothes for the children, staying in the street all day long. Yet I'm always lacking things, Vera doesn't have shoes and she doesn't like to go barefoot. For at least two years I've wanted to buy a meat grinder. And a sewing machine.

[1]*Farinha:* a coarse wheat flour.

I came home and made lunch for the two boys. Rice, beans, and meat, and I'm going out to look for paper. I left the children, told them to play in the yard and not go into the street, because the terrible neighbors I have won't leave my children alone. I was feeling ill and wished I could lie down. But the poor don't rest nor are they permitted the pleasure of relaxation. I was nervous inside, cursing my luck. I collected two sacks full of paper. Afterward I went back and gathered up some scrap metal, some cans, and some kindling wood. As I walked I thought—when I return to the favela there is going to be something new. Maybe Dona Rosa or the insolent Angel Mary fought with my children. I found Vera Eunice sleeping and the boys playing in the street. I thought: it's 2:00. Maybe I'm going to get through this day without anything happening. João told me that the truck that gives out money was here to give out food. I took a sack and hurried out. It was the leader of the Spiritist Center at 103 Vergueiro Street. I got two kilos of rice, two of beans, and two kilos of macaroni. I was happy. The truck went away. The nervousness that I had inside left me. I took advantage of my calmness to read. I picked up a magazine and sat on the grass, letting the rays of the sun warm me as I read a story. I wrote a note and gave it to my boy João to take to Senhor Arnaldo to buy soap, two aspirins, and some bread. Then I put water on the stove to make coffee. João came back saying he had lost the aspirins. I went back with him to look. We didn't find them.

When I came home there was a crowd at my door. Children and women claiming José Carlos had thrown stones at their houses. They wanted me to punish him.

July 17 Sunday A marvelous day. The sky was blue without one cloud. The sun was warm. I got out of bed at 6:30 and went to get water. I only had one piece of bread and three cruzeiros. I gave a small piece to each child and put the beans, that I got yesterday from the Spiritist Center, on the fire. Then I went to wash clothes. When I returned from the river the beans were cooked. The children asked for bread. I gave the three cruzeiros to João to go and buy some. Today it was Nair Mathias who started an argument with my children. Silvia and her husband have begun an open-air spectacle. He is hitting her and I'm disgusted because the children are present. They heard words of the lowest kind. Oh, if I could move from here to a more decent neighborhood!

I went to Dona Florela to ask for a piece of garlic. I went to Dona Analia and got exactly what I expected:

"I don't have any!"

I went to collect my clothes. Dona Aparecida asked me:

"Are you pregnant?"

"No, Senhora," I replied gently.

I cursed her under my breath. If I am pregnant it's not your business. I can't stand these favela women, they want to know everything. Their tongues are like chicken feet. Scratching at everything. The rumor is circulating that I am pregnant! If I am, I don't know about it!

I went out at night to look for paper. When I was passing the São Paulo football stadium many people were coming out. All of them were white and only one black. And the black started to insult me:

"Are you looking for paper, auntie? Watch your step, auntie dear!"

I was ill and wanted to lie down, but I went on. I met several friends and stopped to talk to them. When I was going up Tiradentes Avenue I met some women. One of them asked me:

"Are your legs healed?"

After I was operated on, I got better, thanks to God. I could even dance at Carnival in my feather costume. Dr. José Torres Netto was who operated on me. A good doctor. And we spoke of politics. When a woman asked me what I thought of Carlos Lacerda,[2] I replied truthfully:

"He is very intelligent, but he doesn't have an education. He is a slum politician. He likes intrigues, to agitate."

One woman said it was a pity, that the bullet that got the major didn't get Carlos Lacerda.

"But his day . . . it's coming," commented another.

Many people had gathered and I was the center of attention. I was embarrassed because I was looking for paper and dressed in rags. I didn't want to talk to anyone, because I had to collect paper. I needed the money. There was none in the house to buy bread. I worked until 11:30. When I returned home it was midnight. I warmed up some food, gave some to Vera Eunice, ate and laid down. When I awoke the rays of the sun were coming through the gaps of the shack.

July 18   I got up at 7. Happy and content. Weariness would be here soon enough. I went to the junk dealer and received 60 cruzeiros. I passed by Arnaldo, bought bread, milk, paid what I owed him, and still had enough to buy Vera some chocolate. I returned to a Hell. I opened the door and threw the children outside. Dona Rosa, as soon as she saw my boy José Carlos, started to fight with him. She didn't want the boy to come near her shack. She ran out with a stick to hit him. A woman of 48 years fighting with a child! At times, after I leave, she comes to my window and throws a filled chamber pot onto the children. When I return I find the pillows dirty and the children fetid. She hates me. She says that the handsome and distinguished men prefer me and that I make more money than she does.

[2]Carlos Lacerda: a young energetic politician (current Governor of the State of Guanabara where Rio de Janeiro is located) who is always in the limelight with fiery speeches and ideas for social reform. A newsman as well, he wrote editorials which contributed to the downfall and eventual suicide of Brazil's President Getulio Vargas in 1954. Vargas was a dictator until 1945 and loved by the lower classes. His friends attempted to assassinate Lacerda but killed an army major instead.

Dona Cecilia appeared. She came to punish my children. I threw a right at her and she stepped back. I told her:

"There are women that say they know how to raise children, but some have children in jails listed as delinquents."

She went away. Then came that bitch Angel Mary. I said:

"I was fighting with the banknotes, now the small change is arriving. I don't go to anybody's door, and you people who come to my door only bore me. I never bother anyone's children or come to your shack shouting against your kids. And don't think that yours are saints; it's just that I tolerate them."

Dona Silvia came to complain about my children. That they were badly educated. I don't look for defects in children. Neither in mine nor in others. I know that a child is not born with sense. When I speak with a child I use pleasant words. What infuriates me is that the parents come to my door to disrupt my rare moments of inner tranquillity. But when they upset me, I write. I know how to dominate my impulses. I only had two years of schooling, but I got enough to form my character. The only thing that does not exist in the favela is friendship.

Then came the fishmonger Senhor Antonio Lira and he gave me some fish. I started preparing lunch. The women went away, leaving me in peace for today. They had put on their show. My door is actually a theater. All children throw stones, but my boys are the scapegoats. They gossip that I'm not married, but I'm happier than they are. They have husbands but they are forced to beg. They are supported by charity organizations.

My kids are not kept alive by the church's bread. I take on all kinds of work to keep them. And those women have to beg or even steal. At night when they are begging I peacefully sit in my shack listening to Viennese waltzes. While their husbands break the boards of the shack, I and my children sleep peacefully. I don't envy the married women of the favelas who lead lives like Indian slaves.

I never got married and I'm not unhappy. Those who wanted to marry me were mean and the conditions they imposed on me were horrible.

Take Maria José, better known as Zefa, who lives in shack number nine on "B" street. She is an alcoholic and when she is pregnant she drinks to excess. The children are born and they die before they reach two months. She hates me because my children thrive and I have a radio. One day she asked to borrow my radio. I told her I wouldn't loan it, and as she didn't have any children, she could work and buy one. But it is well known that people who are given to the vice of drink never buy anything. Not even clothes. Drunks don't prosper. Sometimes she throws water on my children. She claims I never punish my kids. I'm not given to violence. José Carlos said:

"Don't be sad, Mama. Our Lady of Aparecida will help you, and when I grow up I'll buy a brick house for you."

I went to collect paper and stayed away from the house an hour. When I returned I saw several people at the river bank. There was a man unconscious from alcohol and the worthless men of the favela were cleaning out his pockets. They stole his money and tore up his documents. It is 5 p.m. Now Senhor Heitor turns on the light. And I, I have to wash the children so they can go to bed, for I have to go out. I need money to pay the light bill. That's the way it is here. Person doesn't use the lights but must pay for them. I left and went to collect paper. I walked fast because it was late. I met a woman complaining about her married life. I listened but said nothing. I tied up the sacks, put the tin cans that I found in another sack, and went home. When I arrived I turned on the radio to see what time it was. It was 11:55. I heated some food, read, undressed, and laid down. Sleep came soon.

Richard M. Elman

Barbara dugan's story

"I wish I could remember when I got this sickle-cell anemia. A lot of us here have got it. They say we got it down South, but when you got it you just don't feel like doing too much. It makes your blood slow. Hard not to do too much when you are on the Welfare. They give you the pills and the special diets, and they send you to homemaking classes if they think it will help you, but they don't help you otherwise, so you still have a lot to do. They is picking up the kids after school because you don't want them walking home alone in a neighborhood like this . . . and they's cooking and shopping and laundry and housecleaning, and then well-baby clinic and sick-baby clinic and the clinic for yourself and that sickle-cell anemia. It's a full day.

"What I mean by a neighborhood like this is they's a lot of junkies and queers around here. Well, you just don't want to take a chance on them. So you carry your kids to school in the morning, and you carry them home after school. My kids live ten blocks away from the school. Ain't no buses down here . . .

"Ain't no lazy people on Welfare. Oh, maybe they is a few, but they ain't many. Seems like you got to pull your lazy butt from one place to the next, and you got to pull your kids with you wherever you go because they ain't no place you can leave them where they be safe . . . And sometimes you just don't feel like doing too much, but you still got to do it if you don't want them to take your kids away from you. *They find you lying in bed with nothing to do that's just what they going to do—sickle-cell anemia and all.* I got two sick kids like me and another in the Kennedy Home in the Bronx . . . I don't know about him . . . and sometimes you get pretty tired, but you just got to do certain things. After all, they say, if you don't take care of these kids, who will? They got a point. Ain't nobody else around here . . . and, after all, they's givin' you a special diet . . .

"But every time you want something extra from them, it's a whole nuisance. Like carfare. Sometimes I got to spend ninety cents for carfare for me and the kids to go off to Bellevue, because, as I told you, you can't leave them alone if you got to go there for some reason. And when I come back from Bellevue clinic, I got to rush over here to 28th Street for that carfare money or else I'm going to run short on food. Well, even so, they don't just give you your money like that. Sometimes they want proof. Sometimes they say they will owe it to you. You got to be careful about the ones who say that. I learned you got to insist right then and there you want that carfare or else you don't get it. So you just got to sit there and wait for the man until he gives it to you. You think they care? Sometimes I think I spend half my life waiting somewhere for ninety cents.

"And what I mean is, if I send my boy to get the money for me, how do I know if the man is going to listen to him? They don't like kids there. You know what they tell my boy when he goes? 'You make sure that gets to your mother. Don't you go spending on yourself.' Shit!

"And if they think they can get away with it, they liable to ask your boy all kinds of questions which they just know they got no business asking. They ask. Nothing private with them . . . Except when you want some money. Then you got a case against them.

"Shit! I could put up with anything if it weren't for the going this place and that. It's just about enough to make me give up everything sometimes, especially when I wake up feeling like I just can't do too much. But you know as well as I do that if you stay that way you are going to end up in a lot of trouble. So it's off to well-baby clinic and sick-baby clinic and now they even got my big girl seeing this psychiatrist. You think I let her go there alone? She goes there with me. Otherwise they say, 'Look at Barbara Dugan. She don't give a good goddamn,' and they try to take my kids away from me.

"Barbara Ann goes to the psychiatrist because they said so at school but if you ask me, it's because we've been pushed down for so long even the kids know it. She cries a lot. I used to be that way. You mustn't believe them when they say we get something for nothing. You may not have to work when you are on the Welfare, but you don't get anything for nothing.

They make it hard as dirt. If you want something, you got to go and get it. And you can't ask the man to help because how should he know. He don't even know you're alive half the time, and the other half it's always so much this and that. Takes a genius to know what anybody is talking about.

"Worse thing of all is when they decide you haven't done right. Then they get awful mean. They'll threaten you. Some of these women get sulky after one of those visits. They get sunk down real low. Every time they's a visit they get that way . . . real low . . . I don't get that way anymore. Any time they get after my tail, I take my kids and march right over here and I just start scuffling. They see me barging in like that, hollering for the man, and they just know I know my rights. You think they would treat me like those others?

"Well, you can't do that every day of the week when you got sickle-cell anemia. Sometimes you just wake up too tired. Sometimes you just don't want to go out looking for bargains. So, when night comes, you send your kids out for some of the *cuchifritos* or maybe delicatessen or a pizza pie and cokes and you just sitting around having an early supper when he comes by.

"He says, 'I just wanted to see how things are coming along.' Or he says, 'I thought I would like to find out how you are getting on.'

And then he looks at all that food and he gets real mean. Gives you a big lecture about how you got sickle-cell anemia and should eat the proper food or what is the use of the special diet anyway. And sure enough, next time you get a check they have taken away that special diet and you got to start all over again at Bellevue with a letter from the doctor.

"Seems like you're always doing the same things over and over again. You get an apartment. You start furnishing it. Then you got to move because of the relocation and it starts all over again. The man won't give you security. The man don't want you to live in that building. You go to look for an apartment and the man say, 'Who's looking after the children?' Seems like they always got to make remarks.

"That's why I don't want my boy to come home from that school. I know Welfare would give me more money. You think I want them snooping around? Kids grow up too fast here. That little Puerto Rican girl next door— she's fifteen and Welfare just give her money for the layette.

"Well, you just can't expect any different from people like us. It is the way people live, I guess. I think they ought to take all the kids away from some of these women. The way they bring up kids. You wouldn't want it to happen to your kid. They just don't know any better, and they afraid to ask without getting into trouble. It's a hard life. Every time you want something they's somebody there to make it hard for you. You say, 'I don't want to cause any trouble. I'll do just as they say.' Then you get a new investigator, and he's changed his mind about everything . . .

"I guess the Seventh Day Adventists do best on Welfare. They just like

Jews. Strict about everything, even food. If I was going to stay on Welfare, I would become a Seventh Day Adventist. But it is hard. You got to keep kosher. I think the Welfare likes these people better than us because you never see one of them getting into any trouble. They know how to live on the Welfare better than anybody else. Don't kid yourself. It must be hard, living like one of them. You can get money for the special diets, but they make you live just like a Jew . . .

"Some of the Puerto Ricans also do good because rice and beans and bananas are cheap, but they don't speak good English many of them, and some of them can't read or write. They can get all fouled up sometimes. I've seen it happen. Seems they will never understand why you don't ever get the same check twice. Well, I don't understand it either. I once asked the man and he said if you got a complaint to make . . . I ain't complaining, I told him. I was just wondering why. You think he ever told me? Probably he don't know himself. Like that time I caught that girl making a mistake in my arithmetic. I told her, 'You know you cheating me for fifty cents?' Well, she give me the money, but she turned red in the face and screamed, 'Keep a civil tongue in your mouth, Barbara!'

"Worst of all, though, are the special men who come at night. Like this one man asked me, 'If you got no man in the house what you got those pills?'[1] Well; I told him they give me them over at the Planned Parenthood two years ago and I ain't used any of them, as he can plainly see. Then he says, 'You make sure you stay that way,' as if there was a law against going to bed with a man—I mean if he is not your husband . . .

"Speaking of husbands, they used to come around to some of these women. Early in the morning you could hear them running down the stairs. You think they'd ask these women when they suspected something? No. They come around asking you. Well, I ain't going to tell on any of these girls when I know I'm likely to get my head split in.

"And what's so wrong if the men do drop by? Most of them got no place else to go. You know it's hard on women too not having their enjoyment once in a while. I don't do any of that stuff any more and I'm used to it. I don't even miss it. Maybe it's this damned anemia. But if I had a man I would want to have a separate room. It's not so nice when you sleep in the same room with your kids. Once I lived in a place. They was plaster falling on us every time. You go tell that to the Welfare. I have three rooms here, but one of them got no heat so we all sleep here in the living room as a practical matter. When I asked the Welfare for a bigger apartment, they said you got enough for just the three of you, and the man told me not to apply.

[1]Welfare agencies commonly attempt to ascertain the presence of a man in the house, capable of providing support, as a way of avoiding or terminating their obligations to women with dependent children.

"And that's the way it goes. You're always asking and being told and going from this place to that place. You're always waiting on lines. And all you ever think about is your Welfare. You're right. The way they got it fixed, it's just like being a junkie. You get your checks twice a month, but you got to keep going over there every few days for that extra little fix, and sometimes when you need it worst of all the man ain't nowhere to be seen.

"Worst of all, though, is when you got kids. They need gym shoes. You got to go to Welfare. They need a doctor's examination for camp, and again you got to arrange it for the Welfare. If you spend the money for food to buy your girl shoes (because she needs them for school and you figure you can save yourself a trip), the next thing you know the man wants to know why you ain't got no money. Kids just don't understand budgets, and when they want something, they really want it. I'd like to see the mother who thinks differently. But it don't work that way on Welfare. I get maybe $4.00 a week for their clothes and for me, but I am always using it to do other things. So then, when I need something, I got to go down and get the money from the Welfare, and they likely to want to know why. When you got kids, it's not a good thing to be on the Welfare.

"Well, nobody wants to get rid of their kids. Least I don't see how they could. So you are always buying now and asking questions later, and then they get angry with you and you catch hell. It's the goddamnedest life. If you buy at the store, they overcharge. If you go to the supermarket, you got to carry all that stuff back—and who's taking care of your kids meanwhile? I tell you it isn't easy when you got sickle-cell anemia . . . And some of these women got worse things than that. My neighbor's daughter is an epileptic . . . so when I asked the doctor for a housekeeper because they give her one, this man say, 'You got anybody with brain damage?' Seems it's different if you got brain damage because this man said if he gives me a housekeeper what am I going to do?

"Yes, seems like they always going to make remarks. I don't care if they white or colored. They make remarks. The colored's the worst sometimes. The young ones are a little better, but the way some of them come sniffing around, you think maybe they looking for the wrong thing. Worst of all is that you got to put up with this every day of the week. Except Sunday. They can't do much to you on Sunday. Last Sunday I took my kids in the subway up to the Bronx because this social worker said I should go to visit that other boy. I made a picnic lunch because it was supposed to be a nice day. Then it rained, and then we had to eat in the classrooms. Anyway, when we got back I only had 50¢, so I made my kids hot cereal with raisins for supper, and early next morning I sent my boy with a note to the Welfare center to get us back some of that money.

"Well, my boy say the man had this white stuff all over his face. He had a bad sunburn. It was the week before school was supposed to close, but he say, 'What are you doing out of school?' So he called the guidance counselor and told him he had my boy in his office, and then I had to come to school the next morning with my boy and explain or else they said they would suspend him. Well, I told that man at the school that we just didn't have any money so I had to send my boy over to the Welfare to get reimbursed because I had all this laundry to do else there wouldn't be clean clothes for anybody. You know what that man say then? He say, 'Next time that happens you just telephone.' Can you imagine? He wants me to telephone. Don't he know they don't give us any money to do that?

"It's like when I first started on the Welfare, and they said I was 'mismanaging.' This nice girl—she was a social worker—heard about me and she said she would take my case. So every time I would get a check from the Welfare, I cashed it and brought the money to her and she would put it in this little metal box in her desk. Then I could come over there every day, and she would give me a few dollars for the shopping because she said it was better to shop every day on what I was earning. She was a good sweet girl and she liked me, I think. It was better leaving the money with her than leaving it at home where I could get robbed. So every day I would come to her and get some of that money. Then one day toward the end of the month I come to her and she says, 'I'm sorry, Barbara, I just haven't got any more money for you,' and she opens up that box and shows me that it is empty. Sure enough, we sit down then and do some figuring, and I've taken out more than there was, but she says it isn't my fault. There just wasn't enough to begin with. And she says, 'Let me give you something from my pocketbook until the end of the month.' But when she opens her purse, she's only got about three or four dollars and some change.

" 'I don't know what we are going to do now,' I say. I look over at this girl. She's crying.

" 'Barbara,' she says, 'I'm sorry. I'm really sorry. If I give you this I just won't have anything.'

"So I had to go out then and buy at the Spanish grocer, and I've been paying him back ever since. You know, because I was short. Well, after that I figured I'll hold onto my money myself because if they ain't enough, they ain't much sense to budgeting. You know what I mean? I mean it's a little silly. Course, things can change. I get this special diet now, and I get a little more money. I don't wish to sound ungrateful. I just wish it wasn't always so hard. You know what I mean. And those remarks all the time. You know what I mean, don't you?"

Claude Brown (1937–   )

Everybody white she saw was mr. charlie

This day that I'd come up to talk was right after a big snowstorm. It was pretty cold; there was a lot of snow in the street. Traffic was moving at a snail's pace, almost at a standstill. Mama was complaining about how cold it was.

"Mama, why don't you complain to the landlord about this?"

"I called the office of the renting agency twice, and they said he wasn't in. When I called the third time, I spoke to him, but he said that it wasn't any of his problem, and I'd have to fix it up myself. I ain't got no money to be gettin' these windows relined."

"Mama, that's a whole lot of stuff. I know better than that. Why don't you go up to the housing commission and complain about it?"

"I ain't got no time to be goin' no place complainin' about nothin'. I got all this housework to do, and all this cookin'; I got to be runnin' after Pimp."

"Look, Mama, let's you and me go up there right now. I'm gonna write out a complaint, and I want you to sign it."

"I got all this washin' to do."

"Mama, you go on and you wash. I'm gon wait for you; I'm gon help you wash."

Mama started washing the clothes. As soon as she finished that, she had to put the pot on the stove. Then she had to fix some lunch. As soon as she finished one thing, she would find another thing that she had to do right away. She just kept stalling for time.

Finally, after waiting for about three hours, when she couldn't find anything else to do, I said, "Look, Mama, come on, let's you and me go out there."

We went over to 145th Street. We were going to take the crosstown bus to Broadway, to the temporary housing-commission office.

We were waiting there. Because of the snowstorm, the buses weren't running well, so we waited there for a long time. Mama said, "Look, we'd better wait and go some other time."

I knew she wanted to get out of this, and I knew if I let her go and put it off to another time, it would never be done. I said, "Mama, we can take a cab."

"You got any money?"

"No."

"I ain't got none either. So we better wait until another time."

"Look, Mama, you wait right here on the corner. I'm going across the street to the pawnshop, and when I get back, we'll take a cab."

She waited there on the corner, and I went over to the pawnshop and pawned my ring. When I came back, we took a cab to Broadway and 145th Street, to the temporary housing-commission office. When I got there, I told one of the girls at the window that I wanted to write out a complaint against a tenement landlord.

She gave me a form to fill out and said I had to make out two copies. I sat down and started writing. It seemed like a whole lot to Mama, because Mama didn't do too much writing. She used a small sheet of paper even when she wrote a letter.

She kept bothering me while I was writing. She said, "Boy, what's all that you puttin' down there? You can't be saying nothin' that ain't the truth. Are you sure you know what you're talking about? Because I'm only complaining about the window, now, and it don't seem like it'd take that much writing to complain about just one window."

"Mama, you're complaining about all the windows. Aren't all the windows in the same shape?"

"I don't know."

"Well, look here, Mama, isn't it cold in the whole house?"

"Yeah."

"When was the last time the windows were lined?"

"I don't know. Not since we lived in there."

"And you been livin' there seventeen years. Look, Mama, you got to do something."

"Okay, just don't put down anything that ain't true." She kept pulling on my arm.

"Look, Mama, I'm gonna write out this thing. When I finish I'll let you read it, and if there's anything not true in it, I'll cross it out. Okay?"

"Okay, but it just don't seem like it take all that just to write out one complaint."

I had to write with one hand and keep Mama from pulling on me with the other hand. When I finished it, I turned in the two complaint forms, and we left. Mama kept acting so scared, it really got on my nerves. I said, "Look, Mama, you ain't got nothin' to be scared of."

She said she wasn't scared, but she just wanted to stay on the good side of the landlord, because sometimes she got behind in the rent.

"Yeah, Mama, but you can't be freezin' and catching colds just because sometimes you get behind in the rent. Everybody gets behind in the rent, even people who live on Central Park West and Park Avenue. They get behind in the rent. They're not freezin' to death just because they're behind in the rent."

"Boy, I don't know what's wrong with you, but you're always ready to get yourself into something or start some trouble."

"Yeah, Mama, if I'm being mistreated, I figure it's time to start some trouble."

"Boy, I just hope to God that you don't get yourself into something one day that you can't get out of."

"Mama, everybody grows into manhood, and you don't stop to think about that sort of thing once you become a man. You just do it, even if it's trouble that you can't get out of. You don't stop to think. Look, forget about it, Mama. Just let me worry about the whole thing."

"Okay, you do the worryin', but the landlord ain't gon come down there in Greenwich Village and put you out. He gon put us out."

"Mama, he ain't gon put nobody out, don't you believe me?" I pinched her on the cheek, and she got a smile out.

After a couple of days, I came back uptown. I asked Mama, "What about the windows?"

"Nothin' about the windows."

"What you mean 'nothin' about the windows'?" I was getting a little annoyed, because she just didn't seem to want to be bothered. I said, "You mean they didn't fix the windows yet? You didn't hear from the landlord?"

"No, I didn't hear from the landlord."

"Well, we're going back up to the housing commission."

"What for?"

"Because we're gon get something done about these windows."

"But something's already been done."

"What's been done, if you didn't hear anything from the landlord?"

"Some man came in here yesterday and asked me what windows."

"What man?"

"I don't know what man."

"Well, what did he say? Didn't he say where he was from?"

"No, he didn't say anything. He just knocked on the door and asked me if I had some windows that needed relining. I said, 'Yeah,' and he asked me what windows, so I showed him the three windows in the front."

"Mama, you didn't show him all the others?"

"No, because that's not so bad, we didn't need them relined."

"Mama, oh Lord, why didn't you show him the others?'

"Ain't no sense in trying to take advantage of a good thing.'

"Yeah, Mama. I guess it was a good thing to you."

I thought about it. I thought about the way Mama would go down to the meat market sometimes, and the man would sell her some meat that was spoiled, some old neck bones or some pig tails. Things that weren't too good even when they weren't spoiled. And sometimes she would say, "Oh, those things aren't too bad." She was scared to take them back, scared to complain until somebody said, "That tastes bad." Then she'd go down there crying and mad at him, wanting to curse the man out. She had all that Southern upbringing in her, that business of being scared of Mr. Charlie. Everybody white she saw was Mr. Charlie.

Julian Mayfield (1928–)

A black woman shall see hard times

"A black woman shall see hard times," Gertrude Cooley quoted to herself as she walked toward Lenox Avenue. A few minutes before, she had discovered her bureau drawer pried open and the seven dollars missing. It was possible that someone might have sneaked into the apartment and stolen the money, but, as Hubert was missing, too, it was more than likely he had taken it. The gas and electric bills were long overdue and Consolidated Edison had already threatened to shut off the power. Gertrude did not know how she could get the money back even if she caught up with Hubert before he bet it, but she had to try. She walked in the general direction of John Lewis's house, hoping she would see him.

Mr. Curtis's candy store was empty except for the old man himself. He was sitting behind the counter reading a newspaper with the help of his steel-rimmed glasses. The store was old and dusty, chock-full of penny candy, comic books, vending machines, notebooks, pencils, and a variety of useless gadgets for children. The few people who patronized the store came from force of habit. Mr. Curtis did not seem to care any more, so long as he kept a roof over his head and was his own boss.

"Mrs. Cooley, ain't seen you in I don't know when. Come on in here. How are you?" He was a short little man, a brown West Indian with a completely bald head. His lively eyes smiled and frowned as their owner's moods changed. "Mister Hubert? No, he ain't been in here since last week sometime." Then he swung to his favorite subject, politics and The Black Man. "Say, did you read this week's *Amsterdam*?" He held the paper up in the air and slapped it with the back of his hand. "The white man's up to the same old tricks. They appointed this fellow Clarkson to the Interior department. You know him—his father owns all those funeral homes. Sent that boy to Harvard. He's supposed to be one of us but he wouldn't give a black man the time of day. He made an Uncle Tom statement about that boy they're trying to frame down there in Florida. But he's supposed to be in Washington representing us. Can you beat that!" He looked over his glasses at Gertrude and saw that she was not listening. "Are you all right, Mrs. Cooley? Something the matter with Mister Hubert?"

"No, nothing's the matter, Mr. Curtis." She walked to the door. "I'll be seeing you."

"If I can do anything to help, Mrs. Cooley," he said, "you just give a yell."

"Nothing's the matter," said Gertrude, "but thanks anyway."

Gertrude walked to Lenox Avenue. The afternoon was hot, but there were quite a few people on the street. Lord, Lord, thought Gertrude, where in the world am I supposed to start looking for that crazy man? Where did I sin to deserve all this misery? I must be about the unhappiest woman alive.

She had known Lenox Avenue for more than thirty years, but now she seemed to see it with new eyes, with deeper, more terrible understanding. Many of the faces were familiar: the young men on the corner laughing and boasting of empty accomplishments; old Slim Thomas who had drunk enough wine for the day and now lay asleep on the sidewalk near the Paradise Bar; the old men and women who sat on their folding chairs outside the stores and shops; the boy with the suit on the hanger stealing into Sol's pawnshop; the girl chewing gum behind the hot-dog stand on the corner; the insurance collectors and the furniture collectors and the salesmen with their bags full of sparkling junk and Bibles and cheap tapestries—all these familiar parts became a whole, complete picture as Gertrude looked at them, and the street with all its superficial color and sound became one flat, bluish gray, a dull, monotonous drone. Among these parts Gertrude saw herself, ungainly and ugly and tired in her work clothes. Most of us are just strivers, Gertrude thought, but strivers who never get anywhere. We just follow one day after another until the end comes, and, thank God, it comes soon. Gertrude knew, as she always had known, that you had to make the best of a bad situation. But today remembering the thirty years of her life spent near Lenox Avenue, years that seemed completely wasted, it was almost too much for her.

Suddenly she wanted to scream. She wanted to put her clenched fists to her head and yell bloody murder at the top of her voice. She wanted to break out of herself and make her voice heard everywhere. You couldn't just sit and take it forever. You had to cry for help. If you were being sucked under, if you were drowning, you screamed for somebody to throw you a lifeline.

She clenched her fists and opened her mouth to give way to that desperate need, but that was all. She was Gertrude Cooley who lived on One hundred and twenty-sixth Street, and everybody in her block knew her. When she walked down the street they said, "Good morning, Mrs. Cooley," and "How are you today, Mrs. Cooley?" They respected her, and women often came to her for advice because they knew she was one of the strong ones. She could not let herself go, not ever. She let her arms hang loose at her sides, and as she relaxed she began to tremble. She felt she had just had a narrow escape from something terrible and unknown.

James Agee (1909–1955)

A man and a woman and children

A man and a woman are drawn together upon a bed and there is a child and there are children:

First they are mouths, then they become auxiliary instruments of labor: later they are drawn away, and become the fathers and mothers of children, who shall become the fathers and mothers of children:

Their father and their mother before them were, in their time, the children each of different parents, who in their time were each children of parents:

This has been happening for a long while: its beginning was before stars:

It will continue for a long while: no one knows where it will end:

While they are still drawn together within one shelter around the center of their parents, these children and their parents together compose a family.

This family must take care of itself; it has no mother or father: there is no other shelter, nor resource, nor any love, interest, sustaining strength or comfort, so near, nor can anything happy or sorrowful that comes to anyone in this family possibly mean to those outside it what it means to those within it: but it is, as I have told, inconceivably lonely, drawn upon itself as tramps are drawn round a fire in the cruelest weather; and thus and in such loneliness it exists among other families, each of which is no less lonely, nor any less without help or comfort, and is likewise drawn in upon itself:

Such a family lasts, for a while: the children are held to a magnetic center:

Then in time the magnetism weakens, both of itself in its tiredness of aging and sorrow, and against the strength of the growth of each child, and against the strength of pulls from outside, and one by one the children are drawn away:

Of those that are drawn away, each is drawn elsewhere toward another: once more a man and a woman, in a loneliness they are not liable at that time to notice, are tightened together upon a bed: and another family has begun:

Moreover, these flexions are taking place every where, like a simultaneous motion of all the waves of the water of the world: and these are the classic patterns, and this is the weaving, of human living: of whose fabric each individual is a part: and of all parts of this fabric let this be borne in mind:

Each is intimately connected with the bottom and the extremest reach of time:

Each is composed of substances identical with the substance of all that surrounds him, both the common objects of his disregard, and the hot centers of stars:

All that each person is, and experiences, and shall never experience, in body and in mind, all these things are differing expressions of himself and of one root, and are identical: and not one of these things nor one of these persons is ever quite to be duplicated, nor replaced, nor has it ever quite had precedent: but each is a new and incommunicably tender life, wounded in every breath, and almost as hardly killed as easily wounded: sustaining, for a while, without defense, the enormous assaults of the universe:

So that how it can be a stone, a plant, a star, can take on the burden of being; and how it is that a child can take on the burden of breathing and how through so long a continuation and cumulation of the burden of each moment one on another, does any creature bear to exist, and not break utterly to fragments of nothing: these are matters too dreadful and fortitudes too gigantic to mediate long and not forever to worship:

Just a half-inch beyond the surface of this wall I face is another surface, one of the four walls which square and collaborate against the air another room, and there lie sleeping, on two iron beds and on pallets on the floor, a man and his wife and her sister, and four children, a girl, and three harmed boys. Their lamp is out, their light is done this long while, and not in a long while has any one of them made a sound. Not even straining, can I hear their breathing: rather, I have a not quite sensuous knowledge of a sort of suspiration, less breathing than that indiscernible drawing-in of heaven by which plants live, and thus I know they rest and the profundity of their tiredness, as if I were in each one of these seven bodies whose sleeping I can almost touch through this wall, and which in the darkness I so clearly see, with the whole touch and weight of my body: George's red body, already a little squat with the burden of thirty years, knotted like oakwood, in its clean white cotton summer union suit that it sleeps in; and his wife's beside him, Annie Mae's, slender, and sharpened through with bone, that ten years past must have had such beauty, and now is veined at the breast, and the skin of the breast translucent, delicately shriveled, and blue, and she and her sister Emma are in plain cotton shifts; and the body of Emma, her sister, strong, thick and wide, tall, the breasts set wide and high, shallow and round, not yet those of a full woman, the legs long thick and strong; and Louise's green lovely body, the dim breasts faintly blown between wide shoulders, the thighs long, clean and light in their line from hip to knee, the head back steep and silent to the floor, the chin highest, and the white shift up to her divided thighs; and the tough little body of Junior, hardskinned and gritty, the feet crusted with sores; and the milky and strengthless littler body of Burt whose veins are so bright in his temples; and the shriveled and hopeless, most pitiful body of Squinchy, which will not grow:

But it is not only their bodies but their postures that I know, and their weight on the bed or on the floor, so that I lie down inside each one as if exhausted in a bed, and I become not my own shape and weight and self, but that of each of them, the whole of it, sunken in sleep like stones; so that I know almost the dreams they will not remember, and the soul and body of each of these seven, and of all of them together in this room in sleep, as if they were music I were hearing, each voice in relation to all the others, and all audible, singly, and as one organism, and a music that cannot be communicated: and thus they lie in this silence, and rest.

Burt half-woke, whimpering before he was awake, an inarticulated soprano speaking through not quite weeping in complaint to his mother as before a sure jury of some fright of dream: the bed creaked and I heard her bare feet slow, the shuffling soles, and her voice, not whispering but stifled and gentle, Go to sleep now, git awn back to sleep, they aint nothin agoin to pester ye, git awn back to sleep, in that cadence of strength and sheltering comfort which anneals all fence of language and surpasses music; and George's grouched, sleepy voice, and hers to him, no words audible; and the shuffling; and a twisting in beds, and grumbling of weak springs; and the whimpering sinking, and expired; and the sound of breathing, strong, not sleeping, now, slowed, shifted across into sleep, now, steadier; and now, long, long, drawn off as lightest lithest edge of bow, thinner, thinner, a thread, a filament; nothing: and once more that silence wherein more deep than starlight this home is foundered.

THE FAMILY

Following the French anthropologist Claude Lévi-Strauss, we can define the family as a group manifesting these characteristics: it finds its origin in marriage; it consists of husband, wife and children born in their wedlock—though other relatives may find their place close to that nuclear group; and the members of the group are united by moral, legal, economic, religious, and social rights and obligations. These include a network of sexual rights and prohibitions and a variety of socially patterned feelings such as love, attraction, piety, awe, and so on. The family is among the few universal institutions of mankind. No known society lacks small kinship groups of parents and children related through the process of reproduction. But recognition of the universality of this institution must immediately be followed by the acknowledgment that its forms are exceedingly varied. The fact that many family organizations are not monogamic, as in the West, led many nineteenth-century observers to the erroneous conclusion that in "early" stages of evolution there existed no families, and that "group marriage," institutionalized promiscuity, prevailed. This is emphatically not the case; even though patterned wife-lending shocked the sensibilities of Victorian anthropologists, such an institution is evidently predicated on the fact that men have wives in the first place. No matter what their specific forms, families in all known societies have performed major social functions —reproduction, maintenance, socialization, and social placement of the young.

Families may be monogamous or polygamous—there are systems where one man is entitled to several wives and others where several husbands share one wife. A society may recognize primarily the small nuclear conjugal unit of husband and wife with their immediate descendants or it may institutionalize the large extended family linking several generations and emphasizing consanguinity more than the conjugal bond. Residence after marriage may be matrilocal, patrilocal or neolocal; exchanges of goods and services between families at the time of marriage may be based on bride price, groom price or an equal exchange; endogamous or exogamous regulations may indicate who is and who is not eligible for marriage; the choice of a mate may be controlled by parents or it may be left in large measure to the young persons concerned. These are but a few of the many differences which characterize family structures in variant societies.

The selections chosen illustrate but a handful of the great number of family patterns. The two selections of China—from the classical Chinese novel, *The Dream of the Red Chamber* by Tsao Hsueh-Chin, and Chin P'ng Mei's ribald sixteenth-century novel *The Adventurous History of Hsi Men and His Six Wives*—are meant to convey the prevailing atmosphere of large extended families in which the role expectations for husbands and wives as well as relatives differ fundamentally from those in the West. The readings indicate that the choice of mates in the oriental family is not left to the young persons concerned but authoritatively determined by their elders; thus the selection from the Japanese novel by Bakin poignantly focuses upon the conflict between youthful inclination and institutionalized requirements. The ancient Indian poem reprinted here emphasizes the importance of male offspring in the oriental family structure.

The short selection from Giovanni Verga's classic Sicilian peasant novel *The House by the Medlar Tree* presents the structure of the European peasant "stem" family which dominated rural Europe till very recently. Tolstoi in *Anna Karenina* succeeds in drawing the period of transition in the European upper and middle classes when the choice of mates slowly shifted from the parents to the children themselves. In the Epilogue to *War and Peace* Tolstoi beautifully describes the interlocking network of emotion and expectation which characterizes a "normal" Western monogamous family. The student might compare this picture point by point with that of oriental families depicted in the earlier selections.

Tsao Hsueh-Chin (? –1764)

The matriarch arranges a wedding

One day Black Jade heard an excited chatter in the Takuanyuan. Purple Cuckoo was sent out to investigate and brought back the report that the begonia trees in the Peony Court had suddenly burst into bloom. The day before, Pao-yu had remarked that he had seen some buds on the branches, but no one had paid any attention to him, as it was nowhere near the begonia season. Now there was no mistake about it; the trees were covered with a mass of bright flowers for all to see. Purple Cuckoo was told that the Peony Court was being tidied up in anticipation of the Matriarch's coming.

The Matriarch was already there when Black Jade arrived at Pao-yu's compound, as were Madame Wang and Madame Hsing. The Matriarch tried to minimize the unnaturalness of the phenomenon before them. "The begonia blooms in the spring," she said, "but it has been known to bloom in warm spells in the autumn. Though we are now in the Eleventh Moon, it is just as warm as in the Tenth, which again is not unlike the Third Moon, the season for begonias."

Madame Wang tried to fall in with the Matriarch's interpretation, and Li Huan suggested that it might be a sign of some happy event in Pao-yu's life. Quest Spring, however, was not deceived by these optimistic interpretations. She said nothing but thought to herself, "This cannot portend anything good, for what follows the way of Heaven prospers and what goes against it perishes. The unnatural phenomenon we are witnessing must be a warning that the family fortune is on the decline."

Black Jade was pleased with what Li Huan said, for Pao-yu's happy event would also be hers, she thought.

Now Chia Sheh and Chia Cheng also arrived on the scene. The former said that some malignant spirit must be behind the strange phenomenon and that the trees should be cut down. Chia Cheng, however, took the Confucian view that the best way to render the evil spirits powerless is to ignore them. The Matriarch was displeased with these unhappy suggestions. She said, "Say no more of portents and evil omens. If it portends good, you can all share it; if it portends evil, let me bear it all."

In changing his clothes to receive the Matriarch, Pao-yu had forgotten to put on his jade. When Pervading Fragrance noticed it and asked what he had done with it, he said he must have left it on the k'ang. The maid looked for it but could not find it. Pao-yu suggested that Musk Moon or

---

Reprinted from *Dream of the Red Chamber* by Tsao Hsueh-Chin, translated by Chi-Chen Wang, by permission of Twayne Publishers, Inc.

some other maid might have hidden the jade as a joke, but they all denied it. Thereupon, Pervading Fragrance made a thorough search of the Peony Court and then every court and compound where Pao-yu had been on that day, but all in vain. After a few days, all hope of recovering the jade was given up. Everyone now knew of the loss except the Matriarch, for no one wanted to distress her unnecessarily.

Pao-yu seemed listless and preoccupied after the loss, but Madame Wang thought this was only natural since he had worn the jade all his life. Besides, she had other things to occupy her thoughts. Her brother had been appointed to a high post in one of the ministries and was on his way back to the Capital. She looked forward eagerly to the reunion. Then the Imperial Concubine suddenly died, and for a month or so, Madame Wang and the Matriarch had to be in attendance at the funeral.

During this time, a gradual but noticeable change had come over Pao-yu. He looked normal enough but acted like one whose soul had left him. He followed the suggestions of Pervading Fragrance; otherwise he did nothing but eat and sleep or stare vacantly into space. The maid realized that he was not merely depressed at the loss of his jade but was really very sick. She went to Black Jade and hinted that perhaps she could divert Pao-yu and cheer him up, but Black Jade refused, believing that she would soon be married to Pao-yu and in the meantime must avoid gossip. Precious Virtue could hardly be expected to visit him, since she had been told of her coming engagement to him. Hsueh Yi-ma went to see him occasionally but she, too, was preoccupied because Hsueh Pan was at the time in prison on a charge of murder and, she was busy arranging for his defense.

After the funeral of the Imperial Concubine, the Matriarch went to the Peony Court to see Pao-yu. She was relieved to find him up and about and looking well but presently she noticed that he was merely following the promptings of Pervading Fragrance. The Matriarch said, "When I first came in, I saw nothing amiss but now I observe that he is very sick indeed. Tell me, how long has he been this way?"

Realizing that the truth could no longer be withheld, Madame Wang told the Matriarch about the loss of the jade. At once, the Matriarch became greatly alarmed and reproached Madame Wang for not having told her earlier. She declared that the jade was Pao-yu's life and must be recovered at any cost. She sent for Chia Cheng and, as he was not home, she gave orders immediately to post a reward of ten thousand taels. She decided to take Pao-yu to her own apartment, saying, "I did not like the strange behavior of the begonia trees. The jade kept the evil spirits from doing any harm, but without it Pao-yu is no longer safe here. That's why I want him taken to my apartment."

"Lao Tai-tai is right," Madame Wang agreed. "Lao Tai-tai's good angels will protect Pao-yu."

"It is not that," the Matriarch said, "but I have many volumes of Buddhist scriptures in my apartment. I'll have them read and keep the evil spirits away. Ask Pao-yu if he doesn't think so."

But Pao-yu only grinned.

It was a dismal New Year at the Yungkuofu. The festivities were half-hearted and perfunctory, owing to the recent death of the Imperial Concubine and Pao-yu's illness. To make things even more depressing, news of the death of Wang Tzu-teng came two days after the Feast of Lanterns. Madame Wang grieved deeply for the loss of her brother and fell ill herself as a consequence.

In the following month, Chia Cheng was appointed Imperial Commissioner of Revenues for the province of Kiangsi. He was not pleased with the new honor, as one might expect. First, he was without the kind of administrative experience needed for the post. Then, the Matriarch was aged and Pao-yu seriously ill. He was thinking about these things when he received a summons from the Matriarch.

Chia Cheng knew that the Matriarch had something important to impart when he saw that Madame Wang was also in the room, in spite of her illness.

"You are going away very soon," the Matriarch said to him. "There is something I would like to see settled before you go, but I don't know whether you will obey my wishes."

Chia Cheng stood up and said, "What is Lao Tai-tai saying! How would her son dare disobey anything Lao Tai-tai commands?"

The Matriarch continued, "I am now eighty-one years old. You have been appointed to a distant provincial post and you cannot decline the appointment because your elder brother is at home to wait upon me. After you are gone, I shall have only Pao-yu to cheer me. Now he is very sick and shows no signs of improvement. Yesterday I sent Lai Ta's wife to consult a fortuneteller who said that Pao-yu will get well only if he marries someone with the gold destiny. I know you do not believe in such things but I thought that under the circumstances you might be willing to forget your prejudices. Now tell me, do you want Pao-yu to get well or don't you."

Chia Cheng answered, "How could Lao Tai-tai ask such a question? For though your son cannot hope to be as solicitous and loving of his son as Lao Tai-tai is of her grandson, yet he is not without parental feelings. Your son may have been somewhat hard with Pao-yu, but that's because he has not tried to be worthy; it is like attempting to make a piece of iron into steel. But if Lao Tai-tai wishes him to get married, how could there be any possible objection? Your son has been concerned with Pao-yu's illness, too, but he has not asked to see him because Lao Tai-tai does not wish it. Would Lao Tai-tai permit her son to see him now?"

At this, the Matriarch bade Pervading Fragrance bring Pao-yu into the room. He inquired after Chia Cheng's health as Pervading Fragrance prompted but otherwise showed no interest in his surroundings. He was thin and emaciated, and his eyes were vacant; it was evident that he did not have full possession of his senses. Chia Cheng was grieved to see his son's condition and bade Pervading Fragrance take him back to his room and let him rest. Then he said to the Matriarch, "Lao Tai-tai knows best what to do to save Pao-yu and must do as she wishes. But has it been made clear to Yi Tai-tai?"

"Yi Tai-tai gave her consent long ago," Madame Wang said, "but we have not broached the subject of an early wedding because of the misfortune that has befallen Pan-er."

"That is an obstacle," Chia Cheng said. "It is hardly proper for a girl to marry while her elder brother is in prison. Moreover, there is the mourning for Her Highness to consider. Though weddings have not been forbidden, Pao-yu still ought to observe the rules governing the mourning for an elder sister, which means nine months. Again, the date for my departure has been set by the Board of Rites. How can matters be arranged in the few days still left?"

But the Matriarch had made up her mind. Everything must be done before Chia Cheng's departure, for it might be a year or two before he returned. So she said to Chia Cheng, "I can manage everything if you want to save Pao-yu's life. We can send Kuo-er to see Pan-er and get his consent; I am sure he will agree to this for Pao-yu's sake. As to the mourning period Pao-yu must observe, that does present an obstacle. But then this need not be a real wedding after all. It can be done quietly, so that it will seem more like a propitiatory service than a wedding ceremony. Pao Ya-tou is a sensible girl and will not mind. After Pao-yu recovers and is out of mourning, we can have a real wedding."

Chia Cheng's sense of propriety was outraged by the irregularity of the procedure outlined by the Matriarch, but he kept his feeling to himself. He said, "Doubtless Lao Tai-tai's judgment is right. But we must be sure to keep the matter secret so as to avoid criticism." He left the Matriarch's presence full of misgivings and melancholy reflections. The series of recent events would not occur in a family whose fortune was in the ascendancy. And now this irregular wedding. But owing to his impending departure, he had no time to see to things himself; the arrangements must be left to the Matriarch, Madame Wang, and Phoenix.

Pao-yu did not hear a word of the discussion, for he fell into a heavy sleep as soon as he returned to the inner room. Pervading Fragrance, however, heard everything. She was happy at the turn of events, for she was sure that Precious Virtue would be a good mistress. But what about Pao-yu? How would he react when he learned the truth? The Matriarch and Madame Wang knew something of the regard Pao-yu and Black Jade felt for each other but they did not know the whole story. Precious

Virtue vividly recalled that summer day when Pao-yu mistook her for Black Jade and the things he said to her. If Pao-yu felt so strongly about Black Jade, would not the knowledge of the approaching marriage make him worse instead of better?

With these thoughts in mind, she went to Madame Wang and confided to her all she knew. She also suggested that the Matriarch and Phoenix should be told, so that measures could be taken to safeguard Pao-yu. Madame Wang agreed, and Phoenix proposed a scheme to resolve the dilemma. First, the engagement was to be kept secret, so that Black Jade would not hear of it; then, Pao-yu was to be told that he was engaged to Black Jade and would soon be married to her.

Chin P'ng Mei (16th Century)

When six wives squabble

Gold Lotus, now that she was the favorite, became more and more domineering and capricious. Distrustful by nature, she could no longer find peace by day or by night. Her suspicions were readily aroused, and she was continually spying and peeping from behind walls and hedges. One day, being put out of temper by some trifling matter, Gold Lotus scolded her maid Spring Plum. Little Spring Plum was rather hot-tempered, and by no means inclined to accept a scolding patiently. She ran out of the pavilion and into the kitchen. There she could give uninterrupted expression to her rage at having been corrected. In a fury, she drummed with her little fists on the tables and benches. Her behavior elicited from Snowblossom, who, as usual, was supervising the work of the kitchen, the would-be playful remark: "You funny little thing, can't you arrange to have your hysterical fits somewhere else?"

Spring Plum, who was already sufficiently provoked, now lost her temper completely.

"I'll have no one make such insolent remarks to me!" she hissed.

Mistress Snowblossom wisely ignored her.

Spring Plum ran to her mistress, who was resting in the front apartment. She railed bitterly against Snowblossom, wildly exaggerating the incident by embellishments of her own.

Reprinted by permission of G. P. Putnam's Sons from Chin P'ng Mei—*The Adventurous History of Hsi Men and His Six Wives.* Copyright 1954 by G. P. Putnam's Sons. Also reprinted by permission of The Bodley Head, Ltd.

"Just think, Mistress, she said that you yourself handed me over to the master so that you might retain his favor!"

Her story naturally caused Gold Lotus no little displeasure.

Gold Lotus was feeling tired and languid. That morning she had risen earlier than usual. Moon Lady was attending a funeral, and Gold Lotus had accompanied her part of the way. She lay down again to sleep. Then she rose and went back to her pavilion. On the way thither she met Jade Fountain.

"Why so listless and silent?" Jade Fountain asked her, unsuspectingly. "Are you tired?"

"I feel a little tired, yes. Where have you been?"

"In the kitchen."

"Did that woman in the kitchen tell you anything?"

"No, I don't think so."

Gold Lotus tried to conceal her annoyance, and was silent. They sat down together, and for a while they passed the time with needlework. Then they decided to play a game of chess. No sooner had they begun to play than Hsi Men entered the room. He gazed with satisfaction at the two lightly, but always carefully dressed women. How attractive was the silver net over their hair! How charming the kiss curls on the temples, the earrings of blue sapphire, the red-embroidered ducks on their slippers! How pleasantly the red and silver of their collars stood out from the white of their thin, silken garments!

"As exquisite as two expensive flower girls, not to be had under a hundred ounces of silver!" he could not help exclaiming, in a jesting tone:

"Please, please! Flower girls, did you say? There may be some elsewhere in your household, but not here!" Gold Lotus retorted sharply.

Jade Fountain rose, tactfully seeking to withdraw. But he caught her and drew her back into the room.

"Where are going? No sooner do I come than she runs away! What have you two been doing while I was out?"

"At all events, nothing wrong. We've been playing chess," Gold Lotus replied. She helped him put the chessmen away. "You're back very early from the funeral."

"Yes, I wanted to escape the ceremonial feed in the temple, and then this oppressive heat! So I got out of it before the end."

"And Moon Lady?" asked Jade Fountain.

"She is coming later in the litter." He sat down. "I see you were in the middle of a game. What stakes were you playing for?"

"Oh, we were simply playing for the sake of the game."

"Good, I'll play a game with each of you, now. The loser must pay an ounce of silver for a feast."

"But we haven't any money on us," objected Gold Lotus.

"That doesn't matter. You can give me a hair clasp as a pledge."

He played first with Gold Lotus. She lost, and he was just about to set the pieces again for a game with Jade Fountain, when Gold Lotus suddenly rose, jostled the board so that the pieces fell over in confusion, and ran out of the room and into the park. Hsi Men followed at her heels. At last he found her hiding under a bough laden with fragrant blossoms. She was leaning on a rock at the edge of the water-lily tank.

"So you've hidden yourself here, my soft-spoken little darling!" he cried, breathless from running.

She looked at him with a roguish twinkle in her eyes.

"Villain, to pursue me so, merely because I've lost! You wouldn't dare do that to her!" Opening her little fist, she playfully cast a handful of blossoms over him. Hsi Men slipped under the boughs, took her amorously in his arms, and gently laid her on the rocky brink. Once again she had succeeded in kindling his desire for her body. In the midst of their lustful tongue play they were surprised by Jade Fountain.

"Get up and go to Moon Lady, she has just come home!" she called to Gold Lotus.

Gold Lotus disengaged herself from Hsi Men, and hurried away with Jade Fountain in order to greet Moon Lady as was incumbent on her.

"You have been able to amuse yourselves?" asked Moon Lady, calm and self-contained as ever.

"Yes, Sister Five lost an ounce of silver playing chess with our revered master, so tomorrow there will be something good to eat. Won't you risk a game, too?"

Gold Lotus soon took her leave, in order to rejoin Hsi Men in the pavilion. She thoughtfully had a hot bath prepared for him, and when evening came they diverted themselves like two merry little fishes in the water.

Although Moon Lady held first rank among Hsi Men's five wives, her delicate health usually prevented her from fulfilling the obligations imposed by her rank. When visits were to be paid, Li Kiao, the Second Wife, usually took her place. It was Li Kiao, Lady Sunflower, who managed the household budget. Snowblossom, the Fourth Wife, supervised the kitchen and the staff of servants. This explanation will enable the reader to understand what follows.

Hsi Men once more spent the night with his favorite, Gold Lotus. In a generous mood, he promised to go immediately after breakfast to the Temple Market to buy Gold Lotus some pearls. When he told Spring Plum to fetch breakfast from the kitchen—ordering lotus-seed tarts and silver carp soup—the little girl suddenly refused. She absolutely would not go to the kitchen.

Gold Lotus explained to Hsi Men: "There is someone in the kitchen who says I induced the little one to let you have your way with her, which proves that my love for you is mere hypocrisy. This person is trying to strike at me by reviling others. You had better not send the little one to the kitchen. Send Autumn Aster instead."

"Who is this person?"

"The question is superfluous. All the cooking pots in the kitchen are witnesses."

Hsi Men sent Autumn Aster to the kitchen. A long time passed; time enough to have cooked and eaten two breakfasts. Autumn Aster did not return. Hsi Men, his patience exhausted, was losing his temper when Gold Lotus decided to send Spring Plum after all.

"Go and see where that creature is loitering. She must be waiting to watch the grass grow."

Unwillingly Spring Plum obeyed. She found Autumn Aster standing in the kitchen, waiting.

"You naughty girl!" Spring Plum scolded her. "Our mistress will have your feet chopped off! What is keeping you here? Master Hsi Men has lost his temper. He is in a hurry to go to the Temple Market. I am to fetch you back at once—"

She was about to say more, when Snowblossom angrily interrupted her.

"Silly wench! A kettle is made of iron, isn't it? Do you think the soup in it will get hot of itself? The tarts, too, are not yet nearly done. One mustn't eat undercooked food; it gives one worms in the stomach!"

"Impudence!" cried Spring Plum, flaring up. "Do you think I came here for pleasure? Master Hsi Men will be furious when I tell him!"

She seized Autumn Aster by the ear, and dragged her out of the kitchen. "I have much more reason to complain of you, you insolent creature!" Snowblossom angrily shouted after her.

"Whether you complain or don't complain, it's all the same to me!" Spring Plum called back. "But you won't succeed in sowing dissension in this house!"

And she rushed off in a fury. Yellow with rage, she dragged Autumn Aster before her mistress.

"What is the matter?" Gold Lotus inquired.

"Ask her! When I came into the kitchen, she was standing about looking on. The other was taking as long to prepare a little breakfast as it takes to make doughnuts. When I told her that the master was in a hurry for his breakfast, that wretch burst out and called me a slave wench, and made other ugly personal remarks, even insulting our master! She seems to think the kitchen is intended for scolding and back-biting instead of for cooking."

"What did I tell you?" cried Gold Lotus, turning to Hsi Men. "We ought not to have sent Spring Plum to the kitchen. That woman tries to quarrel with everybody. She insinuates that Spring Plum and I have appropriated you for ourselves, and won't let you out of our bedchamber. To endure such insults from that woman!"

Her words produced the desired effect. Hsi Men angrily rushed into the kitchen, and kicked Snowblossom repeatedly. "You common, malicious bag of bones!" he cried. "What do you mean by abusing the girl I sent to fetch my breakfast and calling her slave wench? Look at your reflection in your own puddle!"

No sooner was his back turned that the poor woman unbosomed herself to Lai Pao's wife who, was working in the kitchen with her.

"You were here! You saw her come snorting in like an evil spirit! But did I say the least thing to her? She simply runs off with the other maid, tells tales to our master, turns white into black, and encourages him to abuse me for no reason at all! But you just wait, I'll keep a lookout for her! Just let that impudent slave wench come here again! It'll be the worse for her, that's all!"

In her anger she did not stop to consider that her words might be overheard by Hsi Men, who was listening outside the door. Suddenly, convulsed with rage, he stood before her, and soundly boxed her ears.

"You vicious, accursed slave!" he shouted. "You say you didn't insult her? With my own ears I heard how you abused her!"

And he beat and buffeted her again, until she shrieked with pain. Then he stormed out of the kitchen.

Moon Lady, who was having her hair dressed, heard the disturbance in the kitchen, and sent her maid, Little Jewel, to learn the cause of the trouble. Little Jewel came back with the story.

"He never ordered pastries for breakfast before!" said Moon Lady. "But that doesn't matter; they must be made as quickly as possible, and in any case Snowblossom mustn't scold the little girl without reason."

She sent Little Jewel to the kitchen again, to urge Snowblossom to hurry. After this interlude Hsi Men at last got his breakfast, after which he left the house for the Temple Market.

Snowblossom could not get over the treatment she had suffered, and as soon as Hsi Men left the house she went to Moon Lady to vindicate herself. She did not suspect that Gold Lotus was creeping after her, or that she hid herself under the window, where she could overhear everything that Snowblossom said to Moon Lady and to Sunflower, who was also in the room.

"You have no idea what this man-crazy woman, who has monopolized Hsi Men, says and does behind our backs," Gold Lotus heard her declare. "One doesn't blame a woman for carrying on all night with her husband once in a while. But this woman simply can't exist without a man. People like that are capable of anything. Didn't she get rid of her first husband by poisoning him? Who knows what mischief she may hatch against us yet? After all, she can't bear the sight of us, this creature who rolls her black eyes like a cackling hen, at every man she sees!"

"All this began harmlessly," Moon Lady quietly replied. "You only had to send the child back with the breakfast, and everything would have been all right. Why, then, this unreasonable abuse?"

"May I be stricken bald and blind if I ever abused her! Don't you listen to her if she comes here after me! Very likely she'll tell you that I tried to stab her in the back with the kitchen knife! Since she has had Hsi Men in her power she has grown so arrogant and presumptuous . . ."

"The Fifth Wife is outside," Little Jewel warned her; and a moment later Gold Lotus walked in. Looking steadily at her enemy, she began:

"Suppose I really had poisoned my first husband, then you shouldn't have allowed Master Hsi Men to receive me into his household. You would then have reason to complain that I prevent him from enjoying himself with you. As far as Spring Plum is concerned, she is not my property. If it doesn't suit you that she should wait on me, she can wait on Moon Lady again as far as I'm concerned. I shouldn't then feel that I was involved if you chose to quarrel with her. As a matter of fact, it is quite permissible nowadays for a widow to marry again. But I can go, if you wish; I can simply ask him to give me a letter of divorcement when he comes home."

"I don't really understand what you two have against each other," Moon Lady intervened. "But in any case, if you were all a little more sparing of words, everything would go smoothly."

"There you have it!" cried Snowblossom, angrily defending herself. "With a mouth like hers, that spills over like a raging torrent! How can one deal with her? And if her tongue were to be cut out before Hsi Men's very face she could still make him believe the contrary by rolling her eyes! If she had her way, we other women, with the exception of yourself, perhaps, would all be driven out of the house."

Moon Lady listened calmly to the accusations and insults which the two wrangling women hurled at each other. When it seemed that Snowblossom was about to spring at Gold Lotus's throat, Moon Lady ordered Little Jewel to take Snowblossom out of the room. Gold Lotus returned to her pavilion. She threw off her clothes, and washed the rouge and powder from her cheeks. With disheveled hair, a wild look in her eyes, and her flowerlike face stained with tears, she cast herself on the bed. She lay there until evening. At last Hsi Men returned. In perplexity, he asked her what had happened. Sobbing loudly, she told him, and demanded a letter of divorcement.

"When I came here it was not a financial speculation but an impulse of my heart," she protested. "And now I must suffer insult upon insult.

A husband poisoner, that's what she called me to my face. It would be better if I had no one to wait on me, for how can I expect a maid to remain in my service when she has to put up with continual abuse on my account . . . ?"

Hsi Men did not wait for her to finish. His three souls each took a mighty leap, his five senses bounded high as heaven. Like a whirlwind he swept down upon Snowblossom. He seized her by the hair of her head, and his short bamboo cudgel whistled through the air as he dealt her blow after blow, until Moon Lady caught and held his arm.

"You ought, all of you, to exercise a little self-control!" she gently reproached poor Snowblossom. "You shouldn't needlessly provoke your master!"

"You accursed, treacherous bag of bones!" Hsi Men roared at Snowblossom. "I myself heard you insult her in the kitchen! If you molest her again I refuse to be responsible for the consequences!"

He went back to the pavilion to give Gold Lotus the present which he had promised to bring her from the Temple Market. It was a set of pearls weighing four ounces. Gold Lotus was content. He had taken her part and had avenged her. She now stood higher than ever in his favor. She had only to ask for whatever she might crave and she received it tenfold. Had she not reason to rejoice?

Takizawa Bakin (1767–1848)

Shino and hamaji
or when duty is stronger than love

> Shino is being sent away from home by his wicked aunt and uncle (the foster parents of Hamaji) so that they can find a more desirable son-in-law. Shino suspects this, but his desire to restore his family fortunes (impelled by filial piety) causes him to leave the woman to whom he is engaged.

Shino had gone to bed, but could not sleep in his impatience for the dawn. His head was filled with thoughts about the future. He realized that he was alone, that there was no one to stop him from leaving, but he could not

Shino and Hamaji by Takizawa Bakin, translated by Donald Keene, appears in *Anthology of Japanese Literature: From the Earliest Era to the Mid-nineteenth Century;* compiled and edited by Donald Keene; published by Grove Press, Inc. Copyright 1955 by Grove Press, Inc.

help feeling unhappy that he was now to go far from the graves of his parents and the place where he was born. Hamaji, who regretted his departure no less than he, slipped out of bed and, taking care lest her parents now snoring in the back room should waken, those parents toward whom she felt a resentment she could not voice, she soundlessly stepped over the threshold of the barrier of her maiden reserve, which had hitherto kept her from going to Shino. Her knees trembled, and she could scarcely walk. How dreary, sad, bitter, and hateful the inconstant world now seemed.

When Hamaji came close to Shino's pillow, he saw that someone had entered his room. He drew his sword to him and sprang to his feet. "Who is it?" he cried, but no sound answered him. He wondered uneasily whether some enemy had come to observe whether he was asleep, with an intent of stabbing him to death. He grew more and more tense. He flashed the light of the lamp and peered into the darkness. Then he saw that it was Hamaji. Without warning she had appeared, and now lay motionless on the other side of the mosquito netting, seemingly shaken by grief but unwilling to reveal it by her tears.

Shino was a brave soldier who would not flinch before the fiercest enemy, but now he was disturbed. Controlling his emotions, he left the mosquito netting and, unfastening the cords by which the netting hung, drew his pallet to where she lay. "Hamaji, what has brought you here in the middle of the night, when you should be sleeping? Have you never heard the proverb, 'Don't arouse suspicion by tying your shoes in a melon field or lifting your arms to straighten your hat under a plum tree'?" When he had thus admonished her, Hamaji, brushing away her tears, lifted her head in indignation. "How cruel of you to ask me in that impersonal way why I have come! If we were joined but casually, and husband and wife only in name, you might well speak in that way, but were we not wedded with my parents' consent? Whatever might be the proper behavior under normal circumstance, it is heartless of you tonight, our last night for farewells, to order me out with a careless word. You are pretending not to know what I feel because you are afraid that it might bring discredit to you. How hardhearted of you!"

Shino sighed in spite of himself. "I am not made of wood or stone, and whether I wish it or not, I know what tender emotions are. But it can serve no purpose for me to voice my feelings—it will only arouse the antipathy of your parents. I know that you will be true to me, and you must know what lies within my heart. Koga is a bare forty miles from here—it takes no more than three or four days to make the journey there and back. Please wait till I return."

He tried to persuade her, but Hamaji, wiping her eyes, exclaimed, "What you say is false. Once you leave here, what will ever make you return? The bird in the cage longs for the sky because it misses its friends; when a man leaves his home it must be because he is thinking of his advancement. You cannot depend on the likes and dislikes of my parents. They are sending you off now because you are in the way, and they have no desire for your return. Once you leave here, when will you come back? Tonight is the last we have of parting . . ."

"Ever since the seventh moon of last year the little stream of our love has been dammed and its passage cut, but one thing remains unchanged, like the downward flow of water, the sincerity of my heart. Not a day has passed but that I have prayed morning and night for your safety, success, and prosperity, but you remain extremely hard of heart. Is it because of duty to your aunt that you are deserting your wife? If you had in you one-hundredth of the depth of feeling that I have, you would say to me, 'For one reason or another the day of my return may be doubtful. Let us steal off secretly, together.' We are man and wife—who would slander you as being my paramour? But however cruel I think you are, I cannot, with my woman's heart, bear separation from you, kill me with your sword. I shall wait for you in the world to come, a hundred years if need be." To these she added many words of persuasion, relating one after another the painful griefs she bore, and though she kept herself from weeping aloud, a thousand tears coursed down to soak her sleeves.

Shino could not very well say that it would bring embarrassment if her voice were heard outside the room, and since there was no way now to undo the ties that bound them, he could only sigh sadly. He said, with his hands folded on his knees, "Every one of your reproaches is justified, but what can I do, Hamaji? My departure is by command of my uncle and aunt. I know that they are really sending me to a distant place so as to get a new husband for you. The problem is that I am, and yet I am not, your husband. Your parents probably suspect our true feelings. However, if now I let myself be guided by my emotions and take you off with me, what man will not say that it was a deed of lust? It will be painful for you to remain behind, but it will be for my sake. And if I go, though it is difficult for me to do so, will that not also be for your sake? Even if we are parted for a brief while, as long as our hearts remain constant a time will surely come when we can be fully married. Please go back to bed before your parents awaken. Please go quickly."

His words were in vain; she remained as she was and merely shook her head. "Having gone this far, it doesn't matter any longer. If my parents waken to find me here and reprove me for it, I too shall have something to say. I will not move from here unless I hear you say that you want me to go with you. Otherwise, kill me." Weak as is a woman's will, hers was firmly set and would not alter.

Shino was quite at a loss. A note of irritation came into his voice, although he still kept it low. "You still do not understand. As long as we remain alive a time will surely come when we can meet. How can death be the proper state for man? If you interfere with me, now that I have this rare chance of winning success granted to me by my aunt and uncle, you are not my wife. Perhaps you are an enemy from a previous existence."

Hamaji sank deeper in tears. "There is nothing I can do when you make me feel that if I obtain my heart's desire I shall become your enemy. If my thoughts are really selfish, I shall put them aside and remain here. May your journey be a safe one. Be careful lest, these terribly hot days, you get sunstroke on the way. In the winter months when the wind blows down the northern mountains, send me messages about yourself with the wind. I shall think only of the fact that you are alive and safe. If the weakening thread of my life should break, now will be our parting for this existence, and all I shall have to depend upon is the yet unseen world to come. Our ties are certain to endure through both worlds. Please never change your heart." Thus she spoke of uncertainties; however wise her prayers may have seemed, the heart of this innocent maiden was pitiful.

Shino in spite of himself also felt downcast, and unable to comfort her could only nod. There was nothing else for him to say. Just then the first cock-crow announced the dawn, and Shino, pulling himself together, said, "In a few moments your parents will waken. Hurry! Hurry!"

Hamaji at last got up, and recited the poem,

Yo mo akeba	Now that dawn has come
Kitsu ni hamenan	Perhaps the foxes will eat
Kudakake no	Those cursed roosters,
Madaki ni nakite	Crowing in the early morn,
Sena wo yaritsutsu	Chasing you away from me.

"That poem was inspired by the casual love of a traveler, but now is the moment of separation with a departing husband. If the cocks do not crow the sky will not grow light; if the dawn does not come, no one will waken. Oh, hateful crowing of the cock! For us only are there no nights of meeting— between us stands an unyielding barrier. Even the moon at dawn brings only sorrow."

As she murmured these words, about to leave, there was a cough outside the door and a faint rapping on the door. "The cocks have crowed, are you not awake yet?" It was his servant who called. Shino hastily answered and the man withdrew to the kitchen. "Quickly, before he returns!" Shino said, pushing her out. Hamaji, her eyelids swollen from weeping, looked back from the darkness where she stood, but her eyes were too misted with tears for her to see him. She leant against the wall a moment, and then went to weep in her room.

Sadder even than parting at death is parting in life, than which is nothing sadder. Ah, rare indeed is this maiden! Yet has she to share a bedquilt with her husband, yet to range her pillow by his and sleep with entwined arms. Their love was more admirable than that of a century of ordinary husbands and wives. Shino, though drawn by love, does not waver in his heart, but by being faithful to his love, maintains the proper separation between men and women. Those who wander in the maze of the passions show insufficient wisdom and a lack of discrimination. Few of all the many young people who have once approached the brink have escaped being drowned. But here we have a case of a righteous husband and a chaste wife. Hamaji's love was not one of pleasures and lust. Shino's sighs were of sorrow, and not of weakness. Hamaji's love is still to be sought; men like Shino are rarer than ever.

by an unknown Indian author about 600 B.C.

On the importance of having a son

In him a father pays a debt
And reaches immortality,
When he beholds the countenance
Of a son born to him alive.

Then all the joy which living things
In waters feel, in earth and fire,
The happiness that in his son
A father feels is greater far.

At all times fathers by a son
Much darkness, too, have passed beyond:
In him the father's self is born,
He wafts him to the other shore.

Food is man's life and clothes afford protection,
Gold gives him beauty, marriages bring cattle;
His wife's a friend, his daughter causes pity:
A son is like a light in highest heaven.

Translated by Arthur A. Macdonell.

Giovanni Verga (1840–1922)

A patriarch

Once the Malavoglia were as numerous as the stones on the old road to Trezza; there were some even at Ognino and at Aci Castello, and good and brave seafaring folk, quite the opposite of what they might appear to be from their nickname of the Ill-wills, as is but right. In fact, in the parish books they were called Toscani; but that meant nothing, because, since the world was a world, at Ognino, at Trezza, and at Aci Castello they had been known as Malavoglia, from father to son, who had always had boats on the water and tiles in the sun. Now at Trezza there remained only Padron 'Ntoni and his family, who owned the Provvidenza, which was anchored in the sand below the washing-tank by the side of Uncle Cola's Concetta and Padron Fortunato Cipolla's bark. The tempests, which had scattered all the other Malavoglia to the four winds, had passed over the house by the medlar-tree and the boat anchored under the tank without doing any great damage; and Padron 'Ntoni, to explain the miracle, used to say, showing his closed fist, a fist which looked as if it were made of walnut wood, "To pull a good oar the five fingers must help one another." He also said, "Men are like the fingers of the hand—the thumb must be the thumb, and the little finger the little finger."

And Padron 'Ntoni's little family was really disposed like the fingers of a hand. First, he came—the thumb—who ordered the fasts and the feasts in the house; then Bastian, his son, called Bastianazzo because he was as big and as grand as the Saint Christopher which was painted over the arch of the fish-market in town; and big and grand as he was, he went right about at the word of command, and wouldn't have blown his nose unless his father had told him to do it. So he took to wife La Longa when his father said to him "Take her!" Then came La Longa, a little woman who attended to her weaving, her salting of anchovies, and her babies, as a good house-keeper should do; last, the grand-children in the order of their age—'Ntoni, the eldest, a big fellow of twenty, who was always getting cuffs from his grandfather, and then kicks a little farther down if the cuffs had been heavy enough to disturb his equilibrium; Luca, "who had more sense than the big one," the grandfather said; Mena (Filo-mena), surnamed Sant'Agata because she was always at the loom, and the proverb goes, "Woman at the loom, hen in the coop, and mullet in January;" Alessio, our urchin, that was his grandfather all over; and Lia (Rosalia), as yet neither fish nor flesh. On

From *The House by the Medlar Tree* by Giovanni Verga, translated by Mary A. Craig.

Sunday, when they went into church one after another, they looked like a procession.

Padron 'Ntoni was in the habit of using certain proverbs and sayings of old times, for, said he, the sayings of the ancients never lie: "Without a pilot the boat won't go;" "To be pope one must begin by being sacristan," or, "Stick to the trade you know, somehow you'll manage to go;" "Be content to be what your father was, then you'll be neither a knave nor an ass," and other wise saws. Therefore the house by the medlar was prosperous, and Padron 'Ntoni passed for one of the weighty men of the village, to that extent that they would have made him a communal councillor. Only Don Silvestro, the town-clerk, who was very knowing, insisted that he was a rotton codino, a reactionary who went in for the Bourbons, and conspired for the return of Franceschello, that he might tyrannize over the village as he tyrannized over his own house.

Lev Tolstoi

The perils and dilemmas of marital choice

Vronski satisfied all the wishes of the mother. He was very rich, clever, of a distinguished family, on the road to a brilliant military career at court, and an attractive man. One could not expect anything better.

Vronski openly courted Kitty at balls, danced with her, and called at her house, consequently there could be no doubt as to the seriousness of his intentions. But, in spite of that, her mother was all that winter in a terrible unrest and agitation.

The princess herself had married thirty years before, the match having been made by an aunt of hers. The fiancé, of whom everything was known in advance, came and saw the fiancée, and they saw him; the matchmaking aunt found their mutual impressions, and informed both parties of them; the impressions were favourable; then, at an appointed day, the proposal was made to the parents, and they, who had been expecting it, accepted it. Everything took place so easily and so simply. At least it so appeared to the princess. But she had found in the case of her daughters that this seemingly customary affair of getting one's daughters married was not at all such an easy and simple matter. How many frights they had had, how many thoughts they had thought, how much money was spent, and how many conflicts she had had with her husband, when marrying their two eldest daughters, Darya and Natalie! Now, in taking their youngest out into

From *Anna Karenina* by Lev Tolstoi (1876), translated by Leo Wiener.

society, they passed through the same fears, the same doubts, and still greater quarrels, than they had had in the case of the elder daughters.

The old prince was, like all fathers, particularly exacting in reference to the honour and purity of his daughters; he was senselessly jealous of his daughters, and especially of Kitty, who was his favourite, and at every step made scenes with the princess for compromising the daughters. The princess had been used to it from the elder daughters, but now she felt that her husband's exactions had a better foundation. She saw that of late many things had changed in society manners, and that a mother's duties were more difficult than ever. She saw that the girls of Kitty's age formed some kind of societies, attended some kind of university courses, freely kept company with men, drove by themselves in the streets, many of them no longer curtsied, and, what was worse, were firmly convinced that it was their business, and not that of their parents, to choose husbands for themselves. "Nowadays they do not give girls in marriage, as was the case in former days," was what all these young girls, and even all older people, thought and said. But how they gave daughters in marriage these days was what the princess was unable to find out. The French method, which was for the parents to decide the fate of their children, was rejected and criticized; the English custom of granting the girl full liberty was not accepted, either, and was impossible in Russian society. The Russian custom of match-making was regarded as something monstrous,—all laughed at it, even the princess. But how one was to marry or be given in marriage was something which nobody knew anything about. All with whom the princess happened to talk told her the same thing:

"It is about time, I tell you, to give up that old custom. It is the young people who are to marry, and not the parents; consequently it ought to be left to the young people to arrange it as they know best."

It was all right for those to talk that way who had no daughters; but the princess knew that with such intimate relations the daughter might fall in love, and that she might fall in love with one she could not marry, or who was not fit for a husband. No matter how much people tried to impress upon the princess that in our day the young people ought to decide their own fate, she could not believe it, just as she could not believe that at any time loaded revolvers might be good toys for children five years of age. And thus the princess was worried more about Kitty than she had been about her other daughters.

Now she was afraid that Vronski might stop at the mere courting of her daughter. She saw that her daughter was already in love with him, but she consoled herself with the thought that he was an honourable man, and so would not do so. But, at the same time, she knew how, with the present free relations between the sexes, it would be an easy matter to turn a girl's head, how, in general, men thought lightly of such a crime. The previous week Kitty had told her mother the conversation which she had had with Vronski during a mazurka; this conversation partly calmed the princess; but she could not be entirely at rest. Vronski had told Kitty that he and his brother were so accustomed to submit to their mother in everything that they never decided to undertake anything important without first consulting her. "Even now I am waiting for my mother's arrival in St. Petersburg, as for a specially happy event," he had said.

Kitty had told this without ascribing any importance to these words. But the princess understood them differently. She knew that his mother was expected any day, and that she would approve of her son's choice, and it seemed strange to her that he kept from proposing for fear of offending his mother; still, still, she was so anxious to get her daughter married, and, above all, wanted so much to have her agitation allayed, that she believed it. However painful it now was for the princess to see the misfortune of her eldest daughter, Dolly, who was getting ready to leave her husband, the agitation about the impending fate of her youngest daughter absorbed all her feeling. On the present day she had received a new cause for unrest. She was afraid that her daughter, who at one time had had a feeling, she thought, for Levin, from an overscrupulous sense of honesty might refuse Vronski, and, in general, that Levin's arrival might entangle and delay the affair which was so near a solution . . .

When the evening was over, Kitty told her mother of her conversation with Levin, and, in spite of the pity which she felt for him, she was happy at having had a *proposal.* She had no doubt but that she had acted right. But, when she retired, she could not fall asleep for a long time. One impression pursued her persistently. It was Levin's face with the overhanging eyebrows and his kindly eyes grazing gloomily underneath them, when he stood talking to her father and looking at her and Vronski. And she felt so sorry for him that tears came to her eyes. But immediately she thought of him for whom she had exchanged him. She vividly recalled that manly, firm face, that noble calm, and in everything the beaming kindness to everybody; she recalled the love for her felt by him whom she loved, and again she felt joyous, and with a smile of happiness lay down on her pillow. "I am sorry. I am sorry, but what is to be done? It is not my fault," she said to herself; but an inner voice told her something different. She did not know whether she regretted having misled Levin, or having refused him. But her happiness was poisoned by doubts. "O Lord, have mercy, O Lord, have mercy, O Lord, have mercy!" she kept saying to herself, until she fell asleep.

At that time, down-stairs, in the prince's small cabinet, was taking place one of the frequently repeated scenes between the parents on account of their favourite daughter.

"What? Is it this," cried the prince, waving his arms, and immediately wrapping himself in his squirrel-fur morning-gown, "you have no pride, no dignity! You are disgracing and ruining the girl with that base, stupid suit!"

"But, pray, for God's sake, prince, what have I done?" said the princess, almost in tears.

Happy and satisfied after her conversation with her daughter, she had come, as usual, to bid him good night, and, though she had had no intention of speaking to him about Levin's proposal and Kitty's refusal, she hinted to her husband that she thought the affair with Vronski all settled, and that it would be decided as soon as his mother should arrive. It was in response to these words that her husband flew up so and began to shout indecent words.

"What have you done? It is this: in the first place, you entice a fiancé, and all of Moscow will be talking about it, and rightly so. If you give evening entertainments, invite everybody, but not chosen prospective fiancés. Invite all those *puppies*" (thus the prince called all the Moscow young men), "call a piano player, and let them dance, but not as this evening,—fiancés. It makes me sick, sick, I say, to see it, and you have succeeded in turning the girl's head. Levin is a thousand times better man than he. He is a St. Petersburg dandy, such as are turned out by a machine, all of one fashion, and a worthless lot. Even if he were a prince of the blood, my daughter has no need of him."

"But what have I done?"

"It is this—" the prince cried, in anger.

"I know, if we are to listen to you," the princess interrupted him, "we shall never get our daughter married. If so, we had better go into the country."

"It would be better."

"Hold on. I am not currying favour with him, am I? Not in the least. He is a very nice young fellow, and in love, and she, I think—."

"Yes, that's what you think! And she will really fall in love with him, and he has marrying as much in mind as I have! Oh! If my eyes did not see it all! 'Ah, spiritualism! Ah, Nice! Ah, at the ball!' " And the prince imagining that he was impersonating his wife, curtsied at every word. "Yes, when we shall have caused Kitty's misfortune, when indeed she will take it into her head.—"

"Why do you think so?"

"I do not think, I know: that's what we men have eyes for. I see a man who has serious intentions,—that is Levin; and I see a merry bird, like that quill-driver, who thinks only of having a good time."

"When you take something into your head—"

"Yes, you will think of it when it is too late, as with Dolly."

"All right, all right, we shall not speak of it," the princess stopped him, as she thought of unhappy Dolly.

"Very well, and good night!"

And making the sign of the cross over each other and kissing, the two separated, each of them feeling that they persisted in their own opinions.

The princess had been firmly convinced that that evening had decided Kitty's fate, and that there could be no question about Vronski's intentions; but her husband's words troubled her. And upon returning to her chamber, she, like Kitty, in terror before the uncertainty of the future, several times repeated inwardly: "O Lord, have mercy, O Lord, have mercy, O Lord, have mercy!"

Lev Tolstoi

A happy family

Natasha was married in the early spring of 1813, and by 1820 she had three daughters and a son. The latter had been eagerly desired, and she was now nursing him herself. She had grown stouter and broader, so that it was hard to recognise in the robust-looking young mother the slim, mobile Natasha of old days. Her features had become more defined, and wore an expression of calm softness and serenity. Her face had no longer that ever-glowing fire of eagerness that had once constituted her chief charm. Now, often her face and body were all that was to be seen, and the soul was not visible at all. All there was to be seen in her was a vigorous, handsome, and fruitful mother. Only on rare occasions now the old fire glowed in her again. That happened only when, as now, her husband returned after absence, when a sick child recovered, or when she spoke to Countess Marya of Prince Andrey (to her husband she never spoke of Prince Andrey, fancying he might be jealous of her love for him), or on the rare occasions when something happened to attract her to her singing, which she had entirely laid aside since her marriage. And at those rare moments, when the old fire glowed again, she was more attractive, with her handsome, fully-developed figure, than she had ever been in the past.

Since her marriage Natasha and her husband had lived in Moscow, in Petersburg, on their estate near Moscow, and at her mother's; that is to say, at Nikolay's. The young Countess Bezuhov was little seen in society, and those who had seen her there were not greatly pleased with her. She was neither charming nor amiable. It was not that Natasha was fond of solitude (she could not have said whether she liked it or not; she rather supposed indeed that she did not), but, as she was bearing and nursing

From *War and Peace* by Lev Tolstoi (1869), translated by Constance Garnett.

children, and taking interest in every minute of her husband's life, she could not meet all these demands on her except by renouncing society. Every one who had known Natasha before her marriage marvelled at the change that had taken place in her, as though it were something extraordinary. Only the old countess, with her mother's insight, had seen that what was at the root of all Natasha's wild outbursts of feeling was simply the need of children and a husband of her own, as she often used to declare, more in earnest than in joke, at Otradnoe. The mother was surprised at the wonder of people who did not understand Natasha, and repeated that she had always known that she would make an exemplary wife and mother. "Only she does carry her devotion to her husband and children to an extreme," the countess would say; "so much so, that it's positively foolish."

Natasha did not follow the golden rule preached by so many prudent persons, especially by the French, that recommends that a girl on marrying should not neglect herself, should not give up her accomplishments, should think even more of her appearance than when a young girl, and should try to fascinate her husband as she had fascinated him before he was her husband. Natasha, on the contrary, had at once abandoned all her accomplishments, of which the greatest was her singing. She gave that up just because it was such a great attraction. Natasha troubled herself little about manners or delicacy of speech; nor did she think of showing herself to her husband in the most becoming attitudes and costumes, nor strive to avoid worrying him by being overexacting. She acted in direct contravention of all those rules. She felt that the arts of attraction that instinct had taught her to use before would now have seemed only ludicrous to her husband, to whom she had from the first moment given herself up entirely, that is with her whole soul, not keeping a single corner of it hidden from him. She felt that the tie that bound her to her husband did not rest on those romantic feelings which had attracted him to her, but rested on something else undefined, but as strong as the tie that bound her soul to her body.

To curl her hair, put on a crinoline, and sing songs to attract her husband would have seemed to her as strange as to deck herself up so as to please herself. To adorn herself to please others might perhaps have been agreeable to her—she did not know—but she had absolutely no time for it. The chief reason why she could not attend to her singing, nor to her dress, nor to the careful choice of her words was that she simply had no time to think of those things.

It is well known that man has the faculty of entire absorption in one subject, however trivial that subject may appear to be. And it is well known that there is no subject so trivial that it will not grow to indefinite proportions if concentrated attention be devoted to it.

The subject in which Natasha was completely absorbed was her family, that is, her husband, whom she kept such a hold on so that he should belong entirely to her, to his home and her children, whom she had to carry, to bear, to nurse and to bring up.

And the more she put, not her mind only, but her whole soul, her whole being, into the subject that absorbed her, the more that subject seemed to enlarge under her eyes and the feebler and the more inadequate her own powers seemed for coping with it, so that she concentrated them all on that one subject, and still had not time to do all that seemed to her necessary.

There were in those days, just as now, arguments and discussions on the rights of women, on the relations of husband and wife, and on freedom and rights in marriage, though they were not then, as now, called *questions*. But these questions had no interest for Natasha, in fact she had absolutely no comprehension of them.

Those questions, then as now, existed only for those persons who see in marriage only the satisfaction the married receive from one another, that is, only the first beginnings of marriage and not all its significance, which lies in the family.

Such discussions and the questions of to-day, like the question how to get the utmost possible gratification out of one's dinner, then, as now, did not exist for persons for whom the object of dinner is nourishment, and the object of wedlock is the family.

If the end of dinner is the nourishment of the body, the man who eats two dinners obtains possibly a greater amount of pleasure, but he does not attain the object of it, since two dinners cannot be digested by the stomach.

If the end of marriage is the family, the person who prefers to have several wives and several husbands may possible derive a great deal of satisfaction therefrom, but will not in any case have a family. If the end of dinner is nourishment and the end of marriage is the family, the whole question is only solved by not eating more than the stomach can digest and not having more husbands or wives than as many as are needed for the family, that is, one wife and one husband. Natasha needed a husband. A husband was given her; and her husband gave her a family. And she saw no need of another better husband, and indeed, as all her spiritual energies were devoted to serving that husband and his children, she could not picture, and found no interest in trying to picture, what would have happened had things been different.

Natasha did not care for society in general, but she greatly prized the society of her kinsfolk—of Countess Marya, her brother, her mother, and Sonya. She cared for the society of those persons to whom she could rush in from the nursery in a dressing-gown with her hair down; to whom she could, with a joyful face, show a baby's napkin stained yellow instead of green, and to receive their comforting assurances that that proved that baby was now really better.

Natasha neglected herself to such a degree that her dresses, her untidy hair, her inappropriately blurted-out words, and her jealousy—she was jealous of Sonya, of the governess, of every woman, pretty and ugly—were a continual subject of jests among her friends. The general opinion was that Pierre was tied to his wife's apron strings, and it really was so. From the earliest days of their marriage Natasha had made plain her claims. Pierre had been greatly surprised at his wife's view—to him a completely novel idea—that every minute of his life belonged to her and their home. He was surprised at his wife's demands, but he was flattered by them, and he acquiesced in them.

Pierre was so far under petticoat government that he did not dare to be attentive, or even speak with a smile, to any other woman; did not dare go to dine at the club, without good reason, simply for entertainment; did not dare spend money on idle whims, and did not dare to be away from home for any long time together, except on business, in which his wife included his scientific pursuits. Though she understood nothing of the latter, she attached great consequence to them. To make up for all this Pierre had complete power in his own house to dispose of the whole household, as well as of himself, as he chose. In their own home Natasha made herself a slave to her husband; and the whole household had to go on tiptoe if the master were busy reading or writing in his study. Pierre had only to show the slightest preference, for what he desired to be at once carried out. He had but to express a wish and Natasha jumped up at once and ran for what he wanted.

The whole household was ruled by the supposed directions of the master, that is, by the wishes of Pierre, which Natasha tried to guess. Their manner of life and place of residence, their acquaintances and ties, Natasha's pursuits, and the bringing up of the children—all followed, not only Pierre's expressed wishes, but even the deductions Natasha strove to draw from the ideas he explained in conversation with her. And she guessed very correctly what was the essential point of Pierre's wishes, and having once guessed it she was steadfast in adhering to it: even when Pierre himself would have veered round she opposed him with his own weapons.

In the troubled days that Pierre could never forget, after the birth of their first child, they had tried three wet nurses, one after another, for the delicate baby, and Natasha had fallen ill with anxiety. At the time Pierre had explained to her Rousseau's views on the unnaturalness and harmfulness of a child being suckled by any woman but its own mother, and told her he fully agreed with those views. When the next baby was born, in spite of the opposition of her mother, the doctors, and even of her husband himself, who all looked on it as something unheard of, and injurious, she insisted on having her own way, and from that day had nursed all her children herself. It happened very often in moments of irritability that the husband and wife quarrelled; but long after their dispute Pierre had, to his own delight and surprise, found in his wife's actions, as well as words, that very idea of his with which she had quarrelled. And he not only found his own idea, but found it purified of all that was superfluous, and had been evoked by the heat of argument in his own expression of the idea.

After seven years of married life, Pierre had a firm and joyful consciousness that he was not a bad fellow, and he felt this because he saw himself reflected in his wife. In himself he felt all the good and bad mingled together, and obscuring one another. But in his wife, he saw reflected only what was really good; everything not quite good was left out. And this result was not reached by the way of logical thought, but by way of a mysterious, direct reflection of himself.

THE sociology of religion

We might define religion, as does Talcott Parsons, as a set of beliefs, practices, and institutions which men in all known societies have evolved as responses to those parts of life which they felt not to be rationally understandable and controllable, and to which they have attached a significance which includes references to a non-empirical or supernatural order. This order is felt by these believers to have fundamental bearing on man's position in the world and on the ultimate values which give meaning to his life and to those of his fellows. Though religions differ enormously, and though there are many atheistic religions, one may nevertheless isolate a few elements common to them all. All religious systems distinguish between the *sacred* and the *profane*. Sacred objects may not differ materially from objects of ordinary use, but the attitude of the worshipper toward them is crucially different; the sacred is set apart from the ordinary, utilitarian concerns—it is regarded with awe and respect. Religious *beliefs* describe and explain the world of sacred beings, and religious *rituals* anchor these beliefs in the

379

behavior of the worshippers. Religious *symbols* help focus and mobilize feelings and afford means for acting out religious emotions which cannot be expressed directly. Finally, the community of *believers* which shares symbols and practices is an essential element of all religions. There can be no religion without a communion of the faithful sharing ethical values and held together by the same religious and moral orientations.

Herman Melville's *Typee* contains acute observations on religious practices of Tahiti and the Marquesas Islands, some of which are reprinted here. Modern anthropologists would doubtlessly provide somewhat different interpretations, yet Melville's descriptive power succeeds in tracing some central strands in a relatively "primitive" religious system. E. M. Forster, the great British novelist, in *Passage to India* shows a humane understanding for modern Hindu culture which has remained unequalled. The selection here is his detailed account of a central Hindu religious ceremony. James Joyce, in his semi-autobiographical *A Portrait of the Artist*, provides a magnificent picture of the hold of Catholic ritual on an adolescent growing up in his native Ireland. The varieties of Protestant religious life are illustrated by the last two selections. Frances Trollope, the mother of Anthony Trollope and a prolific novelist and essayist in her own right, published a book in 1832 on the *Domestic Manners of the Americans* in which she drew a far from flattering portrait of America as she had seen it in the 1820's. Even though her account of one of those revival meetings which periodically swept America in the eighteenth and nineteenth centuries may not be without bias, it seems to have captured certain predominating features of Protestant revivalism. Sinclair Lewis, on the other hand, describes a very different side of American Protestantism; its gradual secularization and decline into mere do-gooder religiosity—the civic faith of the middle-class booster.

Herman Melville

The varieties of religious experience in polynesia

In one of the most secluded portions of the valley, within a stone's-cast of Fayaway's lake—for so I christened the scene of our island yachting—and hard by a growth of palms, which stood ranged in order along both banks of the stream, waving their green arms as if to do honour to its passage, was the mausoleum of a deceased warrior chief. Like all the other edifices of any note, it was raised upon a small pi-pi of stones, which, being of unusual

From *Typee* by Herman Melville (1846).

height, was a conspicuous object from a distance. A light thatching of bleached palmetto leaves hung over it like a self-supported canopy; for it was not until you came very near that you saw it was supported by four slender columns of bamboo, rising at each corner to a little more than the height of a man. A clear area of a few yards surrounded the pi-pi, and was enclosed by four trunks of cocoa-nut trees resting at the angles on massive blocks of stone. The place was sacred. The sign of the inscrutable taboo was seen in the shape of a mystic roll of white tappa, suspended by a twisted cord of the same material from the top of a slight pole planted within the enclosure.[1] The sanctity of the spot appeared never to have been violated. The stillness of the grave was there, and the calm solitude around was beautiful and touching; the soft shadows of those lofty palm-trees!— I can see them now—hanging over the little temple, as if to keep out the intrusive sun.

On all sides as you approached this silent spot you caught sight of the dead chief's effigy, seated in the stern of a canoe, which was raised on a light frame a few inches above the level of the pi-pi. The canoe was about seven feet in length; of a rich, dark-coloured wood, handsomely carved, and adorned in many places with variegated bindings of stained sinnet, into which were ingeniously wrought a number of sparkling seashells, and a belt of the same shells ran all round it. The body of the figure—of whatever material it might have been made—was effectually concealed in a heavy robe of brown tappa, revealing only the hands and head; the latter skilfully carved in wood, and surmounted by a superb arch of plumes. These plumes, in the subdued and gentle gales which found access to this sequestered spot, were never for one moment at rest, but kept nodding and waving over the chief's brow. The long leaves of the palmetto drooped over the eaves, and through them you saw the warrior holding his paddle with both hands in the act of rowing, leaning forward and inclining his head, as if eager to hurry on his voyage. Glaring at him for ever, and face to face, was a polished human skull, which crowned the prow of the canoe. The spectral figurehead, reversed in its position, glancing backwards, seemed to mock the impatient attitude of the warrior.

When I first visited this singular place with Kory-Kory, he told me—or at least I so understood him—that the chief was paddling his way to the realms of bliss and bread-fruit—the Polynesian heaven—where every moment the breadfruit trees dropped their ripened spheres to the ground, and where there was no end to the cocoa-nuts and bananas: there they reposed through the livelong eternity upon mats much finer than those of Typee; and every day bathed their glowing limbs in rivers of cocoa-nut oil. In that happy land there were plenty of plumes and feathers, and boar's tusks and sperm-whale

---

[1] White appears to be the sacred colour among the Marquesans.

teeth, far preferable to all the shining trinkets and gay tappa of the white men; and, best of all, women far lovelier than the daughters of earth were there in abundance. "A very pleasant place," Kory-Kory said it was; "but, after all, not much pleasanter, he thought, than Typee." "Did he not, then," I asked him, "wish to accompany the warrior?" "Oh no; he was very happy where he was; but supposed that some time or other he would go in his own canoe."

Thus far, I think, I clearly comprehended Kory-Kory. But there was a singular expression he made use of at the time, enforced by as singular a gesture, the meaning of which I would have given much to penetrate. I am inclined to believe it must have been a proverb he uttered; for I afterwards heard him repeat the same words several times, and in what appeared to me to be a somewhat similar sense. Indeed, Kory-Kory had a great variety of short, smart-sounding sentences with which he frequently enlivened his discourse; and he introduced them with an air which plainly intimated that, in his opinion, they settled the matter in question, whatever it might be.

Could it have been, then, that when I asked him whether he desired to go to this heaven of bread-fruit, cocoa-nuts and young ladies, which he had been describing, he answered by saying something equivalent to our old adage, "A bird in the hand is worth two in the bush"? If he did, Kory-Kory was a discreet and sensible fellow, and I cannot sufficiently admire his shrewdness.

Whenever in the course of my rambles through the valley I happened to be near the chief's mausoleum, I always turned aside to visit it. The place had a peculiar charm for me; I hardly know why; but so it was. As I leaned over the railing and gazed upon the strange effigy and watched the play of the feathery headdress, stirred by the same breeze which in low tones breathed amidst the lofty palm-trees, I loved to yield myself up to the fanciful superstition of the islanders, and could almost believe that the grim warrior was bound heavenward. In this mood, when I turned to depart, I bade him "God speed, and a pleasant voyage." Ay, paddle away, brave chieftain, to the land of spirits! To the material eye thou makest but little progress; but with the eye of faith, I see thy canoe cleaving the bright waves, which die away on those dimly looming shores of Paradise.

This strange superstition affords another evidence of the fact, that however ignorant man may be, he still feels within him his immortal spirit yearning after the unknown future.

Although the religious theories of the islands were a complete mystery to me, their practical everyday operation could not be concealed. I frequently passed the little temples reposing in the shadows of the taboo groves and beheld the offerings—mouldy fruit spread out upon a rude altar, or hanging in half-decayed baskets around some uncouth, jolly-looking image; I was present during the continuance of the festival; I daily beheld the grinning idols marshalled rank and file in the hoolah-hoolah ground, and was often in the habit of meeting those whom I supposed to be priests. But the temples seemed abandoned to solitude; the festival had been nothing more than a jovial mingling of the tribe; the idols were quite as harmless as any other logs of wood; and the priests were the merriest dogs in the valley.

In fact, religious affairs in Typee were at a very low ebb. All such matters sat very lightly upon the thoughtless inhabitants; and, in the celebration of many of their strange rites, they appeared merely to seek a sort of childish amusement.

A curious evidence of this was given in a remarkable ceremony in which I frequently saw Mehevi and several other chiefs and warriors of note take part; but never a single female.

Among those whom I looked upon as forming the priesthood of the valley, there was one in particular who often attracted my notice, and whom I could not help regarding as the head of the order. He was a noble-looking man, in the prime of life, and of a most benignant aspect. The authority this man, whose name was Kolory, seemed to exercise over the rest, the episcopal part he took in the Feast of Calabashes, his sleek and complacent appearance, the mystic characters which were tattooed upon his chest, and, above all, the mitre he frequently wore, in the shape of a towering headdress, consisting of part of a cocoa-nut branch, the stalk planted uprightly on his brow, and the leaflets gathered together and passed round the temples and behind the ears, all these pointed him out as Lord Primate of Typee. Kolory was a sort of Knight Templar—a soldier-priest; for he often wore the dress of a Marquesan warrior, and always carried a long spear, which, instead of terminating in a paddle at the lower end, after the general fashion of these weapons, was curved into a heathenish-looking little image. This instrument, however, might perhaps have been emblematic of his double functions. With one end in carnal combat he transfixed the enemies of his tribe: and with the other as a pastoral crook he kept in order his spiritual flock. But this is not all I have to say about Kolory. His martial grace very often carried about with him what seemed to me the half of a broken war-club. It was swathed round with ragged bits of white tappa, and the upper part, which was intended to represent a human head, was embellished with a strip of scarlet cloth of European manufacture. It required little observation to discover that this strange object was revered as a god. By the side of the big and lusty images standing sentinel over the altars of the hoolah-hoolah ground, it seemed a mere pigmy in tatters. But appearances all the world over are deceptive. Little men are sometimes very potent, and rags sometimes cover very extensive pretensions. In fact, this funny little image was the 'crack' god of the island; lording it over all the wooden lubbers who looked so grim and dreadful; its name was Moa Artua.[2] And it was in honour of Moa Artua, and for the entertainment of those who believe in him, that the curious ceremony I am about to describe was observed.

Mehevi and the chieftains of the Ti have just risen from their noontide slumbers. There are no affairs of state to dispose of; and, having eaten two or three breakfasts in the course of the morning, the magnates of the valley feel no appetite as yet for dinner. How are their leisure moments to be occupied? They smoke, they chat, and at last one of their number makes a proposition to the rest, who joyfully acquiescing, he darts out of the house, leaps from the pi-pi, and disappears in the grove. Soon you see him returning with Kolory, who bears the god Moa Artua in his arms, and carries in one hand a small trough, hollowed out in the likeness of a canoe. The priest comes along, dandling his charge as if it were a lachrymose infant he was endeavoring to put into a good humour. Presently, entering the Ti, he seats himself on the mats as composedly as a juggler about to perform his sleight-of-hand tricks; and, with the chiefs disposed in a circle around him, commences his ceremony.

In the first place, he gives Moa Artua an affectionate hug, then caressingly lays him to his breast and finally whispers something in his ear, the rest of the company listening eagerly for a reply. But the baby-god is deaf or dumb, perhaps both, for never a word does he utter. At last Kolory speaks a little louder, and soon growing angry, comes boldly out with what he has to say, and bawls to him. He put me in mind of a choleric fellow, who, after trying in vain to communicate a secret to a deaf man, all at once flies into a passion, and screams it out so that every one may hear. Still Moa Artua remains as quiet as ever; and Kolory, seemingly losing his temper, fetches him a box over the head, strips him of his tappa and red cloth, and, laying him a state of nudity in the little trough, covers him from sight. At this proceeding all present loudly applaud and signify their approval by uttering the adjective 'mortakee,' with violent emphasis. Kolory, however, is so desirous his conduct should meet with unqualified approbation that he inquires of each individual separately whether, under existing circumstances, he has not done perfectly right in shutting up Moa Artua. The invariable response is "Aa, aa" (Yes, yes), repeated over again and again in a manner which ought to quiet the scruples of the most conscientious. After a few moments Kolory brings forth his doll again, and while arraying it very carefully in the tappa and red cloth, alternately fondles and chides it. The toilet being completed, he once more speaks to it aloud. The whole company hereupon show the greatest interest; while the priest, holding Moa Artua to his ear,

[2]The word 'Artua,' although having some other significations, is in nearly all the Polynesian dialects used as the general designation of the gods.

interprets to them what he pretends the god is confidentially communicating to him. Some items of intelligence appear to tickle all present amazingly; for one claps his hands in a rapture; another shouts in merriment; and a third leaps to his feet and capers about like a madman.

What under the sun Moa Artua on these occasions had to say to Kolory I never could find out; but I could not help thinking that the former showed a sad want of spirit in being disciplined into making those disclosures, which at first he seemed bent on withholding. Whether the priest honestly interpreted what he believed the divinity said to him, or whether he was not all the while guilty of a vile humbug, I shall not presume to decide. At any rate, whatever as coming from the god was imparted to those present seemed to be generally of a complimentary nature: a fact which illustrates the sagacity of Kolory, or else the time-serving disposition of this hardly-used deity.

Moa Artua having nothing more to say, his bearer goes to nursing him again, in which occupation, however, he is soon interrupted by a question put by one of the warriors to the god. Kolory hereupon snatches it up to his ear again, and, after listening attentively, once more officiates as the organ of communication. A multitude of questions and answers having passed between the parties, much to the satisfaction of those who propose them, the god is put tenderly to bed in the trough, and the whole company unite in a long chant, led off by Kolory. This ended, the ceremony is over; the chiefs rise to their feet in high good-humour, and my Lord Archbishop, after chatting awhile, and regaling himself with a whiff or two from a pipe of tobacco, tucks the canoe under his arm, and marches off with it.

The whole of these proceedings were like those of a parcel of children playing with dolls and baby houses.

For a youngster scarcely ten inches high, and with so few early advantages as he doubtless had had, Moa Artua was certainly a precocious little fellow if he really said all that was imputed to him; but for what reason this poor devil of a deity, thus cuffed about, cajoled, and shut up in a box, was held in greater estimation than the full-grown and dignified personages of the taboo groves, I cannot divine. And yet Mehevi, and other chiefs of unquestionable veracity—to say nothing of the Primate himself—assured me over and over again that Moa Artua was the tutelary deity of Typee, and was more to be held in honour than a whole battalion of the clumsy idols in the hoolah-hoolah grounds. Kory-Kory—who seemed to have devoted considerable attention to the study of theology, as he knew the names of all the graven images in the valley, and often repeated them over to me—likewise entertained some rather enlarged ideas with regard to the character and pretensions of Moa Artua. He once gave me to understand, with a gesture that there was no misconceiving, that if (Moa Artua) were so minded, he could cause a cocoa-nut tree to sprout out of his (Kory-Kory's) head; and that it would be the easiest thing in life for him (Moa Artua) to take the whole island of Nukuheva in his mouth, and dive down to the bottom of the sea with it.

But, in sober seriousness, I hardly knew what to make of the religion of the valley. There was nothing that so much perplexed the illustrious Cook, in his intercourse with the South Sea islanders, as their sacred rites. Although this prince of navigators was in many instances assisted by inter-preters in the prosecution of his researches, he still frankly acknowledges that he was at a loss to obtain anything like a clear insight into the puzzling arcana of their faith. A similar admission has been made by other eminent voyagers; by Carteret, Byron, Kotzebue, and Vancouver.

For my own part, although hardly a day passed while I remained upon the island that I did not witness some religious ceremony or other, it was very much like seeing a parcel of Freemasons making secret signs to each other; I saw everything, but could comprehend nothing.

On the whole, I am inclined to believe that the islanders in the Pacific have no fixed and definite ideas whatever on the subject of religion. I am persuaded that Kolory himself would be effectually posed were he called upon to draw up the articles of his faith and pronounce the creed by which he hoped to be saved. In truth, the Typees, so far as their actions evince, submitted to no laws, human or divine—always excepting the thrice mys-terious taboo. The 'independent electors' of the valley were not to be brow-beaten by chiefs, priests, idols, or devils. As for the luckless idols, they received more hard knocks than supplications. I do not wonder that some of them looked so grim, and stood so bolt upright, as if fearful of looking to the right or the left lest they should give any one offence. The fact is, they had to carry themselves *pretty straight*, or suffer the consequences. Their worshippers were such a precious set of fickle-minded and irreverent heathens, that there was no telling when they might topple one of them over, break it to pieecs, and, making a fire with it on the very altar itself, fall to roasting the offerings of bread-fruit, and eat them in spite of its teeth.

In how little reverence these unfortunate deities were held by the natives was on one occasion most convincingly proved to me. Walking with Kory-Kory through the deepest recesses of the grove, I perceived a curious-looking image, about six feet in height, which originally had been placed upright against a low pi-pi, surmounted by a ruinous bamboo temple, but having become fatigued and weak in the knees, was now carelessly leaning against it. The idol was partly concealed by the foliage of a tree which stood near, and whose leafy boughs drooped over the pile of stones, as if to protect the rude fane from the decay to which it was rapidly hastening. The image itself was nothing more than a grotesquely-shaped log, carved in the likeness of a portly naked man, with the arms clasped over the head, the jaws thrown wide apart, and its thick, shapeless legs bowed into an arch. It was much decayed. The lower part was overgrown with a bright silky moss. Thin spears of grass sprouted from the distended mouth and fringed the outline of the head and arms. His godship had literally attained a green old age. All its prominent points were bruised and battered, or entirely rotted away. The nose had taken its departure, and from the general appearance of the head it might have been supposed that the wooden divinity, in despair at the neglect of its worshippers, had been trying to beat its own brains out against the surrounding trees.

I drew near to inspect more closely this strange object of idolatry; but halted reverently at the distance of two or three paces, out of regard to the religious prejudices of my valet. As soon, however, as Kory-Kory perceived that I was in one of my inquiring scientific moods, to my astonishment, he sprang to the side of the idol, and, pushing it away from the stones against which it rested, endeavoured to make it stand upon its legs. But the divinity had lost the use of them altogether; and while Kory-Kory was trying to prop it up, by placing a stick between it and the pi-pi, the monster fell clumsily to the ground, and would infallibly have broken its neck had not Kory-Kory providentially broken its fall by receiving its whole weight on his own half-circled back. I never saw the honest fellow in such a rage before. He leaped furiously to his feet, and, seizing the stick, began beating the poor image, every moment or two pausing and talking to it in the most violent manner, as if upbraiding it for the accident. When his indignation had subsided a little he whirled the idol about most profanely, so as to give me an opportunity of examining it on all sides. I am quite sure I never should have presumed to have taken such liberties with the god myself, and I was not a little shocked at Kory-Kory's impiety.

E. M. Forster (1879–1970)

A hindu ceremony

He had not to wait long. In a land where all else was unpunctual, the hour of the Birth was chronometrically observed. Three minutes before it was due, a Brahman brought forth a model of the village of Gokul (the Bethlehem in that nebulous story) and placed it in front of the altar. The model was on a wooden tray about a yard square; it was of clay, and was gaily blue and white with streamers and paint. Here, upon a chair too small for him and with a head too large, sat King Kansa, who is Herod, directing the murder of some Innocents, and in a corner, similarly proportioned, stood the father and mother of the Lord, warned to depart in a dream. The model was not holy, but more than a decoration, for it diverted men from the actual image of the God, and increased their sacred bewilderment. Some of the villagers thought the Birth had occurred, saying with truth that the Lord must have been born, or they could not see Him. But the clock struck midnight, and simultaneously the rending note of the conch broke forth, followed by the trumpeting of elephants; all who had packets of powder threw them at the altar, and in the rosy dust and incense, and clanging and shouts, Infinite Love took upon itself the form of Shri Krishna, and saved the world. All sorrow was annihilated, not only for Indians, but for foreigners, birds, caves, railways, and the stars; all became joy, all laughter; there had never been disease nor doubt, misunderstanding, cruelty, fear. Some jumped in the air, others flung themselves prone and embraced the bare feet of the universal lover; the women behind the purdah slapped and shrieked; the little girl slipped out and danced by herself, her black pigtails flying. Not an orgy of the body; the tradition of that shrine forbade it. But the human spirit had tried by a desperate contortion to ravish the unknown, flinging down science and history in the struggle, yes, beauty herself. Did it succeed? Books written afterwards say "Yes." But how, if there is such an event, can it be remembered afterwards? How can it be expressed in anything but itself? Not only from the unbeliever are mysteries hid, but the adept himself cannot retain them. He may think, if he chooses, that he has been with God, but as soon as he thinks it, it becomes history, and falls under the rules of time.

A cobra of papier-mâché now appeared on the carpet, also a wooden cradle swinging from a frame. Professor Godbole approached the latter with a red silk napkin in his arms. The napkin was God, not that it was, and the image remained in the blur of the altar. It was just a napkin, folded into a shape which indicated a baby's. The Professor dandled it and gave it to the Rajah, who, making a great effort, said, "I name this child Shri Krishna," and tumbled it into the cradle. Tears poured from his eyes, because he had seen the Lord's salvation. He was too weak to exhibit the silk baby to his people, his privilege in former years. His attendants lifted him up, a new path was cleared through the crowd, and he was carried away to a less sacred part of the palace. There in a room accessible to Western science by an outer staircase, his physician, Dr. Aziz, awaited him. His Hindu physician, who had accompanied him to the shrine, briefly reported his symptoms. As the ectasy receded, the invalid grew fretful. The bumping of the steam engine that worked the dynamo disturbed him, and he asked for what reason it had been introduced into his home. They replied that they would enquire, and administered a sedative.

Down in the sacred corridors, joy had seethed to jollity. It was their duty to play various games to amuse the newly born God, and to simulate his sports with the wanton dairymaids of Brindaban. Butter played a prominent part in these. When the cradle had been removed, the principal nobles of the state gathered together for an innocent frolic. They removed their turbans, and one put a lump of butter on his forehead, and waited for it to slide down his nose into his mouth. Before it could arrive, another stole up behind him, snatched the melting morsel, and swallowed it himself. All laughed exultantly at discovering that the divine sense of humour coincided with their own. "God is love!" There is fun in heaven. God can play practical jokes upon Himself, draw chairs away from beneath His own posteriors, set His own turbans on fire, and steal His own petticoats when He bathes. By sacrificing good taste, this worship achieved what Christianity has shirked: the inclusion of merriment. All spirit as well as all matter must participate in salvation, and if practical jokes are banned, the circle is incomplete. Having swallowed the butter, they played another game which chanced to be graceful: the fondling of Shri Krishna under the similitude of a child. A pretty red and gold ball is thrown, and he who catches it chooses a child from the crowd, raises it in his arms, and carries it round to be caressed. All stroke the darling creature for the Creator's sake, and murmur happy words. The child is restored to his parents, the ball thrown on, and another child becomes for a moment the World's desire. And the Lord bounds hither and thither through the aisles, chance, and the sport of chance, irradiating little mortals with His immortality. . . . When they had played this long enough—and being exempt from boredom, they played it again and again, they played it again and again—they took many sticks and hit them together, whack smack, as though they fought the Pandava wars, and threshed and churned with them, and later on they hung from the roof of the temple, in a net, a great black earthenware jar, which was painted here and there with red, and wreathed with dried figs. Now came a rousing sport. Springing up, they struck at the jar with their sticks. It cracked, broke, and a mass of greasy rice and milk poured on to their faces. They ate and smeared one another's mouth and dived between each other's legs for what had been pashed upon the carpet. This way and that spread the divine mess, until the line of schoolboys, who had somewhat fended off the crowd, broke for their share. The corridors, the courtyard, were filled with benign confusion. Also the flies awoke and claimed their share of God's bounty. There was no quarrelling, owing to the nature of the gift, for blessed is the man who confers it on another, he imitates God. And those "imitations," those "substitutions," continued to flicker through the assembly for many hours, awakening in each man, according to his capacity, an emotion that he would not have had otherwise. No definite image survived; at the Birth it was questionable whether a silver doll or a mud village, or a silk napkin, or an intangible spirit, or a pious resolution, had been born. Perhaps all these things! Perhaps none! Perhaps all birth is an allegory! Still, it was the main event of the religious year.

James Joyce (1882–1941)

Discipline, devotion, and catholic ritual

Sunday was dedicated to the mystery of the Holy Trinity, Monday to the Holy Ghost, Tuesday to the Guardian Angels, Wednesday to Saint Joseph, Thursday to the Most Blessed Sacrament of the Altar, Friday to the Suffering Jesus, Saturday to the Blessed Virgin Mary.

Every morning he hallowed himself anew in the presence of some holy image or mystery. His day began with an heroic offering of its every moment of thought or action for the intentions of the sovereign pontiff and with an early mass. The raw morning air whetted his resolute piety; and often as he knelt among the few worshippers at the side altar, following with his interleaved prayer book the murmur of the priest, he glanced up for an instant towards the vested figure standing in the gloom between the two candles, which were the old and the new testaments, and imagined that he was kneeling at mass in the catacombs.

His daily life was laid out in devotional areas. By means of ejaculations and prayers he stored up ungrudgingly for the souls in purgatory centuries of days and quarantines and years; yet the spiritual triumph which he felt in achieving with ease so many fabulous ages of canonical penances did not wholly reward his zeal of prayer since he could never know how much temporal punishment he had remitted by way of suffrage for the agonising souls: and, fearful lest in the midst of the purgatorial fire, which differed from the infernal only in that it was not everlasting, his penance might avail no more than a drop of moisture he drove his soul daily through an increasing circle of works of supererogation.

Every part of his day, divided by what he regarded now as the duties of his station in life, circled its own centre of spiritual energy. His life seemed to have drawn near to eternity; every thought, word and deed, every instance of consciousness could be made to revibrate radiantly in heaven: and at times his sense of such immediate repercussion was so lively that he seemed to feel his soul in devotion pressing like fingers the keyboard of a great cash

From *A Portrait of the Artist* by James Joyce, Copyright 1916 by B. W. Huebsch, 1944, by Nora Joyce. Reprinted by permission of The Viking Press, Inc.

register and to see the amount of his purchase start forth immediately in heaven, not as a number but as a frail column of incense or as a slender flower.

The rosaries, too, which he said constantly—for he carried his beads loose in his trousers' pockets that he might tell them as he walked the streets—transformed themselves into coronals of flowers of such vague unearthly texture that they seemed to him as hueless and odourless as they were nameless. He offered up each of his three daily chaplets that his soul might grow strong in each of the three theological virtues, in faith in the Father Who had created him, in hope in the Son Who redeemed him, and love of the Holy Ghost Who had sanctified him; and this thrice triple prayer he offered to the Three Persons through Mary in the name of her joyful and sorrowful and glorious mysteries.

On each of the seven days of the week he further prayed that one of the seven gifts of the Holy Ghost might descend upon his soul and drive out of it day by day the seven deadly sins which had defiled it in the past; and he prayed for each gift on its appointed day, confident that it would descend upon him, though it seemed strange to him at times that wisdom and understanding and knowledge were so distinct in their nature that each should be prayed for apart from the others. Yet he believed that at some future stage of his spiritual progress his difficulty would be removed when his sinful soul had been raised up from its weakness and enlightened by the Third Person of the Most Blessed Trinity. He believed this all the more, and with trepidation, because of the divine gloom and silence wherein dwelt the unseen Paraclete, Whose symbols were a dove and a mighty wind, to sin against Whom was a sin beyond forgiveness, the eternal, mysterious secret Being to Whom, as God, the priests offered up mass once a year, orbed in the scarlet of the tongues of fire.

The imagery through which the nature and kinship of the Three Persons of the Trinity were darkly shadowed forth in the books of devotion which he read—the Father contemplating from all eternity as in a mirror His Divine Perfections and thereby begetting eternally the Eternal Son and the Holy Spirit proceeding out of the Father and Son from all eternity—were easier of acceptance by his mind by reason of their august incomprehensibility than was the simple fact that God had loved his soul from all eternity, for ages before he had been born into the world, for ages before the world itself had existed.

He had heard the names of the passions of love and hate pronounced solemnly on the stage and in the pulpit, had found them set forth solemnly in books, and had wondered why his soul was unable to harbour them for any time or to force his lips to utter their names with conviction. A brief anger had often invested him, but he had never been able to make it an abiding passion and had always felt himself passing out of it as if his very body were being divested with ease of some outer skin or peel. He had felt a subtle, dark and murmurous presence penetrate his being and fire him with a brief iniquitous lust; it, too, had slipped beyond his grasp leaving his mind lucid and indifferent. This, it seemed, was the only love and that the only hate his soul would harbour.

But he could no longer disbelieve in the reality of love since God himself had loved his individual soul with divine love from all eternity. Gradually, as his soul was enriched with spiritual knowledge, he saw the whole world forming one vast symmetrical expression of God's power and love. Life became a divine gift for every moment and sensation of which, were it even the sight of a single leaf hanging on the twig of a tree, his soul should praise and thank the giver. The world for all its solid substance and complexity no longer existed for his soul save as a theorem of divine power and love and universality. So entire and unquestionable was this sense of the divine meaning in all nature granted to his soul that he could scarcely understand why it was in any way necessary that he should continue to live. Yet that was part of the divine purpose and he dared not question its use, he above all others who had sinned so deeply and so foully against the divine purpose. Meek and abased by this consciousness of the one eternal omnipresent perfect reality his soul took up again her burden of pieties, masses and prayers and sacraments and mortifications, and only then for the first time since he had brooded on the great mystery of love did he feel within him a warm movement like that of some newly born life or virtue of the soul itself. The attitude of rapture in sacred art, the raised and parted hands, the parted lips and eyes as of one about to swoon, became for him an image of the soul in prayer, humiliated and faint before her Creator.

But he had been forewarned of the dangers of spiritual exaltation and did not allow himself to desist from even the least or lowliest devotion, striving also by constant mortification to undo the sinful past rather than to achieve a saintliness fraught with peril. Each of his senses was brought under a rigorous discipline. In order to mortify the sense of sight he made it his rule to walk in the street with downcast eyes, glancing neither to right nor left and never behind him. His eyes shunned every encounter with the eyes of women. From time to time also he balked them by a sudden effort of the will, as by lifting them suddenly in the middle of an unfinished sentence and closing the book. To mortify his hearing he exerted no control over his voice which was then breaking, neither sang nor whistled and made no attempt to flee from noise which caused him painful nervous irritation such as the sharpening of knives on the knifeboard, the gathering of cinders on the fire-shovel and the twigging of the carpet. To mortify his smell was more difficult as he found in himself no instinctive repugnance to bad odours, whether they were the odours of the outdoor world such as those of dung or tar or the odours of his own person among which he had made many curious comparisons and experiments. He found in the end that the only odour against which his sense of smell revolted was a certain stale fishy stink like that of long-standing urine: and whenever it was possible he subjected himself to this unpleasant odour. To mortify the taste he practised strict habits at table, observed to the letter all the fasts of the church and sought by distraction to divert his mind from the savours of different foods. But it was to the mortification of touch that he brought the most assiduous ingenuity of inventiveness. He never consciously changed his position in bed, sat in the most uncomfortable position, suffered patiently every itch and pain, kept away from the fire, remained on his knees all through the mass except at the gospels, left parts of his neck and face undried so that air might sting them and, whenever he was not saying his beads, carried his arms stiffly at his sides like a runner and never in his pockets or clasped behind him.

He had no temptations to sin mortally. It surprised him, however, to find that at the end of his course of intricate piety and selfrestraint he was so easily at the mercy of childish and unworthy imperfections. His prayers and fasts availed him little for the suppression of anger at hearing his mother sneeze or at being disturbed in his devotions. It needed an immense effort of his will to master the impulse which urged him to give outlet to such irritation. Images of the outbursts of trivial anger which he had often noted among his masters, their twitching mouths, closeshut lips and flushed cheeks, recurred to his memory, discouraging him, for all his practice of humility, by the comparison. To merge his life in the common tide of other lives was harder for him than any fasting or prayer, and it was his constant failure to do this to his own satisfaction which caused in his soul at last a sensation of spiritual dryness together with a growth of doubts and scruples. His soul traversed a period of desolation in which the sacraments themselves seemed to have turned into dried up sources. His confession became a channel for the escape of scrupulous and unrepented imperfections. His actual reception of the eucharist did not bring him the same dissolving moments of virginal self-surrender as did those spiritual communions made by him sometimes at the close of some visit to the Blessed Sacrament. The book which he used for these visits was an old neglected book written by Saint Alphonsus Liguori, with fading characters and sere foxpapered leaves. A faded world of fervent love and virginal responses seemed to be evoked for his soul by reading of its pages in which the imagery of the canticles was interwoven with the communicant's prayers. An inaudible voice seemed to caress the soul, telling her names and glories, bidding her arise as for espousal and come away, bidding her look forth, a spouse, from Amana and from the mountains of the leopards; and the soul seemed to answer with the same inaudible voice, surrendering herself: *inter ubera mea commorabitur.*

This idea of surrender had a perilous attraction for his mind now that he felt his soul beset once again by the insistent voices of the flesh which began to murmur to him again during his prayers and meditations. It gave him an intense sense of power to know that he could by a single act of consent, in a moment of thought, undo all that he had done. He seemed to feel a flood slowly advancing towards his naked feet and to be waiting for the first faint timid noiseless wavelet to touch his fevered skin. Then, almost at the instant of that touch, almost at the verge of sinful consent, he found himself standing far away from the flood upon a dry shore, saved by a sudden act of the will or a sudden ejaculation: and, seeing the silver line of the flood far away and beginning again its slow advance towards his feet, a new thrill of power and satisfaction shook his soul to know that he had not yielded nor undone all.

When he had eluded the flood of temptation many times in this way he grew troubled and wondered whether the grace which he had refused to lose was not being filched from him little by little. The clear certitude of his own immunity grew dim and to it succeeded a vague fear that his soul had really fallen unawares. It was with difficulty that he won back his old consciousness of his state of grace by telling himself that he had prayed to God at every temptation and that the grace which he had prayed for must have been given him inasmuch as God was obliged to give it. The very frequency and violence of temptations showed him at last the truth of what he had heard about the trials of the saints. Frequent and violent temptations were a proof that the citadel of the soul had not fallen and that the devil raged to make it fall.

Often when he had confessed his doubts and scruples, some momentary inattention at prayer, a movement of trivial anger in his soul or a subtle wilfulness in speech or act, he was bidden by his confessor to name some sin of his past life before absolution was given him. He named it with humility and shame and repented of it once more. It humiliated and shamed him to think that he would never be freed from it wholly, however holily he might live or whatever virtues or perfections he might attain. A restless feeling of guilt would always be present with him: he would confess and repent and be absolved, confess and repent again and be absolved again, fruitlessly. Perhaps that first hasty confession wrung from him by the fear of hell had not been good? Perhaps, concerned only for his imminent doom, he had not had sincere sorrow for his sin? But the surest sign that his confession had been good and that he had had sincere sorrow for his sin was, he knew, the amendment of his life.

—I have amended my life, have I not? he asked himself.

Frances Trollope (1780–1863)

A revival

We had not been many months in Cincinnati when our curiosity was excited by hearing the "revival" talked of by everyone we met throughout the town. "The revival will be very full"–"We shall be constantly engaged during the revival"–were the phrases we constantly heard repeated, and for a long time, without in the least comprehending what was meant; but at length I learnt that the un-national church of America required to be roused, at regular intervals, to greater energy and exertion. At these seasons the most enthusiastic of the clergy travel the country, and enter the cities and towns by scores, or by hundreds, as the accommodation of the place may admit, and for a week or fortnight, or, if the population be large, for a month; they preach and pray all day, and often for a considerable portion of the night, in the various churches and chapels of the place. This is called a Revival.

I took considerable pains to obtain information on this subject; but in detailing what I learnt I fear that it is probable I shall be accused of exaggeration; all I can do is cautiously to avoid deserving it. The subject is highly interesting, and it would be a fault of no trifling nature to treat it with levity.

These itinerant clergymen are of all persuasions, I believe, except the Episcopalian, Catholic, Unitarian, and Quaker. I heard of Presbyterians of all varieties; of Baptists of I know not how many divisions; and of Methodists of more denominations than I can remember; whose innumerable shades of varying belief, it would require much time to explain, and more to comprehend. They enter all the cities, towns, and villages of the Union, in succession; I could not learn with sufficient certainty to repeat, what the interval generally is between their visits. These itinerants are, for the most part, lodged in the houses of their respective followers, and every evening that is not spent in the churches and meeting-houses, is devoted to what would be called parties by others, but which they designate as prayer meetings. Here they eat, drink, pray, sing, hear confessions, and make converts. To these meetings I never got invited, and therefore I have nothing but hear-say evidence to offer, but my information comes from an eye-witness, and one on whom I believe I may depend. If one half of what I heard may be believed, these social prayer meetings are by no means the most curious, or the least important part of the business.

It is impossible not to smile at the close resemblance to be traced between the feelings of a first-rate Presbyterian or Methodist lady, fortunate enough

From *Domestic Manners of the Americans* by Frances Trollope (1832).

to have secured a favourite Itinerant for her meeting, and those of a first-rate London Blue, equally blest in the presence of a fashionable poet. There is a strong family likeness among us all the world over.

The best rooms, the best dresses, the choicest refreshments solemnize the meeting. While the party is assembling, the load-star of the hour is occupied in whispering conversations with the guests as they arrive. They are called brothers and sisters, and the greetings are very affectionate. When the room is full, the company, of whom a vast majority are always women, are invited, intreated, and coaxed to confess before their brothers and sisters, all their thoughts, faults, and follies.

These confessions are strange scenes; the more they confess, the more invariably are they encouraged and caressed. When this is over, they all kneel, and the Itinerant prays extempore. They then eat and drink; and then they sing hymns, pray, exhort, sing, and pray again, till the excitement reaches a very high pitch indeed. These scenes are going on at some house or other every evening during the revival, nay, at many at the same time, for the churches and meeting-houses cannot give occupation to half the Itinerants, though they are all open throughout the day, and till a late hour in the night, and the officiating ministers succeed each other in the occupation of them.

It was at the principal of the Presbyterian churches that I was twice witness to scenes that made me shudder; in describing one, I describe both, and every one; the same thing is constantly repeated.

It was in the middle of summer, but the service we were recommended to attend did not begin till it was dark. The church was well lighted, and crowded almost to suffocation. On entering, we found three priests standing side by side, in a sort of tribune, placed where the altar usually is, handsomely fitted up with crimson curtains, and elevated about as high as our pulpits. We took our places in a pew close to the rail which surrounded it.

The priest who stood in the middle was praying; the prayer was extravagantly vehement, and offensively familiar in expression; when this ended, a hymn was sung, and then another priest took the centre place, and preached. The sermon had considerable eloquence, but of a frightful kind. The preacher described, with ghastly minuteness, the last feeble fainting moments of human life, and then the gradual progress of decay after death, which he followed through every process up to the last loathsome stage of decomposition. Suddenly changing his tone, which had been that of sober accurate description, into the shrill voice of horror, he bent forward his head, as if to gaze on some object beneath the pulpit. And as Rebecca made known to Ivanhoe what she saw through the window, so the preacher made known to us what he saw in the pit that seemed to open before him. The device was certainly a happy one for giving effect to his description of hell. No image that fire, flame, brimstone, molten lead, or redhot pincers could supply; with flesh, nerves, and sinews quivering under them, was omitted. The perspiration ran in streams from the face of the preacher; his eyes rolled, his lips were covered with foam, and every feature had the deep expression of horror it would have borne, had he, in truth, been gazing at the scene he described. The acting was excellent. At length he gave a languishing look to his supporters on each side, as if to express his feeble state, and then sat down, and wiped the drops of agony from his brow.

The other two priests arose, and began to sing a hymn. It was some seconds before the congregation could join as usual; every up-turned face looked pale and horror struck. When the singing ended, another took the centre place, and began in a sort of coaxing affectionate tone, to ask the congregation if what their dear brother had spoken had reached their hearts? Whether they would avoid the hell he had made them see? "Come, then!" he continued, stretching out his arms towards them, "come to us, and tell us so, and we will make you see Jesus, the dear gentle Jesus, who shall save you from it. But you must come to him! You must not be ashamed to come to him! This night you shall tell him that you are not ashamed of him; we will make way for you; we will clear the bench for anxious sinners to sit upon. Come, then! come to the anxious bench, and we will shew you Jesus! Come! Come! Come!"

Again a hymn was sung, and while it continued, one of the three was employed in clearing one or two long benches that went across the rail, sending the people back to the lower part of the church. The singing ceased, and again the people were invited, and exhorted not to be ashamed of Jesus, but to put themselves upon "the anxious benches," and lay their heads on his bosom. "Once more we will sing," he concluded, "that we may give you time." And again they sung a hymn.

And now in every part of the church a movement was perceptible, slight at first, but by degrees becoming more decided. Young girls arose, and sat down, and rose again; and the pews opened, and several came tottering out, their hands clasped, their heads hanging on their bosoms, and every limb trembling, and still the hymn went on; but as the poor creatures approached the rail their sobs and groans became audible. They seated themselves on the "anxious benches;" the hymn ceased, and two of the three priests walked down from the tribune, and going, one to the right, and the other to the left, began whispering to the poor tremblers seated there. These whispers were inaudible to us, but the sobs and groans increased to a frightful excess. Young creatures, with features pale and distorted, fell on their knees on the pavement, and soon sunk forward on their faces; the most violent cries and shrieks followed, while from time to time a voice was heard in convulsive accents, exclaiming, "Oh Lord!" "Oh Lord Jesus!" "Help me, Jesus!" and the like.

Meanwhile the two priests continued to walk among them; they repeatedly

mounted on the benches, and trumpet-mouthed proclaimed to the whole congregation, "the tidings of salvation," and then from every corner of the building arose in reply, short sharp cries of "Amen!" "Glory!" "Amen!" while
the prostrate penitents continued to receive whispered comfortings, and from
time to time a mystic caress. Violent hysterics and convulsions seized many
of them, and when the tumult was at the highest, the priest who remained
above, again gave out a hymn as if to drown it.

It was a frightful sight to behold innocent young creatures, in the gay
morning of existence, thus seized upon, horror struck, and rendered feeble
and enervated for ever. One young girl, apparently not more than fourteen,
was supported in the arms of another, some years older; her face was pale as
death; her eyes wide open, and perfectly devoid of meaning; her chin and
bosom wet with slaver; she had every appearance of idiotism. I saw a priest
approach her, he took her delicate hand, "Jesus is with her! Bless the Lord!"
he said, and passed on.

Did the men of America value their women as men ought to value their
wives and daughters, would such scenes be permitted among them?

It is hardly necessary to say that all who obeyed the call to place themselves on the "anxious benches" were women, and by far the greater number, very young women. The congregation was, in general, extremely well
dressed, and the smartest and most fashionable ladies of the town were there;
during the whole revival the churches and meeting-houses were every day
crowded with well dressed people.

It is thus the ladies of Cincinnati amuse themselves; to attend the theatre
is forbidden; to play cards is unlawful; but they work hard in their families,
and must have some relaxation. For myself, I confess that I think the
coarsest comedy ever written would be a less detestable exhibition for the
eyes of youth and innocence than such a scene.

Sinclair Lewis (1885–1951)

Babbitt's religion or "christianity incorporated"

Nothing gave Babbitt more purification and publicity than his labors for the
Sunday School.

His church, the Presbyterian, was one of the largest and richest, one
of the most oaken and velvety, in Zenith. The pastor was the Reverend

John Jennison Drew, M.A., D.D., LL.D. (The M.A. and the D.D. were from Elbert University, Nebraska, the LL.D. from Waterbury College, Oklahoma.) He was eloquent, efficient, and versatile. He presided at meetings for the denunciation of unions or the elevation of domestic service and confided to the audiences that as a poor boy he had carried newspapers. For the Saturday edition of the *Evening Advocate* he wrote editorials on "The Manly Man's Religion," and "The Dollars and Cents Value of Christianity," which were printed in bold type surrounded by a wiggly border. He often said that he was "proud to be known as primarily a business man" and that he certainly was not going to "permit the old Satan to monopolize all the pep and punch." He was a thin, rustic-faced young man with gold spectacles and a bang of dull brown hair, but when he hurled himself into oratory he glowed with power. He admitted that he was too much the scholar and poet to imitate the evangelist, Mike Monday, yet he had once awakened his fold to new life, and to larger collections, by the challenge, "My brethren, the real cheap skate is the man who won't lend to the Lord!"

He had made his church a true community center. It contained everything but a bar. It had a nursery, a Thursday evening supper with a short bright missionary lecture afterward, a gymnasium, a fortnightly motion-picture show, a library of technical books for young workmen—though, unfortunately, no young workman ever entered the church except to wash the windows or repair the furnace—and a sewing-circle which made short little pants for children of the poor while Mrs. Drew read aloud from earnest novels.

Though Dr. Drew's theology was Presbyterian, his church-building was gracefully Episcopalian. As he said, it had the "most perdurable features of those noble ecclesiastical monuments of grand Old England which stand as symbols of the eternity of faith, religious and civil." It was built of cheery iron-spot brick in an improved Gothic style, and the main auditorium had indirect lighting from electric globes in lavish alabaster bowls.

On a December morning when the Babbitts went to church, Dr. John Jennison Drew was unusually eloquent. The crowd was immense. Ten brisk young ushers, in morning coats with white roses, were bringing folding chairs up from the basement. There was an impressive musical program, conducted by Sheldon Smeeth, educational director of the Y.M.C.A., who also sang the offertory. Babbitt cared less for this, because some misguided person had taught young Mr. Smeeth to smile, smile, smile, while he was singing, but with all the appreciation of a fellow-orator he admired Dr. Drew's sermon. It had the intellectual quality which distinguished the Chatham Road congregation from the grubby chapels on Smith Street.

"At this abundant harvest-time of all the year," Dr. Drew chanted, "when, though stormy the sky and laborious the path to the drudging wayfarer, yet the hovering and bodiless spirit swoops back o'er all the labors and desires of the past twelve months, oh, then it seems to me there sounds behind all our apparent failures the golden chorus of greeting from those passed happily on; and lo! on the dim horizon we see behind dolorous clouds the mighty mass of mountains—mountains of melody, mountains of mirth, mountains of might!"

"I certainly do like a sermon with culture and thought in it," meditated Babbitt.

At the end of the service he was delighted when the pastor, actively shaking hands at the door, twittered, "Oh, Brother Babbitt, can you wait a jiffy? Want your advice."

"Sure, doctor! You bet!"

"Drop into my office. I think you'll like the cigars there." Babbitt did like cigars. He also liked the office, which was distinguished from other offices only by the spirited change of the familiar wall-placard to "This is the Lord's Busy Day." Chum Frink came in, then William W. Eathorne.

Mr. Eathorne was the seventy-year-old president of the First State Bank of Zenith. He still wore the delicate patches of side-whiskers which had been the uniform of bankers in 1870. If Babbitt was envious of the Smart Set of the McKelveys, before William Washington Eathorne he was reverent. Mr. Eathorne had nothing to do with the Smart Set. He was above it. He was the great-grandson of one of the five men who founded Zenith, in 1792, and he was of the third generation of bankers. He could examine credits, make loans, promote or injure a man's business. In his presence Babbitt breathed quickly and felt young.

The Reverend Dr. Drew bounced into the room and flowered into speech:

"I've asked you gentlemen to stay so I can put a proposition before you. The Sunday School needs bucking up. It's the fourth largest in Zenith, but there's no reason why we should take anybody's dust. We ought to be first. I want to request you, if you will, to form a committee of advice and publicity for the Sunday School; look it over and make any suggestions for its betterment, and then, perhaps, see that the press gives us some attention—give the public some really helpful and constructive news instead of all these murders and divorces."

"Excellent," said the banker.

Babbitt and Frink were enchanted to join him.

*   *   *

If you had asked Babbitt what his religion was, he would have answered in sonorous Boosters'-Club rhetoric, "My religion is to serve my fellow men, to honor my brother as myself, and to do my bit to make life happier for one and all." If you had pressed him for more detail, he would have announced, "I'm a member of the Presbyterian Church, and naturally, I accept its doctrines." If you had been so brutal as to go on, he would have protested, "There's no use discussing and arguing about religion; it just stirs up bad feeling."

Actually, the content of his theology was that there was a supreme being who had tried to make us perfect, but presumably had failed; that if one was a Good Man he would go to a place called Heaven (Babbitt unconsciously pictured it as rather like an excellent hotel with a private garden); but if one was a Bad Man, that is, if he murdered or committed burglary or used cocaine or had mistresses or sold non-existent real estate, he would be punished. Babbitt was uncertain, however, about what he called "this business of Hell." He explained to Ted, "Of course I'm pretty liberal; I don't exactly believe in a fire-and-brimstone Hell. Stands to reason, though, that a fellow can't get away with all sorts of Vice and not get nicked for it, see how I mean?"

Upon this theology he rarely pondered. The kernel of his practical religion was that it was respectable, and beneficial to one's business, to be seen going to services; that the church kept the Worst Elements from being still worse; and that the pastor's sermons, however dull they might seem at the time of taking, yet had a voodooistic power which "did a fellow good—kept him in touch with Higher Things."

His first investigations for the Sunday School Advisory Committee did not inspire him.

He liked the Busy Folks' Bible Class, composed of mature men and women and addressed by the old-school physician, Dr. T. Atkins Jordan, in a sparkling style comparable to that of the more refined humorous after-dinner speakers, but when he went down to the junior classes he was disconcerted. He heard Sheldon Smeeth, educational director of the Y.M.C.A. and leader of the church-choir, a pale but strenuous young man with curly hair and a smile, teaching a class of sixteen-year-old boys. Smeeth lovingly admonished them, "Now, fellows, I'm going to have a Heart to Heart Talk Evening at my house next Thursday. We'll get off by ourselves and be frank about our Secret Worries. You can just tell old Sheldy anything, like all the fellows do at the Y. I'm going to explain frankly about the horrible practices a kiddy falls into unless he's guided by a Big Brother, and about the perils and glory of Sex." Old Sheldy beamed damply; the boys looked ashamed; and Babbitt didn't know which way to turn his embarrassed eyes.

Less annoying but also much duller were the minor classes which were being instructed in philosophy and Oriental ethnology by earnest spinsters. Most of them met in the highly varnished Sunday School room, but there was an overflow to the basement, which was decorated with varicose water-pipes and lighted by small windows high up in the oozing wall. What Babbitt saw, however, was the First Congregational Church at Catawba. He was back in the Sunday School of his boyhood. He smelled again that polite stuffiness to be found only in church parlors; he recalled the case of drab Sunday School books: "Hetty, a Humble Heroine" and "Josephus, a Lad of Palestine;" he thumbed once more the high-colored text-cards which no boy wanted but no boy liked to throw away, because they were somehow sacred; he was tortured by the stumbling rote of thirty-five years ago, as in the vast Zenith church he listened to:

"Now, Edgar, you read the next verse. What does it mean when it says it's easier for a camel to go through a needle's eye? What does this teach us? Clarence! Please don't wiggle so! If you had studied your lesson you wouldn't be so fidgety. Now, Earl, what is the lesson Jesus was trying to teach his disciples? The one thing I want you to especially remember, boys, is the words, 'With God all things are possible.' Just think of that always—Clarence, PLEASE pay attention—just say 'With God all things are possible' whenever you feel discouraged, and, Alec, will you read the next verse; if you'd pay attention you wouldn't lose your place!"

Drone—drone—drone—gigantic bees that boomed in a cavern of drowsiness—

Babbitt started from his open-eyed nap, thanked the teacher for "the privilege of listening to her splendid teaching," and staggered on to the next circle.

After two weeks of this he had no suggestions whatever for the Reverend Dr. Drew.

Then he discovered a world of Sunday School journals, an enormous and busy domain of weeklies and monthlies which were as technical, as practical and forward-looking, as the real-estate columns or the shoe-trade magazines. He bought half a dozen of them at a religious book-shop and till after midnight he read them and admired.

He found many lucrative tips on "Focusing Appeals," "Scouting for New Members," and "Getting Prospects to Sign up with the Sunday School." He particularly liked the word "prospects," and he was moved by the rubric:

The moral springs of the community's life lie deep in its Sunday Schools—its school of religious instruction and inspiration. Neglect now means loss of spiritual vigor and moral power in years to come. . . . Facts like the above, followed by a straight-arm appeal, will reach folks who can never be laughed or jollied into doing their part.

Babbitt admitted, "That's so. I used to skin out of the ole Sunday School at Catawba every chance I got, but same time, I wouldn't be where I am to-day, maybe, if it hadn't been for its training in—in moral power. And all about the Bible. Great literature. Have to read some of it again, one of these days."

How scientifically the Sunday School could be organized he learned from an article in the *Westminster Adult Bible Class:*

The second vice-president looks after the fellowship of the class. She chooses a group to help her. These become ushers. Every one who comes gets a glad hand. No one goes away a stranger. One member of the group stands on the doorstep and invites passers-by to come in.

Perhaps most of all Babbitt appreciated the remarks by William H. Ridgway in the *Sunday School Times:*

If you have a Sunday School class without any pep and get-up-and-go in it, that is, without interest, that is uncertain in attendance, that acts like a fellow with the spring fever, let old Dr. Ridgway write you a prescription. Rx. Invite the Bunch for Supper.

The Sunday School journals were as well rounded as they were practical. They neglected none of the arts. As to music, the *Sunday School Times* advertised that C. Harold Lowden, "known to thousands through his sacred compositions," had written a new masterpiece, "entitled 'Yearning for You.' The poem, by Harry D. Kerr, is one of the daintiest you could imagine and the music is indescribably beautiful. Critics are agreed that it will sweep the country. May be made into a charming sacred song by substituting the hymn words, 'I Heard the Voice of Jesus Say.' "

Even manual training was adequately considered. Babbitt noted an ingenious way of illustrating the resurrection of Jesus Christ:

Model for Pupils to Make. Tomb with Rolling Door.—Use a square covered box turned upside down. Pull the cover forward a little to form a groove at the bottom. Cut a square door, also cut a circle of cardboard to more than cover the door. Cover the circular door and the tomb thickly with stiff mixture of sand, flour and water and let it dry. It was the heavy circular stone over the door the women found "rolled away" on Easter morning. This is the story we are to "Go—tell."

In their advertisements the Sunday School journals were thoroughly efficient. Babbitt was interested in a preparation which "takes the place of exercise for sedentary men by building up depleted nerve tissue, nourishing the brain and the digestive system." He was edified to learn that the selling of Bibles was a hustling and strictly competitive industry, and as an expert on hygiene he was pleased by the Sanitary Communion Outfit Company's announcement of "an improved and satisfactory outfit throughout, including highly polished beautiful mahogany tray. This tray eliminates all noise, is lighter and more easily handled than others and is more in keeping with the furniture of the church than a tray of any other material."

He dropped a pile of Sunday School Journals.

He pondered, "Now, there's a real he-world. Corking!

"Ashamed I haven't sat in more. Fellow that's an influence in the community—shame if he doesn't take part in a real virile hustling religion. Sort of Christianity Incorporated, you might say.

"But with all reverence.

"Some folks might claim these Sunday School fans are undignified and unspiritual and so on. Sure! Always some skunk to spring things like that! Knocking and sneering and tearing-down—so much easier than building up. But me, I certainly hand it to these magazines. They've brought ole George F. Babbitt into camp, and that's the answer to the critics!

"The more manly and practical a fellow is, the more he ought to lead the enterprising Christian life. Me for it! Cut out this carelessness and boozing and—Rone! Where the devil you been? This is a fine time o' night to be coming in!"

RACE RELATIONS

Among animals and plants, breeding with other species reduces fertility. As a matter of fact, biologists use interfertility as a basis of classification of plants or animals into species. But among men, all races are interfertile; men and women from any population in the world are able to produce offspring with unreduced fertility. In this sense, then, one may properly speak of the basic unity of mankind. Biological facts, however, do not coincide with social facts. Racial ideologies which are based on demonstrably false premises may still have important functions. In this respect W. I. Thomas' dictum "If men define situations as real, they are real in their consequences," applies with peculiar force. As an example, racial distinctions have been made the basis of rigid caste systems. In such systems dominant and subordinate castes are distinguished by racial criteria and, as in South Africa or in the South of the United States, any white man, no matter how ignorant or poor, is deemed superior to any colored man and must be treated with appropriate deference. Racial castes, as castes generally, ban intimate social

405

intercourse and intermarriage, and attempt to prevent inter-caste mobility. The imputed inferiority of the subordinate race is upheld through racial ideologies as well as through coercive measures. The strict enforcement of racial etiquette with its elaborate devices for symbolizing inferiority and superiority are an important means for upholding racial distinctions and for maintaining the power of the ruling caste.

The following selections stress the importance of racial etiquette and the means by which conformity to expectations of the dominant group is inculcated in the young members of the dominated race. Richard Wright, the important modern American Negro writer, shows in his moving autobiography *Black Boy*, how he was gradually led to recognize the various subtle as well as brutal ways by which white Southerners "keep Negroes in their place."

Peter Abrahams, the talented South-African Negro writer, provides in his autobiography *Tell Freedom* similar clues to an understanding of the means by the dominant race in its so far successful efforts to maintain the dominated race in subjection and to exact from it the tribute of continuous deference.

James Weldon Johnson, an American Negro writer of the pre-World War I generation, describes in his fictional *Autobiography of an Ex-Colored Man* the traumatic shock experienced by a boy when he is suddenly brought to realize that he is socially classified as a Negro even though his skin is white; he illustrates that racial distinctions are based on social rather than on biological definitions.

The short selection from Mark Twain's *Huckleberry Finn,* though presumably well-known, was nevertheless included here because it is perhaps the most moving description in all American literature of what happens when a member of a superior caste is moved by affection to discard the moral code he has taken for granted in regard to an inferior caste. Huck's conscience, the conscience of a Southern white boy in the middle of the last century, urges him to return Jim to slavery. He solves his problem of deciding between his friendship for Jim and the white code by which he has been brought up, not by doing "right" but by doing "wrong."

In recent years, partly because of the impact of legislative action, but largely because of the militant activism of large sectors of the black population, the American system of racial discrimination has been significantly weakened, though by no means eliminated. The heroic civil rights struggle in the South in the late fifties and early sixties has not yet been depicted in literary treatments worthy of note. But urban racial protest and urban ghetto riots have been depicted with enormous power by the great Negro writer Ralph Ellison. A section from his *The Invisible Man* concludes this section.

Richard Wright (1908–1960)

The price of keeping one's place

The next day at school I inquired among the students about jobs and was given the name of a white family who wanted a boy to do chores. That afternoon, as soon as school had let out, I went to the address. A tall, dour white woman talked to me. Yes, she needed a boy, an honest boy. Two dollars a week. Mornings, evenings, and all day Saturdays. Washing dishes. Chopping wood. Scrubbing floors. Cleaning the yard. I would get my breakfast and dinner. As I asked timid questions, my eyes darted about. What kind of food would I get? Was the place as shabby as the kitchen indicated?

"Do you want this job?" the woman asked.

"Yes, ma'am," I said, afraid to trust my own judgment.

"Now, boy, I want to ask you one question and I want you to tell me the truth," she said.

"Yes, ma'am," I said, all attention.

"Do you steal?" she asked me seriously.

I burst into a laugh, then checked myself.

"What's so damn funny about that?" she asked.

"Lady, if I was a thief, I'd never tell anybody."

"What do you mean?" she blazed with a red face.

I had made a mistake during my first five minutes in the white world. I hung my head.

"No, ma'am," I mumbled. "I don't steal."

She stared at me, trying to make up her mind.

"Now look, we don't want a sassy nigger around here," she said.

"No, ma'am," I assured her. "I'm not sassy."

Promising to report the next morning at six o'clock, I walked home and pondered on what could possibly have been in the woman's mind to have made her ask me point-blank if I stole. Then I recalled hearing that white people looked upon Negroes as a variety of children, and it was only in the light of that that her question made any sense. If I had been planning to murder her, I certainly would not have told her and rationally, she no doubt realized it. Yet habit had overcome her rationality and had made her ask me: "Boy, do you steal?" Only an idiot would have answered: "Yes, ma'am, I steal."

What would happen now that I would be among white people for hours at a stretch? Would they hit me? Curse me? If they did, I would leave at once. In all my wishing for a job I had not thought of how I would be treated, and now it loomed important, decisive, sweeping down beneath every other consideration. I would be polite, humble, saying yes sir and no sir, yes ma'am and no ma'am, but I would draw a line over which they must not step. Oh, maybe I'm just thinking up trouble, I told myself. They might like me. . . .

The next morning I chopped wood for the cook stove, lugged in scuttles of coal for the grates, washed the front porch and swept the back porch, swept the kitchen, helped wait on the table, and washed the dishes. I was sweating. I swept the front walk and ran to the store to shop. When I returned the woman said:

"Your breakfast is in the kitchen."

"Thank you, ma'am."

I saw a plate of thick, black molasses and a hunk of white bread on the table. Would I get more than this? They had had eggs, bacon, coffee. . . . I picked up the bread and tried to break it; it was stale and hard. Well, I would drink the molasses. I lifted the plate and brought it to my lips and saw floating on the surface of the black liquid green and white bits of mold. Goddamn. . . . I can't eat this, I told myself. The food was not even clean. The woman came into the kitchen as I was putting on my coat.

"You didn't eat," she said.

"No, ma'am," I said. "I'm not hungry."

"You'll eat at home?" she asked hopefully.

"Well, I just wasn't hungry this morning, ma'am," I lied.

"You don't like molasses and bread," she said dramatically.

"Oh, yes, ma'am, I do," I defended myself quickly, not wanting her to think that I dared criticize what she had given me.

"I don't know what's happening to you niggers nowadays," she sighed, wagging her head. She looked closely at the molasses. "It's a sin to throw out molasses like that. I'll put it up for you this evening."

"Yes, ma'am," I said heartily.

Neatly she covered the plate of molasses with another plate, then felt the bread and dumped it into the garbage. She turned to me, her face lit with an idea.

"What grade are you in school?"

"Seventh, ma'am."

"Then why are you going to school?" she asked in surprise.

"Well, I want to be a writer," I mumbled, unsure of myself; I had not planned to tell her that, but she had made me feel so utterly wrong and of no account that I needed to bolster myself.

"A what?" she demanded.

"A writer," I mumbled defensively.

"You'll never be a writer," she said. "Who on earth put such ideas into your nigger head?"

"Nobody," I said.

"I didn't think anybody ever would," she declared indignantly.

As I walked around her house to the street I knew that I would not go back. The woman had assaulted my ego; she had assumed that she knew my place in life, what I felt, what I ought to be, and I resented it with all my heart. Perhaps she was right; perhaps I would never be a writer; but I did not want her to say so.

Had I kept the job I would have learned quickly just how white people acted toward Negroes, but I was too naïve to think that there were many white people like that. I told myself that there were good white people, people with money and sensitive feelings. As a whole, I felt that they were bad, but I would be lucky enough to find the exceptions.

Fearing that my family might think I was finicky, I lied to them, telling them that the white woman had already hired a boy. At school I continued to ask about jobs and was directed to another address. As soon as school was out I made for the house. Yes, the woman said that she wanted a boy who could milk a cow, feed chickens, gather vegetables, help serve breakfast and dinner.

"But I can't milk a cow, ma'am," I said.

"Where are you from?" she asked incredulously.

"Here in Jackson," I said.

"You mean to stand there, nigger, and tell me that you live in Jackson and don't know how to milk a cow?" she demanded in surprise.

I said nothing, but I was quickly learning the reality—a Negro's reality—of the white world. One woman had assumed that I would tell her if I stole, and now this woman was amazed that I could not milk a cow, I, a nigger who dared live in Jackson. . . . They were all turning out to be alike, differing only in detail. I faced a wall in the woman's mind, a wall that she did not know was there.

"I just never learned," I said finally.

"I'll show you how to milk," she said, as though glad to be charitable enough to repair a nigger's knowledge on that score. "It's easy." . . .

The next morning I was outside the office of the optical company long before it opened. I was reminding myself that I must be polite, must think before I spoke, must think before I acted, must say "yes sir, no sir," that I must so conduct myself that white people would not think that I thought I was as good as they. Suddenly a white man came up to me.

"What do you want?" he asked me.

"I'm reporting for a job, sir," I said.

"O.K. Come on."

I followed him up a flight of steps and he unlocked the door of the office. I was a little tense, but the young white man's manner put me at ease and

I sat and held my hat in my hand. A white girl came and began punching the typewriter. Soon another white man, thin and gray, entered and went into the rear room. Finally a tall, red-faced white man arrived, shot me a quick glance and sat at his desk. His brisk manner branded him a Yankee.

"You're the new boy, eh?"

"Yes, sir."

"Let me get my mail out of the way and I'll talk with you," he said pleasantly.

"Yes, sir."

I even pitched my voice to a low plane, trying to rob it of any suggestion or overtone of aggressiveness.

Half an hour later Mr. Crane called me to his desk and questioned me closely about my schooling, about how much mathematics I had had. He seemed pleased when I told him that I had had two years of algebra.

"How would you like to learn this trade?" he asked.

"I'd like it fine, sir. I'd like nothing better," I said.

He told me that he wanted to train a Negro boy in the optical trade; he wanted to help him, guide him. I tried to answer in a way that would let him know that I would try to be worthy of what he was doing. He took me to the stenographer and said:

"This is Richard. He's going to be with us."

He then led me into the rear room of the office, which turned out to be a tiny factory filled with many strange machines smeared with red dust.

"Reynolds," he said to a young white man, "this is Richard."

"What you saying there, boy!" Reynolds grinned and boomed at me.

Mr. Crane took me to the older man.

"Pease, this is Richard, who'll work with us."

Pease looked at me and nodded. Mr. Crane then held forth to the two white men about my duties; he told them to break me in gradually to the workings of the shop, to instruct me in the mechanics of grinding and polishing lenses. They nodded their assent.

"Now, boy, let's see how clean you can get this place," Mr. Crane said.

"Yes, sir."

I swept, mopped, dusted, and soon had the office and the shop clean. In the afternoons, when I had caught up with my work, I ran errands. In an idle moment I would stand and watch the two white men grinding lenses on the machines. They said nothing to me and I said nothing to them. The first day passed, the second, the third, a week passed and I received my five dollars. A month passed. But I was not learning anything and nobody had volunteered to help me. One afternoon I walked up to Reynolds and asked him to tell me about the work.

"What are you trying to do, get smart, nigger?" he asked me.

"No, sir," I said.

I was baffled. Perhaps he just did not want to help me. I went to Pease, reminding him that the boss had said that I was to be given a chance to learn the trade.

"Nigger, you think you're white, don't you?"

"No, sir."

"You're acting mighty like it," he said.

"I was only doing what the boss told me to do," I said.

Pease shook his fist in my face.

"This is a *white* man's work around here," he said.

From then on they changed toward me; they said good morning no more. When I was just a bit slow in performing some duty, I was called a lazy black sonofabitch. I kept silent, striving to offer no excuse for worsening of relations. But one day Reynolds called me to his machine.

"Nigger, you think you'll ever amount to anything?" he asked in a slow, sadistic voice.

"I don't know, sir," I answered, turning my head away.

"What do niggers think about?" he asked.

"I don't know, sir," I said, my head still averted.

"If I was a nigger, I'd kill myself," he said.

I said nothing. I was angry.

"You know why?" he asked.

I still said nothing.

"But I don't reckon niggers mind being niggers," he said suddenly and laughed.

I ignored him. Mr. Pease was watching me closely; then I saw them exchange glances. My job was not leading to what Mr. Crane had said it would. I had been humble, and now I was reaping the wages of humility.

"Come here, boy," Pease said.

I walked to his bench.

"You didn't like what Reynolds just said, did you?" he asked.

"Oh, it's all right," I said smiling.

"You didn't like it. I could see it on your face," he said.

I stared at him and backed away.

"Did you ever get into any trouble?" he asked.

"No, sir."

"What would you do if you got into trouble?"

"I don't know sir."

"Well, watch yourself and don't get into trouble," he warned.

I wanted to report these clashes to Mr. Crane, but the thought of what Pease or Reynolds would do to me if they learned that I had "snitched" stopped me. I worked through the days and tried to hide my resentment under a nervous, cryptic smile.

The climax came at noon one summer day. Pease called me to his workbench; to get to him I had to go between two narrow benches and stand with my back against a wall.

"Richard, I want to ask you something," Pease began pleasantly, not looking up from his work.

"Yes, sir."

Reynolds came over and stood blocking the narrow passage between the benches; he folded his arms and stared at me solemnly. I looked from one to the other, sensing trouble. Pease looked up and spoke slowly, so there would be no possibility of my not understanding.

"Richard, Reynolds here tells me that you called me Pease," he said.

I stiffened. A void opened up in me. I knew this was the showdown.

He meant that I had failed to call him Mr. Pease. I looked at Reynolds; he was gripping a steel bar in his hand. I opened my mouth to speak, to protest, to assure Pease that I had never called him simply *Pease*, and that I had never had any intention of doing so, when Reynolds grabbed me by the collar, ramming my head against a wall.

"Now, be careful, nigger," snarled Reynolds, baring his teeth. "I heard you call 'im *Pease*. And if you say you didn't, you're calling me a liar, see?" He waved the steel bar threateningly.

If I had said: No, sir, Mr. Pease I never called you *Pease*, I would have been pleading guilty to the worst insult that a Negro can offer to a southern white man. I stood trying to think of a neutral course that would resolve this quickly risen nightmare, but my tongue would not move.

"Richard, I asked you a question!" Pease said. Anger was creeping into his voice.

"I don't remember calling you *Pease*, Mr. Pease," I said cautiously. "And if I did, I sure didn't mean. . . ."

"You black sonofabitch! You called me *Pease,* then!" he spat, rising and slapping me till I bent sideways over a bench.

Reynolds was on top of me demanding:

"Didn't you call him *Pease*? If you say you didn't, I'll rip your gut string loose with this f———g bar, you black granny dodger! You can't call a white man a liar and get away with it!"

I wilted. I begged them not to hit me. I knew what they wanted. They wanted me to leave the job.

"I'll leave," I promised. "I'll leave right now!"

Peter Abrahams (1919–   )

Learning submission

Thus, hurling curses at each other, we reached the fork. Andries saw them first and moved over to my side of the road.

"White boys," he said.

There were three of them, two of about our own size and one slightly bigger. They had school bags and were coming towards us up the road from the siding.

"Better run for it," Andries said.

"Why?"

"No, that'll draw them. Let's just walk along, but quickly."

"Why?" I repeated.

"Shut up," he said.

Some of his anxiety touched me. Our own scrap was forgotten. We marched side by side as fast as we could. The white boys saw us and hurried up the road. We passed the fork. Perhaps they would take the turning away from us. We dared not look back.

"Hear them?" Andries asked.

"No," I looked over my shoulder. "They're coming," I said.

"Walk faster," Andries said. "If they come closer, run."

"Hey, klipkop!"

"Don't look back," Andries said.

"Hottentot!"

We walked as fast as we could.

"Bloody Kaffir!"

Ahead was a bend in the road. Behind the bend were bushes. Once there, we could run without them knowing it till it was too late.

"Faster," Andries said.

They began pelting us with stones.

"Run when we get to the bushes," Andries said.

The bend and the bushes were near. We would soon be there.

A clear young voice carried to us: "Your fathers are dirty black bastards of baboons!"

"Run!" Andries called.

A violent, unreasoning anger suddenly possessed me. I stopped and turned.

"You're a liar!" I screamed it.

The foremost boy pointed at me. "An ugly black baboon!"
In a fog of rage I went towards him.
"Liar!" I shouted. "My father was better than your father!"
I neared them. The bigger boy stepped between me and the one I was after.
"My father was better than your father! Liar!"
The big boy struck me a mighty clout on the side of the face. I staggered, righted myself, and leaped at the boy who had insulted my father. I struck him on the face, hard. A heavy blow on the back of my head nearly stunned me. I grabbed at the boy in front of me. We went down together.
"Liar!" I said through clenched teeth, hitting him with all my might.
Blows rained on me—on my head, my neck, the side of my face, my mouth —but my enemy was under me and I pounded him fiercely, all the time repeating:
"Liar! Liar! Liar!"
Suddenly stars exploded in my head. Then there was darkness.
I emerged from the darkness to find Andries kneeling beside me.
"God, man! I thought they'd killed you."
I sat up. The white boys were nowhere to be seen. Like Andries, they'd probably thought me dead and run off in panic. The inside of my mouth felt sore and swollen. My nose was tender to the touch. The back of my head ached. A trickle of blood dripped from my nose. I stemmed it with the square of coloured cloth. The greatest damage was to my shirt. It was ripped in many places. I remembered the crackling. I looked anxiously about. It was safe, a little off the road on the grass. I relaxed. I got up and brushed my clothes. I picked up the crackling.
"God, you're dumb!" Andries said. "You're going to get it! Dumb arse!"
I was too depressed to retort. Besides, I knew he was right. I was dumb. I should have run when he told me to.
"Come on," I said.
One of many small groups of children, each child carrying his little bag of crackling, we trod the long road home in the cold winter afternoon.
There was tension in the house that night. When I got back, Aunt Liza had listened to the story in silence. The beating or scolding I expected did not come. But Aunt Liza changed while she listened, became remote and withdrawn. When Uncle Sam came home she told him what had happened. He, too, just looked at me and became more remote and withdrawn than usual. They were waiting for something; their tension reached out to me, and I waited with them, anxious, apprehensive.
The thing we waited for came while we were having our supper. We heard a trap pull up outside.
"Here it is," Uncle Sam said, and got up.

Aunt Liza leaned back from the table and put her hands in her lap, fingers intertwined, a cold, unseeing look in her eyes.

Before Uncle Sam reached the door, it burst open. A tall, broad, white man strode in. Behind him came the three boys. The one I had attacked had swollen lips and a puffy left eye.

"Evening, *baas*," Uncle Sam murmured.

"That's him," the bigger boy said, pointing at me.

The white man stared till I lowered my eyes.

"Well?" he said.

"He's sorry, *baas*," Uncle Sam said quickly. "I've given him a hiding he won't forget soon. You know how it is, *baas*. He's new here, the child of a relative in Johannesburg, and they don't all know how to behave there. You know how it is in the big towns, *baas*." The plea in Uncle Sam's voice had grown more pronounced as he went on. He turned to me. "Tell the *baas* and young *basies* how sorry you are, Lee."

I looked at Aunt Liza and something in her lifelessness made me stubborn in spite of my fear.

"He insulted my father," I said.

The white man smiled.

"See, Sam, your hiding couldn't have been good."

There was a flicker of life in Aunt Liza's eyes. For a brief moment she saw me, looked at me, warmly, lovingly; then her eyes went dead again.

"He's only a child, *baas*," Uncle Sam murmured.

"You stubborn too, Sam?"

"No, *baas*."

"Good. Then teach him, Sam. If you and he are to live here, you must teach him. Well—?"

"Yes, *baas*."

Uncle Sam went into the other room and returned with a thick leather thong. He wound it once round his hand and advanced on me. The man and the boys leaned against the door, watching. I looked at Aunt Liza's face. Though there was no sign of life or feeling on it, I knew suddenly, instinctively, that she wanted to cry.

Bitterly, Uncle Sam said: "You must never lift your hand to a white person. No matter what happens, you must never lift your hand to a white person . . ."

He lifted the strap and brought it down on my back. I clenched my teeth and stared at Aunt Liza. I did not cry with the first three strokes. Then, suddenly, Aunt Liza went limp. Tears showed in her eyes. The thong came down on my back again and again. I screamed and begged for mercy. I grovelled at Uncle Sam's feet, begging him to stop, promising never to lift my hand to any white person . . .

At last the white man's voice said: "All right, Sam."

Uncle Sam stopped. I lay whimpering on the floor. Aunt Liza sat like one in a trance.

"Is he still stubborn, Sam?"

"Tell the *baas* and *basies* you are sorry."

"I'm sorry," I said.

"Bet his father is one of those who believe in equality."

"His father is dead," Aunt Liza said.

"Good night, Sam."

"Good night, *baas*. Sorry about this."

"All right, Sam." He opened the door. The boys went out first, then he followed. "Good night, Liza."

Aunt Liza did not answer. The door shut behind the white folk, and soon we heard their trap moving away. Uncle Sam flung the thong viciously against the door, slumped down on the bench, folded his arms on the table, and buried his head on his arms. Aunt Liza moved away from him, sat down on the floor beside me, and lifted me into her large lap. She sat rocking my body. Uncle Sam began to sob softly. After some time he raised his head and looked at us.

"Explain to the child, Liza," he said.

"You explain," Aunt Liza said bitterly. "You are the man. You did the beating. You are the head of the family. This is a man's world. You do the explaining."

"Please, Liza."

"You should be happy. The whites are satisfied. We can go on now."

With me in her arms, Aunt Liza got up. She carried me into the other room. The food on the table remained half-eaten. She laid me on the bed on my stomach, smeared fat on my back, then covered me with the blankets. She undressed and got into bed beside me. She cuddled me close, warmed me with her own body. With her big hand on my cheek, she rocked me, first to silence, then to sleep.

For the only time during my stay there, I slept on a bed in Elsburg.

When I woke next morning, Uncle Sam was gone. Aunt Liza only once referred to the beating he had given me. It was in the late afternoon, when I returned with the day's cow dung.

"It hurt him," she said. "You'll understand one day."

That night Uncle Sam brought me an orange, a bag of boiled sweets, and a dirty old picture book. He smiled as he gave them to me, rather anxiously. When I smiled back at him, he seemed to relax. He put his hand on my head, started to say something, then changed his mind and took his seat by the fire.

Aunt Liza looked up from the floor, where she dished out the food.

"It's all right, old man," she murmured.

"One day . . ." Uncle Sam said.
"It's all right," Aunt Liza repeated insistently.

The long winter passed. Slowly, day by day, the world of Elsburg became a warmer place. The cracks in my feet began to heal. The spells of bearable, noonday cold gave way to warmth. The noise of the veld at night became a din. The freezing nights changed, became bearable; changed again, became warm. Warm nights and hot days!

Summer had come, and with its coming the world became a softer, kindlier, more beautiful place. Sunflowers began blooming in people's yards. And people themselves began to relax and laugh. When, one evening, as I came in with some washing from the line, I heard Uncle Sam's voice raised in laughter and saw him and Aunt Liza playing, I knew the summer had really come. Later that same evening he went into the other room and returned with a guitar. Aunt Liza beamed.

"Open the door?"

Uncle Sam nodded. He played. Soon people from the other houses came, in ones and twos, till our little room was crowded. Someone sang, with his arms on his wife's shoulders, a love song:

"I'll be your sweetheart
If you will be mine . . ."

Summer had come indeed.

In the long summer afternoons, after my day's work, I went down to the river. Sometimes Andries and some of the other children went with me. Often I went alone.

Often, with others or alone, I climbed the short willows, with their long drooping branches. The touch of willow leaf on the cheek gives a feeling of cool wonder. Often I jumped from stone to stone on the broad bed of the shallow, clear, fast-flowing river. Sometimes I found little pools of idle water, walled off by stones from the flow. I tickled long-tailed tadpoles in these. The sun on the water touched their bodies with myriad colours. Sometimes I watched the springhaas—the wild rabbit of the veld—go leaping across the land, almost faster than my eye could follow. And sometimes I lay on my back on the green grass on the bank of the river and looked up at the distant sky, watching thin, fleecy white clouds form and re-form and trying to associate the shapes with people and things I knew. I loved being alone by the river. It became my special world.

Each day I explored a little more of the river, going farther up- or downstream, extending the frontiers of my world. One day, going farther downstream than I had been before, I came upon a boy. He was on the bank on the other side from me. We saw each other at the same time and stared. He was completely naked. He carried two finely carved sticks of equal size and shape, both about his own height. He was not light brown, like the other children of our location, but dark brown, almost black. I moved nearly to the edge of the river. He called out to me in a strange language.

"Hello!" I shouted.

He called out again, and again I could not understand. I searched for a place with stones, then bounded across. I approached him slowly. As I drew near, he gripped his sticks more firmly. I stopped.

He spoke harshly, flung one stick on the ground at my feet, and held the other ready as though to fight.

"Don't want to fight," I said.

I reached down to pick up the stick and return it to him. He took a step forward and raised the one in his hand. I moved back quickly. He stepped back and pointed at the stick on the ground. I shook my head.

"Don't want to fight."

I pushed the stick towards him with my foot, ready to run at the first sign of attack. I showed my new, stubby teeth in a tentative smile. He said something that sounded less aggressive. I nodded, smiling more broadly. He relaxed, picked up the stick, and transferred both to his left hand. He smacked his chest.

"Joseph! Zulu!"

I smacked my own chest. "Lee—" But I didn't know what I was apart from that.

He held out his hand. We shook. His face lit up in a sunny smile. He said something and pointed downstream. Then he took my arm and led me down.

Far downstream, where the river skirted a hillside, hidden by a cluster of willows, we came on a large clear pool. Joseph flung his sticks on the ground and dived in. He shot through the water like a tadpole. He went down and came up. He shouted and beckoned me to come in. I undressed and went in more tentatively. Laughing, he pulled me under. I came up gasping and spluttering, my belly filled with water. He smacked me on the back, and the water shot out of my mouth in a rush. When he realized I could not swim, he became more careful. We spent the afternoon together, with Joseph teaching me to swim.

At home that evening I stood beside Aunt Liza's washtub.

"Aunt Liza—"

"Yes?"

"What am I?"

"What are you talking about?"

"I met a boy at the river. He said he was Zulu."

She laughed.

"You are Coloured. There are three kinds of people: white people, Coloured people, and black people. The white people come first, then the Coloured people, then the black people."

"Why?"

"Because it is so."

Next day when I met Joseph, I smacked my chest and said: "Lee! Coloured!"

He clapped his hands and laughed.

James Weldon Johnson (1871–1938)

To be a negro

There were some black and brown boys and girls in the school, and several of them were in my class. One of the boys strongly attracted my attention from the first day I saw him. His face was as black as night, but shone as though it were polished; he had sparkling eyes, and when he opened his mouth, he displayed glistening white teeth. It struck me at once as appropriate to call him "Shiny Face," or "Shiny Eyes," or "Shiny Teeth," and I spoke to him often by one of these names to the other boys. These terms were finally merged into "Shiny," and to that name he answered good-naturedly during the balance of his public school days.

"Shiny" was considered without question to be the best speller, the best reader, the best penman—in a word, the best scholar, in the class. He was very quick to catch anything, but, nevertheless, studied hard; thus he possessed two powers very rarely combined in one boy. I saw him year after year, on up into the high school, win the majority of the prizes for punctuality, deportment, essay writing, and declamation. Yet it did not take me long to discover that, in spite of his standing as a scholar, he was in some way looked down upon.

The other black boys and girls were still more looked down upon. Some of the boys often spoke of them as "niggers." Sometimes on the way home from school a crowd would walk behind them repeating:

> Nigger, nigger, never die,
> Black face and shiny eye.

On one such afternoon one of the black boys turned suddenly on his tormentors and hurled a slate; it struck one of the white boys in the mouth, cutting a slight gash in his lip. At sight of the blood the boy who had thrown the slate ran, and his companions quickly followed. We ran after them pelting them with stones until they separated in several directions. I was very

---

From *The Autobiography of an Ex-Colored Man* by James Weldon Johnson (1912). Published by Alfred A. Knopf, Inc.

much wrought up over the affair, and went home and told my mother how one of the "niggers" had struck a boy with a slate. I shall never forget how she turned on me. "Don't you ever use that word again," she said, "and don't you ever bother the coloured children at school. You ought to be ashamed of yourself." I did hang my head in shame, not because she had convinced me that I had done wrong, but because I was hurt by the first sharp word she had ever given me.

My school-days ran along very pleasantly. I stood well in my studies, not always so well with regard to my behaviour. I was never guilty of any serious misconduct, but my love of fun sometimes got me into trouble. I remember, however, that my sense of humour was so sly that most of the trouble usually fell on the head of the other fellow. My ability to play on the piano at school exercises was looked upon as little short of marvellous in a boy of my age. I was not chummy with many of my mates, but, on the whole, was about as popular as it is good for a boy to be.

One day near the end of my second term at school the principal came into our room and, after talking to the teacher, for some reason said: "I wish all of the white scholars to stand for a moment." I rose with the others. The teacher looked at me and, calling my name, said: "You sit down for the present, and rise with the others." I did not quite understand her, and questioned: "Ma'm?" She repeated, with a softer tone in her voice: "You sit down now, and rise with the others." I sat down dazed. I saw and heard nothing. When the others were asked to rise, I did not know it. When school was dismissed, I went out in a kind of stupor. A few of the white boys jeered me, saying: "Oh, you're a nigger too." I heard some black children say: "We knew he was coloured." "Shiny" said to them: "Come along, don't tease him," and thereby won my undying gratitude.

I hurried on as fast as I could, and had gone some distance before I perceived that "Red Head" was walking by my side. After a while he said to me: "Le' me carry your books." I gave him my strap without being able to answer. When we got to my gate, he said as he handed me my books: "Say, you know my big red agate? I can't shoot with it any more. I'm going to bring it to school for you tomorrow." I took my books and ran into the house. As I passed through the hallway, I saw that my mother was busy with one of her customers; I rushed up into my own little room, shut the door, and went quickly to where my looking-glass hung on the wall. For an instant I was afraid to look, but when I did, I looked long and earnestly. I had often heard people say to my mother: "What a pretty boy you have!" I was accustomed to hear remarks about my beauty; but now, for the first time, I became conscious of it and recognized it. I noticed the ivory whiteness of my skin, the beauty of my mouth, the size and liquid darkness of my eyes, and how the long, black lashes that fringed and shaded them produced an effect that was strangely fascinating even to me. I noticed the softness and glossiness of my dark hair that fell in waves over my temples, making my forehead appear whiter than it really was. How long I stood there gazing at my image I do not know. When I came out and reached the head of the stairs, I heard the lady who had been with my mother going out. I ran downstairs and rushed to where my mother was sitting, with a piece of work in her hands. I buried my head in her lap and blurted out: "Mother, mother, tell me, am I a nigger?" I could not see her face, but I knew the piece of work dropped to the floor and I felt her hands on my head. I looked up into her face and repeated: "Tell me, mother, am I a nigger?" There were tears in her eyes and I could see that she was suffering for me. And then it was that I looked at her critically for the first time. I had thought of her in a childish way only as the most beautiful woman in the world; now I looked at her searching for defects. I could see that her skin was almost brown, that her hair was not so soft as mine, and that she did differ in some way from the other ladies who came to the house; yet, even so, I could see that she was very beautiful, more beautiful than any of them. She must have felt that I was examining her, for she hid her face in my hair and said with difficulty: "No, my darling, you are not a nigger." She went on: "You are as good as anybody; if anyone calls you a nigger, don't notice them." But the more she talked, the less was I reassured, and I stopped her by asking: "Well, mother, am I white? Are you white?" She answered tremblingly: "No, I am not white, but you—your father is one of the greatest men in the country—the best blood of the South is in you—" This suddenly opened up in my heart a fresh chasm of misgiving and fear, and I almost fiercely demanded: "Who is my father? Where is he?" She stroked my hair and said: "I'll tell you about him some day." I sobbed: "I want to know now." She answered, "No, not now."

Perhaps it had to be done, but I have never forgiven the woman who did it so cruelly. It may be that she never knew that she gave me a sword-thrust that day in school which was years in healing.

_____   **Mark Twain (1835–1910)**   _____   ·

Huck breaks the white code

Once I said to myself it would be a thousand times better for Jim to be a slave at home, where his family was as long as he'd _got_ to be a slave, and so I'd better write a letter to Tom Sawyer and tell him to tell Miss Watson where he was. But I soon give up that notion for two things; she'd be mad

From _Huckleberry Finn_ by Mark Twain (1885).

and disgusted at his rascality and ungratefulness for leaving her, and so she'd sell him straight down the river again; and if she didn't, everybody naturally despises an ungrateful nigger, and they'd make Jim feel it all the time, and so he'd feel ornery and disgraced. And then think of *me!* It would get all around that Huck Finn helped a nigger to get his freedom; and if I was ever to see anybody from that town again I'd be ready to get down and lick his boots for shame. That's just the way: a person does a low-down thing, and then he don't want to take no consequences of it. Thinks as long as he can hide, it ain't no disgrace. That was my fix exactly. The more I studied about this the more my conscience went to grinding me, and the more wicked and low-down and ornery I got to feeling. And at last, when it hit me all of a sudden that here was the plain hand of Providence slapping me in the face and letting me know my wickedness was being watched all the time from up there in heaven, whilst I was stealing a poor old woman's nigger that hadn't ever done me no harm, and now was showing me there's One that's always on the lookout, and ain't a-going to allow no such miserable doings to go only just so fur and no further, I most dropped in my tracks I was so scared. Well, I tried the best I could to kinder soften it up somehow for myself by saying I was brung up wicked, and so I warn't so much to blame, but something inside of me kept saying, "There was the Sunday school, you could 'a' gone to it; and if you'd 'a' done it they'd 'a' learnt you there that people that acts as I'd been acting about the nigger goes to everlasting fire."

It made me shiver. And I about made up my mind to pray, and see if I couldn't try to quit being the kind of a boy I was and be better. So I kneeled down. But the words wouldn't come. Why wouldn't they? It warn't no use to try and hide it from Him. Nor from *me,* neither. I knowed very well why they wouldn't come. It was because my heart warn't right; it was because I warn't square; it was because I was playing double. I was letting *on* to give up sin, but away inside of me I was holding on to the biggest one of all. I was trying to make my mouth *say* I would do the right thing and the clean thing, and go and write to that nigger's owner and tell where he was; but deep down in me I knowed it was a lie, and He knowed it. You can't pray a lie—I found that out.

So I was full of trouble, full as I could be; and didn't know what to do. At last I had an idea; and I says, I'll go and write the letter—and *then* see if I can pray. Why, it was astonishing, the way I felt as light as a feather right straight off, and my trouble all gone. So I got a piece of paper and a pencil, all glad and excited, and set down and wrote:

Miss Watson, your runaway nigger Jim is down here two miles below Pikesville, and Mr. Phelps has got him and he will give him up for the reward if you send.

Huck Finn

I felt good and all washed clean of sin for the first time I had ever felt so in my life, and I knowed I could pray now. But I didn't do it straight off, but laid the paper down and set there thinking—thinking how good it was all this happened so, and how near I come to being lost and going to hell. And went on thinking. And got to thinking over our trip down the river; and I see Jim before me all the time; in the day and in the nighttime, sometimes moonlight, sometimes storms, and we a-floating along, talking and singing and laughing. But somehow I couldn't seem to strike no places to harden me against him, but only the other kind. I'd see him standing my watch on top of his'n, 'stead of calling me, so I could go on sleeping; and see him how glad he was when I come back out of the fog; and when I come to him again in the swamp, up there where the feud was; and such-like times; and would always call me honey, and pet me, and do everything he could think of for me, and how good he always was; and at last I struck the time I saved him by telling the man we had smallpox aboard, and he was so grateful, and said I was the best friend old Jim ever had in the world, and the *only* one he's got now; and then I happened to look around and see that paper.

It was a close place. I took it up, and held it in my hand. I was a-trembling, because I'd got to decide, forever, betwixt two things, and I knowed it. I studied a minute, sort of holding my breath, and then says to myself:

"All right, then, I'll *go* to hell"—and tore it up.

It was awful thoughts and awful words, but they was said. And I let them stay said; and never thought no more about reforming. I shoved the whole thing out of my head, and said I would take up wickedness again, which was in my line, being brung up to it, and the other warn't. And for a starter I would go to work and steal Jim out of slavery again; and if I could think up anything worse, I would do that, too; because as long as I was in, and in for good, I might as well go the whole hog.

Ralph Ellison (1914–   )

Capable of their own action

"Aw man, don't tell me," Scofield said. "Didn't I see it with my own eyes? About eight o'clock down on Lenox and 123rd this paddy slapped a kid for grabbing a Baby Ruth and the kid's mama took it up and then the paddy slapped her and that's when hell broke loose."

"You were there?" I said.

From *The Invisible Man* by Ralph Ellison. Copyright 1952 by Ralph Ellison. Reprinted by permission of Random House, Inc.

"Same's I'm here. Some fellow said the kid made the paddy mad by grabbing a candy named after a white woman."

"Damn if that's the way I heard it," another man said. "When I come up they said a white woman set if off by trying to take a black gal's man."

"Damn *who* started it," Dupre said. "All I want is for it to last a while."

"It was a white gal, all right, but that wasn't the way it was. She was drunk—" another voice said.

But it couldn't have been Sybil, I thought; it had already started.

"You wahn know who started it?" a man holding a pair of binoculars called from the window of a pawnshop. "You wahn really to know?"

"Sure," I said.

"Well, you don't need to go no further. It was started by that great leader, Ras the Destroyer!"

"That monkey-chaser?" someone said.

"Listen, bahstard!"

"Don't nobody know how it started," Dupre said.

"Somebody has to know," I said.

Scofield held his whiskey toward me. I refused it.

"Hell, man, it just exploded. These is dog days," he said.

"*Dog* days?"

"Sho, this hot weather."

"I tell you they mad over what happen to that young fellow, what's-his-name . . ."

We were passing a building now and I heard a voice calling frantically, "Colored store! Colored store!"

"Then put up a sign, motherfouler," a voice said. "You probably rotten as the others."

"Listen at the bastard. For one time in his life he's glad to be colored," Scofield said.

"Colored store," the voice went on automatically.

"Hey! You sho you ain't got some white blood?"

"No, *sir!*" the voice said.

"Should I bust him, man?"

"For what? He ain't got a damn thing. Let the motherfouler alone."

A few doors away we came to a hardware store. "This is the first stop, men," Dupre said.

"What happens now?" I said.

"Who you?" he said, cocking his thrice-hatted head.

"Nobody, just one of the boys—" I began.

"You sho you ain't somebody I know?"

"I'm pretty sure," I said.

"He's all right, Du," said Scofield. "Them cops shot him."

Dupre looked at me and kicked something—a pound of butter, sending it smearing across the hot street. "We fixing to do something what needs to be done," he said. "First we gets a flashlight for everybody . . . And let's have some organization, y'all. Don't everybody be running over everybody else. Come on!"

"Come on in, buddy," Scofield said.

I felt no need to lead or leave them; was glad to follow; was gripped by a need to see where and to what they would lead. And all the time the thought that I should go to the district was with me. We went inside the store, into the dark glinting with metal. They moved carefully, and I could hear them searching, sweeping objects to the floor. The cash register rang.

"Here some flashlights over here," someone called.

"How many?" Dupre said.

"Plenty, man."

"Okay, pass out one to everybody. They got batteries?"

"Naw, but there's plenty them too, 'bout a dozen boxes."

"Okay, give me one with batteries so I can find the buckets. Then every man get him a light."

"Here some buckets over here," Scofield said.

"Then all we got to find is where he keeps the oil."

"Oil?" I said.

"*Coal* oil, man. And hey, y'all," he called, "don't nobody be smoking in here."

I stood beside Scofield listening to the noise as he took a stack of zinc buckets and passed them out. Now the store leaped alive with flashing lights and flickering shadows.

"Keep them lights down on the floor," Dupre called. "No use letting folks see who we are. Now when you get your buckets line up and let me fill 'em."

"Listen to ole Du lay it down—he's a bitch, ain't he, buddy? He always liked to lead things. And always leading me into trouble."

"What are we getting ready to do?" I said.

"You'll see," Dupre said. "Hey, you over there. Come on from behind that counter and take this bucket. Don't you see ain't nothing in that cash register, that if it was I'd have it myself?"

Suddenly the banging of buckets ceased. We moved into the back room. By the light of a flash I could see a row of fuel drums mounted on racks. Dupre stood before them in his new hip boots and filled each bucket with oil. We moved in slow order. Our buckets filled, we filed out into the street. I stood there in the dark feeling a rising excitement as their voices played around me. What was the meaning of it all? What should I think of it, *do* about it?

"With this stuff," Dupre said, "we better walk in the middle of the street. It's just down around the corner."

Then as we moved off a group of boys ran among us and the men started using their lights, revealing darting figures in blonde wigs, the tails of their stolen dress coats flying. Behind them in hot pursuit came a gang armed with dummy rifles taken from an Army & Navy Store. I laughed with the others, thinking: A holy holiday for Clifton.

"Put out them lights!" Dupre commanded.

Behind us came the sound of screams, laughter; ahead the footfalls of the running boys, distant fire trucks, shooting, and in the quiet intervals, the steady filtering of shattered glass. I could smell the kerosene as it sloshed from the buckets and slapped against the street.

Suddenly Scofield grabbed my arm. "Good God, look-a-yonder!"

And I saw a crowd of men running up pulling a Borden's milk wagon, on top of which, surrounded by a row of railroad flares, a huge woman in a gingham pinafore sat drinking beer from a barrel which sat before her. The men would run furiously a few paces and stop, resting between the shafts, run a few paces and rest, shouting and laughing and drinking from a jug, as she on top threw back her head and shouted passionately in a full-throated voice of blues singer's timbre:

> If it hadn't been for the referee,
> Joe Louis woulda killed
> Jim Jefferie
> Free beer!!

—sloshing the dipper of beer around.

We stepped aside, amazed, as she bowed graciously from side to side like a tipsy fat lady in a circus parade, the dipper like a gravy spoon in her enormous hand. Then she laughed and drank deeply while reaching over nonchalantly with her free hand to send quart after quart of milk crashing into the street. And all the time the men running with the wagon over the debris. Around me there were shouts of laughter and disapproval.

"Somebody better stop them fools," Scofield said in outrage. "That's what I call taking things too far. Goddam, how the hell they going to get her down from there after she gits fulla beer? Somebody answer me that. How they going to get her down? 'Round here throwing away all that good milk!"

The big woman left me unnerved. Milk and beer—I felt sad, watching the wagon careen dangerously as they went around a corner. We went on, avoiding the broken bottles as now the spilling kerosene splashed into the pale split milk. How much has happened? Why was I torn? We moved around a corner. My head still ached.

Scofield touched my arm. "Here we is," he said.

We had come to a huge tenement building.

"Where are we?" I said.

"This the place where most of us live," he said. "Come on."

So that was it, the meaning of the kerosene. I couldn't believe it, couldn't believe they had the nerve. All the windows seemed empty. They'd blacked it out themselves. I saw now only by flash or flame.

"Where will you live?" I said, looking up, up.

"You call *this* living?" Scofield said. "It's the only way to git rid of it, man . . ."

I looked for hesitation in their vague forms. They stood looking at the building rising above us, the liquid dark of the oil simmering dully in the stray flecks of light that struck their pails, bent forward, their shoulders bowed. None said "no," by word or stance. And in the dark windows and on the roofs above I could now discern the forms of women and children.

Dupre moved toward the building.

"Now look ahere, y'all," he said, his triple-hatted head showing grotesquely atop the stoop. "I wants all the women and chillun and the old and the sick folks brought out. And when you takes your buckets up the stairs I wants you to go clean to the top. I mean the *top!* And when you git there I want you to start using your flashlights in every room to make sure nobody gits left behind, then when you git 'em out start splashing coal oil. Then when you git it splashed I'm going to holler, and when I holler three times I want you to light them matches and git. After that it's every tub on its own black bottom!"

It didn't occur to me to interfere, or to question . . . They had a plan. Already I could see the women and children coming down the steps. A child was crying. And suddenly everyone paused, turning, looking off into the dark. Somewhere nearby an incongruous sound shook the dark, an air hammer pounding like a machine gun. They paused with the sensitivity of grazing deer, then returned to their work, the women and children once more moving.

"That's right, y'all. You ladies move on up the street to the folks you going to stay with," Dupre said. "And keep holt them kids!"

Someone pounded my back and I swung around, seeing a woman push past me and climb up to catch Dupre's arm, their two figures seeming to blend as her voice arose, thin, vibrant and desperate.

"Please, Dupre," she said, "*please.* You know my time's almost here . . . you *know* it is. If you do it now, where am I going to go?"

Dupre pulled away and rose to a higher step. He looked down at her, shaking his thrice-hatted head. "Now git on out the way, Lottie," he said patiently. "Why you have to start this now? We done been all over it and you know I ain't go'n change. And lissen here, the resta y'all," he said, reaching into the top of his hip boot and producing a nickel-plated revolver and waving it around, "don't think they's going to be any *mind*-changing either. And I don't aim for no arguments neither."

"You goddam right, Dupre. We wid you!"

"My kid died from the t-bees in that deathtrap, but I bet a man ain't no more go'n be *born* in there," he said. "So now, Lottie, you go on up the street and let us mens git going."

She stood back, crying. I looked at her, in house shoes, her breasts turgid, her belly heavy and high. In the crowd, women's hands took her away, her large liquid eyes turned for a second toward the man in the rubber boots.

What type of man is he, what would Jack say of him? Jack. *Jack!* And where was he in this?

"Let's go, buddy," Scofield said, nudging me. I followed him, filled with a sense of Jack's outrageous unreality. We went in, up the stairs, flashing our lights. Ahead I saw Dupre moving. He was a type of man nothing in my life had taught me to see, to understand, or respect, a man outside the scheme till now. We entered rooms littered with the signs of swift emptying. It was hot, close.

"This here's my own apartment," Scofield said. "And ain't the bedbugs going to get a surprise!"

We slopped the kerosene about, upon an old mattress, along the floor; then moved into the hall, using the flashlights. From all through the building came the sounds of footsteps, of splashing oil, the occasional prayerful protest of some old one being forced to leave. The men worked in silence now, like moles deep in the earth. Time seemed to hold. No one laughed. Then from below came Dupre's voice.

"Okay, mens. We got everybody out. Now starting with the top floor I want you to start striking matches. Be careful and don't set yourself on fire . . ."

There was still some kerosene left in Scofield's bucket and I saw him pick up a rag and drop it in; then came the sputtering of a match and I saw the room leap to flame. The heat flared up and I backed away. He stood there silhouetted against the red flare, looking into the flames, shouting.

"Goddam you rotten sonsabitches. You didn't think I'd do it but there it is. You wouldn't fix it up. Now see how you like it."

"Let's go," I said.

Below us, men shot downstairs five and six steps at a time, moving in the weird light of flash and flame in long, dream-bounds. On each floor as I passed, smoke and flame arose. And now I was seized with a fierce sense of exaltation. They've done it, I thought. They organized it and carried it through alone; the decision their own and their own action. Capable of their own action . . .

Collective behavior— the crowd and revolution

Sociologists, in their preoccupation with social structure and institutionalized types of behavior, often tend to neglect those forms of social behavior which are relatively unorganized and lack the stability and predictability of cohesive social groups. Yet collective behavior arising spontaneously, and not based on pre-established norms and traditions, should be studied closely if only because such behavior may enlighten us as to how an old order dies and a new social order emerges. Mob or crowd behavior arising amidst the decay of previously established systems of social control is the very opposite of institutionalized behavior; it may be considered "abnormal" if a stable social system is taken as a point of reference. But just as on the individual level, study of the abnormal may furnish important clues to an understanding of the normal, so on the social level the study of disorganized, unorganized, and irrational crowd behavior may illuminate the very basis of social order. The following are among the main characteristics of the crowd: It is a temporal and ephemeral group requiring the physical presence of its participants; it rubs out certain distinctive characteristics of individuals and instead brings to the fore crude and generalized emotions. To the extent that interaction in the crowd reduces the usual internalized restraints built into the individual, it tends to produce de-socialized responses and uninhibited behavior. As Kingsley Davis has said, "Because the participants in a crowd are all on one level, because their attention is focused on one thing, because their inhibited impulses find ready release in spontaneous action, the crowd is highly suggestible. The participants react to one another's gestures, postures and cries in an almost automatic animal-like way, with a swiftness that precludes thoughtful interpretation or rational foresight." The following selections are meant to expose some of these traits of crowd behavior. In this area literary treatment has often led to subtle, concrete observations which seem superior in many respects to the theoretically informed findings of sociologists.

The short excerpt from William Faulkner's *Intruder in the Dust* shows the restless, almost random movements of certain marginal elements in a Southern town which, if not checked in time, can be the first steps in the formation of a lynching mob. Emile Zola's masterful and frighteningly realistic depiction of a crowd of striking French miners driven to desperation by hunger and misery and then led into horrible acts of violence, from the novel *Germinal,* illustrates some of the major characteristics of mob action. Note especially Zola's stress on the suggestibility of the crowd. Nathanael West, one of the most talented novelists of the thirties, gives us an almost surrealistic description of the seething violence of a Hollywood mob in *The Day of the Locust.* D. C. Themba, a young South-African novelist closely associated with the courageous South-African Negro magazine *Drum,* pictures the *mob passion* aroused in intertribal conflicts among South-African Negroes; one is especially impressed by the fact that Themba has eschewed the temptation to pass over the potentialities for destructive passions in his own people. He shows that the lurk of violence beneath the veneer of civilization is present among whites and blacks alike; it is a universal human characteristic.

Thomas Carlyle's description of the storming of the Bastille from his *French Revolution* shows the distinctive characteristics of a crowd whose action focuses in an attack on the symbolic embodiment of governmental power. Gustave Flaubert's brilliant depiction of the behavior of a revolutionary crowd attacking the very seat of royal legitimation, the king's palace and his throne, during the Paris revolution of 1848, which is taken from his *Sentimental Education,* completes this section.

William Faulkner (1897–1962)

On the eve

Then suddenly the empty street was full of men. Yet there were not many of them, not two dozen, come suddenly and quietly from nowhere. Yet they seemed to fill it, block it, render it suddenly interdict as though not that nobody could pass them, pass through it, use it as a street but that nobody would dare, would even approach near enough to essay the gambit as people stay well away from a sign saying High Voltage or Explosive. He knew, recognised them all; some of them he had even seen and listened to in the barbershop two hours ago—the young men or men under forty, bachelors, the homeless who had the Saturday and Sunday baths in the barbershop— truckdrivers and garagehands, the oiler from the cotton gin, a sodajerker from the drugstore and the ones who could be seen all week long in or around the poolhall who did nothing at all that anyone knew, who owned automobiles and spent money nobody really knew exactly how they earned on weekends in Memphis or New Orleans brothels—the men who his uncle said were in every little Southern town, who never really led mobs nor even instigated them but were always the nucleus of them because of their mass availability.

Emile Zola (1840–1902)

The natural history of a mob

And the troop went off over the flat plain, white with frost beneath the pale winter sun, and overflowed the path as they passed through the beetroot fields.

From the Fourche-aux-Boeufs, Etienne had assumed command. He cried his orders while the crowd moved on and organized the march. Jeanlin galloped at the head, performing a barbarous music on his horn. Then the women came in the first ranks, some of them armed with sticks: Maheude, with wild eyes, seemed to be seeking afar for the promised city of justice,

Mother Brûlé, the Levaque woman, Mouquette, striding along beneath their rags, like soldiers setting out for the seat of war. If they had any encounters we should see if the police dared to strike women. And the men followed in a confused flock with a roar that grew larger and larger, bristling with iron bars and dominated by Levaque's single ax, with its blade glistening in the sun. Etienne, in the middle, kept Chaval in sight, forcing him to walk before him, while Maheu, behind, gloomily kept an eye on Catherine, the only woman among these men, obstinately trotting near her lover for fear that he would be hurt. Bare heads were disheveled in the air; only the clank of sabots could be heard, like the movement of released cattle, carried away by Jeanlin's wild trumpeting.

But suddenly a new cry arose:

"Bread! Bread! Bread!"

It was midday; the hunger of six weeks on strike was awakening in these empty stomachs, whipped up by this race across the fields. The few crusts of the morning and Mouquette's chestnuts had long been forgotten; their stomachs were crying out, and this suffering was added to their fury against the traitors.

"To the pits! No more work! Bread!"

Etienne, who had refused to eat his share at the settlement, felt an unbearable tearing sensation in his chest. He made no complaint but mechanically took his tin from time to time and swallowed a gulp of gin, shaking so much that he thought he needed it to carry him to the end. His cheeks were heated and his eyes inflamed. He kept his head, however, and still wished to avoid needless destruction.

As they arrived at the Joiselle road a Vandame pikeman, who had joined the band for revenge on his master, impelled the men toward the right, shouting:

"To Gaston-Marie! Must stop the pump! Let the water ruin Jean-Bart!"

The mob was already turning in spite of the protests of Etienne, who begged them to let the pumping continue. What was the good of destroying the galleries? It offended his workman's heart, in spite of his resentment. Maheu also thought it unjust to take revenge on a machine. But the pikeman still shouted his cry of vengeance, and Etienne had to cry still louder:

"To Mirou! There are traitors down there! To Mirou! To Mirou!"

With a gesture he had turned the crowd toward the left road, while Jeanlin, going ahead, was blowing louder than ever. An eddy was produced in the crowd; this time Gaston-Marie was saved.

And the four kilometers which separated them from Mirou were traversed in half an hour, almost at running pace, across the interminable plain. The canal on this side cut it with a long icy ribbon. The leafless trees on the banks, changed by the frost into giant candelabra, alone broke this pale uniformity, prolonged and lost in the sky at the horizon, as in a sea. An undulation of the ground hid Montsou and Marchiennes; there was nothing but bare immensity.

They reached the pit and found a captain standing on a footbridge at the screening shed to receive them. They all well knew Father Quandieu, the doyen of the Montsou captains, an old man whose skin and hair were quite white and who was in his seventies, a miracle of fine health in the mines.

"What have you come after here, you pack of meddlers?" he shouted.

The band stopped. It was no longer a master; it was a mate, and a certain respect held them back before this old workman.

"There are men down below," said Etienne. "Make them come up."

"Yes, there are men there," said Father Quandieu, "some six dozen; the others were afraid of you evil beggars! But I warn you that not one comes up, or you will have to deal with me!"

Exclamations arose; the men pushed; the women advanced. Quickly coming down from the footbridge, the captain now barred the door.

Then Maheu tried to interfere.

"It is our right, old man. How can we make the strike general if we don't force all the mates to be on our side?"

The old man was silent a moment. Evidently his ignorance on the subject of coalition equaled the pikeman's. At last he replied:

"It may be your right; I don't say. But I only know my orders. I am alone here; the men are down till three, and they shall stay there till three."

The last words were lost in hooting. Fists were threateningly advanced; the women deafened him, and their hot breath blew in his face. But he still held out, his head erect and his beard and hair white as snow; his courage had so swollen his voice that he could be heard distinctly over the tumult.

"By God, you shall not pass! As true as the sun shines, I would rather die than let you touch the cables. Don't push any more, or I'm damned if I don't fling myself down the shaft before you!"

The crowd drew back, shuddering and impressed. He went on:

"Where is the beast who does not understand that? I am only a workman like you others. I have been told to guard here, and I'm guarding."

That was as far as Father Quandieu's intelligence went, stiffened by his obstinacy of military duty, his narrow skull and eyes dimmed by the black melancholy of half a century spent underground. The men looked at him, moved, feeling within them an echo of what he said, this military obedience, the sense of fraternity and resignation in danger. He saw that they were hesitating still and repeated:

"I'm damned if I don't fling myself down the shaft before you!"

A great recoil carried away the mob. They all turned and in a rush took the right-hand road, which stretched far away through the fields. Again cries arose:

"To Madeleine! To Crèvecoeur! No more work! Bread! Bread!"

But in the center, as they went on, there was hustling. It was Chaval, they said, who was trying to take advantage of an opportunity to escape. Etienne had seized him by the arm, threatening to do for him if he was planning some treachery. And the other struggled and protested furiously:

"What's all this for? Isn't a man free? I've been freezing the last hour. I want to clean myself. Let me go!"

He was, in fact, suffering from the coal glued to his skin by sweat, and his woolen garment was no protection.

"On you go, or we'll clean you," replied Etienne. "Don't expect to get your life at a bargain."

They were still running, and he turned toward Catherine, who was keeping up well. It annoyed him to feel her so near him, so miserable, shivering beneath her man's old jacket and her muddy trousers. She must be nearly dead of fatigue; she was running, all the same.

"You can go off, you can," he said at last.

Catherine seemed not to hear. Her eyes on meeting Etienne's only flamed with reproach for a moment. She would not stop. Why did he want her to leave her man? Chaval was not at all kind, it was true; he would even beat her sometimes. But he was her man, the one who had had her first, and it enraged her that they should throw themselves on him—more than a thousand of them. She would have defended him without any tenderness at all out of pride.

"Off you go!" repeated Maheu violently.

Her father's order slackened her course for a moment. She trembled, and her eyelids swelled with tears. Then in spite of her fear she came back to the same place again, still running. Then they let her be.

The mob crossed the Joiselle road, went a short distance up the Cron road and then mounted toward Cougny. On this side factory chimneys striped the flat horizon; wooden sheds, brick workshops with large dusty windows, appeared along the street. They passed one after another the low buildings of two settlements—that of the Cent-Quatre-Vingts, then that of the Soixante-Seize—and from each of them, at the sound of the horn and the clamor arising from every mouth, whole families came out—men, women and children—running to join their mates in the rear. When they came up to Madeleine there were at least fifteen hundred. The road descended in a gentle slope; the rumbling flood of strikers had to turn round the pit bank before they could spread over the mine square.

It was now not more than two o'clock. But the captains had been warned and were hastening the ascent as the band arrived. The men were all up; only some twenty remained and were now disembarking from the cage. They fled and were pursued with stones. Two were struck; another left the sleeve of his jacket behind. This man hunt saved the material, and neither the cables nor the boilers were touched. The flood was already moving away, rolling on toward the next pit.

This one, Crèvecoeur, was only five hundred meters away from Madeleine. There, also, the mob arrived in the midst of the ascent. A putter girl was taken and whipped by the women with her breeches split open and her buttocks exposed before the men, who were laughing. The trammer boys had their ears boxed; the pikemen got away, their sides blue from blows and their noses bleeding. And in this growing ferocity, in this old need of revenge which was turning every head with madness, the choked cries went on, death to traitors, hatred against ill-paid work, the roaring of bellies after bread. They began to cut the cables, but the file would not bite, and the task was too long now that the fever was on them for moving onward, forever onward. At the boilers a tap was broken, while the water, thrown by bucketfuls into the stoves, made the metal grating burst.

Outside they were talking of marching on St. Thomas. This was the best-disciplined pit. The strike had not touched it; nearly seven hundred men must have gone down there. This exasperated them; they would wait for these men with sticks, ranged for battle, just to see who would get the best of it. But the rumor ran along that there were gendarmes at St. Thomas, the gendarmes of the morning, whom they had made fun of. How was this known? Nobody could say. No matter! They were seized by fear and decided on Feutry-Cantel. Their giddiness carried them on; all were on the road, clanking their sabots, rushing forward. To Feutry-Cantel! To Feutry-Cantel! The cowards there were certainly four hundred in number, and they would be fun! Situated three kilometers away, this pit lay in a fold of the ground near the Scarpe. They were already climbing the slope of the Plâtrières, beyond the road to Beaugnies, when a voice—no one knew from whom—threw out the idea that the soldiers were perhaps down there at Feutry-Cantel. Then from one end to the other of the column it was repeated that the soldiers were down there. They slackened their march; panic gradually spread in the country, idle without work, which they had been scouring for hours. Why had they not come across the soldiers? This impunity troubled them, at the thought of the repression which they felt to be coming.

Without anyone knowing where it came from, a new word of command turned them toward another pit.

"To the Victoire! To the Victoire!"

Were there then neither soldiers nor police at the Victoire? Nobody knew. All seemed reassured. And turning round, they descended from the Beaumont side and cut across the fields to reach the Joiselle road. The railway line barred their passage, and they crossed it, pulling down the palings. Now they were approaching Montsou; the gradual undulation of the landscape grew less; the sea of beetroot fields enlarged, reaching far away to the black houses at Marchiennes.

This time it was a march of five good kilometers. So strong an impulse pushed them on that they had no feeling of their terrible fatigue or of their bruised and wounded feet. The rear continued to lengthen, increased by mates enlisted on the roads and in the settlements. When they had passed the canal at the Magache bridge and appeared before the Victoire there were two thousand of them. But three o'clock had struck; the ascent was completed; not a man remained below. Their disappointment was spent in vain threats; they could only heave broken bricks at the workmen who had arrived to take their duty at the earth cutting. There was a rush, and the deserted pit belonged to them. And in their rage at not finding a traitor's face to strike they attacked things. A rankling abcess was bursting within them, a poisoned boil of slow growth. Years and years of hunger tortured them with a thirst for massacre and destruction.

Behind a shed Etienne saw some porters filling a wagon with coal.

"Will you just clear out of the bloody place?" he shouted. "Not a bit of coal goes out!"

At his orders some hundred strikers ran up, and the porters only had time to escape. Men unharnessed the horses, which were frightened and set off, struck in the haunches, while others, overturning the wagon, broke the shafts.

Levaque, with violent blows of his ax, had thrown himself on the platforms to break down the footbridges. They resisted, and it occurred to him to tear up the rails, destroying the line from one end of the square to the other. Soon the whole band set to this task. Maheu made the metal chairs leap up, armed with his iron bar which he used as a lever. During this time Mother Brûlé led away the women and invaded the lamp cabin, where their sticks covered the soil with a carnage of lamps. Maheude, carried out of herself, was laying about her as vigorously as the Levaque woman. All were soaked in soil, and Mouquette dried her hands on her skirt, laughing to find herself so dirty. Jeanlin, for a joke, had emptied a lamp down her neck. But all this revenge produced nothing to eat. Stomachs were crying out louder than ever. And the great lamentation dominated still:

"Bread! Bread! Bread!"

A former captain at the Victoire kept a stall near by. No doubt he had fled in fear, for his shed was abandoned. When the women came back and the men had finished destroying the railway, they besieged the stall, the shutters of which yielded at once. They found no bread there; there were only two pieces of raw flesh and a sack of potatoes. But in the pillage they discovered some fifty bottles of gin, which disappeared like a drop of water drunk up by the sand.

Etienne, having emptied his tin, was able to refill it. Little by little·a terrible drunkenness, the drunkenness of the starved, was inflaming his eyes and showing his teeth like a wolf's teeth between his pallid lips. Suddenly he perceived that Chaval had gone off in the midst of the tumult. He swore, and men ran to seize the fugitive, who was hiding with Catherine behind the timber supply.

"Ah, you dirty swine; you are afraid of getting into trouble!" shouted Etienne. "It was you in the forest who called for a strike of the enginemen, to stop the pumps, and now you want to play us a filthy trick! Very well! By God, we will go back to Gaston-Marie. I will have you smash the pump; yes, by God, you shall smash it!"

He was drunk; he was urging his men against this pump which he had saved a few hours earlier.

"To Gaston-Marie! To Gaston-Marie!"

They all cheered and rushed on, while Chaval, seized by the shoulders, was drawn and pushed violently along, while he constantly asked to be allowed to wash.

"Will you take yourself off then?" cried Maheu to Catherine, who had also begun to run again.

This time she did not even draw back but turned her burning eyes on her father and went on running.

Once more the mob plowed through the flat plain. They were retracing their steps over the long straight paths, by the fields endlessly spread out. It was four o'clock; the sun, which approached the horizon, lengthened the shadows of this horde with their furious gestures over the frozen soil.

They avoided Montsou and farther on rejoined the Joiselle road; to spare the journey round Fourche-aux-Boeufs, they passed beneath the walls of Piolaine. The Grégoires had just gone out, having to visit a lawyer before going to dine with the Hennebeaus, where they would find Cécile. The estate seemed asleep with its avenue of deserted limes, its kitchen garden and its orchard bared by the winter. Nothing was stirring in the house, and the closed windows were dulled by the warm steam within. Out of the profound silence an impression of good-natured comfort arose, the patriarchal sensation of good beds and a good table, the wise happiness of the proprietor's existence.

Without stopping the band cast gloomy looks through the grating and at the length of protecting walls, bristling with broken bottles. The cry arose again:

"Bread! Bread! Bread!"

The dogs alone replied by barking ferociously, a pair of big Danes with rough coats, who stood with open jaws. And behind the closed blind there were only the servants. Mélanie, the cook, and Honorine, the house maid, attracted by this cry, pale and perspiring with fear at seeing these savages go by. They fell on their knees and thought themselves killed on hearing a single stone breaking a pane of a neighboring window. It was a joke of Jeanlin's; he had manufactured a sling with a piece of cord and had just sent a little passing greeting to the Grégoires. Already he was again blowing his horn, and the band was lost in the distance, and the cry grew fainter:

"Bread! Bread! Bread!"

They arrived at Gaston-Marie in still greater numbers, more than twenty-five hundred madmen, breaking everything, sweeping away everything, with the force of a torrent which gains strength as it moves. The police had passed here an hour earlier and had gone off toward St. Thomas, led astray by some peasants; in their haste they had not even taken the precaution of leaving a few men behind to guard the pit. In less than a quarter of an hour the fires were overturned, the boilers emptied, the buildings torn down and devastated. But it was the pump which they specially threatened. It was not enough to stop it in the last expiring breath of its steam; they threw themselves on it as on a living person whose life they required.

"The first blow is yours!" repeated Etienne, putting a hammer into Chaval's hand. "Come! You have sworn with the others!"

Chaval drew back, trembling, and in the hustling the hammer fell, while other men, without waiting, murdered the pump with blows from iron bars, blows from bricks, blows from anything they could lay their hands on. Some even broke sticks over it. The nuts leaped off; the pieces of steel and copper were dislocated like torn limbs. The blow of a shovel, delivered with full force, fractured the metal body; the water escaped and emptied itself, and there was a supreme gurgle, like an agonizing death rattle.

That was the end, and the mob found themselves outside again, madly pushing on behind Etienne, who would not let Chaval go.

"Kill him! The traitor! To the shaft! To the shaft!"

The livid wretch, clinging with imbecile obstinacy to his fixed idea, continued to stammer his need of cleaning himself.

"Wait, if that bothers you," said the Levaque woman. "Here! Here's a bucket!"

There was a pond there, an infiltration of the water from the pump. It was white with a thick layer of ice, and they struck it and broke the ice, forcing him to dip his head in this cold water.

"Duck then," repeated Mother Brûlé. "By God, if you don't duck we'll shove you in. And now you shall have a drink of it; yes, yes, like a beast, with your jaws in the trough!"

He had to drink on all fours. They all laughed with cruel laughter. One woman pulled his ears; another woman threw in his face a handful of dung found fresh on the road. His old woolen jacket, in tatters, no longer held together. He was haggard, stumbling, and with struggling movements of his hips he tried to flee.

Maheu had pushed him, and Maheude was among those who grew furious, both of them satisfying their old spite; even Mouquette, who generally remained such good friends with her old lovers, was wild with this one, treating him as good-for-nothing and talking of taking his breeches down to see if he were still a man.

Etienne made her hold her tongue.

"That's enough. There's no need for all to set to it. If you like, you, we will just settle it together."

His fist closed and his eyes were lit up with homicidal fury; his intoxication was turning into the desire to kill.

"Are you ready? One of us must stay here. Give him a knife; I've got mine."

Catherine, exhausted and terrified, gazed at him. She remembered his confidences, his desire to devour a man when he had drunk, poisoned after the third glass, to such an extent had his drunkards of parents put this beastliness into his body. Suddenly she leaped forward, struck him with both her woman's hands and choking with indignation, shouted into his face:

"Coward! Coward! Coward! Isn't it enough then, all these abominations? You want to kill him now that he can't stand upright any longer!"

She turned toward her father and her mother; she turned toward the others.

"You are cowards! Cowards! Kill me then with him! I will tear your eyes out, I will, if you touch him again. Oh, the cowards!"

And she planted herself before her man to defend him, forgetting the blows, forgetting the life of misery, lifted up by the idea that she belonged to him since he had taken her and that it was a shame for her when they so crushed him.

Etienne had grown pale beneath this girl's blows. At first he had been about to knock her down, then after having wiped his face with the movement of a man who is recovering from intoxication, he said to Chaval in the midst of deep silence:

"She is right; that's enough. Off you go."

Immediately Chaval was away, and Catherine galloped behind him. The crowd gazed at them as they disappeared round a corner of the road, but Maheude muttered:

"You were wrong; ought to have kept him. He is sure to be after some treachery."

But the mob began to march on again. Five o'clock was about to strike. The sun, as red as a furnace on the edge of the horizon, seemed to set fire to the whole plain. A peddler who was passing informed them that the military were descending from the Crèvecoeur side. Then they turned. An order ran:

"To Montsou! To the manager! Bread! Bread! Bread!"

*   *   *

It was not Rasseneur, however; it was Etienne, who was dealing blows from his ax at Maigrat's shop. And he went on calling to the men: did not the goods in there belong to the colliers? Had they not the right to take back their property from this thief who had exploited them so long, who was starving them at a hint from the company. Gradually they all left the manager's house and ran up to pillage the neighboring shop. The cry, "Bread! Bread! Bread!" broke out anew. They would find bread behind that door. The rage of hunger carried them away, as if they suddenly felt that they could wait no longer without expiring on the road. Such furious thrusts were made at the door that at every stroke of the ax Etienne feared to wound someone.

Meanwhile Maigrat, who had left the hall of the manager's house, had at first taken refuge in the kitchen; but, hearing nothing there, he imagined some abominable attempt against his shop and came up again to hide behind the pump outside, when he distinctly heard the cracking of the door and shouts of pillage in which his own name was mixed. It was not a nightmare then. If he could not see he could now hear, and he followed the attack with ringing ears; every blow struck him in the heart. A hinge must have given way; five minutes more and the shop would be taken. The thing was stamped on his brain in real and terrible images—the brigands rushing forward, then the drawers broken open, the sacks emptied, everything eaten, everything drunk, the house itself carried away, nothing left, not even a stick with which he might go and beg through the villages. No, he would never allow them to complete his ruin; he would rather leave his life there. Since he had been here he noticed at a window of his house his wife's thin silhouette, pale and confused, behind the panes; no doubt she was watching the blows with her usual silent air of a poor, beaten creature. Beneath there was a shed, so placed that from the villa garden one could climb it from the palings; then it was easy to get onto the tiles up to the window. And the idea of thus returning home now pursued him in his remorse at having left. Perhaps he would have time to barricade the shop with furniture; he even invented other and more heroic defenses—boiling oil, lighted petroleum, poured out from above. But this love of his property struggled against his fear, and he groaned in the battle with cowardice. Suddenly, on hearing a deeper blow of the ax, he made up his mind. Avarice conquered; he and his wife would cover the sacks with their bodies rather than abandon a single loaf.

Almost immediately hooting broke out:

"Look! Look! The tomcat's up there! After the cat! After the cat!"

The mob had just seen Maigrat on the roof of the shed. In his fever of anxiety he had climbed the palings with agility in spite of his weight and without troubling over the breaking wood, and now he was flattening himself along the tiles and endeavoring to reach the window. But the slope was very steep; he was incommoded by his stoutness, and his nails were torn. He would have dragged himself up, however, if he had not begun to tremble with the fear of stones, for the crowd, which he could not see, continued to cry beneath him:

"After the cat! After the cat! Do for him!"

And suddenly both his hands let go at once, and he rolled down like a ball, leaped at the gutter and fell across the middle wall in such a way that by ill chance he rebounded on the side of the road, where his skull was broken open on the corner of a stone pillar. His brain had spurted out. He was dead. His wife up above, pale and confused behind the windowpanes, still looked out.

They were stupefied at first. Etienne stopped short, and the ax slipped from his hands. Maheu, Levaque and the others forgot the shop, with their eyes fixed on the wall along which a thin red streak was slowly flowing down. And the cries ceased, and silence spread over the growing darkness.

All at once the hooting began again. It was the women, who rushed forward, overcome by the drunkenness of blood.

"Then there is a good God after all! Ah, the bloody beast, he's done for!" They surrounded the still-warm body. They insulted it with laughter, abusing his fractured head, the dirty chops, hurling in the dead man's face the long venom of their starved lives.

"I owed you sixty francs; now you're paid, thief!" said Maheude, enraged like the others. "You won't refuse me credit any more. Wait! Wait! I must fatten you once more!"

With her fingers she scratched up some earth, took two handfuls and stuffed it violently into his mouth.

"There! Eat that! There! Eat! Eat! You used to eat us!"

The abuse increased while the dead man, stretched on his back, gazed motionless with his large fixed eyes at the immense sky from which the night was falling. This earth heaped in his mouth was the bread which he had refused to give. And henceforth he would eat of no other bread. It had not brought him luck to starve poor people.

But the women had another revenge to wreak on him. They moved round, smelling him like she-wolves. They were all seeking for some outrage, some savagery, that would relieve them.

Mother Brûlé's shrill voice was heard: "Cut him like a tomcat!"

"Yes, yes after the cat! After the cat! He's done too much, the dirty beast!"

Mouquette was already unfastening and drawing off the trousers, while the Levaque woman raised the legs. And Mother Brûlé, with her dry old hands separated the naked thighs and seized this dead virility. She took hold of everything, tearing with an effort which bent her lean spine and made her long arms crack. The soft skin resisted—she had to try again—and at last carried away the fragment, a lump of hairy and bleeding flesh, which she brandished with a laugh of triumph.

"I've got it! I've got it!"

Shrill voices saluted with curses the abominable trophy.

"Ah, swine! You won't fill our daughters any more!"

"Yes, we've done with paying on your beastly body; we shan't any more have to offer a backside in return for a loaf."

"Here, I owe you six francs; would you like to settle it? I'm quite willing, if you can do it still!"

This joke shook them all with terrible gaiety. They showed each other the bleeding fragment as an evil beast from which each of them had suffered and which they had at last crushed and saw before them there, inert, in their power. They spat on it; they thrust out their jaws, saying over and over again with furious burst of contempt:

"He can do no more! He can do no more! It's no longer a man that they'll put away in the earth. Go and rot then, good-for-nothing!"

Mother Brûlé then planted the whole lump on the end of her stick and, holding it in the air, bore it about like a banner, rushing along the road, followed, helter-skelter, by the yelling troop of women. Drops of blood rained down, and that pitiful flesh hung like a waste piece of meat on a butcher's stall. Up above, at the window, Mme. Maigrat still stood motionless, but beneath the last gleams of the setting sun the confused flaws of the windowpanes distorted her white face, which looked as though it were laughing. Beaten and deceived at every hour, with shoulders bent from morning to night over a ledger, perhaps she was laughing while the band of women rushed along with that evil beast, that crushed beast, at the end of the stick.

This frightful mutilation was accomplished in frozen horror. Neither Etienne nor Maheu nor the others had had time to interfere; they stood motionless before this gallop of Furies. At the door of the Estaminet Tison a few heads were grouped—Rasseneur, pale with disgust; Zacharie and Philomène, stupefied at what they had seen. The two old men, Bonnemort and Mouque, were gravely shaking their heads. Only Jeanlin was making fun, pushing Bébert with his elbow and forcing Lydie to look up. But the women were already coming back, turning round and passing beneath the manager's windows. Behind the blinds the ladies were stretching out their necks. They had not been able to observe the scene, which was hidden from them by the wall, and they could not distinguish well in the growing darkness.

"What is it they have at the end of that stick?" asked Cécile, who had been bold enough to look out.

Lucie and Jeanne declared that it must be a rabbitskin.

"No, no," murmured Mme Hennebeau, "they must have been pillaging a pork butcher's; it seems to be a remnant of a pig."

At this moment she shuddered and was silent. Mme Grégoire had nudged her with her knee. They both remained stupefied. The young ladies, who were very pale, asked no more questions but with large eyes followed this red vision through the darkness.

Etienne once more brandished the ax. But the feeling of anxiety did not disappear; this corpse now barred the road and protected the shop. Many had drawn back. Satiety seemed to have appeased them all. Maheu was standing by gloomily, when he heard a voice whisper in his ear to escape. He turned round and recognized Catherine, still in her old overcoat, black and panting. With a movement he repelled her. He would not listen to her; he threatened to strike her. With a gesture of despair she hesitated and then ran toward Etienne.

"Save yourself! Save yourself! The gendarmes are coming!"

He also pushed her away and abused her, feeling the blood of the blows she had given him mounting to his cheeks. But she would not be repelled; she forced him to throw down the ax and drew him away by both arms with irresistible strength.

"Don't I tell you the gendarmes are coming! Listen to me. It's Chaval who has gone for them and is bringing them, if you want to know. It's too much for me, and I've come. Save yourself; I don't want them to take you."

And Catherine drew him away, while at the same instant a heavy gallop shook the street from afar. Immediately a voice arose, "The gendarmes! The gendarmes!" There was a general breaking up, so mad a rush for life that in two minutes the road was free, absolutely clear, as though swept by a hurricane. Maigrat's corpse alone made a patch of shadow on the white earth. Before the Estaminet Tison, Rasseneur only remained, feeling relieved and with open face applauding the easy victory of the sabers, while in dim and deserted Montsou, in the silence of the closed houses, the bourgeois remained with perspiring skins and chattering teeth, not daring to look out. The plain was drowned beneath the thick night; only the blast furnaces and the coke furnaces were burning against the tragic sky. The gallop of the gendarmes heavily approached; they came up in an indistinguishable, somber mass. And behind them the Marchiennes pastry cook's vehicle, a little covered cart which had been confided to their care, at last arrived, and a small drudge of a boy jumped down and quietly unpacked the crusts for the *vol-au-vent*.

Nathanael West (1906–1940)

Crowds, mobs, and terror in hollywood

When Tod reached the street, he saw a dozen great violet shafts of light moving across the evening sky in wide crazy sweeps. Whenever one of the fiery columns reached the lowest point of its arc, it lit for a moment the rose-colored domes and delicate minarets of Kahn's Persian Palace Theatre. The purpose of this display was to signal the world première of a new picture.

Turning his back on the searchlights, he started in the opposite direction, toward Homer's place. Before he had gone very far, he saw a clock that read a quarter past six and changed his mind about going back just yet. He might as well let the poor fellow sleep for another hour and kill some time by looking at the crowds.

When still a block from the theatre, he saw an enormous electric sign that hung over the middle of the street. In letters ten feet high he read that—

Mr. kahn a pleasure dome decreed

Although it was still several hours before the celebrities would arrive, thousands of people had already gathered. They stood facing the theatre with their backs toward the gutter in a thick line hundreds of feet long. A big squad of policemen was trying to keep a lane open between the front rank of the crowd and the facade of the theatre.

Tod entered the lane while the policeman guarding it was busy with a woman whose parcel had torn open, dropping oranges all over the place. Another policeman shouted for him to get the hell across the street, but he took a chance and kept going. They had enough to do without chasing him. He noticed how worried they looked and how careful they tried to be. If they had to arrest someone, they joked good-naturedly with the culprit, making light of it until they got him around the corner, then they whaled him with their clubs. Only so long as a man was actually part of the crowd did they have to be gentle.

Tod had walked only a short distance along the narrow lane when he began to get frightened. People shouted, commenting on his hat, his carriage, and his clothing. There was a continuous roar of catcalls, laughter and yells, pierced occasionally by a scream. The scream was usually followed by a sudden movement in the dense mass and part of it would surge forward wherever the police line was weakest. As soon as that part was rammed back, the bulge would pop out somewhere else.

The police force would have to be doubled when the stars started to arrive. At the sight of their heroes and heroines, the crowd would turn demoniac. Some little gesture, either too pleasing or too offensive, would start it moving and then nothing but machine guns would stop it. Individually the purpose of its members might simply be to get a souvenir, but collectively it would grab and rend.

A young man with a portable microphone was describing the scene. His rapid, hysterical voice was like that of a revivalist preacher whipping his congregation toward the ecstasy of fits.

"What a crowd, folks! What a crowd! There must be ten thousand excited, screaming fans outside Kahn's Persian tonight. The police can't hold them. Here, listen to them roar."

He held the microphone out and those near it obligingly roared for him. "Did you hear it? It's a bedlam, folks. A veritable bedlam! What excitement! Of all premières I've attended, this is the most . . . the most . . . stupendous, folks. Can the police hold them? Can they? It doesn't look so, folks. . . ."

Another squad of police came charging up. The sergeant pleaded with the announcer to stand further back so the people couldn't hear him. His men threw themselves at the crowd. It allowed itself to be hustled and shoved out of habit and because it lacked an objective. It tolerated the police, just as a bull elephant does when he allows a small boy to drive him with a light stick.

Tod could see very few people who looked tough, nor could he see any working men. The crowd was made up of the lower middle classes, every other person one of his torchbearers.

Just as he came near the end of the lane, it closed in front of him with a heave, and he had to fight his way through. Someone knocked his hat off and when he stooped to pick it up, someone kicked him. He whirled around angrily and found himself surrounded by people who were laughing at him. He knew enough to laugh with them. The crowd became sympathetic. A stout woman slapped him on the back, while a man handed him his hat, first brushing it carefully with his sleeve. Still another man shouted for a way to be cleared.

By a great deal of pushing and squirming, always trying to look as though he were enjoying himself, Tod finally managed to break into the open. After rearranging his clothes, he went over to a parking lot and sat down on a low retaining wall that ran along the front of it.

New groups, whole families, kept arriving. He could see a change come over them as soon as they had become part of the crowd. Until they reached the line, they looked diffident, almost furtive, but the moment they had become part of it, they turned arrogant and pugnacious. It was a mistake to think them harmless curiosity seekers. They were savage and bitter, especially the middle-aged and the old, and had been made so by boredom and disappointment.

All their lives they had slaved at some kind of dull, heavy labor, behind desks and counters, in the fields and at tedious machines of all sorts, saving their pennies and dreaming of the leisure that would be theirs when they had enough. Finally that day came. They could draw a weekly income of ten or fifteen dollars. Where else should they go but California, the land of sunshine and oranges?

Once there, they discover that sunshine isn't enough. They get tired of oranges, even of avocado pears and passion fruit. Nothing happens. They haven't the mental equipment for leisure, the money nor the physical equipment for pleasure. Did they slave so long just to go to an occasional Iowa picnic? What else is there? They watch the waves come in at Venice. There wasn't any ocean where most of them came from, but after you've seen one wave, you've seen them all. The same is true of the airplanes at Glendale. If only a plane would crash once in a while so that they could watch the passengers being consumed in a "holocaust of flame," as the newspapers put it. But the planes never crash.

Their boredom becomes more and more terrible. They realize that they've been tricked and burn with resentment. Every day of their lives they read the newspapers and went to the movies. Both fed them on lynchings, murder, sex crimes, explosions, wrecks, love nests, fires, miracles, revolutions, wars. This daily diet made sophisticates of them. The sun is a joke. Oranges can't titillate their jaded palates. Nothing can ever be violent enough to make taut their slack minds and bodies. They have been cheated and betrayed. They have slaved and saved for nothing.

Tod stood up. During the ten minutes he had been sitting on the wall, the crowd had grown thirty feet and he was afraid that his escape might be cut off if he loitered much longer. He crossed to the other side of the street and started back.

He was trying to figure what to do if he were unable to wake Homer when, suddenly he saw his head bobbing above the crowd. He hurried toward him. From his appearance, it was evident that there was something definitely wrong. . . .

The next thing Tod knew, he was torn loose from Homer and sent to his knees by a blow in the back of the head that spun him sideways. The crowd in front of the theatre had charged. He was surrounded by churning legs and feet. He pulled himself erect by grabbing a man's coat, then let himself be carried along backwards in a long, curving swoop. He saw Homer rise above the mass for a moment, shoved against the sky, his jaw hanging as though he wanted to scream but couldn't. A hand reached up and caught him by his open mouth and pulled him forward and down.

There was another dizzy rush. Tod closed his eyes and fought to keep upright. He was jostled about in a hacking cross surf of shoulders and backs, carried rapidly in one direction and then in the opposite. He kept pushing and hitting out at the people around him, trying to face in the direction he was going. Being carried backwards terrified him.

Using the eucalyptus tree as a landmark, he tried to work toward it by slipping sideways against the tide, pushing hard when carried away from it and riding the current when it moved toward his objective. He was within only a few feet of the tree when a sudden, driving rush carried him far past it. He struggled desperately for a moment, then gave up and let himself be swept along. He was the spearhead of a flying wedge when it collided with a mass going in the opposite direction. The impact turned him around. As the two forces ground against each other, he was turned again and again, like a grain between millstones. This didn't stop until he became part of the opposing force. The pressure continued to increase until he thought he must collapse. He was slowly being pushed into the air. Although relief for his cracking ribs could be gotten by continuing to rise, he fought to keep his feet on the ground. Not being able to touch was an even more dreadful sensation than being carried backwards.

There was another rush, shorter this time, and he found himself in a dead spot where the pressure was less and equal. He became conscious of a terrible pain in his left leg, just above the ankle, and tried to work it into a more comfortable position. He couldn't turn his body, but managed to get his head around. A very skinny boy, wearing a Western Union cap, had his back wedged against his shoulder. The pain continued to grow and his whole leg as high as the groin throbbed. He finally got his left arm free and took the back of the boy's neck in his fingers. He twisted as hard as he could. The boy began to jump up and down in his clothes. He managed to straighten his elbow, by pushing at the back of the boy's head, and so turn half way around and free his leg. The pain didn't grow less.

There was another wild surge forward that ended in another dead spot. He now faced a young girl who was sobbing steadily. Her silk print dress had been torn down the front and her tiny brazziere hung from one strap. He tried by pressing back to give her room, but she moved with him every time he moved. Now and then, she would jerk violently and he wondered if she was going to have a fit. One of her thighs was between his legs. He struggled to get free of her, but she clung to him, moving with him and pressing against him.

She turned her head and said, "Stop, stop," to someone behind her.

He saw what the trouble was. An old man, wearing a Panama hat and horn-rimmed glasses, was hugging her. He had one of his hands inside her dress and was biting her neck.

Tod freed his right arm with a heave, reached over the girl and brought his fist down on the man's head. He couldn't hit very hard but managed to knock the man's hat off, also his glasses. The man tried to bury his face in the girl's shoulder, but Tod grabbed one of his ears and yanked. They started to move again. Tod held on to the ear as long as he could, hoping that it would come away in his hand. The girl managed to twist under his arm. A piece of her dress tore, but she was free of her attacker.

Another spasm passed through the mob and he was carried toward the curb. He fought toward a lamp-post, but he was swept by before he could grasp it. He saw another man catch the girl with the torn dress. She screamed for help. He tried to get to her, but was carried in the opposite direction. This rush also ended in a dead spot. Here his neighbors were all shorter than he was. He turned his head upward toward the sky and tried to pull some fresh air into his aching lungs, but it was all heavily tainted with sweat.

In this part of the mob no one was hysterical. In fact, most of the people seemed to be enjoying themselves. Near him was a stout woman with a man pressing hard against her from in front. His chin was on her shoulder, and his arms were around her. She paid no attention to him and went on talking to the woman at her side.

"The first thing I knew," Tod heard her say, "there was a rush and I was in the middle."

"Yeah. Somebody hollered, 'Here comes Gary Cooper,' and then wham!"

"That ain't it," said a little man wearing a cloth cap and pullover sweater. "This is a riot you're in."

"Yeah," said a third woman, whose snaky gray hair was hanging over her face and shoulders. "A pervert attacked a child."

"He ought to be lynched."

Everybody agreed vehemently.

"I come from St. Louis," announced the stout woman, "and we had one of them pervert fellers in our neighborhood once. He ripped up a girl with a pair of scissors."

"He must have been crazy," said the man in the cap. "What kind of fun is that?"

Everybody laughed. The stout woman spoke to the man who was hugging her.

"Hey, you," she said. "I ain't no pillow."

The man smiled beatifically but didn't move. She laughed, making no effort to get out of his embrace.

"A fresh guy," she said.

The other woman laughed.

"Yeah," she said, "this is a regular free-for-all."

The man in the cap and sweater thought there was another laugh in his comment about the pervert.

"Ripping up a girl with scissors. That's the wrong tool."

He was right. They laughed even louder than the first time.

"You'd a done it different, eh, kid?" said a young man with a kidney-shaped head and waxed mustaches.

The two women laughed. This encouraged the man in the cap and he reached over and pinched the stout woman's friend. She squealed.

"Lay off that," she said good-naturedly.

"I was shoved," he said.

An ambulance siren screamed in the street. Its wailing moan started the crowd moving again and Tod was carried along in a slow, steady push. He closed his eyes and tried to protect his throbbing leg. This time, when the movement ended, he found himself with his back to the theatre wall. He kept his eyes closed and stood on his good leg. After what seemed like hours, the pack began to loosen and move again with a churning motion. It gathered momentum and rushed. He rode it until he was slammed against the base of an iron rail which fenced the driveway of the theatre from the street. He had the wind knocked out of him by the impact, but managed to cling to the rail. He held on desperately, fighting to keep from being sucked back. A woman caught him around the waist and tried to hang on. She was sobbing rhythmically. Tod felt his fingers slipping from the rail and kicked backwards as hard as he could. The woman let go.

Despite the agony in his leg, he was able to think clearly about his picture, "The Burning of Los Angeles." After his quarrel with Faye, he had worked on it continually to escape tormenting himself, and the way to it in his mind had become almost automatic.

As he stood on his good leg, clinging desperately to the iron rail, he could see all the rough charcoal strokes with which he had blocked it out on the big canvas. Across the top, parallel with the frame, he had drawn the burning city, a great bonfire of architectural styles, ranging from Egyptian to Cape Cod colonial. Through the center, winding from left to right, was a long hill street and down it, spilling into the middle foreground, came the mob carrying baseball bats and torches. For the faces of its members, he was using the innumerable sketches he had made of the people who came to California to die; the cultists of all sorts, economic as well as religious, the wave, airplane, funeral and preview watchers—all those poor devils who can only be stirred by the promise of miracles and then only to violence. A super "Dr. Know-All Pierce-All" had made the necessary promise and they were marching behind his banner in a great united front of screwballs and screwboxes to purify the land. No longer bored, they sang and danced joyously in the red light of the flames.

In the lower foreground, men and women fled wildly before the vanguard of the crusading mob. Among them were Faye, Harry, Homer, Claude and himself. Faye ran proudly, throwing her knees high. Harry stumbled along behind her, holding on to his beloved derby hat with both hands. Homer seemed to be falling out of the canvas, his face half-asleep, his big hands clawing the air in anguished pantomime. Claude turned his head as he ran to thumb his nose at his pursuers. Tod himself picked up a small stone to throw before continuing his flight.

He had almost forgotten both his leg and his predicament, and to make his escape still more complete he stood on a chair and worked at the flames in an upper corner of the canvas, modeling the tongues of fire so that they licked even more avidly at a corinthian column that held up the palmleaf roof of a nutburger stand.

He had finished one flame and was starting on another when he was brought back by someone shouting in his ear. He opened his eyes and saw a policeman trying to reach him from behind the rail to which he was clinging. He let go with his left hand and raised his arm. The policeman caught him by the wrist, but couldn't lift him. Tod was afraid to let go until another man came to aid the policeman and caught him by the back of his jacket. He let go of the rail and they hauled him up and over it.

When they saw that he couldn't stand, they let him down easily to the ground. He was in the theatre driveway. On the curb next to him sat a woman crying into her skirt. Along the wall were groups of other disheveled people. At the end of the driveway was an ambulance. A policeman asked him if he wanted to go to the hospital. He shook his head no. He then offered him a lift home. Tod had the presence of mind to give Claude's address.

He was carried through the exit to the back street and lifted into a police car. The siren began to scream and at first he thought he was making the noise himself. He felt his lips with his hands. They were clamped tight. He knew then it was the siren. For some reason this made him laugh and he began to imitate the siren as loud as he could.

D. C. Themba

Mob passion

This short story deals with riots which broke out near Johannesburg, South Africa, a few years ago between Basuto gangs calling themselves "Russians" and "Civil Guards" recruited from other tribes.

There was a thick crowd on Platform 2, rushing for the 'All Stations' Randfontein train. Men, women and children were pushing madly to board the train. They were heaving and pressing, elbows in faces, bundles bursting, weak ones kneaded. Even at the opposite side people were balancing precariously to escape being shoved off the platform. Here and there deft fingers were exploring unwary pockets. Somewhere an outraged dignity was shrieking stridently, vilely cursing someone's parentage. Fuller and fuller the carriages became. With a jerk the electric train moved out of the station.

"Whew!" panted Linga Sakwe. He gathered his few parcels upon his lap, pressing his elbows to his side pockets. He did not really have any valuables in these pockets; only long habit was working instinctively now.

Linga was a tall, slender fellow, more man than boy. He was not par-

---

Mob Passion by D. C. Themba is reproduced by permission of Drum Publications.

ticularly handsome; but he had those tense eyes of the young student who was ever inwardly protesting against some wrong or other. In fact, at the moment he was not a student at all. He was working for a firm of lawyers in Market Street. He hoped to save enough money in a year or two to return to university to complete an arts degree which he had been forced by circumstances to abandon.

People were still heaving about in the train; but Linga was not annoyed. He knew that by Langlaagte, or perhaps Westbury, most of these folk would be gone and he would be able to breathe again. At Braamfontein many people alighted; but he was not thinking of his discomfort any more. He was thinking of Mapula now. She had promised that she would be in time for his train. That depended, of course, on whether she succeeded to persuade the staff nurse in charge of the ward in which she worked to let her off a few minutes before time.

The train slowed down. Industria. Linga anxiously looked outside. Sure enough, there she was! He gave a wolf-whistle, as if he was admiring some girl he did not know. She hurried to his carriage, stepped in and sat beside him. They did not seem to know each other from Adam. An old man nearby was giving a lively narration in the grimmest terms of the murders committed at Newclare.

At Westbury the atmosphere was tense. Everybody crowded at the windows to see. Everywhere there were white policemen, heavily armed. The situation was "under control," but every one knew that in the soul of almost every being in this area raved a seething madness, wild and passionate, with the causes lying deep. No cursory measures can remedy; no superficial explanation can illuminate. These jovial faces that can change into masks of bloodlust and destruction with no warning, on smallest provocation! There is a vicious technique faithfully applied in these riots. Each morning these people quietly rise, and with a business-like manner hurry to their work. Each evening they return to a Devil's Party, uncontrollably drawn into hideous orgies. Sometimes the violence would subside for weeks or months, and then suddenly would flare up at some unexpected spot, on some unexpected pretext.

At Newclare, too, from the train all seemed quiet. But Linga and Mapula knew the deceptive quiet meant the same even here. The train skimmed on, emptier. Only when they had passed Maraisburg did these two venture to speak to each other. Linga was Xhosa and Mapula Sotho. A Letebele[1] and a Russian! They had to be very careful. Love in its mysterious, often ill-starred ways had flung them together.

Linga spoke first.

[1]A contemptuous word applied by all Sotho groups to the Nguni groups (Zulu, Xhosa, Swazi, etc.). Originally the term referred to the followers of Mzilikazi who broke away from Chaka and who later harassed the Sothos. The plural of Letebele is Matabele.

"Sure you saw no one who might know you?" he asked softly.

"Eh—eh," she replied.

She fidgeted uneasily with the strap of her handbag. His hand went out and closed over her fingers. They turned simultaneously to look at each other.

A sympathetic understanding came into Linga's eyes. He smiled.

"Rather tense, isn't it?" he said.

She looked past him through the window.

"Witpoortje!" she exclaimed. "Come, let's go."

They rose and went to the door. The train stopped and they went out. Together they walked to a bridge, went over the line and out by a little gate. For some two hundred yards they walked over flat stubbly ground. Then they went down a mountain-cleft at the bottom of which ran a streamlet. They found a shady spot and sat down on the green grass. Then suddenly they fled into each other's arms like frightened children. The time-old ritual, ancient almost as the hills, always novel as the ever-changing skies; long they clung to each other, long and silent. Only the little stream gurgled its nonsense; these two daring hearts were lost in each other. The world, too—good, bad or indifferent—was forgotten in the glorious flux of their souls meeting and mingling.

At last Mapula spoke—half cried:

"Oh Linga! I'm afraid."

"Here where the world is quiet?" he quoted, with infinite softness. "No, dear, nothing can reach and harm us here." Then with a sigh: "Still, the cruelest thing they do is to drive two young people like guilty things to sneak off only to see each other. What is wrong with our people, Mapula?"

She did not answer. He lay musing for a long time. She could see that he was slowly getting angry. Sometimes she wished she could understand the strange indignation of his spirit and the great argument by which he explained life. Most times she only yearned for his love.

"They do not see! They do not see!" he continued vehemently. "They butcher one another, and they seem to like it. Where there should be brotherhood and love, there are bitter animosities. Where there should be co-operation in common adversity, there are barriers of hostility, steeling a brother's heart against a brother's misery. Sometimes, 'Pule, I understand it. We have had so many dishonest leaders, and we have so often had our true leaders left in the lurch by weak-kneed colleagues and lukewarm followers that no one wishes to stick his neck out too far. Where is the courage to weld these suicidal factions into a nation? The trouble is, very few of us have a vision comprehensive enough of our destiny! I believe God has a few of us to whom He whispers in the ear! Our true history is before us, for we yet have to build, to create, to achieve. Our very oppression is the flower of opportunity. If not for History's Grand Finale, why, then, does God hold us back? Hell! and here we are, feuding in God's dressing-room even before the curtain rises. Oh!—" He covered his face and fell into her lap, unable to say any more.

Instinctively, Mapula fingered his hair. "In God's dressing-room" she thought. "What does it mean?" But his anguish stabbed at her heart. Trying to forget herself, she only sought within her tenderness to quell the bitter wretchedness she had heard in his voice.

"Linga, no! Let me show you something else—something that I understand. It is no more so long before you and I can marry. I dream about the home that we are going to have. I . . . I want that home, Linga. You taught me that woman's greatest contribution to civilization so far has been to furnish homes where great men and great ideas have developed. Moreover, there's our problem. Let us rather think of ways of handling my father. No, no; not now. Let us think now of now."

Thabo was running faster now that he was nearing home. His mind was in a whirl; but he knew that he had to tell his father. The lopsided gate was in the far corner, so he smartly leaped over the fence where it was slack. He stopped abruptly at the door. He always did when there were people. But now, he soon realized, these people were his two uncles—Uncle Alpheus and Uncle Frans. He knew how great news always brings a glory of prestige on the head of the bringer. Thabo felt himself almost a hero now; for these two men were die-hard stalwarts in the Russian cause. Uncle Alpheus was a romantic firebrand. Uncle Frans was a scheming character of the power-behind-the-throne variety. They were complementary to each other: together a formidable team.

"Father, where is he?" hissed Thabo, breathing hard. The excitement in his voice aroused every one.

"Holy Shepherd! What's the matter, boy?" cried Uncle Alpheus.

"Mapula, Mapula. She loves with a Letebele."

"What!" exploded Uncle Alpheus. "Where is she?" Then more calmly: "Come'n, boy. Tell us everything more quietly; your father is out there?"

"J-J-Jonas t-t-tells me—J-Jonas is a boy who works with me—Jonas tells me that Mapula loves with a Letebele. They always meet at the hospital; but never in the sitting-room. He hopes to marry her."

"Never!" barked Alpheus. Just then the door burst open. A party of men carried in the limp form of Thabo's father. He was unconscious, and blood streamed all over his face. Beyond them, just outside the door, a crowd had gathered. Everyone was at once asking what had happened. As the news spread, ugly moods swept the crowd. Ra-Thabo was carried into the bedroom and tended by the women. Alpheus and Frans returned to the fore-room and conferred.

"What now?" Alpheus asked Frans.

"Of course, we must take revenge. You will talk to the people—the women. Talk fire into them. Connect it with the Mapula business; that'll warm them. Suggest drugs—a Letebele must use drugs, mustn't he? I'll be in the house. Just when they begin to get excited I'll arrange to carry Ra-Thabo out—to the hospital, you know. See if we can't get them bad!" He smiled cheerlessly.

Outside, the crowd—mostly women—was thickening. Even in the streets they could be seen coming along in groups, blanketed men and women. From the house Thabo and his little sister, Martha, joined the crowd. It was obvious that their uncles were going to do something about it.

Alpheus stepped on to the little mud wall. He raised his left hand and the blanket over it rose with it. That moment was most dramatic. In a few moments the crowd moved closer to him and became silent. Then he began to speak. He began in a matter-of-fact voice, giving the bare fact that Ra-Thabo, their leader, had been hurt. Warming gradually, he discussed the virtues of this man. Then he went on to tell of how this man had actually been hurt. Not confused fighting nor cowardly brutalities rose in the mind as this man spoke, but a glorious picture of crusaders charging on in a holy cause behind their lion-hearted leader. Oh, what a clash was there! The Matabele were pushed beyond Westbury station. There the heroes met a rested, reinforced enemy. For a moment all that could be seen was the head of Ra-Thabo going down among them. The clang of battle could be heard; the furious charge could be seen, in the words of this man who was not there. The Basutos fought desperately and won so much ground that their all but lost leader could be rescued and carried back home. And what finds he there? Alpheus's voice went down, softer and heavier, touching strings of pathos, rousing tragic emotions which the hearts present had never before experienced. There was an automatic movement in the crowd as everybody strained forward to hear. In awful, horror-filled whispers he told of Ra-Thabo's daughter giving herself to a Letebele. "The thing is not possible!" he hissed. "It would not have happened if the maid had not been bewitched with drugs. Are you going to brook it!" he cracked. "No!" all the throats roared. "Are you ready for vengeance!" "Now!" thundered the mob. Someone in the crowd shouted "Mule!"[2] Then the women took up their famous war-cry, chilling to a stranger, but driving the last doubting spirit there to frenzy and fury.

Ee!—le!—le!—le!—le!—le! le!—Eu! Eu! Eu!

Now they were prancing and swaying in uninterpretable rhythms. A possessed bard in their midst was chattering the praises of the dead, the living, and the unborn; his words clattering like the drumsticks of a fiend.

"Let us go past Maraisburg and attack them from the rear!" yelled Alpheus over the din.

[2]Sotho for "hit" or "strike."

At that moment the door of the house went open. The mob which had been on the point of dashing out recoiled. The sight they saw stunned them. Frans and two other men were carrying out Ra-Thabo, besmeared with blood. Thabo saw Uncle Alpheus leaping with trailing blanket and yelling. "To Maraisburg!" Again he leaped over the fence into the street. The mob followed hard on his heels.

As the last blanket swept round the corner, Frans turned back to the injured man. His two helpers had also been drawn in by the irresistible suction of mob-feeling. With a smile, he said to the unhearing Ra-Thabo: "I'll have to get a taxi to take you to hospital, brother." Then he carried him back into the house.

Late in the afternoon the train from Randfontein suddenly stopped at Maraisburg. Everybody was surprised. Something must be wrong. This train never stops at Maraisburg. Then suddenly!

"All Change! All Change!" And more brusquely: "Come'n, puma! Puma!"[3]

Linga and Mapula hurried out. News had arrived that trouble had started again at Newclare; more seriously than usual. All trains from Randfontein were being stopped here and sent back.

Shrugging his shoulders, Linga drew Mapula away, and arm-in-arm they strolled along the platform, out by the little gate, into some suburban area. For a time they walked on in silence. Then Mapula spoke.

"I hope I'll get back in time," she said.

"Let's walk faster, then. We might get a lift outside the suburb." They walked into the open country. Linga knew that if he could only find a certain golf-course somewhere around here, he would know where the road was. Meanwhile, they had to stumble on over rough country, and Mapula's cork-heel shoes were tormenting her toes. She limped on as stoically as she could. Linga did not notice her suffering as he was looking out for familiar landmarks. Those trees looked suspiciously like the golf-course to him.

When they reached the trees Mapula said: "Linga, let us rest here; my toes are suffering."

"All right," he replied. "But I must look for the road. Let's look for a cool place where you may rest, while I search for the golf-course."

"Mm."

He led her amongst the trees. She sat down and pulled off her shoes.

When he thought he saw a shadow of distress flit across her brow, he bent down, took her hand, pressed it, and then muttered: "Back in a moment, sweet." He rose slowly, looked at her indecisively, then turned away slowly and walked off.

He did not search far before he noticed a torn and faded flag. The hole was nearby. Suddenly he emerged from the cluster of trees, and came across

---

[3]Zulu for "get out."

the road. But his attention was caught by a horde of Russians pursuing a woman who came flying towards Linga. Should he chance it: he wondered. He spoke fluent Sesotho and believed he could pass as a Masatho, possibly as a Russian. He quickly drew a white handkerchief from his trouser-pocket and tied it round his head. This made him, he knew, an active supporter of the Russian cause. Skirts flying, the woman sped past him. Facing the mob, he shouted:

"Helele!"[4]

All its wrath spent, the mob crowded round out of sheer curiosity. Some were even in a jocular mood now; one playing lustily on a concertina. But here and there Linga could see deadly weapons, snatched up in their hasty exodus from Newclare. He spoke to them in fluent Sesotho, taking his idiom from Teya-teyaneng. He asked if that was the road to Newclare; he said that he worked in Roodepoort, but was going to Newclare because his uncle there wanted more man-power in the house. Won't they please tell him where this road is?

"Che! It is no Letebele this; this is a child of at home," remarked Alpheus.

"Kgele! You speak it, man," said a burly fellow. Then everyone directed Linga how to get to Newclare.

As Fate would have it, just then Mapula came running, shoes in hand and stockings twisted round her neck.

"Linga! Linga, darling mine! What are they doing to you?" she screamed, as she forced her way through the crowd. Linga stiffened. When she came to him she flung her arm around him and clung to him with all her strength, crying all the time. Then she saw her uncle stupefied like the rest of them, standing there. She fled to him and begged him to save her lover. He pushed her aside and walked up to Linga. He stood before him, arms akimbo.

"Ehe! So you are a Letebele, after all. You lie so sleekly that I can understand why my niece thinks she loves you." Then he swung round, his blanket trailing in an arc: "Friends, we need go no further. This is the dog that bewitched my brother's child. Let's waste no time with him. Tear him to pieces!" The mob rushed upon Linga: "Mmate! Mmate!"[5]

"Uncle! Uncle!" cried Mapula. But even as she cried she knew that nothing could be done. She had courted the contempt of her people; and she understood now that all her entreaties were falling on deaf ears. Whether from convenience or superstition—it did not signify which—she was considered the victim of the Letebele's root-craft.

From the scuffling mob suddenly flew an axe which fell at her feet. In a flash she knew her fate. Love, frustrated beyond bearing, bent her mind to the horrible deed.

[4]Sotho for "hail."

[5]Sotho for "strike him."

Mapula acted. Quickly she picked up the axe whilst the mob was withdrawing from its prey, several of them bespattered with blood. With the axe in her hand, Mapula pressed through them until she reached the inner, sparser group. She saw Alpheus spitting upon Linga's battered body. He turned with a guttural cackle—He-he-he! He-he-he!—into the descending axe. It sank into his neck and down he went. She stepped on his chest and pulled out the axe. The blood gushed all over her face and clothing. That evil-looking countenance she gradually turned to the stunned crowd, half lifting the axe and walking slowly but menacingly towards the largest group. They retreated—a hundred and twenty men and women retreated before this devil-possessed woman with the ghastly appearance. But then she saw the mangled body of the man she loved and her nerve snapped. The axe slipped from her hand and she dropped on Linga's body, crying piteously:

"Jo-o! Jo-o! Jo-na-jo! Jo-na-jo!"

Someone came and lifted her up. Someone else was dragging Alpheus's bleeding corpse by the collar so that his shoes sprang out one after the other.

The crowd was going back now. All the bravado gone, they were quiet and sulky. Only the agonized wailing of Mapula. Every breast was quelled by a sense of something deeply wrong, a sense of outrage. The tumult in every heart, feeling individually now, was a human protest insistently seeking expression, and then that persistent wail of the anguished girl, torturing the innermost core of even the rudest conscience there. The men felt themselves before God; the women heard the denunciations of thwarted love. Within they were all crying bitterly:

"Jo-l! Jo-o! Jo-nana-jo!"

Thomas Carlyle (1795–1881)

How the bastille was stormed

To describe this Siege of the Bastille (thought to be one of the most important in History) perhaps transcends the talent of mortals. Could one but, after infinite reading, get to understand so much as the plan of the building! But there is the open Esplanade, at the end of the Rue Saint-Antoine; there are such Forecourts, *cour avancé, cour de l'orme*, arched Gateway (where Louis Tournay now fights); then new drawbridges, dormant-bridges, rampart-bastions, and the grim Eight Towers: a labyrinthic Mass, high-frowning there, of all ages from twenty years to four hundred and twenty;— beleaguered, in this its last hour, as we said, by mere Chaos come again! Ord-

From *The French Revolution* by Thomas Carlyle (1837).

nance of all calibres; throats of all capacities; men of all plans, every man his own engineer: seldom since the war of Pygmies and Cranes was there seen so anomalous a thing. Half-pay Elie is home for a suit of regimentals; no one would heed him in colored clothes: half-pay Hulin is haranguing Gardes Francaises in the Place de Grève. Frantic Patriots pick up the grape-shots; bear them, still hot (or seemingly so), to the Hotel-de-Ville:—Paris, you perceive, is to be burnt! Flesselles is "pale to the very lips;" for the roar of the multitude grows deep. Paris wholly has got to the acme of its frenzy; whirled, all ways, by panic madness. At every street-barricade, there whirls simmering a minor whirlpool,—strengthening the barricade, since God knows what is coming; and all minor whirlpools play distractedly into that grand Fire-Mahlstrom which is lashing round the Bastille.

And so it lashes and it roars. Cholat the wine-merchant has become an impromptu cannoneer. See Georget, of the Marine Service, fresh from Brest, ply the King of Siam's cannon. Singular (if we were not used to the like): Georget lay, last night, taking his ease at his inn; the King of Siam's cannon also lay, knowing nothing of *him*, for a hundred years. Yet now, at the right instant, they have got together, and discourse eloquent music. For, hearing what was toward, Georget sprang from the Brest Diligence, and ran. Gardes Francaises also will be here, with real artillery: were not the walls so thick!—Upwards from the Esplanade, horizontally from all neighboring roofs and windows, flashes one irregular deluge of musketry, without effect. The Invalides lie flat, firing comparatively at their ease from behind stone; hardly through port-holes show the tip of a nose. We fall, shot; and make no impression!

Let conflagration rage; of whatsoever is combustible! Guardrooms are burnt, Invalides mess-rooms. A distracted "Perukemaker with two fiery torches" is for burning "the saltpetres of the Arsenal;"—had not a woman run screaming; had not a Patriot, with some tincture of Natural Philosophy, instantly struck the wind out of him (butt of musket on pit of stomach), overturned barrels, and staved the devouring element. A young beautiful lady, seized escaping in these Outer Courts, and thought falsely to be De Launay's daughter, shall be burnt in De Launay's sight; she lies swooned on a paillasse: but again a Patriot, it is brave Aubin Bonnemère the old soldier, dashes in, and rescues her. Straw is burnt; three cartloads of it, hauled thither, go up in white smoke; almost to the choking of Patriotism itself; so that Elie had, with singed brows, to drag back one cart; and Réole the "gigantic haberdasher" another. Smoke as of Tophet; confusion as of Babel; noise as of the Crack of Doom!

Blood flows; the aliment of new madness. The wounded are carried unto houses of the Rue Cerisaie; the dying leave their last mandate not to yield till the accursed Stronghold fall. And yet, alas, how fall? The walls are so thick! Deputations, three in number, arrive from the Hotel-de-Ville; Abbé

Fauchet (who was of one) can say, with what almost superhuman courage of benevolence. These wave their Town-flag in the arched Gateway; and stand, rolling their drum; but to no purpose. In such Crack of Doom, De Launay cannot hear them, dare not believe them: they return, with justified rage, the whew of lead still singing in their ears. What to do? The Firemen are here, squirting with their fire-pumps on the Invalides cannon, to wet the touch-holes; they unfortunately cannot squirt so high; but produce only clouds of spray. Individuals of classical knowledge purpose *catapults*. Santerre, the sonorous Brewer of the Suburb Saint-Antoine, advises rather that the place be fired, by a "mixture of phosphorus and oil-of-turpentine spouted up through forcing-pumps:" O Spinola-Santerre, hast thou the mixture *ready?* Every man his own engineer! And still the fire-deluge abates not; even women are firing, and Turks; at least one woman (with her sweetheart), and one Turk. Gardes Francaises have come: real cannon, real cannoneers. Usher Maillard is busy; half-pay Elie, half-pay Hulin rage in the midst of thousands.

How the great Bastille Clock ticks (inaudible) in its Inner Court there, at its ease, hour after hour; as if nothing special, for it or the world, were passing! It tolled One when the firing began; and is now pointing towards Five, and still the firing slakes not.—Far down, in their vaults, the seven Prisoners hear muffled din as of earthquakes; their Turnkeys answer vaguely.

Woe to thee, De Launay, with thy poor hundred Invalides! Broglie is distant, and his ears heavy: Besenval hears, but can send no help. One poor troop of Hussars has crept, reconnoitring, cautiously along the Quais, as far as the Pont Neuf. "We are come to join you," said the Captain; for the crowd seems shoreless. A large-headed dwarfish individual, of smoke-bleared aspect, shambles forward, opening his blue lips, for there is sense in him; and croaks: "Alight then, and give up your arms!" The Hussar-Captain is too happy to be escorted to the Barriers, and dismissed on parole. Who the squat individual was? Men answer, It is M. Marat, author of the excellent pacific *avis au peuple!* Great truly, O thou remarkable Dogleech, is this day of emergence and new-birth: and yet this same day come four years—! But let the curtains of the Future hang.

What shall De Launay do? One thing only De Launay could have done: what he said he would do. Fancy him sitting, from the first, with lighted taper, within arm's-length of the Powder-Magazine; motionless, like old Roman Senator, or Bronze Lamp-holder; coldly apprising Thuroit, and all men, by a slight motion of his eye, what his resolution was:—Harmless he sat there, while unharmed; but the King's Fortress, meanwhile, could, might, would, or should in nowise be surrendered, save to the King's Messenger: one old man's life is worthless, so it be lost with honor; but think, ye brawling *canaille,* how will it be when a whole Bastille springs skyward!—in such statuesque, taper-holding attitude, one fancies De Launay might have left

Thuriot, the red Clerks of the Basoche, Curé of Saint-Stephen and all the tagrag-and-bobtail of the world, to work their will.

And yet, withal, he could not do it. Hast thou considered how each man's heart is so tremulously responsive to the hearts of all men; hast thou noted how omnipotent is the very sound of many men? How their shriek of indignation palsies the strong soul; their howl of contumely withers with unfelt pangs? The Ritter Gluck confessed that the ground-tone of the noblest passage, in one of his noblest Operas, was the voice of the Populace he had heard at Vienna, crying to their Kaiser: Bread! Bread! Great is the combined voice of men; the utterance of their *instincts*, which are truer than their *thoughts:* it is the greatest of man encounters, among the sounds and shadows which make up this World of Time. He who can resist that, has his footing somewhere *beyond* Time. De Launay could not do it. Distracted, he hovers between two; hopes in the middle of despair; surrenders not his Fortress; declares that he will blow it up, seizes torches to blow it up, and does not blow it. Unhappy old De Launay, it is the death-agony of thy Bastille and thee! Jail, Jailering and Jailer, all three, such as they may have been, must finish.

For four hours now has the World-Bedlam roared: call it the World-Chimera, blowing fire! The poor Invalides have sunk under their battlements, or rise only with reversed muskets: they have made a white flag of napkins; go beating the *chamade*, or seeming to beat, for one can hear nothing. The very Swiss at the Portcullis look weary of firing; disheartened in the fire-deluge: a port-hole at the drawbridge is opened, as by one that would speak. See Huissier Maillard, the shifty man! On his plank, swinging over the abyss of that stone Ditch; plank resting on parapet, balanced by weight of Patriots,—he hovers perilous: such a Dove toward such an Ark! Deftly, thou shifty Usher: one man already fell; and lies smashed, far down there, against the masonry! Usher Maillard falls not: deftly, unerring he walks, with outspread palm. The Swiss holds a paper through his port-hole; the shifty Usher snatches it, and returns. Terms of surrender: Pardon, immunity to all! Are they accepted?—*"foi d'officier,* On the word of an officer," answers half-pay Hulin,—or half-pay Elie, for men do not agree on it,—"they are!" Sinks the drawbridge,—Usher Maillard bolting it when down; rushes in the living deluge: The Bastille is fallen! *Victoire! La Bastille est prise!*

Gustave Flaubert (1821–1880)

A throne is toppled

Suddenly the "Marseillaise" resounded. Hussonnet and Frederick bent over the balusters. It was the people. They rushed up the stairs, shaking with a dizzying, wave-like motion bare heads, or helmets, or red caps, or else bayonets or human shoulders with such impetuosity that some people disappeared every now and then in this swarming mass, which was mounting up without a moment's pause, like a river compressed by an equinoctial tide, with a continuous roar under an irresistible impulse. When they got to the top of the stairs, they were scattered, and their chant died away. Nothing could any longer be heard but the tramp of all the shoes intermingled with the chopping sound of many voices. The crowd not being in a mischievous mood, contented themselves with looking about them. But, from time to time, an elbow, by pressing too hard, broke through a pane of glass, or else a vase or a statue rolled from a bracket down on the floor. The wainscotings cracked under the pressure of people against them. Every face was flushed; the perspiration was rolling down their features in large beads. Hussonnet made this remark:

"Heroes have not a good smell."

"Ah! you are provoking," returned Frederick.

And, pushed forward in spite of themselves, they entered an apartment in which a daïs of red velvet rose as far as the ceiling. On the throne below sat a representative of the proletariat in effigy with a black beard, his shirt gaping open, a jolly air, and the stupid look of a baboon. Others climbed up the platform to sit in his place.

"What a myth!" said Hussonnet. "There you see the sovereign people!"

The armchair was lifted up on the hands of a number of persons and passed across the hall, swaying from one side to the other.

"By Jove, 'tis like a boat! The Ship of State is tossing about in a stormy sea! Let it dance the cancan! Let it dance the cancan!"

They had drawn it towards a window, and in the midst of hisses, they launched it out.

"Poor old chap!" said Hussonnet, as he saw the effigy falling into the garden, where it was speedily picked up in order to be afterwards carried to the Bastille and burned.

Then a frantic joy burst forth, as if, instead of the throne, a future of boundless happiness had appeared; and the people, less through a spirit of vindictiveness than to assert their right of possession, broke or tore the

From *Sentimental Education* by Gustave Flaubert (1869).

glasses, the curtains, the lustres, the tapers, the tables, the chairs, the stools, the entire furniture, including the very albums and engravings, and the corbels of the tapestry. Since they had triumphed, they must needs amuse themselves! The common herd ironically wrapped themselves up in laces and cashmeres. Gold fringes were rolled round the sleeves of blouses. Hats with ostriches' feathers adorned blacksmiths' heads, and ribbons of the Legion of Honour supplied waistbands for prostitutes. Each person satisfied his or her caprice; some danced, others drank. In the queen's apartment a woman gave a gloss to her hair with pomatum. Behind a folding-screen two lovers were playing cards. Hussonnet pointed out to Frederick an individual who was smoking a dirty pipe with his elbows resting on a balcony; and the popular frenzy redoubled with a continuous crash of broken porcelain and pieces of crystal, which, as they rebounded, made sounds resembling those produced by the plates of musical glasses.

Then their fury was overshadowed. A nauseous curiosity made them rummage all the dressing-rooms, all the recesses. Returned convicts thrust their arms into the beds in which princesses had slept, and rolled themselves on the top of them, to console themselves for not being able to embrace their owners. Others, with sinister faces, roamed about silently, looking for something to steal, but too great a multitude was there. Through the bays of the doors could be seen in the suite of apartments only the dark mass of people between the gilding of the walls under a cloud of dust. Every breast was panting. The heat became more and more suffocating; and the two friends, afraid of being stifled, seized the opportunity of making their way out.

In the antechamber, standing on a heap of garments, appeared a girl of the town as a statue of Liberty, motionless, her grey eyes wide open—a fearful sight.

They had taken three steps outside the château when a company of the National Guards, in greatcoats, advanced towards them, and, taking off their foraging-caps, and, at the same time, uncovering their skulls, which were slightly bald, bowed very low to the people. At this testimony of respect, the ragged victors bridled up. Hussonnet and Frederick were not without experiencing a certain pleasure from it as well as the rest.

They were filled with ardour. They went back to the Palais-Royal. In front of the Rue Fromanteau, soldiers' corpses were heaped up on the straw. They passed close to the dead without a single quiver of emotion, feeling a certain pride in being able to keep their countenance.

The Palais overflowed with people. In the inner courtyard seven piles of wood were flaming. Pianos, chests of drawers, and clocks were hurled out through the windows. Fire-engines sent streams of water up to the roofs. Some vagabonds tried to cut the hose with their sabres. Frederick urged a pupil of the Polytechnic School to interfere. The latter did not understand him, and, moreover, appeared to be an idiot. All around, in the two galleries, the populace, having got possession of the cellars, gave themselves up to a horrible carouse. Wine flowed in streams and wetted people's feet; the mudlarks drank out of the tail-ends of the bottles, and shouted as they staggered along.

"Come away out of this," said Hussonnet; "I am disgusted with the people."

All over the Orleans Gallery the wounded lay on mattresses on the ground, with purple curtains folded round them as coverlets; and the small shop-keepers' wives and daughters from the quarter brought them broth and linen.

"No matter!" said Frederick; "for my part, I consider the people sublime."

The great vestibule was filled with a whirlwind of furious individuals. Men tried to ascend to the upper storys in order to put the finishing touches to the work of wholesale destruction. National Guards, on the steps, strove to keep them back. The most intrepid was a chasseur, who had his head bare, his hair bristling, and his straps in pieces. His shirt caused a swelling between his trousers and his coat, and he struggled desperately in the midst of the others. Hussonnet, who had sharp sight, recognised Arnoux from a distance.

Then they went into the Tuileries garden, so as to be able to breathe more freely. They sat down on a bench; and they remained for some minutes with their eyes closed, so much stunned that they had not the energy to say a word. The people who were passing came up to them and informed them that the Duchesse d'Orleans had been appointed Regent, and that it was all over. They were experiencing that species of comfort which follows rapid *dénouements,* when at the windows of the attics in the château appeared men-servants tearing their liveries to pieces. They flung their torn clothes into the garden, as a mark of renunciation. The people hooted at them, and then they retired.

The attention of Frederick and Hussonnet was distracted by a tall fellow who was walking quickly between the trees with a musket on his shoulder. A cartridge-box was pressed against his pea-jacket; a handkerchief was wound round his forehead under his cap. He turned his head to one side. It was Dussardier; and casting himself into their arms:

"Ah! what good fortune, my poor old friends!" without being able to say another word, so much out of breath was he with fatigue.

He had been on his legs for the last twenty-four hours. He had been engaged at the barricades of the Latin Quarter, had fought in the Rue Rabu-teau, had saved three dragoons' lives, had entered the Tuileries with Colonel Dunoyer, and, after that, had repaired to the Chamber, and then to the Hôtel de Ville.

"I have come from it! all goes well! the people are victorious! the work-men and the employers are embracing one another. Ha! if you knew what I have seen! what brave fellows! what a fine sight it was!"

And without noticing that they had no arms:

"I was quite certain of finding you there! This has been a bit rough—no matter!"

A drop of blood ran down his cheek, and in answer to the questions put to him by the two others:

"Oh! 'tis nothing! a slight scratch from a bayonet!"

"However, you really ought to take care of yourself."

"Pooh! I am substantial! What does this signify? The Republic is proclaimed! We'll be happy henceforth! Some journalists, who were talking just now in front of me, said they were going to liberate Poland and Italy! No more kings! You understand? The entire land free! the entire land free!"

And with one comprehensive glance at the horizon, he spread out his arms in a triumphant attitude. But a long file of men rushed over the terrace on the water's edge.

"Ah, deuce take it! I was forgetting. I must be off. Good-bye!"

He turned round to cry out to them while brandishing his musket:

"Long live the Republic!"

Deviant behavior

The term *deviant behavior* or *deviance*, as it is used in most recent American sociological writings, refers to behavior that violates patterned expectations, that is, departures from norms considered legitimate within a society. *Deviance* here refers to the social rather than the personality structure; behavior which might be considered pathological from a psychiatric point of view may not be considered deviant if it does not lead to a violation of institutionalized norms. Much of what is considered deviant, as criminal behavior for example, is engaged in by persons who are relatively "normal" and "well-adjusted." Despite the variety of mechanisms which enforce conformity to society's demands, no society is free from some deviations. Nor is this altogether to be deplored; although upsetting to the community, deviant behavior may also stir it into activity, goad it into a re-examination of its moral standards, and entice it to depart from automatic reliance on precedent and tradition. Such reliance often would prevent it from responding to the challenge of new conditions. Deviant behavior, and this is sometimes forgotten, consists not only of criminal and other self-interested departures from the norms, but also of actions of disinterested innovators and dissenters who call upon a society to break from accustomed systems of wont and use in order to respond creatively to the challenges of new social and moral values.

Deviance may often be traced to psychological sources, but sociological explanations need not refer to innate instincts, hereditary tendencies or other psychological entities. Just like normal behavior, it is learned by individuals in their differential association with others. The fact that the frequency of deviant behavior varies among different social structures and with position within such structures indicates that these, to quote Robert K. Merton, "exert a definite pressure upon certain persons in the society to engage in non-conforming rather than in conforming conduct." Though each murderer or delinquent has a private biography which indeed furnishes psychological understanding of his action, the rates of murder or delinquency cannot be accounted for simply by adding up individual motivations. They must be explained in terms of the social structure in which they occur.

The selections cover only a small fraction of the wide variety of deviant behavior in modern societies. Guy de Maupassant's gripping story of sexual pathology and the inversion of sexual roles stresses the crucial importance of the definition of the situation provided by the community for patterning deviant behavior. Sherwood Anderson's story, "The Philosopher," from his portrayal of "grotesques" in a small Midwest town, *Winesburg, Ohio,* shows the ways that narrow codes of conventional behavior cause eccentric departures from them. Voltaire's scintillating discussion of suicide with its emphasis on the importance of cultural and societal variations in its incidence reads almost like an adumbration of Durkheim's later sociological treatment. Bertolt Brecht's moving poem, "Concerning the Infanticide Marie Farrar," links criminal behavior to class position and attempts to explain it in terms of economic and cultural deprivation. Nelson Algren, a leading contemporary novelist, in the selection from *The Man with the Golden Arm,* focuses his discussion of drug addiction upon the interaction between the addict and the "pusher." Rousseau's almost clinical description of his theft, and his subsequent accusation of an innocent person in the famous "ribbon incident" from his *Confessions* highlights the complex interplay between internalized norms and external expectations. Finally, the modern American poet William Carlos Williams reveals in his moving short story, "The Insane," the ambivalent reactions of those deemed normal towards those whom the community has stigmatized as pathological.

Guy de Maupassant (1850–1893)

Mademoiselle

He had been registered under the names of Jean Marie Mathieu Valot, but he was never called anything but "Mademoiselle." He was the idiot of the district, but not one of those wretched, ragged idiots who live on public charity. He lived comfortably on a small income which his mother had left him, and which his guardian paid him regularly, and so he was rather envied than pitied. And then, he was not one of those idiots with wild looks and the manners of an animal, for he was by no means an unpleasing object, with his half-open lips and smiling eyes, and especially in his constant make-up in female dress. For he dressed like a girl, and showed by that how little he objected to being called Mademoiselle.

And why should he not like the nickname which his mother had given him affectionately, when he was a mere child, so delicate and weak, and with a fair complexion—poor little diminutive lad not as tall as many girls of the same age? It was in pure love that, in his earlier years, his mother whispered that tender Mademoiselle to him, while his old grandmother used to say jokingly:

"The fact is, that as for the male element in him it is really not worth mentioning in a Christian—no offense to God in saying so." And his grandfather, who was equally fond of a joke, used to add: "I only hope it will not disappear as he grows up."

And they treated him as if he had really been a girl and coddled him, the more so as they were very prosperous and did not require to toil to keep things together.

When his mother and grandparents were dead, Mademoiselle was almost as happy with his paternal uncle, an unmarried man, who had carefully attended the idiot, and who had grown more and more attached to him by dint of looking after him; and the worthy man continued to call Jean Marie Mathieu Valot, Mademoiselle.

He was called so in all the country round as well, not with the slightest intention of hurting his feelings, but, on the contrary, because all thought they would please the poor gentle creature who harmed nobody in doing so.

The very street boys meant no harm by it, accustomed as they were to call the tall idiot in a frock and cap by the nickname; but it would have struck them as very extraordinary, and would have led them to rude fun, if they had seen him dressed like a boy.

"Mademoiselle" from *Short Stories of the Tragedy and Comedy of Life* by Guy de Maupassant.

Mademoiselle, however, took care of that, for his dress was as dear to him as his nickname. He delighted in wearing it, and, in fact, cared for nothing else, and what gave it a particular zest was that he knew that he was not a girl, and that he was living in disguise. And this was evident by the exaggerated feminine bearing and walk he put on, as if to show that it was not natural to him. His enormous, carefully filled cap was adorned with large variegated ribbons. His petticoat, with numerous flounces, was distended behind by many hoops. He walked with short steps, and with exaggerated swaying of the hips, while his folded arms and crossed hands were distorted into pretensions of comical coquetry.

On such occasions, if anybody wished to make friends with him, it was necessary to say:

"Ah! Mademoiselle, what a nice girl you make."

That put him into a good humor, and he used to reply, much pleased:

"Don't I? But people can see I only do it for a joke."

But, nevertheless, when they were dancing at village festivals in the neighborhood, he would always be invited to dance as Mademoiselle, and would never ask any of the girls to dance with him; and one evening when somebody asked him the reason for this, he opened his eyes wide, laughed as if the man had said something very stupid, and replied:

"I cannot ask the girls, because I am not dressed like a lad. Just look at my dress, you fool!"

As his interrogator was a judicious man, he said to him:

"Then dress like one, Mademoiselle."

He thought for a moment, and then said with a cunning look:

"But if I dress like a lad, I shall no longer be a girl; and then, I am a girl"; and he shrugged his shoulders as he said it.

But the remark seemed to make him think.

For some time afterward, when he met the same person, he would ask him abruptly:

"If I dress like a lad, will you still call me Mademoiselle?"

"Of course, I shall," the other replied. "You will always be called so."

The idiot appeared delighted, for there was no doubt that he thought more of his nickname than he did of his dress, and the next day he made his appearance in the village square, without his petticoats and dressed as a man. He had taken a pair of trousers, a coat, and a hat from his guardian's clothespress. This created quite a revolution in the neighborhood, for the people who had been in the habit of smiling at him kindly when he was dressed as a woman, looked at him in astonishment and almost in fear, while the indulgent could not help laughing, and visibly making fun of him.

The involuntary hostility of some, and the too evident ridicule of others, the disagreeable surprise of all, were too palpable for him not to see it, and to be hurt by it, and it was still worse when a street urchin said to him in a jeering voice, as he danced round him:

"Oh! oh! Mademoiselle, you wear trousers! Oh! oh! Mademoiselle!"

And it grew worse and worse, when a whole band of these vagabonds were on his heels, hooting and yelling after him, as if he had been somebody in a masquerading dress during the Carnival.

It was quite certain that the unfortunate creature looked more in disguise now than he had formerly. By dint of living like a girl, and by even exaggerating the feminine walk and manners, he had totally lost all masculine looks and ways. His smooth face, his long flax-like hair, required a cap with ribbons, and became a caricature under the high chimney-pot hat of the old doctor, his grandfather.

Mademoiselle's shoulders, and especially her swelling stern, danced about wildly in this old-fashioned coat and wide trousers. And nothing was as funny as the contrast between his quiet dress and slow trotting pace, the winning way he used his head, and the conceited movements of his hands, with which he fanned himself like a girl.

Soon the older lads and girls, the old women, men of ripe age and even the Judicial Councilor, joined the little brats, and hooted Mademoiselle, while the astonished idiot ran away, and rushed into the house with terror. There he took his poor head between both hands, and tried to comprehend the matter. Why were they angry with him? For it was quite evident that they were angry with him. What wrong had he done, and whom had he injured, by dressing as a boy? Was he not a boy, after all? For the first time in his life, he felt a horror for his nickname, for had he not been insulted through it? But immediately he was seized with a horrible doubt.

"Suppose that, after all, I am a girl?"

He would have liked to ask his guardian about it but he did not like to, for he somehow felt, although only obscurely, that he, worthy man, might not tell him the truth, out of kindness. And, besides, he preferred to find out for himself, without asking anyone.

All his idiot's cunning, which had been lying latent up till then, because he never had any occasion to make use of it, now came out and urged him to a solitary and dark action.

The next day he dressed himself as a girl again, and made his appearance as if he had perfectly forgotten his escapade of the day before, but the people, especially the street boys, had not forgotten it. They looked at him sideways, and, even the best of them, could not help smiling, while the little blackguards ran after him and said:

"Oh! oh! Mademoiselle, you had on a pair of breeches!"

But he pretended not to hear, or even to guess to what they were alluding. He seemed as happy and glad to look about him as he usually did, with half-open lips and smiling eyes. As usual, he wore an enormous cap with variegated ribbons, and the same large petticoats; he walked with short, mincing steps, swaying and wriggling his hips and gesticulating like a coquette, and licked his lips when they called him Mademoiselle, while really he would have liked to have jumped at the throats of those who called him so.

Days and months passed, and by degrees those about him forgot all about his strange escapade. But he had never left off thinking about it, or trying to find out—for which he was ever on the alert—how he could ascertain his qualities as a boy, and how to assert them victoriously. Really innocent, he had reached the age of twenty without knowing anything or without ever having any natural impulse, but being tenacious of purpose, curious and dissembling, he asked no questions, but observed all that was said and done.

Often at their village dances, he had heard young fellows boasting about girls whom they had seduced, and girls praising such and such a young fellow, and often, also, after a dance, he saw the couples go away together, with their arms round each other's waists. They had no suspicions of him, and he listened and watched, until, at last, he discovered what was going on.

And then, one night, when dancing was over, and the couples were going away with their arms round each other's waists, a terrible screaming was heard at the corner of the woods through which those going to the next village had to pass. It was Josephine, pretty Josephine, and when her screams were heard, they ran to her assistance, and arrived only just in time to rescue her, half strangled, from Mademoiselle's clutches.

The idiot had watched her and had thrown himself upon her in order to treat her as the other young fellows did the girls, but she resisted him so stoutly that he took her by the throat and squeezed it with all his might until she could not breathe, and was nearly dead.

In rescuing Josephine from him, they had thrown him on the ground, but he jumped up again immediately, foaming at the mouth and slobbering, and exclaimed:

"I am not a girl any longer, I am a young man, I am a young man, I tell you."

Sherwood Anderson

The philosopher

Doctor Parcival was a large man with a drooping mouth covered by a yellow mustache. He always wore a dirty white waistcoat out of the pockets of which protruded a number of the kind of black cigars known as stogies. His teeth were black and irregular and there was something strange about his eyes. The lid of the left eye twitched; it fell down and snapped up; it was exactly as though the lid of the eye were a window shade and someone stood inside the doctor's head playing with the cord.

Doctor Parcival had a liking for the boy, George Willard. It began when George had been working for a year on the *Winesburg Eagle* and the acquaintanceship was entirely a matter of the doctor's own making.

In the late afternoon Will Henderson, owner and editor of the *Eagle*, went over to Tom Willy's saloon. Along an alleyway he went and slipping in at the back door of the saloon began drinking a drink made of a combination of sloe gin and soda water. Will Henderson was a sensualist and had reached the age of forty-five. He imagined the gin renewed the youth in him. Like most sensualists he enjoyed talking of women, and for an hour he lingered about gossiping with Tom Willy. The saloon keeper was a short, broad-shouldered man with peculiarly marked hands. That flaming kind of birthmark that sometimes paints with red the faces of men and women had touched with red Tom Willy's fingers and the backs of his hands. As he stood by the bar talking to Will Henderson he rubbed the hands together. As he grew more and more excited the red of his fingers deepened. It was as though the hands had been dipped in blood that had dried and faded.

As Will Henderson stood at the bar looking at the red hands and talking of women, his assistant, George Willard, sat in the office of the *Winesburg Eagle* and listened to the talk of Doctor Parcival.

Doctor Parcival appeared immediately after Will Henderson had disappeared. One might have supposed that the doctor had been watching from his office window and had seen the editor going along the alleyway. Coming in at the front door and finding himself a chair, he lighted one of the stogies and crossing his legs began to talk. He seemed intent upon convincing the boy of the advisability of adopting a line of conduct that he was himself unable to define.

"If you have your eyes open you will see that although I call myself a doctor I have mighty few patients," he began. "There is a reason for that. It is not an accident and it is not because I do not know as much of medicine as anyone here. I do not want patients. The reason, you see, does not appear on the surface. It lies in fact in my character, which has, if you think about it, many strange turns. Why I want to talk to you of the matter I don't know. I might keep still and get more credit in your eyes. I have a desire to make you admire me, that's a fact. I don't know why. That's why I talk. It's very amusing, eh?"

Sometimes the doctor launched into long tales concerning himself. To the boy the tales were very real and full of meaning. He began to admire the fat unclean-looking man and, in the afternoon when Will Henderson had gone, looked forward with keen interest to the doctor's coming.

Doctor Parcival had been in Winesburg about five years. He came from Chicago and when he arrived was drunk and got into a fight with Albert Longworth, the baggage-man. The fight concerned a trunk and ended by the doctor's being escorted to the village lockup. When he was released he rented a room above a shoe-repairing shop at the lower end of Main Street and put out the sign that announced himself as a doctor. Although he had but few patients and these of the poorer sort who were unable to pay, he seemed to have plenty of money for his needs. He slept in the office that was unspeakably dirty and dined at Biff Carter's lunch room in a small frame building opposite the railroad station. In the summer the lunch room was filled with flies and Biff Carter's white apron was more dirty than his floor. Doctor Parcival did not mind. Into the lunch room he stalked and deposited twenty cents upon the counter. "Feed me what you wish for that," he said laughing. "Use up food that you wouldn't otherwise sell. It makes no difference to me. I am a man of distinction, you see. Why should I concern myself with what I eat."

The tales that Doctor Parcival told George Willard began nowhere and ended nowhere. Sometimes the boy thought they must all be inventions, a pack of lies. And then again he was convinced that they contained the very essence of truth.

"I was a reporter like you here," Doctor Parcival began. "It was in a town in Iowa—or was it in Illinois? I don't remember and anyway it makes no difference. Perhaps I am trying to conceal my identity and don't want to be very definite. Have you ever thought it strange that I have money for my needs although I do nothing? I may have stolen a great sum of money or been involved in a murder before I came here. There is food for thought in that, eh? If you were a really smart newspaper reporter you would look me up. In Chicago there was a Doctor Cronin who was murdered. Have you heard of that? Some men murdered him and put him in a trunk. In the early morning they hauled the trunk across the city. It sat on the back of an expresswagon and they were on the seat as unconcerned as anything. Along they went through quiet streets where everyone was asleep. The sun was just coming up over the lake. Funny, eh—just to think of them smoking pipes and chattering as they drove along as unconcerned as I am now. Perhaps I was one of those men. That would be a strange turn of things, now wouldn't it?" Again Doctor Parcival began his tale: "Well, anyway there I was, a reporter on a paper just as you are here, running about and getting little items to print. My mother was poor. She took in washing. Her dream was to make me a Presbyterian minister and I was studying with that end in view.

"My father had been insane for a number of years. He was in an asylum over at Dayton, Ohio. There you see I have let it slip out! All of this took place in Ohio, right here in Ohio. There is a clew if you ever get the notion of looking me up.

"I was going to tell you of my brother. That's the object of all this. That's what I'm getting at. My brother was a railroad painter and had a job on the Big Four. You know that road runs through Ohio here. With other men he lived in a box car and away they went from town to town painting the railroad property—switches, crossing gates, bridges, and stations.

"The Big Four paints its stations a nasty orange color. How I hated that color! My brother was always covered with it. On pay days he used to get ⟨drunk and come home wearing his paint-covered clothes and bringing his money with him. He did not give it to mother but laid it in a pile on our kitchen table.

"About the house he went in the clothes covered with the nasty orange colored paint. I can see the picture. My mother, who was small and had red, sad-looking eyes, would come into the house from a little shed at the back. That's where she spent her time over the washtub scrubbing people's dirty clothes. In she would come and stand by the table, rubbing her eyes with her apron that was covered with soap-suds.

" 'Don't touch it! Don't you dare touch that money,' my brother roared, and then he himself took five or ten dollars and went tramping off to the saloons. When he had spent what he had taken he came back for more. He never gave my mother any money at all but stayed about until he had spent it all, a little at a time. Then he went back to his job with the painting crew on the railroad. After he had gone things began to arrive at our house, groceries and such things. Sometimes there would be a dress for mother or a pair of shoes for me.

"Strange, eh? My mother loved my brother much more than she did me, although he never said a kind word to either of us and always raved up and down threatening us if we dared so much as touch the money that sometimes lay on the table three days.

"We got along pretty well. I studied to be a minister and prayed. I was a regular ass about saying prayers. You should have heard me. When my father died I prayed all night, just as I did sometimes when my brother was in town drinking and going about buying the things for us. In the evening after supper I knelt by the table where the money lay and prayed for hours. When no one was looking I stole a dollar or two and put it in my pocket. That makes me laugh now but then it was terrible. It was on my mind all the time. I got six dollars a week from my job on the paper and always took it straight home to mother. The few dollars I stole from my brother's pile I spent on myself, you know, for trifles, candy and cigarettes and such things.

"When my father died at the asylum over at Dayton, I went over there. I borrowed some money from the man for whom I worked and went on the train at night. It was raining. In the asylum they treated me as though I were a king.

"The men who had jobs in the asylum had found out I was a newspaper reporter. That made them afraid. There had been some negligence, some carelessness, you see, when father was ill. They thought perhaps I would write it up in the paper and make a fuss. I never intended to do anything of the kind.

"Anyway, in I went to the room where my father lay dead and blessed the dead body. I wonder what put that notion into my head. Wouldn't my brother, the painter have laughed, though. There I stood over the dead body and spread out my hands. The superintendent of the asylum and some of his helpers came in and stood about looking sheepish. It was very amusing. I spread out my hands and said, 'Let peace brood over this carcass.' That's what I said."

Jumping to his feet and breaking off the tale, Doctor Parcival began to walk up and down in the office of the *Winesburg Eagle* where George Willard sat listening. He was awkward and, as the office was small, continually knocked against things. "What a fool I am to be talking," he said. "That is not my object in coming here and forcing my acquaintanceship upon you. I have something else in mind. You are a reporter just as I was once and you have attracted my attention. You may end by becoming just such another fool. I want to warn you and keep on warning you. That's why I seek you out."

Doctor Parcival began talking of George Willard's attitude toward men. It seemed to the boy that the man had but one object in view, to make everyone seem despicable. "I want to fill you with hatred and contempt so that you will be a superior being," he declared. "Look at my brother. There was a fellow, eh? He despised everyone, you see. You have no idea with what contempt he looked upon mother and me. And was he not our superior? You know he was. You have not seen him and yet I have made you feel that. I have given you a sense of it. He is dead. Once when he was drunk he lay down on the tracks and the car in which he lived with the other painters ran over him."

One day in August Doctor Parcival had an adventure in Winesburg. For a month George Willard had been going each morning to spend an hour in the doctor's office. The visits came about through a desire on the part of the doctor to read to the boy from the pages of a book he was in the process of writing. To write the book Doctor Parcival declared was the object of his coming to Winesburg to live.

On the morning in August before the coming of the boy, an incident had happened in the doctor's office. There had been an accident on Main Street. A team of horses had been frightened by a train and had run away. A little girl, the daughter of a farmer, had been thrown from a buggy and killed.

On Main Street everyone had become excited and a cry for doctors had gone up. All three of the active practitioners of the town had come quickly but had found the child dead. From the crowd someone had run to the office of Doctor Parcival who had bluntly refused to go down out of his office to the dead child. The useless cruelty of his refusal had passed unnoticed. Indeed, the man who had come up the stairway to summon him had hurried away without hearing the refusal.

All of this, Doctor Parcival did not know and when George Willard came to his office he found the man shaking with terror. "What I have done will arouse the people of this town," he declared excitedly. "Do I not know human nature? Do I not know what will happen? Word of my refusal will be whispered about. Presently men will get together in groups and talk of it. They will come here. We will quarrel and there will be talk of hanging. Then they will come again bearing a rope in their hands."

Doctor Parcival shook with fright. "I have a presentiment," he declared emphatically. "It may be that what I am talking about will not occur this morning. It may be put off until to-night but I will be hanged. Everyone will get excited. I will be hanged by a lamp-post on Main Street."

Going to the door of his dirty little office, Doctor Parcival looked timidly down the stairway leading to the street. When he returned the fright that had been in his eyes was beginning to be replaced by doubt. Coming on tip-toe across the room he tapped George Willard on the shoulder. "If not now, sometime," he whispered, shaking his head. "In the end I will be crucified, uselessly crucified."

Doctor Parcival began to plead with George Willard, "You must pay attention to me," he urged. "If something happens perhaps you will be able to write the book that may never get written. The idea is very simple, so simple that if you are not careful you will forget it. It is this—that everyone in the world is Christ, and they are all crucified. That's what I want to say. Don't you forget that. Whatever happens, don't you dare let yourself forget."

Voltaire (1694–1778)

Suicide

Philip Mordaunt, cousin-german to the famous earl of Peterborough, who was so well known in all the courts of Europe, and who made his boast that he had seen more postilions, and more crowned heads, than any other man in the world; this Philip Mordaunt, I say, was a young man about twenty-seven, handsome, well made, rich, of an illustrious family, and one who might pretend to anything; and, what was more than all the rest, he was passionately beloved by his mistress. However, this man took a distaste to life, discharged all that he owed, wrote to his friends to take leave of them, and even composed some verses upon the occasion, which concluded thus, that "though opium might be some relief to a wise man, if disgusted with the world, yet in his opinion a pistol, and a little resolution, were much more effectual remedies." His behavior was suitable to his principles; and he despatched himself with a pistol, without giving any other reason for it than that his soul was weary of his body, and that when we dislike our house we ought to quit it. One would imagine he chose to die because he was weary of being happy.

One Richard Smith has lately exhibited a most extraordinary instance of this nature to the world. This Smith was tired of being really unhappy; he had been rich, and was reduced to poverty; he had been healthy, and had become infirm; he had a wife, to whom he had nothing to give but a share in his misfortunes; and an infant in the cradle was the only thing he had left. Richard Smith and his wife, Bridget, then, after having affectionately embraced, and given each a formal kiss to their child, first cut the poor little creature's throat, and then hanged themselves at the foot of their bed. I do not remember to have heard anywhere of such a scene of horrors committed in cold blood; but the letter which these unhappy wretches wrote to their cousin, Mr. Brindley, before their death, is as remarkable as the manner of their death. "We are certain," said they, "of meeting with forgiveness from God. . . . We put an end to our lives because we were miserable, without any prospect of relief; and we have done our child that service to put it out of life, for fear it should have been as miserable as ourselves. . . ." It is to be observed that these people, after having murdered their child out of their paternal affection, wrote to a friend, recommending their dog and cat to his care. They thought, probably, that it was easier to make their dog and cat

---

From *The English Letters* by Voltaire (1733), translated by W. F. Fleming.

happy in this world than their child, and that keeping them would not be any great expense to their friend.[1]

The earl of Scarborough has lately quitted life with the same indifference as he did his place of master of the horse. Having been told in the house of lords that he sided with the court, on account of the profitable post he held in it, "My lords," said he, "to convince you that my opinion is not influenced by any such consideration, I will instantly resign." He afterward found himself perplexed between a mistress he was fond of, but to whom he was under no engagements, and a woman whom he esteemed, and to whom he had made a promise of marriage. My lord Scarborough, therefore, killed himself to get rid of difficulty.

The many tragical stories of this nature, with which the English newspapers abound, have made the greater part of Europe imagine that the English are fonder of killing themselves than any other people; and yet I question much whether there are not as many madmen at Paris as at London; and if our newspapers were to keep an exact register of those who have either had the folly, or unhappy resolution to destroy themselves, we might in this respect be found to vie with the English. But our compilers of news are more prudent; the adventures of private persons are never set forth to public scandal in any of the papers licensed by the government; however, I believe I may venture to affirm that this rage of suicide will never become epidemic. Nature has sufficiently guarded against it, and hope and fear are the powerful curbs she makes uses of to stop the hand of the wretch uplifted to be his own executioner.

I know it may be said, that there have been countries where a council was established to give license to the people to kill themselves, when they could give sufficient reasons for doing it. To this I answer, that either the fact is false, or that such council found very little employment.

There is one thing indeed which may cause some surprise, and which I think deserves to be seriously discussed, which is, that almost all the great heroes among the Romans, during the civil wars, killed themselves when they lost a battle, and that we do not find an instance of a single leader, or great man, in the disputes of the League, the Fronde, or during the troubles of Italy and Germany, who put end to his life with his own hand. It is true, that these latter were Christians, and that there is great difference between a Christian soldier and a Pagan; and yet, how comes it that those very men who were so easily withheld by Christianity, from putting an end to their own lives, should be restrained either by that or any other consideration,

---

[1]Richard Smith was a bookbinder, and a prisoner for debt within the liberty of the King's Bench; and this shocking tragedy was acted in 1732. Smith and his wife had been always industrious and frugal, invincibly honest, and remarkable for conjugal affection.

when they had a mind to poison, assassinate, or publicly execute a vanquished enemy? Does not the Christian religion forbid this manner of taking away the life of a fellow-creature, if possible more than our own? The advocates for suicide tell us that it is very allowable to quit our house when we are weary of it. Agreed: but most men had rather lie in a bad house than sleep in the open fields.

I one day received a circular letter from an Englishman, in which he proposes a premium to the person who should the most clearly demonstrate that it was allowable for a man to kill himself. I made him no answer, for I had nothing to prove to him, and he had only to examine within himself if he preferred death to life.

But then let us ask why Cato, Brutus, Cassius, Antony, Otho, and so many others gave themselves death with so much resolution, and that our leaders of parties suffered themselves to be taken alive by their enemies, or waste the remains of a wretched old age in a dungeon? Some refined wits pretend to say that the ancients had no real courage; that Cato acted like a coward in putting an end to his own life; and that he would have showed more greatness of soul in crouching beneath the victorious Caesar. This may be very well in an ode, or as a figure in rhetoric; but it is very certain there must be some courage to resign a life coolly by the edge of a sword, some strength of mind thus to overcome the most powerful instinct of nature; in a word, that such an act shows a greater share of ferocity than weakness. When a sick man is in a frenzy, we cannot say he has no strength, though we may say it is the strength of a madman.

Self-murder was forbidden by the Pagan as well as by the Christian religion. There was even a place allotted in hell to those who put an end to their own lives. Witness these lines of the poet.

> Then crowds succeed, who prodigal of breath,
> Themselves anticipate the doom of death;
> Though free from guilt, they cast their lives away,
> And sad and sullen hate the golden day.
>
> Oh! with what joy the wretches now would bear
> Pain, toil, and woe, to breathe the vital air!
> In vain! by fate forever are they bound
> With dire Avernus, and the lake profound;
> And Styx with nine wide channels roars around.
>   —Pitt.

This was the religion of the heathens; and notwithstanding the torments they were to endure in the other world, it was esteemed an honor to quit this by giving themselves death by their own hands; so contradictory are the manners of men! Is not the custom of dueling still unhappily accounted honorable among us, though prohibited by reason, by religion, and by all laws, divine and human? If Cato and Caesar, Antony and Augustus, did not challenge each other to a duel, it was not that they were less brave than ourselves. If the duke of Montmorency, Marshal Marillac, de Thou, Cinq-Mars, and many others, rather chose to be dragged to execution like the vilest miscreants, than put an end to their own lives like Cato and Brutus, it was not that they had less courage than those Romans; the true reason is, that it was not then the fashion at Paris to kill oneself on such occasions; whereas it was an established custom with the Romans.

The women on the Malabar coast throw themselves alive into the flames, in which the bodies of their dead husbands are burning. Is it because they have more resolution than Cornelia? No; but the custom of the country is for wives to burn themselves.

> Custom and fancy of our fate decide,
> And what is this man's shame is t'other's pride.

Bertolt Brecht (1898–1956)

Concerning the infanticide marie farrar

Marie Farrar, born in April,
No marks, a minor, rachitic, both parents dead,
Allegedly, up to now without police record,
Committed infanticide, it is said,
As follows: in her second month, she says,
With the aid of a barmaid she did her best
To get rid of her child with two douches,
Allegedly painful but without success.
But you, I beg you, check your wrath and scorn
For man needs help from every creature born.

She then paid out, she says, what was agreed
And continued to lace herself up tight.
She also drunk liquor with pepper mixed in it
Which purged her but did not cure her plight.

Her body distressed her as she washed the dishes,
It was swollen now quite visibly.
She herself says, for she was still a child,
She prayed to Mary most earnestly.
But you, I beg you, check your wrath and scorn
For man needs help from every creature born.

Her prayers, it seemed, helped her not at all.
She longed for help. Her trouble made her falter
And faint at early mass. Often drops of sweat
Broke out in anguish as she knelt at the altar.
Yet until her time had come upon her
She still kept secret her condition.
For no one believed such a thing had happened,
That she, so unenticing, had yielded to temptation.
But you, I beg you, check your wrath and scorn
For man needs help from every creature born.

And on that day, she says, when it was dawn,
As she washed the stairs it seemed a nail
Was driven into her belly. She was wrung with pain.
But still she secretly endured her travail.
All day long while hanging out the laundry
She racked her brains till she got it through her head
She had to bear the child and her heart was heavy.
It was very late when she went up to bed.
But you, I beg you, check your wrath and scorn
For man needs help from every creature born.

She was sent for again as soon as she lay down:
Snow had fallen and she had to go downstairs.
It went on till eleven. It was a long day.
Only at night did she have time to bear.
And so, she says, she gave birth to a son.
The son she bore was just like all others.
She was unlike to others but for this
There is no reason to despise this mother.
You, too, I beg you, check your wrath and scorn
For man needs help from every creature born.

Accordingly I will go on with the story
Of what happened to the son that came to be.
(She says she will hide nothing that befell)
So let it be a judgment upon both you and me.

She says she had scarcely gone to bed when she
Was overcome with sickness and she was alone,
Not knowing what would happen, yet she still
Contrived to stifle all her moans.
And you, I beg you, check your wrath and scorn
For man needs help from every creature born.

With her last strength, she says, because
Her room had now grown icy cold, she then
Dragged herself to the latrine and there
Gave birth as best she could (not knowing when)
But toward morning. She says she was already
Quite distracted and could barely hold
The child for snow came into the latrine
And her fingers were half numb with cold.
You too, I beg you, check your wrath and scorn
For man needs help from every creature born.

Between the latrine and her room, she says,
Not earlier, the child began to cry until
It drove her mad so that she says
She did not cease to beat it with her fists
Blindly for some time till it was still.
And then she took the body to her bed
And kept it with her there all through the night:
When morning came she hid it in the shed.
But you, I beg you, check your wrath and scorn
For man needs help from every creature born.

Marie Farrar, born in April,
An unmarried mother, convicted, died in
The Meissen penitentiary,
She brings home to you all men's sin.
You who bear pleasantly between clean sheets
And give the name "blessed" to your womb's weight
Must not damn the weakness of the outcast,
For her sin was black but her pain was great.
Therefore, I beg you, check your wrath and scorn
For man needs help from every creature born.

Nelson Algren (1909–   )

The monkey on the back

By the time Frankie got inside the room he was so weak Louie had to help him onto the army cot beside the oil stove. He lay on his back with one arm flung across his eyes as if in shame; and his lips were blue with cold. The pain had hit him with an icy fist in the groin's very pit, momentarily tapering off to a single probing finger touching the genitals to get the maximum of pain. He tried twisting to get away from the finger: the finger was worse than the fist. His throat was so dry that, though he spoke, the lips moved and made no sound. But Fomorowski read such lips well.

"Fix me. Make it stop. Fix me."

"I'll fix you, Dealer," Louie assured him softly.

Louie had his own bedside manner. He perched on the red leather and chrome bar stool borrowed from the Safari, with the amber toes of his two-tone shoes catching the light and the polo ponies galloping down his shirt. This was Nifty Louie's Hour. The time when he did the dealing and the dealer had to take what Louie chose to toss him in Louie's own good time.

He lit a match with his fingertip and held it away from the bottom of the tiny glass tube containing the fuzzy white cap of morphine, holding it just far enough away to keep the cap from being melted by the flame. There was time and time and lots of time for that. Let the dealer do a bit of melting first; the longer it took the higher the price. "You can pay me off when Zero pays you," he assured Frankie. There was no hurry. "You're good with me any time, Dealer."

Frankie moaned like an animal that cannot understand its own pain. His shirt had soaked through and the pain had frozen so deep in his bones nothing could make him warm again.

"Hit me, Fixer. Hit me."

A sievelike smile drained through Louie's teeth. This was his hour and this hour didn't come every day. He snuffed out the match's flame as it touched his fingers and snapped the head of another match into flame with his nail, letting its glow flicker one moment over that sievelike smile; then brought the tube down cautiously and watched it dissolve at the flame's fierce touch. When the stuff had melted he held both needle and tube in one hand, took the dealer's loose-hanging arm firmly with the other and pumped it in a long, loose arc. Frankie let him swing it as if it were attached to someone else. The cold was coming *up* from within now: a colorless cold spreading through stomach and liver and breathing across the heart like an odorless gas. To make the very brain tighten and congeal under its icy touch. "Warm. Make me warm."

And still there was no rush, no hurry at all. Louie pressed the hypo down to the cotton; the stuff too high these days to lose the fraction of a drop. "Don't vomit, student," he taunted Frankie to remind him of the first fix he'd had after his discharge—but it was too cold to answer. He was falling between glacial walls, he didn't know how anyone could fall so far away from everyone else in the world. So far to fall, so cold all the way, so steep and dark between those morphine-colored walls of Private McGantic's terrible pit.

He couldn't feel Louie probing into the dark red knot above his elbow at all. Nor see the way the first blood sprayed faintly up into the delicate hypo to tinge the melted morphine with blood as warm as the needle's heated point.

When Louie sensed the vein he pressed it down with the certainty of a good doctor's touch, let it linger a moment in the vein to give the heart what it needed and withdrew gently, daubed the blood with a piece of cotton, tenderly, and waited.

Louie waited. Waited to see it hit.

Louie liked to see the stuff hit. It meant a lot to Louie, seeing it hit.

"Sure I like to watch," he was ready to acknowledge any time. "Man, their *eyes* when that big drive hits 'n goes tinglin' down to the toes. They retch, they sweat, they itch—then the big drive hits 'n here they come out of it cryin' like a baby 'r laughin' like a loon. *Sure* I like to watch. *Sure* I like to see it hit. Heroin got the drive awright—but there's not a tingle to a ton—you got to get M to get that tingle-tingle."

It hit all right. It hit the heart like a runaway locomotive, it hit like a falling wall. Frankie's whole body lifted with that smashing surge, the very heart seemed to lift up-up-up then rolled over and he slipped into a long warm bath with one long orgasmic sigh of relief. Frankie opened his eyes.

He was in a room. Somebody's dust-colored wavy-walled room and he wasn't quite dead after all. He had died, had felt himself fall away and die but now he wasn't dead any more. Just sick. But not too sick. He wasn't going to be really sick, he wasn't a student any more. Maybe he wasn't going to be sick at all, he was beginning to feel just right.

Then it went over him like a dream where everything is love and he wasn't even sweating. All he had to do the rest of his life was to lie right here feeling better and better with every beat of his heart till he'd never felt so good in all his life.

"Wow," he grinned gratefully at Louie, "that was one good *whan.*"

"I seen it," Louie boasted smugly. "I seen it was one good *whan*"—and lapsed into the sort of impromptu jargon which pleases junkies for no reason

they can say—"vraza-s'vraza-s'vraza—it was one good *whan-whan-whan.*"
He dabbed a silk handkerchief at a blob of blood oozing where the needle
had entered Frankie's arm.

"There's a silver buck and a buck 'n a half in change in my jacket pocket,"
Frankie told him lazily. "I'm feelin' too good to get up 'n get it myself."

Louie reached in the pocket with the handkerchief bound about his palm
and plucked the silver out. Two-fifty for a quarter grain wasn't too high.
He gave Frankie the grin that drained through the teeth for a receipt. The
dealer was coming along nicely these days, thank you.

The dealer didn't know that yet, of course. That first fix had only cost him
a dollar, it had quieted the everlasting dull ache in his stomach and sent him
coasting one whole week end. So what was the use of spending forty dollars in the bars when you could do better at home on one? That was how
Frankie had it figured *that* week end. To Louie, listening close, he'd already
talked like a twenty-dollar-a-day man.

Given a bit of time.

And wondered idly now where in the world the dealer would get that kind
of money when the day came that he'd need half a C just to taper off. He'd
get it all right. They always got it. He'd seen them coming in the rain, the
unkjays with their peculiarly rigid, panicky walk, wearing some policeman's
castoff rubbers, no socks at all, a pair of Salvation Army pants a size too
small or a size too large and a pajama top for a shirt—but with twenty dollars
clutched in the sweating palm for that big twenty-dollar fix.

"Nothing can take the place of junk—just junk"—the dealer would learn.
As Louie himself had learned long ago.

Louie was the best fixer of them all because he knew what it was to need
to get well. Louie had had a big habit—he was one man who could tell you
you lied if you said no junkie could kick the habit once he was hooked.
For Louie was the one junkie in ten thousand who'd kicked it and kicked
it for keeps.

He'd taken the sweat cure in a little Milwaukee Avenue hotel room cutting
himself down, as he put it, "from monkey to zero." From three full grains a
day to one, then a half of that and a half of that straight down to zero, though
he'd been half out of his mind with the pain two nights running and was so
weak, for days after, that he could hardly tie his own shoelaces.

Back on the street at last, he'd gotten the chuck horrors: for two full days
he'd eaten candy bars, sweet rolls and strawberry malteds. It had seemed
that there would be no end to his hunger for sweets.

Louie never had the sweet-roll horrors any more. Yet sometimes himself
sensed that something had twisted in his brain in those nights when he'd
gotten the monkey off his back on Milwaukee Avenue.

"*Habit? Man,*" he liked to remember. "I had a great *big* habit. One time
I knocked out one of my own teet' to get the gold for a fix. You call that

bein' hooked or not? *Hooked?* Man, I wasn't hooked, I was *crucified.* The monkey got so big he was carrying *me.* 'Cause the way it starts is like this, students: you let the habit feed you first 'n one morning you wake up 'n you're feedin' the habit.

"But don't tell *me* you can't kick it if you *want* to. When I hear a junkie tell me he wants to kick the habit but he just can't I know he lies even if *he* don't know he does. He *wants* to carry the monkey, he's punishin' hisself for somethin' 'n don't even know it. It's what I was doin' for six years, punishin' myself for things I'd done 'n thought I'd forgot. So I told myself how I wasn't to blame for what I done in the first place, I was only tryin' to live like everyone else 'n doin' them things was the only way I had of livin'. Then I got forty grains 'n went up to the room 'n went from monkey to nothin' in twenny-eight days 'n that's nine-ten years ago 'n the monkey's dead."

"The monkey's never dead, Fixer," Frankie told him knowingly.

Louie glanced at Frankie slyly. "You know that awready, Dealer? You know how he don't die? It's what they say awright, the monkey never dies. When you kick him off he just hops onto somebody else's back." Behind the film of glaze that always veiled Louie's eyes Frankie saw the twisted look. "*You* got my monkey, Dealer? You take my nice old monkey away from me? Is that my monkey ridin' your back these days, Dealer?"

The color had returned to Frankie's cheeks, he felt he could make it almost any minute now. "No more for me, Fixer," he assured Louie confidently. "Somebody else got to take your monkey. I had the Holy Jumped-up-Jesus Horrors for real this time—'n I'm one guy knows when he got enough. I learned my lesson but *good*. Fixer—you just give the boy with the golden arm his very latest fix."

Jean Jacques Rousseau (1712–1778)   --------------

The stolen ribbon

Would that I had finished all that I had to say about my stay at Madame de Vercellis's! But, although my condition apparently remained the same, I did not leave the house as I entered it. I carried away from it lasting recollections of crime and the insupportable weight of remorse, which, after forty years, still lies heavy on my conscience; while the bitterness of it, far from growing weaker, makes itself more strongly felt with my advancing years. Who would believe that a childish fault could have such cruel con-

From *Confessions* by Jean Jacques Rousseau (1783).

sequences? For these more than probable consequences my heart is inconsolable. I have, perhaps, caused the ruin of an amiable, honest, and estimable girl, who certainly was far more worthy than myself, and doomed her to disgrace and misery.

It was almost unavoidable that the break up of an establishment should cause some confusion in the house, and that several things should get lost; however, the servants were so honest, and the Lorenzis so watchful, that nothing was missing when the inventory was taken. Only Mademoiselle Pontal had lost a piece of old red and silver-coloured ribbon. Many other things of greater value were at my disposal; this ribbon alone tempted me; I stole it, and, as I took no trouble to conceal it, it was soon found. They wanted to know how it had come into my possession. I became confused, stammered, blushed, and at last said that Marion had given it to me. Marion was a young girl from Maurienne, whom Madame de Vercellis had taken for her cook, when she left off giving dinners and discharged her own, as she had more need of good soup than of fine stews. Marion was not only pretty but had a fresh colour, only found on the mountains, and, above all, there was something about her so gentle and modest, that it was impossible for anyone to see her without loving her; in addition to that, she was a good and virtuous girl, and of unquestionable honesty. All were surprised when I mentioned her name. We were both equally trusted and it was considered important to find out which of us two was really the thief. She was sent for; a number of people were assembled, amongst them the Comte de la Roque. When she came, the ribbon was shown to her. I boldly accused her; she was astounded, and unable to utter a word; looked at me in a manner that would have disarmed the Devil himself, but against which my barbarous heart was proof. At last, she denied the theft firmly, but without anger, addressed herself to me, exhorted me to reflect, and not to disgrace an innocent girl who had never done me any harm; but I, with infernal impudence, persisted in my story, and declared to her face that she had given me the ribbon. The poor girl began to cry, and only said to me: "Ah! Rousseau, I thought you were a good man. You make me very unhappy, but I should not like to be in your place." That was all. She proceeded to defend herself with equal simplicity and firmness, but without allowing herself to utter the slightest reproach against me. This moderation, contrasted with my decided tone, did her harm. It did not seem natural to suppose, on the one side, such devilish impudence, and, on the other, such angelic mildness. Although the matter did not appear to be absolutely settled, they were prepossessed in my favor. In the confusion which prevailed, they did not give themselves time to get to the bottom of the affair; and the Comte de la Roque, in dismissing us both, contented himself with saying that the conscience of the guilty one would amply avenge the innocent. His prediction has been fulfilled; it fulfills itself everyday.

I do not know what became of the victim of my false accusation; but it is not likely that she afterwards found it easy to get a good situation. She carried away with her an imputation upon her honesty which was in every way cruel. The theft was only a trifling one, but still it was a theft, and, what is worse, made use of to lead a young man astray; lastly, lying and obstinacy left nothing to be hoped from one in whom so many vices were united. I do not even consider misery and desertion as the greatest danger to which I exposed her. At her age, who knows to what extremes discouragement and the feeling of ill-used innocence may have carried her? Oh, if my remorse at having, perhaps, made her unhappy is unendurable, one may judge what I feel at the thought of having, perhaps, made her worse than myself!

This cruel remembrance at times so sorely troubles and upsets me, that in my sleepless hours I seem to see the poor girl coming to reproach me for my crime, as if it had been committed only yesterday. As long as I have lived quietly, it has tormented me less; but in the midst of a stormy life it robs me of the sweet consolation of persecuted innocence, it makes me feel what I think I have said in one of my books, that "Remorse goes to sleep when our fortunes are prosperous, and makes itself felt more keenly in adversity." However, I have never been able to bring myself to unburden my heart of this confession to a friend. The closest intimacy has never led me so far with anyone, not even with Madame de Warens. All that I have been able to do has been to confess that I had to reproach myself with an atrocious act, but I have never stated wherein it consisted. This burden has remained to this day upon my conscience without alleviation; and I can affirm that the desire of freeing myself from it in some degree, has greatly contributed to the resolution I have taken of writing my Confessions.

I have behaved straightforwardly in the confession which I have just made, and it will assuredly be found that I have not attempted to palliate the blackness of my offence. But I should not fulfil the object of this book, if I did not at the same time set forth my inner feelings, and hesitated to excuse myself by what is strictly true. Wicked intent was never further from me than at that cruel moment; and when I accused the unhappy girl, it is singular, but it is true, that my friendship for her was the cause of it. She was present to my thoughts; I threw the blame on the first object which presented itself. I accused her of having done what I meant to do, and of having given me the ribbon, because my intention was to give it to her. When I afterwards saw her appear, my heart was torn; but the presence of so many people was stronger than repentance. I was not afraid of punishment, I was only afraid of disgrace; and that I feared more than death, more than crime, more than anything else in the world. I should have rejoiced if the earth had suddenly opened, swallowed me up and suffocated me; the unconquerable fear of shame overcame everything, and alone made me impudent. The greater my crime, the more the dread of confessing it made me fearless. I saw nothing but the horror of being recognised and publicly declared, in my own presence, a thief, liar, and slanderer. Complete embarrassment deprived me of every other feeling. If I had been allowed to recover myself I should have assuredly confessed everything. If M. de la Roque had taken me aside and said to me: "Do not ruin this poor girl; if you are guilty, confess it to me," I should have immediately thrown myself at his feet, of that I am perfectly certain. But, when I needed encouragement, they only intimidated me. And yet it is only fair to consider my age. I was little more than a child, or rather, I still was one. In youth real crimes are even more criminal than in riper years; but that which is only weakness is less so, and my offence was at bottom scarcely anything else. Thus the recollection of it afflicts me not so much by reason of the evil in itself as on account of its evil consequences. It has been done me the good of securing me for the rest of my life against every act tending to crime, by the terrible impression which I have retained of the only offence that I have ever committed; and I believe that my horror of a lie is due in great measure to my regret at having been capable myself of telling one so shameful. If it is a crime that can be expiated, as I venture to believe, it must be expiated by all the unhappiness which has overwhelmed the last years of my life, by forty years of honourable and upright conduct in difficult circumstances; and poor Marion finds so many avengers in this world, that, however great my offence against her may have been, I have little fear of dying without absolution. This is what I have to say on this matter; permit me never to speak of it again.

_____   **William Carlos Williams (1883–   )**   _____

The insane

What are they teaching you now, son? said the old Doc brushing the crumbs from his vest.

Have one, Dad? Yeah. Throw it to me. I got matches.

I wish you wouldn't do that, said his wife trying hard to scowl. It was the usual Saturday evening dinner, the young man, a senior in medical school, out for his regular weekend siesta, in the suburbs.

I'm curious, said the old Doc glancing at his wife. Then to his son, Anything new? She placed an ash tray at his elbow.

I go on Medicine Monday, said the boy. We finished Pediatrics and Psychiatry today.

Psychiatry, eh? That's one you won't regret, said his father. Or do you like it, maybe?

Not particularly. But what can we learn in a few weeks? The cases we get are so advanced, just poor dumb clucks, there's nothing to do for them anyway. I can see though that there must be a lot to it.

What are you two talking about? said his mother.

Insanity, Ma.

Oh.

Any new theories as to cause? said the older man. I mean, not the degenerative cases, with a somatic background, but the schizophrenics especially. Have they learned anything new about that in recent years?

Oh, Dad, there are all sorts of theories. It starts with birth in most cases, they tell us. Even before birth sometimes. That's what we're taught. Unwanted children, conflicts of one sort or another. You know.

No. I'm curious. What do they tell you about Freud?

Sex as the basis for everything? The boy's mother looked up at him a moment and then down again.

It's largely a reflection of his own personality, most likely. I mean it's all right to look to sex as a cause, but that's just the surface aspect of the thing. Not the thing itself. Don't you think?

That's what I'm asking you.

But everybody has a different theory. One thing I can understand though, even from my little experience, and that is why insanity is increasing so rapidly here today.

Really? said his mother.

I mean from my Pediatric work. He paused. Of the twenty-five children I saw in the clinic this week only two can be said to be really free from psychoneurotic symptoms. Two! Out of twenty-five. And maybe a more careful history would have found something even in those two.

Do you mean that those children all showed signs of beginning insanity? said his mother.

Potentially, yes.

Not a very reassuring comment on modern life, is it?

Go ahead, son, said his father.

Take a funny-faced little nine-year-old guy with big glasses I saw in the clinic this afternoon. His mother brought him in for stealing money.

How old a child, did you say?

Nine years. The history was he'd take money from her purse. Or if she sent him to the store to buy something, he'd come back without it and use the money for something he wanted himself.

Do you have to treat those cases too? asked his mother.

Anything that comes in. We have to get the history, do a physical, a complete physical—you know what that means, Dad—make a diagnosis and prescribe treatment.

What did you find?

The story is this. The lad's father was a drunk who died two years ago when the boy was just seven. A typical drunk. The usual bust up. They took him to the hospital and he died.

But before that—to go back, this boy had been a caesarian birth. He has a brother, three years younger, an accident. After that the woman was sterilized. But I'll tell you about him later.

Anyhow, when she came home, on the ninth day after her caesarian, she found her husband under the influence, dead drunk as usual and he started to take her over—that's the story.

What's that?

Oh, you know, Mother. Naturally she put up a fight and as a result he knocked her downstairs.

What! Nine days after her confinement?

Yes, nine days after the section. She had to return to the hospital for a check up. And naturally when she came out again she hated her husband and the baby too because it was his child.

Terrible.

And the little chap had to grow up in that atmosphere. They were always battling. The old man beat up his wife regularly and the child had to witness it for his entire existence up to two years ago.

As I say, she had a second child—three years old now, which, though she hated it, came between the older boy and his mother forcing them apart still further. That one has tuberculosis which doesn't make things any easier.

Imagine such people!

They're all around you, Mother, if you only knew it. Oh, I forgot to tell you the older kid was the dead spit of his dad who had always showered all kinds of attentions on him. His favorite. All the love the kid ever knew came from his old man.

So when the father died the only person the boy could look to for continued affection was his mother—who hated him.

Oh, no!

As a result the child doesn't eat, has lost weight, doesn't sleep, constipation and all the rest of it. And in school, whereas his marks had always been good—because he's fairly bright—after his father died they went steadily down, down and down to complete failure.

Poor baby.

And then he began to steal—from his mother—because he couldn't get the love he demanded of her. He began to steal from her to compensate for what he could not get otherwise, and which his father had given him formerly.

Interesting. Isn't it, dear?

So young!

The child substitutes his own solution for the reality which he needs and cannot obtain. Unreality and reality become confused in him. Finally he loses track. He doesn't know one from the other and we call him insane.

What will become of him in this case? asked the mother.

In this case, said her son, the outcome is supposed to be quite favorable. We'll explain the mechanism to the woman—who by the way isn't in such good condition herself—and if she follows up what she's told to do the boy is likely to be cured.

Strange, isn't it? said the old Doc.

But what gets me, said his son. Of course we're checked up on all these cases; they're all gone over by a member of the staff. And when we give a history like that, they say, Oh those are just the psychiatric findings. That gripes me. Why, it's the child's life.

Good boy, said his father. You're all right. Stick to it.

ANOMIE

The term *anomie* was introduced into the language of modern sociology by the great French theorist Emile Durkheim, although it had already been coined earlier. He took it to mean a condition of relative normlessness or moral anarchy, a situation of crisis in which the customary norms governing the conduct of individuals have broken down. An eminent American sociologist, Robert K. Merton, further developed this concept in his classic essay "Social Structure and Anomie," where he directed attention to strains toward anomie operating unevenly throughout certain types of societies "when there is an acute disjunction between the cultural norms and goals and the socially structured capacities of members of the group to act in accord with them." Finally, certain contemporary theorists, Robert MacIver, for example, have elaborated a psychological concept of anomie, stressing states of mind rather than states of the social structure. To MacIver anomie is "a state of mind in which the individual's sense of social cohesion—the mainspring of his morale—is broken or fatally weakened."

The selection from the great metaphysical poet John Donne, from the elegy "An Anatomy of the World," reflects the spiritual anguish of an age in which the truth of faith was challenged by the truth of science so that "all coherence [seemed] gone." William Butler Yeats in "The Second Coming" expresses a similar disjunction of norms and beliefs in the modern world. The French Romantic poet, Alfred de Musset, describes, in the passages from his *Confessions of a Child of the Century,* the breakdown of the moral coherence of French society after the successive shocks to political and ethical sensibilities of the French Revolution, the Napoleonic era and the Restoration.

Diderot's *Rameau's Nephew* is perhaps the first and certainly among the most literary creations evoking the anomic man, cut loose from all the moorings to which norms of conduct are anchored. Dostoevski's "underground man"—in *Notes from the Underground*—may be said to be his lineal descendent. He is a man who has lost the capacity for moral choice, even for acting on the basis of his own emotion; cut off from all meaningful action, he subsists in a cosmic void.

F. Scott Fitzgerald's autobiographical essay, "The Crack-Up," describes a related experience of meaninglessness toward the close of his life, when after an extremely successful career he seemed suddenly to have come to the conclusion that he was at the end of his artistic as well as his human resources.

The final three readings, from Charles Dickens, from the American satirist and short-story writer Ambrose Bierce, and from Dostoevski, illustrate conflicts of cultural values, as well as discrepancies between cultural values and social relations, that lead to anomic "innovations" when institutionally prescribed success goals are attained by institutionally proscribed means.

John Donne (1573–1631)

All cohaerence gone

And new Philosophy calls all in doubt,
The Element of fire is quite put out;
The Sun is lost, and the earth, and no man's wit
Can well direct him where to looke for it.
And freely men confesse that this world's spent,
When in the Planets, and the Firmament
They seeke so many new; they see that this

From *The First Anniversary* by John Donne (1611).

Is crumbled out againe to his Atomies.
'Tis all in peeces, all cohaerence gone;
All just supply, and all Relation:
Prince, Subject, Father, Sonne, are things forgot,
For every man alone thinkes he hath got
To be a Phoenix, and that then can bee
None of that kinde, of which he is, but hee.
This is the worlds condition now, and now
She that should all parts to reunion bow,
She that had all Magnetique force alone,
To draw, and fasten sundred parts in one;
She whom wise nature had invented then
When she observed that every sort of men
Did in their voyage in this worlds Sea stray,
And needed a new compasse for their way;
She that was best, and first originall
Of all faire copies, and the generall
Steward to Fate; she whose rich eyes, and brest
Guilt the West Indies, and perfumed the East;
Whose having breath'd in this world, did bestow
Spice on those Iles, and bade them still smell so,
And that rich Indie which doth gold interre,
Is but as single money, coyn'd from her;
She to whom this world must it selfe refer,
As Suburbs, or the Microcosme of her,
Shee, shee is dead; shee's dead: when thou knowst this,
Thou knowst how lame a cripple this world is.
And learn'st thus much by our Anatomy,
That this worlds generall sickenesse doth not lie
In any humour, or one certain part;
But as thou sawest it rotten at the heart,
Thou seest a Hectique feaver hath got hold
Of the whole substance, not to be contrould,
And that thou hast but one way, not t'admit
The worlds infection, to be none of it.
For the worlds subtilst immateriall parts
Feele this consuming wound, and ages darts.
For the worlds beauty is decai'd, or gone,
Beauty, that's colour, and proportion.

William Butler Yeats (1865–1939)

The second coming

Turning and turning in the widening gyre
The falcon cannot hear the falconer;
Things fall apart; the centre cannot hold;
Mere anarchy is loosed upon the world,
The blood-dimmed tide is loosed, and everywhere
The ceremony of innocence is drowned;
The best lack all conviction, while the worst
Are full of passionate intensity.

Surely some revelation is at hand;
Surely the Second Coming is at hand.
The Second Coming! Hardly are those words out
When a vast image out of *spiritus mundi*
Troubles my sight: somewhere in sands of the desert
A shape with lion body and the head of a man,
A gaze blank and pitiless as the sun,
Is moving its slow thighs, while all about it
Reel shadows of the indignant desert birds.
The darkness drops again; but now I know
That twenty centuries of stony sleep
Were vexed to nightmare by a rocking cradle,
And what rough beast, its hour come round at last,
Slouches towards Bethlehem to be born?

Alfred de Musset (1810–1857)

Things were drifting toward the abyss

It was a denial of all heavenly and earthly facts that might be termed disenchantment, or if you will, despair; as if humanity in lethargy had been

From *Confessions of a Child of the Century* by Alfred de Musset (1836).

pronounced dead by those who felt its pulse. Like a soldier who is asked: "In what do you believe?" and who replies: "In myself," so the youth of France, hearing that question, replied: "In nothing."

Then formed two camps: on one side the exalted spirits, sufferers, all the expansive souls who yearned toward the infinite, bowed their heads and wept; they wrapped themselves in unhealthful dreams and nothing could be seen but broken reeds in an ocean of bitterness. On the other side the materialists remained erect, inflexible, in the midst of positive joys, and cared for nothing except to count the money they had acquired. It was but a sob and a burst of laughter, the one coming from the soul, the other from the body.

This is what the soul said:

"Alas! Alas! religion has departed; the clouds of heaven fall in rain; we have no longer either hope or expectation, not even two little pieces of black wood in the shape of a cross before which to clasp our hands. The star of the future is loath to appear; it can not rise above the horizon, it is enveloped in clouds, and like the sun in winter its disc is the color of blood, as in '93. There is no more love, no more glory. What heavy darkness over all the earth! And death will come ere the day breaks."

This is what the body said:

"Man is here below to satisfy his senses; he has more or less of white or yellow metal, by which he merits more or less esteem. To eat, to drink, and to sleep, that is life. As for the bonds which exist between men, friendship consists in loaning money; but one rarely has a friend whom he loves enough for that. Kinship determines inheritance: love is an exercise of the body; the only intellectual joy is vanity."

Like the Asiatic plague exhaled from the vapors of the Ganges, frightful despair stalked over the earth. Already Chateaubriand, prince of poesy, wrapping the horrible idol in his pilgrim's mantle, had placed it on a marble altar in the midst of perfumes and holy incense. Already the children were clenching idle hands and drinking in a bitter cup the poisoned brewage of doubt. Already things were drifting toward the abyss, when the jackals suddenly emerged from the earth. A deathly and infected literature, which had no form but that of ugliness, began to sprinkle with fetid blood all the monsters of nature.

Who will dare to recount what was passing in the colleges? Men doubted everything: the young men denied everything. The poets sang of despair; the youth came from the schools with serene brow, their faces glowing with health, and blasphemy in their mouths. Moreover, the French character, being by nature gay and open, readily assimilated English and German ideas; but hearts too light to struggle and to suffer withered like crushed flowers. Thus the seed of death descended slowly and without shock from the head to the bowels. Instead of having the enthusiasm of evil we had only the negation of the good; instead of despair, insensibility. Children of fifteen, seated listlessly under flowering shrubs, conversed for pastime on subjects which would have made shudder with terror the still thickets of Versailles. The Communion of Christ, the Host, those wafers that stand as the eternal symbol of divine love, were used to seal letters; the children spit upon the Bread of God.

Happy they who escaped those times! Happy they who passed over the abyss while looking up to Heaven. There are such, doubtless, and they will pity us.

It is unfortunately true that there is in blasphemy a certain outlet which solaces the burdened heart. When an atheist, drawing his watch, gave God a quarter of an hour in which to strike him dead, it is certain that it was a quarter of an hour of wrath and of atrocious joy. It was the paroxysm of despair, a nameless appeal to all celestial powers; it was a poor, wretched creature squirming under the foot that was crushing him; it was a loud cry of pain. Who knows? In the eyes of Him who sees all things, it was perhaps a prayer.

Thus these youth found employment for their idle powers in a fondness for despair. To scoff at glory, at religion, at love, at all the world, is a great consolation for those who do not know what to do; they mock at themselves, and in doing so prove the correctness of their view. And then it is pleasant to believe one's self unhappy when one is only idle and tired. Debauchery, moreover, the first result of the principles of death, is a terrible millstone for grinding the energies.

The rich said: "There is nothing but riches, all else is a dream; let us enjoy and then let us die." Those of moderate fortune said: "There is nothing real but oblivion, all else is a dream; let us forget and let us die." And the poor said: "There is nothing real but unhappiness, all else is a dream; let us blaspheme and die."

Denis Diderot

An anomic man

I: "If the expedient I have suggested does not suit you then have courage enough to be a penniless beggar."

He: "It's hard to be penniless while there are so many wealthy fools at whose expense one might live. And then, self-contempt is so unbearable."

I: "Is that a feeling you've experienced?"

From *Rameau's Nephew* by Denis Diderot, in *Diderot, Interpreter of Nature*, translated by Jean Stewart and Jonathan Kemp. Copyright by International Publishers, 1943.

He: "Have I experienced it! How many times have I said to myself: What, Rameau, there are ten thousand good tables in Paris, each laid for fifteen or twenty, and of all those places not one is for you! There are purses full of gold being shed right and left, and not one coin falls to you! A thousand petty wits, without talent or merit; a thousand little wenches, without any charms; a thousand dull intriguers go well-clad, and shall you go naked? Must you be foolish to that extent? Couldn't you flatter as well as anyone? Couldn't you lie, swear, perjure yourself, make promises, keep or break them as well as anyone? Couldn't you crawl on all fours as well as anyone? Couldn't you assist Madame's intrigue and carry Monsieur's *billet-doux* as well as anyone? Couldn't you encourage this young man to speak to Mademoiselle, and persuade Mademoiselle to listen to him, as well as anyone . . .?"

"What! possessing that talent, you lack bread? Aren't you ashamed, you wretch? I remembered a crowd of rascals, who didn't come up to my ankle, and who were overflowing with riches. I wore a coat of coarse cloth, and they were clad in velvet; they leaned on sticks with golden knobs and curbed handles; and they had Aristotle and Plato engraved on the signet-rings they had on their fingers. And yet what used they to be? Wretched tenth-rate musicians for the most part; now they're as good as lords. Then I felt brave, high-hearted, keen-minded, capable of anything. But it seems that this happy condition did not endure; for up till now, I've not succeeded in making any real progress. However that may be, that is the text of my frequent soliloquies, which you may paraphrase as you please; provided that you conclude therefrom that I do know self-contempt, that torment of the conscience which springs from the uselessness of the gifts that Heaven has allotted to us; it is the most cruel of all torments. A man might almost as well not have been born."

I listened to him, and while he was acting the scene between the procurer and the young girl whom he seduces, my soul was disturbed by two contrary impulses; I did not know whether to give way to a longing to laugh or to a fit of indignation. I was in distress. A score of times a burst of laughter would prevent my anger from breaking out; a score of times the anger rising within my heart ended in a burst of laughter. I was astounded at such shrewdness allied with such baseness; such sound ideas alternating with such falseness; such a general perversity of feeling, such utter corruption, together with such uncommon frankness. He noticed the struggle that was going on within me, and said: "What is the matter?"

I: "Nothing."

He: "You seem distressed."

I: "So I am."

He: "But tell me, what do you advise me to do?"

I: "To change the subject. Unfortunate creature, to what an abject state you have fallen!"

He: "I admit it. Nevertheless don't be too much upset about my state. I did not intend, when I confided in you, to distress you. I saved some money at these people's: remember that I needed nothing, absolutely nothing, and that I was allowed so much for pocket money."

(Then he began once more to beat his brow with his fist, to bite his lip, and to roll his eyes wildly to the ceiling, adding:)

"But it's all over and done with. I have set something aside. Time has passed; and that's always something saved."

I: "You mean something lost."

He: "No, no, saved. Every instant one grows rich. One day less to live, or one crown to the good, it comes to the same thing. The important point is to go easily, freely, pleasantly, copiously, to the closet every evening: *o stercum pretiosum!* That is the great end of life, for all conditions of men. At the last moment, we are all equally rich; Samuel Bernard who by dint of thefts, plunder, and bankruptcies leaves twenty-seven million in gold, and Rameau who leaves nothing at all; Rameau for whom charity will provide a bit of packing cloth for a shroud. The dead man hears no bells tolling. In vain do a hundred priests sing themselves hoarse for him; in vain does a long procession of burning torches go before and behind him; his soul is not walking beside the master of ceremonies. Whether you rot under marble or under the earth, you still rot. Whether you have round your coffin children in red and children in blue, or no one at all, it makes no difference."

Fedor Dostoevski

A voice from the underground

I am a sick man . . . I am a spiteful man. I am an unattractive man. I believe my liver is diseased. However, I know nothing at all about my disease, and do not know for certain what ails me. I don't consult a doctor for it, and never have, though I have a respect for medicine and doctors. Besides, I am extremely superstitious, sufficiently so to respect medicine, anyway (I am well educated enough not to be superstitious, but I am superstitious). No, I refuse to consult a doctor from spite. That you will probably not understand. Well, I understand it though. Of course, I can't explain who it is pre-

From *Notes from the Underground* by Fedor Dostoevski (1864), translated by Constance Garnett.

cisely that I am mortifying in this case by my spite: I am perfectly well aware that I cannot "pay out" the doctors by not consulting them; I know better than any one that by all this I am only injuring myself and no one else. But still, if I don't consult a doctor it is from spite. My liver is bad, well—let it get worse!

I have been going on like that for some time—twenty years. Now I am forty. I used to be in the government service, but am no longer. I was a spiteful official. I was rude and took pleasure in being so. I did not take bribes, you see, so I was bound to find a recompense in that, at least. (A poor jest, but I will not scratch it out. I wrote it thinking it would sound very witty; but now that I have seen myself that I only wanted to show off in a despicable way, I will not scratch it out on purpose!)

When petitioners used to come for information to the table at which I sat, I used to grind my teeth at them, and felt intense enjoyment when I succeeded in making anybody unhappy. I almost always did succeed. For the most part they were all timid people—of course, they were petitioners. But of the uppish ones there was one officer in particular I could not endure. He simply would not be humble, and clanked his sword in a disgusting way. I carried on a feud with him for eighteen months over that sword. At last I got the better of him. He left off clanking it. That happened in my youth, though.

But do you know, gentlemen, what was the chief point about my spite? Why, the whole point, the real sting of it lay in the fact that continually, even in the moment of the acutest spleen, I was inwardly conscious with shame that I was not only not a spiteful but not even an embittered man, that I was simply scaring sparrows at random and amusing myself by it. I might foam at the mouth, but bring me a doll to play with, give me a cup of tea with sugar in it, and maybe I should be appeased. I might even be genuinely touched, though probably I should grind my teeth at myself afterwards and lie awake at night with shame for months after. That was my way.

I was lying when I said just now that I was a spiteful official. I was lying from spite. I was simply amusing myself with the petitioners and with the officer, and in reality I never could become spiteful. I was conscious every moment in myself of many, very many elements absolutely opposite to that. I felt them positively swarming in me, these opposite elements. I knew that they had been swarming in me all my life and craving some outlet from me, but I would not let them, would not let them, purposely would not let them come out. They tormented me till I was ashamed: they drove me to convulsions and—sickened me, at last, how they sickened me! Now, are not you fancying gentlemen, that I am expressing remorse for something now, that I am asking your forgiveness for something? I am sure you are fancying that . . . However, I assure you I do not care if you are . . .

It was not only that I could not become spiteful, I did not know how to become anything: neither spiteful nor kind, neither a rascal nor an honest man, neither a hero nor an insect. Now, I am living out my life in my corner, taunting myself with the spiteful and useless consolation that an intelligent man cannot become anything seriously, and it is only the fool who becomes anything. Yes, a man in the nineteenth century must and morally ought to be pre-eminently a characterless creature; a man of character, an active man is pre-eminently a limited creature. That is my conviction of forty years. I am forty years old now, and you know forty years is a whole lifetime; you know it is extreme old age. To live longer than forty years is bad manners, is vulgar, immoral. Who does live beyond forty? Answer that, sincerely and honestly. I will tell you who do: fools and worthless fellows. I tell all old men that to their face, all these venerable old men, all these silver-haired and reverend seniors! I tell the whole world that to its face! I have a right to say so, for I shall go on living to sixty myself. To seventy! To eighty! . . . Stay, let me take a breath . . .

You imagine no doubt, gentlemen, that I want to amuse you. You are mistaken in that, too. I am by no means such a mirthful person as you imagine, or as you may imagine; however, irritated by all this babble (and I feel that you are irritated) you think fit to ask me who I am—then my answer is, I am a collegiate assessor. I was in the service that I might have something to eat (and solely for that reason), and when last year a distant relation left me six thousand roubles in his will I immediately retired from the service and settled down in my corner. I used to live in this corner before, but now I have settled down in it. My room is a wretched, horrid one in the outskirts of the town. My servant is an old country-woman, ill-natured from stupidity, and, moreover, there is always a nasty smell about her. I am told that the Petersburg climate is bad for me, and that with my small means it is very expensive to live in Petersburg. I know all that better than all these sage and experienced counsellors and monitors . . . But I am remaining in Petersburg; I am not going away from Petersburg! I am not going away because . . . ech! Why, it is absolutely no matter whether I am going away or not going away.

But what can a decent man speak of with most pleasure?

Answer: Of himself.

Well, so I will talk about myself.

I want now to tell you, gentlemen, whether you care to hear it or not, why I could not even become an insect. I tell you solemnly, that I have many times tried to become an insect. But I was not equal even to that. I swear, gentlemen, that to be too conscious is an illness—a real thoroughgoing illness. For man's everyday needs, it would have been quite enough to have the ordinary human consciousness, that is, half or a quarter of the amount which falls to the lot of a cultivated man of our unhappy nineteenth century, especially one who has the fatal ill-luck to inhabit Petersburg, the most theoretical and intentional town on the whole terrestrial globe. (There are intentional and unintentional towns). It would have been quite enough, for instance, to have the consciousness by which all so-called direct persons and men of action live. I bet you think I am writing all this from affectation, to be witty at the expense of men of action; and what is more, that from ill-bred affectation, I am clanking a sword like my officer. But, gentlemen, whoever can pride himself on his diseases and even swagger over them?

Though, after all, every one does do that; people do pride themselves on their diseases, and I do, may be, more than any one. We will not dispute it; my contention was absurd. But yet I am firmly persuaded that a great deal of consciousness, every sort of consciousness, in fact, is a disease. I stick to that. Let us leave that, too, for a minute. Tell me this: why does it happen that at the very, yes, at the very moment when I am most capable of feeling every refinement of all that is "good and beautiful," as they used to say at one time, it would, as though of design, happen to me not only to feel but to do such ugly things, such that . . . Well, in short, actions that all, perhaps, commit; but which, as though purposely, occurred to me at the very time when I was most conscious that they ought not to be committed. The more conscious I was of goodness and of all that was "good and beautiful," the more deeply I sank into my mire and the more ready I was to sink in it altogether. But the chief point was that all this was, as it were, not accidental in me, but as though it were bound to be so. It was as though it were my most normal condition, and not in the least disease or depravity, so that at last all desire in me to struggle against this depravity passed. It ended by my almost believing (perhaps actually believing) that this was perhaps my normal condition. But at first, in the beginning, what agonies I endured in that struggle! I did not believe it was the same with other people, and all my life I hid this fact about myself as a secret. I was ashamed (even now, perhaps, I am ashamed): I got to the point of feeling a sort of secret abnormal, despicable enjoyment in returning home to my corner on some disgusting Petersburg night, acutely conscious that that day I had committed a loathsome action again, that what was done could never be undone, and secretly, inwardly gnawing, gnawing at myself for it, tearing and consuming myself till at last the bitterness turned into a sort of shameful accursed sweetness, and at last—into positive real enjoyment! Yes, into enjoyment, into enjoyment! I insist upon that. I have spoken of this because I keep wanting to know for a fact whether other people feel such enjoyment? I will explain; the enjoyment was just from the too intense consciousness of one's own degradation; it was from feeling oneself that one had reached the last barrier, that it was horrible, but that it could not be otherwise; that there was no escape for you; that you never could become a different man; that even if time and faith were still left you to change into something different you would most likely not wish to change; or if you did wish to, even then you would do nothing; because perhaps in reality there was nothing for you to change into.

And the worst of it was, and the root of it all, that it was all in accord with the normal fundamental laws of over-acute consciousness, and with the inertia that was the direct result of those laws, and that consequently one was not only unable to change but could do absolutely nothing. Thus it would follow, as the result of acute consciousness, that one is not to blame in being a scoundrel: as though that were any consolation to the scoundrel once he has come to realize that he actually is a scoundrel. But enough . . . Ech, I have talked a lot of nonsense, but what have I explained? How is enjoyment in this to be explained? But I will explain it. I will get to the bottom of it! That is why I have taken up my pen . . .

I, for instance, have a great deal of amour propre. I am as suspicious and prone to take offence as a humpback or a dwarf. But upon my word I sometimes have had moments when if I had happened to be slapped in the face I should perhaps, have been positively glad of it. I say, in earnest, that I should probably have been able to discover even in that a peculiar sort of enjoyment—the enjoyment, of course, of despair; but in despair there are the most intense enjoyments, especially when one is very acutely conscious of the hopelessness of one's position. And when one is slapped in the face— why then the consciousness of being rubbed into a pulp would positively overwhelm one. The worst of it is, look at it which way one will, it still turns out that I was always the most to blame in everything. And what is most humiliating of all, to blame for no fault of my own but, so to say, through the laws of nature. In the first place, to blame because I am cleverer than any of the people surrounding me. (I have always considered myself cleverer than any of the people surrounding me, and sometimes, would you believe it, have been positively ashamed of it. At any rate, I have all my life, as it were, turned my eyes away and never could look people straight in the face.) To blame, finally, because even if I had had magnanimity, I should only have had more suffering from the sense of its uselessness. I should certainly have never been able to do anything from being magnanimous—neither to forgive, for my assailant would perhaps have slapped me from the laws of nature, and one cannot forgive the laws of nature; nor to forget, for even if it were owing to the laws of nature, it is insulting all the same. Finally, even if I had wanted to be anything but magnanimous, had desired on the contrary to revenge myself on my assailant, I could not have revenged myself on any one for anything because I should certainly never have made up my mind to do anything, even if I had been able to. Why should I not have made up my mind? About that in particular I want to say a few words.

F. Scott Fitzgerald

The crack-up

Of course all life is a process of breaking down, but the blows that do the dramatic side of the work—the big sudden blows that come, or seem to come, from outside—the ones you remember and blame things on and, in moments of weakness, tell your friends about, don't show their effect all at once. There is another sort of blow that comes from within—that you don't feel until it's too late to do anything about it, until you realize with finality that in some regard you will never be as good a man again. The first sort of breakage seems to happen quick—the second kind happens almost without your knowing it but is realized suddenly indeed.

Before I go on with this short history, let me make a general observation— the test of a first-rate intelligence is the ability to hold two opposed ideas in the mind at the same time, and still retain the ability to function. One should, for example, be able to see that things are hopeless and yet be determined to make them otherwise. This philosophy fitted into my early adult life, when I saw the improbable, the implausible, often the "impossible," come true. Life was something you dominated if you were any good. Life yielded easily to intelligence and effort, or to what proportion could be mustered of both. It seemed a romantic business to be a successful literary man—you were not ever going to be as famous as a movie star but what note you had was probably longer-lived—you were never going to have the power of a man of strong political or religious convictions but you were certainly more independent. Of course within the practice of your trade you were forever unsatisfied—but I, for one, would not have chosen any other.

As the twenties passed, with my own twenties marching a little ahead of them, my two juvenile regrets—at not being big enough (or good enough) to play football in college, and at not getting overseas during the war—resolved themselves into childish waking dreams of imaginary heroism that were good enough to go to sleep on in restless nights. The big problems of life seemed to solve themselves, and if the business of fixing them was difficult, it made one too tired to think of more general problems.

Life, ten years ago, was largely a personal matter. I must hold in balance the sense of the futility of effort and the sense of the necessity to struggle; the conviction of the inevitability of failure and still the determination to "succeed"—and, more than these, the contradiction between the dead hand of the past and the high intentions of the future. If I could do this through the common ills–domestic, professional and personal–then the ego would continue as an arrow shot from nothingness to nothingness with such force that only gravity would bring it to earth at last.

For seventeen years, with a year of deliberate loafing and resting out in the center–things went on like that, with a new chore only a nice prospect for the next day. I was living hard, too, but: "Up to forty-nine it'll be all right," I said. "I can count on that. For a man who's lived as I have, that's all you can ask."

–And then, ten years this side of forty-nine, I suddenly realized that I had prematurely cracked.

Now a man can crack in many ways–can crack in the head–in which case the power of decision is taken from you by others! or in the body, when one can but submit to the white hospital world; or in the nerves. William Seabrook in an unsympathetic book tells, with some pride and a movie ending, of how he became a public charge. What lead to his alcoholism or was bound up with it, was a collapse of his nervous system. Though the present writer was not so entangled–having at the time not tasted so much as a glass of beer for six months–it was his nervous reflexes that were giving way– too much anger and too many tears.

Moreover, to go back to my thesis that life has a varying offensive, the realization of having cracked was not simultaneous with a blow, but with a reprieve.

Not long before, I sat in the office of a great doctor and listened to a grave sentence. With what, in retrospect, seems quite equanimity, I had gone on about my affairs in the city where I was then living, not caring much, not thinking how much I had left undone, or what would become of this and that responsibility, like people do in books; I was well insured and anyhow I had been only a mediocre caretaker of most of the things left in my hands, even of my talent.

But I had a strong sudden instinct that I must be alone. I didn't want to see any people at all. I had seen so many people all my life–I was an average mixer, but more than average in a tendency to identify myself, my ideas, my destiny, with those of all classes that I came in contact with. I was always saving or being saved–in a single morning I would go through the emotions ascribable to Wellington at Waterloo. I lived in a world of inscrutable hostiles and inalienable friends and supporters.

But now I wanted to be absolutely alone and so arranged a certain insulation from ordinary cares.

It was not an unhappy time. I went away and there were fewer people. I found that I was good-and-tired. I could lie around and was glad to, sleeping or dozing sometimes twenty hours a day and in the intervals trying resolutely not to think–instead I made lists–made lists and tore them up, hundreds of lists; of cavalry leaders and football players and cities, and popular tunes and pitchers, and happy times, and hobbies and houses lived in and how many suits since I left the army and how many pairs of shoes (I didn't count the suit I bought in Sorrento that shrunk, nor the pumps and dress shirt and collar that I carried around for years and never wore, because the pumps got damp and grainy and the shirt and collar got yellow and starch-rotted). And lists of women I liked, and of the times I had let myself be snubbed by people who had not been my betters in character or ability.

—And then suddenly, surprisingly, I got better.

—And cracked like an old plate when I heard the news.

This is the real end of this story. What was to be done about it will have to rest in what used to be called the "womb of time." Suffice it to say that after about an hour of solitary pillow-hugging, I began to realize that for two years my life had been a drawing on resources that I did not possess, that I had been mortgaging myself physically and spiritually up to the hilt. What was the small gift of life given back in comparison to that?—when there had once been a pride of direction and a confidence in enduring independence.

I realized that in those two years, in order to preserve something—an inner hush maybe, maybe not—I had weaned myself from all the things I used to love—that every act of life from the morning tooth-brush to the friend at dinner had become an effort. I saw that for a long time I had not liked people and things, but only followed the rickety old pretense of liking. I saw that even my love for those closest to me was become only an attempt to love, that my casual relations—with an editor, a tobacco seller, the child of a friend, were only what I remembered I should do, from other days. All the same month I became bitter about such things as the sound of the radio, the advertisements in the magazines, the screech of tracks, the dead silence of the country—contemptuous at human softness, immediately (if secretively) quarrelsome toward hardness—hating the night when I couldn't sleep and hating the day because it went toward night. I slept on the heart side now because I knew that the sooner I could tire that out, even a little, the sooner would come that blessed hour of nightmare which, like the catharsis, would enable me to better meet the new day.

There were certain spots, certain faces I could look at. Like most Middle Westerners, I have never had any but the vaguest race prejudices—I have always had a secret yen for the lovely Scandinavian blondes who sat on porches in St. Paul but hadn't emerged enough economically to be a part of what was then society. They were too nice to be "chickens" and too quickly off the farmlands to seize a place in the sun, but I remember going round blocks to catch a single glimpse of shining hair—the bright shock of a girl I'd never know. This is urban, unpopular talk. It strays afield from the fact that in these latter days I couldn't stand the sight of Celts, English, Politicians, Strangers, Virginians, Negroes (light or dark), Hunting People, or retail clerks, and middlemen in general, all writers (I avoided writers very carefully because they can perpetuate trouble as no one else can)—and all the classes as classes and most of them as members of their class . . .

Trying to cling to something, I liked doctors and girl children up to the age of about thirteen and well-brought-up boy children from about eight years old on. I could have peace and happiness with these few categories of people. I forgot to add that I liked old men—men over seventy, sometimes over sixty if their faces looked seasoned. I liked Katherine Hepburn's face on the screen, no matter what was said about her pretentiousness, and Miriam Hopkins' face, and old friends if I only saw them once a year and could remember their ghosts.

All rather inhuman and undernourished, isn't it? Well, that, children, is the true sign of cracking up.

It is not a pretty picture. Inevitably it was carted here and there within its frame and exposed to various critics. One of them can only be described as a person whose life makes other people's lives seem like death—even this time when she was cast in the usually unappealing role of Job's comforter. In spite of the fact that this story is over, let me append our conversation as a sort of postscript:

"Instead of being so sorry for yourself, listen—" she said. (She always says "Listen," because she thinks while she talks—really thinks.) So she said: "Listen. Suppose this wasn't a crack in you—suppose it was a crack in the Grand Canyon."

"The crack's in me," I said heroically.

"Listen! The world only exists in your eyes—your conception of it. You can make it as big or as small as you want to. And you're trying to be a little puny individual. By God, if I ever cracked, I'd try to make the world crack with me. Listen! the world only exists through your apprehension of it, and so it's much better to say that it's not you that's cracked—it's the Grand Canyon."

"Baby et up all her Spinoza?"

"I don't know anything about Spinoza. I know—" She spoke, then, of old woes of her own, that seemed, in the telling, to have been more dolorous than mine, and how she had met them, over-ridden them, beaten them.

I felt a certain reaction to what she said, but I am a slow-thinking man, and it occurred to me simultaneously that of all natural forces, vitality is the incommunicable one. In days when juice came into one as an article without duty, one tried to distribute it—but always without success; to further mix metaphors, vitality never "takes." You have it or you haven't it, like health or brown eyes or a baritone voice. I might have asked some of it from her, neatly wrapped and ready for home cooking and digestion, but I could have never have got it—not if I'd waited around for a thousand hours with the tin cup of self-pity. I could walk from her door, holding myself very carefully liked cracked crockery, and go away into the world of bitterness, where I was making a home with such materials as are found there—and quote to myself after I left her door:

"Ye are the salt of the earth. But if the salt hath lost its savour, wherewith shall it be salted?"

Matthew 5-13.

Charles Dickens

"Smart" dealings in america

Another prominent feature is the love of "smart" dealing: which gilds over many a swindle and gross breach of trust; many a defalcation, public and private; and enables many a knave to hold his head up with the best, who well deserves a halter: though it has not been without its retributive operation, for this smartness has done more in a few years to impair the public credit, and to cripple the public resources, than dull honesty, however rash, could have effected in a century. The merits of a broken speculation, or a bankruptcy, or of a successful scoundrel, are not gauged by its or his observance of the golden rule, "Do as you would be done by," but are considered with reference to their smartness. I recollect, on both occasions of our passing that ill-fated Cairo on the Mississippi, remarking on the bad effects such gross deceits must have when they exploded, in generating a want of confidence abroad, and discouraging foreign investment: but I was given to understand that this was a very smart scheme by which a deal of money had been made: and that its smartest feature was, that they forgot these things abroad, in a very short time, and speculated again, as freely as ever. The following dialogue I have held a hundred times: "Is it not a very disgraceful circumstance that such a man as So and So should be acquiring a large property by the most infamous and odious means, and notwithstanding all the crimes of which he has been guilty, should be tolerated and abetted by your Citizens? He is a public nuisance, is he not?"—"Yes, sir."— "A convicted liar?"—"Yes, sir."—"He has been kicked, and cuffed, and caned?"—"Yes, sir."—"And he is utterly dishonourable, debased, and profligate?"—"Yes, sir." "In the name of wonder, then, what is his merit?"— "Well, sir, he is a smart man."

From *American Notes* by Charles Dickens (1842).

Ambrose Bierce

Crime and its correctives

The good American is, as a rule, pretty hard upon roguery, but he atones for his austerity by an amiable toleration of rogues. His only requirement is that he must personally know the rogues. We all "denounce" thieves loudly enough if we have not the honor of their acquaintance. If we have, why, that is different—unless they have the actual odor of the slum or the prison about them. We may know them guilty, but we meet them, shake hands with them, drink with them, and, if they happen to be wealthy, or otherwise great, invite them to our houses, and deem it an honor to frequent theirs. We do not "approve their methods"—let that be understood; and thereby they are sufficiently punished. The notion that a knave cares a pin what is thought of his ways by one who is civil and friendly to himself appears to have been invented by a humorist. On the vaudeville stage of Mars it would probably have made his fortune.

I know men standing high in journalism who to-day will "expose" and bitterly "denounce" a certain rascality and to-morrow will be hobnobbing with the rascals whom they have named. I know legislators of renown who habitually raise their voices against the dishonest schemes of some "trust magnate," and are habitually seen in familiar conversation with him. Indubitably these be hypocrites all. Between the head and the heart of a man of this objectionable kind is a wall of adamant, and neither knows what the other is doing.

If social recognition were denied to rogues they would be fewer by many. Some would only the more diligently cover their tracks along the devious paths of unrighteousness, but others would do so much violence to their consciences as to renounce the disadvantages of rascality for those of an honest life. An unworthy person dreads nothing so much as the withholding of an honest hand, the slow, inevitable stroke of an ignoring eye.

We have rich rogues because we have "respectable" persons who are not ashamed to take them by the hand, to be seen with them, to say that they know them. For such it is treachery to censure them; to cry out when robbed by them is to turn state's evidence.

One may smile upon a rascal (most of us do so many times a day) if one does not know him to be a rascal, and has not said he is; but knowing him to be, or having said he is, to smile upon him is to be a hypocrite—just a plain hypocrite or a sycophantic hypocrite, according to the station in life of the rascal smiled upon. There are more plain hypocrites than sycophantic ones,

---

From *The Collected Works of Ambrose Bierce* (1891).

for there are more rascals of no consequence than rich and distinguished ones, though they get fewer smiles each. The American people will be plundered as long as the American character is what it is; as long as it is tolerant of successful knaves; as long as American ingenuity draws an imaginary distinction between a man's public character and his private—his commercial and his personal. In brief, the American people will be plundered as long as they deserve to be plundered. No human law can stop it, none ought to stop it, for that would abrogate a higher and more salutary law: "As ye sow ye shall reap."

In a sermon by the Rev. Dr. Parkhurst is the passage following:

"The story of all our Lord's dealings with sinners leaves upon the mind the invariable impression, if only the story be read sympathetically and earnestly, that He always felt kindly towards the transgressor, but could have no tenderness of regard toward the transgression. There is no safe and successful dealing with sin of any kind save as that distinction is appreciated and made a continual factor in our feelings and efforts."

If Dr. Parkhurst will read his New Testament more understandingly he will observe that Christ's kindly feeling to transgressors was not to be counted on by sinners of every kind, and it was not always in evidence; for example, when he flogged the money-changers out of the temple. Nor is Dr. Parkhurst himself any too amiably disposed toward the children of darkness. It was not by mild words and gentle means that he hurled the mighty from their seats and exalted them of low degree. Such revolutions as he set afoot are not made with spiritual rosewater; there must be the contagion of a noble indignation fueled with harder wood than abstractions. The people can not be mustered and incited to action by the spectacle of a man fighting something that does not fight back. It was men that Dr. Parkhurst was trouncing—not their crimes—not Crime. He may fancy himself "dowered with the hate of hate, the scorn of scorn," but in reality he does not hate hate but hates the hateful, and scorns, not scorn but the scornworthy.

It is singular with what tenacity this amusing though mischievous superstition keeps its hold upon the human mind—this grave, *bona fide* personification of abstractions and the funny delusion that it is possible to hate or love them. Sin is not a thing; there is no existing object corresponding to any of the mere counter-words that are properly named abstract nouns. One can no more hate sin or love virtue than one can hate a vacuum (which Nature—itself imaginary—was once by the scientists of the period solemnly held to do) or love one of the three dimensions. We may think that while loving a sinner we hate the sin, but that is not so; if anything is hated it is other sinners of the same kind, who are not quite so close to us.

The French have a saying to the effect that to know all is to pardon all; and doubtless with an omniscient insight into the causes of character we should find the field of moral responsibility pretty thickly strewn with extenuating circumstances very suitable indeed for consideration by a god who has had a hand in besetting "with pitfall and with gin," the road we are to "wander in." But I submit that universal forgiveness would hardly do as a working principle. Even those who are most apt and facile with the incident of the woman taken in adultery commonly cherish a secret respect for the doctrine of eternal damnation; and some of them are known to pin their faith to the penal code of their state. Moreover, there is some reason to believe that the sinning woman, being "taken," was penitent—they usually are when found out.

"But," says Citizen Goodheart, who thinks with difficulty, "shall I throw over my friend when he is 'in trouble'?" Yes, when convinced that he deserves to be in trouble; throw him all the harder and the further because he is your friend. In addition to his particular offense against society he has disgraced *you*. If there are to be lenity and charity let them go to the criminal who has foreborne to involve you in his shame. It were a pretty state of affairs if an undetected scamp, fearing exposure, could make you a co-defendant by so easy a precaution as securing your acquaintance and regard. Don't throw the first stone, of course, but when convinced that your friend is a proper target, heave away with a right hearty good-will, and let the stone be of serviceable weight and delivered with a good aim.

I care nothing for principles—they are lumber and rubbish. What concerns our happiness and welfare, as affectable by our fellowmen, is conduct. "Principles, not men," is a rogue's cry; rascality's counsel to stupidity, the noise of the duper duping on his dupe. He shouts it most loudly and with the keenest sense of its advantage who most desires attention to his own conduct, or to that forecast of it, his character. As to sin, that has an abundance of expounders and is already universally known to be wicked. What more can be said against it, and why go on repeating that? The thing is a trifle wordworn, whereas the sinner cometh up as a flower every day, fresh, ingenuous and inviting. Sin is not at all dangerous to society; what does all the mischief is the sinner. Crime has no arms to thrust into the public treasury and the private; no hands with which to cut a throat; no tongue to wreck a reputation withal. I would no more attack it than I would attack an isoceles triangle, or Hume's "phantasm floating in a void." My chosen enemy must be something that has a skin for my switch, a head for my cudgel—something that can smart and ache. I have no quarrel with abstractions; so far as I know they are all good citizens.

Fedor Dostoevski

The christmas tree and the wedding

The other day I saw a wedding . . . But no! I would rather tell you about a Christmas tree. The wedding was superb. I liked it immensely. But the other incident was still finer. I don't know why it is that the sight of the wedding reminded me of the Christmas tree. This is the way it happened:

Exactly five years ago, on New Year's Eve, I was invited to a children's ball by a man high up in the business world, who had his connections, his circle of acquaintances, and his intrigues. So it seemed as though the children's ball was merely a pretext for the parents to come together and discuss matters of interest to themselves, quite innocently and casually.

I was an outsider, and, as I had no special matters to air, I was able to spend the evening independently of the others. There was another gentleman present who like myself had just stumbled upon this affair of domestic bliss. He was the first to attract my attention. His appearance was not that of a man of birth or high family. He was tall, rather thin, very serious, and well dressed. Apparently he had no heart for the family festivities. The instant he went off into a corner by himself the smile disappeared from his face, and his thick dark brows knitted into a frown. He knew no one except the host and showed every sign of being bored to death, though bravely sustaining the role of thorough enjoyment to the end. Later I learned that he was a provincial, had come to the capital on some important, brain-racking business, had brought a letter of recommendation to our host, and our host had taken him under his protection, not at all *con amore*. It was merely out of politeness that he had invited him to the children's ball.

They did not play cards with him, they did not offer him cigars. No one entered into conversation with him. Possibly they recognized the bird by its feathers from a distance. Thus, my gentleman, not knowing what to do with his hands, was compelled to spend the evening stroking his whiskers. His whiskers were really fine, but he stroked them so assiduously that one got the feeling that the whiskers had come into the world first and afterwards the man in order to stroke them.

There was another guest who interested me. But he was of quite a different order. He was a personage. They called him Julian Mastakovich. At first glance one could tell he was an honoured guest and stood in the same relation to the host as the host to the gentleman of the whiskers. The host and hostess said no end of amiable things to him, were most attentive, wining

---

"The Christmas Tree and the Wedding," from *White Nights, and Other Stories* by Fedor Dostoevski (1848).

him, hovering over him, bringing guests up to be introduced, but never leading him to any one else. I noticed tears glisten in our host's eyes when Julian
Mastakovich remarked that he had rarely spent such a pleasant evening.
Somehow I began to feel uncomfortable in this personage's presence. So,
after amusing myself with the children, five of whom, remarkably well-fed
young persons, were our host's, I went into a little sitting-room, entirely
unoccupied, and seated myself at the end that was a conservatory and took
up almost half the room.

The children were charming. They absolutely refused to resemble their
elders, notwithstanding the efforts of mothers and governesses. In a jiffy
they had denuded the Christmas tree down to the very last sweet and had
already succeeded in breaking half of their playthings before they even
found out which belonged to whom.

One of them was a particularly handsome little lad, dark-eyed, curly-
haired, who stubbornly persisted in aiming at one with his wooden gun. But
the child that attracted the greatest attention was his sister, a girl of about
eleven, lovely as a Cupid. She was quiet and thoughtful, with large, full,
dreamy eyes. The children had somehow offended her, and she left them
and walked into the same room that I had withdrawn into. There she seated
herself with her doll in a corner.

"Her father is an immensely wealthy business man," the guests informed
each other in tones of awe. "Three hundred thousand rubles set aside for
her dowry already."

As I turned to look at the group from which I heard this news item issuing,
my glance met Julian Mastakovich's. He stood listening to the insipid chatter in an attitude of concentrated attention, with his hands behind his back
and his head inclined to one side.

All the while I was quite lost in admiration of the shrewdness our host
displayed in the dispensing of the gifts. The little maid of the many-rubled
dowry received the handsomest doll, and the rest of the gifts were graded in
value according to the diminishing scale of the parents' stations in life. The
last child, a tiny chap of ten, thin, red-haired, freckled, came into possession of a small book of nature stories without illustrations or even head and
tail pieces. He was the governess's child. She was a poor widow, and her
little boy, clad in a sorry-looking little nankeen jacket, looked thoroughly
crushed and intimidated. He took the book of nature stories and circled
slowly about the children's toys. He would have given anything to play with
them. But he did not dare to. You could tell he already knew his place.

I like to observe children. It is fascinating to watch the individuality in
them struggling for self-assertion. I could see that the other children's things
had tremendous charm for the red-haired boy, especially a toy theatre, in
which he was so anxious to take a part that he resolved to fawn upon the
other children. He smiled and began to play with them. His one and only

apple he handed over to a puffy urchin whose pockets were already crammed with sweets, and he even carried another youngster pickaback—all simply that he might be allowed to stay with the theatre.

But in a few moments an impudent young person fell on him and gave him a pummelling. He did not dare even to cry. The governess came and told him to leave to interfering with the other children's games, and he crept away to the same room the little girl and I were in. She let him sit down beside her, and the two set themselves busily to dressing the expensive doll.

Almost half an hour passed, and I was nearly dozing off, as I sat there in the conservatory half listening to the chatter of the red-haired boy and the dowered beauty, when Julian Mastakovich entered suddenly. He had slipped out of the drawing-room under cover of a noisy scene among the children. From my secluded corner it had not escaped my notice that a few moments before he had been eagerly conversing with the rich girl's father, to whom he had only just been introduced.

He stood still for a while reflecting and mumbling to himself, as if counting something on his fingers.

"Three hundred—three hundred—eleven—twelve—thirteen—sixteen—in five years! Let's say four per cent—five times twelve—sixty, and on these sixty—. Let us assume that in five years it will amount to—well, four hundred. Hmhum! But the shrewd old fox isn't likely to be satisfied with four per cent. He gets eight or even ten, perhaps. Let's suppose five hundred, five hundred thousand, at least, that's sure. Anything above that for pocket money—hm—"

He blew his nose and was about to leave the room when he spied the girl and stood still. I, behind the plants, escaped his notice. He seemed to me to be quivering with excitement. It must have been his calculations that upset him so. He rubbed his hands and danced from place to place, and kept getting more and more excited. Finally, however, he conquered his emotions and came to a standstill. He cast a determined look at the future bride and wanted to move toward her, but glanced about first. Then, as if with a guilty conscience, he stepped over to the child on tiptoe, smiling, and bent down and kissed her head.

His coming was so unexpected that she uttered a shriek of alarm.

"What are you doing here, dear child?" he whispered, looking around and pinching her cheek.

"We're playing."

"What, with him?" said Julian Mastakovich with a look askance at the governess's child. "You should go into the drawing-room, my lad," he said to him.

The boy remained silent and looked up at the man with wide-open eyes. Julian Mastakovich glanced round again cautiously and bent down over the girl.

"What have you got, a doll, my dear?"

"Yes, sir." The child quailed a little, and her brow wrinkled.

"A doll? And do you know, my dear, what dolls are made of?"

"No, sir," she said weakly, and lowered her head.

"Out of rags, my dear. You, boy, you go back to the drawing-room, to the children," said Julian Mastakovich, looking at the boy sternly.

The two children frowned. They caught hold of each other and would not part.

"And do you know why they gave you the doll?" asked Julian Mastakovich, dropping his voice lower and lower.

"No."

"Because you were a good, very good little girl the whole week."

Saying which, Julian Mastakovich was seized with a paroxysm of agitation. He looked round and said in a tone faint, almost inaudible with excitement and impatience:

"If I come to visit your parents will you love me, my dear?"

He tried to kiss the sweet little creature, but the red-haired boy saw that she was on the verge of tears, and he caught her hand and sobbed out loud in sympathy. That enraged the man.

"Go away! Go away! Go back to the other room, to your playmates."

"I don't want him to. I don't want him to! You go away!" cried the girl. "Let him alone! Let him alone!" She was almost weeping.

There was a sound of footsteps in the doorway. Julian Mastakovich started and straightened up his respectable body. The red-haired boy was even more alarmed. He let go the girl's hand, sidled along the wall, and escaped through the drawing-room into the dining-room.

Not to attract attention, Julian Mastakovich also made for the dining-room. He was red as a lobster. The sight of himself in a mirror seemed to embarrass him. Presumably he was annoyed at his own ardour and impatience. Without due respect to his importance and dignity, his calculations had lured and pricked him to the greedy eagerness of a boy, who makes straight for his object—though this was not as yet an object; it only would be so in five years' time. I followed the worthy man into the dining-room, where I witnessed a remarkable play.

Julian Mastakovich, all flushed with vexation, venom in his look, began to threaten the red-haired boy. The red-haired boy retreated farther and farther until there was no place left for him to retreat to, and he did not know where to turn in his fright.

"Get out of here! What are you doing here? Get out, I say, you good-for-nothing! Stealing fruit, are you? Oh, so, stealing fruit! Get out, you freckle face, go to your likes!"

The frightened child, as a last desperate resort, crawled quickly under the table. His persecutor, completely infuriated, pulled out his large linen handkerchief and used it as a lash to drive the boy out of his position.

Here I must remark that Julian Mastakovich was a somewhat corpulent man, heavy, well-fed, puffy-cheeked, with a paunch and ankles as round as nuts. He perspired and puffed and panted. So strong was his dislike (or was it jealousy?) of the child that he actually began to carry on like a madman.

I laughed heartily. Julian Mastakovich turned. He was utterly confused and for a moment, apparently, quite oblivious of his immense importance. At that moment our host appeared in the doorway opposite. The boy crawled out from under the table and wiped his knees and elbows. Julian Mastakovich hastened to carry his handkerchief, which he had been dangling by the corner, to his nose. Our host looked at the three of us rather suspiciously. But, like a man who knows the world and can readily adjust himself, he seized upon the opportunity to lay hold of his very valuable guest and get what he wanted out of him.

"Here's the boy I was talking to you about," he said, indicating the red-haired child. "I took the liberty of presuming on your goodness in his behalf."

"Oh," replied Julian Mastakovich, still not quite master of himself.

"He's my governess's son," our host continued in a beseeching tone. "She's a poor creature, the widow of an honest official. That's why, if it were possible for you—"

"Impossible, impossible!" Julian Mastakovich cried hastily. "You must excuse me, Philip Alexeyevich, I really cannot. I've made inquiries. There are no vacancies, and there is a waiting list of ten who have a greater right— I'm sorry."

"Too bad," said our host. "He's a quiet, unobtrusive child."

"A very naughty little rascal, I should say," said Julian Mastakovich, wryly. "Go away, boy. Why are you here still? Be off with you to the other children."

Unable to control himself, he gave me a sidelong glance. Nor could I control myself. I laughed straight in his face. He turned away and asked our host, in tones quite audible to me, who that odd young fellow was. They whispered to each other and left the room, disregarding me.

I shook with laughter. Then I, too, went to the drawing-room. There the great man, already surrounded by the fathers and mothers and the host and the hostess, had begun to talk eagerly with a lady to whom he had just been introduced. The lady held the rich little girl's hand. Julian Mastakovich went into fulsome praise of her. He waxed ecstatic over the dear child's beauty, her talents, her grace, her excellent breeding, plainly laying himself out to flatter the mother, who listened scarcely able to restrain tears of joy, while the father showed his delight by a gratified smile.

The joy was contagious. Everybody shared in it. Even the children were obliged to stop playing so as not to disturb the conversation. The atmosphere was surcharged with awe. I heard the mother of the important little girl, touched to her profoundest depths, ask Julian Mastakovich in the choicest language of courtesy, whether he would honour them by coming to see them. I heard Julian Mastakovich accept the invitation with unfeigned enthusiasm. Then the guests scattered decorously to different parts of the room, and I heard them, with veneration in their tones, extol the daughter, and, especially, Julian Mastakovich.

"Is he married?" I asked out loud of an acquaintance of mine standing beside Julian Mastakovich.

Julian Mastakovich gave me a venomous look.

"No," answered my acquaintance, profoundly shocked by my-intentional-indiscretion. . . .

Not long ago I passed the Church of ——. I was struck by the concourse of people gathered there to witness a wedding. It was a dreary day. A drizzling rain was beginning to come down. I made my way through the throng into the church. The bridegroom was a round, well-fed, pot-bellied little man, very much dressed up. He ran and fussed about and gave orders and arranged things. Finally word was passed that the bride was coming. I pushed through the crowd, and I beheld a marvellous beauty whose first spring was scarcely commencing. But the beauty was pale and sad. She looked distracted. It seemed to me even that her eyes were red from recent weeping. The classic severity of every line of her face imparted a peculiar significance and solemnity to her beauty. But through that severity and solemnity, through the sadness, shone the innocence of a child. There was something inexpressibly naive, unsettled and young in her features, which, without words, seemed to plead for mercy.

They said she was just sixteen years old. I looked at the bridegroom carefully. Suddenly I recognised Julian Mastakovich, whom I had not seen again in all those five years. Then I looked at the bride again.—Good God! I made my way as quickly as I could, out of the church. I heard gossiping in the crowd about the bride's wealth—about her dowry of five hundred thousand rubles—so and so much for pocket money.

"Then his calculations were correct," I thought, as I pressed out into the street.